Handbook of
Research in
School Consultation

Edited by

William P. Erchul • Susan M. Sheridan

Routledge
Taylor & Francis Group
New York   London

D1472885

First published by
Lawrence Erlbaum Associates,
10 Industrial Avenue
Mahwah, New Jersey 07430

Reprinted 2009 by Routledge

Routledge
Taylor & Francis Group
270 Madison Avenue
New York, NY 10016

Routledge
Taylor & Francis Group
2 Park Square
Milton Park, Abingdon
Oxon OX14 4RN

© 2008 by Taylor & Francis Group, LLC

Printed in the United States of America on acid-free paper
10 9 8 7 6 5 4 3 2

International Standard Book Number-13: 978-0-8058-5336-0 (Softcover) 978-0-8058-5335-3 (Hardcover)

No part of this book may be reprinted, reproduced, transmitted, or utilized in any form by any electronic, mechanical, or other means, now known or hereafter invented, including photocopying, microfilming, and recording, or in any information storage or retrieval system, without written permission from the publishers.

Trademark Notice: Product or corporate names may be trademarks or registered trademarks, and are used only for identification and explanation without intent to infringe.

Library of Congress Cataloging-in-Publication Data

Handbook of research in school consultation / editors, William P. Erchul, Susan M. Sheridan.
    p. cm.
   Includes bibliographical references and index.
   ISBN-13: 978-0-8058-5336-0 (alk. paper)
   ISBN-10: 0-8058-5336-7 (alk. paper)
   ISBN-13: 978-0-8058-5335-3 (alk. paper)
   ISBN-10: 0-8058-5335-9 (alk. paper)
   1. Educational consultants--United States. 2. School psychology--United States. I. Erchul, William P. II. Sheridan, Susan M.

LB2799.2.H36 2008
371.4--dc22
                                               2007014055

Visit the Taylor & Francis Web site at
http://www.taylorandfrancis.com

Contents

Foreword

Psychologists who focus their practice on children are faced with the daunting challenge of developing expertise across a number of knowledge and skill domains and contexts. In addition to understanding learning, and typical and atypical physical, social, and emotional development, they must have skills in navigating the important systems that care for children, especially families and schools. In fact, it is likely that children are often best served through the adult systems that are charged with their care. Children, though not passive within developmental and environmental influences, are seldom in positions to change the contexts that mold their behaviors so powerfully.

This perspective has served as a primary rationale for the use of consultation as a method of mental health service delivery for children. Consultation in schools has the potential advantage of indirectly reaching most children and adolescents to offer universal, selective, and targeted interventions. Many educational professionals see the link between learning, achievement, and positive mental health. In addition, educators are often faced with troubling dilemmas related to young people's behavior, learning, adjustment, and peer and family relationships and seek out expert input to solve problems.

The practice of school-based consultation has been fueled by these analyses along with the awareness that there will never be enough psychologists to engineer all the daily environments or instructional tasks for children. The need to increase and support the effectiveness of care providers who have greater access to children is evident.

Bill Erchul and Sue Sheridan's work to develop the *Handbook of Research in School Consultation*, focused on the extant and nagging research lacuna associated with school consultation, is timely. Students, families, and educators are interacting within a high-stakes academic environment. The standards movement with its associated state and national testing programs has fueled a long-overdue accountability for equitable learning outcomes for all children. The demand that every child reach proficient levels of skill in core academic subjects may be unrealistic, but it also represents an unprecedented opportunity to stretch the limits of our educational system.

Children who arrive at school with an accumulation of risk factors such as poverty, single-parent households, poorly educated parents, low proficiency in English or their native language, and many siblings but few adult supports have rarely fared well in our educational system. The demands for achievement in the current context can reinforce consulting psychologists' participation with educators and families in new ways to build a system that is responsive to these learning barriers. The motivation to do so is now quite high. The time may be right to expand consultation services in schools.

Consultation is a process meant to bring new expertise, capacity, persistence, and care into a system, but does it really work that way? Do we have evidence that we can rely on skillful application of consultation as a reliable way to help teachers and students thrive in the 21st century context of tremendous linguistic, economic, ethnic, and values pluralism? This context has sharpened the reality that individual teachers are rarely, if ever, capable of meeting the academic, social, and emotional needs of all children. Is greater reliance on consultation the preferred strategy to meet educators' needs?

This volume takes the reader on a carefully planned and expertly implemented journey by reviewing what is known about the effectiveness of various models of consultation, exploring new and well-established research methods to further the research enterprise, and identifying what is missing in our evidence base. An additional strength of the volume is the analysis provided by commentary authors at the end of each section.

As the need for innovative strategies to buoy public education's success with all children grows, so does the need to build an evidence base associated with all intervention approaches that are applied. The ethics of practice demand that we continuously build a foundation for confident application. This volume brings us up to the moment on what is known and lays out a path for sophisticated further study. Every psychologist who intends to focus on school practice will benefit from a careful reading and analysis of the *Handbook of Research in School Consultation: Empirical Foundations for the Field*. The authors and editors represent eminent members of the research and practice communities. They have created an important resource for every psychologist who works for child and family welfare.

Jane Close Conoley

Dean, Gevirtz Graduate School of Education
University of California at Santa Barbara

Preface

The challenge of providing effective educational and psychological interventions to child and adolescent clients—even under ideal circumstances—is well documented. However, delivering these services through an intermediary (e.g., teacher, parent) rather than directly by a highly trained specialist (e.g., psychologist), and within complex organizational settings (e.g., U.S. public schools), multiplies the difficulty of the task considerably. Professionals employed by schools to offer consultation to others regarding child and adolescent treatment issues face this challenge on a regular, if not daily, basis.

We live in an era of heightened accountability within education, brought about in part by major federal legislation governing school-based services, shrinking funding scenarios for many school systems, and great student diversity. At the same time, as specialists in education and psychology, we strive to reach high standards for practice, often promoted under the banner of "evidence-based interventions" (EBIs). Given these and other contemporary forces, it seems an appropriate time to fully embrace a scientist-practitioner perspective and critically examine the empirical foundations for consultation as an essential service provided by school-based professionals.

How does one consult "effectively" in schools? Is there an evidence base to inform the practice of school consultation? If so, are the directives for "best practice" grounded in methodologically sound research? Is consultation, in fact, an EBI? What has research uncovered thus far about school consultation and effective consulting practices? What areas require further empirical study, and consequently, what future research directions can one expect to see? How, for that matter, is research on school consultation conducted? What topics and constructs are regarded as important to study? What are the hallmark characteristics of exemplary consultation research studies? It is questions such as these that led us to develop the *Handbook of Research in School Consultation: Empirical Foundations for the Field*.

In essence, the handbook is a volume for both producers and consumers of school consultation research that attempts to lay the groundwork for approaches to practice that are based on the best available empirical evidence. We believe the handbook's chapters together provide an exhaustive review of the current research literature and therefore specify what is known and what needs to be known about school consultation research. The intended audience includes researchers, graduate students, and practitioners from various human service disciplines, including psychology, counseling, special education, and social work. Chapter authors, nearly all of whom are school psychologists, have contributed to the school consultation research literature for many years and collectively are recognized for their ability to translate scientific findings into implications for practice.

Structurally, the *Handbook of Research in School Consultation* consists of five major sections. In addition to the introductory and epilogue sections, the three others offer content related to (a) methodological, measurement, and statistical foundations of consultation research; (b) process/outcome results from five recognized school consultation models; and (c) process/outcome results from four thematic research perspectives that inform consultative practice. Features unique to the handbook include (a) Chapter 2, by Jennifer Frank and Thomas Kratochwill, which sets the stage for school consultation to be scrutinized as an intervention; and (b) three commentary chapters (Chapters 6, 12, and 17), which provide integrative critiques at the end of the major sections of the handbook.

As coeditors, we are greatly indebted to all of the contributors, who generously gave of their time and talent to the handbook. We feel fortunate to have learned so much from them over the course of this multiyear project. Lane Akers and the staff at Lawrence Erlbaum Associates, Inc. and Marsha Hecht of the Taylor & Francis Group are thanked for their insights and skills displayed throughout the process of bringing these ideas to print. We also wish to acknowledge the clerical support of Holly Sexton and Stephanie Asbeck as well as the encouragement and support of Ann Schulte and Steve Statz. Finally, we would like to thank the many consultants, teachers, parents, and children whose participation in research studies ultimately made the *Handbook of Research in School Consultation: Empirical Foundations for the Field* possible.

William P. Erchul
Susan M. Sheridan

Contributors

Jennifer D. Burt, MEd, Department of Educational Psychology, School Psychology Program, University of Nebraska-Lincoln, Lincoln, NE

Michelle Buss, MS, Department of Educational Psychology, School Psychology Program, Texas A&M University, College Station, TX

Brandy L. Clarke, MA, Department of Educational Psychology, School Psychology Program, University of Nebraska-Lincoln, Lincoln, NE

Amanda Smith Collins, EdS, Department of Counseling and Psychological Services, School Psychology Program, Georgia State University, Atlanta, GA

Jane Close Conoley, PhD, Gevirtz Graduate School of Education, University of California at Santa Barbara, Santa Barbara, CA

Florence D. DiGennaro, PhD, Department of Psychology, School Psychology Program, Syracuse University, Syracuse, NY

Kirsten M. Ellingsen, MS, School of Education, School Psychology Program, University of North Carolina at Chapel Hill, Chapel Hill, NC

William P. Erchul, PhD, Department of Psychology, School Psychology Program, North Carolina State University, Raleigh, NC

Susan G. Forman, PhD, Graduate School of Applied and Professional Psychology, Rutgers University, Piscataway, NJ

Jennifer L. Frank, PhD, Department of Pediatrics, Center for Child Development, Vanderbilt University, Nashville, TN

Kimberly C. Getty, PhD, Department of Psychology, School Psychology Program, North Carolina State University; Wake County Public School System, Raleigh, NC

Todd A. Gravois, PhD, Department of Counseling and Personnel Services, Laboratory for Instructional Consultation Teams, University of Maryland, College Park, MD

Frank M. Gresham, PhD, Department of Psychology, School Psychology Program, Louisiana State University, Baton Rouge, LA

Priscilla F. Grissom, PhD, Department of Psychology, School Psychology Program, North Carolina State University, Raleigh, NC

Jan N. Hughes, PhD, Department of Educational Psychology, School Psychology Program, Texas A&M University, College Station, TX

Robert J. Illback, PsyD, R.E.A.C.H. of Louisville, Inc., Louisville, KY

Colette L. Ingraham, PhD, Department of Counseling and School Psychology, San Diego State University, San Diego, CA

Maureen Kanuika, MA, School of Education, School Psychology Program, University of North Carolina at Chapel Hill, Chapel Hill, NC

Steven E. Knotek, PhD, School of Education, School Psychology Program, University of North Carolina at Chapel Hill, Chapel Hill, NC

Thomas R. Kratochwill, PhD, Department of Educational Psychology, School Psychology Program, University of Wisconsin-Madison, Madison, WI

Emilia C. Lopez, PhD, Department of Educational and Community Programs, Graduate Program in School Psychology, Queens College of the University of New York, Flushing, NY

Linda Loyd, BS, Department of Educational Psychology, School Psychology Program, Texas A&M University, College Station, TX

Brian K. Martens, PhD, Department of Psychology, School Psychology Program, Syracuse University, Syracuse, NY

Adena B. Meyers, PhD, Department of Psychology, School Psychology Program, Illinois State University, Normal, IL

Joel Meyers, PhD, Department of Counseling and Psychological Services; School Psychology Program; Center for Research on School Safety, School Climate and Classroom Management; Georgia State University, Atlanta, GA

Bonnie K. Nastasi, PhD, School Psychology Program, Walden University, Minneapolis, MN

George H. Noell, PhD, Department of Psychology, School Psychology Program, Louisiana State University, Baton Rouge, LA

Margaret A. Pennington, MSSW, R.E.A.C.H. of Louisville, Inc., Louisville, KY

Sylvia A. Rosenfield, PhD, Department of Counseling and Personnel Services, School Psychology Program, Laboratory for Instructional Consultation Teams, University of Maryland, College Park, MD

Ann C. Schulte, PhD, Department of Psychology, School Psychology Program, North Carolina State University, Raleigh, NC

Susan M. Sheridan, PhD, Department of Educational Psychology, School Psychology Program; Nebraska Center for Research on Children, Youth, Families, and Schools; University of Nebraska-Lincoln, Lincoln, NE

Arlene Silva, MA, Department of Counseling and Personnel Services, School Psychology Program, University of Maryland, College Park, MD; Nashua School District, Nashua, NH

Stephen D. Truscott, PsyD, Department of Counseling and Psychological Services, School Psychology Program, Georgia State University, Atlanta, GA

Amanda M. VanDerHeyden, PhD, Counseling, Clinical, and School Psychology Programs, University of California at Santa Barbara, Santa Barbara, CA

Mike Vanderwood, PhD, Graduate School of Education, School Psychology Program, University of California at Riverside, Riverside, CA

Kristen Varjas, PsyD, Department of Counseling and Psychological Services; School Psychology Program; Center for Research on School Safety, School Climate and Classroom Management; Georgia State University, Atlanta, GA

Joseph C. Witt, PhD, Department of Psychology, School Psychology Program, Louisiana State University, Baton Rouge, LA

Joseph E. Zins, EdD, Department of Early Childhood Education and Special Education, University of Cincinnati, Cincinnati, OH (deceased)

A

INTRODUCTION

D1472915

1

Overview

The State of Scientific Research in School Consultation

WILLIAM P. ERCHUL

North Carolina State University

SUSAN M. SHERIDAN

University of Nebraska-Lincoln

The overall state of scientific research in school consultation may be best characterized as promising but underdeveloped at present. However, it is decidedly not the goal of this chapter to provide a comprehensive review of the school consultation research literature that supports this assessment, largely because other handbook chapters successfully accomplish this goal. Instead, the two major purposes of chapter 1 are to establish an overall context for the handbook and to offer a preview of the book's content. To achieve these purposes, we present background issues, delineate significant influences on school consultation research and practice, specify the purpose of the handbook, and introduce its contents.

BACKGROUND ISSUES

Consultation within the human service professions represents an indirect model of delivering educational and mental health services by which a professional with specialized expertise (i.e., consultant) and a staff member (i.e., consultee) work together to optimize the functioning of a client in the staff member's setting. Consultation is regarded as an *indirect* helping approach because a consultant generally does not work directly with clients but rather helps clients through direct interactions with consultees. The two fundamental goals of consultation are to enhance services to clients and to increase consultees' capacities to deal with similar situations in the future (Gutkin & Curtis, 1999; Zins, Kratochwill, & Elliott, 1993).

There are several traditional aspects of consultation that distinguish it from other helping processes, such as supervision, teaching, and counseling (Caplan, 1970; Conoley & Conoley, 1982). These aspects include the

- triadic nature of consultation, involving a consultant and one or more consultees and clients;
- assumption of the optimal working relationship between a consultant and consultee (described as coordinate and nonhierarchical);
- direct focus of consultation on consultee work-related problems rather than personal problems;

- retention of ultimate responsibility for client welfare by a consultee;
- freedom of accepting or rejecting consultant guidance by a consultee; and
- communication between a consultant and consultee regarded as confidential (within specified limits).

Owing to the evolution of consultation within the human services, variations on these aspects can be found in different consultative approaches (e.g., Brown, Pryzwansky, & Schulte, 2006; Erchul & Martens, 2002; Sheridan & Kratochwill, 2007). Given these many variations, a universally accepted definition of *consultation* understandably does not exist.

Psychologists and other educational and mental health professionals have been active as school consultants in the manner described since the 1960s, when consultation first appeared in a formal sense in U.S. schools (Alpert and Associates, 1982; Sarason, 1971). Accounts of the practice of school consultation occurring some 40 years ago typically are narrative case studies of external consultants who, after negotiating entry with the school principal, proceeded to work with teacher consultees, either individually or in small groups (e.g., Newman, 1967; Weinstein, 1982). Often, the overt focus on a particular student client served as a springboard for discussion of a wide range of issues pertinent to teachers' professional functioning and development. Due to the prominence of psychoanalytic thought at the time, there is a strong presence of mental health consultation (Caplan, 1964, 1970) in these case studies.

In the 1970s, the rise of behaviorism saw the development and greater use of behavioral consultation approaches (e.g., Bergan, 1977; Tharp & Wetzel, 1969), a trend still evident in the schools (Kratochwill, Elliott, & Stoiber, 2002). The relative popularity of school-based behavioral consultation has been attributed to its well-operationalized interview procedures and reliance on applied behavior-analytical techniques, which have been shown to be effective in intervening with children's academic and adjustment problems (Martens, 1993). Of course, other models besides mental health consultation and behavioral consultation have been evident in schools over time.

Many graduate training programs in school psychology, special education, school counseling, counseling psychology, clinical psychology, and community psychology offer training in consultation, and most professionals currently practicing in these specialties spend some portion of their day engaged in consultation. For example, surveys of practitioners indicate that about 20% of the typical school psychologist's time is spent on activities related to consultation (Fagan & Wise, 2000), and the practitioner would prefer to spend more time (i.e., 31–40%) on consultation (Costenbader, Swartz, & Petrix, 1992). As in earlier times, school psychologists today consult with classroom teachers on students' academic, behavioral, and social problems. Though less common, school psychologists also consult at higher systems levels by working with administrators and other personnel to develop policies and programs that affect teachers, parents, students, and others (Erchul & Martens, 2002).

Despite the documented prevalence of consultation in schools, however, its research base has lagged considerably behind its practice (e.g., Gresham & Kendell, 1987; Gutkin, 1993) and therein lies the raison d'être for the *Handbook of Research in School Consultation: Empirical Foundations for the Field*. In essence, as a volume for both producers and consumers of school consultation research, the handbook attempts to lay a foundation for approaches to school consultation that are based on the best-available empirical evidence.

SCHOOL CONSULTATION: INFLUENCES ON RESEARCH AND PRACTICE

That school consultation is here to stay is not in dispute. Therefore, rather than building a case for why it should continue to exist, we proceed by acknowledging some of the forces that shape practice and research trends in school consultation. Drawing mainly from a school psychology perspective, we offer some examples of notable influences on the present and future of school consultation. This selective listing is built around philosophical, legislative, and empirical influences.

Philosophical Influences

From early (Caplan, 1964) to more contemporary writings (e.g., Zins & Erchul, 2002), a significant undercurrent in the consultation literature is that consultation is concerned with the prevention of mental illness and educational failure. Although the terms primary, secondary, and tertiary prevention essentially have been replaced by the labels universal, selective, and indicated prevention, respectively (Gordon, 1987), the consistent message is that consultants work with consultees on existing problems mainly in the service of preventing the occurrence of future problems. Evidence supporting school consultation's primary/universal prevention purpose generally has been documented by reductions in number of referrals for special education services following consultation (e.g., Ponti, Zins, & Graden, 1988). This evidence is limited, however, to the point that it perhaps is more accurate to conclude that school consultation serves a secondary/selective or tertiary/indicated purpose rather than a primary/universal one (Zins, 1995). Thus, consistently attaining the elusive, perhaps aspirational, goal of primary/universal prevention via school consultation still remains a challenge.

A second philosophical influence on school consultation is the "paradox of school psychology" (Conoley & Gutkin, 1986; Gutkin & Conoley, 1990). The paradox holds that, "to serve children effectively, school psychologists must, first and foremost, concentrate their attention and professional expertise on *adults*" (emphasis added; Gutkin & Conoley, p. 212). Though seemingly running counter to the way many individuals perceive the field of school psychology, these authors construct a defensible argument indicating that, with the exception of remedial services (e.g., individual child assessment), almost all services that school psychologists offer either are indirect services (e.g., consultation) or result in indirect services (e.g., program evaluation). The implications of the paradox of school psychology are considerable and extend well beyond the scope of this chapter. However, there is great value in researching adult-to-adult interactions (i.e., those found in school consultation) to strengthen educational and psychological services provided to child clients.

A third philosophical influence on school consultation, based on both a prevention orientation and the paradox of school psychology, is a bold new vision for school psychology for the 21st century (Sheridan & Gutkin, 2000). These authors first specify the problems inherent to current school psychological services (e.g., reliance on medical model, ineffectual special education practices) and then propose a new comprehensive services model for the field. Their new model recognizes systemic realities of school-based services and, using ecological theory, promotes connections within schools, societal contexts, and families. Sheridan and Gutkin advocate that activities such as consultation, prereferral intervention, parent and teacher training, program planning and evaluation, organizational development, and family therapy be emphasized to address the paradox of school psychology successfully because these services "facilitate relationship building, and intensive, ongoing, and collaborative communication between school psychologists and strategic adults in children's lives" (p. 499). It is clear that effective consultation practices figure highly in operationalizing this new perspective.

Legislative Influences

School psychology as a professional specialty has been greatly affected by federal legislation, from most notably the Education for All Handicapped Children Act of 1975 (Pub. L. No. 94-142), through its recent reauthorization, the Individuals With Disabilities Education Improvement Act (IDEIA) of 2004 (Pub. L. No. 108-446). The regulations for IDEIA 2004 Part B, released in August 2006 for implementation during the 2006–2007 academic year, have several implications for school consultation; two of these implications involve response to intervention (RTI) and positive behavior support (PBS).

Regarding documenting a suspected learning disability, IDEIA 2004 Part B regulations permit an RTI approach to substitute for the well-known IQ/achievement discrepancy eligibility determination. RTI can be described straightforwardly as a series of steps: (a) the student is presented with effective/research-based instruction by the classroom teacher; (b) the student's academic progress is monitored; (c) if the student does not respond (i.e., improve academic performance), then the intervention is intensified; (d) the student's progress is again monitored; and (e) if the student still does not respond, the student qualifies for special education services or for a formal psychoeducational evaluation that may lead to special education placement (Fuchs, Mock, Morgan, & Young, 2003). It is clear that RTI, which places intervention ahead of formal eligibility assessment, will elevate the stature of consultation as a means to deliver research-based interventions in schools.

IDEIA 2004, like its predecessor, the Individuals With Disabilities Education Act (IDEA) 1997, emphasizes the importance of PBS. PBS typically is conceptualized as a proactive, schoolwide intervention effort that promotes discipline through "defining, teaching, and supporting appropriate student behaviors to create positive school environments" (Office of Special Education Programs, n.d.). Within PBS, the goal is to create and sustain universal (i.e., schoolwide), selective (i.e., small-group), and indicated (i.e., individual) support systems that improve lifestyle results for all children by minimizing the impact of problem behavior and maximizing the functionality of desired behavior. PBS is somewhat similar to RTI in that both are based on the same problem-solving framework and system of hierarchical interventions (Dee & Cowan, 2006). PBS's preventive orientation and systemwide focus is highly consistent with the overall aims of school consultation, and this consistency will serve to increase the prominence of school consultation.

Empirical Influences

As scientist-practitioners, we strongly believe that school consultants' actions should be guided by the best-available empirical evidence, and it is primarily this belief that led to the development of the *Handbook of Research in School Consultation*. Two specific ways that empiricism has influenced school consultation are through the (a) conduct of research studies of school consultation that link processes (i.e., independent variables) to outcomes (i.e., dependent variables) and (b) accumulation of this empirical knowledge through literature reviews, methodological reviews, and meta-analyses of consultation outcomes. Table 1.1 contains a list of major reviews and meta-analyses published since 1975 that have focused on outcomes of school consultation.

It is not our intent to summarize the results or themes found in these 17 sources, which together provide a comprehensive picture of school consultation research across time. We will, however, state a basic conclusion: Despite the methodological limitations that plague the consultation outcome research literature in general, the overall consensus is that much of the time the implementation of school consultation results in improved outcomes for clients and consultees. Certainly, other contributors to the handbook elaborate on this straightforward conclusion as well as draw out its subtleties.

What may be equally important to emphasize is the *datedness* of the references displayed in Table 1.1. For example, the most recently published meta-analysis of consultation outcomes (i.e., Reddy, Barboza-Whitehead, Files, & Rubel, 2000) — now 8 years old — examined outcome studies published from 1986 to 1997. Among other things, this scenario unfortunately suggests the field

Table 1.1   Major Published Research Reviews and Meta-Analyses of School Consultation Outcome Studies

Mannino and Shore (1975)
Medway (1979)
Medway (1982)
Alpert and Yammer (1983)
Medway and Updyke (1985)
Pryzwansky (1986)
Gresham and Kendell (1987)
West and Idol (1987)
Duncan and Pryzwansky (1988)
Kratochwill, Sheridan, and VanSomeren (1988)
Fuchs, Fuchs, Dulan, Roberts, and Fernstrom (1992)
Gresham and Noell (1993)
Gutkin (1993)
Busse, Kratochwill, and Elliott (1995)
Sheridan, Welch, and Orme (1996)
Reddy, Barboza-Whitehead, Files, and Rubel (2000)
Lewis and Newcomer (2002)

may be basing its conclusions for the current practice of school consultation on the study of past practice. Regarding the issue of empiricism, we believe the school consultation research enterprise needs to be more forward looking than it is currently.

In our view, a forward-looking perspective applied to school consultation research includes an evidence-based intervention (EBI) orientation. Also known by the terms *empirically supported treatment, empirically validated therapy,* and *evidence-based practice,* an EBI approach holds that a professional's actions should be informed by the best-available scientific evidence. The EBI orientation was clearly in its infancy at the time Reddy et al. (2000) conducted their meta-analysis, yet today its centrality to the fields of mental health (e.g., Norcross, Beutler, & Levant, 2006), professional psychology (e.g., APA Presidential Task Force on Evidence-based Practice, 2006), and school psychology (e.g., Kratochwill & Stoiber, 2002) cannot be underestimated. As a specific process of helping, school consultation will clearly benefit from more careful scrutiny within an EBI framework, and authors of several handbook chapters undertake this challenge.

A perspective on school consultation research that is focused on the future naturally will need to incorporate other scientific concepts in addition to EBIs. A sampling of the possibilities includes advanced statistical techniques (e.g., structural equation modeling), specialized computer programs (e.g., Sequential Data Interchange Standard-Generalized Sequential Courier; Bakeman & Quera, 1995), and less commonly seen data collection and analysis strategies (e.g., ethnographic methods). Again, handbook chapter authors address these and other concepts associated with the empirical study of school consultation.

PURPOSE OF THE HANDBOOK

Given the preceding context, the *Handbook of Research in School Consultation: Empirical Foundations for the Field* intends to accomplish several goals. Specifically, as coeditors we have attempted to develop a single volume that

- offers critical, integrative, and progressive coverage of the state of the art of school consultation research;
- plots the future of the field by advancing cutting-edge research agendas, thereby pushing researchers to maximize research methodologies to explore important new questions;
- strikes a balance between offering content relevant to those who are consultation researchers and those who wish to learn more about the research literature to become more evidence based in their approach to consultation;
- promotes a scientist-practitioner framework by providing guidance for consultation practice that is based on research findings when defensible within this framework;
- considers the essence of school consultation to be a process of helping that produces significant outcomes for consultees and clients and therefore focuses explicitly on the specification of, and linkages between, the processes and outcomes of consultation;
- identifies the aspects of consultation practice that have not been adequately researched to date; and
- ultimately offers a forward-looking perspective on the enterprise of school consultation, thereby moving it closer to other recognized treatment approaches (e.g., psychotherapy) for which a strong evidence base exists currently.

In short, the 18 chapters comprising the *Handbook of Research in School Consultation* together provide an exhaustive review of the current research literature and specify what we know and what we need to know about school consultation research. An overview of the handbook and brief descriptions of individual chapters follow.

DESCRIPTION OF THE CONTENTS

This edited volume is comprised of five major parts. Besides the introductory and conclusion sections, the three others respectively provide content corresponding to methodological, measurement, and statistical foundations of school consultation research; process/outcome findings from five consultation models utilized in schools; and process/outcome results from four consultation research perspectives that inform — or have the potential to inform — school practice. At the end of each of these three parts are commentary chapters that integrate themes found in the section's chapters and propose future research issues and directions.

Section A, Introduction, consists of this overview chapter and a stage-setting chapter by Jennifer Frank and Thomas Kratochwill. Frank and Kratochwill's chapter 2 functions essentially as the substantive introductory chapter one typically encounters in a lengthy edited volume. Some provocative questions raised by these authors include the following: Is problem-solving consultation an intervention? If so, is it an EBI? How can research on effective consultation practices and EBIs be integrated to advance research and practice in both areas? Their answers are at times surprising and lead to a thoughtful consideration of how a consultation research agenda may progress using multitier prevention and levels-of-evidence frameworks.

In Section B, Methodological Foundations, there are four chapters that inform the reader of the primary methods or "tools" at the disposal of the consultation researcher, how these tools may be used, and implications of their use. Chapter 3, by Ann Schulte, focuses on the many psychological measurement issues present in school consultation research. Unique to Schulte's presentation is her consideration of perspectives offered by several sources reporting current standards or best practices in treatment research and her application of these perspectives to consultation research. Frank Gresham and Mike Vanderwood's chapter 4 offers a comprehensive review of quantitative research methods and designs in consultation, with a special emphasis on single-case experimental designs. They also highlight the importance of several sets of research standards as applied to the enterprise of consultation research.

Chapter 5, contributed by Joel Meyers, Stephen Truscott, Adena Meyers, Kristen Varjas, and Amanda Smith Collins, describes and critiques qualitative and mixed-method designs. The authors build a strong case for the application of these approaches to school consultation research and in particular argue for greater use of action research models. In chapter 6, Amanda VanDerHeyden and Joseph Witt comment on the preceding chapters, focusing on the scientific evidence that is needed to declare consultation an evidence-based practice and what makes a consultant effective.

Section C, What We Know: Process/Outcome Findings From Selected Models of Practice, is the lengthiest section of the handbook, perhaps reflecting that "consultation model" as a categorical scheme has been a time-honored way to organize the field's literature. The models considered are mental health consultation (MHC) and consultee-centered consultation (C-CC); behavioral consultation (BC); conjoint behavioral consultation (CBC); instructional consultation (IC) and instructional consultation teams (ICTs); and organizational development consultation (ODC). Each chapter in section C concludes with an extensive research agenda for the particular consultation model reviewed.

Chapter 7, by Steven Knotek, Maureen Kanuika, and Kirsten Ellingsen, describes and evaluates MHC, the original model of human services consultation, and C-CC, a modern version of MHC that appears well suited to the daily realities of schools. These authors discuss the future of C-CC relative to the model's effectiveness, transportability, and dissemination. In chapter 8, Brian Martens and Florence DiGennaro review BC, summarizing its past and posing future challenges to ensure the model will remain highly relevant to school-based practice. In their analysis, Martens and DiGennaro emphasize the importance of direct service components (e.g., client interventions, functional behavioral assessments) within BC.

Chapter 9, coauthored by Susan Sheridan, Brandy Clarke, and Jennifer Burt, offers a comprehensive look at CBC, the only model included in this volume that has a distinct home-school focus. Sheridan et al. summarize the model's growing empirical literature and conclude with a detailed research agenda that encourages CBC researchers to consider new settings, diverse clients, relationship effects, long-term outcomes, preventive aspects, and different methodological designs. In chapter 10, Sylvia Rosenfield, Arlene Silva, and Todd Gravois present ongoing research and program evaluation on IC and ICTs, two problem-solving consultation approaches that deal explicitly with the instructional context. As ICTs have been implemented in over 200 schools in the United States, these authors address the challenges inherent in moving from research to practice.

Chapter 11, by Robert Illback and Margaret Pennington, reviews the literature and research associated with organizational development and ODC. Although school-based ODC efforts generally have a limited empirical basis, Illback and Pennington note that PBS is one area that presents encouraging outcome data. Finally, in chapter 12, Emilia Lopez and Bonnie Nastasi offer their comments on the five other chapters in the section, noting integrative themes across consultation models and advancing issues for future study.

Section D, What We Know: Process/Outcome Findings From Selected Research Perspectives, is comprised of five chapters. In chapter 13, Colette Ingraham addresses the complicated topic of how to study multicultural aspects of school consultation. She reviews the literature through both content and methodological lenses and concludes by presenting sensible ways that cultural perspectives may be integrated into consultation research. Chapter 14, co-authored by William Erchul, Priscilla Grissom, and Kim Getty, centers on the role of social influence in school consultation as it plays out within consultant and consultee face-to-face interactions. Their review is constructed around the social power base and relational communication perspectives.

In chapter 15, George Noell points out the centrality of treatment plan implementation (TPI) to school consultation. Key questions he addresses are as follows: What are meaningful and practical methods for assessing TPI? How does TPI influence treatment outcome? What variables significantly influence TPI? Chapter 16, contributed by Jan Hughes, Linda Loyd, and Michelle Buss, revisits Caplan's (1970) model of mental health consultation. These authors review school consultation outcome research; present an updated version of MHC; and conclude with a discussion of implications of the model for training, practice, and research. Finally, in chapter 17 Susan Forman and Joseph Zins discuss themes found in the chapters of the section and highlight the importance of the consultee, context, and intervention implementation and sustainability issues within school consultation.

In Section E, the epilogue chapter, we attempt to integrate critical issues and offer some predictions about the future of school consultation research and its potential to guide practice. Although an optimistic note is sounded, considerable work remains to be done.

CONCLUSIONS

It has been stated that empirical research in consultation lags 20 to 30 years behind comparable research in psychotherapy (Meade, Hamilton, & Yuen, 1982) and 15 to 20 years behind comparable research in interpersonal communication (Erchul, 1993). On a related theme, we conclude this chapter by emphasizing that the practice of school consultation has developed at a much faster rate than the research base that should logically support it. Therein lies a central challenge and intended contribution of this handbook: to lessen the divide between practice and research in school consultation. We hope that the chapters that follow stimulate considerable thought and action, resulting in a greatly expanded scientific knowledge base that ultimately will lead to more efficacious and effective consulting practices in schools.

AUTHOR NOTE

It is with our heartfelt appreciation that we dedicate this chapter to Joseph E. Zins, who passed away unexpectedly in March 2006. During his career, Joe made many notable contributions to the science and practice of school consultation. Among these contributions was his service as editor of the *Journal of Educational and Psychological Consultation* and consulting psychologist to the Beechwood, Kentucky, Independent Schools. Perhaps most relevant to us was Joe's role as senior editor of the *Handbook of Consultation Services for Children* (Zins et al., 1993), the most direct predecessor to this handbook. Joe Zins was an ardent supporter of our professional efforts, and his impact on the field of school consultation will surely continue.

REFERENCES

Alpert, J. L., and Associates. (1982). *Psychological consultation in educational settings: A casebook for working with administrators, teachers, students, and community.* San Francisco: Jossey-Bass.

Alpert, J. L., & Yammer, M. D. (1983). Research in school consultation: A content analysis of selected journals. *Professional Psychology: Research and Practice, 14,* 604–612.

APA Presidential Task Force on Evidence-based Practice. (2006). Evidence-based practice in psychology. *American Psychologist, 61,* 271–285.

Bakeman, R., & Quera, V. (1995). *Analyzing interaction: Sequential analysis with SDIS and GSEQ.* New York: Cambridge University Press.

Bergan, J. R. (1977). *Behavioral consultation.* Columbus, OH: Merrill.

Brown, D., Pryzwansky, W. B., & Schulte, A. C. (2006). *Psychological consultation and collaboration: Introduction to theory and practice* (6th ed.). Boston: Pearson/Allyn & Bacon.

Busse, R. T., Kratochwill, T. R., & Elliott, S. N. (1995). Meta-analysis for single-case outcomes: Applications to research and practice. *Journal of School Psychology, 33*, 269–285.

Caplan, G. (1964). *Principles of preventive psychiatry.* New York: Basic Books.

Caplan, G. (1970). *The theory and practice of mental health consultation.* New York: Basic Books.

Conoley, J. C., & Conoley, C. W. (1982). *School consultation: A guide to practice and training.* Elmsford, NY: Pergamon Press.

Conoley, J. C., & Gutkin, T. B. (1986). School psychology: A reconceptualization of service delivery realities. In S. N. Elliott & J. C. Witt (Eds.), *The delivery of psychological services in schools: Concepts, processes, and issues* (pp. 393–424). Hillsdale, NJ: Erlbaum.

Costenbader, V., Swartz, J., & Petrix, L. (1992). Consultation in the schools: The relationship between preservice training, perception of consultation skills, and actual time spent in consultation. *School Psychology Review, 21*, 95–108.

Dee, C. C., & Cowan, K. C. (2006, October). Focus on mental health: Positive behavior supports. *NASP Communique, 35*(2), 44.

Duncan, C., & Pryzwansky, W. B. (1988). Consultation research: Trends in doctoral dissertations, 1978–1985. *Journal of School Psychology, 26*, 107–119.

Erchul, W. P. (1993). Selected interpersonal perspectives in consultation research. *School Psychology Quarterly, 8*, 38–49.

Erchul, W. P., & Martens, B. K. (2002). *School consultation: Conceptual and empirical bases of practice* (2nd ed.). New York: Kluwer Academic/Plenum.

Fagan, T. K., & Wise, P. S. (2000). *School psychology: Past, present, and future* (2nd ed.). Bethesda, MD: National Association of School Psychologists.

Fuchs, D., Fuchs, L. S., Dulan, J., Roberts, H., & Fernstrom, P. (1992). Where is the research on consultation effectiveness? *Journal of Educational and Psychological Consultation, 3*, 151–174.

Fuchs, D., Mock, D., Morgan, P. L., & Young, C. L. (2003). Responsiveness-to-intervention: Definitions, evidence, and implications for the learning disabilities construct. *Learning Disabilities Research & Practice, 18*, 157–171.

Gordon, R. (1987). An operational classification of disease prevention. In J. A. Steinberg & M. M. Silverman (Eds.), *Preventing mental disorder* (pp. 20–26). Rockville, MD: U.S. Department of Health and Human Services.

Gresham, F. M., & Kendell, G. K. (1987). School consultation research: Methodological critique and future research directions. *School Psychology Review, 16*, 306–316.

Gresham, F. M., & Noell, G. H. (1993). Documenting the effectiveness of consultation outcomes. In J. E. Zins, T. R. Kratochwill, & S. N. Elliott (Eds.), *Handbook of consultation services for children: Applications in educational and clinical settings* (pp. 249–273). San Francisco: Jossey-Bass.

Gutkin, T. B. (1993). Conducting consultation research. In J. E. Zins, T. R. Kratochwill, & S. N. Elliott (Eds.), *Handbook of consultation services for children: Applications in educational and clinical settings* (pp. 227–248). San Francisco: Jossey-Bass.

Gutkin, T. B., & Conoley, J. C. (1990). Reconceptualizing school psychology from a service delivery perspective: Implications for practice, training, and research. *Journal of School Psychology, 28*, 203–223.

Gutkin, T. B., & Curtis, M. J. (1999). School-based consultation theory and practice: The art and science of indirect service delivery. In C. R. Reynolds & T. B. Gutkin (Eds.), *Handbook of school psychology* (3rd ed., pp. 598–637). New York: Wiley.

Kratochwill, T. R., Elliott, S. N., & Stoiber, K. C. (2002). Best practices in school-based problem-solving consultation. In A. Thomas & J. Grimes (Eds.), *Best practices in school consultation IV* (pp. 583–608). Bethesda, MD: National Association of School Psychologists.

Kratochwill, T. R., Sheridan, S. M., & VanSomeren, K. R. (1988). Research in behavioral consultation: Current status and future directions. In J. F. West (Ed.), *School consultation: Interdisciplinary perspectives on theory, research, training, and practice* (pp. 77–102). Austin, TX: Association of Educational and Psychological Consultants.

Kratochwill, T. R., & Stoiber, K. C. (2002). Evidence-based interventions in school psychology: Conceptual foundations of the Procedural and Coding Manual of Division 16 and the Society for the Study of School Psychology Task Force. *School Psychology Quarterly, 17*, 341–389.

Lewis, T. J., & Newcomer, L. L. (2002). Examining the efficacy of school-based consultation: Recommendations for improving outcomes. *Child & Family Behavior Therapy, 24*, 165–181.

Mannino, F. V., & Shore, M. F. (1975). The effects of consultation: A review of the literature. *American Journal of Community Psychology, 3,* 1–21.

Martens, B. K. (1993). A behavioral approach to consultation. In J. E. Zins, T. R. Kratochwill, & S. N. Elliott (Eds.), *Handbook of consultation services for children: Applications in educational and clinical settings* (pp. 65–86). San Francisco: Jossey-Bass.

Meade, C. J., Hamilton, M. K., & Yuen, R. K. (1982). Consultation research: The time has come, the walrus said. *Counseling Psychologist, 10,* 39–51.

Medway, F. J. (1979). How effective is school consultation? A review of recent research. *Journal of School Psychology, 17,* 275–282.

Medway, F. J. (1982). School consultation research: Past trends and future directions. *Professional Psychology, 13,* 422–430.

Medway, F. J., & Updyke, J. F. (1985). Meta-analysis of consultation outcome studies. *American Journal of Community Psychology, 13,* 489–505.

Newman, R. G. (1967). *Psychological consultation in the schools.* New York: Basic Books.

Norcross, J. C., Beutler, L. E., & Levant, R. F. (Eds.). (2006). *Evidence-based practices in mental health: Debate and dialogue on the fundamental questions.* Washington, DC: American Psychological Association.

Office of Special Education Programs Technical Assistance Center on Positive Behavioral Interventions and Supports. (n.d.). *School-wide PBS.* Retrieved October 30, 2006, from http://www.pbis.org/schoolwide.htm.

Ponti, C. R., Zins, J. E., & Graden, J. L. (1988). Implementing a consultation-based service delivery system to decrease referrals for special education: A case study of organizational considerations. *School Psychology Review, 17,* 89–100.

Pryzwansky, W. B. (1986). Indirect service delivery: Considerations for future research in consultation. *School Psychology Review, 15,* 479–488.

Reddy, L. A., Barboza-Whitehead, S., Files, T., & Rubel, E. (2000). Clinical focus of consultation outcome research with children and adolescents. *Special Services in the Schools, 16,* 1–22.

Sarason, S. B. (1971). *The culture of the school and the problem of change.* Boston: Allyn & Bacon.

Sheridan, S. M., & Gutkin, T. B. (2000). The ecology of school psychology: Examining and changing our paradigm for the 21st century. *School Psychology Review, 29,* 485–502.

Sheridan, S. M., & Kratochwill, T. R. (2007). *Conjoint behavioral consultation: Promoting family-school connections and interventions* (2nd ed.). New York: Springer.

Sheridan, S. M., Welch, M., & Orme, S. F. (1996). Is consultation effective? A review of outcome research. *Remedial and Special Education, 17,* 341–354.

Tharp, R. G., & Wetzel, R. J. (1969). *Behavior modification in the natural environment.* San Diego: Academic Press.

Weinstein, R. S. (1982). Establishing a mental health team in a middle school. In J. L. Alpert and Associates, *Psychological consultation in educational settings: A casebook for working with administrators, teachers, students, and community* (pp. 85–107). San Francisco: Jossey-Bass.

West, J. F., & Idol, L. (1987). School consultation (part I): An interdisciplinary perspective on theory, models, and research. *Journal of Learning Disabilities, 20,* 388–408.

Zins, J. E. (1995). Has consultation achieved its primary prevention potential? *Journal of Primary Prevention, 15,* 285–301.

Zins, J. E., & Erchul, W. P. (2002). Best practices in school consultation. In A. Thomas & J. Grimes (Eds.), *Best practices in school psychology IV* (pp. 625–643). Bethesda, MD: National Association of School Psychologists.

Zins, J. E., Kratochwill, T. R., & Elliott, S. N. (Eds.). (1993). *Handbook of consultation services for children: Applications in educational and clinical settings.* San Francisco: Jossey-Bass.

2

School-Based Problem-Solving Consultation
Plotting a New Course for Evidence-Based Research and Practice in Consultation

JENNIFER L. FRANK

Vanderbilt University

THOMAS R. KRATOCHWILL

University of Wisconsin-Madison

For decades, the consultation problem-solving approach to intervention has been the driving force in school psychology practice (Allen & Graden, 2002; Bergan & Kratochwill, 1990; Chalfant & Pysh, 1989; Graden, Casey, & Christenson, 1985; Zins, 1996; Zins & Erchul, 2002). Although variations of problem solving have emerged in consultation literature and practice, most psychologists adhere to a stage-based model that emphasizes the need for collaboration with professionals and parents, functional problem definition, assessment for intervention, ongoing progress monitoring, and evaluating outcomes to determine intervention effectiveness (Bergan & Kratochwill, 1990; Kratochwill, Elliott, & Stoiber, 2002).

Because consultation has been a vehicle for the delivery of various effective social/emotional and academic interventions, it is often presented in the literature as an effective form of intervention independent of the intervention embedded in the consultation problem-solving process. Indeed, one might see various advocates of problem-solving consultation noting that "consultation is effective" in addressing X, Y, and Z problems. With the evolution of the evidence-based intervention movement in psychology and education (see Kratochwill & Shernoff, 2004, for an overview), a natural question to ask is: Is consultation supported by a comprehensive research base? The question of whether problem-solving consultation can be considered an evidence-based intervention, based on a literature review or meta-analysis of the problem-solving literature, is challenging on two counts. First, although reviews of the problem-solving consultation literature have found it to be a generally effective model for directing both individual and team-based school intervention service delivery processes (e.g., Medway & Updyke, 1985; Sheridan, Welch, & Orme, 1996), the methodological rigor of some research included in these reviews casts doubt on the validity of this assumption (Gresham & Kendell, 1987; Kratochwill & Stoiber, 2002).

Improving the quality of empirical evidence available for reviewers to draw from is only the first step toward establishing an evidence base for problem-solving consultation. Other more complex conceptual issues loom large for scholars eager to establish consultation models or processes as evidence based. Whether effective consultative practices can now or could really ever be considered an evidence-based intervention depends greatly on how the field of school psychology stands in relation to what we believe to be the critical questions at hand:

1. Is problem-solving consultation an intervention? If so, how is it similar to or different from other types of interventions?
2. When examining student- or systems-level outcomes, can we separate the effect of the problem-solving process from the effect due to the content of the intervention itself?
3. How can research on effective consultation practices and evidence-based interventions be integrated to advance research and practice in both areas?

Consideration of these critical conceptual issues, yet unexplored within either the consultation or evidence-based intervention literatures, has unfortunately taken a back seat to the ongoing call to arms to enhance the methodological quality of consultation research generally. Although enhancing the quality of consultation research is a necessary and important goal, focusing attention on only the quality of evidence for problem-solving consultation diverts attention from the more complex, and arguably more interesting, questions raised as we consider the current or future status of problem-solving consultation as an evidence-based intervention. Although we cannot answer these questions entirely at this juncture, it is our hope that addressing these critical conceptual questions directly will stimulate much-needed discussion of the broader goals related to what school psychology as a field hopes to accomplish with its expanding consultation and evidence-based intervention knowledge base and finite resources needed to implement these programs and practices. This chapter is dedicated to exploring these critical questions in greater depth, beginning what we hope to become an ongoing dialogue within the field of school psychology regarding the current and future of research on evidence-based interventions and consultation.

IS PROBLEM-SOLVING CONSULTATION AN INTERVENTION?

Consideration of problem-solving consultation as an intervention raises some interesting questions regarding how a school-based intervention should be defined and what necessary and sufficient intervention components must be in place before we can say that an intervention has occurred at all. Scholarship over the past quarter century has provided a strong foundation for judging the relative quality of experimental intervention research, but these criteria do not necessarily differentiate an intervention from a simple reaction or response to a given problem or issue.

This question is important from both professional and practical standpoints. First, the question of what is, and is not, an intervention within a given helping profession is vitally important as it is intimately linked to professional identity and legitimacy of claims to specialized knowledge. Historically, helping professions that fail to articulate clearly what it is they know how to do, how it is different from what other professions know how to do, how they know it works, and how they regulate the applied use of this specialized knowledge are co-opted by professions that have a more readily understandable, identifiable, and organized professional paradigm in place (Abbott, 1988, 2001). Therefore, defining what is, and is not, an intervention within our profession is an arguably worthwhile endeavor from both scholarly and practical standpoints.

Using Logic Models to Operationalize Intervention Components and Design Tests of Intervention Theories of Action

A useful conceptual tool for clarifying and organizing intervention-related information is through the use of a logic model. A logic model specifies the theory of action or established links between interven-

Evidence-Based Intervention Logic Model

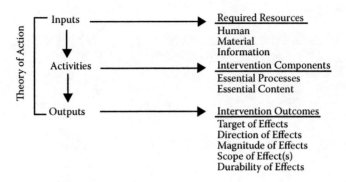

Figure 2.1   Structure of intervention logic model.

tion inputs, activities, and outcomes. A logic model specifies which types of inputs are required for an intervention to work and how these inputs are used to engage in necessary intervention activities that ultimately result in the intervention outcomes we observe. In essence, logic models are a tool to operationalize the necessary and sufficient components of an intervention in a purely empirical and atheoretical fashion. Because they are atheoretical, logic models do not necessarily explain why the intervention works. In fact, one (or more) theories can be evoked to explain why a given input may result in a given output. However, because they are atheoretical they are powerful for organizing and synthesizing complex interventions that may be understood from multiple (and sometimes competing) theories.

Figure 2.1 provides an overview of what we believe to be a widely generalizable logic model for organizing the essential intervention components of an evidence-based intervention. Table 2.1 illustrates how this generic model might be applied to a specific intervention. As the figure implies, distinctions between different types of evidence-based interventions on the basis of their (a) required inputs (i.e., required human, material, and informational resources); (b) required activities (i.e., required processes or intervention content that is delivered); and (c) expected outputs (i.e., observed intervention outcomes classified according to changes in the direction, magnitude, scope, or durability of intervention effects). Although there is some variation in the names and degree of subdivision within each category (e.g., whether short-term or long-term outputs are considered), most are used to describe the relationship among resources (inputs), components (necessary activities and content), and outputs (important outcomes of interest) (McLaughlin & Jordan, 1999). When intervention essential components include both processes and content, making conceptual and experimental distinctions between the two is critical.

Considered from this perspective, for problem-solving consultation to be considered an intervention, it must have stable and observable intervention components and required inputs, activities, and outputs. For problem-solving consultation to be considered evidence based, the theory of action or assumed links among inputs, activities, and outputs must be validated experimentally. To do this, we must be able to operationalize, manipulate, and observe the effects of manipulating the essential components of the intervention in question. Our confidence in this theory of action grows as different intervention components are subjected to experimental evaluation over a period of many years and by many different researchers. Throughout this process, it is critical that the necessary and sufficient program components remain the focus of any experimental efficacy, effectiveness, or dissemination efforts. Failure to ensure that the necessary and sufficient program components have either been controlled for or fully manipulated within experimental designs is an incomplete test of the intervention's theory of action.

Table 2.1   Proposed Taxonomy to Organize Consultation Research

Design	Level of Intervention	Mediator
Efficacy	Universal	Dyad
		Team
		System
	Selected	Dyad
		Team
		System
	Indicated	Dyad
		Team
		System
Transportability	Universal	Dyad
		Team
		System
	Selected	Dyad
		Team
		System
	Indicated	Dyad
		Team
		System
Dissemination	Universal	Dyad
		Team
		System
	Selected	Dyad
		Team
		System
	Indicated	Dyad
		Team
		System
Systems evaluation	Universal	Dyad
		Team
		System
	Selected	Dyad
		Team
		System
	Indicated	Dyad
		Team
		System

SIMILARITIES AND DIFFERENCES BETWEEN MEDIATOR-BASED AND NON-MEDIATOR-BASED INTERVENTIONS: DEFINING THE INTERVENTION COMPONENTS OF THE CONSULTATION PROCESS

Operationalizing the active intervention components of the consultation process as an evidence-based intervention is particularly difficult. This is due to the (a) lack of specificity regarding the necessary and sufficient intervention inputs, including assessment information and material intervention resources; (b) conceptual and experimental overlap between the process and content features of consultation; and (c) difficulty controlling for the various mediator and moderator variables known to have an impact on the efficacy of student interventions delivered through a consultative process.

Required Inputs of Problem-Solving Consultation

Problem-solving consultation is not typically implemented as a "packaged" intervention, and there is no single manual that describes completely what a problem-solving team or individual consultant must do to ensure results. Thus, the required inputs of problem-solving consultation are not clearly known.

Required Activities of Problem-Solving Consultation

Although the inputs of problem-solving consultation may be less than clear at this point, there is ample evidence to support the efficacy and effectiveness of the activity components or process features of problem-solving consultation. In fact, the process features are among the best-articulated features of problem-solving consultation and have been fairly well studied in the existing empirical literature.

Essential Process Components of Problem-Solving Consultation

The intervention process features of problem-solving consultation include the relationships and interactions between consultant and consultee and are typically prescriptive in directing consultants to perform specific behaviors (Kratochwill & Pittman, 2002). For example, the need to establish and maintain a collaborative relationship has been a frequently cited critical component defining the process features of problem-solving consultation and is prescribed in virtually all models of consultation.

Although variations of problem-solving consultation have emerged in the consultation literature and practice, most adhere to a stage-based model that emphasizes processes such as the need for collaboration with professionals and parents, use of functional problem definition, assessment to design the intervention, ongoing progress monitoring, and evaluation of outcomes to determine intervention efficacy. As a framework for the process of consultation, consider the phases outlined by Kratochwill, Elliott, and Carrington Rotto (1995): (a) relationship building, (b) problem identification, (c) problem analysis, (d) intervention implementation, and (e) program evaluation. A review of the literature to support the effectiveness of each of these intervention components is considered next.

Relationship Building

The first stage of the problem-solving process typically involves some type of relationship building. During this stage, a consultant focuses on applying strategies to develop rapport and build trust with the consultee. A considerable amount of research has shown that the benefits of consultation depend largely on the relationship that is established between the consultant and the consultee (e.g., Gutkin & Curtis, 1999; Martin, 1978). Consultants who do not actively work to create a supportive, encouraging climate in consultation meetings may render less-than-optimal outcomes when consultees are expected to implement the intervention program independently. Findings from this area of research have led to a set of tasks that help to form a good relationship between the consultant and the consultee. According to Allen and Graden (2002), relationship building within a consultant-consultee relationship can be enhanced by (a) establishing and maintaining a sense of rapport, trust, and respect; (b) clarifying expectations, roles, and responsibilities from the outset; (c) discussing relevant legal and ethical guidelines early in the process; (d) establishing a preferred means of communication; (e) making certain that all members understand the problem-solving process and are supportive of it; (f) using language that is familiar to everyone involved, without the use of technical jargon; (g) sharing valuable information between team members; and (h) incorporating team members' perspectives and opinions (Colton & Sheridan, 1998; Sheridan & Kratochwill, 1992).

Problem Identification

During the problem identification stage, a consultant works to define the target behavior in observable terms and describe the topography of the behavior in terms of frequency, duration, or intensity. Conducting team-based problem solving often involves coming to a consensus regarding the specific problems or keystone behaviors that need to be addressed. An important outcome of this process is to establish a baseline measure of behavioral data and to use this information to construct operational goals and temporal benchmarks for achieving those goals. Ideally, the behavioral assessment data used to establish the baseline for performance is continually gathered throughout the duration of the intervention, thus providing the consultant with a continuous picture of changes in student behavior before, during, and after intervention.

Problem Analysis

During the problem analysis stage, a consultant typically uses various assessment methods to identify critical child-environment interactions responsible for maintaining the target behavior and develops a plan to remove the contingencies. This process may involve conducting a functional behavioral assessment, observing the student in the classroom, or administering student, parent, or teacher interviews. During this stage of the problem-solving process, the consultant and consultee work together to try to understand the antecedents and consequences maintaining the identified problem. Consultants who use complicated or technical terminology often damage the collaborative, cooperative nature of the consultant-consultee relationship (Bergan & Kratochwill, 1990).

Intervention Implementation

During the intervention implementation stage, a consultant typically monitors the implementation of the intervention plan and provides assistance as needed to ensure that the intervention is implemented with integrity. For those embracing an evidence-based approach, a key consideration at this stage is to identify an evidence-based intervention known to be effective in treating the target behaviors in question (Kratochwill & Stoiber, 2002). A consultant, in turn, may need to train consultees in how to implement the evidence-based intervention with integrity.

Program Evaluation

During the problem evaluation phase, a consultant typically evaluates the effectiveness of the intervention and determines if the intervention should be adapted to enhance intervention effectiveness or integrity. This process involves observing the teacher or student in classroom or other natural settings to determine if the intervention has been successful. If the intervention has not been successful, then the consultant can determine if the lack of success was due to an integrity problem or if the intervention itself did not work for the particular student. Depending on the perceived reason for failure to obtain successful outcomes, the consultant can cycle back through any of the previous steps, reanalyze the student's problem, select a different intervention, or review procedures for administering the intervention with integrity.

Systematic reviews of problem solving within the consultation literature suggest that problem solving results in more effective intervention outcomes for students and systems when the process features of problem solving are implemented (e.g., Medway & Updyke, 1985; Sheridan et al., 1996). However, researchers conducting consultation efficacy or effectiveness studies have seldom examined the various features or components of the problem-solving consultation process systematically to examine possible differential contributions to student outcomes. Thus, when we examine the literature reviews of consultation, we do not find answers to questions about the contribution of various process (or content) components of the problem-solving process.

Essential Content Components of Problem-Solving Consultation

Within the problem-solving literature, the connection between the content of consultation and actual interventions delivered has been discussed in a somewhat general way. Discussions of problem solving have suggested that intervention selection (whether by teams or individual consultants) is primarily informed by problem severity and the degree of resources needed to address problems.

Although some researchers have examined contextual variables that facilitate or inhibit the success of intervention teams' implementation of problem-solving processes, none thus far have examined whether adherence to a problem-solving model necessarily encourages the identification and implementation of evidence-based interventions, which in turn results in superior intervention outcomes. Stated differently, although effective consultation practices are a necessary component of effective interventions within an indirect service delivery model, probably they are by no means sufficient.

Can We Separate the Effect of Essential Problem-Solving Processes from Intervention Content?

An important assumption of evidence-based interventions is that critical components of the intervention interact with client characteristics to result in effective intervention outcomes. In theory, the process of consultation provides the structure and organization necessary so that evidence-based interventions can be delivered with sufficient dosage to have an impact on client target behaviors. Certainly, other indirect beneficial factors associated with the use of problem-solving consultation could be cited, but from a purely evidence-based perspective, the critical contribution of consultation is to ensure the delivery and appropriate dosage of effective intervention components. The assumption that problem-solving consultation results in an increased likelihood of identifying or implementing evidence-based interventions has yet to be tested experimentally. Indeed, the interrelationship between specific process components and specific content components is poorly understood.

Mediators Influencing the Link Between Intervention Activities and Outputs

Although the majority of studies on problem-solving consultation processes have occurred in the field as effectiveness trials, systematic investigation of key mediating variables that have an impact on the implementation of problem-solving consultation processes, and how these processes are linked to outcomes and sustainability, are few and far between. Among these, the most consistently identifiable variables with a clear and definite link to student- or system-level outcomes include integrity and acceptability. Certainly, other important factors have been identified, but the important link among integrity, acceptability, and consultation outcomes has been the most widely studied and replicated. What we are beginning to learn about the operation of these two variables is described next.

Integrity of Interventions Delivered Through Problem-Solving Consultation

Although problem-solving consultation can promote the adoption of interventions, the ultimate effectiveness of mediator-based interventions has been found to depend largely on the consultee's ability to implement the selected intervention with integrity (Sanetti & Kratochwill, 2005). If an intervention is not implemented as intended, then it is difficult to determine the cause of any resulting outcomes (Gresham, 1989; Gresham, Gansle, Noell, Cohen, & Rosenblum, 1993; Sterling-Turner, Watson, & Moore, 2002). Bergan and Kratochwill (1990) and Sheridan, Welch et al. (1996) suggested that consultation can work to promote high treatment integrity among consultees, and several researchers have tried to identify the specific techniques that promote high treatment integrity (Sanetti & Kratochwill, 2005). The following suggestions have resulted from that line of study: (a) make use of treatment scripts (Erhardt, Barnett, Lentz, Stollar, & Reifin, 1996); (b) implement consultee goal-setting and feedback procedures (Martens et al., 1997); (c) incorporate performance feedback interviews (Noell, Witt, Gilbertson, Ranier, & Freeland, 1997); (d) directly train teachers on treatment integrity for each intervention (Sterling-Turner, Watson, & Moore, 2002); and (e) make use of interventions that have high treatment acceptability for the teachers (Finn & Sladeczek, 2001; Rones & Hoagwood, 2000).

Intervention Acceptability

Adoption of an intervention is intimately tied to treatment acceptability. Several researchers have tried to determine how to make the interventions proposed in consultation more acceptable to teachers (for reviews, see Cowan & Sheridan, 2003; Eckert & Hintze, 2000; Elliott, 1988; Reimers, Wacker, & Koeppl, 1987). Some of the preliminary findings suggest that interventions will be more likely to be accepted by teachers if they are (a) positive rather than negative (Elliott, Witt, Galvin, & Peterson, 1984; Kazdin, 1980; Witt, Elliott, & Martens, 1984; Witt & Robbins, 1985); (b) simple rather than complex (Elliott, 1988; Reimers et al., 1987); (c) in response to severe, rather than mild, child behavior (Elliott et al., 1984; Witt, Moe, Gutkin, & Andrews, 1984); (d) implemented with high integrity (Witt & Elliott, 1985); and (e) considered effective (Witt & Elliott, 1985).

Overall, although we are beginning to understand more about key mediators and moderators of consultation outcomes and factors that have an impact on the idealized processes that connect program inputs, outputs, and outcomes, a variety of other interesting mediators and moderators could be the subject of a fruitful line(s) of research (see Noell, chapter 15, this volume). Additional focused qualitative studies of problem-solving consultation processes in various types of schools or among different team configurations could provide further examples of important unexplored variables worthy of further experimental investigation. However, the current consultation literature is replete with investigator footnotes and discussion sections referencing client, consultant, team, and contextual factors with operation and impact on consultation outcomes that is yet unknown.

Outputs of Problem-Solving Consultation

Problem solving, like many mediator-based interventions, has evolved over time in response to a number of complex professional and political trends. However, because studies have not reliably specified how different types of outputs are reliably related (or unrelated) to changes in intervention activities or required inputs, we cannot say with certainty that the same theory of action was tested in each study. However, some reliably observed outcome effects are consistently cited across the consultation literature.

Efficiency in Service Delivery
School-based problem-solving approaches evolved within the behavioral consultation literature as an alternative to expert-based models of consultation (Telzrow, McNamara, & Hollinger, 2000). This transition from expert consultant to collaborator was concurrent with a number of shifts in school demographics, theoretical and assessment technologies, graduate-level training content, special education law, and accountability requirements that made problem solving an attractive model for delivering school-based consultation services. In particular, the indirect nature of school-based problem solving has long been promoted as a more time-effective approach to service delivery because intervention providers could affect many more children than could be reached with traditional direct approaches (Gutkin, 1996; Gutkin & Curtis, 1999; Kratochwill, Elliott, & Busse, 1995; Zins & Erchul, 2002). Considered in this light, problem-solving consultation could be conceptualized as an intervention that targets school psychology practitioners with the intervention goal, or output, more time-efficient service delivery.

Ecologically Valid Assessment Results
Many early proponents of the problem-solving model argued that interventions were most effective when student assessment, intervention, and outcomes evaluation took into account unique student characteristics and local context. School-based problem solving gained popularity as many states and districts began to promote a functional classroom-based philosophy that embraced the notion that understanding the interaction between the child and environment is critical to developing effective interventions (Reschly & Tilly, 1999; Shinn, Good, & Parker, 1999; Ysseldyke & Marston, 1999). Therefore, a second goal or output of problem-solving consultation might reasonably be considered to be the production and use of ecologically valid assessment results in school psychological practice.

Context for Multidisciplinary Collaboration
The adoption of problem solving as a model for school-based teams has been driven in part by several important pieces of legislation, and developments in best practice standards have increased the need for interdisciplinary collaboration in providing intervention services. For example, the Title V of the 1973 Rehabilitation Act included the provision of a "free and appropriate education" as a right for all students. This provision required that public schools admit students with disabilities who previously would have been denied access to the general education system. A variety of regulations emerging from the 1997 reauthorization of the Individuals With Disabilities Education Act (IDEA) also significantly increased the need for consultative services in schools. Of particular relevance is the fact that IDEA requires that (a) schools serve students with disabilities in the least-restrictive environment (often, the regular classroom); (b) schools develop Individual Education Plans (IEPs) for any student identified as in need of special services, and that the IEP contains plans for intervention strategies and supports specifically designed to address each student's particular needs; and (c) IEP teams conduct a functional behavioral assessment, develop a positive behavior support plan, and identify goals for outcome evaluation. Therefore, a third goal or output of problem-solving consultation might rightfully be considered a process to enhance interdisciplinary collaboration and direct school-based team activities through a sequential organized process consistent with federal regulations and due process requirements.

Achieving Intervention Goals

Like many other mediator-based interventions, goals of problem-solving consultation focused on individual (vs. system-level) outcomes are client rather than intervention (in this case, problem-solving) specific. Because problem solving does not have a consistent unitary goal or outcome measure at the individual level that transcends clients, treatment contexts, and time, it necessarily lacks a single logic model and associated theory of action that can be tested experimentally and identified as evidence based or not evidence based. Considered together, if we cannot say with certainty what problem-solving consultation is (and is not) intended to accomplish for an individual student, then it is difficult to judge the relative quantity or quality of associated evidence for individual student-level effects.

IS PROBLEM-SOLVING CONSULTATION AN EVIDENCE-BASED INTERVENTION?

Whether considered as a systems-level or individual-level intervention, fitting problem-solving consultation into an evidence-based intervention framework is difficult despite a considerable and diverse array of literature attesting to its multiple and varied effects. First, problem-solving consultation has highly variable intervention inputs, and the effects of required (or optional) inputs in terms of human, material, or informational resources on intervention activities and outcomes are only partially understood. Second, separating the necessary and sufficient process and content components of problem-solving consultation is conceptually and experimentally challenging. Although such investigations may be technically possible, to date no such studies have been undertaken. Finally, in the absence of a consistent logic model to operationalize the problem-solving consultation construct across studies, we cannot say with certainty whether the same theory of action has been experimentally tested, replicated, and extended across all of these studies.

Considered together, although the question of whether school-based problem solving is an evidence-based intervention is intriguing, it is an ill-posed question that may not be possible to answer easily from a purely empirical standpoint. Given the current status of our knowledge base, a far more researchable set of questions might be: How and under which conditions do school-based problem-solving consultation processes enhance the effectiveness of evidence-based interventions? Which features of problem-solving facilitate the identification of appropriate interventions? Which features facilitate or inhibit intervention integrity? How do consultants and mediators adapt intervention components to fit the local context? What are the implications of such adaptations?

How Can Research on Effective Consultation Practices and Evidence-based Interventions Be Integrated To Advance Research and Practice In Both Areas?

Despite the aforementioned limitations, school psychology's wealth of knowledge about effective school-based consultation models and practices is foundational for understanding the means to transport evidence-based interventions to school settings. In this respect, school-based consultation models such as problem solving could be thought of as the missing chapter in many evidence-based intervention manuals on how to get interventions to work in complex and sometimes resistant school settings.

Problem-Solving Consultation and Systems Change: Consultation as a Component of Multitier Prevention Models and Response to Intervention

Since its early conceptualizations, the consultation paradigm has been linked to the concept of prevention. The prevention concept has been central to conceptual models of both mental health (e.g.,

Caplan & Caplan, 1993) and behavioral consultation (e.g., Bergan & Kratochwill, 1990). One of the stated advantages of consultation is that it can contribute to teacher competencies and thereby prevent future problems from occurring (e.g., Gutkin & Curtis, 1999). Yet, consultation researchers have been guided by a heavy focus on outcome research that embraces an effectiveness model by which "prereferral" problems are addressed. To help advance the research agenda, a broader and more complex model of intervention (read prevention) could be considered as a framework for future research that makes systematic distinctions among universal, selected, and indicated levels of preventive intervention (Gordon, 1987; Institute of Medicine, 1994).

Universal Preventive Interventions

Universal preventive interventions target the general or a whole student population that has not been identified on the basis of individual risk. Universal programs may address a group as large as the entire school-age population in a district or may be more narrowly directed at children in a specific grade level or a specific group identified by characteristics unrelated to risk. Exemplars of universal school-based programs in which consultation processes could be relevant might include school-based drug prevention programs or schoolwide positive behavior support.

Selective Preventive Interventions

Selective interventions target individuals or subgroups (based on biological or social risk factors) whose risk of developing academic or mental health disorders is significantly higher than average. Examples of selective intervention programs include home visitation and infant day care for low birth weight children, preschool programs for all children from poor neighborhoods, and support groups for children who have suffered losses/traumas. Studies examining beneficial modifications or adaptations to traditional problem-solving consultation processes when used with specific groups of individuals with specific needs or intervention issues could be yet another fruitful area of future research.

Indicated Preventive Interventions

Indicated preventive interventions target individuals who are identified as having early signs or symptoms or biological markers related to academic or mental health disorders but who do not yet meet diagnostic criteria. Providing social skills or parent-child interaction training for children who have early behavioral problems is an example of an indicated intervention.

Benefits of a Multitier Prevention Focus

Linking problem-solving processes to these more descriptive levels of intervention offers a number of advantages over traditional conceptualizations of problem-solving intervention levels. First, consultation research could expand in scope to consider how variations in consultation inputs and activities result in differential effectiveness when applied across multiple levels of service delivery (rather than simply focus on the effects of mediator-based individual intervention through a teacher or parent). Second, multitier models are inherently more focused on prevention and early intervention service provision. Reframing consultation research in accordance with a multitier framework would allow for an expanded research agenda by which consultation outputs could include outcome indicators related to both problem solving and problem prevention. Finally, the multitier model of intervention allows consultation researchers and practitioners to link their work to a much larger literature base on evidence-based interventions and prevention science (see Weisz,

Doss, & Hawley, 2005). Indeed, those in the field of school psychology are well poised to share their consultation expertise with investigators from a variety of disciplines and areas of study. The potential theoretical, methodological, and practical advances that could arise from the formation of such interdisciplinary partnerships cannot be underestimated.

Agenda for Reconfiguring the Design of Consultation Research:
Systematic Progression Through Levels of Evidence

Experimental studies of the effectiveness of problem-solving consultation processes varies greatly regarding design, operationalization of key constructs, selection of dependent variables, and control of important mediators and moderators of intervention outcomes (for critiques of the literature, see Erchul & Martens, 2002; Sheridan, Welch, et al., 1996; West & Idol, 1990; Witt, Gresham, & Noell, 1996). In future consultation research, it will be useful to make some distinctions that have been made in development of evidence-based interventions. Traditional distinctions in the evidence-based intervention research literature involve the concepts of effectiveness and efficacy (Chambless et al., 1998; Fonagy, Target, Cottrell, Phillips, & Kurtz, 2002; Nathan & Gorman, 2002). *Efficacy* is the standard for evaluating interventions in controlled research; *effectiveness* is the standard for evaluating interventions in a practice context. Efficacy studies are generally conducted in laboratories or clinical research facilities and use methodologies intended to ensure group equivalence among other features; they are usually designated as randomized controlled trials. In contrast, effectiveness studies focus on the generalizability of the intervention to practice contexts. Both efficacy and effectiveness studies are critical to establish the evidence base of interventions. Expanding on these critical distinctions, Chorpita (2003) grouped research designed to advance evidence-based practice into the following four types: efficacy, transportability, dissemination, and system evaluation studies.

Type I: Efficacy Studies

Efficacy studies evaluate interventions in a controlled research context. Efficacy studies could prove useful in clarifying the necessary and sufficient components of consultation and validating the theory of action of consultation models.

Type II: Transportability Studies

Transportability studies examine not only the degree to which intervention effects generalize from research to practice settings, but also the feasibility of implementing and the acceptability of evidence-based interventions in practice settings (Schoenwald & Hoagwood, 2001). In applied settings, practitioners are faced with administrative, logistical, and ethical issues (to name just a few) that may not be part of the efficacy research agenda (Backer, Liberman, & Kuehnel, 1986; Kazdin et al., 1986). Thus, transportability studies allow for the examination of how various contextual issues (e.g., training requirements, characteristics of the treatment provider, training resources, acceptability of treatments, cost and time efficiency, and administrative supports) facilitate or constrain the effective transport of evidence-based interventions into practice settings (e.g., Hoagwood, Burns, Kiser, Ringeisen, & Schoenwald, 2001). Here, transportability studies could be used to examine important mediator and moderator variables within a consultative logic model and identify important adaptations and modifications with effects that should be studied experimentally prior to more widespread dissemination.

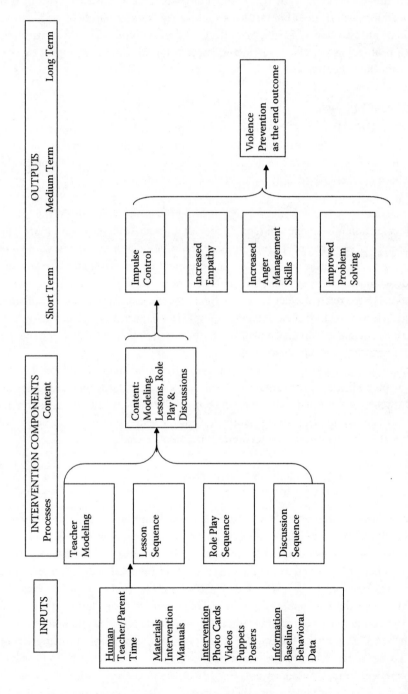

Figure 2.2   Logic model of hypothetical school-based violence prevention program.

Type III: Dissemination Studies

Dissemination studies use intervention agents that are part of the system of services — in our case, the school. In this type of research, an intervention protocol would be deployed in the school and carried out, for example, by school psychologists serving either as direct intervention agents or as mediators working with consultees such as teachers or parents (see Kratochwill & Pittman, 2002, for an overview of mediator options). Because Type III research still involves a formal research protocol, researcher control and supervision may have an impact on the intervention and its ultimate effectiveness.

Type IV: System Evaluation Studies

To establish independence from the "investigator effect" present in dissemination studies, another type of research — system evaluation studies — can be undertaken. Establishing the additive effects of consultation to intervention outcomes would be the last stage in establishing empirically what works in consultation to achieve specific ends.

Given these distinctions, the most productive melding of consultation within the broader evidence-based intervention movement will require consultation research to strike a more equal balance between studies of effectiveness of specific consultation models and processes, and questions of how consultation can be used to enhance the acceptability, effectiveness, and sustainability of specific evidence-based interventions in specific school settings. For example, at each level of research, variations in the relative effectiveness of different consultation processes could be studied at the universal, selected, or indicated prevention levels (see Figure 2.2). Studies at each of these levels could then be further subdivided according to the type of mediator delivering the intervention (e.g., dyad, team, or whole school system).

Although the implications of this transition may be that consultation research takes on the character of a chapter within a much larger intervention-focused text, the increased relevance and specificity of this scientific knowledge increases the probability that consultation research in school psychology will become required reading for anyone with a vested interest in developing, implementing, or evaluating evidence-based intervention in school settings.

PROBLEM-SOLVING CONSULTATION AS A PRACTICE GUIDELINE: AN ALTERNATIVE PROPOSAL

In this chapter, we have noted that there is growing empirical support for the effectiveness of various interventions that have been delivered in consultation, and many of these studies have been summarized in literature reviews of the field, as referenced in our discussion. There is also support for a growing number of interventions in the educational and mental health domains, but many of these procedures have not been implemented within a structured problem-solving model of consultation. Moreover, there is support for a variety of features of consultation that make it more effective as a process and likely contribute to effective client and consultee outcomes.

However, there are gaps in the literature in each of these areas, and the integration of these domains into a packaged intervention program has not been tested in research to provide a clear guideline for practice. In fact, based on our analysis of the current situation, it is questionable whether problem-solving consultation, or any particular model of consultation, might rightly be referred to as an intervention as we have defined it.

Therefore, instead of considering problem-solving consultation as an intervention, we would advance the notion that the process and content components of problem-solving consultation can be the framework for a practice guideline in school-based educational and mental health services. Unlike highly structured, component-driven interventions, practice guidelines are flexible recommendations endorsed by a profession for how to treat (or prevent) a given problem or issue. Practice guidelines have been used in medicine for more than 50 years (Woolf, Grol, Hutinson, Eccles, & Grimshaw, 1999), and their application in other fields, such as education and mental health, is growing. Most practice guidelines include comprehensive literature reviews undertaken by content experts (Atezaz-Saeed, 2004) and an evaluation of empirical evidence for treatment efficacy, known mechanisms of action, appropriate training necessary to administer the treatment effectively, potential risks, and factors to consider when trying to determine the appropriate intensity or dosage of a given treatment (White & Kratochwill, 2005).

Considered in this light, rather than as an intervention, the five research-supported stages of problem-solving consultation (i.e., relationship building, problem identification, problem analysis, intervention implementation, and program evaluation) might be thought of as a general practice guideline for how to implement specific evidence-based interventions in actual school settings. We realize that advancing this concept is a somewhat radical proposition; however, if we return to our initial question from the beginning of this chapter regarding what we as a field hope to accomplish with our expanding knowledge of effective interventions and consultation processes, it is a rather interesting prospect indeed.

Consider the following: Imagine a time in which researchers in the field of consultation know with the utmost certainty everything there is to know about effective consultation processes and practices. We know exactly what worked, why it worked, for whom it worked, and under what conditions it worked. Then, imagine experts in the field of school-based consultation were commissioned to write a summary of what works in consultation for current and future practitioners in the field. What would such a summary look like? How would the various sections be organized and main headings divided?

Based on our analysis of the scope and content of the consultation literature, we believe such a document would be organized much like a practice guideline: an organized, sequential set of recommended practices, considerations, and activities that ultimately culminate in the delivery of effective interventions to children in schools. Rather than organization like an evidence-based intervention with specific inputs, well-defined process and content components, and consistent outputs, consultation might be more easily understood as an effective — yet flexible — set of guidelines for transporting various interventions into school settings. Although the particular features of the consultation process that result in effective transport are likely to vary according to the particular level of intervention (e.g., universal, selected, or indicated) and nature of the intervention in question, this knowledge could prove vastly useful to practitioners working at a variety of levels within a given school organization. It would also likely prove useful to researchers with a variety of prevention- and intervention-related interests, training backgrounds, and professional associations.

However, if the field were commissioned to produce such a piece today, it would likely be rather disjointed and incomplete. Certain sections would be missing and some thoughts left unfinished, whereas some chapters would seem to go on forever. Worse yet, it is possible that a reader might get through the entire text and still be left wondering what exactly they should _do_ — step by step — to promote positive outcomes for the students and systems with whom and with which they work. We believe that the research agenda outlined in this chapter could prove useful in addressing these gaps and providing greater coherence and sense of focus to the consultation researcher.

REFERENCES

Abbott, A. (1988). *The system of professions: An essay on the division of expert labor*. Chicago: University of Chicago Press.

Abbott, A. (2001). *Chaos of the professions*. Chicago: University of Chicago Press.

Allen, S. J., & Graden, J. L. (2002). Best practices in collaborative problem-solving for intervention design. In A. Thomas & J. Grimes (Eds.), *Best practices in school psychology* (4th ed., pp. 414–435). Bethesda, MD: National Association of School Psychologists.

Atezaz-Saeed, S. (2004). An overview of clinical decision-making parameters. In C. E. Stout & R. A. Hayes (Eds.), *The evidence-based practice: Methods, models, and tools for mental health professionals* (pp. 111–118). Hoboken, NJ: Wiley.

Backer, T. E., Liberman, R. P., & Kuehnel, T. G. (1986). Dissemination and adoption of innovative psychosocial interventions. *Journal of Consulting and Clinical Psychology, 54*, 111–118.

Bergan, J. R., & Kratochwill, T. R. (1990). *Behavioral consultation and therapy*. New York: Plenum.

Caplan, G., & Caplan, R. B. (1993). *Mental health consultation and collaboration*. San Francisco: Jossey-Bass.

Chalfant, J. C., & Pysh, V. (1989). Teacher assistance teams: Five descriptive studies on 96 teams. *Remedial and Special Education, 10*, 49–58.

Chambless, D. L., Baker, M. J., Baucom, D. H., Beutler, L. E., Calhoun, K. S., Crits-Christoph, P., et al. (1998). Update on empirically validated therapies, II. *The Clinical Psychologist, 51*, 3–16.

Chorpita, B. F. (2003). The frontier of evidence-based practice. In A. E. Kazdin & J. R. Weisz (Eds.), *Evidence-based psychotherapies for children and adolescents* (pp. 42–59). New York: Guilford.

Colton, D., & Sheridan, S. (1998) Conjoint behavioral consultation and social skills training: Enhancing the play behaviors of boys with attention deficit hyperactivity disorder. *Journal of Educational and Psychological Consultation, 9*, 3–28.

Cowan, R. J., & Sheridan, S. M. (2003). Investigating the acceptability of behavioral interventions in applied conjoint behavioral consultation: Moving from analog conditions to naturalistic settings. *School Psychology Quarterly, 18*, 1–21.

Eckert, T. L., & Hintze, J. M. (2000). Behavioral conceptualizations and applications of treatment acceptability: Issues related to service delivery and research methodology. *School Psychology Quarterly, 15*, 123–148.

Elliott, S. N. (1988). Acceptability of behavioral treatments: Review of variables that influence treatment selection. *Professional Psychology: Research and Practice, 19*, 68–80.

Elliott, S. N., Witt, J. C., Galvin, G., & Peterson, R. (1984). Acceptability of positive and reductive interventions: Factors that influence teachers' decisions. *Journal of School Psychology, 22*, 353–360.

Erchul, W. P., & Martens, B. K. (2002). *School consultation: Conceptual and empirical bases of practice* (2nd Ed.). New York: Plenum.

Erhardt, K. E., Barnett, D. W., Lentz, F. E., Stollar, S. A., & Reifin, L. H. (1996). Innovative methodology in ecological consultation: Use of scripts to promote treatment acceptability and integrity. *School Psychology Quarterly, 11*, 149–168.

Finn, C. A., & Sladeczek, I. E. (2001). Assessing the social validity of behavioral interventions: A review of treatment acceptability measures. *School Psychology Quarterly, 16*, 176–206.

Fonagy, P., Target, M., Cottrell, D., Phillips, J., & Kurtz, Z. (2002). *What works for whom? A critical review of treatments for children and adolescents*. New York: Guilford.

Gordon, R. (1987). An operational classification of disease prevention. In J. A. Steinberg & M. M. Silverman (Eds.), *Preventing mental disorders: A research perspective* (pp. 20–26) (DHHS Publication No. ADM 87-1492). Washington, DC: U.S. Government Printing Office.

Graden, J. L., Casey, A., & Christenson, S. (1985). Implementing a prereferral intervention system part I: The model. *Exceptional Children, 51*, 377–384.

Gresham, F. M. (1989). Assessment of treatment integrity in school consultation and prereferral intervention. *School Psychology Review, 18*, 37–50.

Gresham, F. M., Gansle, K. A., Noell, G. H., Cohen, S., & Rosenblum, J. (1993). Treatment integrity of school-based behavioral intervention studies. *School Psychology Review, 22*, 254–272.

Gresham, F. M., & Kendell, G. K. (1987). School consultation research: Methodological critique and future research directions. *School Psychology Review, 16*, 306–316.

Gutkin, T. (1996). Patterns of consultant and consultee verbalizations: Examining communication leadership during initial consultation interviews. *Journal of School Psychology, 34,* 199–219.

Gutkin, T. B., & Curtis, M. J. (1999). School-based consultation: The art and science of indirect service delivery. In C. R. Reynolds & T. B. Gutkin (Eds.), *The handbook of school psychology* (3rd ed., pp. 598–637). New York: Wiley.

Hoagwood, K., Burns, B. J., Kiser, L., Ringeisen, H., & Schoenwald, S. K. (2001). Evidence-based practice in child and adolescent mental health services. *Psychiatric Services, 52,* 1179–1189.

Institute of Medicine. (1994). *Clinical practice guidelines: Directions for a new program.* Washington, DC: National Academy Press.

Kazdin, A. E. (1980). Acceptability of alternative treatments for deviant child behavior. *Journal of Applied Behavior Analysis, 13,* 259–273.

Kazdin, A. E. (1996). Developing effective treatments for children and adolescents. In E. D. Hibbs & P. S. Jensen (Eds.), *Psychosocial treatments for child and adolescent disorders: Empirically based strategies for clinical practice* (pp. 9–18). Washington, DC: American Psychological Association.

Kratochwill, T. R., Elliott, S. N., & Busse, R. T. (1995). Behavior consultation: A five-year evaluation of consultant and client outcomes. *School Psychology Quarterly, 10,* 87–117.

Kratochwill, T. R., Elliott, S. N., & Rotto, P. C. (1995). Best practices in school-based behavioral consultation. In A. Thomas & J. Grimes (Eds.), *Best practices in school psychology III* (pp. 519–535). Bethesda, MD: NASP.

Kratochwill, T. R., Elliott, S. N., Loitz, P. A., Sladeczek, I., & Carlson, J. S. (2003). Conjoint behavioral consultation using self-administered manual and videotape parent-teacher training: Effects on children's behavioral difficulties. *School Psychology Quarterly, 18,* 269–302.

Kratochwill, T. R., Elliott, S. N., & Stoiber, K. C. (2002). Best practices in school-based problem-solving consultation. In A. Thomas & J. Grimes (Eds.), *Best practices in school psychology* (4th ed., pp. 583–608). Bethesda, MD: National Association of School Psychologists.

Kratochwill, T. R., & Pittman, P. H. (2002). Expanding problem-solving consultation training: Prospects and frameworks. *Journal of Educational and Psychological Consultation, 13,* 69–95.

Kratochwill, T. R., & Shernoff, E. S. (2004). Evidence-based practice: Promoting evidence-based interventions in school psychology. *School Psychology Review, 33,* 34–48.

Kratochwill, T. R., & Stoiber, K. C. (2002). Evidence-based interventions in school psychology: Conceptual foundations of the procedural and coding manual of Division 16 and the Society for the Study of School Psychology Task Force. *School Psychology Quarterly, 17,* 341–389.

Martens B. K., Hiralall, A. S., & Bradley, T. A. (1997). A note to teacher: Improving student behavior through goal setting and feedback. *School Psychology Quarterly, 12,* 33–41.

Martin, R. P. (1978). Expert and referent power: A framework for understanding and maximizing consultation effectiveness. *Journal of School Psychology, 16,* 49–55.

McLaughlin, J. A., & Jordan, J. B. (1999). Logic models: A tool for telling your program's performance story. *Evaluation and Program Planning, 22,* 65–72.

Medway, F. J., & Updyke, J. F. (1985) Meta-analysis of consultation outcome studies. *American Journal of Community Psychology, 13,* 489–505.

Nathan, P., & Gorman, J. (2002). *A guide to treatments that work (2nd ed.).* Oxford, England: Oxford University Press.

Noell, G. H., Witt, J. C., Gilbertson, D. N., Ranier, D. D., & Freeland, J. T. (1997). Increasing teacher intervention implementation in general education settings through consultation and performance feedback. *School Psychology Quarterly, 12,* 77–88.

Reimers, T. M., Wacker, D. P., & Koeppl, G. (1987). Acceptability of behavioral interventions: A review of the literature. *School Psychology Review, 20,* 530–550.

Reschly, D. J., & Tilly, W. D. (1999). Reform trends and system design alternatives. In D. J. Reschly, W. D. Tilly, & J. P. Grimes (Eds.), *Special education in transition: Functional assessment and noncategorical programming* (pp. 19–48). Longmont, CO: Sopris West.

Rones, M., & Hoagwood, K. (2000). School-based mental health services: A research review. *Clinical Child and Family Psychology Review, 3,* 223–241.

Sanetti, L. H., & Kratochwill, T. R. (2005). Treatment integrity assessment within a problem-solving model. In R. Brown-Chidsey (Ed.), *Assessment for intervention: A problem solving approach* (pp. 304–325). New York: Guilford Press.

Schoenwald, S. K., & Hoagwood, K. R.(2001). Effectiveness, transportability, and dissemination of interventions: What matters when? *Psychiatric Services, 52,* 1190–1197.

Sheridan, S. M., Dee, C. C., Morgan, J. C., McCormick, M. E., & Walker, D. (1996). A multi-method intervention for social skills deficits in children with ADHD and their parents. *School Psychology Review, 25,* 57–76.

Sheridan, S. M., & Kratochwill, T. R. (1992). Behavioral parent-teacher consultation: Conceptual and research considerations. *Journal of School Psychology, 30,* 117–139.

Sheridan, S., Welch, M., & Orme, S. F. (1996). Is consultation effective? A review of outcome research. *Remedial and Special Education, 17,* 341–354.

Shinn, M., Good III, R. H., & Parker, C. (1999). Noncategorical special education services with students with severe achievement deficits. In J. Reschly, W. D. Tilly, & J. P. Grimes (Eds.), *Special education in transition: Functional assessment and noncategorical programming* (pp. 81–106). Longmont, CO: Sopris West.

Sterling-Turner, H. E., Watson, T. S., & Moore, J. W. (2002). The effects of direct training and treatment integrity on treatment outcomes in school consultation. *School Psychology Quarterly, 17,* 115–119.

Telzrow, C. E., McNamara, K., & Hollinger, C. L. (2000). Fidelity of problem-solving implementation and relationship to student performance. *School Psychology Review, 29,* 443–461.

Weisz, J. R., Doss, A. J., & Hawley, K. M. (2005). Youth psychotherapy outcome research: A review and critique of the evidence base. *Annual Review of Psychology, 56,* 337–342.

West, J. F., & Idol, L. (1990). Collaborative consultation in the education of mildly handicapped and at-risk students. *Remedial and Special Education, 11,* 22–31.

White, J. L., & Kratochwill, T. R. (2005). Practice guidelines in school psychology: Issues and directions for evidence-based interventions in practice and training. *Journal of School Psychology, 43,* 99–115.

Witt, J. C., & Elliott, S. N. (1985). Acceptability of classroom management strategies. In T. R. Kratochwill (Ed.), *Advances in school psychology* (Vol. 4, pp. 251–288). Hillsdale, NJ: Erlbaum.

Witt, J. C., Elliott, S. N., & Martens, B. K. (1984). Assessing the acceptability of behavioral interventions used in classrooms: The influence of amount of teacher time, severity of behavior problem, and type of intervention. *Behavioral Disorders, 9,* 95–104.

Witt, J. C., Gresham, F. M., & Noell, G. H. (1996). What's behavioral about behavioral consultation? *Journal of Educational and Psychological Consultation, 7,* 327–344.

Witt, J. C., Moe, G., Gutkin, T. B., & Andrews, L. (1984). The effect of saying the same thing in different ways: The problem of language and jargon in school-based consultation. *Journal of School Psychology, 22,* 361–367.

Witt, J. C., & Robbins, J. R. (1985). Acceptability of classroom interventions strategies. In T. R. Kratochwill (Ed.), *Advances in school psychology* (Vol. 4, pp. 251–288). Mahwah, NJ: Erlbaum.

Woolf, S. H., Grol, R., Hutinson, A., Eccles, M., & Grimshaw, J. (1999). Clinical guidelines: Potential benefits, limitations, and harms of clinical guidelines. *British Medical Journal, 318,* 527–530.

Ysseldyke, J. E., & Marston, D. (1999). Origins of categorical special education services in schools and a rationale for changing them. In D. J. Reschly, W. D. Tilly, & J. P. Grimes (Eds.), *Special education in transition.* Longmont, CO: Sopris West.

Zins, J. E. (1996). Editor's comments. *Journal of Educational and Psychological Consultation, 7,* 209–210.

Zins, J. E., & Erchul, W. P. (2002). Best practices in school consultation. In A. Thomas & J. Grimes (Eds.), *Best practices in school psychology* (4th ed., pp. 625–643). Bethesda, MD: National Association of School Psychologists.

B

METHODOLOGICAL FOUNDATIONS

3

Measurement in School Consultation Research

Ann C. Schulte

North Carolina State University

Measurement plays an important role in intervention research. It also takes many forms. Sometimes, it involves simple counting. For example, knowing the number of participants in a study is useful in evaluating the confidence that can be placed in the results. More frequently, measurement in treatment research is complex. For example, assessing the fidelity of intervention implementation or quantifying how much participants improved as a result of the treatment both require the operationalization and scaling of complex, multidimensional constructs.

This chapter discusses a broad array of measurement issues in school consultation research, from the simple to the complex. To limit the chapter's length and breadth, the choice of measurement topics includes those that are central to one of the most important challenges facing school consultation researchers: demonstrating that school consultation is an effective treatment that merits more widespread use and support. The increased focus on the use of evidenced-based or empirically supported treatments in schools offers an unprecedented opportunity to further develop and promote consultation as a viable and cost-effective treatment mode. However, capitalizing on this opportunity will only be possible if future school consultation research can meet the rigorous and evolving research standards that are part of the move toward evidence-based treatments in a number of human services fields.

The chapter begins with a brief summary of the evidence-based treatment movement and its roots in medicine. It then moves to a discussion of what should be measured in consultation research and how, focusing on three major aspects of school consultation research: (a) describing the participants, (b) documenting the consultation process, and (c) assessing client outcomes. The chapter concludes with recommendations related to increasing the rigor of measurement in school consultation research and reducing the extent to which measurement issues may distort or attenuate the findings supporting school consultation. In keeping with the emphasis on consultation as a treatment, the focus is on research concerning triadic case-centered consultation in schools, in which the consultant (typically a psychologist, counselor, or specialist) meets with a direct service provider (teacher) to address a concern about a client (child), with the primary focus on improving the functioning of the client rather than the consultee.

EVIDENCE-BASED INTERVENTIONS IN SCHOOLS

The research base that supports the use of psychological and educational treatments has come under increased scrutiny. As part of a broad-based effort to encourage the use of interventions that have been shown to be effective in methodologically sound studies, a number of groups have begun to review systematically the quality of scientific evidence for psychological and educational treatments (e.g., Chambless et al., 1998; Kratochwill & Stoiber, 2002; Nathan & Gorman, 1998; National Institute of Child Health and Human Development, NIH, DHHS, 2000; Spirito, 1999).

These groups' activities are part of a larger movement that began in the United Kingdom in the early 1990s (Chambless & Ollendick, 2001; Spring, Pagoto, Altman, & Thorn, 2005). However, the roots of the movement can be traced to the 1970s (Cochrane Collaboration, n.d.) or even earlier (Sackett, Rosenberg, Gray, Haynes, & Richardson, 1996). Initially termed *evidence-based medicine* (Chambless & Ollendick, 2001), the major goals of this movement are to make summaries of the evidence supporting various treatments easily available to clinicians and consumers and to promote the integration of high-quality research evidence and individual clinical expertise in clinical decision making (Sackett et al., 1996).

Within medicine, this movement has had a profound impact (Bernstein, 2004). Its most well-known outcome is the Cochrane Collaboration (http://www.cochrane.org/). This international organization, founded in 1993, uses meta-analysis to review systematically the effects of health care interventions. It then makes the results of these reviews available to professionals and consumers through the Cochrane Database of Systematic Reviews (www3.interscience.wiley.com/cgi-bin/mrwhome/106568753/HOME). To date, the Cochrane Collaboration has published more than 2,000 reviews of treatment research in specific areas (Cochrane Collaboration, n.d.).

Although the evidence-based movement began with a focus on medical treatments, as it gained momentum other human service areas began to examine the research support for their practices (Spring et al., 2005). For example, in 1993 Division 12 (Clinical Psychology) of the American Psychological Association appointed the first of two task forces to review the evidence for a number of psychological interventions for adults and children (e.g., Chambless et al., 1998; Lonigan, Elbert, & Johnson, 1998; Spirito, 1999). Later, Division 16 (School Psychology) of the American Psychological Association joined with the Society for the Study of School Psychology to support the formation of the Task Force on Evidence-Based Interventions in School Psychology (Kratochwill & Stoiber, 2002; hereafter called the Task Force on EBI).

In 1999, the Campbell Collaboration, a sibling to the Cochrane Collaboration, was established "to help policymakers, practitioners, and the public make well informed decisions about policy interventions by preparing, maintaining, and disseminating systematic reviews of the effectiveness of social and behavioural interventions in education, crime and justice, and social welfare" (Davies & Boruch, 2001, p. 294). In 2002, the U.S. Department of Education partnered with the Campbell Collaboration and established the What Works Clearinghouse to study and report on the effectiveness of educational interventions (U.S. Department of Education, n.d.).

This chronology does not provide a complete list of organizations examining the research bases of medical, psychosocial, and educational practices but illustrates the breadth of this movement. One result of these systematic reviews of research evidence has been increased scrutiny of the overall quality of treatment research methodology and reporting. For example, an outgrowth of the Cochrane Collaboration (Wormold & Oldfield, 1998) has been the Consolidated Standards of Reporting Trials or CONSORT statement (Begg et al., 1996). This document is a checklist of essential items that are to be included when reporting the results of randomized controlled trials. The document was developed by an international group of journal editors and investigators when it became apparent that incomplete reporting of the methodology used in published clinical trials was a major barrier to systematic reviews of the evidence for health care interventions (Altman et al., 2001).

These original CONSORT guidelines have since been revised, and their use appears to have improved the quality of reporting in published treatment outcome studies (Moher, Schulz, & Altman, 2001). Both the Revised CONSORT reporting template (Moher et al., 2001) and the accompanying explanation and rationale for each of its components (Altman et al., 2001) are valuable resources for anyone designing research to investigate psychological or educational treatments.

Other groups have also articulated specific standards against which to judge the quality of the available research studies investigating different treatments. For example, the Task Force on EBI has drafted the *Procedural and Coding Manual for Review of Evidence-Based Interventions* (Task Force on EBI, 2003; hereafter, the *EBI Procedural and Coding Manual*). This document articulates specific guidelines for use in judging the strength of evidence to support psychological and educational treatments used in schools. Studies are rated on eight key methodological dimensions (Lewis-Snyder, Stoiber, & Kratochwill, 2002).

Not surprisingly, measurement has been one focus of this increased scrutiny on treatment research methodology. Categorization, quantification, and description play a critical role in the design, implementation, and evaluation of treatment research. For example, the first domain in the *EBI Procedural and Coding Manual* (Task Force on EBI, 2003) is the quality of the measures used to assess outcomes. The careful scrutiny of measurement issues in treatment research appears merited. In an extensive methodological meta-analysis of over 16,000 psychological and educational treatment studies, Wilson and Lipsey (2001) found that how constructs were measured contributed as much to the variance in treatment effect sizes as what was measured. Hunter and Schmidt (2004) also have shown that measurement error, including unreliability and poor construct validity, contributes substantially to variability in outcomes across studies, often obscuring our knowledge of which treatments are effective and ineffective.

In sum, there is an increasing emphasis on the use of evidence-based practices in psychology and education. This emphasis is likely to result in a stronger demand for high-quality intervention research, and a key to high-quality intervention research is adequate measurement of important study variables and components.

WHAT SHOULD BE MEASURED IN SCHOOL CONSULTATION RESEARCH AND HOW?

As noted, when treatment literature has been systematically reviewed, it has become evident that not all the information needed to fully assess the quality of, and empirical support for, various medical and psychosocial treatments is available in published reports (Altman et al., 2001). Problems with the quality of reporting in the consultation research literature have also been noted (e.g., Gresham, 1989; Gresham & Kendell, 1987; Gresham & Noell, 1993; Sheridan, Welch, & Orme, 1996). Given these findings, this section focuses on information that should be included in research reports and the measurement issues that arise in efforts to obtain this information.

In presenting which variables are important to include in school consultation research and how they should be measured, four publications that address issues related to conducting and reporting treatment research are used here as primary sources: (a) the Revised CONSORT statement (Altman et al., 2001; Moher et al., 2001); (b) Weisz, Doss, and Hawley's (2005) methodological review and critique of the youth psychotherapy research; (c) the guidelines contained in the *EBI Procedural and Coding Manual* proposed by school psychology's Task Force on EBI (2003); and (d) Gresham and Noell's (1993) chapter concerning issues in documenting treatment outcomes in consultation research. Commonalities among these sources are used as a basis for inferring current standards or best practices in treatment research, either because the sources have explicitly stated standards for reporting or evaluating treatment research (the Revised CONSORT statement and the *EBI Procedural and Coding Manual*) or they have evaluated the quality of current treatment research on a number of dimensions (Gresham & Noell, 1993; Weisz et al., 2005). These particular sources were selected because of their widespread use in the treatment literature (the Revised CONSORT statement), their relevance to child treatment research (Weisz et al., 2005), or their direct relevance to school consultation research (Gresham & Noell, 1993; Task Force on EBI, 2003). Although the focus of both the Revised CONSORT statement and Weisz et al.'s methodological review was randomized controlled trials, many of the methodological and measurement concerns raised in those sources are relevant to consultation research regardless of the design.

The discussion of which variables should be measured in school consultation research is divided into three sections, each addressing a major area of treatment research design. First, key considerations in the description of participants are addressed. Second, measurement issues involved in documenting the consultation process are discussed. Finally, issues relevant to the measurement of client outcomes are presented. For each of these topics, salient reporting or measurement issues from the four methodological sources (Altman et al., 2001; Gresham & Noell, 1993; Task Force on EBI, 2003; Weisz et al., 2005) are discussed. When appropriate, the state of practice in the school consultation research literature, as indicated by comprehensive reviews (Fuchs, Fuchs, Dulan, Roberts, & Fernstrom, 1992; Reddy, Barboza-Whitehead, Files, & Rubel, 2000; Sheridan, Welch, & Orme, 1996), is compared to the state of practice in the youth psychotherapy research literature, as portrayed in Weisz et al.'s (2005) comprehensive review of this research area. Such a comparison is useful because it provides a normative perspective on the state of school consultation research.

Description of Study Participants

A key component of any report of research is a description of the number and characteristics of the participants. Knowledge of sample size is important in assessing a study's statistical power (Cohen, 1988). A complete description of the participants is important in understanding the study's generalizability or external validity (Task Force on EBI, 2003) and identifying potential variables that may moderate treatment outcomes (Weisz et al., 2005).

Sample Size

A count of participants would seem to be one of the simplest measurement tasks facing researchers. In fact, it seems so simple that it may be difficult even to think of sample size as a measurement issue in consultation research. However, a serious problem found in much of the overall treatment literature is the failure to report changes in sample size from the beginning to the end of treatment and to report the number of participants included or excluded in calculations of treatment outcomes (Moher et al., 2001). When interventions take place across a significant time interval, it is likely that the number of participants remaining, as well as the number complying with the intervention protocol, will change over the course of the study. Under these circumstances, it can be difficult to determine how to count participants because the number may vary over time and with the criteria used to define study participation.

School consultation research presents particular problems in counting participants because continued study participation depends not only on the client's continued willingness to participate in treatment, but also on the consultee's continued willingness. For example, in the classic behavioral consultation study by Bergan and Tombari (1976), 806 cases were referred to consultants for psychological services. Of these, consultation was initiated in only 43% of the cases. Consultation proceeded to the plan implementation phase for 31% of the original cases. In only 30% of the original referral cases did problem solution occur. Considerable drops in participants from referral to treatment completion do not seem to be unusual in consultation research (e.g., Hughes, Hasbrouck, Serdahl, Heidgerken, & McHaney, 2001; Schulte, Osborne, & McKinney, 1990), but the implications of this phenomenon for assessing consultation's overall efficacy or effectiveness are not often recognized.

The Revised CONSORT statement (Altman et al., 2001) provides a template for reporting the flow of participants through phases of a study, including reports of the number of persons assessed for eligibility for study participation, assigned to treatment groups, receiving the intended treatment(s), completing the study protocol, and included in the primary outcome analysis. Similarly, the *EBI Procedural and Coding Manual* (Task Force on EBI, 2003) requires an examination of study attrition by treatment group and the manner in which study attrition was handled in data analysis procedures. These standards suggest that it is important for consultation researchers to track and report study sample sizes carefully from initial entry into treatment through follow-up.

When sample sizes differ across intervention phases, researchers must decide which participants to include in the calculation of study outcomes. In an intention-to-treat analysis, data from all of the participants originally assigned to a treatment condition are included in the analysis of treatment outcomes. In an on-treatment or per protocol analysis, only participants who followed the intended study protocol are included in the outcome analysis (Altman et al., 2001). If the total number of participants in a treatment study varies markedly by these two types of analyses, then the choice of analysis strategy also is likely to affect the odds of obtaining a statistically significant result and the magnitude of the effect reported.

Kratochwill, Elliott, and Busse's (1995) report of a 5-year evaluation of consultant training provides an example of how the choice of analysis and, consequently, who is counted as a participant in calculating outcomes can affect study results. Of the 44 consultation cases initiated by trainees, 9 were terminated prior to case completion. In 23 of the remaining 35 cases, data were collected in a way that allowed calculation of effect sizes. The average effect size for these cases was 0.95. If an effect size of 0 were coded for each of the 9 early terminations[1] and these cases were included in the determination of average effect size, then the average effect size would drop to 0.68.

There are good arguments for using both types of analyses, particularly in studies in which both a treatment and comparison or control group are used (Altman et al., 2001; McCall & Green, 2004). However, the important point is that in reporting consultation research, the number of participants at each study phase and the type of analysis used in reporting treatment effects should be documented. When individual studies vary in the proportion of participants they use in reporting effect sizes, it is likely that some of the variance in consultation outcomes across studies will be a result of whose data have been included in the determination of treatment outcomes rather than any true variation in consultation outcome.

In sum, given the likelihood of substantial participant attrition in consultation studies, routine use of a reporting template such as that provided in the Revised CONSORT statement should be part of school consultation research to provide accurate counts of participants at each phase of a study. The basis for calculating effect sizes should also be reported.

Participant Characteristics

All four of the methodological sources (Altman et al., 2001; Gresham & Noell, 1993; Task Force on EBI, 2003; Weisz et al., 2005) delineated key variables that are important in describing participants in reports of treatment studies. For school consultation research, there are typically three distinct groups of participants: clients, consultees, and consultants. Issues in describing each group of participants are discussed next.

Clients

A description of the client sample, including key demographic variables and client clinical status before treatment, is an important component of any description of consultation research. Among the demographic variables most frequently mentioned across the four methodological sources were age, gender, ethnicity, family income or socioeconomic status, and grade level in school.

These client characteristics would seem to pose few measurement challenges for the consultation researcher. Despite relative ease of measurement, it appears that even this basic information about client characteristics is not always included in treatment research reports. In their review of the youth psychotherapy research literature, Weisz et al. (2005) expressed concern that 60% of the psychotherapy studies they reviewed did not provide information on client ethnicity, and 70% did not provide information on family income or socioeconomic status. A similar situation appears to exist within the consultation treatment literature. In their meta-analysis of 35 school consultation outcome studies, Reddy et al. (2000) reported that only 10 provided information on client ethnicity. Given the increasing diversity of the U.S. school population (Federal Interagency Forum on Child and Family Statistics, 2005), information about the extent to which any school-based intervention has been tested and found to be effective with a diverse student body is an important component of establishing its efficacy.

In developing the *EBI Procedural and Coding Manual*, the Task Force on EBI (2003) aimed to incorporate a finer-grain approach to assessing and describing participants than typically had been used in treatment research (when this information is reported at all). They reasoned that more detailed information would permit better assessments of the extent to which an intervention generalized across diverse groups (Kratochwill & Stoiber, 2002). Although their work in this area is still in progress (Kratochwill & Stoiber, 2002), the present version of the manual (Task Force on EBI, 2003) calls for intervention and control samples to be described on several dimensions of diversity, including ethnic identity, acculturation, and primary language. It is unclear how some of these dimensions could be efficiently assessed for each participant in treatment research (e.g., ethnic identity and acculturation), although a general characterization of the treatment sample on these dimensions would be helpful in assessing to whom an intervention is likely to generalize. As the Task Force on EBI and other groups grapple with providing researchers with more sophisticated and sensitive ways of defining diversity and assessing the generalizability of interventions across different contexts and groups (Kratochwill & Stoiber, 2002), measurement options for describing participants that move beyond gross categorizations by ethnic group and socioeconomic status are likely to become more widely available. In the meantime, it is important to report basic demographic information about clients in consultation research studies.

If the research population of interest is students with a particular clinical diagnosis, then another important issue is verification that the research sample met the criteria for the disorder or displayed the symptoms characteristic of the disorder to a significant degree. This information is important in ensuring the external validity of an intervention study's findings. Three of the four methodological sources discussed issues related to the assessment of participants' clinical status. The Revised CONSORT statement (Altman et al., 2001) calls for including a delineation of the eligibility criteria for selecting participants as well as the baseline clinical characteristics of the participants in reports of treatment research. In its listing of external validity indicators, the *EBI Procedural and Coding Manual* (Task Force on EBI, 2003) asks reviewers to judge the extent to which participants are described in a way that permits other researchers to determine an intervention's generalizability to its intended participants and the extent to which the study inclusion criteria are related to the goal of the intervention. For example, if a study examines consultation as a treatment for school phobia, then some participant inclusion criteria should be related to documenting the presence of this disorder or its symptoms.

In their examination of the youth psychotherapy outcome research, Weisz et al. (2005) assessed youth psychotherapy studies on a number of dimensions related to documentation of a client's initial clinical status. These included whether studies used formal diagnoses based on established diagnostic criteria for various disorders, used a formal clinical cutoff on a standardized clinical measure, or used standardized continuous measures of psychopathology. They found that more than half of the studies of youth psychotherapy in their review identified study participants based on nonstandard measures completed by parents or teachers or through advertisements or requests for youths with particular problems. When formal diagnoses or clinical cutoffs on standardized measures were used, which was less than 40% of the time, they were typically based on the use of nonstandard measures with unknown validity.

In their consultation meta-analysis, Reddy et al. (2000) reported that only 57% of consultation studies provided diagnostic or classification information for their client samples. The authors did not report on the types of measures used in these studies and whether standardized instruments with known reliability and validity were used.

When clinical populations are of interest, it is important for consultation researchers to consider carefully how the clinical status of clients is assessed and, whenever possible, use published, standardized measures of the disorder. The data reported by Weisz et al. (2005) and Reddy et al. (2000) suggest adequate documentation of the extent to which study samples represent the clinical populations may be a problem in both psychotherapy and consultation research.

Studies examining consultation as a treatment alternative for students identified for special education face a unique difficulty regarding verifying that study samples meet special education criteria for the classification in question (e.g., learning disability, behavioral/emotional disturbance). Federal special education law provides a number of specific disability categories, but the identification criteria for the categories vary by state. Furthermore, the manner in which identification criteria are implemented can vary from community to community (Singer, Palfrey, Butler, & Walker, 1989). For this reason, consultation researchers investigating treatments for students in special education should provide a clear statement of the classification criteria employed and documentation that their sample met these criteria, as well as a description of the sample on key dimensions related to the disability category in question (e.g., IQ and adaptive behavior for students with mental retardation), using published (vs. experimenter-designed) scales. Without this information, the extent to which a sample is comparable to the special education population in different communities and states will remain in question.

In sum, the current state of school consultation research appears to mirror the current state of youth treatment research. In both areas, client-descriptive information is scant, with insufficient information about the demographic and clinical characteristics of study participants. Current reporting standards (e.g., the *EBI Procedural and Coding Manual,* Task Force on EBI, 2003) and the need to ensure that interventions are valid across cultural groups (Sue, 1999) are likely to create a press for much more detailed information in reports of treatment outcome studies.

Consultees
All four methodological sources (Altman et al., 2001; Gresham & Noell, 1993; Task Force on EBI, 2003; Weisz et al., 2005) mentioned the provision of relevant information about treatment

agents as an important component of complete intervention outcome reports. The most relevant of these sources to the discussion of consultee characteristics is Gresham and Noell's (1993) listing of variables likely to moderate consultation treatment outcomes. In addition to basic demographic characteristics (e.g., gender, ethnicity, grade level taught if teachers are consultees), they listed level of training, experience, classroom management style, attitudes toward consultation, knowledge of classroom interventions, and referral rates for special education and consultation as potential moderators.

Although there is considerable discussion in the consultation literature of the potential impact that consultee characteristics may have on outcomes (e.g., Brown, Pryzwansky, & Schulte, 2006; Gibbs, 1980; Gresham & Noell, 1993), consultation studies often fail to report even basic demographic information on consultees (Reddy et al., 2000). Unfortunately, the lack of routine reporting of basic information about consultees suggests that any systematic variation in outcomes across consultation studies due to consultee characteristics will be less readily detectable in future meta-analyses.

Despite the failure of many consultation studies to describe consultees adequately, two consultee variables that have been assessed in a number of school consultation studies are level of experience and attitudes toward consultation. In school consultation research, consultee experience has typically been measured in terms of number of years of teaching experience (e.g., Dunson, Hughes, & Jackson, 1994; Gutkin & Bossard, 1984; Hughes et al., 2001). However, Gutkin and Bossard (1984) found that number of years teaching and number of years at the same school had opposing effects on consultees' attitudes toward consultation, suggesting that both may be important to assess in consultation research studies.

At least two measures, the Preference for Consultation Scale from the Pupil Problem Behavior Inventory (Gutkin, Singer, & Brown, 1980) and the Consultation Preference Questionnaire (Babcock & Pryzwansky, 1983), have been used in multiple consultation studies to assess consultee attitudes toward consultation (Babcock & Pryzwansky, 1983; Buysse, Schulte, Pierce, & Terry, 1994; Gutkin & Ajchenbaum, 1984; Gutkin et al., 1980; Schulte, Osborne, & Kauffman, 1993; West, 1985). Both assess teacher consultees' preferences for using consultation over referral to a specialist for children's problems, although the Consultation Preference Questionnaire also assesses preference for three models of consultation. Internal consistency reliability figures are available for both instruments. In addition, the Preference for Consultation Scale has been shown to be sensitive to changes in attitudes toward consultation following experience working with a consultant (Gutkin et al., 1980; Schulte et al., 1993).

Consultants
Consultants are the final group of participants considered in this section. As stated in the section discussing consultee characteristics, all four methodological sources (Altman et al., 2001; Gresham & Noell, 1993; Task Force on EBI, 2003; Weisz et al., 2005) call for the reporting of basic demographic characteristics of treatment agents (e.g., number used in the study, age, ethnicity, gender), as well as other characteristics that might be important in assessing the generalizability of the intervention, such as consultant vocation, experience, training, and education, or potential moderators of treatment outcome.

Weisz et al. (2005) found that over a quarter of all youth psychotherapy studies failed to report who had provided the intervention. In their review of consultation outcome research, Reddy et al. (2000) found that less than 10% of studies reported data on consultant ethnicity, 40% on consultant gender, and 60% on their educational level. It appears that in both the child psychotherapy and consultation research areas, descriptions of treatment providers are quite limited.

Summary

Characteristics of the client, consultee, and consultant are likely to affect consultation outcomes (Gresham & Noell, 1993). Given the limited information available about consultation participants, the conclusions of Weisz et al. (2005) concerning the state of youth psychotherapy research appear to also apply to school consultation research:

> Our review suggests that the critical first step toward moderator assessment — i.e., collecting information on participant characteristics that might moderate effects — has not been taken in a remarkably large percentage of studies. ... A related problem noted in our review is the high percentage of studies in which no data were reported for important variables such as who carried out the treatment and in what setting the treatment took place. Given the potential value of all these types of information to the field, and the lost opportunities for moderator assessment once data sets are no longer available, it seems desirable to encourage greater consistency in the kinds of information required by journals prior to acceptance of manuscripts for publication. (p. 358)

In light of the *EBI Procedural and Coding Manual* (Task Force on EBI, 2003) and the revised CONSORT statement (Moher et al., 2001), the evolving standards for reporting treatment research call for more detailed descriptions of study participants and settings than has been true in the past. At present, the most salient problem in describing school consultation participants is not a lack of available measures but failure to include descriptive information even on easily measured variables. However, as school consultation research moves beyond basic questions about potential moderator variables, there will be a need for more refined ways of describing participants on a wider range of dimensions. One important direction for future research will be the development of measures that allow researchers to ask more sophisticated questions about moderators, once these moderators are identified. For example, it may be possible to examine whether consultation treatments are differentially effective by client ethnic group and whether this difference is explained by cultural, language, background experience, or socioeconomic factors.

Measurement of Consultation Process

The term *consultation process* is used here to refer to actions of the consultant or consultee that have an impact (or are thought to have an impact) on the outcome of consultation. It is the "what" and "how" of consultation. The primary focus of this section is measurement issues related to describing what constituted the treatment in a consultation study and assessing the extent to which that treatment was implemented as planned (treatment integrity). Other topics of interest to consultation researchers within the area of the consultation process, such as consultant/consultee interaction from a relational perspective (e.g., Erchul, Covington, Hughes, & Meyers, 1995) and consultant facilitative characteristics (e.g., Schowengerdt, Fine, & Poggio, 1976), are only touched on here. These issues are less central to the primary concern of the chapter, which focuses on measurement issues related to increasing support for school consultation as an evidence-based treatment. Readers are referred to this volume's chapter 14 by Erchul, Grissom, and Getty and chapter 9 by Sheridan, Clarke, and Burt for more on these topics.

Describing and Documenting Treatments

Until recently, published reports of treatment outcome studies focused primarily on describing who received the treatment and the extent to which the treatment alleviated the problem of interest (Miller & Binder, 2002). A detailed and verifiable description of the actual treatment typically was not provided. For example, early reports of psychological treatment research frequently characterized the treatment under study with only brief descriptions of its sequence (e.g., White & Fine, 1976). If further documentation of treatment was provided, then it consisted of a description of the actions the researchers had taken to ensure that the treatment agent was competent in the implementation of the treatment model and adhered to it throughout treatment (Waltz, Addis, Koerner, & Jacobson, 1993). These early practices were criticized because they (a) failed to clearly specify the treatment and (b) did not directly measure whether treatment was implemented as intended (Gresham, 1989; Gresham & Kendell, 1987; Moncher & Prinz; 1991; Peterson, Homer, & Wonderlich, 1982; Waltz et al., 1993). This criticism has led to a greater focus on defining and documenting procedures employed in treatment studies (Sass, Twohig, & Davies, 2004; Weisz et al., 2005).

Although all four methodological sources mention the importance of adequately specifying the independent variable in treatment studies (Altman et al., 2001; Gresham & Noell, 1993; Task Force on EBI, 2003; Weisz et al., 2005), only two of the sources explicitly discuss procedures for describing and documenting psychological treatments. Both Weisz et al. (2005) and the *EBI Procedural and Coding Manual* (Task Force on EBI, 2003) put considerable emphasis on the use of treatment manuals. This emphasis is not surprising as treatment manuals have come to be the predominant means of specifying interventions (Miller & Binder, 2002).

Although treatment manuals make replication of psychological interventions much easier, their use does not fully address the concerns raised about the specification of the independent variable in treatment research. Without direct measurement of the extent to which the treatment providers adhered to the procedures described in the manual, we have no evidence that the intervention described was the intervention implemented (Sass et al., 2004; Waltz et al., 1993) and no way to assess variability in how a treatment was implemented across participants. Thus, adequate assessment of treatment integrity requires measures of intervention adherence by providers. Others have also suggested that competence in delivering the intervention should also be assessed (Miller & Binder, 2002; Waltz et al., 1993).

Added to the usual challenges in assessing treatment integrity for educational and psychological treatments, consultation researchers face the problems posed by the two-tier nature of the consultative services. The consultant interacts with the consultee, who then provides the treatment to the client. As such, school consultation research must provide information not only about the model of consultative problem solving and how it was implemented (typically by describing interactions between the consultant and consultee) but also about how the consultee implemented the planned intervention with the client.

Noell (chapter 15, this volume) provides a thorough discussion of issues of treatment fidelity in school consultation research in the context of this two-tier model. Reflecting the two-tier nature of consultation processes, he uses the term *consultation procedural integrity* to refer to the extent to which consultation procedures were implemented as designed and the term *treatment plan implementation* to refer to the integrity with which a treatment plan developed in consultation was implemented. In this section, issues related to the measurement of these two aspects of treatment fidelity are discussed separately.

Consultation Procedural Integrity

Although treatment manuals are only a first step in ensuring that an intervention is adequately described (Waltz et al., 1993), even this first step is not yet a universal in treatment research. Despite considerable emphasis on treatment manuals in the youth psychotherapy literature, Weisz et al. (2005) found only about half of youth psychotherapy studies used treatment manuals, although an additional one third used a structured treatment protocol consisting of a detailed listing of the steps involved in intervention.

The percentage of consultation outcome studies using manuals is unknown as their use has not been tracked in any comprehensive review. Sheridan, Welch, and Orme's (1996) finding that only 26% of school consultation studies used any procedures to describe the consultation process (either procedural or treatment integrity) suggests that the figure is low. However, a number of consultation treatments within the behavioral model have been "manualized," providing specific procedures that should be followed by the consultant to implement consultative problem solving. Bergan's (1977) initial book, *Behavioral Consultation*, and its successor, *Behavioral Consultation and Therapy* (Bergan & Kratochwill, 1990), each provide a detailed set of instructions that the consultant is to follow in implementing consultative problem solving. In addition, Sheridan, Kratochwill, and Bergan (1996) have published a manual for conjoint behavioral consultation, a model of behavioral consultation that has been expanded to include home and school caregivers as joint consultees. Fuchs and his colleagues (1989) also have published a manual for their application of Bergan's (1977) model to prereferral assessment. Finally, the *Consultant Evaluation Rating Form (CERF) Scoring Manual* (Hughes & Hasbrouck, 1997) for Hughes and colleagues' responsive systems consultation model (Hughes et al., 2001) is sufficiently detailed that it could serve as both a treatment manual and a procedural integrity tool for implementing this model of consultation.

To the extent that treatment manuals constitute an explicit statement of how the treatment process should proceed, they then provide the basis for developing measures of adherence and competence in implementing the model (Waltz et al., 1993). Although adherence can be assessed in a variety of ways, including self-report, case notes, and objective measures (Noell, chapter 15, this volume; Waltz et al., 1993), consultation researchers appear to have most frequently assessed consultation procedural integrity by having independent judges compare a list of objectives for each stage of consultation problem to audiotapes of consultation sessions. Typically, the objectives have been taken (or created) from a treatment manual, and the number of objectives achieved has been divided by the total number of objectives stated, converted to a percentage, and used as a measure of consultation procedural integrity. Equal weight is given to each objective.

For example, in Galloway and Sheridan's (1994) report of a series of case studies using the conjoint behavioral consultation model, two independent coders assessed consultants' adherence to interview objectives. The authors reported adherence in terms of a percentage of interview objectives met and reported a point-by-point interrater agreement reliability of 84%, as well as a kappa value for interrater agreement. Kratochwill et al. (1995) used similar procedures in their evaluation of consultant and client outcomes for behavioral consultation training. In other cases, the consultant's coding of his or her own behavior using a checklist of objectives has served as one set of ratings, and then a second, independent coder has listened to audiotapes of the session to verify the consultant's self-ratings (e.g., Jones, Wickstrom, & Friman, 1997; Sterling-Turner, Watson, & Moore, 2002).

Within a study, the number of sessions coded to establish the percentage of consultation objectives achieved has ranged from about 50% (e.g., Jones et al., 1997; Kratochwill et al., 1995; Noell et al., 2000) to 100% (e.g., Sterling-Turner et al., 2002). When less than 100% of interviews are coded, there is presently no empirical basis for judging the adequacy of the sampling strategy.

Only a few studies have reported the criteria they used for judging that adherence to interview objectives was adequate (e.g., Kratochwill et al., 1995), and in some cases, the results of the adherence checks have not been reported, only that the adherence checks were done (e.g., Jones et al., 1997). However, when adherence has been reported, it is generally in the 85–100% range.

At present, the use of checklists with a simple calculation of the percentage of treatment objectives achieved appears to be the widest practice in assessing consultant adherence as it relates to consultation procedural integrity. Advantages of this method are that it is objective, and its reliability can be determined. However, to advance the technology for assessing procedural integrity advances, it may be useful to consider whether some objectives should be weighted more heavily than others and to develop an empirical basis for determining what constitutes adequate model adherence. In terms of weighting some objectives more heavily, most persons would view obtaining a behavioral description of the client behavior in a problem analysis interview as more critical than setting a date for the next interview. However, because both are objectives listed for the problem identification interview in behavioral consultation, they have been given equal weight in assessing model adherence in the current coding schemes (Bergan & Kratochwill, 1990; Wickstrom, Jones, LaFleur, & Witt, 1998).

Another strategy employed in the measurement of consultant adherence and procedural integrity is statement-by-statement coding of consultant and consultee verbal behaviors during consultation interviews. For example, the Consultation Analysis Record (CAR; Bergan, 1977) has been used extensively in behavioral consultation research to assess a variety of dimensions of consultant verbal behavior and their relation to client outcomes (e.g., Busse, Kratochwill, & Elliott, 1999; Hughes & DeForest, 1993). Although measures derived from the information coded on the CAR are clearly related to adherence to the behavioral consultation model, this measure has been used less as an assessment of consultant procedural integrity, perhaps because it is not clear where cut points might be set for variables derived from the CAR in terms of assessing consultant adherence.

In a thoughtful discussion of the measurement of treatment integrity, Waltz et al. (1993) suggested that measures of treatment adherence would be improved by using manuals that specify *all* aspects of treatment agent competence, including nonspecific ones such as warmth and nurturance. They also suggested that adherence be assessed relative to treatment agent actions that are (a) unique to a treatment modality; (b) essential but not unique; (c) compatible but neither necessary nor unique; and (d) proscribed. As an example, they suggested that assigning homework would be essential and unique to behavioral therapy but proscribed in psychodynamic therapy. In contrast, empathetic listening would be essential to both modalities but not unique.

Waltz et al.'s (1993) recommendations have many implications for school consultation research. First, articulating and assessing consultant behaviors in these four categories would provide an explicit basis for characterizing consultation models in terms of commonalities and differences. Second, such a listing would provide a basis for developing consultation process integrity measures that assess specific and nonspecific aspects of consultant behavior and allow for assessment of errors of inclusion or exclusion by consultants in treatment studies. A detailed articulation of consultation process would also help in examining overlap between models of consultation in treatment comparisons and operationalizing ill-defined constructs such as collaborative, which may have many different meanings across consultation models and researchers (Schulte & Osborne, 2003).

Another important issue relevant to consultation procedural integrity is treatment agent competence. Both Waltz et al. (1993) and Miller and Binder (2002) have suggested that adherence and competence may be separate dimensions of treatment integrity, and empirical investigations of these dimensions in psychotherapy have provided support for this proposition (Bein et al., 2000; Carroll et al., 2000). Waltz et al. defined competence in terms of the extent to which the treatment agent took relevant aspects of therapeutic context into account and responded to these appropriately within each treatment case. Taking into account relevant contextual factors in consultation might include adapting procedures to the (a) knowledge and skill level of the consultee, (b) degree of consultee distress, or (c) particular client problem. For example, proceeding through a problem identification interview while a stressed consultee cries in frustration over her difficulties managing a client would constitute an example of adequate adherence to behavioral consultation but consultant incompetence. Alternately, a consultant and consultee might achieve all objectives related to developing a treatment plan in a consultation interview (high adherence) yet develop a plan that is unlikely to succeed in changing client behavior (low competence; see Fuchs & Fuchs, 1989).

Although procedures for assessing consultant competence are less developed than those for assessing adherence, there are some studies that have examined consultant competence. For example, Kratochwill et al. (1995) used tests of knowledge of learning theory and behavior consultation to assess consultant trainees' competence prior to their first consultation case. However, contextually sensitive deployment of behavioral knowledge during actual consultation cases was not assessed. In an early attempt to assess consultant competence in a way that did take into account consultation context, Bergan and Tombari (1976) examined the variety of psychological principles applied by consultants across consultation cases, hypothesizing that the consultant who applied a broad range of psychological principles would be more effective than a consultant who only used a narrow range of principles. Working from case reporting forms filled out by consultants, they coded which change procedures were incorporated into client treatment plans developed by consultant and consultees (e.g., modeling, positive reinforcement, task alteration). An index of consultant flexibility was then calculated for each consultant based on the number of different principles used in plans and the proportions of cases in which each psychological principle was employed. They found that consultant flexibility was a predictor of successful problem resolution. Although Bergan and Tombari's procedures did not measure contextually sensitive deployment of consultant strategies directly, presumably the consultant who used a range of psychological principles would be more able to respond to the unique aspects of the client's difficulty.

Hughes et al. (2001) used the Consultant Evaluation Rating Form (Hughes & Hasbrouck, 1997) to evaluate consultants' implementation of her responsive systems consultation model. This measure explicitly defines and measures consultant competence on both task-oriented and interpersonal dimensions of the consultation process, including effectiveness of the intervention plan, consultant nonverbal behavior, and consultant sensitivity to consultee needs. The reliability and validity data for the measure are promising (Hughes et al., 2001). Within consultation, this coding system appears to come the closest to the recommendations for developing treatment agent adherence and competence measures recommended by Waltz et al. (1993).

Treatment Plan Implementation

The second component of treatment fidelity in consultation is implementation of the intervention plan by the consultee (Noell, chapter 15, this volume). In most models of consultation, providing the intervention is the responsibility of the consultee. Given that researchers exercise less control over the integrity of consultees than consultants, treatment implementation is more likely to vary among cases. As such, measurement of treatment plan implementation is particularly important in documenting that consultative problem solving is responsible for client change. Measurement issues associated with both treatment adherence and consultee competence are addressed next.

Treatment plan adherence has not always been routinely assessed in consultation research (Gresham, 1989; Gresham & Kendell, 1987; Lentz & Daly, 1996; Noell, chapter 15, this volume; Sheridan, Welch, & Orme, 1996). However, when assessed, it has been measured in a variety of ways, including consultee self-report (e.g., Galloway & Sheridan, 1994); assessment of permanent products (e.g., Noell, Witt, Gilbertson, Ranier, & Freeland, 1997); and direct observation (e.g., Jones et al., 1997).

Not surprisingly, self-reports of treatment plan adherence are viewed as problematic (Waltz et al., 1993). However, consultee accuracy may depend on the form of self-report. For instance, in a study consisting of a series of three case studies in consultation, Robbins and Gutkin (1994) simply asked consultees if they had implemented the treatment plan developed in consultation. All consultees reported they had implemented the treatment plan; however, observations of the frequency with which one of the central components of the intervention was implemented indicated that implementation frequency was low. In contrast, Ehrhardt, Barnett, Lentz, Stollar, and Reifin (1996) developed intervention scripts collaboratively with parent and teacher consultees. The scripts were designed to provide guidance in implementing interventions in consultees' own words. The scripts were then adapted to a checklist format that allowed consultees to carry out the intervention and monitor their own degree of implementation of the treatment at the same time. Comparisons of consultees' self-ratings and independent observers' ratings indicated high compliance with the treatment plan and high accuracy in self-report.

Although some forms of self-report may be accurate, they are probably best viewed as a supplement to an independent measure of treatment plan implementation rather than the sole measure of treatment plan implementation in treatment research. However, when a self-monitoring method serves as a reminder of the correct implementation sequence for the consultee, it may be useful both as an assessment tool and as a means of promoting treatment plan adherence.

Permanent product assessment of treatment plan implementation in consultation was suggested by Gresham (1989) and has been used extensively by Noell in his studies investigating variables that affect consultee treatment plan implementation (Noell et al., 1997, 2000, 2005). With this technique, the intervention designed in consultation is broken down into smaller steps such that each implementation of each step results in the generation of a permanent product. For example, daily ratings of student behavior on a home-school report card might be used as an indicator that a teacher had consistently evaluated a student's behavior, and the parent's signature on the report card would indicate that the report card had been brought home and the agreed-on consequence for a particular rating was implemented by the parent.

Three advantages of this measurement method are that it is likely to be less reactive than observations (Noell, chapter 15, this volume), is low cost, and does not require sampling because a measure of treatment plan implementation is generated each time the treatment is used. However, the use of permanent products does not lend itself to the assessment of implementation for all types of treatment. For example, it would be difficult to envision how a permanent product assessment could be generated for a treatment plan in which a teacher ignores inappropriate behavior, particularly if the inappropriate behavior had a high frequency.

One potential advantage of the increasing use of computers and the Internet in the home and classroom is that permanent product measures that do not require extra time or effort from the consultee can be incorporated into the intervention. For example, the online reading instructional system Headsprout (www.headsprout.com/) generates online performance reports that could be used to indicate the extent to which reading instruction in a specific area was carried out. As computerized and Internet-based interventions become more sophisticated and inexpensive, their use in plans developed in consultation may increase because of the ease with which treatment plan implementation can be documented with them. They may be particularly valuable if the move to a response-to-intervention model of special education eligibility (Fuchs, Mock, Morgan, & Young, 2003) gains more momentum.

Direct observation of treatment plan implementation, the final method of assessing plan implementation, is adaptable to a wide range of interventions. However, unless the intervention is only delivered on an infrequent basis, it is likely to be an expensive and intrusive method of monitoring plan adherence. One option for reducing the cost of observation is sampling only a proportion of the times in which the intervention is to be implemented. For instance, Robbins and Gutkin (1994) observed consultees for 30 minutes each day to assess their use of contingent praise. Similarly, Sterling-Turner et al. (2002) assessed consultees' adherence with treatment plans that involved ignoring inappropriate behavior, administering reinforcers, and providing prompts, with classroom observations lasting 20 to 40 minutes per day. However, unless the treatment is only implemented for that brief period each day, the data collected with these types of sampling plans reflect only a small portion of the school day. The generalizability of the results obtained during the observation period to the entire day is not known.

In most cases when consultee adherence has been assessed, whether it is through self-monitoring, permanent product measures, or observation, its measurement has taken the form of the percentage of required steps implemented per day or the percentage of the opportunities for the treatment to be implemented in which it was implemented. For example, Noell et al. (2000) calculated the percentage of intervention steps implemented per day of treatment by consultee, and Wickstrom et al. (1998) calculated the percentage of time that a target behavior exhibited by the client was followed by a programmed consequence.

Although there have been many calls for the inclusion of treatment plan implementation data in consultation studies (e.g., Gresham, 1989; Sheridan, Welch, & Orme, 1996), it is not clear what level of treatment plan implementation is expected or necessary to conclude that the intervention was satisfactorily implemented (Gresham, 1989). For example, Sterling-Turner et al. (2002) found that, for two of their four consultees, relatively low levels of treatment implementation in one phase of their study were associated with behavior change for the clients in question. In one of the cases, treatment plan implementation averaged less than 80% per day and for another case less than 40%. Sterling-Turner et al. speculated that when the consultee demonstrated the lowest level of treatment plan implementation, other aspects of the plan, such as client self-monitoring, accounted for the change in the client's behavior.

However, Sterling-Turner et al.'s (2002) speculation about the reasons for the lack of correspondence between their measure of treatment plan implementation and client improvement points out another difficulty in measuring treatment plan adherence. When adherence for only one component of a complex intervention plan is assessed, rather than adherence across all components, the measure may not be a valid indicator of the degree of treatment plan implementation. Treatment plan implementation measurement technology is still in its infancy. Although studies are beginning to assess plan implementation, we have relatively little understanding of the reliability and validity of measurement procedures in this domain. Specifically, validating a particular treatment plan implementation measure will require documentation of the extent to which the measure (a) represents the intervention (content validity); (b) generalizes across time intervals, situations, and settings in which the treatment is used; (c) converges with other measures of treatment implementation; and (d) discriminates between adequate and inadequate adherence (Gresham, 1989). As more consultation researchers develop treatment implementation measures and provide data about the relationship between consultee adherence and client outcomes, this technology should develop considerably.

Despite the fact that consultation researchers still face many challenges in developing consultee treatment plan adherence measures, we do have examples of these measures in the present consultation literature (e.g., Noell et al., 2000; Sterling-Turner et al., 2002). However, measures of consultee competence in implementing the treatment plan are much more difficult to find. Again, the distinction made in the psychotherapy literature between therapist adherence and competence is between accomplishing specified objectives or exhibiting certain frequencies of desired behaviors (adherence) and examining the adequacy with which these objectives were accomplished or how sensitively particular behaviors were deployed given the context (competence). For consultation, it is conceivable that consultees might adhere to intervention plans but show low competence. For example, a consultee might use contingent praise so frequently as to disrupt instruction or draw unwanted attention to a child.

It may be that adequate specification of all the components of an intervention would result in complete overlap between a measure of consultee adherence and competence. This situation would simplify the measurement of both constructs. Given that most assessments of treatment agent competence involve the use of expert raters (Kazantzis, 2003), one potential test that a treatment plan adherence measure also assesses consultee competence might be a high correlation of the treatment adherence measure with expert ratings of videotapes of the consultee implementing the intervention.

Summary

Treatment integrity in consultation can be divided into two distinct components: consultation procedural integrity and treatment plan implementation. Each of these components can be considered along two dimensions: adherence and competence. At present, both components of treatment integrity have been assessed in consultation research, but not routinely. This situation parallels the state of research in youth psychotherapy research (Weisz et al., 2005). For both components of treatment integrity in consultation, adherence has been assessed much more frequently than competence.

The development of treatment fidelity measures for consultation is still in its beginning stages. There remain many unanswered questions about the frequency and form of measurement needed for reliable and valid assessments of consultation procedural integrity and treatment plan implementation. Consultation researchers should consider the comprehensive framework proposed by Waltz et al. (1993) in developing measures of treatment fidelity, particularly measures of consultation procedural integrity. This framework includes specification of behaviors that are (a) unique to a treatment modality; (b) essential but not unique; (c) compatible but neither necessary nor unique; and (d) proscribed. When employed in the consultation context, such a framework would result in clearer descriptions of models; allow delineation of overlap between models; and promote specification of frequently studied but poorly defined variables in consultation, such as collaboration.

Measurement OF Client Outcomes

In any type of intervention outcome research, accurately assessing the impact of treatment is a critical issue. Three aspects of outcome assessment are considered in this section: (a) what should be measured in assessing client outcomes in consultation, (b) how it should be measured, and (c) methods for measuring consultation outcomes when studies address a diverse set of referral concerns.

What to Measure

The four methodological sources (Altman et al., 2001; Gresham & Noell, 1993; Task Force on EBI, 2003; Weisz et al., 2005) discuss a number of potential areas that are relevant to evaluating the impact of consultation. All sources mention the importance of assessing the problem specifically targeted for treatment, whether it is a clinical condition or specific target behavior. Additional areas of outcome assessment are (a) client symptoms outside the primary focus of treatment; (b) functional impact of the treatment (e.g., improved grades, fewer school suspensions, change in educational placement); (c) consumer satisfaction (or social validation of treatment effects); (d) environmental impact (e.g., reduced parenting stress or increased instructional time when a student's disruptive behavior is controlled); and (e) adverse effects of treatment. Also discussed are generalization of behavior changes over settings and maintenance of behavior change after the cessation of treatment (Task Force on EBI, 2003).

Weisz et al. (2005) reported that the typical psychotherapy outcome study employed a total of 12 participant measures. All studies had at least 1 measure of the target problem, with the average study including 5. Of the studies, 78% included a measure of symptoms outside the primary focus of treatment, and 28% included one or more measures of the functional impact of treatment. Less than 10% of the studies included a measure of consumer satisfaction or environmental impact of treatment. Weisz and colleagues did not tabulate studies' use of measures to assess adverse effects of treatment or generalization and long-term maintenance of gains, although Weisz, Weiss, Han, Granger, and Morton (1995) reported that a third of youth psychotherapy studies included follow-up measures.

There have been no examinations of the breadth of outcome areas assessed in consultation research in the detailed manner of Weisz et al. (2005). However, in their discussion of consultation research, Gresham and Noell (1993) characterized consultation research as employing dependent variables that were "limited in scope, univariate, and ecologically invalid" (p. 257). Sheridan, Welch, & Orme (1996) tabulated the percentage of consultation research studies that assessed consumer satisfaction, long-term maintenance of treatment gains, and generalization of treatment effects across persons, settings, or behaviors. They found that 37% of the studies had assessed consumer satisfaction, and 26% had assessed long-term maintenance of treatment gains. Less than 5% of studies had included measures to assess the generalization of treatment gains. The more frequent use of consumer satisfaction measures in the consultation literature compared to the youth psychotherapy literature (37% vs. <10%) may reflect the indirect nature of consultation service delivery. When others are delivering the treatment, their perceptions of its impact and satisfaction with the treatment may be more likely to be measured. Reddy et al. (2000) reported that the majority of consultation studies in their meta-analysis had employed more than one outcome measure, suggesting that breadth and depth in the measurement of outcomes in consultation research may be increasing.

How to Measure

Across the four methodological sources (Altman et al., 2001; Gresham & Noell, 1993; Task Force on EBI, 2003; Weisz et al., 2005), recommended practices for assessing outcomes include the use of measures that (a) are objective, (b) demonstrate high reliability and evidence of validity, (c) include assessment of normalization, and (d) allow assessment of each treatment construct with a multi-method, multisource approach. These four characteristics of high-quality outcome measurement are discussed next. In addition, the issue of how to measure outcomes across referral problems, a particular problem in consultation research, is addressed.

Objective Measurement

The strongest evidence that a treatment is effective is produced when (a) assessors are blind to the participant's treatment status; (b) the clients are unaware or unable to influence the ratings; or (c) independent life events, such as arrests or high school dropout rate, are used as outcome measures (Altman et al., 2001; Weisz et al., 2005). When the child or those involved in treatment serve as informants or are able to influence the intervention assessment, the evidence of an intervention effect is weakened because factors other than actual behavior change may have influenced the assessment. The preference for objective measurement does not mean that teacher's and parents' views of whether treatment has resulted in changes in child symptoms or behavior are unimportant. Rather, these assessments should be viewed as a component of social validation (Finn & Sladeczek, 2001) or consumer satisfaction rather than as the primary indicator of treatment outcome.

Weisz et al. (2005) reported that approximately 63% of youth psychotherapy studies had included behavioral observations among their outcome measures. Less than half of these, or a third of all studies reviewed, had used "blind" observers to collect the behavioral observations. Approximately 14% of all studies had used independent life data as an outcome measure. Using a somewhat different definition of direct observation, Sheridan, Welch, & Orme (1996) reported that direct observation was used in 44% of consultation outcome studies. They did not report the percentage of consultation studies using blind observers or independent life data. Although direct comparisons of the two treatment literatures are not possible, it appears that less than half of all studies of either treatment modality employed objective observers in assessing client improvement.

Although the use of independent observers helps to ensure assessments of treatment outcome are unbiased, results from independent observations often are based on considerably fewer observation opportunities than measures completed by study participants. There are several studies in which positive effects of consultation on pupil behavior have been found with teacher ratings, but the gains have not been confirmed by independent observers blind to participant treatment status (Dunson et al., 1994; Fuchs & Fuchs, 1989; Fuchs, Fuchs, & Bahr, 1990). Expectancy effects may explain the discrepancy. However, another explanation is that the assessments completed by objective observers were based on much more limited amounts of data than those completed by consultation participants. For example, in the Fuchs, Fuchs, and Bahr (1990) study, classroom observations took place twice before and twice after the completion of consultation, and each session lasted 20 minutes.

Given that Lomax (1982) found that several hours of classroom observation are needed to obtain stable estimates of pupil behavior, it is unlikely that the amount of classroom observation used in many consultation studies would yield comparisons between treatments conditions that were sensitive to anything but large changes in pupil behavior. This fact does not diminish the importance of objective outcome measures but suggests that consultation researchers consider carefully the frequency and length of behavioral observations that will be needed to ensure that a treatment effect will be detected.

High Reliability and Evidence of Validity
One of the eight features of studies examined in evaluating the quality of the evidence to support a treatment in the *EBI Procedural and Coding Manual* (Task Force on EBI, 2003) is the use of outcome measures that produce reliable and valid scores. The highest rating, "strong evidence," in the coding system's key feature of measurement requires the use of measures for each outcome construct with reliability coefficients above .85 and evidence of validity.

To date, no review has characterized outcome measures across studies in youth psychotherapy or consultation studies in terms of their reliability and validity. However, it seems reasonable to assert that many of the outcome measures used in school consultation studies would meet the criteria outlined in the *EBI Procedural and Coding Manual* (Task Force on EBI, 2003). That is, most published consultation studies have provided evidence that their outcome measures are reliable across at least one facet of measurement (e.g., observers, items) and relate in some way to the construct assessed (e.g., through construct, content, or concurrent validity). However, it is also true that there is considerable variability in outcome measures across consultation studies, even when the same outcome construct is assessed. For example, student on-task behavior has been assessed through standardized observational systems (Dunson et al., 1994); researcher-designed observational systems with data collected over all instructional activities (Jones et al., 1997); researcher-designed observational codes with data collected during seat work only (Robbins & Gutkin, 1994); teacher ratings of frequency, severity, and duration of off-task behavior (Fuchs, Fuchs, & Bahr, 1990); and norm-referenced teacher ratings of attentional behavior (Dunson et al., 1994). Although assessing the same construct, these measures are likely to vary in a number of ways. This variability is likely to contribute to differences in treatment outcomes and estimates of consultation effect size across studies.

As noted, Wilson and Lipsey (2001) provided evidence that how a treatment outcome is measured contributes as much in the variability in treatment outcomes across studies as what is measured. In addition, two comprehensive reviews have found that intervention effects are likely to be larger when researcher-designed measures rather than published or standardized measures are used (Marshall et al., 2000; Wilson & Lipsey, 2001). Taken together, these findings suggest that moving toward the use of a small number of standardized, published instruments for common targets of consultation treatment (e.g., achievement, on-task behavior) would likely yield more consistent and generalizable estimates of intervention effects for consultation. If the same instruments were used with other interventions aimed at the same problems, then this strategy would also allow comparisons among treatment approaches.

More consistent use of the same outcome measures in consultation studies with similar treatment targets would also make psychometric studies of these measures more cost-effective. For example, given the discussion of the limited amount of occasions typically sampled when observational measures are used in consultation studies, it would be useful to know the number and length of observational sessions that would be needed to have a reasonable likelihood of obtaining a generalizable or stable estimate of on-task behavior when planning a consultation study.

Normalization
One way of assessing the educational or clinical significance of a change in client behavior is the extent to which the client's behavior is normalized by treatment. Both the *EBI Procedural and Coding Manual* (Task Force on EBI, 2003) and Gresham and Noell (1993) discussed the importance of including measures that allow this type of assessment as part of treatment studies.

Neither Weisz et al. (2005) nor any of the comprehensive consultation reviews that have been conducted to date (Fuchs et al., 1992; Reddy et al., 2000; Sheridan, Welch, & Orme, 1996) have examined the extent to which client normalization has been assessed in youth psychotherapy or consultation outcome studies. However, examples of normalization assessment are present in the consultation literature.

For example, Sheridan, Kratochwill, and Elliott (1990) compared the social initiations of withdrawn children and their nonreferred classroom peers in assessing the impact of behavioral consultation on withdrawn children's social functioning. This strategy employs local "micronorms" (Gresham & Noell, 1993) as the basis for a normative comparison. Two other strategies for normative comparisons are examining the number of clients who no longer meet diagnostic criteria following treatment or assessing the number of clients who score within normal limits (e.g., within one standard deviation) on a norm-referenced measure of the target behavior before and after treatment.

Multisource, Multimethod Approach
Both the *EBI Procedural and Coding Manual* (Task Force on EBI, 2003) and Gresham and Noell (1993) advocate the use of multisource, multimethod approaches to assessing treatment outcomes.

The use of multiple measures to establish treatment efficacy presents an interesting methodological dilemma. On the one hand, measuring the same construct through multiple methods and sources helps ensure that the treatment effect is robust and not dependent on the way it is measured (Cook, 2000). On the other hand, this practice increases the Type I error rate unless the researcher adjusts the alpha level required for significance to reflect the use of multiple measures. The increased alpha level in turn requires a larger sample size to achieve adequate power. When resources are limited, the researcher may need to sacrifice power to meet the demand for multiple measures.

An alternative strategy, endorsed in the Revised CONSORT statement (Altman et al., 2001) is careful a priori designation of one or two measures (or a composite) as the primary outcomes. A limited number of other measures also may be specified a priori as secondary measures, but study power is calculated based on the primary measure. This strategy not only allows the use of fewer participants but also prevents researchers from using multiple outcome measures or assessment points to cast a broad net and subsequently focusing only on those measures or time points when significant results were obtained (Altman et al., 2001; Feise, 2002) in reporting results. An important criterion for selection of a single primary outcome measure would be objectivity, given the discussion about treatment expectancy bias when treatment participants rate degree of client improvement.

Dunson et al. (1994) provides a good illustration of both the promise and problems associated with the use of a multisource, multimethod approach to assessing outcomes in consultation. The authors assessed the impact of behavioral consultation on students who were displaying symptoms consistent with attention deficit/hyperactivity disorder. Ten students were randomly assigned to receive teacher consultation; ten students were assigned to a no-treatment control group. Consultation outcomes were assessed with teacher ratings of problem severity and hyperactivity as well as behavioral observations using a published observation system and observers blind to children's treatment status. The observational system assessed four categories of student behavior (on-task, scanning, social, and disruptive behavior).

Dunson et al.'s (1994) methodology is consistent with the multisource, multimethod approach advocated in the *EBI Procedural and Coding Manual* (Task Force on EBI, 2003) and Gresham and Noell (1993). However, with 10 participants per condition, their power to detect effects using significance levels that controlled for familywise error rate and six dependent measures was extremely low (Cohen, 1992). Given the difficulty conducting consultation research and the high participant attrition observed in many consultation studies, increasing consultation study rigor through the use of a single, high-quality, objective primary outcome measure, as endorsed in the Revised CONSORT statement, seems the preferred strategy. Additional measures, such as teacher ratings, might provide supplemental information about treatment effects but would not be used in the primary test of the intervention's efficacy.

Measuring Consultation Outcomes Across Referral Problems

School consultation is often viewed as a preventive strategy for addressing academic and behavioral problems that typically occur in the classroom (Bergan, 1977; Brown et al., 2006). Perhaps it is this view that has led many researchers to examine consultation's impact on more than one type of referral problem within a single study (e.g., Bergan & Tombari, 1976; Fuchs, Fuchs, & Bahr, 1990; Fuchs, Fuchs, Bahr, Fernstrom, & Stecker, 1990; Galloway & Sheridan, 1994; Sterling-Turner et al., 2002). Although such a strategy increases studies' external validity, it presents a measurement difficulty because client improvement must be assessed in relation to different target behaviors for each client. A similar issue arises when researchers attempt to cumulate consultation outcomes across studies in meta-analyses.

At least five strategies have been employed in consultation studies to cumulate and characterize outcomes across different referral problems. These strategies are to (a) characterize the outcome for each consultation case using a binary scale (goal met, goal not met); (b) employ "generic" rating scales or (c) "generic" behavioral observational procedures across referral problems; (d) use Goal Attainment Scaling (GAS); and (e) quantify case outcomes with effect sizes.

Binary coding, the first strategy, was employed by Bergan and Tombari (1976). Consultants coded cases as 1 or 0 depending on whether the problem identified in consultation was considered solved in the final interview. No reliability figures were reported for consultants' coding of cases. Generic rating scales, the second strategy, were used by Fuchs and colleagues in a series of studies concerning consultation as a prereferral strategy (Fuchs & Fuchs, 1989; Fuchs, Fuchs, & Bahr, 1990; Fuchs, Fuchs, Bahr, Fernstrom, et al., 1990), as well as by Wickstrom et al. (1998) and Sheridan, Eagle, Cowan, and Mickelson (2001). In the Fuchs studies, teachers rated each child's target problem in terms of its manageability, severity, and tolerability on three 5-point scales. Scores on the three scales were summed to examine changes in consultees' perceptions of whether the target behaviors had changed from pre- to posttesting for the treatment or control groups. Sheridan et al. (2001) made minor modifications to the Effectiveness scale of the Behavior Intervention Rating Scale (Von Brock & Elliott, 1987) and then used this scale to assess parent and teacher perceptions of problem resolution across referral problems. Internal consistency reliabilities for the measures used in the Fuchs and Sheridan studies were good.

The three Fuchs studies mentioned (Fuchs & Fuchs, 1989; Fuchs, Fuchs, & Bahr, 1990; Fuchs, Fuchs, Bahr, Fernstrom, et al., 1990) also used the third strategy, an observational measure that allowed results to be cumulated across target behaviors. For each student participating in the consultative treatment, the student and two randomly selected same-sex peers were observed before and after consultation. The mean percentage of intervals in which students exhibited the particular behavior that had been targeted for intervention in the treated student was then recorded, and the discrepancy between the target pupil's behavior and his or her peer's behavior was used as the measure of the target pupil's functioning. Although the observers were not blind to the treatment condition of participants, independent coders who did not know the participants' treatment condition assignment were used in reliability checks, and agreement between both types of observers was high (Fuchs, Fuchs, Bahr, Fernstrom, et al., 1990).

The fourth strategy, GAS (Kiresuk, Smith, & Cardillo, 1994), was used by Kratochwill et al. (1995), Sheridan et al. (2001), and Hughes et al. (2001) to cumulate results across consultation cases that addressed different referral problems. With this technique, individual goals for each client are scaled on 5-point scales, typically ranging from –2 to +2. Negative scores (–2, –1) indicate poor outcomes, and positive scores (+1, +2) indicate good outcomes. The midpoint of each scale, 0, represents client functioning at baseline (no change) or the expected outcome at the close of treatment, depending on which variant of GAS is used (Hughes et al., 2001; Kiresuk et al., 1994). Persons completing the scales for clients can be independent judges or persons participating in the treatment under study. There is support for both the reliability and the validity of GAS (Kiresuk et al., 1994; Shefler, Canetti, & Wiseman, 2001), although concerns have been raised about scale-weighting procedures and whether the scale points should be treated as equal-interval data (MacKay & Somerville, 1996).

The final strategy for cumulating outcomes across different types of target problems is the conversion of treatment outcomes to effect sizes. A variety of ways of calculating effect sizes is available, and these ways are appropriate for single-subject, within-subject group (repeated measures), and between-group designs (Busk & Serlin, 1992; Durlak, Meerson, & Foster, 2003; Hunter & Schmidt, 2004; Task Force on EBI, 2003). Both Kratochwill et al. (1995) and Sheridan et al. (2001) used effect sizes as an outcome measure for a series of single-subject case studies that addressed diverse referral problems. For example, Sheridan et al. calculated 66 effect sizes for 52 children whose parents and teachers participated in conjoint behavioral consultation. Referral problems included academic, behavioral, or social difficulties. Mean effect sizes for interventions in home and school settings were calculated, and confidence intervals were used to estimate the "true" population mean effect size for conjoint behavioral consultation in each setting. In addition, the effect sizes were used as the criterion in a regression equation examining the extent to which client age, case complexity, and symptom severity and the interactions of these variables predicted effect size.

The five strategies just described differ in terms of their advantages and disadvantages for cumulating and characterizing outcomes across different referral problems. In terms of precision, strategies in which information is retained about the magnitude of client change are preferable. This criterion is met by all the strategies with the exception of the goal met/not met strategy of Bergan and Tombari (1976). In terms of rigor, not all of the strategies employed objective observers, but each could be modified to use objective observers rather than treatment participants.

Compared to the other strategies, the peer-discrepancy observational strategy (Fuchs & Fuchs, 1989; Fuchs, Fuchs, & Bahr, 1990; Fuchs, Fuchs, Bahr, Fernstrom, et al., 1990) offers the advantage of providing information about the extent to which the consultation normalized client behavior compared to peers. However, the use of a discrepancy score introduces unreliability (Cone & Wilson, 1981). This problem may be lessened by the fact that the scores used in calculating the discrepancy are based on observations of the client and the client's peers. High correlations increase the measurement error, and discrepancy scores that are based on two scores from different persons are less likely to be highly correlated than those based on two scores from the same person. Nevertheless, there is likely to be a correlation between the peer's and target pupil's behavior because they are observed in the same setting.

Effect sizes are widely used in characterizing the impact of treatment and cumulating results across subjects or studies (e.g., DuPaul & Eckert, 1997; Lipsey & Wilson, 1993; Weisz et al., 1995), and are now a standard way of characterizing study outcomes in research reports (American Psychological Association, 2001). However, caution is needed in using and interpreting effect sizes as a means of summarizing treatment outcomes across different referral problems. The magnitude of effect sizes is dependent on both the manner in which they are calculated and the type of study design on which they are based (Durlak et al., 2003; Matyas & Greenwood, 1990; Parker et al., s2005; Rosenthal, 2000). This fact has sometimes been ignored in reporting and interpreting the meaning of effect sizes within and across consultation studies (e.g., Reddy et al., 2000; Sheridan et al., 2001). Effect sizes that are based on repeated measures of the same person or group without the use of a control group will be inflated by autocorrelation relative to effect sizes calculated from between-group designs (Busk & Marascuilo, 1992). Thus, mean effect sizes from different designs must be reported separately (Durlak et al., 2003), and effect sizes calculated on single-subject or within-group designs cannot be interpreted using Cohen's (1992) criteria for small, medium, and large effect sizes.

Summary

The limited breadth and quality of outcome measurement in consultation research has been a focus of criticism (e.g., Gresham & Noell, 1993). As a research area, consultation appears to lag behind youth treatment research in the number of measures used and the range of outcomes assessed. Although consultation studies are likely to include reliable and valid measures, suggested steps for improving the quality of the outcome measure in consultation studies are the use of objective measures and the inclusion of measures assessing normalization. A multisource, multimethod approach is recommended by two of the methodological sources. However, this approach may dilute the power of studies to detect treatment effects unless it is combined with a specification of a primary outcome measure.

FUTURE DIRECTIONS

As the evidence-based treatment movement begins to exert its impact on school-based practice, consultation researchers have an opportunity to strengthen the body of empirical studies that support consultation. Increasing breadth, consistency, and accuracy in the measurement of participants, processes, and outcomes in future consultation research will be critical in providing evidence of consultation's efficacy and effectiveness.

Weisz et al.'s (2005) characterization of the methodology used in youth psychotherapy research studies provides a useful yardstick for examining the state of current consultation research. Although direct comparisons are not possible because the consultation research methodology has not been reviewed as recently or as comprehensively as the youth psychotherapy research, the similarity in methodological issues and weaknesses in the two treatment approaches is striking. It is clear that there are many aspects of research design and reporting for which "best practice," as it is defined by emerging cross-disciplinary standards for evaluating treatment studies, must be more consistently implemented by researchers investigating both psychological treatments. In addition, there are a number of areas in which measurement technology is not yet well developed and further research is needed.

Table 3.1 presents a number of short- and long-term suggestions for improving the quality of measurement in consultation literature. The suggestions are organized around the three domains covered in this chapter. *Basic considerations* are actions that can be easily achieved in the short term given the current state of consultation treatment manuals and measures. *Future directions* are actions that will increase the rigor of consultation research in the long term by improving our tools or increasing our understanding of measurement issues.

In conclusion, this chapter has covered a wide range of topics related to strengthening the research base for school consultation by improving the accuracy of measurement related to describing study participants, validating the study process, and documenting treatment outcomes. Many topics related to measurement, such as the assessment of consultee skill development as a result of consultation, were not discussed. The length and complexity of this chapter, despite these omissions, is a testament to the difficulty involved in designing and conducting treatment research, particularly when studying an indirect treatment mode such as consultation.

Researchers face an unending battle to increase the signal-to-noise ratio in psychological treatment research (Hunter & Schmidt, 2004). If Wilson and Lipsey's (2001) assertion is correct, and how a construct is measured contributes as much variance in outcome research as what is measured, then attention to measurement issues by consultation researchers should yield great dividends in documenting consultation's usefulness as an intervention strategy. With the future of school consultation at stake as the evidence-based treatment movement moves forward, it is time to reap these dividends.

NOTE

1. In an intention-to-treat analysis, the last data point collected is carried forward in subsequent assessments. With baseline data comprising both the pre- and posttreatment assessments, the effect size would be 0.

Table 3.1   Basic Considerations and Future Directions for Improving Measurement and Reporting in Consultation Treatment Studies

Basic Considerations	Future Directions
Participant Characteristics	
Report the number of participants at each phase of a consultation treatment study and report the type of analysis used in reporting outcomes (e.g., intention to treat vs. per protocol). Report basic client demographic characteristics, including age, gender, ethnicity, socioeconomic status, and grade. Report basic consultee and consultant characteristics, including age, gender, ethnicity, occupation, years of experience, and training in profession and consultation. If results are intended to generalize to a clinical population, then use established clinical criteria and formal measures to verify diagnoses. When school-identified special education students are study participants, provide a statement of classification criteria used by the schools and independently assess "caseness" or describe the sample on key dimensions related to the disability classification.	Consider adoption of the Revised CONSORT Statement reporting template or an adaptation for journals reporting psychological treatments to allow uniform assessment of participant attrition. Develop more appropriate means of characterizing participants on diversity dimensions, such as acculturation and ethnic identity. Move toward consensus in child clinical and school psychology on participant and setting characteristics that should be included in journal reports.
Consultation Process	
Use a treatment manual to describe consultation procedures. Include measures of both consultation procedural integrity and treatment plan implementation that can be verified by independent observers.	Refine the technology for assessing consultation procedural integrity through delineation of (a) unique, (b) essential but not unique, (c) compatible but neither necessary nor unique, and (d) proscribed consultant behaviors within each model of consultation. Conduct comparative studies of the reliability, generalizability, and validity of consultation procedural and treatment plan integrity measures to provide better understanding of cost-effective strategies and sampling plans. Continue development of consultant and consultee measures that assess competence as well as adherence.
Consultation Outcomes	
Include measures of the primary treatment target (e.g., disruptive behavior), nontarget behaviors or symptoms, functional impact, environmental impact, potential adverse effects, and normalization. Designate, a priori, the primary measure that will be used in determining consultation treatment efficacy in each treatment domain. Include additional measures to allow multisource, multimethod assessment of consultation outcomes within each treatment domain. Restrict the use of participant-completed measures to social validation. Restrict consultation cases to single referral problems within a study to facilitate comparison of direct and indirect treatment strategies. Interpret obtained effect sizes within, not across, study design types.	Move toward more uniform measurement of frequent treatment targets across studies with common assessment instruments. Conduct a meta-analysis to ascertain typical effect sizes within study design types for a better understanding of large, medium, and small effect sizes within consultation.

REFERENCES

Altman, D. G., Schulz, K. F., Moher, D., Egger, M., Davidoff, F., Elbourne, D., et al. (2001). The Revised CON-SORT statement for reporting randomized trials: Explanation and elaboration [Electronic version]. *Annals of Internal Medicine, 134,* 663–694. Retrieved March 6, 2006, from http://www.annals.org/cgi/reprint/134/8/663.pdf

American Psychological Association. (2001). *Publication manual of the American Psychological Association.* Washington, DC: Author.

Babcock, N., & Pryzwansky, W. B. (1983). Models of consultation: Preferences of educational professionals at five stages of service. *Journal of School Psychology, 21,* 359–366.

Begg, C., Cho, M., Eastwood, S., Horton, R., Moher, D., Okin, I., et al. (1996). Improving the quality of reporting of randomized controlled trials. The CONSORT statement [Electronic version]. *Journal of the American Medical Association, 276,* 637–639.

Bein, E., Anderson, T., Strupp, H. H., Henry, W. P., Schacht, T. E., Binder, J. L., et al. (2000). The effects of training in time-limited dynamic psychotherapy: Changes in therapeutic outcome. *Psychotherapy Research, 10,* 119–132.

Bergan, J. R. (1977). *Behavioral consultation.* Columbus, OH: Merrill.

Bergan, J. R., & Kratochwill, T. R. (1990). *Behavioral consultation and therapy.* New York: Plenum.

Bergan, J. R., & Tombari, M. L. (1976). Consultant skill and efficiency and the implementation and outcomes of consultation. *Journal of School Psychology, 14,* 3–14.

Bernstein, J. (2004). Evidence-based medicine [Electronic version]. *Journal of the American Academy of Orthopaedic Surgeons, 12,* 80–88.

Brown, D., Pryzwansky, W. B., & Schulte, A. C. (2006). *Psychological consultation and collaboration: Introduction to theory and practice* (6th ed.). Boston: Pearson.

Busk, P. L., & Marascuilo, L. A. (1992). Statistical analysis in single-case research: Issues, procedures, and recommendations, with applications to multiple behaviors. In T. R. Kratochwill & J. R. Levin (Eds.), *Single-case research design and analysis: New directions for psychology and education* (pp. 159–185). Hillsdale, NJ: Erlbaum.

Busk, P. L., & Serlin, R. C. (1992). Meta-analysis for single-case research. In T. R. Kratochwill & J. R. Levin (Eds.), *Single-case research design and analysis: New directions for psychology and education* (pp. 187–212). Hillsdale, NJ: Erlbaum.

Busse, R. T., Kratochwill, T. R., & Elliott, S. N. (1999). Influences of verbal interactions during behavioral consultations on treatment outcomes. *Journal of School Psychology, 37,* 117–143.

Buysse, V., Schulte, A. C., Pierce, P. P., & Terry, D. (1994). Models and styles of consultation: Preferences of professionals in early intervention. *Journal of Early Intervention, 18,* 302–310.

Carroll, K. M., Nich, C., Sifry, R. L., Nuro, K. F., Frankforter, T. L., Ball, S. A., et al. (2000). A general system for evaluating therapist adherence and competence in psychotherapy research in the addictions [Electronic version]. *Drug and Alcohol Dependence, 57,* 225–238.

Chambless, D. L., Baker, M. J., Baucom, D. H., Beutler, L. E., Calhoun, K. S., Crits-Christoph, P., et al. (1998). Update on empirically validated therapies, II [Electronic version]. *Clinical Psychologist, 51,* 3–16.

Chambless, D. L., & Ollendick, T. H. (2001). Empirically supported psychological interventions: Controversies and evidence. *Annual Review of Psychology, 52,* 685–716.

Cochrane Collaboration. (n.d.). *Chronology of the Cochrane Collaboration.* Retrieved July 19, 2005, from http://www.cochrane.org/docs/cchronol.htm

Cohen, J. (1988). *Statistical power analysis for the behavioral sciences* (2nd ed.). Hillsdale, NJ: Erlbaum.

Cohen, J. (1992). A power primer. *Psychological Bulletin, 112,* 155–159.

Cone, T. E., & Wilson, L. R. (1981). Quantifying a severe discrepancy: A critical analysis. *Learning Disability Quarterly, 4,* 359–371.

Cook, T. D. (2000). Toward a practical theory of external validity. In L. Bickman (Ed.), *Validity and social experimentation* (pp. 3–43). Thousand Oaks, CA: Sage.

Davies, P., & Boruch, R. (2001). The Campbell Collaboration [Electronic version]. *British Medical Journal, 323,* 294–295.

Dunson, R. M., Hughes, J. N., & Jackson, T. W. (1994). Effect of behavioral consultation on student and teacher behavior. *Journal of School Psychology, 32,* 247–266.

DuPaul, G. J., & Eckert, T. L. (1997). The effects of school-based interventions for attention-deficit hyperactivity disorder: A meta-analysis. *School Psychology Review, 26*, 5–27

Durlak, J. A., Meerson, I., & Foster, C. J. E. (2003). Meta-analysis. In J. C. Thomas, & M. Hersen (Eds.), *Understanding research in clinical and counseling psychology* (pp. 243–267). Mahwah, NJ: Erlbaum.

Ehrhardt, K. E., Barnett, D. W., Lentz, F. E., Stollar, S. A., & Reifin, L. H. (1996). Innovative methodology in ecological consultation: Use of scripts to promote treatment acceptability and integrity. *School Psychology Quarterly, 11*, 149–168.

Erchul, W. P., Covington, C. G., Hughes, J. N., & Meyers, J. (1995). Further explorations of request-centered relational communication within school consultation. *School Psychology Review, 24*, 621–632.

Federal Interagency Forum on Child and Family Statistics. (2005). *America's children: Key national indicators of well-being, 2005*. Washington, DC: U.S. Government Printing Office. Retrieved January 19, 2006, from http://childstats.gov/amchildren05/index.asp.

Feise, R. J. (2002). Do multiple outcome measures require p-value adjustment? *BMC Medical Research Methodology, 2*, 8–11. Retrieved March 6, 2006, from http://www.biomedcentral.com/content/pdf/1471-2288-2-8.pdf

Finn, C. A., & Sladeczek, I. E. (2001). Assessing the social validity of behavioral interventions: A review of treatment acceptability measures. *School Psychology Quarterly, 16*, 176–206.

Fuchs, D., & Fuchs, L. S. (1989). Exploring effective and efficient prereferral interventions: A component analysis of behavioral consultation. *School Psychology Review, 18*, 260–283.

Fuchs, D., Fuchs, L. S., & Bahr, M. W. (1990). Mainstream assistance teams: A scientific basis for the art of consultation. *Exceptional Children, 57*, 128–139.

Fuchs, D., Fuchs, L. S., Bahr, M. W., Fernstrom, P., & Stecker, P. M. (1990). Prereferral intervention: A prescriptive approach. *Exceptional Children, 56*, 493–513.

Fuchs, D., Fuchs, L. S., Dulan, J., Roberts, H., & Fernstrom, P. (1992). Where is the research on consultation effectiveness? *Journal of Educational and Psychological Consultation, 3*, 151–174.

Fuchs, D., Fuchs, L., Reeder, P., Gilman, S., Fernstrom, P., Bahr, M., et al. (1989). *Mainstream assistance teams: A handbook on prereferral intervention*. Nashville, TN: Peabody College, Vanderbilt University.

Fuchs, D., Mock, D., Morgan, P. L., & Young, C. L. (2003). Responsiveness-to-intervention: Definitions, evidence, and implications for the learning disabilities construct. *Learning Disabilities Research & Practice, 18*, 157–171.

Galloway, J., & Sheridan, S. M. (1994). Implementing scientific practices through case studies: Examples using home-school interventions and consultation. *Journal of School Psychology, 32*, 385–413.

Gibbs, J. T. (1980). The interpersonal orientation in mental health consultation: Toward a model of ethnic variations in consultation. *Journal of Community Psychology, 8*, 195–207.

Gresham, F. M. (1989). Assessment of treatment integrity in school consultation and prereferral intervention. *School Psychology Review, 18*, 37–50.

Gresham, F. M., & Kendell, G. K. (1987). School consultation research: Methodological critique and future research directions. *School Psychology Review, 16*, 306–316.

Gresham, F. M., & Noell, G. H. (1993). Documenting the effectiveness of consultation outcomes. In J. E. Zins, T. R. Kratochwill, & S. N. Elliott (Eds.), *Handbook of consultation services for children* (pp. 249–273). San Francisco: Jossey-Bass.

Gutkin, T. B., & Ajchenbaum, M. (1984). Teachers' perception of control and preferences for consultative services. *Professional Psychology: Research and Practice, 15*, 565–570.

Gutkin, T. B., & Bossard, M. D. (1984). The impact of consultant, consultee, and organizational variables on teacher attitudes toward consultative services. *Journal of School Psychology, 22*, 251–258.

Gutkin, T. B., Singer, J. H., & Brown, R. (1980). Teacher reactions to school-based consultative services. *Journal of School Psychology, 18*, 126–134.

Hughes, J. N., & DeForest, P. A. (1993). Consultant directiveness and support as predictors of consultation outcomes. *Journal of School Psychology, 31*, 355–373.

Hughes, J. N., & Hasbrouck, J. (1997). *Consultant Evaluation Rating Form (CERF) scoring manual*. Unpublished manuscript. College Station, TX: Texas A & M University.

Hughes, J. N., Hasbrouck, J. E., Serdahl, E., Heidgerken, A., & McHaney, L. (2001). Responsive systems consultation: A preliminary evaluation of implementation and outcomes. *Journal of Educational and Psychological Consultation, 12*, 179–201.

Hunter, J. E., & Schmidt, F. L., (2004). *Methods of meta-analysis: Correcting error and bias in research findings* (2nd ed.). Thousand Oaks, CA: Sage.

Jones, K. M., Wickstrom, K. F., & Friman, P. C. (1997). The effects of observational feedback on treatment integrity in school-based behavioral consultation. *School Psychology Quarterly, 12*, 316–326.

Kazantzis, N. (2003). Therapist competence in cognitive-behavioural therapies: Review of the contemporary empirical evidence. *Behaviour Change, 20*, 1–12.

Kiresuk, T. J., Smith, A., & Cardillo, J. E. (Eds.). (1994). *Goal Attainment Scaling: Applications, theory, and measurement*. Hillsdale, NJ: Erlbaum.

Kratochwill, T. R., Elliott, S. N., & Busse, R. T. (1995). Behavior consultation: A 5-year evaluation of consultant and client outcomes. *School Psychology Quarterly, 10*, 87–117.

Kratochwill, T. R., & Stoiber, K. C. (2002). Evidence-based interventions in school psychology: Conceptual foundations of the *Procedural and Coding Manual* of Division 16 and the Society for the Study of School Psychology Task Force. *School Psychology Quarterly, 17*, 341–389.

Lentz, F. E., & Daly, E. J. (1996). Is the behavior of academic change agents controlled metaphysically? An analysis of the behavior of those who change behavior. *School Psychology Quarterly, 11*, 337–352.

Lewis-Snyder, G., Stoiber, K. C., & Kratochwill, T. R. (2002). Evidence-based interventions in school psychology: An illustration of task force coding criteria using group-based research design. *School Psychology Quarterly, 17*, 423–465.

Lipsey, M. W., & Wilson, D. B. (1993). The efficacy of psychological, educational, and behavioral treatment: Confirmation from meta-analysis. *American Psychologist, 48*, 1181–1209.

Lomax, R. G. (1982). An application of generalizability theory to observational research. *Journal of Experimental Education, 51*, 22–30.

Lonigan, C. J., Elbert, J. C., & Johnson, S. B. (Eds.). (1998). Empirically supported psychosocial interventions for children [Special section]. *Journal of Clinical Child Psychology, 27*, 138–226.

MacKay, G., & Somerville, W. (1996). Reflections on Goal Attainment Scaling (GAS): Cautionary notes and proposals for development. *Educational Research, 38*, 161–172.

Marshall, M., Lockwood, A., Bradley, C., Adams, C., Joy, C., & Fenton, M. (2000). Unpublished rating scales: A major source of bias in randomized controlled trials of treatments for schizophrenia. *British Journal of Psychiatry, 176*, 249–252.

Matyas, T. A., & Greenwood, K. M. (1990). Visual analysis of single-case time series: Effects of variability, serial dependence, and magnitude of intervention effects. *Journal of Applied Behavior Analysis, 23*, 341–341.

McCall, R. B., & Green, B. L. (2004). Beyond the methodological gold standards of behavioral research: Considerations for practice and policy [Electronic version]. *Social Policy Report, 18*(2), 3–12. Retrieved July 16, 2005, from http://www.srcd.org/Documents/Publications/SPR/spr18-2.pdf.

Miller, S. J., & Binder, J. L. (2002). The effects of manual-based training on treatment fidelity and outcome: A review of the literature on adult individual psychotherapy. *Psychotherapy: Theory/Research/Practice/Training, 39*, 184–198.

Moher, D., Schulz, K. F., & Altman, D. G. (2001). The CONSORT Statement: Revised recommendations for improving the quality of reports of parallel group randomized trials [Electronic version]. *Annals of Internal Medicine, 134*, 657–662. Retrieved March 6, 2006, from http://www.consort-statement.org/Statement/annals.pdf

Moncher, F. J., & Prinz, R. J. (1991). Treatment fidelity in outcome studies. *Clinical Psychology Review, 11*, 247–266.

Nathan, P. E., & Gorman, J. M. (1998). *A guide to treatments that work*. New York: Oxford University Press.

National Institute of Child Health and Human Development, NIH, DHHS. (2000). *Report of the National Reading Panel: Teaching children to read: Reports of the subgroups* (NIH Publication No. 00-4754). Washington, DC: U.S. Government Printing Office.

Noell, G. H., Witt, J. C., Gilbertson, D. N., Ranier, D. D., & Freeland, J. T. (1997). Increasing teacher intervention implementation in general education settings through consultation and performance feedback. *School Psychology Quarterly, 12*, 77–88.

Noell, G. H., Witt, J. C., LaFleur, L. H., Mortenson, B. P., Ranier, D. D., & LeVelle, J. (2000). Increasing intervention implementation in general education following consultation: A comparison of two follow-up strategies. *Journal of Applied Behavior Analysis, 33*, 271–284.

Noell, G. H., Witt, J. C. Slider, N. J., Connell, J. E., Gatti, S. L., Williams, K. L., et al. (2005). Treatment implementation following behavioral consultation in schools: A comparison of three follow-up strategies. *School Psychology Review, 34,* 87–106.

Parker, R. I., Brossart, D. F., Vannest, K. J., Long, J. R., De-Alba, R. G., Baugh, F. G., et al. (2005). Effect sizes in single case research: How large is large? *School Psychology Review, 34,* 116–132.

Peterson, L., Homer, A. L., & Wonderlich, S. A. (1982). The integrity of independent variables in behavior analysis. *Journal of Applied Behavior Analysis, 15,* 477–492.

Reddy, L., Barboza-Whitehead, S., Files, T., & Rubel E. (2000). Clinical focus of consultation outcome research with children and adolescents. *Special Services in the Schools, 16,* 1–22.

Robbins, J. R., & Gutkin, T. B. (1994). Consultee and client remedial and preventive outcomes following consultation: Some mixed empirical results and directions for future researchers. *Journal of Educational and Psychological Consultation, 5,* 149–167.

Rosenthal, R. (2000). Effect sizes in behavioral and biomedical research: Estimation and interpretation. In L. Bickman (Ed.), *Validity and social experimentation* (pp. 121–139). Thousand Oaks, CA: Sage.

Sackett, D. L., Rosenberg, W. M. C., Gray, J. A. M., Haynes, R. B., & Richardson, W. S. (1996). Editorial: Evidence based medicine: What it is and what it isn't. *British Medical Journal, 312,* 71–72.

Sass, D. A., Twohig, M. P., & Davies, W. H. (2004). Defining the independent variables and ensuring treatment integrity: A comparison across journals of different theoretical orientations. *Behavior Therapist, 27,* 172–174.

Schowengerdt, R. V., Fine, M. J., & Poggio, J. P. (1976). An examination of some bases of teacher satisfaction with school psychological services. *Psychology in the Schools, 13,* 269–275.

Schulte, A. C., & Osborne, S. S. (2003). When assumptive worlds collide: A review of definitions of collaboration in consultation. *Journal of Educational and Psychological Consultation, 14,* 109–138.

Schulte, A. C., Osborne, S. S., & Kauffman, J. M. (1993). Teacher responses to two types of consultative special education services. *Journal of Educational and Psychological Consultation, 4,* 1–28.

Schulte, A. C., Osborne, S. S., & McKinney, J. D. (1990). Academic outcomes for students with learning disabilities in consultation and resource programs. *Exceptional Children, 57,* 162–175.

Shefler, G., Canetti, L., & Wiseman, H. (2001). Psychometric properties of goal-attainment scaling in the assessment of Mann's time-limited psychotherapy. *Journal of Clinical Psychology, 57,* 971–979.

Sheridan, S. M., Eagle, J. W., Cowan, R. J., & Mickelson, W. (2001). The effects of conjoint behavioral consultation: Results of a 4-year investigation. *Journal of School Psychology, 39,* 361–385.

Sheridan, S. M., Kratochwill, T. R., & Bergan, J. R. (1996). *Conjoint behavioral consultation: A procedural manual.* New York: Plenum Press.

Sheridan, S. M., Kratochwill, T. R., & Elliott, S. N. (1990). Behavioral consultation with parents and teachers: Delivering treatment for socially withdrawn children at home and school. *School Psychology Review, 19,* 33–52.

Sheridan, S., Welch, M., & Orme, S. F. (1996). Is consultation effective? A review of outcome research. *Remedial and Special Education, 17,* 341–354.

Singer, J. D., Palfrey, J. S., Butler, J. A., & Walker, D. K. (1989). Variation in special education classification across school districts: How does where you live affect what you are labeled? *American Educational Research Journal, 26,* 261–281.

Spirito, A. (Ed.). (1999). Empirically supported treatments in pediatric psychology [Special issue]. *Journal of Pediatric Psychology, 24*(2).

Spring, B., Pagoto, S., Altman, S., & Thorn, B. (2005). An evidence-based practice glossary: Unscrambling alphabet soup [Electronic version]. *Health Psychologist, 27*(2), 3, 15–16.

Sterling-Turner, H. E., Watson, T. S., & Moore, J. W. (2002). The effects of direct training and treatment integrity on treatment outcomes in school consultation. *School Psychology Quarterly, 17,* 47–77.

Sue, S. (1999). Science, ethnicity, and bias: Where have we gone wrong? *American Psychologist, 54,* 1070–1077.

Task Force on Evidence-Based Interventions. (2003). *Procedural and coding manual for review of evidence-based interventions.* Retrieved July 3, 2005, from http://www.sp-ebi/documents/_workingfiles/EBImanual1.pdf.

U.S. Department of Education. (n.d.). *What Works Clearinghouse: Who we are.* Retrieved July 3, 2005, from http://www.whatworks.ed.gov/whoweare/overview.html

Von Brock, M., & Elliott, S. N. (1987). The influence of treatment effectiveness information on the acceptability of classroom interventions. *Journal of School Psychology, 28,* 27–37.

Waltz, J., Addis, M. E., Koerner, K., & Jacobson, N. S. (1993). Testing the integrity of a psychotherapy protocol: Assessment of adherence and competence. *Journal of Consulting and Clinical Psychology, 61,* 620–630.

Weisz, J. R., Doss, A. J., & Hawley, K. M. (2005). Youth psychotherapy outcome research: A review and critique of the evidence base [Electronic version]. *Annual Review of Psychology, 56,* 337–63.

Weisz, J. R., Weiss, B., Han, S. S., Granger, D. A., & Morton, T. (1995). Effects of psychotherapy with children and adolescents revisited: A meta-analysis of treatment outcome studies. *Psychological Bulletin, 117,* 450–468.

West, J. F. (1985). *Regular and special educators' preferences for school-based consultation models: A statewide study* (Technical Rep. No. 101). Austin, TX: Research and Training Institute on School Consultation, The University of Texas at Austin.

White, P. L., & Fine, M. J. (1976). The effects of three school psychological consultation modes on selected teacher and pupil outcomes. *Psychology in the Schools, 13,* 414–420.

Wickstrom, K. F., Jones, K. M., LaFleur, L. H., & Witt, J. C. (1998). An analysis of treatment integrity in school-based behavioral consultation. *School Psychology Quarterly, 13,* 141–154.

Wilson, D. B., & Lipsey, M. W. (2001). The role of method in treatment effectiveness research: Evidence from meta-analysis. *Psychological Methods, 6,* 413–429.

Wormold, R., & Oldfield, K. (1998). Evidence based medicine, the Cochrane Collaboration, and the CONSORT statement. *British Journal of Ophthalmology, 82,* 597–598.

4

Quantitative Research Methods and Designs in Consultation

Frank M. Gresham

Louisiana State University

Mike Vanderwood

University of California–Riverside

Research in school-based consultation has lagged behind the advances made in other areas of intervention research, such as applied behavior analysis, psychotherapy, and counseling, in terms of both quality and methodological sophistication. Gresham and Kendell (1987) noted that most consultation research at that time was elementary, unsophisticated, and descriptive relative to the knowledge produced by intervention research published in other areas of psychology and education. Unfortunately, there has not been a substantial improvement in the quality of school-based consultation research since that time relative to advances that have been made in other areas of intervention research. For example, the volume edited by Kazdin (2003) stands as a testament to the sophistication of methodological issues and strategies in clinical research. Stoiber and Kratochwill (2000) noted that there is an increasing movement toward developing and utilizing evidence-based practices in psychology, psychiatry, and pediatric psychology. However, similar advances are not apparent in the consultation research base.

Almost all areas of applied psychology (e.g., clinical, counseling, school, and pediatric) that utilize interventions to deliver services have embraced the notion of evidence-based practice to bridge the research-to-practice gap in these areas (see Kazdin & Weisz, 2003; Kratochwill & Stoiber, 2000; Stoiber & Kratochwill, 2000). Similarly, the field of special education has evolved into adopting scientific methods as the basis for evidence-based practices in the field (Odom et al., 2005). Although evidence-based practices are becoming the coin of the realm in most applied areas, there remains a huge chasm between the existence of research findings and their utilization by practitioners (Gutkin, 1993; Stoiber & Kratochwill, 2000).

In psychotherapy research, surveys of practicing psychotherapists have indicated that they perceive research questions as not relevant, the variables investigated are not thought to be representative of typical clinical practice, and the manner in which results are presented does not represent clinically important changes in behavior or psychological functioning (Morrow-Bradley & Elliott, 1986). Some have argued that most controlled psychotherapy research lacks, if not totally sacrifices, external validity in favor of internal validity (Parloff, 1979; Persons, 1991). In short, controlled psychotherapy research is perceived by many practitioners as not focusing on the types of clients seen in practice and not involving the type of therapy delivered by therapists in their practices. It is likely school-based practitioners could say the same about the utilization of consultation research.

Despite the above opinions, it remains that any scientific field cannot progress without paying close attention to research methodology to establish what is and is not known about phenomena of interest. This chapter focuses on quantitative research methodology as a means of establishing a knowledge base in school-based consultation. The primary goal of research methodology is to allow professionals to draw valid inferences from controlled research that are not confounded or otherwise disconfirmed by plausible rival hypotheses.

The scope of research topics addressed in school-based consultation is quite large. Topics in consultation research include the reciprocal relationships between consultant and consultee verbal interactions (Erchul & Chewning, 1990), effects of behavioral consultation on client academic performance (Rosenfield, 1995), the use of performance feedback in enhancing the treatment integrity of consultee-delivered interventions (Noell, Witt, Gilbertson, Ranier, & Freeland, 1997), the use of the Consultation Analysis Record in training consultants in behavioral consultation (Bergan & Kratochwill, 1990), treatment integrity in school consultation (Gresham, 1989), and a host of others. One thing all of these topics have in common is that they were investigated using well-established principles of research methodology. These principles constitute the focus of this chapter.

GROUP EXPERIMENTAL AND QUASI-EXPERIMENTAL DESIGNS

Experimental design involves a scheme of assigning participants to conditions (i.e., the independent variables) and the subsequent statistical analyses of that scheme. Kirk (1995) indicated that an experimental design is comprised of a number of interrelated activities, which are shown in Table 4.1.

In school-based consultation research, these activities might look something like the following: *Research hypothesis*: Consultees provided with performance feedback on their delivery of behavioral interventions will have higher treatment integrity than those who are not provided with performance feedback. *Independent variable*: The independent variable will be whether participants are assigned to either the performance feedback or control conditions (one independent variable with two levels). The *dependent variable* is the level of integrity with which interventions are implemented. The *nuisance variable* is the complexity of the interventions implemented by teachers. The *number of participants* will be 30 teachers (15 teachers per condition) that will be *randomly assigned* to either the performance feedback or control conditions. *Statistical analysis* will be a one-way

Table 4.1   Activities in Planning an Experimental Design

Formulating a research question

Formulating a research hypothesis

Formulating a statistical hypothesis

Identifying independent variables to be used

Identifying dependent variables to be used

Identifying potential nuisance variables

Controlling potential nuisance variables

Deciding on type of research strategy (true experiment or quasi-experiment)

Deciding on type of research strategy (cross-sectional or longitudinal)

Deciding on type of research strategy (retrospective or prospective)

Determining appropriate statistical analyses

analysis of covariance (ANCOVA) using treatment complexity as a covariate (the nuisance variable). It should be noted that blocking treatments according to complexity in a randomized blocks design could also be used to control the treatment complexity nuisance variable. In this case, the statistical analysis would be a 2 (Group) × 3 (Blocks) analysis of variance with 10 participants per block (high complexity, moderate complexity, or low complexity).

Hyatt and colleagues conducted an experimental study of the effects of jargon usage in consultation on treatment acceptability of a time-out intervention by undergraduate students and teachers (Hyatt, Tingstrom, & Edwards, 1991). Thus, the design of this study was a 2 (Condition) × 2 (Group) between-subjects arrangement. Participants were randomly assigned to either a jargon or no jargon condition. Results showed that teachers preferred the jargon presentation of the time-out intervention relative to the no jargon presentation, whereas undergraduates showed no preference for either presentation.

Not all research in consultation can be characterized as involving "true" experimental or even quasi-experimental designs. In fact, most research in school-based consultation is either descriptive or correlational (Gresham & Kendell, 1987; Zins & Erchul, 2002). *Descriptive research*, as the name implies, involves a description of phenomena as they exist and does not involve any control or manipulation of independent variables. Erchul and colleagues provided a good example of descriptive research in their survey of gender differences in social power bases in teacher consultation (Erchul, Raven, & Wilson, 2004). *Correlational research* involves the determination of a relationship between variables in consultation. For example, Martens and colleagues found that consultees' satisfaction with the consultation process was highly correlated with consultants' agreement statements with consultees (Martens, Lewandowski, & Houk, 1989).

Quasi-experimental designs are those designs that use intact groups rather than random assignment of experimental units to experimental conditions. Quasi-experiments are used when it is impractical, unfeasible, or unethical to use random assignment to conditions. Much research conducted in schools uses quasi-experimental designs because of the constraints on random assignment of participants to experimental conditions. An example of a quasi-experimental design follows.

A consultation researcher is interested in the effects of behavioral consultation with teachers on reducing office discipline referrals. The researcher cannot randomly assign schools to the behavioral consultation versus the control conditions and therefore must use intact groups. School A is designated as the behavioral consultation school, and School B is the control school. Office discipline referrals are collected before, immediately after, and 3 months after the behavioral consultation intervention for both schools. Data were analyzed using a 2 (School) × 3 (Time) repeated-measures analysis of variance. Results showed that School A had lower rates of office discipline referrals than School B at immediate posttest and follow-up. The researcher concludes that behavioral consultation is an effective intervention for improving school discipline. Quasi-experimental research of this nature, although valuable, creates some issues in experimental validity (see Gersten et al., 2005). These issues are discussed in the following section.

VALIDITY CONSIDERATIONS IN CONSULTATION RESEARCH

The purpose of research methodology is to design studies that uncover relations among variables that might not be readily apparent by casual observation. Research design assists in simplifying a situation in which many variables are operating concurrently and in helping the researcher to isolate the variable of interest (Kazdin, 1992). Research designs thus aid the researcher in ruling out alternative explanations for the data that are collected. The extent to which any given research design is successful in ruling out plausible rival hypotheses in not absolute but rather is a matter of degree. In particular, researchers use validity arguments to assist them in ruling out alternative explanations for their data. Four types of validity are typically considered: internal, external, construct, and statistical conclusion (Campbell & Stanley, 1963; Shadish, Cook, & Campbell, 2002).

Internal Validity

Internal validity refers to the degree to which a researcher can attribute changes in a dependent variable to an independent variable while simultaneously ruling out alternative explanations (Campbell & Stanley, 1963). An experiment or study that does not have adequate internal validity suffers from competing rival hypotheses that could explain the obtained results of a given study. Shadish et al. (2002) enumerated a number of potential threats to the internal validity of research studies. These threats include history, maturation, instrumentation, statistical regression, selection biases, attrition, and interaction of selection biases with other threats to internal validity (e.g., Selection × Attrition, Selection × History, Selection × Maturation). Several of these threats are illuminated as they pertain to school-based consultation research.

History and maturation are two major threats to the internal validity of research studies. History and maturation refer to changes occurring over time because of events in the environment (history) and within the individual (maturation) that could explain changes in the dependent variable rather than the unique effects of the independent variable (Kazdin, 2003). For example, a consultation researcher is interested in the effects of collaborative consultation with teachers on teachers' knowledge and implementation of behavioral intervention strategies in the classroom. The researcher administers a pretest of knowledge and implementation and subsequently consults with a group of teachers over a period of 10 weeks, during which principles of behavioral intervention and implementation are emphasized. At the end of 10 weeks, the researcher administers a posttest of teachers' knowledge of behavioral principles and implementation strategies and concludes that consultation increased in teachers' knowledge of these principles.

This study is particularly susceptible to history and maturation threats to internal validity. Because the study did not include a control group (i.e., it was a one-group pretest/posttest design), the researcher cannot rule out alternative explanations for the increase in teacher knowledge. There is no way to know from this study that the independent variable (consultation) was responsible for changes in the dependent variable (increased teacher knowledge).

The study also suffers from the internal validity threats of selection biases and testing as alternative explanations for the results. Selection bias could explain the results rather than the effects of consultation per se. For example, the researcher may have simply selected a group of teachers who were brighter or better informed than another group who might have been selected. Also, because the study involved a pretest/posttest condition, simply taking the pretest may have affected performance on the posttest (pretest sensitization).

How might this consultation researcher have designed the study to protect against these threats to internal validity? The answer is straightforward: include a no-treatment control group in addition to the consultation treatment group and randomly assign teachers to either the treatment or control group and evaluate changes in knowledge at the conclusion of 10 weeks. In a quasi-experiment using intact groups, the researcher could have matched the two groups on relevant variables (e.g., experience, education). Any changes in knowledge for the treatment group could then be attributed to the independent variable (consultation) and not history, maturation, selection biases, or testing. Consultation studies using group experimental or quasi-experimental designs must be planned with these potential threats to internal validity in mind.

External Validity

External validity refers to the generalizability of the results of a research study. It asks the question, To what extent can the results of a study be generalized to other populations, settings, treatment variables, and measurement variables (Campbell & Stanley, 1966)? The issue of external validity is about the boundary conditions or limits of research findings (Kazdin, 1992). Whereas internal validity is concerned with attributing changes in a dependent variable to an independent variable, external validity is concerned with demonstrating the extent to which that same effect would be obtained with other participants in other settings, using other treatments, and measuring outcomes using other methods.

External validity concerns the interactions between a treatment and other conditions (e.g., testing, selection, setting, history, multiple treatments). Several threats to external validity have been identified and can be classified into four broad categories: sample, stimulus, contextual, and assessment characteristics (Bracht & Glass, 1968).

A research finding demonstrated with a particular sample may not be demonstrated with another sample. Thus, *sample characteristics* may limit the generalizability of research findings to other samples that might differ on key variables. For example, Kazdin (1980) investigated the acceptability of four alternative behavioral treatments by undergraduate college students who responded to written vignettes that described each of the four interventions and then rated the acceptability of each treatment. In general, this investigation found that positive treatments were rated more favorably than reductive treatments. This study raises several questions regarding external validity. Would the same results be found with a sample of parents or teachers? Would the same results be found in home or classroom environments? Would acceptability ratings change after individuals implemented the interventions (posttreatment rather than pretreatment acceptability)?

Another external validity threat deals with the extent to which the findings of a given research study can be generalized to other stimulus characteristics. In this sense, *stimulus characteristics* refer to different settings, consultants, consultees, clients, or other characteristics or features to which research participants are exposed. A good example of a program of research that suffers from external validity threats concerns treatment acceptability (Cavell, Frentz, & Kelley, 1986; Elliott, Witt, Galvin, & Peterson, 1984; Witt, Martens, & Elliott, 1984). All of these studies were conducted in analogue settings in which teachers read vignettes of various behavioral interventions and rated their acceptability on a behavior rating scale. This research program indicated that interventions requiring more time, that focused on less-severe problems, and that involved reductive techniques were rated relatively lower in acceptability. Unfortunately, the extent to which these findings can be generalized to natural settings with real clients and behavior problems has not been demonstrated (an external validity problem).

Yet another threat to external validity has to do with assessment characteristics in the experimental situation, specifically, *reactivity of assessment* procedures. Participants who are aware that their performance is under assessment may react to these obtrusive assessments. An example from the consultation literature is the research on consultee treatment integrity in which the degree to which consultation plans are implemented as intended are assessed. Wickstrom and colleagues showed that 33 of 33 teachers implemented consultation-based interventions with less than 10% integrity (measured by unobtrusive direct observation), although these same teachers reported much higher levels of integrity (70% or higher) (Wickstrom, Jones, LaFleur, & Witt, 1998). Thus, teachers reacted to the obtrusive self-report of treatment integrity and thereby limited the external validity of the findings.

Construct Validity

Construct validity refers to the basis for interpreting the causal relation between an independent variable and a dependent variable. Remember that internal validity is concerned with whether an independent variable is responsible for change in a dependent variable. In contrast, construct validity focuses on the reason or interpretation of the change in the dependent variable brought about by the independent variable. For example, suppose a number of consultants are randomly assigned to Consultation Method A (traditional behavioral consultation with teachers) and other consultants are randomly assigned to Consultation Method B (conjoint behavioral consultation with teachers and parents). At the conclusion of the study, it is shown that Method B is superior to Method A in producing behavior change in clients. One might presume that Method B is superior because it includes parents as consultees in addition to teacher consultees (construct validity interpretation). However, because consultants are nested within method (A and B), one cannot separate the consultation methods from consultants because consultants were nested within each method. It may well be the case that consultants in Method B were simply better consultants than the consultants in Method A (a Consultant × Method confound).

Kazdin (1992) characterized the construct validity of an experiment based on two questions: What is the intervention? and, What explains the causal mechanism for change in the dependent variable? Many consultation-based interventions are embedded within other conditions that might account for changes in the dependent variable. For example, behavioral consultation is embedded or confounded by the skill and knowledge of the consultant as well as the social influence the consultant has on the consultee. It is difficult in cases like this to disentangle the effects of behavioral expertise from the social influence of the consultant to determine the most important mechanisms of change. Construct validity is important because it affects the field's interpretation of the reasons for behavior and attitudinal change produced by the consultation process.

Statistical Conclusion Validity

Statistical conclusion validity refers to threats to drawing valid inferences that result from random error and the poor selection of statistical procedures (Kirk, 1995). In other words, statistical conclusion validity deals with those aspects of the statistical evaluation of a study that affect the conclusions drawn from the experimental conditions and their effect on the dependent variable. There are several threats to statistical conclusion validity. These include (but are not limited to) low statistical power, reliability of treatment implementation, reliability of dependent measures, random irrelevancies in the experimental setting, and random heterogeneity of respondents (see Kirk, 1995). These are briefly described in the following paragraphs.

Low statistical power refers to the failure to reject the null hypothesis because of small sample size, failure to control irrelevant sources of variation, and inefficient test statistics (Kirk, 1995). *Power* is the probability of rejecting the null hypothesis when the null hypothesis is false. Power is a function of (a) sample size, (b) significance level, and (c) effect size (Cohen, 1992). Thus, a power analysis specifies the required sample size N that is required to obtain a given level of significance α for a given effect size (small, medium, or large). The most straightforward way to increase power is to increase the sample size. However, this may be difficult to accomplish in applied consultation research, particularly when consultants are the participants in a consultation research study. Many studies in both psychology and education produce either nonsignificant or weak results because of low statistical power of the studies (Maxwell, 2004).

Another threat to statistical conclusion validity deals with the *reliability of treatment implementation* or what is known as *treatment integrity*. Failure to implement an intervention as planned or intended may lead to inaccurate conclusions regarding the effects of a given intervention. This is particularly problematic in consultation research because interventions are typically implemented by consultees (Gresham, 1989). For example, consultation-based interventions can produce null results because the interventions were implemented without integrity rather than because the intervention itself is ineffective. In this case, the researcher would commit a Type II error by concluding the intervention was ineffective when in fact it was potentially effective but its effectiveness was compromised by poor integrity.

Another threat to statistical conclusion validity is the *unreliability of dependent measures* used to index consultation outcomes. Measures with poor reliability inflate error variance and reduce the effect size, thereby leading to inflated Type II error rates (Kirk, 1995). Researcher-constructed measures that are not subjected to reliability analyses are likely to suffer from this threat to statistical conclusion validity.

Yet another threat to statistical conclusion validity is *random irrelevancies* in the experimental setting. Variation in classroom environments (e.g., physical, behavioral) in which a consultation-based intervention is implemented inflates error variance, thereby leading to Type II errors (Kirk, 1995). For instance, interventions implemented in chaotic classroom environments are likely to be less effective than those same interventions implemented in better-controlled classrooms. Any comparison of the relative effectiveness of these two interventions is confounded by the characteristics of the respective classrooms in which they were implemented.

Finally, the *random hetereogeneity of respondents* (consultees) poses a threat to statistical conclusion validity. That is, differing characteristics of consultees may inflate error variance leading to a Type II error. For example, some consultees are brighter, better trained, and easier to work with than other consultees. Other consultees are not as bright, are poorly trained, and are more difficult to work with in the consultation process. Comparisons of the effectiveness of consultation interventions thus can be compromised by the characteristics of the consultees that lead to an inaccurate retention of the null hypothesis (a Type II error).

SINGLE-CASE EXPERIMENTAL DESIGNS

Background and Description

There are basically two paradigms of experimental research available to researchers in consultation. The most common approach uses group or nomothetic data to make statements about average differences between two or more groups. The approach uses repeated measures of behavior collected on either a single or several individuals to make statements about differences in behavior between baseline and experimental conditions. These two research paradigms differ in their goals, assumptions, and inferences made about the effects of independent variables on dependent variables (Gresham, 1998). The purpose of this section is to describe the latter of these two research paradigms.

In single-case designs, controlling for chance occurrences is accomplished by observing repeated patterns of behavior under repeated and alternated baseline and experimental conditions. If a behavior pattern under the baseline condition systematically differs from a behavior pattern under the experimental condition, then one can conclude that differences in these behavior patterns are not caused by chance.

A central concern in single-case research is obtaining a sufficient number of observations to obtain a representative sample of behavior and to assess steady-state responding. *Steady-state responding* can be defined as a pattern of behavior that exhibits relatively little variability in its measured dimensional quantities over time (Johnston & Pennypacker, 1993). Thus, in single-participant research, the researcher repeatedly exposes each participant to a condition (e.g., baseline and intervention) to control extraneous influences and to obtain a stable pattern of responding. This is an essential aspect of single-case research because it is used to evaluate the degree of experimental control in an investigation.

In single-case designs, Type I errors are not as precisely computable as they are in group experimental designs. The single-case researcher uses visual inspection of repeated differences between baseline and treatment conditions to guard against Type I errors. As a result, single-case researchers assume they will make few Type I errors and a correspondingly larger number of Type II errors (Baer, 1977). Single-case researchers are interested in discovering strong treatments and are willing to conclude that a treatment was not a functional one in changing behavior when, in fact, it might have been (a Type II error).

Single-case experimental designs are often underutilized in clinical research and practice relative to group experimental designs (Morgan & Morgan, 2001). Gresham and Kendell (1987) made a similar observation regarding research and practice of school-based consultation. Some 26 years ago, Hayes (1981) noted several reasons for the infrequent use of single-case methodology in clinical psychology: (a) It is either untaught or undertaught in most training programs; (b) it has not been directed toward the practicing clinician and is therefore perceived as impractical; (c) it is typically associated with behavioral approaches, although it is theoretically neutral; and (d) many researchers think only in terms of group comparison research.

The reasons for the underutilization of single-case research specified by Hayes (1981) remain true today. Only a relatively small number of researchers are trained in single-case methodology, and the overwhelming majority of them are applied behavior analysts. Single-case research has been accepted as a methodological means of establishing evidence-based practices in child clinical (Lonigan, Elbert, & Johnson, 1998) and school psychology (Kratochwill & Stoiber, 2000; Stoiber & Kratochwill, 2000) as well as special education research (R. H. Horner et al., 2005).

Principles of Single-Case Methodology

Single-case experimental designs compare the same individual's performance or that of several individuals under baseline and treatment conditions, with each individual serving as his or her own control. Single-participant research is experimental (as opposed to descriptive or correlational) and seeks to isolate functional relations between independent and dependent variables. Data evaluation in this type of research is based on the extent to which behavioral performance varies reliably under baseline and intervention conditions. There are several core elements that distinguish single-case research from traditional group experimental designs. These core elements have been discussed by others and enjoy consensual agreement from most experts in the field of behavior therapy and applied behavior analysis (Barlow & Hersen, 1984; Hayes, 1981; Johnston & Pennypacker, 1993; Kazdin, 1992; Kennedy, 2005). These core elements are (a) repeated measurement, (b) analysis of behavioral variability, (c) dynamic experimental design, (d) specification of experimental conditions, and (e) replication. These core elements are discussed briefly in the following paragraphs.

Repeated measurement of dependent variables in single-participant research both within and across baseline and treatment conditions is used to identify patterns of behavior. These repeated measurements of behavior are based on precise, operational definitions of behavior that remain constant throughout the experiment. A central concern in single-case design is obtaining a sufficient number of measurements of the dependent variable under baseline and treatment conditions because these measurements are the basis for judging the effects of treatment. Repeated measurements of the dependent variable accomplish four objectives in single-case experimental designs: (a) an evaluation of steady-state or stable responding, (b) evaluation of the degree of experimental control, (c) comparisons between baseline and treatment conditions, and (d) assessment of trends or changes in behavior over time (Gresham, 1998).

Analysis of behavioral variability is a central feature of single-case research, and it represents the context in which levels and trends of repeatedly measured behavior are evaluated. Intrasubject variability is the window through which the single-case researcher views what is occurring in an experiment, and it serves as the basis for evaluating the effects of treatment. Intrasubject variability is treated as *error* in group experimental designs (within-subjects variance), whereas it is considered an extremely valuable source of information in single-case research. Graphic displays of this intrasubject variability during different phases of the experiment allow for certain conclusions to be drawn from the data.

Dynamic experimental design is a core feature of single-case research in which the design is always flexible and subject to change depending on how the participants respond to various experimental arrangements. With group designs, the design, number of participants, and statistical analysis strategy are planned before the experiment is conducted and are not changed. By contrast, single-case designs are tentative and may be changed depending on how participants respond to the treatment.

Specification of experimental conditions is another hallmark of single-case designs. Treatment specification is extremely important to assess the treatment integrity of the independent variable. *Treatment integrity* refers to the extent to which a treatment (the independent variable) is implemented as planned and is concerned with the accuracy and consistency with which treatments are implemented (Gresham, 1989; Gresham, Gansle, & Noell, 1993). Treatments that are not well specified cannot be subjected to integrity assessments, and conclusions regarding the effects of treatment are compromised.

Replication is central to all scientific investigation because the results of any experimental manipulation should be repeatable by the same researcher and by other researchers to have scientific credibility. In single-case experimental designs, replications can occur within phases of the experiment (within baseline and treatment conditions) as well as across two or more baseline and treatment conditions (e.g., in withdrawal designs).

Replication can also occur across baseline and intervention conditions for participants, settings, or behaviors, as in a multiple-baseline design. Replication may also take place between two or more intervention conditions that are rapidly alternated or changed, as in a multielement design. Replication in this sense establishes the internal validity of the single case design.

Replication can also occur across different experiments, different experimenters, different consultants, and different clients. Replication in this sense establishes the external validity of findings of an experiment.

Experimental Design Models

As in group experimental design methodology, there are a number of combinations of single-case experimental designs that can be used to evaluate the effects of an independent variable on a dependent variable. Hayes (1981) suggested that all single-case experimental designs could be classified into three core elements organized by the logic of their data comparisons. These design features are (a) within-series strategies, (b) between-series strategies, and (c) combined-series strategies. These

Table 4.2   Research Questions and Single-Case Experimental Designs
Does an intervention work?
ABAB withdrawal design
Multielement design
Changing criterion design
Multiple-baseline design
Does one intervention work better than another one?
ABAC withdrawal design (simple phase change)
Multielement design
Do different elements interact or combine to produce behavior change?
ABB+CACB+C design (complex phase change)
Multielement design (comparing BB+CC elements)
Do intervention effects maintain after treatment is withdrawn?
Sequential withdrawal design
Partial-withdrawal design
Partial-sequential withdrawal design
Complex phase change with withdrawals (B/B+C/B/A)
Multiple-baseline designs (with withdrawals)
Does the intervention work with different individuals?
Multiple-baseline designs across subjects
Replicated ABAB designs with different individuals
Replicated multielement designs with different individuals
Changing criterion designs with different individuals

design strategies parallel the within-subjects, between-subjects, and combined- (mixed-) group experimental designs; however, the sampling units are different (Kirk, 1995). In group designs, the sampling units are usually persons who are exposed to one or more conditions, depending on whether it is a within-subjects, between-subjects, or mixed design. In single-case designs, the sampling units are samples of repeatedly measured behavior of the same person over time within and across baseline and experimental conditions (Gresham, 1998).

Theoretically, there are an infinite number of experimental designs that could be constructed to answer research questions from these three core strategies. Table 4.2 lists some examples of frequently used single-case experimental designs and research questions that they address. The logic and examples of each approach are described in the following sections.

Within-Series Strategies

One of the most common experimental arrangements in single-case designs compares changes within a series of data points under at least two baseline and two experimental conditions. The most frequently used within-series strategy is known as a *withdrawal design*. The withdrawal design (sometimes called a reversal design) consists of observing behavior under baseline (A) and experimental (B) conditions to note A-to-B changes in behavior. This sequence is replicated by returning to baseline (A) and experimental (B) conditions. Thus, one has an ABAB withdrawal design in which the treatment (B conditions) is withdrawn to demonstrate experimental control.

Within-series designs may involve either a simple phase change or a complex phase change. In a simple phase change design, treatment effects are evaluated against changes from baseline to intervention levels of performance, such as in an ABAB design. It is also possible to compare two or more treatments using simple phase changes such as ABAC or BCBC in which B and C represent two different treatments. There are, however, better ways of determining which of two treatments is more effective, such as using a multielement design (described in the between-series strategies section).

DuPaul and Henningson (1993) utilized a withdrawal or ABAB design with a simple phase change to evaluate the effects of classwide peer tutoring for on-task, fidgeting, and math accuracy behaviors in a child with attention deficit/hyperactivity disorder (ADHD). In this study, a consultant trained an above-average math student in the class to work with the child with ADHD at a specific time during the school day. Thus, in this design, the A conditions represented the baseline conditions (teacher-mediated instruction), and the B conditions represented the treatment conditions (classwide peer tutoring).

Designs using complex phase changes seek to determine the combined or interactive effects of two or more treatments. The purpose of these designs is to evaluate and analyze the effects of two or more treatments separately and in combination and replicate these findings across experimental phases (Barlow & Hersen, 1984). These designs use the same logic as the simple phase change but add and subtract treatment components in various sequences to determine experimental effects. For example, a consultant may be interested in the unique and combined effects of overcorrection and response cost on inappropriate verbalizations in a classroom. This experimental design might take the following sequence: A/B/B+C/B/A/B+C where A is baseline, B is overcorrection, C is response cost, and B+C is a combination of overcorrection and response cost.

Gresham (1979) used a withdrawal design with a complex phase change in a consultation study focusing on reducing problem behaviors in a special education setting. In this design, the A conditions represented the baselines against which the B (response cost) and C (time-out) and B + C (response cost + time-out) conditions were compared. This design allowed for the investigation of the main effects of the two intervention strategies as well as the interactive effects of the combined strategies.

Withdrawal designs can also be used to assess response maintenance after experimental control has been established (Rusch & Kazdin, 1981). There are three variations of the withdrawal design: (a) sequential withdrawal, (b) partial withdrawal, and (c) partial sequential withdrawal. In the *sequential withdrawal design*, components of a multicomponent treatment are withdrawn one at a time until all have been withdrawn. In a *partial withdrawal design*, one component of a multicomponent treatment or the entire treatment is withdrawn from one of several baselines in a multiple-baseline design. In a *partial sequential withdrawal design*, an entire multicomponent treatment or a component of that treatment from one of the baselines in a multiple-baseline design is withdrawn.

Between-Series Strategies

Between-series designs make comparisons between a series of data points across time to establish experimental control. Between-series strategies compare rapid and repeated alterations of treatment conditions. Unlike within-series strategies, there is no need to determine stability, level, and trend within baseline or treatment phases because a given data point may be preceded or followed by measurement of other treatment conditions (Hayes, 1981). Between-series designs are particularly useful for comparing the effects of two or more treatments and do not suffer the same threats to internal validity as simple and complex phase designs that compare two or more treatments.

The most common between-series strategy is the *multielement* design (sometimes called the *alternating treatments* design). The basic logic of this design is the rapid alteration of two or more treatment conditions so that responding under these different conditions can be compared. For example, a researcher might be interested in comparing the effects of differential reinforcement of other behavior (DRO) versus noncontingent reinforcement (NCR) in reducing rates of disruptive behavior in a classroom. The researcher will run the intervention for 10 days and will randomly assign DRO and NCR conditions to days. Thus, the DRO condition may take place on Days 1, 4, 7, 8, and 10, and the NCR condition will be implemented on Days 2, 3, 5, 6, and 9. The relative effectiveness of DRO and NCR can be compared using this type of design.

Multielement designs such as the one above have several advantages over within-series strategies. First, these designs typically produce effects more rapidly than withdrawal designs. Second, there is no need to establish a stable baseline or to be concerned with increasing or decreasing trends within phases because a data point is associated with a given condition and is not part of a consecutive series of data points. Third, these designs are especially useful in functional analytic work in which specific conditions (e.g., social attention, escape, alone) can be rapidly alternated.

Heckaman and colleagues used a multielement design to evaluate the effects of different intervention conditions designed to decrease the disruptive behaviors of a child with autism (Heckaman, Alber, Hooper, & Heward, 1998). The two intervention conditions were teacher-delivered instruction on easy tasks (A conditions) versus difficult tasks (B conditions). The teacher was instructed to alternate between the easy and difficult task conditions a total of six times. Disruptive behavior was always higher under the difficult task conditions and lower under the easy task conditions. Unlike withdrawal designs, the intervention conditions in a multielement design are rapidly alternated to evaluate the effects of an intervention.

Combined-Series Strategies

Combined-series strategies make comparisons both within and between a series of data points to determine experimental control. The most common of these strategies is the *multiple-baseline design* that allows for sequential comparisons between baseline and treatment conditions for persons, settings, or behaviors. In this design, two or more baselines are concurrently established, and the intervention is implemented sequentially across baselines. Multiple-baseline designs control for weaknesses in simple phase change designs by reducing the likelihood that extraneous events could be responsible for experimental effects.

Musser and colleagues used a multiple-baseline design across students in a consultation study to decrease disruptive classroom behavior for students with emotional and behavioral disorders (Musser, Bray, Kehle, & Jenson, 2001). In another consultation study, Matheson and Shriver (2005) examined the effects of effective command training for increasing compliance and academic engagement in a multiple-baseline-across-teachers design. Finally, Noell, Duhon, Gatti, and Connell (2002) investigated the impact of consultation procedures to increase levels of treatment integrity in a multiple-baseline design across three teachers.

Another combined-series strategy is known as the *changing criterion design,* which is a variation of the multiple-baseline design that allows for comparisons both within and between a series of data points (Hartmann & Hall, 1976). In this design, baseline data are collected on a target behavior. The first treatment phase involves setting a criterion for performance (e.g., 50% correct spelling words) that will result in reinforcement. The second treatment phase involves setting a higher criterion for reinforcement (e.g., 60% correct spelling words). The third phase involves yet a higher criterion for reinforcement (e.g., 70% correct spelling words). These phases continue until the desired final criterion of performance is attained (e.g., 100%). If the target behavior changes in relation to the criteria, then experimental control is demonstrated. Changing criterion designs are particularly well suited for certain academic behaviors in which the target behaviors are expressed as accuracy or amount of work completion (i.e., expressed as percentages).

Ray, Skinner, and Watson (1999) used an accelerating changing criterion design in a parent-and-teacher consultation study designed to increase compliance in a 5-year-old boy with autism. Each of the phases in the study represented various combinations of high- and low-probability commands issued by the parent and the teacher. This study showed that the boy's compliance rate increased from baseline levels of about 10% to intervention levels of almost 95% for teacher commands. Parental compliance increased from baseline levels of 60% to treatment levels of approximately 85%.

Changing criterion designs can also be *decelerating*, in which the goal is to reduce the frequency of a target behavior from baseline levels. For example, the goal of an intervention may be to reduce the number of disruptive behaviors from a baseline average of 5 per day to 0 per day. A changing criterion design in which criterion levels for reinforcement are systematically reduced could be used to demonstrate that the intervention was responsible for behavior change. Gresham (1980) used a decelerating changing criterion design in a parent consultation study designed to decrease occurrences of childhood enuresis. In this study, variations of differential reinforcement of low rates of behavior were used to reduce bedwetting occurrences.

There are several variations of the multiple-baseline design. R. D. Horner and Baer (1978) described a variation of the multiple-baseline design for studying acquisition behavior called the *multiple-probe technique*. This design does not require continuous baseline measurement, and instead "probes" of responding are obtained. Multiple-probe designs are appropriate when (a) extended baselines may be reactive, (b) it is impractical to collect continuous multiple baselines, and (c) there are strong a priori assumptions of stability of responding. Multiple-probe designs are useful for investigating chains or successive approximations of behavior (e.g., reading, language acquisition, social skills).

Quantitative Analysis

One issue that has not been satisfactorily resolved in single-case design concerns the most appropriate way of quantifying effects of intervention. With group experimental designs, conventionally accepted statistical methods are used to test the significance of between-groups or between-treatments analysis by using within-group variability as "error." There is no consensus regarding how to best quantify the effects of single-case experimental designs. Four methods of quantitative analysis of single-case design effects are described next: (a) visual inspection, (b) effect size estimates, (c) statistical analyses, and (d) social validation.

Visual Inspection

Visual inspection of graphed data is by far the most common way of evaluating data from single-case experimental designs (Johnston & Pennypacker, 1993; Kennedy, 2005). Effects of intervention are determined by comparing baseline levels of performance to postintervention levels of performance to detect treatment effects. Unlike complex statistical analyses, this method uses the "interocular" test of significance. There are several advantages to visual analysis of graphed data: (a) It does not require advanced training in complex statistical analyses, (b) it identifies strong effects, (c) it forces the researcher to look at behavioral variability within and across phases of an experiment, and (d) it does not have to meet stringent statistical assumptions.

Some, however, have criticized visual inspection of graphed data because it is an insensitive method of determining treatment effects (Kazdin, 1984). Visual inspection identifies only large effects and fails to detect subtle, and perhaps cumulative, changes in the dependent variable and would therefore create a Type II error. There is a considerable body of research suggesting that even highly trained behavior analysts cannot obtain consensus in evaluating single-case data using visual inspection (Center, Skiba, & Casey, 1985; DeProspero & Cohen, 1979; Knapp, 1983; Matyas & Greenwood, 1990, 1991; Ottenbacher, 1990).

The investigation by DeProspero and Cohen (1979) is particularly informative in this regard. These authors created 36 single-case graphs that depicted ideal effects (12 graphs), inconsistent effects (12 graphs), and irreversible effects (12 graphs). These 36 graphs were sent to 215 reviewers of articles submitted to the *Journal of Applied Behavior Analysis* and 35 reviewers of articles submitted to the *Journal of Experimental Analysis of Behavior*. The average concordance rate for these expert reviewers was only $r = 0.61$, suggesting rather poor interobserver agreement. It appears that the following plague the visual inspection of graphed data: (a) Detection of reliable effects is compromised by "noisy" data (i.e., variability within and between phases); (b) experts are no better than novices in judging effects using visual analysis; (c) Type II error rates may be unacceptably high; (d) newer statistical analytic techniques (e.g., conditional probabilities, sequential analyses) may be more informative; and (e) visual inspection of graphed data is more complex than argued by its proponents.

Baer's (1977) position regarding Type I and Type II error rates in single-case and group experimental designs was discussed in the background section on single-case designs. Baer suggested that visual inspection produces low Type I error rates and relatively higher Type II error rates than do group experimental designs. Along these lines, Matyas and Greenwood (1990) showed that Type I error rates ranged from 16% to 84% with autocorrelated data. A subsequent study by these authors showed that data from studies published in the *Journal of Applied Behavior Analysis* demonstrated a Type I error rate of approximately 10% (Matyas & Greenwood, 1991). These results do not support Baer's (1977) contention that visual inspection of single-case data produces few Type I errors. As such, other methods have been proposed to supplement the visual inspection method of data in single-case experimental designs.

Effect Size Estimates

Another way of quantifying effects in single-case designs is through the use of effect sizes. Effect sizes are used in meta-analytic research that integrates bodies of research by converting results of independent investigations to a common metric using Cohen's *d* (Cohen, 1988). This metric is calculated by subtracting the mean of a control group from the mean of the treatment group and dividing by the standard deviation of the control group (Rosenthal, 1991). The effect size is expressed as a *z* score having a mean of 0 and a standard deviation of 1.

Busk and Serlin (1992) proposed an approach for calculating an effect size in single-case studies. The effect size is calculated by subtracting the mean of data points in the intervention phases from the mean of data points in the baseline phase and dividing by the standard deviation of the baseline data points. Effect sizes calculated in this manner can be interpreted in the same way as traditional effect sizes. The effect size can be used to interpret the results of a single study or for synthesizing results from numerous single-case studies in a meta-analysis. A major problem with this effects size estimate is that it often leads to extremely large effect size estimates that cannot be interpreted parametrically. Parker et al. (2005) reanalyzed data from 77 published single-participant studies and showed that effect size estimates yielded highly variable results depending on the effect size estimate used (Parker et al., 2005). Moreover, few effect size estimates met Cohen's (1988) criteria for small, medium, or large effect sizes.

Effect sizes can also be computed by calculating the *percentage of nonoverlapping data points* (PND) between baseline and treatment phases (Scruggs & Mastropieri, 1998). Indicating the number of treatment data points that exceed the highest or lowest baseline data point in an expected direction and dividing by the total number of data points in the treatment phase computes PND. For example, if 10 of 15 treatment data points exceed the highest baseline data point, then PND would be 67%. PND can be distorted by variability in baseline trends, nonorthogonal slope changes, and floor/ceiling effects. For example, if the lowest baseline data point were 0 words spoken at school in a study of selective mutism, then PND would be indeterminate.

Another metric that can be used in single-case design to determine the clinical significance for individuals is the reliable change index (RCI), first proposed by Nunnally and Kotsch (1983). The RCI is calculated by subtracting the posttest score from the pretest score and dividing by the standard error of difference between posttest and pretest scores (Christensen & Mendoza, 1986; Jacobson, Follette, & Revenstorf, 1984). The standard error of difference is the spread or variation in the distribution of change scores that would be expected if no change from pre- to posttest had occurred.

In single-case designs, the RCI would be calculated from the means of baseline and intervention phases of the design. For example, in a withdrawal design (ABAB), pretest scores would be computed from the initial baseline mean (A_1), and posttest scores would be computed from the mean of the two intervention phases ($B_1+B_2/2$). In a multiple-baseline design, pretest scores would be calculated from the mean of the baselines for each subject (setting or behavior) and posttest scores from the respective intervention phases. The standard error of difference would be based on the autocorrelation and variation of baseline and intervention phases. The RCI in a multielement design would be calculated from the means of the different interventions divided by the standard error of difference.

Perhaps the easiest and most relevant index to quantify the magnitude of behavior change in single-participant research is to calculate the percentage of behavior change from baseline to intervention levels of performance. This index is calculated by taking the median data point in baseline and comparing that value to the median data point in the intervention phases. The median is used rather than the mean because it is less susceptible to outlier effects. For example, if a child's median number of negative social interactions on the playground during baseline was 8 occurrences and the median level of negative social interactions during intervention was 2, then the percentage reduction in disruptive behavior would be 75%. This metric is not unlike the methods used by physicians to quantify weight loss or reductions in blood cholesterol levels. The difference is, however, that there are well-established medical standards for ideal weights and cholesterol levels but not for problem social behaviors such as negative social interactions on the playground. Yet another method is required to determine whether changes in behavior are important ones. This requires the process of social validation, described in a separate section.

Statistical Analyses

Statistical analyses of data produced in single-participant research are a controversial topic because they appear to conflict with the purposes and goals of single-case research. Advocates of single-participant research argue that identification of reliable effects does not require statistical analyses, and that reliable effects can be detected by a simple visual inspection of graphed data described in this chapter (Baer, 1977; Franklin, Gorman, Beasley, & Allison, 1996; Johnston & Pennypacker, 1993; Michael, 1974; Sidman, 1960). The logic of single-case design relies on ongoing experimental control based on steady-state responding rather than statistical control. Single-case data provide a wide range of quantitative data involving changes, variability, and stability, whereas statistical analyses involve averaging data over individuals, thereby masking the natural variability in behavior.

Others argue that visual inspection of graphed data is an insensitive method for detecting reliable treatment effects, and that statistical analyses constitute a viable supplement for interpreting graphed data (Gentile, Roden, & Klein, 1972; Hartmann et al., 1980; Jones, Vaught, & Weinrott, 1977). Moreover, there are sufficient data to suggest that experts in applied behavior analysis do not agree at high levels on the magnitude of treatment effects using visual inspection (DeProspero & Cohen, 1979), that experts make more rather than fewer errors when interpreting trend lines (Greenspan & Fisch, 1992), and that untrained raters perform almost as well as journal reviewers (Harbst, Ottenbacher, & Harris, 1991).

There are several characteristics of single-case data, however, that influence the choice of statistical analytic techniques. An important characteristic is the serial dependence in time series data produced by single-participant designs. *Serial dependence* refers to a variable with a future that is predicted to some degree by its own values and is quantified by patterns of autocorrelation and partial autocorrelation among a series of data points (Johnston & Pennypacker, 1993; Matyas & Greenwood, 1997).

Autocorrelation refers to the extent to which values of measured behavior at one point in time are correlated with values of that behavior at other points in time. For example, in a series of data points, autocorrelation is computed by correlating values of adjacent data points throughout the entire time series (e.g., 1 with 2, 2 with 3, 3 with 4, 4 with 5). These are called Lag 1 autocorrelations. Lag 2 autocorrelations are computed by correlating data points that are two intervals apart (e.g., 1 with 3, 2 with 4, 4 with 6). Lag 3 and Lag 4 autocorrelations are computed by correlating data points separated by three and four intervals, respectively. *Partial autocorrelations* are analogous to partial correlation and reflect the correlation between two variables (X and Y) with a third variable (Z) held constant. For example, a partial autocorrelation could be computed between Lag 2 and Lag 3 autocorrelations with Lag 1 autocorrelations held constant or removed.

Why does serial dependence matter in time series data? One reason is that graphical judgment using visual analysis is substantially affected by serial dependence (Franklin et al., 1996; Matyas & Greenwood, 1997). For example, research suggests that time series data showing higher autocorrelations produce higher false-positive rates than lower autocorrelated data (Matyas & Greenwood, 1997). In addition, medium-to-high autocorrelated data result in the least-accurate visual judgment (Matyas & Greenwood, 1990). The presence and pattern of serial dependence indicate a nonrandom structure in a time series and thus the predictability of behavior over time.

A second reason to be concerned with serial dependence is that serial dependence does not affect the mean or level in a time series across phases but does affect estimates of error variance. As such, statistical tests based on mean comparisons (t and F tests) are invalidated by serial dependence because distributions that are serially dependent do not have serially independent residuals that violate the independence or error assumption (see Hartmann, 1974). Although interrupted time series analysis can cope with serially dependent data, this approach requires far too many data points to be practically useful in typical single-participant research studies (Hartmann et al., 1980; Jones et al., 1977).

The field awaits further research to determine the most accurate and practical statistical methods for detecting reliable treatment effects in single-participant research in consultation. One promising approach is the use of hierarchical linear models (HLM) that conceptualizes measurement occasions as nested within participants and participants as nested within conditions (see Raudenbush & Bryk, 2002). Thus, a simple HLM for single-case data consisting of baseline and intervention conditions would estimate an overall intercept that is equivalent to the baseline mean and coefficient indicator that represents the overall effect of the intervention. Van den Noortgate and Onghena (2003) provided an informative and illustrative description of HLM for combining the results of single-participant research that can be extended to the individual level to analyze autocorrelated time series data.

Social Validation

Practical approaches to establishing the clinical or social validity of behavior change such as percentage of change in behavior between baseline and treatment phases have been reported in the literature for a number of years. Social validity deals with three fundamental questions faced by school-based consultants: What should we change? How should we change it? How will we know it was effective? There are sometimes disagreements between consultants and consultees on these three fundamental questions. Wolf (1978) is credited with originating the notion of social validity, and it has become common parlance among many researchers and practitioners, particularly those operating out of an applied behavior analysis perspective. Gresham and Lopez (1996) outlined the social validation process for the practice of school-based consultation.

Social validity refers to the assessment of the social significance of the goals of an intervention (What should we change?), the social acceptability of intervention procedures to attain those goals (How should we change it?), and the social importance of the effects produced by the intervention (How will we know it was effective?).

Kazdin (1977) recommended three methods of social validation interventions. First, consultants can use subjective evaluations to determine the social importance of intervention effects. These subjective evaluations consist of treatment consumers (teacher or parents) rating the qualitative aspects of the child's behavior. These global evaluations of behavior assess how the child is functioning after intervention and provide an overall assessment of performance. Another approach in social validation is to use social comparisons in which the behavior of the target child is compared to that same behavior of a comparison peer in the classroom. If the intervention moved the target child's behavior into the same range of functioning as the comparison peer, then the intervention produced socially valid results. Finally, one can use combined social validation procedures consisting of both subjective evaluations and social comparisons.

In using single-case experimental designs, there are several methods of quantifying effects of interventions, ranging from visual inspection to the calculation of reliable change indices. As discussed, none of these techniques is without conceptual and measurement difficulty. Whichever metric is used to quantify treatment effects, we argue that these effects always should be socially validated using combined social validation procedures of subjective evaluation and social comparison.

RESEARCH STANDARDS

Since the early 1990s, the quality of educational research has received increased scrutiny, and in many cases was found to be inadequate (Atkinson & Jackson, 1992). In fact, some suggested that increases in the quality of education research are needed to further advance the quality and impact of schooling (Levin & O'Donnell, 1999). In the field of medicine, randomized controlled trials (RCTs) are considered essential to maintain high-quality research and improve medical science by providing unbiased comparisons between treatment and control groups (Bennett, 2005). Comprehensive guidelines, the Consolidated Standards of Reporting Trials (CONSORT; Moher, Schultz, & Altman, 2003), are one mechanism used to guide implementation and publication of

RCT studies and have led to an increase in the quality of research published in many medical journals (Devereaux, Manns, Ghali, Quan, & Guyatt, 2002).

To address these concerns in education, several organizations have developed guidelines to help develop and implement evidence-based practices and to increase scientific-based research in education. Responding to the perceived need to increase the quality of education research, the federal government reorganized its Department of Education research funding organizations to place more emphasis on supporting rigorous research design and methodology that can lead to more informed classroom practices (Odom et al., 2005).

As part of the reorganization, the Department of Education's Institute of Education Sciences developed the What Works Clearinghouse (WWC) (www.whatworks.ed.gov) to promote scientific-based practice in education. The WWC places strong emphasis on determining causality for intervention effects and will only evaluate RCTs, quasi-experiment (QED), or regression discontinuity (RD) designs. For an intervention to be labeled "meets evidence standards," the study must be either an RCT or RD design without problems related to attrition or disruption. Studies that use QED designs can at best be labeled "meets evidence standards with reservations" and must have comparison groups and meet several other WWC standards (WWC, 2005). The WWC standards also focus on intervention fidelity, quality of outcome measures, issues related to internal validity, and statistical analysis and reporting.

Although most of the federal government's emphasis on research standards is fairly new, the American Psychological Association (APA) was one of the first groups connected to education to pursue the development and implementation of research standards. Besides creating the *Criteria for Evaluating Treatment Guidelines* (APA, 2002), leaders in Division 12 (Clinical Psychology) and then Division 16 (School Psychology) of the APA created standards for research in their respective communities. The Task Force on Evidence-Based Interventions in School Psychology sponsored by APA's Division 16 and the Society for the Study of School Psychology produced a manual to code and identify evidence-based interventions (EBIs) for group and single-subject research that address behavioral, academic, and emotional problems (Kratochwill & Stoiber, 2000; Frank & Kratochwill, chapter 2, this volume) (see www.sp-ebi.org for a copy of the manual). A task force of the Division for Research of the Council for Exceptional Children (CEC) produced a special issue of the journal *Exceptional Children* that focused on criteria for evidence-based practice in special education for group experimental and quasi-experimental (Gersten et al., 2005), correlational (Thompson, Diamond, McWilliam, Snyder, & Snyder, 2005), single-subject (R. H. Horner et al., 2005), and qualitative (Brantlinger, Jimenez, Klingner, Pugach, & Richardson, 2004) research.

An obvious question is the extent to which RCT is currently used in consultation and intervention research. In a review of empirical studies published in five school psychology and special education journals (*Journal of Special Education, Exceptional Children, Learning Disabilities Research and Practice, Journal of Learning Disabilities, School Psychology Review*) from 1999 to 2004, only 4.22% of the 806 studies used random assignment (Seethaler & Fuchs, 2005). The authors concluded that RCT is underrepresented in the research literature studying math and reading interventions.

The common theme across all the research standards organizations is a desire to establish a system to evaluate the quality of research and to suggest guidelines about what should be called empirically supported practice. Not surprisingly, these organizations have focused their standards on areas they believe are the most important for their respective fields. The next two sections of this chapter more closely examine the recommendations from APA Division 16 and CEC task forces that can be applied to consultation research.

Evidence-Based Interventions in School Psychology

The Task Force on Evidence-Based Interventions in School Psychology (EBI Task Force) provides standards for group and single-subject design intervention studies that can be used to evaluate the quality of research. These guidelines are especially relevant for consultation outcome studies designed to compare consultation models and provide data about the effectiveness of each approach (Schulte, chapter 3, this volume; Frank & Kratochwill, chapter 2, this volume). Several authors have suggested that most studies comparing consultation models have significant design and methodological flaws (Gresham & Kendell, 1987; Gutkin, 1993; Kratochwill, Sheridan, & VanSomeren, 1988). Many aspects of the EBI criteria were recommended earlier by Kratochwill and colleagues (1988) as part of a research agenda to improve the knowledge base regarding consultation effectiveness and comparisons of consultation models.

The coding manual focuses on the studies' general characteristics, key features, and supplemental descriptive information. Issues of design, type of program, stage of program, and intervention exposure are coded as general characteristics for single-case designs, and the same areas plus power and unit of analysis are added for group designs. For each of the eight key features that are evaluated, studies are given classifications of strong (3), promising (2), or weak (1) evidence. The standards are specific and are similar across both group and single-case designs. For example, to receive the classification of strong evidence for the category of measurement, multiple methods and sources of outcome data are necessary, and the reliability of the measures must be greater than .85. This point is especially critical for consultation research given that a significant amount of outcome variables is based on self-report (Witt, Gresham, & Noell, 1996). This requirement is fairly easy to meet when using established measures like the Intervention Rating Profile (IRP-15; Witt & Martens, 1983) but becomes a more complex challenge for measures that are developed for a specific study or project.

To gain a rating of 3 for the key variable of comparison groups, studies must include at least one active control group along with ensuring group equivalency (e.g., random assignment) and similar attrition rates. The lack of use of experimental design in consultation outcome studies has consistently been defined as a limitation of consultation research (Gutkin, 1993; Kratochwill et al., 1988) and in an examination of research over an entire decade was used less than half the time (Sheridan, Welch, & Orme, 1996). Recent research suggests that when an experimental design is used to compare consultation approaches, behavioral consultation appears to produce the strongest outcomes (Reddy, Barboza-Whitehead, Files, & Rubel, 2000).

Given the multivariate nature of the consultation process, multiple measures and methods should be used to assess consultation outcomes (Gresham & Kendell, 1987; Gutkin, 1993). To assess significance, a demonstration of a moderate effect as measured by an effect size index (Ottenbacher, 1990) for at least 75% of the outcome measures is necessary, in addition to a demonstration of clinical significance (Kazdin, 1977). Many of the statistical validity issues raised in this chapter are also examined as part of the process of determining significance.

The standards place a clear emphasis on demonstrating the cause for the intervention outcomes, including requiring clear evidence that all components of the intervention were necessary to obtain the demonstrated outcomes. As part of this process, studies are only given the classification as demonstrating strong evidence for "implementation fidelity" if a manual is used and two forms of treatment integrity data are collected (e.g., videotapes, observation, coding sessions). This topic is of particular importance for consultation research and one that has received recent attention. For example, Noell and colleagues (G. H. Noell et al., 2005) compared the impact of three follow-up strategies to determine which approach had the most impact on treatment implementation. The authors found that performance feedback was better at improving treatment integrity than weekly interviews or interviews with a focus on maintaining commitment to the treatment.

The task force clearly encourages replication by considering it a key variable that can be coded a 3 only if the study is a replication by an independent evaluator with the same target problem and intervention that were used in a previous study. Of particular importance for consultation research is the focus on the site of implementation as a key variable. Strong evidence is given only if a study was conducted in a public or alternative school. The final key variable of follow-up assessment requires assessment with the entire original sample over multiple intervals after the intervention to be classified as strong evidence. The current trend to use repeated measures of performance (i.e., progress monitoring) to evaluate response to intervention would meet this requirement if the data collection continues for several weeks after the intervention period.

In addition to the key variables just described, the EBI Task Force also recommends examining several supplemental variables. External validity variables such as sampling, participant characteristics, and evidence of generalization are described to allow the reader to consider these variables before selecting an intervention. In addition, intervention costs, length, feasibility, intensity, and characteristics of the interventionist are also described.

Evidence-Based Practice in Special Education

One goal of the CEC Division for Research Task Force was to produce evidence-based practice standards that reflect the complexity of special education and take into account the unique aspects of conducting research with such a diverse group. Although the authors acknowledged that randomized clinical trials are the gold standard of science, they also suggested that not all questions in special education can be addressed through this method (Odom et al., 2005). As mentioned, the committee generated suggestions for evidence-based practice for experimental and quasi-experimental, correlational, single-case, and qualitative research. The recommendations are similar to those of the APA Division 16 task force (especially for single-case designs), yet there are differences in both focus and depth of the standards.

One of the biggest differences is the increase in focus by the CEC task force on the conceptualization of the study and the description of the sample. Six of the 14 essential indicators for proposals and 3 of the 10 essential indicators for articles from group experimental or quasi-experimental research address conceptualization of the study or sample characteristics (Gersten et al., 2005). Similar to the APA task force, a substantial focus was placed on measurement of the outcome variables, with particular attention placed on addressing the error inherent in educational and psychological assessment. The confidence intervals for the outcome data, sample statistics, and effect sizes were all recommended as quality indicators for correlational research (Thompson et al., 2005). The authors also attempted to address some common analytic mistakes such as (a) inappropriate use of univariate methods for multivariate questions, (b) using univariate tests as post hoc methods for multivariate analysis, and (c) mistakenly converting interval data to nominal scales (Thompson et al., 2005).

SUMMARY

A number of areas in applied psychology are now calling for the use of EBIs to deliver services to their respective clienteles. In addition, the fields of general education and special education are now advocating for scientific, evidence-based practices in schools. Unfortunately, there is a large gulf between the existence of evidence-based practices and their utilization by practitioners in these various fields. This chapter focused on characteristics and standards of quantitative research methods as a means of providing evidence-based research in school-based consultation practice. The major goal of quantitative research methodology is to allow professionals the means by which they can draw valid inferences from controlled research and to rule out plausible rival hypotheses.

The chapter reviewed various quantitative research methodologies, including true experimental designs, quasi-experimental designs, and single-case research designs. Various threats to valid inference making were reviewed and include discussions of internal validity, external validity, statistical conclusion validity, and construct validity. The chapter concluded with a discussion of research standards espoused by various organizations, such as the Institute of Educational Science, the APA, the CEC, and Division 16 (Division of School Psychology) of the APA. The standards can be used to help design research proposals, develop research reports and manuscripts, and evaluate the quality of research.

REFERENCES

American Psychological Association. (2002). Criteria for evaluating treatment guidelines. *American Psychologist, 57,* 1052–1059.

Atkinson, R. C., & Jackson, G. B. (Eds.). (1992). *Research and education reform: Roles for the office of educational research and improvement.* Washington, DC: National Academy of Sciences.

Baer, D. M. (1977). Perhaps it would be better not to know everything. *Journal of Applied Behavior Analysis, 10,* 167–172.

Barlow, D., & Hersen, M. (1984). *Single case experimental design: Strategies for studying behavior change* (2nd ed.). New York: Pergamon.

Bennett, J. A. (2005). The Consolidated Standards of Reporting Trials (CONSORT): Guidelines for reporting randomized trials. *Nursing Research, 54,* 128–132.

Bergan, J. R., & Kratochwill, T. R. (1990). *Behavioral consultation and therapy.* New York: Plenum.

Bracht, G.H., & Glass, G.V. (1968). The external validity of experiments. *American Educational Research Journal, 5,* 437–474.

Brantlinger, E., Jimenez, R., Klingner, J., Pugach, M., & Richardson, V. (2004). Qualitative studies in special education. *Exceptional Children, 71,* 195–207.

Busk, P. L., & Serlin, R. C. (1992). Meta-analysis for single-case research. In T. R. Kratochwill & J. R. Levin (Eds.), *Single-case research design and analysis: New directions for psychology and education* (pp. 187–212). Hillsdale, NJ: Erlbaum.

Campbell, D., & Stanley, J. (1963). Experimental and quasi-experimental designs for research and teaching. In N. L. Gage (Ed.), *Handbook of research on teaching* (pp. 171–246). Chicago: Rand McNally.

Cavell, T. A., Frentz, C. E., & Kelley, M. L. (1986). Consumer acceptability of the single case withdrawal design: Penalty for early withdrawal? *Behavior Therapy, 17,* 82–87.

Center, B. A., Skiba, R. J., & Casey, A. (1985). A methodology for the quantitative synthesis of intra-subject design research. *Journal of Special Education, 19,* 387–400.

Christensen, L., & Mendoza, J. (1986). A method of assessing change in a single subject: An alteration of the RC index. *Behavior Therapy, 17,* 305–308.

Cohen, J. (1988). *Statistical power analysis for the behavioral sciences* (2nd ed.). Hillsdale, NJ: Erlbaum.

Cohen, J. (1992). A power primer. *Psychological Bulletin, 112,* 155–159.

DeProspero, A., & Cohen, S. (1979). Inconsistent visual analyses of intrasubject data. *Journal of Applied Behavior Analysis, 12,* 573–579.

Devereaux, P. J., Manns, B. J., Ghali, W. A., Quan, H., & Guyatt, G. H. (2002). The reporting of methodological factors in randomized controlled trials and the association with a journal policy to promote adherence to the Consolidated Standards of Reporting Trials (CONSORT) checklist. *Controlled Clinical Trials, 23,* 380–388.

DuPaul, G. J., & Henningson, P. N. (1993). Peer tutoring effects on the classroom performance of children with attention deficit hyperactivity disorder. *School Psychology Review, 22,* 134–143.

Elliott, S. N., Witt, J. C., Galvin, G. A., & Peterson, R. (1984). Acceptability of positive and reductive behavioral interventions: Factors that influence teachers' decisions. *Journal of School Psychology, 22,* 353–360.

Erchul, W. P., & Chewning, T. G. (1990). Behavioral consultation from a request-centered relational communication perspective. *School Psychology Quarterly, 5*, 1–20.

Erchul, W. P., Raven, B. H., & Wilson, K. E. (2004). The relationship between gender of consultant and social power perceptions within school consultation. *School Psychology Review, 33*, 582–590.

Franklin, R. D., Gorman, B. S., Beasley, T. M., & Allison, D. B. (1996). Graphical display and visual analysis. In R. D. Franklin, D. B. Allison, & B. S. Gorman (Eds.), *Design and analysis of single-case research* (pp. 119–158). Hillsdale, NJ: Erlbaum.

Gentile, J. R., Roden, A. H., & Klein, R. D. (1972). An analysis-of-variance model for the intrasubject replication design. *Journal of Applied BehaviorAnalysis, 5*, 193–198.

Gersten, R., Fuchs, L. S., Compton, D., Coyne, M., Greenwood, C., & Innocenti, M. S. (2005). Quality indicators for group experimental and quasi-experimental research in special education. *Exceptional Children, 71*, 149–164.

Greenspan, P., & Fisch, G.S. (1992). Visual inspection of data: A statistical analysis behavior. *Proceeding of the Annual Meeting of the American Statistical Association* (pp. 79–82). Alexandria, VA: American Statistical Association.

Gresham, F. M. (1979). Comparison of response cost and timeout in a special education setting. *Journal of Special Education, 13*, 199–208.

Gresham, F. M. (1980). Preliminary evidence on the use of DRL schedules in treating childhood enuresis: A case study via parental consultation. *Psychological Reports, 47*, 115–120.

Gresham, F. M. (1989). Assessment of treatment integrity in school consultation and prereferral intervention. *School Psychology Review, 18*, 37–50.

Gresham, F. M. (1998). Designs for evaluating behavior change: Conceptual principles of single case methodology. In T. S. Watson & F. M. Gresham (Eds.), *Handbook of child behavior therapy. Issues in clinical child psychology* (pp. 23–40). New York: Plenum.

Gresham, F. M., Gansle, K. A., & Noell, G. H. (1993). Treatment integrity in applied behavior analysis with children. *Journal of Applied Behavior Analysis, 26*, 257–263.

Gresham, F. M., & Kendell, G. K. (1987). School consultation research: Methodological critique and future research directions. *School Psychology Review, 16*, 306–316.

Gresham, F. M., & Lopez, M. F. (1996). Social validation: A unifying concept for school-based consultation research and practice. *School Psychology Quarterly, 11*, 204–227.

Gutkin, T. B. (1993). Conducting consultation research. In J. E. Zins, T. R. Kratochwill, & S. N. Elliott (Eds.), *Handbook of consultation services for children: Applications in educational and clinical settings* (pp. 227–248). San Francisco: Jossey-Bass.

Harbst, K. B., Ottenbacher, K. J., & Harris, S. R. (1991). Interrater reliability of therapists' judgments of graphed data. *Physicial Therapy, 71*, 107–115.

Hartmann, D. P. (1974). Forcing square pegs into round holes: Some comments on "An analysis-of-variance model for the intrasubject design." *Journal of Applied Behavior Analysis, 7*, 635–638.

Hartmann, D. P., Gottman, J. M., Jones, R. R., Gardner, W., Kazdin, A. E., & Vaught, R. S. (1980). Interrupted time-series analysis and its application to behavioral data. *Journal of Applied Behavior Analysis, 13*, 543–559.

Hartmann, D., & Hall, R. V. (1976). The changing criterion design. *Journal of Applied Behavior Analysis, 9*, 527–532.

Hayes, S. C. (1981). Single case experimental design and empirical clinical practice. *Journal of Consulting and Clinical Psychology, 49*, 193–211.

Heckaman, K. A., Alber, S., Hooper, S., & Heward, W. L. (1998). A comparison of least-to-most prompts and progressive time delay on the disruptive behavior of students with autism. *Journal of Behavioral Education, 8*, 171–201.

Horner, R. D., & Baer, D. M. (1978). Multiple-probe technique: A variation of the multiple baseline. *Journal of Applied Behavior Analysis, 11*, 189–196.

Horner, R. H., Carr, E. G., Halle, J., McGee, G., Odom, S., & Wolery, M. (2005). The use of single-subject research to identify evidence-based practice in special education. *Exceptional Children, 71*, 165–179.

Hyatt, S. P., Tingstrom, D. H., & Edwards, R. (1991). Jargon usage in intervention presentation during consultation: Demonstration of a facilitative effect. *Journal of Educational and Psychological Consultation, 2*, 49–58.

Jacobson, N. S., Follette, W. C., & Revenstorf, D. (1984). Psychotherapy outcome research: Methods for reporting variability and evaluating clinical significance. *Behavior Therapy, 15,* 336–352.

Johnston, J. M., & Pennypacker, H. S. (1993). *Strategies and tactics of behavioral research* (2nd ed.). Hillsdale, NJ: Erlbaum.

Jones, R. R., Vaught, R. S., & Weinrott, M. (1977). Time-series analysis in operant research. *Journal of Applied Behavior Analysis, 10,* 151–166.

Kazdin, A. E. (1977). Assessing the clinical or applied significance of behavior change through social validation. *Behavior Modification, 1,* 427–452.

Kazdin, A. E. (1980). Acceptability of alternative treatments for deviant child behavior. *Journal of Applied Behavior Analysis, 13,* 259–273.

Kazdin, A. (1984). Statistical analyses for single-case experimental designs. In D. Barlow & M. Hersen (Eds.), *Single case experimental designs: Strategies for studying behavior change* (pp. 285–324). New York: Pergamon.

Kazdin, A. E. (Ed.). (1992). *Methodological issues and strategies in clinical research.* Washington, DC: American Psychological Association.

Kazdin, A. E. (Ed.). (2003). *Methodological issues and strategies in clinical research* (3rd ed.). Washington, DC: American Psychological Association.

Kazdin, A. E., & Weisz, J. R. (Eds.). (2003). *Evidence-based psychotherapies for children and adolescents.* New York: Guilford.

Kennedy, C. H. (2005). *Single-case design for educational research.* Boston: Allyn and Bacon.

Kirk, R. E. (1995). *Experimental design: Procedures for the behavioral sciences* (3rd ed.). Belmont, CA: Brooks/Cole.

Knapp, T. J. (1983). Behavior analysts' visual appraisal of behavior change in graphic display. *Behavioral Assessment, 5,* 155–164.

Kratochwill, T. R., & Callan Stoiber, K. (2000). Empirically supported interventions and school psychology: Conceptual and practice issues — Part II. *School Psychology Quarterly, 15,* 233–253.

Kratochwill, T. R, Sheridan, S. M., & VanSomeren, K. R. (1988). Research in behavioral consultation: Current status and future directions. In F. West (Ed.), *School consultation interdisciplinary perspectives on theory, research, training, and practice* (pp. 77–102). Austin, TX: Association of Educational and Psychological Consultants.

Levin, J. R., & O'Donnell, A. M. (1999). What do about education's credibility gap? *Issues in Education: Contributions From Educational Psychology, 5,* 177–229.

Lonigan, C. J., Elbert, J. C., & Johnson, S. B. (1998). Empirically supported psychosocial interventions for children: An overview. *Journal of Clinical Child Psychology, 27,* 138–145.

Martens, B. K., Lewandowski, L. J., & Houk, J. L. (1989). Correlational analysis of verbal interactions during the consultative interview and consultees' subsequent perceptions. *Professional Psychology: Research and Practice, 20,* 334–339.

Matheson, A. S., & Shriver, M. D. (2005). Training teachers to give effective commands: Effects on student compliance and academic behaviors. *School Psychology Review, 34,* 202–219.

Matyas, T. A., & Greenwood, K. M. (1990). Visual analysis of single-case time series: Effects of variability, serial dependence, and magnitude of intervention effects. *Journal of Applied Behavior Analysis, 23,* 341–351.

Matyas, T. A., & Greenwood, K. M. (1991). Problems in the estimation of autocorrelation in brief time series and some implications for behavioral data. *Behavioral Assessment, 13,* 137–157.

Matyas, T. A., & Greenwood, K. M. (1997). Serial dependency for single-case data. In R. Franklin, D. Allison, & B. Gorman (Eds.), *Design and analysis of single-case research* (pp. 245–278). Mahwah, NJ: Erlbaum.

Maxwell, S. E. (2004). The persistence of underpowered studies in psychological research: Causes, consequences, and remedies. *Psychological Methods, 9,* 147–163.

Michael, J. (1974). Statistical inference for individual organism research: Mixed blessing or curse? *Journal of Applied Behavior Analysis, 7,* 647–653.

Moher, D., Schultz, K. F., & Altman, D. G. (2003). The CONSORT statement: Revised recommendations for improving the quality of reports of parallel-group randomized trials. *Clinical Oral Investigations, 7,* 2–7.

Morgan, D. L., & Morgan, R. K. (2001). Single-participant research design: Bringing science to managed care. *American Psychologist, 56,* 119–127.

Morrow-Bradley, C., & Elliott, R. (1986). Utilization of psychotherapy research by practicing psychotherapists. *American Psychologist, 41*, 188–197.

Musser, E. H., Bray, M. A., Kehle, T. J., & Jenson, W. R. (2001). Reducing disruptive behaviors in students with serious emotional disturbance. *School Psychology Review, 30*, 294–304.

Noell, G. H., Duhon, G. J., Gatti, S. L., & Connell, J. E. (2002). Consultation, follow-up, and implementation of behavior management interventions in general education. *School Psychology Review, 31*, 217–234.

Noell, G. H., Witt, J. C., Gilbertson, D., Ranier, D., & Freeland, J. (1997). Increasing teacher intervention implementation in general education settings through consultation and performance feedback. *School Psychology Quarterly, 12*, 77–88.

Noell, G. H., Witt, J. C., Slider, N. J., Connell, J. E., Gatti, S. L., Williams, K. L., et al. (2005). Treatment implementation following behavioral consultation in schools: A comparison of three follow-up strategies. *School Psychology Review, 34*, 87–106.

Nunnally, J. C., & Kotsch, W. E. (1983). Studies of individual subjects: Logic and methods of analysis. *British Journal of Clinical Psychology, 22*, 83–93.

Odom, S. L., Brantlinger, E., Gersten, R., Horner, R. H., Thompson, B., & Harris, K. R. (2005). Research in special education: Scientific methods and evidence-based practices. *Exceptional Children, 71*, 137–148.

Ottenbacher, K. J. (1990). When is a picture worth a thousand p values? A comparison of visual and quantitative methods to analyze single subject data. *Journal of Special Education, 23*, 436–449.

Palincsar, A. S., & Brown, A. L. (1984). Reciprocal teaching of comprehension-fostering and comprehension-monitoring activities. *Cognition and Instruction, 1*, 117–175.

Parker, R. I., Brossart, D. F., Vannest, K. J., Long, J. R., De-Alba, R. G., Baugh, F. G., et al. (2005). Effect sizes in single case research: How large is large? *School Psychology Review, 34*, 116–132.

Parloff, M. B. (1979). Can psychotherapy research guide the policymaker? A little knowledge may be a dangerous thing. *American Psychologist, 34*, 296–306.

Persons, J. B. (1991). Psychotherapy outcome studies do not accurately represent current models of psychotherapy: A proposed remedy. *American Psychologist, 46*, 99–106.

Raudenbush, S. W., & Bryk, A. S. (2002). *Hierarchical linear models: Applications and data analysis methods.* Thousand Oaks, CA: Sage.

Ray, K. P., Skinner, C. H., & Watson, T. S. (1999). Transferring stimulus control via momentum to increase compliance in a student with autism: A demonstration of collaborative consultation. *School Psychology Review, 28*, 622–628.

Reddy, L., Barboza-Whitehead, S., Files, T., & Rubel, E. (2000). Clinical focus of consultation outcome research with children and adolescents. *Special Services in the Schools, 16*, 1–22.

Rosenfield, S. (1995). Instructional consultation: A model for service delivery in the schools. *Journal of Educational and Psychological Consultation, 6*, 297–316.

Rosenthal, R. (1991). *Meta-analytic procedures for social research* (rev. ed.). Thousand Oaks, CA: Sage.

Rusch, F. R., & Kazdin, A. E. (1981). Toward a methodology of withdrawal designs for the assessment of response maintenance. *Journal of Applied Behavior Analysis, 14*, 131–140.

Schwartz, I. S., & Baer, D. M. (1991). Social validity assessments: Is current practice state of the art? *Journal of Applied Behavior Analysis, 24*, 189–204.

Scruggs, T. E., & Mastropieri, M. A. (1998). Summarizing single-subject research: Issues and applications. *Behavior Modification, 22*, 221–242.

Seethaler, P., & Fuchs, L. (2005). A drop in the bucket: Randomized controlled trials testing reading and math interventions. *Learning Disabilities Research and Practice, 20*, 98–102.

Shadish, W. R., Cook, T. D., & Campbell, D. T. (2002). *Experimental and quasi-experimental designs for generalized causal inference.* Boston: Houghton Mifflin.

Sheridan, S. M., Welch, M., & Orme, S. F. (1996). Is consultation effective? A review of outcome research. *Remedial and Special Education, 17*, 341–354.

Sidman, M. (1960). *Tactics of scientific research.* Oxford, UK: Basic Books.

Skinner, B. F. (1953). *Science and human behavior.* New York: Free Press.

Stoiber, K. C., & Kratochwill, T. R. (2000). Empirically supported interventions and school psychology: Rationale and methodological issues — Part I. *School Psychology Quarterly, 15*, 75–105.

Thompson, B., Diamond, K. E., McWilliam, R., Snyder, P., & Snyder, S. (2005). Evaluating the quality of evidence from correlational research for evidence-based practice. *Exceptional Children, 71*, 181–194.

Van den Noortgate, W., & Onghena, P. (2003). Combining single-case experimental data using hierarchical linear models. *School Psychology Quarterly, 18,* 325–346.

What Works Clearinghouse. (2005). *WWC review standards.* Retrieved March 15, 2005, from http://www. whatworks.ed.gov/reviewprocess/studystandards_final.pdf

Wickstrom, K. F., Jones, K. M., LaFleur, L. H., & Witt, J. C. (1998). An analysis of treatment integrity in school-based behavioral consultation. *School Psychology Quarterly, 13,* 141–154.

Witt, J. C., Gresham, F. M., & Noell, G. H. (1996). What's behavioral about behavioral consultation? *Journal of Educational and Psychological Consultation, 7,* 327–344.

Witt, J. C., & Martens, B. K. (1983). Assessing the acceptability of behavioral interventions used in classrooms. *Psychology in the Schools, 20,* 510–517.

Witt, J. C., Martens, B. K., & Elliott, S. N. (1984). Factors affecting teachers' judgments of the acceptability of behavioral interventions: Time involvement, behavior problem severity, and type of intervention. *Behavior Therapy, 15,* 204–209.

Witt, J. C., Noell, G. H., LaFleur, L. H., & Mortenson, B. P. (1997). Teacher usage of interventions in general education: Measurement and analysis of the independent variable. *Journal of Applied Behavior Analysis, 30,* 693–696.

Wolf, M. M. (1978). Social validity: The case for subjective measurement or how applied behavior analysis is finding its heart. *Journal of Applied Behavior Analysis, 11,* 203–214.

Zins, J. E., & Erchul, W. P. (2002). Best practices in school consultation. In A. Thomas & J. Grimes (Eds.), *Best practices in school psychology* (4th ed., pp. 625–644). Bethesda, MD: National Association of School Psychologists.

5

Qualitative and Mixed-Methods Designs in Consultation Research

Joel Meyers and Stephen D. Truscott

Georgia State University

Adena B. Meyers

Illinois State University

Kristen Varjas and Amanda Smith Collins

Georgia State University

The literature in professional psychology and education has discussed consultation as a method of delivering services since the 1950s. Early discussions focused on mental health, behavioral, and organizational consultation (see J. Meyers, Parsons, & Martin, 1979). Although there has been some research on consultation throughout much of this period (e.g., see Gutkin & Curtis, 1999), numerous questions remain to be addressed. The purpose of this chapter is to illustrate how qualitative and mixed methods may help to enhance knowledge about processes and outcomes of consultation in educational settings. The chapter includes the following sections: a rationale for qualitative methodology; an overview of the history of qualitative methods; a description of key elements of qualitative methodology; a review of the previous research about consultation that has been conducted using qualitative and mixed methods; and future directions for using qualitative and mixed methods in research on school based consultation.

RATIONALE FOR USING QUALITATIVE AND MIXED METHODS IN CONSULTATION RESEARCH

Overview of Consultation

Consultation can be defined as an indirect method of delivering psychological and educational services to children and by which the consultant works with a consultee or group of consultees (e.g., parent, teacher or other educational personnel) to help them work more effectively with an individual student (or group of students). Because the consultee has regular contact with the student, this is conceptualized as a potentially efficient approach to service delivery that allows the consultant to reach a maximum number of students and emphasizes preventive services (e.g., see J. Meyers et al., 1979; Parsons & Meyers, 1984).

Several key elements of consultation must be understood to conceptualize the most promising approaches to research in this field. These elements include (a) the interpersonal process of consultation; (b) the problem-solving process in consultation (i.e., consultation stages); (c) the ecological and sociopolitical context of consultation; (d) preventive goals of consultation; and (e) outcomes of consultation. These factors have complex interrelationships that can make it difficult to answer important research questions about consultation.

Consultation is an interpersonal process that requires relationship-building skills that enable consultants to obtain clear problem descriptions, maintain positive relationships, and support consultees' active involvement and feelings of ownership during problem solving. Effective consultation requires systematic use of problem-solving steps that include entry, problem definition, data collection to clarify problem definition, intervention development and implementation, and evaluation. In addition, when the consultation process takes place in schools, this adds complex ecological and sociopolitical layers that can influence the processes and outcomes of consultation. These include culture, classroom climate, school climate, family structure, community values, as well as local, state, and national politics. Further, consultation represents a unique approach to intervention because it often has multiple goals. One type of consultation goal is to solve the immediate referral problem (e.g., to improve academic performance, reduce disruptive behavior, or remediate social-emotional difficulties). This type of goal is consistent with tertiary or secondary prevention because the aim is to remediate an existing or emerging problem. At the same time, consultation often has a primary prevention goal of averting future problems by strengthening the instructional and behavior management skills of consultees.

Often, it is necessary to evaluate multiple levels of outcomes based on goals that are congruent with primary, secondary, and tertiary prevention. In addition, the evaluation of outcomes must be understood within an ecological system that includes multiple cultures; the settings of school, family, and community; and the sociopolitical layers that influence all of these factors. Further, effective consultation must follow systematic problem-solving stages to generate effective intervention plans. Finally, it is typically the consultee rather than the consultant who carries out interventions developed through consultation. In this context, interpersonal processes are of utmost importance in creating circumstances that maximize the chances that consultees will implement interventions systematically and effectively. The field of consultation demands research methodologies that have the potential to illuminate these dynamics. Qualitative and mixed methods are well suited to this endeavor.

The Need for Qualitative and Mixed Methods

Most qualitative research methodologies are rooted in the context studied, deliberately incorporate into the findings the ecological variables that affect the investigation, offer a recursive process of ongoing interactions between the researcher and participants, require the persistent observation of the setting to better engage participants and understand their perspectives, and can be focused on the interactions and processes inherent in the setting studied. Qualitative research, therefore, is appropriate for studying the process variables of consultation in the context of particular settings and can provide insight about consultation outcome variables that are often difficult to quantify.

The qualitative research methods discussed in this chapter use field-based observations, interviews, and document examinations to observe social interactions in much the same way that naturalists such as Darwin used repeated and extended observations of nature to understand the biological world. However, the qualitative methods that we discuss focus on human interactions involving social transactions. To understand these transactions, researchers must also understand the participants' interpretations of the interactions, which leads to another central theme of qualitative research: findings from qualitative research are "phenomenological," reflecting the perspectives and contexts of the participants.

Making sharp distinctions between qualitative research and quantitative research can be misleading because many approaches to qualitative methods produce data that can be counted (e.g., Schensul & LeCompte, 1999). Mixed methods (e.g., using qualitative, quantitative, or small-n designs in the same study) could enhance the concurrent examination of process variables, qualitative outcomes, and quantitative outcomes such as student progress. Qualitative data obtained from open-ended data sources can be reported in narrative form by describing the major findings and using the words of the participants to convey the central themes as well as the connections between themes. Meanwhile, the use of closed-ended and structured data collection strategies may be analyzed quantitatively using frequency counts, means, and so forth. In addition, narrative data obtained from open-ended data collection can be coded and transformed into quantitative data by counting the frequency of various themes found in the data. There are times when it may even be appropriate to use statistical techniques to analyze qualitative data that have been coded. An example is the use of factor analysis to determine the structure of qualitatively derived codes (e.g., see Gelzheiser, Meyers, & Pruzek, 1997; Gelzheiser, Meyers, Slesinski, Douglas, & Lewis, 1997; Hitchcock et al., 2005).

Mixed methods have not been used widely to date in school-based consultation research. Nevertheless, qualitative and mixed-method designs offer school-based consultation researchers additional options beyond what have been described as the experimental and correlational traditions in psychology (Reschly & Ysseldyke, 2002). Qualitative and mixed-method designs offer researchers the possibility of adding naturalistic or ecological approaches to understand better the processes and contexts of consultation. Further, qualitative and mixed-method designs may offer school-based consultants the opportunity to integrate seamlessly research with practice. Such methods have rich histories in other fields (e.g., anthropology and sociology) and were foundational to early psychology (e.g., Piaget's studies of his children) but have been neglected until recently in contemporary American psychology.

HISTORY OF QUALITATIVE RESEARCH AND MIXED METHODS

Qualitative research became a tangible method of social inquiry around the turn of the 19th century when several researchers and journalists attempted to understand and describe the situations of poor people and poor children in urban settings (e.g., see Bogdan & Biklen, 2003). The "Chicago school" of sociology beginning around 1900 represented the institutionalization of qualitative inquiry as a means to understand social interactions (Bogdan & Biklen). Key precepts of early qualitative research included field-based research, focus on specific cases, data that were not easily quantifiable, and efforts to understand the contexts of participants (Bogdan & Biklen).

Several researchers extended early qualitative research through the first half of the 20th century, including beginning efforts to use qualitative methods to understand educational systems. Two threads of qualitative research that are important to the ideas presented in this chapter began about midcentury: Anthropologists became interested in education (e.g., see Bogdan & Biklen, 2003), and a formal link was established between qualitative research and social action (Lewin, 1948). Anthropologists studied education to understand better the perspectives of teachers and students (Bogdan & Biklen). Among other things, this was deemed to be important because there was increasing interest in finding out why schools did not seem to provide urban, poor, and minority children with the tools needed to move up in society. To find out why public education was not working as the great equalizer, some researchers thought it was necessary to understand the phenomenological experience of those directly involved in schools. Classic studies of racial factors in classrooms (e.g., Rist, 1970), urban teachers' experiences (E. Fuchs, 1969), and students' perceptions of school (Kozol, 1967) originated from this interest in the participants' perspectives.

For some researchers, chronicling the perspectives and situations of different sections of society was not enough; some action was needed to attempt to rectify the problems identified in such studies. Although there were earlier efforts to link action with social research, Kurt Lewin (1948) is credited with a formal model of action research. Lewin was a social psychologist who thought that "research that produces nothing but books will not suffice" (1948, p. 203). He conducted several action research projects and developed a spiral model of action research that he described as nonlinear. In simple terms, Lewin's action research model is comprised of identification of a general idea, fact finding, planning, action, evaluation, plan amendation, action, and so on. In retrospect, Lewin's action research model is remarkably close to the general problem-solving models proposed by many consultation theorists, and it was a formative model leading to the development of organization development consultation.

This action research model also has strong connections to qualitative research methods (e.g., Schensul & LeCompte, 1999). Contemporary researchers have adapted this methodology to consultation-focused qualitative research (e.g., Nastasi, Bernstein-Moore, & Varjas, 2004; Truscott, Cosgrove, Meyers, & Eidle-Barkman, 2000). Other qualitative research models such as ethnography and microethnography (e.g., Knotek, 2003; Westby & Ford, 1993), interview studies (e.g., Behring, Cabello, Kushida, & Murguia, 2000), and mixed-method studies (e.g., Conwill, 2003) have been used recently to study consultation. Many of these researchers use variations of grounded theory methods for data analysis (Strauss & Corbin, 1998). This research is discussed in greater detail in this chapter. First, we present critical issues required for effective implementation of qualitative research to learn about school-based consultation.

KEY ELEMENTS OF QUALITATIVE METHODOLOGY FOR SCHOOL-BASED CONSULTATION RESEARCH

Philosophical Frameworks

Several underlying philosophical frameworks are important to the success of consultation and have great potential when applied to consultation research. Three with particular implications for qualitative research methods are empowerment, constructivism, and ecological theory.

Empowerment

Empowerment (Rappaport, 1981) provides one conceptual framework for qualitative methodology. Empowerment suggests that participants in consultation research be given the opportunity to exert control over consultation and the research. This is a dramatic departure from approaches to consultation research by which the researcher controls the process of consultation as well as the design and implementation of the research about consultation. Application of this approach to consultation research would result in a radical reconceptualization of the relationship among consultants, consultees, clients, and researchers so that the participants' values, rather than only the researchers' values, would influence the approach to research and consultation (e.g., see Alpert, 1985). This may increase the likelihood that consultation and related research will have the maximum opportunity to advance relevant knowledge, augment the effective performance of consultants and consultees, and modify the attitudes and behavior of students who are targets of consultation.

Constructivism

Vygotsky's (1978) theoretical rationale describes the interrelationship among thought, speech and language, social conditions, and contexts. From this perspective, language serves a social function that can help to solve problems and develop intellectual thought. According to this perspective, knowledge is constructed by the individual in the context of social or cultural circumstances (Sexton & Griffin, 1997). Several principles are particularly important when applying social-constructivist principles to qualitative research about consultation, and these are discussed in the remainder of this section (see also Sexton & Griffin).

Because knowledge is conceptualized as constructed by the individual, it requires active engagement of the learner (Sexton & Griffin, 1997). This principle suggests that participants in research on consultation (e.g., consultant, consultee, client, and researcher) need to be actively involved in the research. Because knowledge is constructed in social contexts, this principle assumes that participants must be actively involved in a collaborative manner to produce research that has the greatest potential to create knowledge that is meaningful and applicable to consultation practice (Sexton & Griffin).

This framework views prior knowledge as organized in unique cognitive structures referred to as *schemas* (Vygotsky, 1978). The social context provides unique meaning to knowledge (schemas) that is shared by the social or cultural group. This shared cultural knowledge can be exchanged between cultures (or may be difficult to exchange) based on the extent to which the cultures are similar. This is important for research about consultation because it involves multiple cultural groups, including consultant, consultee, client, researcher, ethnicity, socioeconomic status, gender, and so forth (Ingraham, 2000).

New knowledge developed from the collaboration of researchers, consultants, consultees, or students must be within the realm of the conceivable (zone of proximal development), or it will be discounted by one or more of the participants and the groups that they represent (Vygotsky, 1978). In the context of consultation research, the zone of proximal development is the place where new knowledge is developed through social mediation that occurs in formal and informal interactions among the participants in consultation research.

Learning can be influenced by providing support for the learner in the area just beyond their existing knowledge (i.e., the zone of proximal development). This support is referred to as *scaffolding* to convey the notion that new knowledge is built on prior knowledge. Further, *accommodation* refers to the individual's active attempts to create meaning from new information that is obtained through scaffolding. Importantly, this view suggests that new knowledge must be acted on to be incorporated into the individual's schemas. This implies the need for active participation of participants in consultation and in the research process to create new knowledge that can be incorporated into schemas of all participants.

Ecological Theory

Ecological theory is congruent with the assumption that the most effective interventions address interactions between the person and the setting (Bronfenbrenner, 1989; J. Meyers & Nastasi, 1999). A good example is found in research on curricula that teach social competence. Positive and sustained results are most likely when curricula to enhance social competence have been combined systematically with environmental variables (e.g., when environmental supports are provided by educators and parents to help children implement new social competencies in real situations in the classroom, at home, or in the community; J. Meyers & Nastasi; Shure, 1988).

Qualitative researchers who study consultation must understand the importance of ecological theory in practice and research. If researchers incorporate ecological variables into research designs, then this will support consultants' and consultees' use of methods that encourage environmental supports to reinforce students' use of skills that were taught.

Cultural Issues in Consultation and Qualitative Methodology

Research suggests increasingly that cultural factors can have a significant impact on the process and outcome of school consultation (Ingraham, 2000) and consultation with families (Sheridan, 2000). Cultural factors are important in qualitative methodology (Creswell, 1998; Lincoln & Guba, 1985; Merriam, 1998; Schensul & LeCompte, 1999; Strauss & Corbin, 1990) and should be a factor in qualitative research about consultation.

Culture includes a range of factors in addition to ethnicity or race (e.g., socioeconomic status, acculturation status, gender, professional role, sexual orientation, disability status). Culture has been discussed as an "organized framework of thoughts, beliefs, and norms for interaction and communication patterns" (Ingraham, 2000). We believe that consultants and qualitative researchers must display attitudes, skills, and knowledge relevant to multicultural practice, including awareness of their own and other cultures, and skills in cross-cultural communication and collaboration. This is an area that needs further investigation (see also Ingraham, chapter 13, this volume).

Strong Objectivity: A Link Among Consultation, Culture, and Prevention in Consultation Research
It has been argued previously that strong objectivity has the potential to strengthen multicultural consultation (Henning-Stout & Meyers, 2000). *Strong objectivity* is a perspective on science (Harding, 1991) suggesting that the most objective, undistorted, and untainted perspectives on any mainstream theory come from the most marginalized people in the system or culture that generated the theory. As applied to consultation research, the least powerful and most disenfranchised participants would help to provide an objective perspective, leading to research methods and consultation strategies that are most responsive and relevant and that have great potential to result in successful outcomes (Henning-Stout & Meyers). Because this perspective assumes and provides for the maximum inclusion of the people who are marginal to the consultation-research system, it encourages the active involvement of consultees, clients, and others who have traditionally lacked power in consultation research.

These relatively powerless groups have been referred to elsewhere as the "missing voices" (B. Meyers, Dowdy, & Paterson, 2000). Examples of groups with relatively limited power and voice in consultation research might include parents, other family members, teachers, bus drivers, custodians, student clients, peers, and so forth. Consultation and related research might be more effective in relationship to multicultural issues if these missing voices were encouraged to be active and influential participants in consultation and research. This needs to be a systematic focus of future consultation investigations, and it is a research focus that is congruent with qualitative methods.

Culture and Consultation With Families

Because families represent one missing voice in consultation, one approach to strengthen consultation and related research in the context of multiple cultures is to investigate efforts to strengthen bonds between schools and families while providing consultation that includes families. This approach is found in recent discussions of home-school collaboration (Christenson & Sheridan, 2001) and conjoint behavioral consultation (Sheridan, 2000; Sheridan & Kratochwill, in press; Sheridan, Kratochwill, & Bergan, 1996). Qualitative approaches to consultation research can have maximal effects by actively involving families in the design and implementation of consultation research. This enhances the possibilities of expanding the knowledge base about effective multicultural approaches to consultation that involves family members.

Stages of Qualitative Methodology With Implications for Consultation Research

The literature on qualitative methodology rarely includes an explicit discussion of problem-solving stages. One potential reason for this is that a strict interpretation of a stage model may be inappropriate for qualitative methodologies that rely on recursive procedures in which research questions (e.g., statement of problem) are followed by data collection and preliminary data analyses that are used to refine research questions and additional data collection. By interspersing data analysis and preliminary interpretation of data throughout the research process, it may be considered inappropriate to conceptualize a linear model of problem solving in qualitative research. On the other hand, it is useful to delineate the research steps that serve an important function to ensure that qualitative research proceeds systematically. This section provides a description of research steps that are most important in our approach to qualitative research, even though we acknowledge that qualitative researchers continually cycle back and forth through these steps rather than implement them in a fixed sequence.

Before presenting the six research steps, it is important to acknowledge that beginning from the first step and continuing throughout the research process, most qualitative researchers seek to create and maintain the active involvement of the research participants. Researchers actively engage participants in all phases of the research, including developing the problem statement and research goals, collecting data, interpreting findings, as well as developing, implementing, and evaluating interventions.

Research Step 1: Entry Into the Research System

A critical step in research involves strategies to enter the system and develop productive, collaborative relationships with the research participants. This facilitates a thorough understanding of the cultural, ecological, and political circumstances that surround the phenomenon under study (Lincoln & Guba, 1985; Schensul & LeCompte, 1999). Entry can include efforts to negotiate an agreement about the research with all relevant parties and subgroups in the system, including those at the highest levels of administration who are relevant to the investigation. As a part of this process, effective qualitative researchers seek to align themselves with key participants such as gatekeepers (see Lincoln & Guba). Early negotiations with all relevant constituent groups will seek to identify potential impediments to the research process and can facilitate researchers' efforts to include participants in research to a maximum extent.

Research Step 2: Initial Definition of Research Goals/Problem

Our model of qualitative research begins with a clear statement of the research goals that are communicated to research participants. Frequently, these research goals are tied closely to a problem that research participants believe needs attention in their setting. Although this statement of research goals helps initiate the research process, it is expected that the goals and any related problem statements may change as data are collected throughout the research process (Hunt et al., 2002).

Research Step 3: Needs Assessment

Early in the research process, it is recommended that researchers conduct a needs assessment to obtain input from a maximum number of participants to help shape the research goals, the problem statement, and the research methodology. Needs assessments can be conducted using mixed methods, including interviews, observations, surveys, and a review of extant records. Further, these methods can use a mixture of open- and closed-ended data collection methods (Hunt et al., 2002).

Research Step 4: Recursive Process

Perhaps the most important component of qualitative methodology is its use of a recursive process that integrates data collection, data analysis, and interpretation throughout the research process. This requires that after initial data are collected, preliminary data analysis creates tentative interpretations that are used to influence future data collection. This process is enhanced when member checking is built into the process so that data and interpretations are presented to research participants whose feedback is used to further refine interpretations and to suggest new data collection when needed. This ongoing process can be conceptualized as follows: (a) collect data; (b) conduct preliminary analysis of data; (c) collect new data based on prior analyses; (d) analyze and interpret new data; (e) continue this process until clear understanding of data is achieved; (f) present data and interpretations to participants for feedback (i.e., member checking); (g) collect new data as needed (based on participant feedback) and present new data and interpretations to participants to develop consensus about findings; and (h) continue this recursive process as needed to reach clarity about problems, goals, and interventions.

Research Step 5: Develop, Implement, and Sustain Interventions

Any interventions that are derived from the research process are designed to collaborate with research participants to change school structures and culture so that the intervention can be both effective and sustained. For example, research on consultation might result in changes to the child study team process to ensure that it has the proper membership and sufficient time to solve consultation problems that have preventive goals. Further, to ensure the likelihood that interventions developed from such research can be sustained, it will be important to provide ongoing training so that those implementing new methods are continually up to date about procedures. It will be important to maintain ongoing, effective communication to relevant constituent groups so that those who need the information are continuously informed about research findings and interventions.

Research Step 6: Evaluate Outcome, Acceptability, and Integrity

The research process requires a systematic evaluation of acceptability, integrity, and outcomes of any interventions that are implemented (Elliott, Witt, & Kratochwill, 1991). Evaluation should focus on data that reflect the outcomes and efficacy of interventions. In addition, evaluation should examine participant perceptions of the acceptability of interventions and research methods. Finally, evaluation should be conducted to determine how interventions are implemented and what changes are made to the intervention protocol.

Components of Research Design Using Qualitative and Mixed Methodology

A number of methods can be used to design strong qualitative investigations that have great potential to produce findings that will make meaningful contributions to the literature. These approaches have been discussed frequently in the literature on qualitative methodology (e.g., Creswell, 1998; Lincoln & Guba, 1985; Merriam, 1998; Nastasi & Schensul, 2005; Schensul & LeCompte, 1999; Strauss & Corbin, 1990). Researchers using qualitative methods to investigate school-based consultation need to have a clear understanding of these principles so that they can design the strongest possible investigations.

Recursive Methodology and Persistent Observation

One component of qualitative methodology is the use of persistent observation to provide in-depth and detailed information about the phenomena studied (see Lincoln & Guba, 1985). Persistent observation is best accomplished using recursive methodology by which the researcher continuously mixes data collection and analysis to develop an increasingly focused understanding of the problem. A hallmark of our model of consultation research is to use recursive methods as noted in the presentation of qualitative research steps. This process is referred to by Nastasi and Schensul (2005) as an *interactive process*.

Unexpected Findings

To develop an in-depth understanding of the phenomena studied, it is necessary to look for unexpected findings that are inconsistent with the emerging findings and hypotheses. This has been referred to as *negative case analysis* (Lincoln & Guba, 1985) and as *unintended outcomes* (Nastasi & Schensul, 2005). As unexpected findings are obtained, the researcher is forced to challenge emerging conclusions and hypotheses that will lead to more focused data collection and more valid conclusions. It is important that consultation researchers using qualitative and mixed methods show evidence of how they have systematically sought out unexpected findings and how they have used those findings to enhance validity.

Extent of Engagement

Researchers must be involved with the research setting over a sufficient period of time to maximize the scope and depth of data collection. Prolonged engagement with the setting ensures that data are collected over a long enough time period to produce credible data that are interpreted in a manner that leads to accurate conclusions. This ensures that a sufficient period of time is spent in the research setting to allow for recursive methods by which data collected early in the research process are analyzed, leading to modifications in future data collection and ongoing analyses, leading to progressively accurate findings (Lincoln & Guba, 1985; Nastasi & Schensul, 2005; Schensul & LeCompte, 1999).

Triangulation

Triangulation applies to both data collection and data analysis. Frequently, this refers to data collection using multiple sources of information (e.g., consultants, consultees, students, parents, and other educators in the system) or multiple data collection methods (e.g., interviews, surveys, observations, extant records, and so forth). In addition, triangulation can refer to the use of multiple researchers to collect (i.e., multiple interviewers, observers) and analyze data (i.e., multiple coders) (Lincoln & Guba, 1985; Nastasi & Schensul, 2005; Schensul & LeCompte, 1999).

Cultural-Contextual Sensitivity

Data collection methods are designed to ensure that data are collected in a manner that facilitates analysis of individual and group variations based on cultural experiences and the culture of the setting. Examples include open-ended questioning or interviewing that encourages elaborated responses, ethnographic surveys designed specifically for the group that is the focus of research, and in-depth description of the context (Lincoln & Guba, 1985; Nastasi & Schensul, 2005; Schensul & LeCompte, 1999).

Sampling Methods

A number of sampling strategies can be used in qualitative and mixed methodology. These can include random sampling, convenience sampling, and a range of approaches to criterion-based selection (e.g., see Schensul & LeCompte, 1999). Several criterion-based approaches to sampling have been described by Schensul and LeCompte, with selection relevant to the context and research questions. These methods include (a) extreme/dichotomous selection to reflect the ends of a continuum, (b) typical case selection to reflect a typical case, (c) reputational case selection based on referral from community experts, (d) ideal case selection to reflect the optimum conditions for the phenomenon under study, (e) comparable case selection to reflect specific characteristics of interest in the research, and (f) targeted selection of participants to reflect systematically known groups from the study population.

In addition, sampling decisions must include a focus on all relevant participant groups. In consultation, these might include the consultants, consultees (e.g., teachers, family members), clients (e.g., students), and other key stakeholders (e.g., administrators). For example, in consultation research designed to investigate the impact of consultee-centered consultation, it might be important to select participants carefully to ensure that the consultation cases studied involved consultee-centered rather than client-centered issues. If a particular approach to consultee-centered consultation is under investigation (e.g., mental health consultation), then it would be important to pick participants for whom the teacher's problem lends itself to a mental health approach (e.g., teacher anger or ambiguity about teacher role) and the use of consultation is congruent with the philosophy of the consultant. Regardless of the approach selected, it is important that researchers describe and justify the sampling methods used.

Sample Size

Sample size is an important issue that must be addressed clearly in qualitative research. Decisions about sample size often pose a dilemma because it is desirable to have a large enough sample to provide sufficient opportunity to observe variability, yet the sample must also be small enough to allow intensive and recursive study of the phenomenon (Schensul & LeCompte, 1999). It is important for researchers to report the number of participants and provide a clear rationale for the sample size (Nastasi & Schensul, 2005). Because the goal is to develop a valid, in-depth understanding of the phenomenon under local conditions, rather than create broad generalized findings, it is often appropriate to use small samples that are studied in detail.

Member Checking/Negotiated Interpretation

Member checking is an approach by which feedback from research participants is obtained regarding the collected data, data analyses, and interpretations (Lincoln & Guba, 1985). For example, member checking might involve asking consultees to read a transcript of their interviews to ensure that the transcript is accurate, to indicate whether emerging codes accurately reflect the consultation process, and to provide feedback on emerging interpretations and conclusions. In this way,

Table 5.1   Components for Intensive Data Analysis in Qualitative Research

Component	Brief Description
1. Prepare data for analysis	Create transcripts of interviews/observations. Create summaries for data sources that are not transcribed.
2. Brainstorm themes	Write initial ideas about findings in transcript margins or summaries attached to documents.
3. Create coding manual	Include the definition and quotations to illustrate each code.
4. Code and summarize	Use manual to code and summarize tentative findings for each data source, one at a time.
5. Confirm and revise codes	Use constant comparison. Confirm codes, determine their application to new data, and revise codes as needed.
6. Structure analysis	Use research questions to structure analysis by creating codes that are confirmed across data sources.
7. Pattern coding	Examine relationships among codes/themes based on participants' suggestions, co-occurrence of important codes, and sequences of events and codes in data.
8. Create grounded theory	Use data to create grounded theory in narrative form. Be clear how this answers research questions and is data based.
9. Graphic representation	Use figures, charts, and tables to illustrate findings.
10. Check accuracy of analysis	Check accuracy with input from multiple researchers.
11. Computer programs	Use qualitative analysis computer programs to manage/analyze data.

the participants are asked to participate in data analysis to create a negotiated interpretation of the findings (see Nastasi & Schensul, 2005).

Intensive Data Analysis

Several approaches to data analysis have been reported in the literature on qualitative research (e.g., see Creswell, 1998; Miles & Huberman, 1994; Schensul & LeCompte, 1999; Strauss & Corbin, 1990). We emphasize 11 components in data analysis, which are described briefly in Table 5.1. After transcripts and summaries of documents are prepared (Component 1), brainstorming is used to create initial ideas about themes based on reading the transcripts. This brainstorming results in a list of initial ideas about themes, potentially significant findings and interpretations (Component 2). Sometimes, it is useful to write these ideas directly on the transcripts.

In Components 3 and 4, the researchers create a coding manual to guide analyses and then apply the manual procedures to the data. Component 5 is the recursive process of modifying the manual and analyses as new data suggest new interpretations. This has been referred to as the *constant comparative method* (e.g., see Lincoln & Guba, 1985; Schensul & LeCompte, 1999; Strauss & Corbin, 1990).

Components 6, 7, and 8 are used to create sophisticated interpretations by determining how themes are interrelated, answer research questions, and create theory. This is done with pattern coding (Schensul & LeCompte, 1999) and the use of data to create grounded theory (Strauss & Corbin, 1990). The last three components (Components 9–11) provide approaches to assist with ensuring accuracy of coding (agreement among researchers) as well as management and presentation of data (computer programs designed for qualitative data and graphic displays of data).

Peer Debriefing

Peer debriefing is an approach through which the researcher obtains feedback from an independent peer who is not one of the researchers. This feedback can be focused on research questions, research design, data collection methods, data analysis, and conclusions (Lincoln & Guba, 1985). This goal can be attained, in part, through the use of research teams in which team members are encouraged to provide multiple perspectives on the data. However, research teams may not include disinterested peers because all team members have a common goal. We recommend the creation of research communities consisting of researchers who are interested in common topics and methodologies (e.g., see Cochran-Smith & Lytle, 1993). The members of such communities would be from multiple research teams and would provide each other feedback as they plan and design investigations, collect and analyze data, and write reports based on findings.

Audit Trail

An audit trail is used to obtain peer feedback from an independent researcher regarding the adequacy of methods used and the extent to which conclusions are justifiable and likely to be confirmed. Prior to asking someone outside the research team to conduct an audit of research methods, it is necessary for the researchers to work systematically to create an audit trail by collecting materials that reflect what was done throughout the research, including data collection procedures, personal researcher notes (i.e., memos), organization of data, approaches to data analysis, description of the data and findings, and description of emerging and final interpretations. The audit trail includes copies of all research materials. In addition to serving as a basis for obtaining input on the adequacy of methods and conclusions, establishing an audit trail helps the researcher maintain clear records of the research process that can assist in data management (Lincoln & Guba, 1985; Schwandt, 2001).

REVIEW OF QUALITATIVE RESEARCH ABOUT SCHOOL-BASED CONSULTATION

The systematic study of school-based consultation is a recent endeavor. Caplan's (1970) descriptions of mental health consultation led to adaptations of consultation to different settings (e.g., schools) and the development of new models (e.g., Bergan, 1977; J. Meyers, 1973). There is now a substantial body of literature on at least some elements of consultation, although the existing research is heavily skewed toward positivist (quantitative) notions and methods.

Henning-Stout (1994) argued cogently that consultation as studied is not typical of consultation as practiced. Her call for research that reflects authentic practice is consistent with other authors' identification of the potential contributions that qualitative and naturalistic research could make toward understanding the complex interplay of consultation processes, contexts, relationships, and outcomes (Athanasiou, Geil, Hazel, & Copeland, 2002; J. Meyers, Meyers, & Grogg, 2004; Pryzwansky & Noblit, 1990; Truscott et al., 2000). Yet, a body of such systematic qualitative studies of consultation is just beginning to emerge. Although nascent, both the number and rigor of qualitative studies about consultation have increased substantially over the past 5 to 7 years as the methods become more accepted and the researchers more proficient. This section reviews some of the existing literature, highlighting the predominant methods, foci, and contributions featured in consultation-focused qualitative research to date.

Qualitative Case Studies

Qualitative case studies are detailed descriptions of a specific setting, event, or subject (Bogdan & Biklen, 2003) that examines something within a "bounded" context (Miles & Huberman, 1994). Case studies comprised a substantial part of the early consultation literature. For example, Newman (1967) described a psychodynamic consultation model and provided case examples. Caplan's 1970 book also contained case examples. In 1976, J. Meyers and Pitt described a case of using consultation to implement a schoolwide bereavement process in response to the deaths of two children. Conoley (1981) reported results of a case study of students who were learning to be consultants. Alpert (1982) edited an early book in which chapter authors described cases focusing on particular elements or targets of consultation. A number of authors illustrated applications of organizational psychology to school-based consultation through case examples (e.g., Broskowski, 1973; Curtis & Metz, 1986; Lennox, Flanagan, & Meyers, 1979). Some of these early case descriptions had many elements that would now be required for strong qualitative research (e.g., Cherniss, Trickett, D'Antonio, & Tracy, 1982), and all provided important information for the developing knowledge base. In 1990, Pryzwansky and Noblit called for the systematic study of the complexities in consultation using qualitative case studies and described how such case studies could be useful for theory generation, understanding the consultation processes, and training. Only a few such case studies have been published since then (e.g., Alpert & Taufique, 2002; Denton, Hasbrouck, & Sekaquaptewa, 2003; Goldberg, 1995; B. Meyers, 2002; Salmon & Fenning, 1993).

A case study can provide a detailed description of a particular consultation case. Multiple-case studies can be used to compare cases that share an essential element and provide an opportunity to observe variation on one or more key variables. Athanasiou et al. (2002) provided an example of a qualitative multiple case study of the consultation process in which four cases shared a focus on individual consultation between school psychologists and elementary school teachers. These cases were examined to determine similarities and differences across cases regarding the participants' beliefs about the causes of the client's behavior, the linkage between causal attributions and intervention preferences, the teachers' perceived role in consultation, and the participants' beliefs about the process and efficacy of consultation. The researchers collected individual interviews, focus group interviews, questionnaires, and transcriptions of consultation sessions over a 4-week time period. These data were supplemented with observations from consultant training sessions and meetings. Their findings provide important information about teachers' efforts to intervene for their students, their reactions to frustration when students do not respond to interventions, the information and behavior changes that teachers value, and their perceptions of the consultation process.

Both Ingraham (2003) and Lopez (2000) used qualitative multiple-case methodology to examine multicultural issues in consultation. Ingraham's investigation focused on novice consultants' use of multicultural consultee-centered consultation (MCCC) with experienced teachers. Data from the class portfolios of three consultants-in-training were used to examine the process of using MCCC, factors associated with success and failure of the consultations, and strategies consultants used to address cultural issues relevant to the referral problem. Two of the interesting findings were that a co-constructed understanding of the multicultural aspects of the case was associated with successful consultation outcomes, and that bilingual teachers may be particularly open to MCCC methods.

Lopez (2000) analyzed field notes from five consultation cases involving instructional consultation with high school students with limited English proficiency. Her study focused on the influence of interpreters on the consultation process and found that the pace of consultation, clarity of communication, and interpersonal relationships were each affected in various ways. These studies illustrate how qualitative research can contribute to the literature by examining complex contexts and processes.

Ethnographies

Ethnographies are detailed descriptions of cultures or aspects of a culture (Bogdan & Biklen, 2003). Ethnographers typically engage in extended contact with the studied setting, examine multiple elements of the day-to-day interactions within the community, and may participate directly or indirectly in local activities (Miles & Huberman, 1994). Often, the research focuses on the perceptions of members of the culture of which the researcher is a participant observer.

Milofsky (1989) conducted an important ethnographic study of school psychologists in Chicago area schools. He followed school psychologists, observing and interviewing them using prolonged engagement and periodic member checking to ensure the accuracy of findings. He identified two distinct approaches to school psychology practice. *Activist* school psychologists tried to influence the system to provide a range of services, consider the child in context, and offer insights about children's behavior (i.e., approaches similar to consultation). In contrast, *administratively* oriented school psychologists performed a function of the school organization by administering tests to provide information about student placements. This large urban district tended to attract administratively oriented school psychologists for whom the administrative role is well defined. The activist school psychologists in this urban setting found that their change efforts were neither supported nor valued.

Milofsky (1989) also documented practitioners' concerns about becoming overwhelmed by the immense problems faced by their urban students, communities, and schools. This often led to feelings of vulnerability and helplessness and resulted in the continual use of school psychology practices that failed to employ effective consultation. According to Milofsky, "The contemporary dilemma faced by good people who work in bureaucratic settings is that they do not know what they can do to stop practices they find abhorrent or unethical. ... School psychologists either choose not to see that there is a problem or they pass the blame onto regular educators" (p. 178). This conclusion begins to explain how school psychologist/consultants often blame the consultee (teacher) just as teacher-consultees often blame difficult children. When people are frustrated, they tend to blame the other person for lack of progress (e.g., see Parsons & Meyers, 1984).

Ethnographies and microethnographies have focused directly on school consultation. Knotek and colleagues (Knotek 2003; Knotek, Babinski, & Rogers, 2002; Knotek, Rosenfield, Gravois, & Babinski, 2003, Webster, Knotek, Babinski, Rogers, & Barnett, 2003) used observations, interviews, field notes, participant observer notes, group interviews, and member checks to study new teacher groups and problem-solving teams. This research focused generally on how language is used to transmit cultural knowledge (e.g., Knotek, 2003) and how it can be used as a consultation tool to affect change in these groups (e.g., Knotek, 2003; Knotek et al., 2002; Webster et al., 2003).

This body of work demonstrates how qualitative research can extend our understanding of verbal dynamics in consultation, which has been studied previously using various a priori coding schemes (e.g., Erchul, 1999). This research also supports consultee-centered mental health consultation techniques (e.g., "one-downsmanship") and the use of questions to clarify understanding of consultees' perceptions.

Henning-Stout (1999) used ethnographic methods to study how novice consultants perceived the process of learning to consult. Several cohorts of students enrolled in an advanced consultation class kept detailed logs of their consultation experiences. A content analysis of the logs, instructor comments, and final papers from a sample of eight students was conducted. She concluded that there is substantially more to the consultation learning process than following a set of procedures.

In general, students followed the basic stages of consultation but altered those stages to fit the situation and sometimes required corrective direction from the instructor. The students sometimes extended their practice by adding appropriately some procedural and relationship elements that were not covered in class. The students also attended consistently to the systemic and interpersonal variables that affect the consultation relationship. This study is important because it documents that learning to be a consultant is a process as well as a set of skills.

Slonski-Fowler and Truscott (2004) conducted an ethnographic study about referring teachers' perceptions of the prereferral intervention team (PIT) process in two suburban elementary schools. Data were collected from interviews, team observations, classroom observations, and surveys over the course of one school year, and cases were followed from referral to the end of the year. Results suggested three critical barriers (or, conversely, facilitators) to teachers' active participation in prereferral problem solving and intervention implementation: (a) devaluation of the teachers' input in the problem-solving process; (b) disconnected, vague, or redundant interventions to address the problem presented; or (c) lack of team accountability for outcomes and follow-up on recommendations. These barriers resulted in teachers who were likely to withdraw from the prereferral process, either actually or by not implementing PIT recommendations. Among other things, the results provide a potentially useful model for understanding why teachers sometimes choose not to implement prereferral recommendations.

Action Research

Collaborative and action research projects are conducted by both external researchers and internal system members, using systematic qualitative and quantitative methods to obtain research findings and create social change (Bogdan & Biklen, 2003). This type of research is common in the community psychology and organizational development literature (e.g., Prilleltensky, Peirson, & Nelson, 1997; Schmuck, 1995). Action research is common in education (e.g., McConaughy, Kay, & Fitzgerald, 1998), but there are only a few examples in the consultation literature.

Nastasi, Varjas, Bernstein, and Jayasena (2000) described an action research project focused on developing school-based mental health services in Sri Lanka. The project used ethnographic and action research methods embedded within an interactive consultation model that the authors called participatory culture-specific consultation (PCSC). The researchers collected qualitative and quantitative data from various sources to identify the culture-specific needs of individuals and systems. These data were then examined by the researchers and local participants to plan and modify general consultation interventions to fit the local situation. As the project progressed, the researchers and local participants collected ongoing formative data about the implementation, modifications, and acceptability of the interventions. These data were used to inform the continued intervention effort and to work toward institutionalization of the mental health interventions resulting from the project. The authors posited that the PCSC model is applicable to school-based consultation in general.

Truscott et al. (2000) engaged in a collaborative action research project with preventive intervention teams (PITs). The researchers worked with the PIT members to collect data from interviews, observations, record reviews, surveys, and team meetings over an 18-month project. In a recursive process, data were presented periodically to the teams for their interpretation of the findings and to plan later rounds of data collection. Team members and researchers collaboratively examined the teams' processes, interventions, and structures. Teachers' and administrators' perceptions of the teams were also collected. Truscott et al. reported that the teams used the data to alter their team practices, membership, and interventions. The teams also planned new systemic responses to some of the identified referral issues and exhibited later signs that the process had resulted in acceptable and lasting changes that were incorporated in the teams' functioning despite some obstacles.

Grounded Theory

As noted, grounded theory (Strauss & Corbin, 1998) refers to a method of data collection and analysis that is often used in the context of qualitative research and can be applied to various types of investigations, including case studies, interview studies, and ethnographies (Merriam, 1998). In general, the goal of this inductive approach is to generate, build, or refine theory based on themes and patterns in the data. Hylander (2003) argued that this approach is especially useful for studying the complex interpersonal processes of consultee-centered consultation. Hylander illustrated this in her investigation of consultants and consultees working in several school and daycare settings in Sweden. She analyzed data from focus groups, tapes of consultation sessions, interviews, and open-ended survey responses to generate a theory about the process of change in consultee-centered consultation. Her conclusions focused on the theoretical concept of "turnings" or changes in the consultant or consultee's conceptualization of a problem situation. The theoretical concept of approach/closeness versus distance (between clients and consultees and between consultees and consultants) was used to explain the turnings. For example, consultees often changed their representations of problems by either approaching or distancing themselves from the client. Grounded theory has also been applied to the study of complex organizational and systems issues in consultation service delivery (e.g., Peirson & Prilleltensky, 1994).

Interview Studies

Interviews and focus groups have occasionally been used to study consultation when the methods used include qualitative interviews or focus groups with no clear connection to a particular model of qualitative research. Interview studies use transcripts of interviews and focus groups as the primary data sources (Bogdan & Biklen, 2003). The participants' own words form the basis of the research and give the researchers insight into the participants' perceptions of their world. Interview questions can range from open-ended invitations to talk about the participants' perceptions in general (e.g., "Can you tell me about your experience with consultation?") or questions designed to elicit information about a specific item of interest (e.g., "What do people mean when they say the student is 'emotionally disturbed'?").

Wilson, Gutkin, Hagen, and Oats (1998) interviewed elementary teachers to find out how teachers attempt to work with students who are difficult to teach. They found that the interviewed teachers knew little about classroom-based interventions, and that they consulted only infrequently with school specialists (e.g., school psychologists) prior to referring students to special education.

Truscott, Cohen, Sams, Sanborn, and Frank (2005) interviewed 170 PIT members to find out about common PIT practices and interventions. Among other things, the researchers found that none of the five most commonly reported PIT interventions (i.e., peer tutors/buddies, individual or group counseling, out-of-classroom remediation, change the child's seat, and decrease the amount of work) required the classroom teacher to alter instruction. Only about 12% of the respondents identified providing consultation to the teacher as a PIT response to referrals.

Mixed-Method Studies

Mixed-method studies include both qualitative and quantitative data (Tashakkori & Teddlie, 2002). These data can be analyzed either sequentially (e.g., using qualitative data to inform the design of a quantitative instrument) or concurrently (e.g., using qualitative process and quantitative outcome data). Frequently, qualitative data are coded and quantified for at least descriptive purposes. Mixed methods are common in the program evaluation literature (Caracelli & Greene, 1997), and some of that literature is applicable to consultation (e.g., Welch, Richards, Okada, Richards, & Prescott, 1995). Although mixed-method studies are potentially promising ways to address process and outcome issues simultaneously in consultation, only a few such studies exist in the literature. For example, Conwill (2003) examined the process and outcomes for one consultation case regarding a child with ongoing behavior disorders in a special school setting. Case notes were presented as qualitative data about the process and teachers', parents', and staff's reactions to the consultation methods. Quantitative data from a functional analysis of the child's behavior and ongoing behavioral intervention were presented as outcome data. It was apparent that providing ongoing information to the teacher and parents was instrumental in developing their ownership of the intervention and sustained implementation of the program. It was also apparent that the child responded positively to the implemented program.

Some mixed-method studies have been used to examine school personnel's attitudes and preferences about consultation. For example, Schulte, Osborne, and Kauffman (1993) used quantitative rating scales and qualitative interviews to study teachers' preferences for consultation. Teachers preferred sharing services with consultant-specialists in ongoing collaboration. Rankin and Aksamit (1994) studied prereferral teams using mixed methods, including open interviews, narrative observations, and a quantitative survey. They found that educators' perceptions of the teams varied by level (e.g., elementary or high school) and the participants' role in the process (team member or teacher). Still, the promise of mixed-method designs in consultation has yet to be realized.

Contributions to the Consultation Literature from Qualitative Research

Although we believe that qualitative and mixed methods have much to offer and will contribute significantly to the literature over time, it is fair to say that to date the contributions have been limited. Although case studies, ethnographies, grounded theory, interview studies, and mixed-method studies have begun to contribute to consultation research, research with these methods is at an early stage. In addition, other qualitative research methods with great potential, such as narrative inquiry, discourse analysis, feminist inquiry, and critical event analyses, have not been used widely in consultation research.

There are some areas that qualitative research has begun to elucidate. The first is team- and group-based consultation. The methods used by these teams, the parameters of consultation provided by teams, and the recommendations commonly made by teams have all been examined in qualitative research (e.g., Knotek, 2003; B. Meyers, Valentino, Meyers, Boretti, & Brent, 1996; Truscott et al., 2000). Team members' and teachers' perceptions of the process are well represented in the qualitative literature on teams (e.g., Mamlin & Harris, 1998; Rankin & Aksamit, 1994; Slonski-Fowler & Truscott, 2004), documenting limitations and problems with team-based consultation. It will be important for researchers to identify what works well in team- and group-based consultation, perhaps by defining and studying effective teams with naturalistic methods and combining these findings with quantitative outcome data for the consultation cases.

Qualitative methods have added substantial information about consultation participants' perceptions of the process. In particular, teachers' perceptions of consultation have been a focus for qualitative researchers. Babinski and Rogers (1998), Webster et al. (2003), Knotek (2003), Slonski-Fowler and Truscott (2004), Athanasiou et al. (2002), Mamlin and Harris (1998), and others have all contributed to our understanding of teachers' perceptions of consultation. It has been found not only that teachers usually care about their students and try many interventions prior to referral, but also that they face difficult dilemmas about accountability for teaching the group while trying to meet the needs of difficult individual students.

Novice consultants' perceptions of consultation and training have also received attention. Conoley (1981), Henning-Stout (1999), Lopez (2000), and Ingraham (2003) found that training is complex and entails learning some specific skills that must be applied to a variety of situations and modified to meet the demands of the setting and case. Learning to consult may be conceptualized as a gradual process of gaining confidence and tailoring learning from many sources as well as developing a set of discrete skills (e.g., problem-solving interviews and multicultural competencies).

Less has been written about consultants' perspectives on process. Knotek (2003) examined one consultant's strategic use of language to implement consultee-centered consultation interventions with problem-solving teams, and Athanasiou et al. (2002) examined concurrent consultant and teacher perceptions of the process. Conwill (2003) examined some of the consultation strategies used with a special school consultation case involving a child with serious behavioral problems. Still, there is a tremendous need for research on how experienced consultants choose consultation tactics and assess the results of those tactics as cases progress. Qualitative methods could be used to gain a much better understanding of these issues.

Finally, qualitative researchers have begun to acquire a better understanding of the ecological factors that impede or facilitate consultation. Milofsky's (1989) study of school psychology provides a well-documented picture of the situational barriers to consultation in a large urban school district and the critical importance of interactions between systemic factors and personal preferences for role functions. Rankin and Aksamit (1994) identified barriers to effective problem-solving team practices in secondary schools. Rubinson (2002) identified structural barriers and facilitators to implementing effective problem-solving teams in urban high schools. It will be important for consultation researchers to continue building a more nuanced understanding of factors that impede and facilitate consultative efforts in schools.

The initial efforts to apply qualitative methodologies to consultation have provided a rich and detailed view of consultation as it is actually conducted in schools. It will be important to continue that work and to expand the topics to include more about the factors that facilitate effective consultation.

AGENDA FOR CONSULTATION RESEARCH USING QUALITATIVE METHODS

Qualitative and mixed method studies of school-based consultation have contributed to our knowledge about team-based consultation in authentic settings, participants' perceptions of the consultation process, novice consultants' thinking and perceptions as they learn to consult, the ecological factors and contexts that impinge on the consultation process, as well as a little about consultants' rationales and strategic actions. Still, we believe that qualitative and mixed methods will help shed light on a number of important and yet unanswered questions about a variety of complex phenomena related to consultation processes and outcomes. Ethnographic methods, action research, and comparative case study techniques seem particularly well suited to these efforts. Mixed-method studies have the potential to link familiar quantitative outcome variables (e.g., outcome variables used in small-n quantitative designs) with qualitative investigations of the consultation process. The caveat for future researchers is that it will be important to use careful sampling and focused investigations; to identify settings, personal characteristics, and consultant strategies that facilitate the consultation process; and to provide detailed information about the interplay of these variables. Next, we outline a research agenda that includes questions about (a) consultation in the age of responsiveness to intervention (RTI); (b) aptitude-by-treatment interactions; (c) process variables in consultation; (d) treatment integrity and acceptability; and (e) an emphasis on action research.

Responsiveness to Intervention

School-based consultation is increasingly overlapped with school improvement. This overlap will increase as special services for students with challenging academic and behavioral issues begin to shift focus from identifying within-child deficits to measuring changes in academic and behavioral functioning that occur in response to targeted interventions (i.e., RTI) (e.g., D. Fuchs, Mock, Morgan, & Young, 2003). In this context, serious attention must be given to classroom, instructional, and climate issues in the schools. Qualitative and mixed-method studies can enhance understanding of RTI models and various ecological elements that impede and facilitate effective RTI service delivery. Insufficient attention has been paid to the specific contexts in which school-based consultation is conducted and contextual effects of RTI models. Because qualitative designs focus directly on contextual variables and ecological factors, they are well suited to studying consultation in the context of RTI.

Under RTI models, regular classroom teachers may be called on to deliver more individualized instructional and behavioral interventions, and consultants may in turn be called on to support teachers in these efforts. As such, attention to preventive consultation and capacity building with consultees is an RTI-related area that could become a focus for qualitative and mixed-method research on consultation. Consultee-centered consultation has always had the goal of improving the consultees' work with later clients, but this has seldom been investigated systematically, in part because it is difficult to measure. Qualitative research could be used to document consultee changes and could be supplemented with large- and small-scale quantitative measures of such things as student outcomes and teacher referral rates. The qualitative nature of such work would allow for some examination of the intangibles often identified as issues in consultation, such as goals to enhance consultee confidence or objectivity.

Aptitude-by-Treatment Interactions

It is not enough to know whether school-based consultation strategies are effective. Of equal importance is research that can help determine which approaches are likely to be effective under various circumstances. This problem may be understood in the context of the historic dichotomy in psychological research between correlational and experimental methods (e.g., see Cronbach & Snow, 1977; Reschly & Ysseldyke, 2002). Whereas experimental methods have traditionally sought to eliminate error associated with individual variation in an effort to determine the treatment that works most effectively for the populations studied, correlational methods have sought to study these individual differences. Cronbach and Snow pointed out this division between experimental and correlational methods and argued for research that combines these approaches. Based on the assumption that the best outcomes would be obtained if treatments were refined and targeted to different subgroups defined by individual difference variables (e.g., ability, motivation, social-emotional variables), they called for research designs that could uncover aptitude-by-treatment interactions.

Although questions have been raised about the success of research on aptitude-by-treatment interactions (e.g., Reschly & Ysseldyke, 2002), it is premature to conclude that such interactions do not exist. An alternative explanation is that the designs used to discover aptitude-by-treatment interactions are not sufficiently complex and do not allow for systematic examination of the multiple factors that simultaneously influence intervention in real-world settings. Because they are designed to study complex phenomena in natural settings, qualitative methodologies represent a promising means to address this shortcoming in the literature.

Interactive Effects of Process Variables

Although research about consultation outcomes is important, it is equally important to study the process of consultation. Knowledge about process can provide guidance about how to implement consultation effectively to solve various problems under a range of ecological conditions. Despite limited research on the consultation process, there have been some recent investigations addressing the interpersonal process of consultation (e.g., Erchul, 1999; Gutkin & Curtis, 1999). See Erchul, Grissom, and Getty's chapter 14 of this volume for more discussion of this issue. More research is needed in this area, and qualitative methodology is well suited to studying the richness and complexity of interpersonal processes in consultation.

There is some evidence that implementation of consultation stages (e.g., entry and contract negotiation, relationship building, problem identification, data collection, problem definition, collaborative development of interventions, implementation of interventions and evaluation, termination) can contribute to the efficacy of consultation (Bergan & Tombari, 1975; Flugum & Reschly, 1994; Truscott et al., 2000). Still, there is a need for more research to develop an understanding of how this works in practice and how implementation of stages is understood within the context of ecological variables, roles of consultant and consultee, cultural factors, and so forth. For example, it is possible that interpersonal process variables have a differential impact at different stages of the consultation process, and it is possible that the types of modifications needed for effective intervention may vary based on cultural and ecological circumstances. Qualitative methods can provide the in-depth information needed to learn about such interactive effects.

Expanding the Conceptions of Treatment Acceptability and Treatment Integrity

One useful framework for considering the process of consultation is to differentiate between treatment acceptability and treatment integrity (e.g., see Elliott et al., 1991; Kazdin, 2000; Wolf, 1978). *Treatment acceptability* refers to the perceptions that participants have about an intervention's potential effectiveness and whether the intervention is reasonable to implement (i.e., consumer satisfaction). Elliott et al. defined *treatment integrity* as the degree to which the program is implemented as intended (i.e., adherence to intervention protocol). These constructs have been widely discussed as important components of applied research, and there has been a good deal of relevant research (Reimers, Wacker, & Koeppl, 1987).

Recent research has explored the connection between treatment acceptability and treatment integrity, examining whether participants who view an intervention favorably (i.e., high treatment acceptability) will be more likely to have high levels of adherence to the treatment (i.e., high treatment integrity). Although two behavioral investigations have failed to find support for this connection (i.e., Sterling-Turner & Watson, 2002; Wickstrom, Jones, & LaFleur, 1998), there is a need for research investigating the relationship between treatment integrity and treatment acceptability using a range of intervention models and alternative research designs (see chapter 15 of this volume for Noell's discussion of these issues).

Several factors suggest that qualitative and mixed methods provide a promising direction for research investigating treatment acceptability and treatment integrity in school-based consultation. Qualitative methods can illuminate the subjective perspectives of research participants. In the area of treatment acceptability, such methods may contribute to a more complete understanding of how various stakeholders (including teachers, parents, and children) view consultation and the interventions that emerge from it. Applying an inductive, qualitative approach to research on treatment acceptability might enable these potentially important concepts and themes to emerge from the data.

Finally, the concept of treatment integrity assumes that changes to intervention protocols are undesirable. However, effective practice often requires treatment implementation to vary with local circumstances. Thus, treatment integrity may be more usefully conceptualized as explicit information about how the intervention is modified during implementation. This approach is consistent with the situation-specific emphasis of qualitative research. If we are interested in understanding phenomena in context, then we cannot necessarily expect to repeat a procedure the same way over and over again. Rather than using reliability and replicability (both of which are related to the traditional conceptualization of treatment integrity), the integrity of interventions and rigor of qualitative methods can be demonstrated through the use of an "audit trail" that documents how, when, and why changes to an intervention protocol are made.

CONCLUSIONS ABOUT THE FUTURE OF QUALITATIVE AND MIXED METHODS IN CONSULTATION RESEARCH

Qualitative and mixed methods have already made some contributions to the research literature on school consultation, and it is apparent that these contributions are growing. In addition, consultation research programs using a mixture of qualitative and quantitative methods have great potential to add substantially to consultation research. Qualitative methods can be useful early in studying a phenomenon and can generate theory (e.g., Straus & Corbin, 1990). Elements of the theory can then be tested using quantitative methods to produce generalizable knowledge. Conversely, qualitative methods can facilitate understanding of unexpected findings from quantitative methods. For example, if a consultation intervention works despite poor fidelity to the original plan, then a qualitative case study might lead to a better understanding of exactly which elements of the intervention are critical and which are not.

Changes in educational legislation, emphasis on cross-disciplinary services for students, and increasing interest in a variety of research approaches make this an exciting time to consider qualitative and mixed-method approaches to consultation research. Prior work has produced some knowledge about consultation and sophisticated guidelines for judging the adequacy and rigor of future qualitative studies. Many complex questions require research. The answers to those questions have substantive potential to have an impact on children's lives. Qualitative and mixed-method studies of school-based consultation will play an increasingly important role in the literature for the foreseeable future.

An Emphasis on Action Research Models

In this chapter, we have included a rationale for qualitative methods in consultation research and reviewed the relevant research. In addition, we have presented our approach for implementing qualitative methods. Throughout this discussion, we have emphasized that consultation research must address questions relevant to consultation practice and situated in natural, local contexts. One important direction for the future is to blur distinctions between research and practice and to emphasize research as a method that leads to meaningful change in schools. Action research as described in this chapter provides a vehicle for moving in this direction.

One systematic way to implement action research when investigating school-based consultation is the participatory culture-specific intervention model (PCSIM) developed by Nastasi et al. (2004). The PCSIM was designed to ensure explicit attention to culture in consultation through the use of qualitative methodology and to facilitate construction of culture- and context-specific interventions, particularly through ethnography, within a mixed-methods approach.

Similar to the research model proposed in this chapter, PCSIM is grounded in concepts, methods, and procedures from the fields of applied anthropology, education, and school psychology. For example, critical to effective use of PCSIM is a recursive process involving reflective integration of research, intervention, and consultation, similar to the recursive process in the qualitative research model presented in this chapter. Also embedded throughout the PCSIM is a partnership process in which stakeholders (consultants, researchers, and others with vested interests or resources) participate in all phases of program development (design, implementation, evaluation). Thus, the PCSIM may provide a mechanism for embedding the qualitative research process proposed in this chapter with both consultation and intervention in school settings.

A primary goal of PCSIM is development of culture-specific interventions that reflect the shared language, ideas, beliefs, values, and behavioral norms of the members of the target culture. This is consistent with the qualitative research model presented in this chapter as PCSIM includes a formal phase of "learning the culture," in which ethnographic methods are used to study the target culture (e.g., relevant to a specific community, context, group) in relationship to the intervention goals. These data are used to create a culture-specific (local) theory that guides development of quantitative culture-specific instruments (e.g., culture-specific surveys; Hitchcock et al., 2005) and culture-specific interventions (i.e., creating new or adapting existing interventions). The attention to cultural and contextual specificity continues throughout the process of program implementation and evaluation using a recursive research ←→ intervention process. Furthermore, the involvement of key stakeholders (partners) facilitates an ongoing consultation process (Nastasi et al., 2004).

The PCSIM addresses issues related to institutionalization and translation of intervention. In addition to a focus on sustainability of the target intervention, PCSIM prepares stakeholders to develop culture- and context-specific interventions that target other goals. Thus, the process of change becomes institutionalized within the system. This provides a vehicle for using qualitative research methods that have the potential to learn about and support sustained implementation of interventions resulting from consultation. The final phases of PCSIM are focused on dissemination of information to facilitate translation of the target program to other settings and populations through repetition of the PCSIM process.

The PCSIM provides a roadmap for implementing action research to study school-based consultation in a comprehensive manner. It provides a systematic approach that combines intervention approaches with research and can be used to help accomplish our stated goal of blurring distinctions between research and practice. The result can be researchers who are more effective in developing a knowledge base that has meaningful effects on practice and practitioners who contribute to research, understand its results, and sustain implementation of meaningful interventions that result from research.

REFERENCES

Alpert, J. L. (Ed.). (1982). *Psychological consultation in educational settings.* San Francisco: Jossey-Bass.
Alpert, J. L. (1985). Change within a profession: Change, future, prevention, and school psychology. *American Psychologist, 40,* 1112–1121.

Alpert, J. L., & Taufique, S. R. (2002). Consultation training: 26 years and three questions. *Journal of Educational and Psychological Consultation, 13*, 13–33.

Athanasiou, M. S., Geil, M., Hazel, C. E., & Copeland, E. P. (2002). A look inside school-based consultation: A qualitative study of the beliefs and practices of school psychologists and teachers. *School Psychology Quarterly, 17*, 258–298.

Babinski, L. M., & Rogers, D. L. (1998). Supporting new teachers through consultee-centered group consultation. *Journal of Educational and Psychological Consultation, 9*, 285–308.

Behring, S. T., Cabello, B., Kushida, D., & Murguia, A. (2000). Cultural modifications to current school-based consultation approaches reported by culturally diverse beginning consultants. *School Psychology Review, 29*, 354–367.

Bergan, J. R. (1977). *Behavioral consultation.* Columbus, OH: Merrill.

Bergan, J. R., & Tombari, M. L. (1975). The analysis of verbal interaction occurring during consultation. *Journal of School Psychology, 13*, 209–226.

Bogdan, R. C., & Biklen, S. K. (2003). *Qualitative research for education: An introduction to theory and methods* (4th ed.). Boston: Allyn & Bacon.

Bronfenbrenner, U. (1989). Ecological systems theory. In R. Vasta (Ed.), *Annals of child development* (Vol. 6, pp. 187–249). Greenwich, CT: JAI Press.

Broskowski, A. (1973). Concepts of teacher-centered consultation. *Professional Psychology, 4*, 50–58.

Caplan, G. (1970). *The theory and practice of mental health consultation.* New York: Basic Books.

Caracelli, V. J., & Greene, J. C. (1997). Crafting mixed-method evaluation designs. *New Directions for Evaluation, 74*, 19–32.

Cherniss, C., Trickett, E. J., D'Antonio, M., & Tracy, K. (1982). Involving students in organizational change in a high school. In J. L. Alpert (Ed.), *Psychological consultation in educational settings* (pp. 108–142). San Francisco: Jossey-Bass.

Christenson, S. L., & Sheridan, S. M. (2001). *Schools and families: Creating essential connections for learning.* New York: Guilford.

Cochran-Smith, M., & Lytle, S. L. (1993). *Inside outside: Teacher research and knowledge.* New York: Teachers College Press.

Conoley, J. C. (1981). *Consultation in schools: Theory, research, and procedures.* New York: Academic Press.

Conwill, W. L. (2003). Consultation and collaboration: An action research model for the full-service school. *Consulting Psychology Journal, 55*, 239–248.

Creswell, J. W. (1998). *Qualitative inquiry and research design: Choosing among five traditions.* Thousand Oaks, CA: Sage.

Cronbach, L. J., & Snow, R. E. (1977). *Aptitudes and instructional methods.* New York: Wiley.

Curtis, M. J., & Metz, L. W. (1986). System level intervention in a school for handicapped children. *School Psychology Review, 15*, 510–518.

Denton, C. A., Hasbrouck, J. E., & Sekaquaptewa, S. (2003). The consulting teacher: A descriptive case study in responsive systems consultation. *Journal of Educational & Psychological Consultation, 14*, 41–73.

Elliott, S. N., Witt, J. C., & Kratochwill, T. R. (1991). Selecting, implementing, and evaluating classroom interventions. In G. Stoner, M. R. Shinn, & H. M. Walker (Eds.), *Interventions for achievement and behavior problems* (pp. 99–136). Silver Spring, MD: National Association of School Psychologists.

Erchul, W. P. (1999). Two steps forward, one step back: Collaboration in school-based consultation. *Journal of School Psychology, 37*, 191–203.

Flugum, K. R., & Reschly, D. J. (1994). Prereferral interventions: Quality indices and outcomes. *Journal of School Psychology, 32*, 1–14.

Fuchs, D., Mock, D., Morgan, P. L., & Young, C. L. (2003). Responsiveness-to-intervention: Definitions, evidence, and implications for the learning disabilities construct. *Learning Disabilities Research & Practice, 18*, 157–171.

Fuchs, E. (1969). *Teachers talk: Views from inside city schools.* Garden City, NY: Doubleday.

Gelzheiser, L. M., Meyers, J., & Pruzek, R. M. (1997). A novel methodology for describing integration practices. *Exceptionality, 7*, 263–266.

Gelzheiser, L. M., Meyers, J., Slesinski, C., Douglas, C., & Lewis, L. (1997). Patterns in general education teachers' integration practices. *Exceptionality, 7*, 207–228.

Goldberg, I. (1995). Implementing the consultant teacher model: Interfacing multiple linking relationships and roles with systemic conditions. *Journal of Educational and Psychological Consultation, 6,* 175–190.

Gutkin, T. B., & Curtis, M. J. (1999). School-based consultation theory and practice: The art and science of indirect service delivery. In C. R. Reynolds & T. B. Gutkin (Eds.), *Handbook of school psychology* (3rd ed., pp. 598–637). New York: Wiley.

Harding, S. (1991). *Whose science? Whose knowledge? Thinking from women's lives.* Ithaca, NY: Cornell University Press.

Henning-Stout, M. (1994). Consultation and connected knowing: What we know is determined by the questions we ask. *Journal of Educational and Psychological Consultation, 5,* 81–97.

Henning-Stout, M. (1999). Learning consultation: An ethnographic analysis. *Journal of School Psychology, 37,* 73–98.

Henning-Stout, M., & Meyers, J. (2000). Consultation and human diversity: First things first. *School Psychology Review, 29,* 419–425.

Hitchcock, J. H., Nastasi, B. K., Dai, D. Y., Newman, J., Jayasena, A., Bernstein-Moore, R., et al. (2005). Illustrating a mixed-method approach for validating culturally specific constructs. *Journal of School Psychology, 43,* 259–278.

Hunt, M. H., Meyers, J., Davies, G., Meyers, B., Rogers, K., & Neel, J. (2002). A comprehensive needs assessment to facilitate prevention of school dropout and violence. *Psychology in the Schools, 39,* 399–416.

Hylander, I. (2003). Toward a grounded theory of the conceptual change process in consultee-centered consultation. *Journal of Educational and Psychological Consultation, 14,* 263–280.

Ingraham, C. L. (2000). Consultation through a multicultural lens: Multicultural and cross-cultural consultation in schools. *School Psychology Review, 29,* 320–343.

Ingraham, C. L. (2003). Multicultural consultee-centered consultation: When novice consultants explore cultural hypotheses with experienced teacher consultees. *Journal of Educational and Psychological Consultation, 14,* 329–362.

Kazdin, A. E. (2000). Perceived barriers to treatment participation and treatment acceptability among antisocial children and their families. *Journal of Child and Family Studies, 9,* 157–174.

Knotek, S. E. (2003). Making sense of jargon during consultation: Understanding consultees' social language to effect change in student study teams. *Journal of Educational and Psychological Consultation, 14,* 181–207.

Knotek, S. E., Babinski, L. M., & Rogers, D. L. (2002). Consultation in new teacher groups: School psychologists facilitating collaboration among new teachers. *California School Psychologist, 7,* 39–50.

Knotek, S. E., Rosenfield, S. A., Gravois, T. A., & Babinski, L. M. (2003). The process of fostering consultee development during instructional consultation. *Journal of Educational and Psychological Consultation, 14,* 303–328.

Kozol, J. (1967). *Death at an early age: The destruction of the hearts and minds of Negro children in the Boston public schools.* Boston: Houghton Mifflin.

Lennox, N., Flanagan, D., & Meyers, J. (1979). Organizational consultation to facilitate communications within a school staff. *Psychology in the Schools, 16,* 520–526.

Lewin, K. (1948). *Resolving social conflicts: Selected papers on group dynamics* (G. W. Lewin, Ed.). New York: Harper & Row.

Lincoln, Y. S., & Guba, E. G. (1985). *Naturalistic inquiry.* Beverly Hills, CA: Sage.

Lopez, E. (2000). Conducting instructional consultation through interpreters. *School Psychology Review, 29,* 378–388.

Mamlin, N., & Harris, K. R. (1998). Elementary teachers' referral to special education in light of inclusion and preferral: "Every child is here to learn … but some of these children are in real trouble." *Journal of Educational Psychology, 90,* 385–396.

McConaughy, S. H., Kay, P. J., & Fitzgerald, M. (1998). Preventing SED through parent-teacher action research and social skills instruction: First year outcomes. *Journal of Emotional and Behavioral Disorders, 6,* 81–93.

Merriam, S. B. (1998). *Qualitative research and case study applications in education* (2nd ed.). San Francisco: Jossey-Boss.

Meyers, B. (2002). The contract negotiation stage of a cross-cultural consultation: A case study. *Journal of Educational and Psychological Consultation, 13,* 151–183.

Meyers, B., Dowdy, J., & Paterson, T. (2000). Missing voices: Perspectives of the least visible families and their willingness and capacity for school involvement. *Current Issues in Middle Level Education, 7,* 59–79.

Meyers, B., Valentino, C. T., Meyers, J., Boretti, M., & Brent, D. (1996). Implementing prereferral intervention teams as an approach to school-based consultation in an urban school system. *Journal of Educational and Psychological Consultation, 7,* 119–149.

Meyers, J. (1973). A consultation model for school psychological services. *Journal of School Psychology, 11,* 5-15.

Meyers, J., Meyers, A. B., & Grogg, K. (2004). Prevention through consultation: A model to guide future developments in the field of School Psychology. *Journal of Educational and Psychological Consultation, 15,* 257–276.

Meyers, J., & Nastasi, B. (1999). Primary prevention as a framework for the delivery of psychological services in the schools. In T. Gutkin & C. Reynolds (Eds.), *Handbook of school psychology* (3rd ed., pp. 764–799). New York: Wiley.

Meyers, J., Parsons, R. D., & Martin, R. P. (1979). *Mental health consultation in the schools.* San Francisco: Jossey Bass.

Meyers, J., & Pitt, N. (1976). A consultation approach to help a school cope with the bereavement process. *Professional Psychology, 7,* 559–564.

Miles, M. B., & Huberman, A. M. (1994). *Qualitative data analysis: A sourcebook of new methods.* Beverly Hills, CA: Sage.

Milofsky, C. (1989). *Testers and testing: The sociology of school psychology.* New Brunswick, NJ: Rutgers University Press.

Nastasi, B. K., Bernstein-Moore, R., & Varjas, K. (2004). *School-based mental health service: Creating comprehensive and culturally specific programs.* Washington, DC: American Psychological Association.

Nastasi, B. K., & Schensul, S. (2005). Contributions of qualitative research to the validity of intervention research. *Journal of School Psychology, 43,* 177–195.

Nastasi, B. K., Varjas, K., Bernstein, R., & Jayasena, A. (2000). Conducting participatory culture-specific consultation: A global perspective on multicultural consultation. *School Psychology Review, 29,* 401–413.

Newman, R. G. (1967). *Psychological consultation in the schools.* New York: Basic Books.

Parsons, R. D., & Meyers, J. (1984). *Developing consultation skills.* San Francisco: Jossey Bass.

Peirson, L., & Prilleltensky, I. (1994). Understanding school change to facilitate prevention: A study of change in a secondary school. *Canadian Journal of Community Mental Health, 13,* 127–143.

Prilleltensky, I., Peirson, L., & Nelson, G. (1997). The application of community psychology values and guiding concepts to school consultation. *Journal of Educational and Psychological Consultation, 8,* 153–173.

Pryzwansky, W. B., & Noblit, G. W. (1990). Understanding and improving consultation practice: The qualitative case study approach. *Journal of Educational and Psychological Consultation, 5,* 293–307.

Rankin, J. L., & Aksamit, D. L. (1994). Perceptions of elementary, junior high, and high school student assistant team coordinators, team members, and teachers. *Journal of Educational and Psychological Consultation, 5,* 229–256.

Rappaport, J. (1981). In praise of paradox: A social policy of empowerment over prevention. *American Journal of Community Psychology, 9,* 1–25.

Reimers, T. M.., Wacker, D. P., & Koeppl, G. (1987). Acceptability of behavioral interventions: A review of the literature. *School Psychology Review, 16,* 212–227.

Reschly, D. J., & Ysseldyke, J. E. (2002). Paradigm shift: The past is not the future. In A. Thomas & J. Grimes (Eds.), *Best practices in school psychology IV* (pp. 3–20). Washington, DC: National Association of School Psychologists.

Rist, R. C. (1970). Student social class and teacher expectations: The self-fulfilling prophecy in ghetto education. *Harvard Education Review, 40,* 411–451.

Rubinson, F. (2002).Lessons learned from implementing problem-solving teams in urban high schools. *Journal of Educational and Psychological Consultation, 13,* 185–217.

Salmon, D., & Fenning, P. (1993). A process of mentorship in school consultation. *Journal of Educational and Psychological Consultation, 4,* 69–87.

Schensul, J. J., & LeCompte, M. D. (1999). *Ethnographer's toolkit.* Walnut Creek, CA: Altamira Press.

Schmuck, R. A. (1995). Process consultation and organization development. *Journal of Educational and Psychological Consultation, 6,* 199–205.

Schulte, A. C., Osborne, S. S., & Kauffman, J. M. (1993). Teacher responses to two types of consultative special education services. *Journal of Educational and Psychological Consultation, 4,* 1–27.

Schwandt, T. A. (2001). *Dictionary of qualitative inquiry* (2nd ed.). Thousand Oaks, CA: Sage.

Sexton, T. L., & Griffin, B. L. (Eds.). (1997). *Constructivist thinking in counseling practice, research and training.* New York: Teachers College Press.

Sheridan, S. M. (2000). Considerations of multiculturalism and diversity in behavioral consultation with parents and teachers. *School Psychology Review, 29,* 344–353.

Sheridan, S. M., & Kratochwill, T. R. (2007). *Conjoint behavioral consultation: Promoting family-school connections and interventions.* New York: Springer.

Sheridan, S. M., Kratochwill, T. R., & Bergan, J. R. (1996). *Conjoint behavioral consultation: A procedural manual.* New York: Plenum.

Shure, M. B. (1988). How to think, not what to think: A cognitive approach to prevention. In L. A. Bond & B. M. Wagner (Eds.), *Families in transition: Primary prevention programs that work* (pp. 170–199). Newbury Park, CA: Sage.

Slonski-Fowler, K. E., & Truscott, S. D. (2004). General education teachers' perceptions of the prereferral intervention team process. *Journal of Educational and Psychological Consultation, 15,* 1–39.

Sterling-Turner, H. E., & Watson, T. S. (2002). An analog investigation of the relationship between treatment acceptability and treatment integrity. *Journal of Behavioral Education, 11,* 39–50.

Strauss, A., & Corbin, J. (1998). *Basics of qualitative research: Techniques and procedures for developing grounded theory* (2nd ed.). Thousand Oaks, CA: Sage.

Tashakkori, A., & Teddlie, C. (Eds.). (2002). *Handbook of mixed methods in social and behavioral research.* Thousand Oaks, CA: Sage.

Truscott, S. D., Cohen, C., Sams, D. P., Sanborn, K., & Frank, A. (2005). The current state(s) of prereferral intervention teams: A national survey of state regulations and existing prereferral intervention teams. *Remedial and Special Education, 26,* 130–140.

Truscott, S. D., Cosgrove, G., Meyers, J., & Eidle-Barkman, K. A. (2000). The acceptability of organizational consultation with prereferral intervention teams. *School Psychology Quarterly, 15,* 172–206.

Vygotsky, L. (1978). *Mind in society.* Cambridge, MA: Harvard University Press.

Webster, L., Knotek, S. E., Babinski, L. M., Rogers, D. L., & Barnett, M. M. (2003). Mediation of consultees' conceptual development in new teacher groups: Using questions to improve coherency. *Journal of Educational and Psychological Consultation, 14,* 281–301.

Welch, M., Richards, G., Okada, T., Richards, J., & Prescott, S. (1995). A consultation and paraprofessional pull-in system of service delivery: A report of student outcomes and teacher satisfaction. *Remedial and Special Education, 16,* 16–28.

Westby, C. E., & Ford, V. The role of team culture and intervention. *Journal of Education and Psychological Consultation, 4,* 319–341.

Wickstrom, K. F., Jones, K. M., & LaFleur, L. H. (1998). An analysis of treatment integrity in school-based behavioral consultation. *School Psychology Quarterly, 13,* 141–154.

Wilson, C. P., Gutkin, T. B., Hagen, K. M., & Oats, R. G. (1998). General education teachers knowledge and self-reported use of classroom interventions for working with difficult-to-teach students: Implications for consultation, prereferral intervention and inclusive services. *School Psychology Quarterly, 13,* 45–62.

Wolf, M. M. (1978). Social validity: The case for subjective measurement or how applied behavioral analysis is finding its heart. *Journal of Applied Behavioral Analysis, 11,* 203–214.

6

Section Commentary on Effective Consultation

AMANDA M. VANDERHEYDEN

University of California at Santa Barbara

JOSEPH C. WITT

Louisiana State University

During the past three decades, consultation has been formalized and recognized as a process that is relevant to school psychology. Yet, fundamental questions exist about consultation in the schools. For example, what are the unique and specific components of consultation? Are these components equally weighted or equally important to outcomes? How do we know when consultation has occurred (relative to some other process)? Can similar outcomes be obtained using strategies other than consultation, and if so, what is the relative cost/benefit analysis? Do teachers recognize and value consultation with school psychologists? What makes a consultant effective? And more broadly, is it necessary to invoke theories and principles that are not measurable? Finally, what is the purpose of consultation?

In this commentary, we provide perspectives on consultation research in the context of what constitutes scientifically based practices. We also consider data that are needed to further demonstrate the empirical value of consultation, the consultant's role in ensuring effective consultation, and consultation as a context for understanding and promoting system change.

IS CONSULTATION AN EVIDENCE-BASED PRACTICE?

Developing an evidence base has been described as an iterative process of idea development, empirical investigation, peer scrutiny, and self-correction (Feuer, Towne, & Shavelson, 2002). The tremendous variation in schools has been noted as a challenge to identifying generalizable findings and ultimately building a coherent knowledge base that can be consumed readily by policymakers and practitioners. The lack of consensus that occurs naturally as part of the scientific process is difficult for consumers and perhaps intolerable to policymakers. Hence, some have argued that there is a need for some consensus of thought related to what constitutes evidence, while protecting freedom in scientific method and allowing an adherence to the ideals of science (Feuer et al., 2002; National Research Council, 2002). Feuer et al. (2002) further warned that in the absence of consensus, policymakers may impose on the scientific process in their efforts to identify evidence-based practices and guide their decision making. Whereas continuity of thought often occurs naturally within various factions in the community of educational researchers (e.g., on journal editorial boards, training programs, publications within certain journals), there is not a tradition of identifying themes and trends that transcend individual study to rise to the level of conventionally accepted standards for effective practices (Burkhardt & Schoenfeld, 2003). Within such systems, few contingencies exist to support dissemination outside the school of thought to which one subscribes as an academician. Certainly, few, if any, contingencies exist to support the application of such findings in schools.

This lack of consensus in research findings creates a challenge for those who wish to reach conclusions, for example, about what constitutes effective instructional strategies. There does seem to be consensus, however, among several task forces regarding the challenges faced in translating educational research findings into practice. For example, the mathematics and science initiative (U.S. Department of Education, 2003) identified barriers to research that included a lack of integration among research activities; absence of alignment between and among instruction, curriculum, and assessment; paucity of comprehensive, well-integrated, long-term programs of research; lack of a coherent theory; lack of agreement about the goals of education; and tremendous variation across settings and programs. These barriers affect those who wish to implement programs and practices that are of demonstrated effectiveness.

The cultural and belief systems of schools also impede changing practices irrespective of research findings (U.S. Department of Education, 2003). Whether the idea of using data to inform practice will endure depends in part on the translation of so-called evidence into practical application in settings that share certain commonalities but have perhaps many more differences, where an allegiance to data cannot be assumed, and in which there have been long learning histories of philosophy-driven programs and ever-changing policy. When actual applications bear little resemblance to prescribed applications, effectiveness will suffer.

Scholars in school psychology and special education have identified the importance of accumulating knowledge and building an accessible base of evidence that translates into practices in schools that enhance outcomes for children. School psychology and special education have explicitly acknowledged the need for high-quality scholarship that effectively addresses how to most effectively identify, intervene, monitor outcomes, and promote sustainability for children and families; see *Exceptional Children* (71) and Kratochwill and Shernoff (2004) for further discussion. During the multisite conference, the Future of School Psychology in 2002, multiple themes were identified as outcome goals for the conference (and relevant to the future of school psychology), including a focus on ecological assessment, early identification and intervention, use of evidence-based interventions, a focus on family involvement, and enhanced collaboration between education and psychological specialty areas; see *School Psychology Review* (33) and Dawson et al. (2004) for more information. These recommendations are consistent with recent legislative mandates (Individuals With Disabilities Education Improvement Act reauthorization of 2004, No Child Left Behind Act [NCLB]) that acknowledge the importance of these goals, increase accountability, and have created a need to focus considerable attention on exactly how to bring evidence to improve learning and learning trajectories for school-aged children.

Relative to school consultation specifically, Frank and Kratochwill (chapter 2, this volume) pose an intriguing question: Is consultation an intervention? Because consultation is directed toward specific outcomes (i.e., the solution of a problem), consultation arguably is an intervention. Consultation traditionally has been viewed as a consultant working with a second person to bring about changes in a third person (e.g., the student). Hence, consultation is ultimately one of the strategies available to schools to improve student performance. Therefore, consultation appears to qualify as an intervention or intervention component that can be used potentially to enhance student out-

Scientifically based research:

The term "scientifically based research:"

1. Means research that involves the application of rigorous, systematic, and objective procedures to obtain reliable and valid knowledge relevant to education activities and programs; and

2. Includes research that--

    a. Employs systematic, empirical methods that draw on observation or experiment;

    b. Involves rigorous data analyses that are adequate to test the stated hypotheses and justify the general conclusions drawn;

    c. Relies on measurements or observational methods that provide reliable and valid data across evaluators and observers, across multiple measurements and observations, and across studies by the same or different investigators;

    d. Is evaluated using experimental or quasi-experimental designs in which individuals, entities, programs, or activities are assigned to different conditions and with appropriate controls to evaluate the effects of the condition of interest, with a preference for random-assignment experiments, or other designs to the extent that those designs contain within-condition or across-condition controls;

    e. Ensures that experimental studies are presented in sufficient detail and clarity to allow for replication or, at a minimum, offer the opportunity to build systematically on their findings; and

    f. Has been accepted by a peer-reviewed journal or approved by a panel of independent experts through a comparably rigorous, objective, and scientific review [Title IX, Part A, section 9101(37)].

Figure 6.1   Definition of scientifically based research provided in No Child Left Behind Act, 2002 (Pub. L. 107–110, Title IX, Part A, Section 9101, Subsection 37).

comes. If consultation is an intervention, then, in this era of accountability, consultation must be examined to determine whether it meets the standards of a scientifically based practice (see Figure 6.1 for the NCLB definition of scientifically based research). Empiricism as a guide to practice requires the use of assessment and intervention strategies that have been shown to work, are likely to produce better results (i.e., enhance effectiveness), and minimize the allocation of precious professional resources to strategies that are not likely to produce results (i.e., enhance efficiency).

Is consultation a scientifically based procedure that has been linked to student outcomes, or is it a costly use of professional time that could be reallocated to engagement in activities that more effectively produce improved student outcomes? This volume is a testament to advancements in the science of consultation. There is evidence that consultation, properly designed and used, does lead to improvements in student outcomes (e.g., Noell et al., 2005).

Gresham and Kendell (1987) asserted that there were no experts in consultation, partly because there was not a body of scientific research defining and supporting consultation. Like much education research, consultation research languished in the world of self-report, in which the prevailing philosophy seemed to be if the consultee liked the consultation "experience," then it was a strategy or approach worthy of use in schools. Gresham and Kendell alleged that consultation seemed to have been invented by consultants to justify the existence of a person in a school who lacked content expertise but who could facilitate a "problem-solving" process and, as a bonus, could bring about a sense of empowerment in the consultee. Much progress has been made since Gresham and Kendell's comment; however, much remains to be done.

WHAT IS NEEDED FOR CONSULTATION TO BE AN EVIDENCE-BASED PRACTICE?

In this volume, Frank and Kratochwill (chapter 2), Schulte (chapter 3), Gresham and Vanderwood (chapter 4), and Meyers et al. (chapter 5) point to methods for measurement and for research to improve our ability to know if consultation is effective. Schulte and Frank and Kratochwill situate their examination of consultation in the context of evidence-based practice. Schulte provides an excellent overview of the evolution of evidence-based practice in school psychology and provides a research "task list" of ways to immediately enhance our ability to know whether consultation is effective (see Table 3.1 in chapter 3, this volume). Frank and Kratochwill chart a new and exciting course for consultation that is highly related to problem-solving response-to-intervention (RTI) models of assessment and capitalizes on much of the evidence indicating that a problem-solving approach in consultation advances child and system outcomes. Gresham and Vanderwood provide a thorough review of quantitative methodologies that permit the building of a base of findings to know whether a practice may be empirically supported. Interestingly, each of the four chapters notes an explicit focus on consequential validity (Messick, 1995), and Schulte and Gresham and Vanderwood directly indicate that a standard of effectiveness ought to represent normalized outcomes or postintervention performances that are similar to children who never were in need of intervention. This recommendation is visionary and offers intervention researchers an opportunity to aim at the right target (Macmann & Barnett, 1999) and directly examine the social validity of the outcomes of interventions (Wolf, 1978). Meyers and colleagues similarly acknowledge the need for empirical scrutiny of consultation practices and describe the potential contribution of qualitative methodologies to identifying what works in consultation. Meyers et al. identify some outcome variables that differ from those identified in the quantitative methods and measurement chapters and tackle questions related to cultural sensitivity, equity, and consumer satisfaction in consultation.

Consultation effectiveness is influenced by a wide array of variables. In any particular study or situation, researchers often theorize about why certain behavior change efforts failed or why certain data patterns were observed. These discussions are useful as they often set the stage for future research investigations, and systematic replication presumably leads to patterns of evidence that can inform practice in ways that enhance desired outcomes. Consultation does not denote a particular set of procedures implemented in particular ways with established data interpretation guidelines. The behaviors that constitute consultative activities are variable, as are the goals and outcome measures. This variability makes it difficult to think about demonstrating the carte blanche effectiveness of consultation as a science or model of practice. To quantify consultation effectiveness, some criterion for what constitutes consultation must be determined, and some standard criterion of effectiveness must be agreed on. Because consultation is a broad term that denotes a variety of processes and desired outcomes loosely organized by delivery format (i.e., a consultant works with a second person to bring about change in a client), consensus about specific processes and desired outcomes may be difficult to obtain and ultimately may lack utility. For a practice to be evidence based, a level of precision is needed to identify which procedures implemented in which ways reliably result in outcomes of a given effect size. Conclusions may be reached over time not so much about consultation globally, but about consultation delivered in a particular way and under particular conditions. There is also a surprising lack of information regarding which procedures can be implemented under specific conditions to attain particular outcomes. A rich description of what occurs during consultation is not sufficient to permit consistently replicable effects in varied settings with different practitioners (Gresham & Vanderwood, chapter 4, this volume).

Frank and Kratochwill (chapter 2, this volume) offer the problem-solving framework as an organizing heuristic for consultation, which creates a framework within which consultation outcomes might be evaluated. Methods guided by inductive logic (e.g., single-subject design) seek to understand all sources of variation, including what might be called error as a meaningful source of variation. Methods guided by deductive logic allocate certain variation to error and subsequently remove that error from consideration or analysis. Inductive logic can lead to detailed explanations and understandings that are so specific to certain circumstances that they might have little applied utility under different conditions or with different people. Yet, if effective components are identified and replicated across settings and individuals, conceptual systems can be developed and a science of consultation produced that is more than a "bag of tricks" (Baer, Wolf, & Risley, 1968). Frank and Kratochwill argue that this degree of precision of understanding is necessary to permit successful adaptation across environments without compromising effectiveness. Detailed understanding permits effective application, and systematic replication permits generalization and the development of conceptual systems.

In consultation research and intervention research in general, it is particularly important to identify the floor and ceiling of the independent variable as well as the dependent variable (Baer, Wolf, & Risley, 1987). A rich description of the independent and dependent variables, however, is insufficient (Carnine, 2000). An empirical understanding of the "active ingredients" of consultation is necessary to assert that consultation is an evidence-based practice. Component analyses examining cause and effect are needed in addition to program evaluation studies. The standard should be that if the consultant implements a particular procedure under particular conditions, a certain effect (and effect size) may be anticipated (Gresham & Vanderwood, chapter 4, this volume). Practicing consultants (as opposed to consultation researchers) will benefit themselves and children when they can anticipate that an intervention will be effective when implemented a certain way in a certain context for a specific problem. Also, relative weight or value of treatment components should be examined. The elements of parsimony and efficiency should be primary, and these elements should be operationalized variables on the research agenda (Power, 2006).

Interestingly, one of the few active ingredients identified empirically and replicated systematically by multiple authors over several years is intervention integrity. Each of the preceding four chapters refers to intervention integrity as a primary active ingredient in effective consultation. There was not another key component that was similarly recognized across chapters, and yet, intervention integrity is not the only variable in consultation that has been empirically linked to outcomes. If Frank and Kratochwill's framework of consultation is adopted, then studies examining the reliability of problem identification and treatment strategy selection will be needed. Future research in treatment plan implementation is needed to identify the most meaningful ways to measure implementation integrity, to specify thresholds of integrity that influence outcomes, and to identify how treatment components that are not equally weighted (i.e., equally important or detrimental to the outcomes) can best be quantified (Noell & Gansle, 2006). Finally, decision making within consultation and at the end of consultation must be examined. Concerning the formative use of data and decision making, Olson, Daly, Anderson, Turner, and LeClair (in press) have noted that the consultant's or interventionist's responsiveness to the data is central to ensuring improved outcomes.

WHAT MAKES A CONSULTANT EFFECTIVE?

A related but different question about consultation effectiveness is, What makes a consultant effective? In thinking about how the literature might inform a response to this question and future research investigations, we would like to share an anecdote. Recently, the first author was working at a school to implement a schoolwide RTI problem-solving model. At this particular school, schoolwide screening had occurred successfully, and follow-up assessments had been conducted with 122 children. Classwide interventions were under way in reading or math in several classrooms. Individual interventions were under way with a handful of children, with strong support for successful intervention implementation. Deliberate efforts had been made and were in progress to build the school's capacity and to function collaboratively with teachers. Teachers appeared happy. The school psychologist was happy. All was going well until the supply of digital timers ran out. The timers were an integral part of the intervention process, so the lack of timers brought the entire intervention process to a halt. No individual interventions could be started. The school psychologist said, "Well, maybe the teachers could use the wall clock." Knowing that providing all needed materials to run the intervention is related to intervention integrity, this solution was not tenable. Functionally, the effect of running out of timers was to stop intervention efforts. Intervention is critical to obtaining desired changes in academic performance (i.e., delivering the results that the system cares about). Yet, the system had struggled to get enough timers ordered and present at the school despite 2 months of working toward that goal. In this case, the effective consultant was literally one who could quickly remove that barrier by going out and purchasing timers.

We share this anecdote because we believe there are critical decision points that occur during assessment and intervention, despite proper planning, at which either the process is halted because specific variables interfere with implementation or alterations are made to the process to deal with these barriers and the alterations adversely affect outcomes. We can think of numerous other examples that we have encountered in our own work in the schools.

One popular example is negotiating and changing components of an intervention that are systematically related to intervention outcomes. For example, one teacher may want to modify task difficulty, another may be opposed to the use of incentives for academic performance, and a third may disagree with the behavior that should be targeted for intervention. Some components of interventions can be modified without reducing intervention effectiveness, but many variables cannot. It is the consultant's job to have a system for evaluating variables that affect intervention outcomes and to negotiate and collaborate with the teacher with that in mind. Often during consultation, particular resource barriers interfere with effective implementation and have to be resolved. Other times, personal beliefs, learning history, system politics, and other less-measurable or less-explicit barriers operate to halt correct implementation. Effective consultants must be able to correctly identify barriers and work to remove those variables quickly so that implementation can continue.

One simple answer to the question of what makes a consultant effective is that an effective consultant is able to define problems, introduce strategies, facilitate correct implementation, and attain desired outcomes. This answer is outcome oriented and may be somewhat inconsistent with the conclusions reached by Meyers et al. (chapter 5, this volume). From our perspective, a consultant is someone who can deliver results. Delivering results as a consultant is not easy because there are multiple variables over which the consultant has no control and perhaps little influence. In our collective experience (and we have no formal data), a consultant must be humble and approachable, knowledgeable about effective instructional techniques, aware of the multiple constraints of the system, and operate and prioritize efforts with efficiency and effectiveness in mind. Consultants should think in terms of substituting efforts rather than requesting new added effort from the teacher. Consultants are people who know which data need to be collected and can quickly demonstrate that those data are meaningful to particular benchmark indicators of progress toward a valued goal for the system. Effective consultants know how to identify what the desired outcomes or the reinforcers are for the system. These reinforcers often are not explicitly stated and must be assessed by the consultant.

Because consultants operate in the context of the school environment, consultants must be able to work within the system to promote positive change. Each of the chapters we reviewed identified facets of research methodology related to identifying effective consultation practices and procedures. Further, each chapter identified treatment plan implementation or integrity as a cornerstone of effective consultation. We believe that the effective consultant brings the behaviors and skills needed to ensure adequate treatment plan implementation. This individual must have considerable content expertise (Gresham & Kendell, 1987) and must be able to integrate information rapidly within a system to identify and remove barriers to effective consultation, promote identified effective consultation practices, and systematically plan for sustainability over time. These capabilities eventually create system change, and we allege that system change must occur for child outcomes to improve, and that the processes of system change need not happen separately or linearly but rather must occur simultaneously through behavioral shaping processes.

CONTEXTUALIZED DECISION MAKING: UNDERSTANDING THE CONSULTATION CONTEXT

The degree to which the consultant can properly contextualize the problem within a school system and classroom will influence outcomes. Schools and school systems have many unwritten rules, and to function effectively, consultants must learn these rules. Errors made as the consultant attempts to learn the unwritten rules that operate in a school environment can be detrimental to system change or behavior change efforts. Questions posed by teachers or other educators such as, "How many second grade classes have you taught?" or "Isn't this intervention the same as what I am already doing that is not working?" are indicative of this phenomenon. What we have learned informally in our work with schools is that these types of questions are not asked because the question-asker wants an answer. Rather they indicate that the question-asker is resistant and questions the consultant's credibility or the intervention's potential to deliver results in their unique environment or circumstance. Consultants who do not recognize the intent of this question may answer the question directly but not respond appropriately to the situation. What we have learned (in our efforts to answer this question early on) is that often there is a series of follow-up questions (e.g., "How many years did you teach second grade? Did you teach second grade in this state/county/city/district/school/era of accountability?"). The questions continue until the consultant recognizes the underlying concern and validates that setting variations can be challenging and may require slight alterations to procedures in ways that do not adversely affect the desired outcomes (Neef, 1995). This type of answer requires more than just graciousness and humility; it requires a deep understanding on the part of the consultant that credibility comes only through delivering results. Hence, the consultant must be a good psychologist with a great deal of content expertise.

The effective consultant is also one who can persist in behavior change efforts in a questioning and anxious environment. Consultants whose efforts are reinforced by obtaining desired results will have the most success in these types of environments. Consultants who retreat from behavior change efforts because the system has an initial negative reaction may not get anything done or get anything done well, and this can be detrimental to the success and sustainability of the consultation process. Consultants must identify which behaviors to attend to and which to ignore so that the process can move forward.

Prioritizing intervention targets at the child, consultee, and system levels should occur within the consultant's scientific framework. For example, a consultant who uses an RTI problem-solving model to guide academic intervention ultimately evaluates academic performance to determine when changes should be made to the intervention program and systematically makes changes based on that primary dependent variable. The dependent variable selected should be one that (a) represents the desired outcome, (b) is valued by consumers of the behavior change effort, and (c) provides the greatest gain for the student in the setting in which the student must function. As consultation proceeds, and at routine intervals, the consultant should attend to variables that interfere with attaining these goals.

Whether consultation is effective may depend on actions of the consultant that include (a) identifying an appropriate intervention target, (b) selecting an effective intervention, (c) ensuring correct implementation of the intervention, and (d) correctly monitoring the effectiveness of the intervention and responding formatively to facilitate effectiveness. Frank and Kratochwill seem to suggest a redefinition of consultation to include these major activities of the consultant. Whether a consultant can correctly complete each step may depend on a host of contextualized variables (e.g., characteristics of the school, the teacher, the behavior targeted for intervention) and consultant variables in isolation (e.g., consultant skill; ability to persist in the face of resistance, absence of reinforcement, or presence of negative consequences; consultant demeanor) or as they interact with the consultee (e.g., consultee preference for collaborative input). Meyers et al. (chapter 5, this volume) recognize the need for empirical attention to each of these contextual and interpersonal characteristics that may account for variance in consultation outcomes. In this way, qualitative research is consistent with a movement toward problem-solving and RTI methods that are highly contextualized decision-making models. However, major differences arise between and among qualitative, quantitative, and problem-solving models in how the desired outcomes are defined and therefore operationalized and measured.

Because school psychologists must operate in contexts in which different schedules of contingencies (sometimes in direct conflict) operate simultaneously, the ability to articulate consultant behaviors that are critical to enhance child learning and behavior outcomes (as indicated ideally by multiple direct indicators of child learning and behavior) will be essential for effective consultation. The movement in school psychology toward contextualized decision making is creating a need for evolved models of technical adequacy for assessment and, more recently, for intervention under RTI models (i.e., because intervention generates assessment data, intervention activities must meet certain criteria to preserve the meaningfulness of decisions based on those data). In the current era of RTI models of decision making, consultation has become an activity on which high-stakes decisions may be based. Hence, basic studies of the reliability with which specific procedures can be conducted and linked to particular decisions about what to do next will be primary to demonstrating the technical adequacy of decisions made during consultation. Evolved models will consider facets of the independent variables (sufficiently selected, defined, and implemented) and the dependent variables (sufficiently selected, defined, and measured). Because the process is dynamic, requiring a sequence of data collection, data interpretation, and implementation of the next step, an analysis of the accuracy and reliability of decisions reached and the degree to which this sequence was carried out will be fundamental to questions of effectiveness and adequacy. These characteristics are not totally unique to current consultation practices; rather, they have always operated to affect intervention outcomes. Evolved technical adequacy models will permit more precise conclusions about the variables affecting intervention outcomes.

CONSULTATION AND SYSTEMS CHANGE: CHANGING THE CONSULTATION CONTEXT

Effective system change agents are proactive in their efforts to identify system goals and move the system toward attaining that goal. Wolf (1978) and Schwartz and Baer (1991) identified the importance of measuring and ensuring that the outcome of a behavior change program will be an outcome that is valued by consumers of the behavior change effort. Many researchers and practitioners have attempted to meet this goal by having teachers, parents, and occasionally children complete ratings of their satisfaction with the behavior change effort. More recently, researchers and practitioners are recognizing that this goal is so important that it merits multiple sources of measurement (American Educational Research Association/American Psychological Association/National Council on Measurement in Education, 1999) and recommending direct measurement of the degree to which intervention outcomes approximate the performance of meaningful comparison samples or functional criteria (Gresham & Vanderwood, chapter 4, this volume). Efforts to measure the degree to which the outcomes of consultation result in desired outcomes for children reflect an underlying core value that what we do should be valued by those we intend to help or inform (Baer et al., 1968; Wolf, 1978). Social validation is a meaningful effect size estimate (Messick, 1995). Meyers et al. (chapter 5, this volume) and Frank and Kratochwill (chapter 2, this volume) all alluded to the importance of direct measurement of social and consequential validity.

The great challenge of consultation research is the immense complexity of its process. Perhaps we can learn from the psychotherapy researchers who have reframed the basic question. Instead of merely asking, What works? recent psychotherapy research has focused on, What works for whom and in what context? Given the myriad of consultant-addressed topics, ranging from student academic concerns to mental health issues of the consultee, the future success of consultation may rely on the ability to know what works for which types of problems, in which situations, and at what point in time. This commentary began by mentioning the need for practices to be scientifically based. Viewing consultation as a potential evidence-based practice has political, empirical, and practical value. Quantifying the relative efficacy of consultation practices requires operationalization of independent variables, specification of consultation goals, and adequate selection and measurement of dependent measures. Evolved models of technical adequacy will be important to advance research in consultation and other areas of school psychology and education that examine interventions in schools. Most particularly, contextualized analyses of consultation will permit researchers, practitioners, and policymakers to anticipate which behaviors conducted under which circumstances will produce desired outcomes.

REFERENCES

American Educational Research Association, American Psychological Association, and National Council on Measurement in Education. (1999). *Standards for educational and psychological testing* (3rd ed.). Washington, DC: American Psychological Association.

Baer, D. M., Wolf, M. M., & Risley, T. R. (1968). Some current dimensions of applied behavior analysis. *Journal of Applied Behavior Analysis, 1,* 91–97.

Baer, D. M., Wolf, M. M., & Risley, T. R. (1987). Some still-current dimensions of applied behavior analysis. *Journal of Applied Behavior Analysis, 20,* 313–327.

Burkhardt, H., & Schoenfeld, A. H. (2003). Improving educational research: Toward a more useful, more influential, and better-funded enterprise. *Educational Researcher, 32,* 3–14.

Carnine, D. (2000). *Why education experts resist effective practices (and what it would take to make education more like medicine).* Retrieved March 16, 2004, from http://www.edexcellence.net/foundation/publication/publication.cfm?id=46

Dawson, M., Cummings, J. A., Harrison, P. L., Short, R. J., Gorin, S., & Palomares, R. (2004). The 2002 multisite conference on the future of school psychology: Next steps. *School Psychology Review, 33,* 115–125.

Feuer, M. J., Towne, L., & Shavelson, R. J. (2002). Scientific culture and educational research. *Educational Researcher, 31,* 4–14.

Gresham, F. M., & Kendell, G. K. (1987). School consultation research: Methodological critique and future research directions. *School Psychology Review, 16,* 306–316.

Kratochwill, T. R., & Shernoff, E. S. (2004). Evidence-based practice: Promoting evidence-based interventions in school psychology. *School Psychology Review, 33,* 34–48.

Macmann, G. M., & Barnett, D. W. (1999). Diagnostic decision making in school psychology: Understanding and coping with uncertainty. In C. R. Reynolds & T. B. Gutkin (Eds.), *The handbook of school psychology* (3rd ed., pp. 519–548). New York: Wiley.

Messick, S. (1995). Validity of psychological assessment: Validation of inferences from persons' responses and performances as scientific inquiry into score meaning. *American Psychologist, 50,* 741–749.

National Research Council. (2002). *Scientific research in education.* In R. J. Shavelson & L. Towne (Eds.), Committee on Scientific Principles for Educational Research. Washington, DC: National Academy Press.

Neef, N. A. (1995). Research on training trainers in program implementation: An introduction and future directions. *Journal of Applied Behavior Analysis, 28,* 297–299.

Noell, G. H., & Gansle, K. A. (2006). Assuring the form has substance: Treatment plan implementation as the foundation of assessing response to intervention. *Assessment for Effective Intervention, 32,* 32–39.

Noell, G., Witt, J., Slider, N., Connell, J., Gatti, S., Williams, K., et al. (2005). Treatment implementation following behavioral consultation in schools: A comparison of three follow-up strategies. *School Psychology Review, 34,* 87–106.

Olson, S. C., Daly, E. J., III, Anderson, M., Turner, A., & LeClair, C. (in press). Assessing student response to intervention. In S. R. Jimerson, M. K. Burns, & A. M. VanDerHeyden (Eds.), *Handbook of response to intervention: The science and practice of assessment and intervention.* New York: Springer.

Power, T. J. (2006). School psychology review: 2006–2010. *School Psychology Review, 35,* 3–10.

Schwartz, I. S., & Baer, D. M. (1991). Social validity assessments: Is current practice state of the art? *Journal of Applied Behavior Analysis, 24,* 189–204.

U.S. Department of Education. (2003). *Mathematics and science initiative concept paper.* Retrieved November 20, 2003, from http://www.ed.gov/rschstat/research/progs/mathscience/concept_paper.pdf

Wolf, M. M. (1978). Social validity: The case for subjective measurement or how applied behavior analysis is finding its heart. *Journal of Applied Behavior Analysis, 11,* 203–214.

C

WHAT WE KNOW: PROCESS/OUTCOME FINDINGS FROM SELECTED MODELS OF PRACTICE

7

Mental Health Consultation and Consultee-Centered Approaches

STEVEN E. KNOTEK, MAUREEN KANIUKA,
AND KIRSTEN ELLINGSEN

University of North Carolina

As a young psychiatrist in Israel in the late 1940s, Gerald Caplan was confronted with the problem of having few resources to meet the mental health needs of children who had survived the Holocaust. Caplan and a small staff of trained mental health professionals were responsible for upward of a 1,000 referrals a year (Caplan, Caplan, & Erchul, 1995). Given the breadth and depth of the children's mental health needs, it was not feasible to use the direct services Caplan was trained to deliver to process these referrals. Out of necessity, Caplan established an approach to indirect service, mental health consultation (MHC), by which he would enhance the abilities of other caregivers to meet, and ideally prevent, children's psychological problems. Caplan developed consultation as a form of primary (i.e., universal) prevention to support mental health outcomes for underserved children with mental illness.

DISTINGUISHING FEATURES OF MENTAL HEALTH CONSULTATION

Caplan's formulation of this intervention took the unique approach of meeting children's mental health needs by supporting and enhancing the professional functioning of their caretakers. As Caplan (Caplan & Caplan, 1993) conceived it, consultation is a work-related, problem-solving process that takes place between a consultant and a consultee. Four types of consultation may occur: (a) client-centered case consultation, (b) consultee-centered case consultation, (c) program-centered administrative consultation, and (d) consultee-centered administrative consultation. Each of these types of mental health consultation has similar core characteristics (Brown, Pryzwansky, & Schulte, 2006); they are voluntary, are coordinate, have a psychodynamic orientation, are concerned with mental health issues, and are preventive via generalization of problem solving to future cases (Erchul & Schulte, 1993). Since Caplan's model of mental health consultation first appeared, psychologists and mental health professionals in the United States and other countries have adapted the method to a wide variety of settings with consultees functioning in many work roles (Lambert, 2004). Mental health consultation has been used successfully in clinical settings; however, its use has been more restricted in schools.

EMPIRICAL SUPPORT FOR MENTAL HEALTH CONSULTATION

School-based consultation was defined by Medway (1979) as collaborative problem solving between a consultant and consultee to provide psychological assistance to a client with the goals of addressing the presenting problem of the client and increasing consultee effectiveness. As such, a measure of success for school-based consultation is successful remediation of the primary concern. Continued support for this broad definition of school-based consultation was presented by Gutkin and Curtis (1999). Although this broad definition shares characteristics with consultee-centered consultation (C-CC), there is a critical difference in terms of the primary goal. Specifically, within C-CC, the main goal is the increase in consultee functioning. As such, when examining the literature base for school-based consultation, it is important to differentiate between school-based consultation in general and specific forms of school-based consultation, including behavioral consultation and C-CC.

Within the current research base, a greater emphasis has been placed on behavioral consultation within the schools than C-CC. Alpert and Yammer (1983) attributed the lack of focus on mental health consultation (compared to behavioral consultation) to behavioral consultation's relative ease of empirical analysis due to the fact that data are embedded in the process. Gutkin and Curtis (1999) presented many studies showing favorable results for school-based consultation; however, the research base they cited is comprised predominantly of behavioral consultation studies. As such, the studies described in this section were selected because the consultation method specified was clearly consultee centered based on methodological description and the primary goal of consultee change.

Beginning in the mid-1980s, several meta-analyses have been conducted to ascertain the empirical support for school consultation in general, with several findings specific to mental health consultation. Medway and Updyke (1985) included 54 studies in their meta-analysis, resulting in an overall mean effect size of .47 in terms of behavioral, attitudinal, and achievement effects for those receiving mental health, behavioral, or organizational development consultation. Their meta-analysis showed mental health consultation to be more effective on consultee than client measures, with effect sizes of .68 and .28, respectively. In addition, the analysis resulted in an effect size of .89 for mental health consultation in changing consultee behavior. These results are consistent with and supportive of the primary goal of C-CC.

In a comprehensive review, Sheridan, Welch, and Orme (1996) revisited the outcomes research for consultation and applied more stringent criteria to the inclusion of research studies conducted between 1985 and 1995. Of those studies, 76% supported positive outcomes in at least one area, with the outcomes examined consumer satisfaction, social validity, process integrity, follow-up, and generalization. Of the studies, 11% were categorized as mental health consultation, with a positive outcome in at least one area reported in 60% of the mental health consultation studies, considerably less than the 95% reported for behavioral consultation.

The lack of well-defined, empirical studies to validate mental health consultation in the schools has been discussed for decades (Hughes, 1994; Kratochwill, Sheridan, & VanSomeren, 1988; Meade, Hamilton, & Yuen, 1982; Pryzwansky, 1986). Much of the available literature is theoretical and much that has been studied has focused on interpersonal variables rather than efficacy and effectiveness. For example, Medway and Forman (1980) found teachers rated behavioral consultation as more effective than mental health consultation, despite the preference school psychologists indicated for mental health consultation. Maitland, Fine, and Tracy (1985) examined the impact of the interpersonally based problem-solving process used in mental health consultation and found a positive impact when examining consultee satisfaction, problem resolution, and professional growth. Similarly, in comparing teachers' reactions to behavioral and mental health consultants,

Slesser, Fine, and Tracy (1990) found the consultants to be equally facilitative; however, there was an overall higher degree of teacher-rated satisfaction, professional competence, and problem resolution for behavioral consultation. Although quantitatively derived, the aforementioned studies did not examine outcome measures beyond consultee rating of effectiveness and primarily focused on relational aspects of consultation. Finally, Meyers, Brent, Faherty, and Modafferi (1993) put forth an extensive research agenda to improve the body of research examining the effectiveness of mental health consultation. The recommendations are as valid today as they were at that time and include the need to establish empirical support to determine the role of gender in mental health consultation and the role of internal versus external consultants and its effect on process and outcomes and to examine the multiple facets of mental health consultation, including decision-making frameworks, modeling as a consultation technique, the preventive effects of mental health consultation, and best-practice methods in mental health consultation.

LIMITATIONS OF MENTAL HEALTH CONSULTATION IN SCHOOL-BASED SETTINGS

Despite the fact that Caplanian mental health consultation has received considerable attention in the literature since its inception, its use in schools has been limited for theoretical, practical, and empirical reasons. For example, the psychodynamic orientation of the model is seen as overly narrow and its techniques too focused on unconscious mechanisms to be meaningful in schools (Dougherty, 2000). Also, in practice, mental health consultation does not address critical school-related academic issues, traditionally has relied on an external consultant, and does not allow for joint consultant-consultee responsibility during the phases of problem solving (Brown et al., 2006). Finally, mental health consultation has been the least empirically supported consultation model (Gutkin & Curtis, 1999; Meyers, 1995). Although these concerns restrict the use and application of mental health consultation in schools, several school-based variants of Caplan's model address the first two limitations listed and have been developed, researched, and utilized (e.g., Ingraham, 2000; Knotek & Sandoval, 2003; Meyers, 1981; Rosenfield & Gravois, 1996).

Establishing evidence-based support for the consultation models that have developed from mental health consultation is difficult, if not impossible, to achieve due to a lack of agreement about core definitions and characteristics within and across forms (Kratochwill & Pittman, 2002). This lack of accord on basic operational definitions has hindered past research efforts in mental health consultation and, if not addressed, will continue to negatively impact future efforts. Fortunately, a consensus has emerged on definitional and operational issues for a new type of consultation, C-CC (Lambert, Hylander, & Sandoval, 2004), which has evolved from Caplan's original model. This chapter focuses on this model because there is a consensus on its definitions and parameters, and there are several examples of school-based applications (e.g., instructional consultation, Rosenfield & Gravois, 1996; multicultural consultee-centered consultation, Ingraham, 2000).

CONSULTEE-CENTERED CONSULTATION

C-CC is conceptualized as comprising the following definitional features (Knotek & Sandoval, 2003):

1. C-CC emphasizes a nonhierarchical helping role relationship between a resource (consultant) and a person or group (consultee) who seeks professional help with a work problem involving a third party (client).
2. This work problem is a topic of concern for the consultee, who has a direct responsibility for the learning, development, or productivity of the client.

3. The primary task of the consultant is to help the consultee pinpoint critical information and then consider multiple views about well-being; development; and intrapersonal, interpersonal, and organizational effectiveness appropriate to the consultee's work setting. Ultimately, the consultee may reframe his or her prior conceptualization of the work problem.

4. The goal of the consultation process is the joint development of a new way of conceptualizing the work problem so that the repertoire of the consultee is expanded and the professional relationship between the consultee and the client is restored or improved. As the problem is jointly reconsidered, new ways of approaching the problem may lead to acquiring new means to address the work dilemma.

Differences from Caplan's Model

C-CC differs from classical mental health consultation in three significant ways: theoretical foundation, consultant's role with respect to the organization, and content of the consultation. Relative to theoretical basis, the psychodynamic underpinnings of Caplan's model can be traced to the theory's dominant stature during his training and early practice as a psychiatrist in the 1940s and 1950s (Erchul & Schulte, 1993). At the time, Freud's work was the most widely used explanatory perspective in mental health. In contrast, C-CC uses a constructivist perspective as its core explanatory perspective, in which conceptual change becomes the intrapsychic goal of the consultation process (Sandoval, 2003). Conceptual change in the consultant and the consultee are hallmarks of the problem-solving process (Sandoval, 1996).

A second difference between C-CC and traditional mental health consultation is the reality of the practice of school-based consultation, in which the consultant is usually an internal member of the system. This places limits on the practice of traditional mental health consultation because schools typically do not have the funds to hire external consultants on a sustained basis. However, it also creates opportunities for an expanded role for the consultant. For example, Pryzwansky (1986) and Rosenfield and Gravois (1996) have proposed models in which the consultant and consultee jointly assume responsibility for various aspects of consultation. The reciprocal nature of the problem-solving process is central to C-CC.

Third, the content of Caplan's version of consultation is narrowly delineated in its name — mental health. Caplan (1970) described the origins of his model as occurring in settings in which (a) clients had mental health disorders or personality idiosyncrasies, (b) the goal was the promotion of mental health in the client, and (c) a consultee's work was less effective with particular groups of children. However, as Caplan's model, especially his special instance of consultee-centered case consultation, was adopted by consultants in schools and daycare centers, it evolved to better fit the needs of the clients and consultees encountered within these particular environments. The work problems encountered by teachers, principals, and other school personnel may range from academic concerns to behavioral concerns to staffing issues. The newly described C-CC thus is content neutral, and the consultee is free to bring whichever work-focused issue to the table the consultee considers important.

Consultee-Centered Consultation Research

C-CC, like its predecessor mental health consultation, has an intuitive appeal to consultants who view their professional practice through a prevention lens. It is assumed that not only can consultation have an impact on clients, but also it may support the development of consultees' abilities to solve work problems and subsequently allow the consultee to successfully attend to similar issues in the future. What is the evidence that these three goals are attainable? What evidence would be necessary to prove or disprove the underlying assumptions of C-CC? Issues and goals related to forms of evidence needed to investigate and evaluate C-CC have been offered by Hylander (2004) and Sandoval (2004).

Hylander (2004) discussed the benefits and shortcomings of using three traditional research paradigms to investigate C-CC. Accordingly, the effectiveness of consultation in general, and C-CC in particular, must be established through the triangulation of investigations across the three major research paradigms in consultation research:

> Three main research perspectives give three different types of information: hypothetico-deductive methodology, giving information about the probability of occurrence of a certain hypothesis; interpretative methodology, giving descriptions and deeper understanding of a phenomenon; and theory generating methodology, giving probable explanations for complex interactions and social processes. (p. 374)

First, hypothetico-deductive studies are necessary but not sufficient in C-CC research given the goals and processes of the practice. For example, the core C-CC process of nonprescriptive, joint problem identification does not lend itself well to randomized evaluation studies that measure the effectiveness of C-CC on particular types of referral problems. In C-CC, the consultation problem is not necessarily understood, defined, or identified prior to consultation; therefore, it would not be possible to assign a case randomly to an experimental or control group by referral problem. Second, investigative methods associated with the interpretive perspective are better suited to explore "complex processes characterized by ambiguity where simple relationships of cause and effect through the manipulation of a single variable are not likely to be found" (Hylander, 2004, p. 378). Investigational means such as case studies and ethnographies are needed to understand, analyze, and interpret C-CC processes. Finally, theory-generating perspectives are well suited to the constructivist framework in C-CC. Theory generating is a research approach that is "particularly suitable when a researcher wants to explore a new field or give a new perspective on an old field" (Hylander, 2004, p. 380). The nonprescriptive nature of C-CC, combined with its status as an emerging model of consultation, lends itself to investigation from a theory-generating perspective, whereas the design of research should be guided by actual practice.

Sandoval (2004) proposed that C-CC research should target changes in (a) client behaviors and (b) consultee behavior, attitude and affect, and conceptualizations. The impact of C-CC on client behavior should assess the impact not only on clients associated with the immediate consultation, but also with a range of future clients as well. If C-CC produces "horizontal transfer of learning" (Gagne, 1977), then successful consultation would support change within some range of the consultee's clients. Consultee behavioral changes may be assessed indirectly through supervisors, peers, or clients (e.g., through questionnaires) and within the consultation process (e.g., through changes in the thread of discussion about the presentation and representation of the consultation problem). Affect and attitude can be observed through nonverbal behaviors, such as relaxed body language, increased sense of humor, decreased confusion, and decreased anxiety with similar clients. Finally, Sandoval proposed examining changes in consultees' conceptualizations through consultee mapping, an adaptation of the process of concept mapping (Novak & Gowin, 1984). In this process, concept maps are generated preconsultation to reveal misconceptions and then generated postconsultation to map any conceptual development.

Both authors emphasized that, although client outcomes are important in all forms of consultation, C-CC inherently demands additional research and evaluation of consultation's impact on the consultee. As Sandoval (2004) stated, in C-CC "improvement occurs because effective consultation interventions work to bring about changes in consultee perceptions and attitudes and then, in turn, changes in consultee-client behavior and, finally, changes in client behavior and performance" (p. 393).

Many of the defining features of C-CC have also prompted the use of qualitative study as the primary research methodology. For example, Ingraham (2000) emphasized the role of co-construction of case conceptualization in multicultural C-CC. In addition, through microethnographic studies, effective questioning has been supported as a means of developing the consultee's conceptual understanding of and approach to the work problem (Knotek, Rosenfield, Gravois, & Babinski, 2003; Webster, Knotek, Babinski, Rogers, & Barnett, 2003). However, according to Gresham and Kendell (1987), the qualitative methodology used in these studies results in rationally derived conclusions and requires additional quantitative analysis to be empirically supported. This notion is examined within the framework of efficacy and effectiveness in establishing evidence-based interventions (EBIs) in school psychology.

EVIDENCE-BASED INTERVENTIONS IN SCHOOL PSYCHOLOGY

Prevention science has demonstrated that effective early intervention is crucial to decreasing the range and depth of impact of numerous behavioral, academic, and developmental problems in students (Allington & Walmsley, 1995; Durlak & Wells, 1997). Marked improvement in outcomes may occur when students with, for example, reading and attention problems are provided with interventions in early, crucial periods (Simeonsson, 1994). Given the benefits that occur with targeted action and combined with the risk of negative outcomes associated with delayed intervention, it is incumbent on psychological professionals to implement interventions with proven efficacy and effectiveness. Surmounting the challenge of providing effective early intervention is of great importance to the field of school psychology. It is critical that the profession continue to develop improved means to meet the academic and behavioral needs of our nation's students. The professional response to this challenge is the implementation of EBIs. Simply put, interventions that are deemed evidence based have been systematically evaluated according to a professionally cogent process.

Characteristics of Evidence-based Practice in School Psychology

In response to the general need for a framework to guide investigations into the efficacy of school-based interventions, a Task Force on Evidence-Based Interventions in School Psychology was formed (Stoiber & Kratochwill, 2000). One of the task force's responsibilities was to conceptualize specifically what constitutes evidence-based practice. Because of several factors, including the range of contextual issues confronting any widely applied school-based intervention, the task force took a "broad, inclusive view of evidence-based practice" (Stoiber, 2002, p. 541). Stoiber (2002) reported that two considerations framed the adoption of the task force's broad-based framework on the use of research methods to evaluate interventions: (a) the need to use sound science and (b) the need to consider context. Accordingly, several types of methodologies were deemed integral to the investigation of intervention efficacy and effectiveness.

Sound Science

The task force cited the need for evidence to consider both intervention's efficacy and effectiveness (Kratochwill & Stoiber, 2002; Nathan & Gorman, 1998). *Efficacy* refers to an intervention's baseline empirical support and is determined through the use of randomized, between-group clinical trials, and if appropriate, within-group, single-case research (Weisz & Hawley, 1999). *Effectiveness* refers to "evaluating interventions in a practice context" (Kratochwill & Stoiber, 2002, p. 369). Research methodologies that are deemed appropriate to investigate effectiveness include quasi-experimental and single-subject designs (Christenson, Carlson, & Valdez, 2002), as well as qualitative research procedures and confirmatory program evaluation (Kratochwill, 2002).

Context

Schools are among the nation's most pluralistic cultural institutions. Although schools' quality may differ, no matter a child's geographic location, ethnicity, handicapping condition, social status, or family background, the child is legally required to have formal access to a public education. This grand scale of educational access means that schooling occurs in myriad, sometimes contrasting, contexts, such as in rural versus urban settings, well-funded versus poorly funded school districts, systems with highly credentialed staff versus systems with staff who are less well trained, and classrooms with predominantly English language-proficient students versus classrooms with predominantly second-language learners. Given this range of contextual factors, it should be expected that an intervention's effectiveness will vary across schools, classrooms, and contexts. An intervention's evidence base should include studies that use research designs that can investigate a program's effectiveness in various contexts (Christenson et al., 2002; Kratochwill, 2002; Stoiber, 2002). For example, the effectiveness of an early intervention program that requires the establishment of a reflective "community of learners" should be assessed in both supportive and punitive organizational structures.

Research-to-Practice Gap in Consultee-Centered Consultation

Although it is important that different types of consultation establish empirical support under the basic EBI framework, it is important to note that EBI status in and of itself will not guarantee that a consultation approach will actually work in "real" environments. Interventions that work under controlled circumstances in carefully selected environments may not successfully bridge the research-to-practice gap (Schoenwald & Hoagwood, 2001). Consultation within a school site includes not only the successful application of the core consultation skills but also a reckoning with systemic issues such as administrative buy-in, access to time resources, and credibility with school staff. Taken together, these issues are reflective of the challenge of intervention implementation (Adelman & Taylor, 2003).

Core assumptions of the C-CC approach are that students will be better served and consultees will improve their ability to meet future work-related problems when teachers and allied professionals engage in a mediated problem-solving process. However, research on this seemingly straightforward process, talking with a teacher about a student's academic or behavioral functioning, becomes complicated as it is applied in actual settings (Glisson, 2002). For example, laboratory studies have not addressed such important issues as when and where school-based consultation will occur (e.g., in an office or hallway) and how the practice will meaningfully be incorporated into a consultant's professional duties (e.g., added to or replacing existing responsibilities). However, researchers have identified key challenges to the problem of implementation: (a) efficacy, (b) effectiveness and transportability, and (c) dissemination and transportability (Kratochwill & Shernoff, 2004; Schoenwald & Hoagwood, 2001).

Efficacy

The efficacy of an intervention is often established in an ideal setting that promotes maximum effect and allows for control of variables (Burns & Hoagwood, 2002). Sometimes, these studies take place out of context (e.g., in a university lab), and other times they occur in carefully selected sites at which multiple variables can be controlled. Accordingly, efficacy trials of a consultation method may limit the range and depth of the presenting issues (e.g., they may focus only on attention-seeking behavior problems or be limited to sites at which administrators have self-selected in response to a researcher's offer to provide teacher consultations).

Of course, the evaluation process must begin by first establishing the efficacy of an intervention in a setting in which possible confounding variables are known, identified, and controlled, with a focus on understanding the basic functioning of core components of the intervention. However, too often research has begun and ended with efficacy studies within these controlled settings, in which the experimental conditions may bear little resemblance to the vagaries of real-life settings. For example, at a most basic level, the priorities of a consultation researcher may have little in common with the core vision of the stakeholders within a district, school, or grade level. Thus, what the researcher finds to be essential may in fact be considered incidental to a teacher or principal. Furthermore, a researcher's priorities may not be shared by the power holders who possess influence within the actual sites at which an intervention is intended to be used. In addition, evidence-based laboratory research may not translate to success in the larger world.

The ecological realities inherent in ordinary schools may contain complexities that fatally interfere with the implementation of an intervention. The literature on medicine trials in animals is replete with examples of "miracle cures" in the lab failing to have efficacy when used with humans. In consultation research, a model that worked in a well-funded experimental trial in which teacher's classes were staffed during consultation may not work during implementation because the consultation requires a consultee to give up several of his or her planning periods.

Effectiveness and Transportability

The American educational landscape is full of once-popular, yet ultimately ineffective, programs and interventions that promised to ameliorate, if not outright solve, the identified problem. Veteran educators can recite buzzwords such as "new math" (Bosse, 1995) and "just say 'no'" (Kanof, 2003; Thombs, 2000) that were related to interventions that promised to somehow improve student circumstances. Although each of the aforementioned interventions undoubtedly had supporters, both are widely seen as having serious shortcomings because they lacked effectiveness or because they could not be effectively implemented in schools.

Throughout time, teachers and administrators have expressed reluctance to engage in a new type of intervention. When the first author began his first consultation internship in an inner city high school, he had a conversation about the benefits of the emerging model of C-CC with the district's oldest teacher, who was then in his early 70s. The teacher told the would-be consultant, "Wow, that [consultation] is old news; we tried that approach when I first started teaching [after the war]. It's amazing how everything in education is recycled. It didn't work before because it took too much time. Teachers have seen this before, I think you're going to have a hard time getting them [teachers] to commit to this." The veteran teacher's comments may be seen as related to the issue of research-to-practice gap or transportability.

Transportability is "the movement of efficacious interventions to usual care settings" (Schoenwald & Hoagwood, 2001, p. 1192). Modern schools are complex environments with functioning that is impinged on by macrosystemic (e.g., state of the economy, current legislative mandates), mesosystemic (e.g., interactions between police and schools), and microsystemic (e.g., current class size) issues. Within this context, Schoenwald and Hoagwood described six dimensions in which there may be contrast between research and practice settings: intervention characteristics, practitioner characteristics, client characteristics, service delivery characteristics, organizational characteristics, and service system mandates. Intervention development has not traditionally focused on bridging the research-to-practice gap to ensure an intervention's transportability (i.e., implementation has often been left to chance) (Hoagwood & Johnson, 2002).

The most exquisitely designed consultation model will be useless if it cannot be practically employed as designed in its intended settings (Walker, 2004). If a model's design does not lend itself to a straightforward translation from lab to school, then it will likely face the prospect of improper implementation. Development of a consultation model that can only be properly implemented in a restricted range of circumstances will yield inconsistent integrity. Treatment efficacy is linked to treatment acceptability (Truscott, Cosgrove, Eidle, & Meyers, 2000), such that intervention models will be more likely to be implemented with integrity when delivery can be consistent and core aspects of the model are put to use as intended (Gresham, 1989). Given the time and proficiency needed to correctly implement school-based consultation, each model must explicitly address and attend to how its component processes should individually and collectively be implemented.

These questions touch on some of the salient questions related to implementation integrity: Who has training in evaluation? Who should be responsible for carrying out the evaluation step? Can the intervention be adopted as originally designed (Hoagwood, 2003–2004; Schoenwald & Hoagwood, 2001)? The implementation of C-CC may need to begin with the basic question of professional responsibility and contain some mechanism to support the transfer of knowledge and skill between professions.

Dissemination and Transportability

Dissemination refers to whether interventions are sustained beyond their original adoption within settings of normal practice (Burns & Hoagwood, 2002; Rones & Hoagwood, 2000). To realize dissemination within schools, C-CC must include a planned, directed path that addresses how sustainability will be achieved. How will the goals of a consultation service model become a part of the school's goals? Which processes will be used to facilitate training, buy-in, and organizational support? Who will conduct the consultation, under what circumstances, and to what effect (Schoenwald & Hoagwood, 2001)? Factors known to be important to dissemination include comprehensive training (Knoff & Batsche, 1993), participatory action and collaboration (Nastasi, 1998), and supervision and monitoring (McDougal, Clonan, & Martens, 2000).

Consultee-centered consultants must address issues beyond efficacy and actively plan for transportability, effectiveness, and dissemination to enter schools successfully and establish a long-term presence. Programmatic content cannot simply be downloaded into schools via single-session workshops or through administrative mandate (Gravois, Knotek, & Babinski, 2002). Transportability of C-CC to school environments requires an embedded diffusion process that at a minimum takes into account professional development needs, adaptation to the school's unique ecological context, a workable evaluation process, and a means to encourage system buy-in.

As mentioned, the available research base for C-CC primarily focuses on relational aspects of consultation, without emphasis on primary or secondary goal attainment. Although those measures provide insight into core characteristics, they lack focus on outcomes. Without some measure of goal attainment, it would seem that C-CC is lacking support in terms of both efficacy and effectiveness, a conclusion that revisits criticism put forth for mental health consultation for several decades. Given the current state of research about the effectiveness and efficacy of C-CC, what critical dimensions need to be further explored? The final section uses a research agenda proposed by

Kratochwill and Shernoff (2003, 2004) to outline some research issues that may be considered to investigate C-CC within an EBI framework.

FUTURE RESEARCH

Any agenda for future research on school-based EBIs must take into account issues related to efficacy and effectiveness and the overall research-to-practice gap. Kratochwill and Shernoff (2004) offered a four-level agenda to guide research on EBIs that was developed within the context of the task force and in consideration of research-to-practice issues raised by Hoagwood (2001) and others. The four levels take into account context and implementation: (a) Type I efficacy studies, (b) Type II transportability studies, (c) Type III dissemination studies, and (d) Type IV system evaluation studies. The implementation and utility of C-CC will benefit from study in each of these areas. After a brief discussion of the dual uses of C-CC as intervention and "metaintervention," a research agenda is proposed.

C-CC is unique in that it both can be used as an intervention and can serve in a meta fashion to facilitate the application, integration, and effect of other interventions. In other words, given that a core quality of C-CC is the process of problem solving, it may be used as (a) an intervention in its own right and (b) a metaintervention that can be drawn on to problem solve the implementation of other interventions within the unique context of schools.

Consultation may be used directly to help a consultee gain a new perspective on a work problem using only prior knowledge and an in-depth problem identification process (Knotek, 2003a). Consultation can also be used indirectly in a meta sense to support consultees' implementation of some other intervention within the distinctive climate of their own classroom. For example, some scientifically designed reading interventions presuppose that students will be at a certain minimum level of reading fluency. However, this assumption can prove disastrous for students who fall below the assumed grade-level norm of reading ability. Metaconsultation can be used to help a teacher consultee consider how to adapt and implement a reading EBI to be effective within the context of the teacher's classroom comprised of below grade-level readers. These dual qualities of consultation, as intervention and intervention catalyst, give it promise as a means to support the transportability and dissemination of prevention programs into the complex ecological environments of school systems.

C-CC was described in this chapter as possessing many of the core processes and content found in other well-established models, such as consultation unfolding in stages, relying heavily on interpersonal communication, and using data-based decision making. Although aspects of these core processes still need to be further researched, this discussion focuses on describing research needs across the four levels (Kratochwill & Shernoff, 2003) that are more specific to issues central to C-CC: (a) joint responsibility for the problem-solving process (cf. Sheridan, 1992), (b) consultee outcomes, and (c) prevention outcomes for clients.

CONSULTATION AS INTERVENTION

Type I Research

Although C-CC shares some general assumptions and structures with other forms of consultation, it has only recently emerged as a distinct form of consultation (Knotek & Sandoval, 2003), and its unique attributes have therefore only begun to be empirically investigated. At the level of efficacy, research on C-CC should focus on validating that the consultation process leads to the anticipated outcomes of changes in consultees' conceptual development.

Studies are needed to assess which, if any, outcomes are present within a consultee's conceptual understanding of the work-related problem and in the consultee's problem-solving approach to new instances of the issue. With C-CC's emphasis on the establishment of an equitable, nonhierarchical relationship between the consultant and consultee, the interpersonal process of C-CC is sufficiently different from other models of consultation to warrant investigation into the efficacy of the process (Daniels & DeWine, 1991; Erchul, 1992; Knotek, 2003b). Consultee's conceptual development might be investigated through several approaches, including concept mapping, discourse analysis, and brain imaging.

Concept mapping is a technique pioneered by Novak (Novak & Gowin, 1984) that uses diagramming to represent individuals' conceptions about the relationships between associated ideas. In a concept map, lines and arrows are drawn to highlight connections between related words and conceptions. This approach has been used both to facilitate learning and to evaluate instruction (Yin & Shavelson, 2004). For example, concept maps have been used to assess the effect of medical training on the conceptual framework of physician residents (West, Pomeroy, Park, Gerstenberger, & Sandoval, 2000). Sandoval (2004) proposed the use of consultee mapping to investigate "changes in a consultee's conceptualizations and understandings" (p. 397). Consultee maps may be used pre- and postintervention to investigate the process of conceptual development and to determine the overall impact of consultation on consultee conceptual development. Future studies could use consultee mapping to investigate issues such as the efficacy of C-CC to have an impact on consultees' problem conceptualization across differing issues (e.g., behavioral vs. academic), trends in consultees' misperceptions (Sandoval, 2004), and transfer of effect across different students.

In consultation, we typically come to understand and mutually explore consultees' conceptions through dialogue (Erchul, 2003; Knotek, 2003b; Rosenfield, 2004). Consultants may therefore gain access to consultees' impressions by undertaking discourse analysis of communication in consultation. As Wetherell, Taylor, and Yates (2001) wrote, "Discourse research offers routes into the study of meanings, a way of investigating the back-and-forth dialogues which constitute social action, along with the patterns of signification and representation which constitute culture" (p. i). Discourse analysis provides researchers with several investigational approaches with which to describe, analyze, and gauge the impact of consultation on the conceptual development of consultees. Methods of discourse analysis relevant to the study of conceptual development in consultation may be found within each of the three core research paradigms described by Hylander (2004): (a) hypothetico-deductive, (b) interpretive, and (c) grounded theory.

Analysis of both verbal and written representations allows researchers to understand the impact of consultation on the mind and to ascertain development of consultees' knowledge and understandings. New brain imaging methods, especially functional magnetic resonance imaging (fMRI), may allow researchers to expand the range of our knowledge by investigating C-CC's impact on the consultee's brain.

By definition, fMRI is "used to demonstrate correlations between physical changes (as in blood flow) in the brain and mental functioning (as in performing cognitive tasks)" (*Merriam-Webster*, 2002). This technology is based on differentiating oxygenated and deoxygenated hemoglobin in the brain, which allows researchers experimentally to examine brain-based differences in cognitive functioning among individuals and to document specific areas of brain function (Uttal, 2001). Researchers have used fMRI to "uncover the underlying neural signatures of complex causal reasoning" (Fugelsang & Dunbar, 2004, p. 1749), to study moral reasoning (Greene, Sommerville, Nystrom, Darley, & Cohen, 2001), to explore the process of insight (Bowden & Jung-Beeman, 2003), and to distinguish between efficient and inefficient problem solving (Reichle, Carpenter, & Just,

2000). Several types of studies may be useful to assess the impact of C-CC on consultees' mental functioning. Research possibilities include investigating (a) differences in brain efficiency between expert consultants and novices, (b) differences in pre/post brain efficiency in problem identification with consultees, (c) experimental/control group comparisons of efficiency in problem identification, and (d) networks of the brain that are involved with processing evidence that is both consistent and inconsistent with the consultation problem and whether consultation has an impact on the hypothesized biological filters (Fugelsang & Dunbar, 2005).

Whatever the focus, studies stemming from Hylander's (2003) three research paradigms are needed to address the issue of the efficacy of C-CC on consultee conceptions. Studies of effectiveness — the efficacy of consultation in actual settings — should focus on further extending the understanding of the impact of C-CC on changes in behavior as well.

Type II Research

An intervention that is shown to have efficacy in the lab or in carefully controlled school settings may not be transportable and effective in actual practice. Efficacy does not automatically confer effectiveness; interventions must also be investigated for their utility and success in the authentic world of students, teachers, and administrators. Type II research poses such questions as "how the intervention works in real settings, who can and will conduct the intervention, under what conditions and to what effect" (Kratochwill & Shernoff, 2004; Schoenwald & Hoagwood, 2001). Even if C-CC is shown to be efficacious in facilitating the conceptual development of consultees in narrowly defined, highly advantageous experimental conditions, effectiveness trials must also be undertaken to discover which factors in the ecology of the school setting support or inhibit C-CC. Type II investigations of effectiveness in usual school settings may focus on three of Schoenwald and Hoagwood's (2001) research-to-practice dimensions: intervention, practitioner characteristics, and client characteristics.

Intervention Characteristics

C-CC is less structured, more ambiguous (Hylander, 2004), and less directive than other types of consultation. Consequently, the impact of these characteristics on C-CC's processes and outcomes in school settings should be investigated. Meeting time is a valuable and often-scarce resource in school settings, such that teachers often have a restricted ability to meet outside the classroom on a regular basis. Research questions include, What is the impact of time restrictions on the implementation of C-CC? What levels of time are necessary to achieve high levels of fidelity? How can consultants and consultees leverage necessary amounts of time from the school day?

The assumption that consultees are competent and can problem solve difficult issues in their professional work setting is central to the practice of C-CC. Consultees have demands placed on them that include responsibility for important aspects of the problem-solving process. Although the C-CC consultant has expertise in facilitating this process, the consultee is presumed to have relevant professional expertise and better knowledge of the work environment. Given this assumption of responsibility, how well does C-CC work when consultees expect to "give away" the problem? For example, if a regular education teacher believes that he or she is powerless to help a child in his or her classroom and that the child will only benefit from special education services, then how receptive will the teacher be to C-CC? Will this teacher take on the responsibilities of the consultee in C-CC? Effectiveness studies should examine the utility, in conjunction with teacher expectations, of C-CC for particular types of referral issues.

Practitioner Characteristics

Level II research on practitioner characteristics should focus on the basic question, Who can do this? What personal skills, temperament, professional roles, and training are associated with successful consultee-centered consultants? C-CC requires its practitioners to have "a keen sense of the importance of recognizing the expertise of the consultee" (Lambert, 2004, p. 15) so that he or she might successfully facilitate "the joint development of a new way of conceptualizing the work problem" (Lambert, p. 12). The assumption is that although the content expertise and theoretical orientation of C-CC consultants may vary, their appreciation of consultee competence should be evident in their attitude, cognitions, and behavior. This belief should be empirically validated to ascertain which aspects of these elements are possessed by experienced C-CC consultants and how variations in them have an impact on the process and outcome of consultation in school settings.

Client Characteristics

In the case of consultation, the Schoenwald and Hoagwood (2001) definition of client would apply to the person receiving the intervention (i.e., consultee). However, for the purpose of this discussion, *client* refers to both consultee (i.e., teacher) and client (i.e., student). Hylander (2004) suggested that effectiveness studies should investigate consultee conceptions and expected changes in the consultee-client interaction, especially behaviors.

Conceptual changes in the client may be studied using the previously discussed methods of concept mapping, discourse analysis, and fMRI in field-based trials in usual care settings. The investigations should seek not only to document changes but also to discover congruencies/incongruencies between results obtained from the well-controlled environments of efficacy trials and the more random environments associated with effectiveness trials. Crucial context variables may become evident in such a research-to-practice comparison. In addition, teacher characteristics such as preferences, experiences, affect, and ethnic background (Brown et al., 2006) should be evaluated for their impact on the effectiveness of C-CC.

Consultee behaviors may be observed or reported by the consultee, consultant, peers, supervisors, investigators, or students. Sandoval (2004) suggested that observable behaviors such as a shift toward learner-centered practices (Lambert & McCombs, 1998), in which teachers become more responsive to learners and less encumbered by curriculum, may be used as a measure of the impact of C-CC on consultees. Outcome measures should be given immediately after consultation as well as in future cases to determine if there has been any transfer of learning across students or situations. Outcome data about client/student behaviors may come from many sources, including behavioral and achievement data, consultee reports about the client, and evaluations of changes in teacher/student interactions.

Type III Research

Dissemination research is concerned with the movement of an intervention beyond the boundaries of its efficacy and effectiveness trials and reaching across classrooms, schools, and systems. The range of topics is varied and includes the (a) professionals or intervention agents who are responsible for implementing and overseeing the intervention (Kratochwill & Pittman, 2002) and (b) three research-to-practice dimensions of service delivery, organizational characteristics, and service system mandates (Schoenwald & Hoagwood, 2001) that are related to differences in the conditions across settings. Research agendas for each of these areas are discussed next.

Training

When a program has been developed to the level of effectiveness in usual practice, the next step is to train the school personnel or intervention agents to be responsible for its delivery and ongoing evaluation. A critical Type III issue is to develop a training program that allows for programmatic responsibility to shift from the lab to the school. What C-CC training issues might be important to investigate?

Because the C-CC model is designed to be egalitarian, it may conflict with the prior training of the school personnel who serve as consultants. It is likely that school personnel will be familiar with the expert approach to consultation in which the primary goal is to influence client change but will be less familiar with the goal of facilitating consultee change. Therefore, consultants will likely need to have intensive on-the-job training. Important research questions include (a) What level of training will be needed to allow the consultant to independently undertake this type of consultation? (b) Will 1- or 2-day symposia suffice? and (c) Will consultants need training that provides not only an intellectual framework but also structured on-site practice? (Walker, 2004).

Research methods that could contribute to answering these questions include experimental, quasi-experimental, single-participant, and case study methods. The experimental approach will help to answer basic questions about training efficacy, and single-participant and case study designs will help to understand the role of context in dissemination.

Setting Characteristics

Psychological climate and organizational culture are two important variables that may have an impact on the effectiveness and, ultimately, dissemination of interventions. James and James (1989) defined psychological climate as "the individual's perception of the psychological impact of the work environment or his or her own well-being" (cited in Glisson, 2002, p. 235). Components of psychological climate that are important to C-CC include role conflict, role clarity, cooperation, fairness, and emotional exhaustion. Organizational culture is defined as "normative beliefs and shared behavioral expectations in an organization or work unit" (Cooke & Szumal, 1993, p. 1314). A factor analysis by Glisson and James (2002) found two core types of culture: (a) constructive, characterized by support and positive work attitudes; and (b) passive-defensive, characterized by dependence and conformity. It would be reasonable to expect consultation conducted in schools with a supportive climate to fare better than consultation conducted in schools with a punitive organizational climate.

Investigations of the dissemination of C-CC across school settings should seek to understand how the unique qualities of the model are implemented. For example, C-CC relies on an interpersonal relationship in which the core characteristics of genuineness, respect, and trust are demonstrated by the consultant for the consultee to be able to look at the work-related problem without fear of judgment or harsh evaluation. Problem solving requires the consultant and consultee to be able to widen the problem space through a focused problem identification process. Research questions include how variations in climate (i.e., cooperation, fairness) and culture (i.e., support, subservience) have an impact on C-CC service delivery across settings. Quasi-experimental methods using a matched design could be used to compare the effect of climate and culture across schools that use C-CC. Qualitative methods such as case studies and ethnographies of communication could be used to describe and explain how the unique climate or cultural context of a school impinges on or supports the application of C-CC.

Type IV Research

Research into the utility of an intervention should not stop when the researchers have phased themselves out of overseeing or structuring the implementation and have returned to the lab. The ultimate test of an intervention's usefulness is what happens when it is handed over to school personnel to implement independently. Type IV research investigates the sustainability of interventions as they are authentically practiced in schools. Sustainability research into C-CC should evaluate how the essential qualities of the practice are adopted, freestanding, in the context of individual schools and describe what outcomes occur in real situations.

Type IV research questions are related to consultee and client outcomes. What evidence is there to indicate that consultees acquire new conceptualizations and problem-solving strategies? What evidence is there to show that newly acquired understandings and strategies are used to solve similar work situations, with similar clients, in the future? In what contexts and situations is there a high degree of implementation and consultee transfer to similar situations? Longitudinal studies that focus on consultee, client, and school-level outcomes will be needed to evaluate the ultimate sustainability of C-CC. Case studies will be useful to discover the organizational dynamics and interpersonal processes that contribute to sustainability.

Consultation as Metaintervention

Implementation of an intervention is a daunting task that requires major thought, planning, and effort. As the EBI research protocols have described (Kratochwill & Stoiber, 2002), interventions are not necessarily ready for dissemination or sustainability simply by virtue of statistical significance in studies of effectiveness. Interventions that aim to have a national, or even regional, impact will have to thoughtfully consider and plan for transportability and diffusion. The research-to-practice gap will have to be accounted for in a systematic and programmatic fashion. As discussed, C-CC may be useful as a metaintervention to support the transportability and dissemination of other interventions to the unique context of individual schools. C-CC may support the implementation of new interventions by explicitly addressing the problem of conceptual mismatch between the consultee's preexisting beliefs and the intervention's programmatic assumptions. The consultant and consultee may use the process jointly to reconceptualize the work problem and to expand the repertoire of the consultee to handle implementation of the new intervention.

The research agenda to understand and support the utility of C-CC as a metaintervention is twofold: (a) conduct independent investigations of efficacy and effectiveness to determine how to best use C-CC to support sustainability and implementation and (b) include the application of C-CC as a metaintervention in Level II–IV trials of other interventions that use it to support effectiveness, transportability, and dissemination.

In conclusion, mental health consultation and its descendants, such as C-CC, are notable not only for focusing on fostering client change but also for emphasizing consultee development. Many practitioners find that the approach has an intuitive appeal, and it is valued for its presumed prevention effects. However, for C-CC to meet the criteria of an EBI, its outcomes must be investigated through efficacy and effectiveness research.

REFERENCES

Adelman, H. S., & Taylor, L. (2003). On sustainability of project innovations as systemic change. *Journal of Educational and Psychological Consultation, 14,* 1–25.

Allington, R. L., & Walmsley, S. A. (1995). *No quick fix.* New York: Teachers College Press.

142 STEVEN E. KNOTEK, MAUREEN KANIUKA, AND KIRSTEN ELLINGSEN

Alpert, J. L., & Yammer, M. D. (1983). Research in school consultation: A content analysis of selected journals. *Professional Psychology: Research and Practice, 14*, 604–612.

Bosse, M. (1995). The NCTM standards in light of the new math movement: A warning! *Journal of Mathematical Behavior, 14*, 171–201.

Bowden, E. M., & Jung-Beeman, M. (2003). Aha! Insight experience correlates with solution activation in the right hemisphere. *Psychonomic Bulletin Review, 10*, 730–737.

Brown, D., Pryzwansky, W. B., & Schulte, A. C. (2006). *Psychological consultation and collaboration: Introduction to theory and practice* (6th edition). Boston: Allyn & Bacon.

Burns, B., & Hoagwood, K. (2002). *Community treatment for youth: Evidence-based interventions for severe emotional and behavioral disorders.* New York: Oxford University Press.

Caplan, G. (1970). *The theory and practice of mental health consultation.* New York: Basic Books.

Caplan, G., & Caplan, R. B. (1993). *Mental health consultation and collaboration.* San Francisco: Jossey Bass.

Caplan, G., Caplan, R., & Erchul, W. P. (1995). A contemporary view of mental health consultation: Comments on "Types of Mental Health Consultation." *Journal of Educational and Psychological Consultation, 6*, 23–30.

Christenson, S. L., Carlson, C., & Valdez, C. R. (2002). Evidence-based interventions in school psychology: Opportunities, challenges, and cautions. *School Psychology Quarterly, 17*, 466–474.

Cooke, R. A., & Szumal, J. L. (1993). Measuring normative beliefs and shared behavioral expectations in organizations: The reliability and validity of the Organizational Culture Inventory. *Psychological Reports, 72*, 1299–1330.

Daniels, T. D., & DeWine, S. (1991). Communication process as target and tool for consultancy intervention: Rethinking a hackneyed theme. *Journal of Educational and Psychological Consultation, 2*, 303–322.

Dougherty, M. A. (2000). *Psychological consultation and collaboration in school and community settings* (3rd ed). Belmont, CA: Wadsworth.

Durlak, J., & Wells, A. (1997). Primary prevention mental health programs for children and adolescents: A meta-analytic review. *American Journal of Community Psychology, 25*, 115–152.

Erchul, W. P. (1992). On dominance, cooperation, teamwork, and collaboration in school-based consultation. *Journal of Educational and Psychological Consultation, 3*, 363–366.

Erchul, W. P. (2003). Communication and interpersonal processes in consultation: Guest editor's comments. *Journal of Educational and Psychological Consultation, 14*, 105–107.

Erchul, W. P., & Schulte, A. C. (1993). Gerald Caplan's contributions to professional psychology: Conceptual underpinnings. In W. P. Erchul (Ed.), *Consultation in community, school, and organizational practice: Gerald Caplan's contributions to professional psychology* (pp. 3–39). Washington, DC: Taylor & Francis.

Fugelsang, J. A., & Dunbar, K. N. (2004). A cognitive neuroscience framework for understanding causal reasoning and the law. *Philosophical Transactions of the Royal Society B: Biological Sciences, 359*, 1749–1754.

Fugelsang, J. A., & Dunbar, K. N. (2005). Brain-based mechanisms underlying complex causal thinking. *Neuropsychologia, 48*, 1204–1213.

Gagne, R. (1977). *The conditions of learning* (3rd ed.). New York: Holt, Rinehart & Winston.

Glisson, C. (2002). The organizational context of children's mental health services. *Clinical Child and Family Psychology Review, 5*, 233–253.

Glisson, C., & James, L. R. (2002). The cross-level effects of culture and climate in human service teams. *Journal of Organizational Behavior, 23*, 767–794.

Gravois, T. A., Knotek, S. E., & Babinski, L. M. (2002). Educating practitioners as consultants: The instructional consultation team consortium. *Journal of Educational and Psychological Consultation, 13*, 113–132.

Greene, J. D., Sommerville, B., Nystrom, L., Darley, J., & Cohen, J. (2001). An fMRI investigation of emotional engagement in moral judgment. *Science, 293*, 2105–2108.

Gresham, F. M. (1989). Assessment of treatment integrity in school consultation and prereferral intervention. *School Psychology Review, 17*, 211–226.

Gresham, F. M., & Kendell, G. K. (1987). School consultation research: Methodological critique and future research directions. *School Psychology Review, 16*, 306–316.

Gutkin, T. B., & Curtis, M. J. (1999). School-based consultation: Theory and techniques. In C. R. Reynolds & T. B. Gutkin (Eds.), *The handbook of school psychology* (3rd ed., pp. 598–637). New York: Wiley.

Hoagwood, K. (2001). Evidence-based practice in children's mental health services: What do we know? Why aren't we putting it to use? *Emotional & Behavioral Disorders in Youth, 1,* 84–87.

Hoagwood, K. (2003–2004). Evidence-based practice in child and adolescent mental health: Its meaning, application, and limitations. *Emotional & Behavioral Disorders in Youth, 4,* 7–8.

Hoagwood, K., & Johnson, J. (2002). School psychology: A public health framework I. From evidence-based practices to evidence-based policies. *Journal of School Psychology, 41,* 3–21.

Hughes, J. N. (1994). Back to basics: Does consultation work? *Journal of Educational and Psychological Consultation, 5,* 77–84.

Hylander, I. (2003). Toward a grounded theory of the conceptual change process in consultee-centered consultation. *Journal of Educational and Psychological Consultation,14,* 263–280.

Hylander, I. (2004). Identifying change in consultee-centered consultation. In N. Lambert, I. Hylander, & J. Sandoval (Eds.), *Consultee-centered consultation: Improving the quality of professional services in schools and community organizations* (pp. 373–389). Mahwah, NJ: Erlbaum.

Ingraham, C. L. (2000). Consultation through a multicultural lens: Multicultural and cross-cultural consultation in schools. *School Psychology Review, 29,* 320–343.

James, L. A., & James, L. R. (1989). Integrating work environment perceptions: Explorations into the measurement of meaning. *Journal of Applied Psychology, 74,* 739–751.

Kanof, M. E. (2003). Youth illicit drug use prevention: DARE long-term evaluations and federal efforts to identify effective programs. Washington, DC: General Accounting Office.

Knoff, H., M., & Batsche, G. M. (1993). A school reform process for at-risk students: Applying Caplan's organizational consultation principles to guide prevention, intervention, and home-school cooperation. In W. P. Erchul (Ed.), *Consultation in community, school, and organizational practice: Gerald Caplan's contributions to professional psychology* (pp. 123–147). Washington, DC: Taylor & Francis.

Knotek, S. E. (2003a). Bias in problem solving and the social process of student study teams: A qualitative investigation of two SST's. *Journal of Special Education, 37,* 2–14.

Knotek, S. E. (2003b). Making sense of jargon during consultation: Understanding consultees' social language to effect change in student study teams. *Journal of Educational and Psychological Consultation, 14,* 181–208.

Knotek, S. E., Rosenfield, S. A., Gravois, T. A., & Babinski, L. M. (2003). The process of fostering consultee development during instructional consultation. *Journal of Educational and Psychological Consultation, 14,* 303–328.

Knotek, S. E., & Sandoval, J. (2003). Current research in consultee-centered consultation. *Journal of Educational and Psychological Consultation, 14,* 243–250.

Kratochwill, T. R. (2002). Evidence-based interventions in school psychology: Thoughts on a thoughtful commentary. *School Psychology Quarterly, 17,* 518–532.

Kratochwill, T. R., & Pittman, P. (2002). Defining constructs in consultation: An important training agenda. *Journal of Educational and Psychological Consultation, 13,* 69–95.

Kratochwill, T. R., Sheridan, S. M., & VanSomeren, K. R. (1988). Research in behavioral consultation: Current status and future directions. In J. F. West (Ed.), *School consultation.* Austin, TX: University of Texas at Austin, Research and Training Project on School Consultation.

Kratochwill, T. R., & Shernoff, E. S. (2003). Evidence-based practice: Promoting evidence-based interventions in school psychology. *School Psychology Quarterly, 18,* 389–408.

Kratochwill, T., & Shernoff, E. S. (2004). Evidence-based practice: Promoting evidence-based interventions in school psychology. *School Psychology Review, 33,* 34–48.

Kratochwill, T. R., & Stoiber, K. C. (2002). Evidence-based interventions in school psychology: Conceptual foundations of the procedural and coding manual of Division 16 and the Society for the Study of School Psychology Task Force. *School Psychology Quarterly, 17,* 341–389.

Lambert, N. M. (2004). Consultee-centered consultation: An international perspective on goals, process, and theory. In N. Lambert, I. Hylander, & J. Sandoval (Eds.), *Consultee-centered consultation: Improving the quality of professional services in schools and community organizations* (pp. 3–20). Mahwah, NJ: Erlbaum.

Lambert, N. M. Hylander, I., & Sandoval, J. (Eds.). (2004). *Consultee-centered consultation: Improving the quality of professional services in schools and community organizations.* Mahwah, NJ: Erlbaum.

Lambert, N. M., & McCombs, B. L. (1998). *How students learn: Reforming schools through learner-centered education.* Washington, DC: American Psychological Association.

Maitland, R. E., Fine, M. J., & Tracy, D. B. (1985). The effects of an interpersonally based problem-solving process on consultation outcomes. *Journal of School Psychology, 23,* 337–345.

McDougal, J. L., Clonan, S. M., & Martens, B. K. (2000). Using organizational change procedures to promote the acceptability of prereferral interventions services: The school-based intervention team project. *School Psychology Quarterly, 15,* 149-171.

Meade, C. J., Hamilton, M. K., & Yuen, R. K. (1982). Consultation research: The time has come, the walrus said. *The Counseling Psychologist, 10,* 39–51.

Medway, F. J. (1979). How effective is school consultation? A review of recent research. *Journal of School Psychology, 17,* 275–282

Medway, F. J., & Forman, S. G. (1980). Psychologists' and teachers' reactions to mental health and behavioral school consultation. *Journal of School Psychology, 18,* 338–348.

Medway, F. J., & Updyke, J. F. (1985). Meta-analysis of consultation outcome studies. *American Journal of Community Psychology, 13,* 489–505.

Merriam-Webster. (2002). *Merriam-Webster's desk medical dictionary.* Springfield, MA: Author.

Meyers, J. (1981). Mental health consultation. In J. C. Conoley (Ed.), *Consultation in schools* (pp. 35–58). New York: Academic Press.

Meyers, J. (1995). A consultation model for school psychological services: 20 years later. *Journal of Educational and Psychological Consultation, 6,* 73–81.

Meyers, J., Brent, D., Faherty, E., & Modafferi, C. (1993). Caplan's contributions to the practice of psychology in schools. In W. P. Erchul (Ed.), *Consultation in community, school, and organizational practice: Gerald Caplan's contributions to professional psychology* (pp. 99–122). Washington, DC: Taylor & Francis.

Nathan, P. E., & Gorman, J. M. (Eds.) (1998). *A guide to treatments that work.* New York: Oxford.

Nastasi, B. K. (1998). A model for mental health programming in schools and communities: Introduction to the mini-series. *School Psychology Review, 27,* 165–174.

Novak J. D., & Gowin, D. B. (1984). *Learning how to learn.* New York: Cambridge University Press.

Pryzwansky, W. B. (1986). Indirect service delivery: Considerations for future research in consultation. *School Psychology Review, 15,* 479–488.

Reichle, E. D., Carpenter, P. A., & Just, M. A. (2000). The neural bases of strategy and skill in sentence-picture verification. *Cognitive Psychology, 40,* 261–295.

Rones, M., & Hoagwood, K. (2000). School-based mental health services: A research review. *Clinical Child and Family Psychology Review, 3,* 223–241.

Rosenfield, S. A. (2004). Consultation as dialogue: The right words at the right time. In N. M. Lambert, I. Hylander, & J. Sandoval (Eds.), *Consultee-centered consultation: Improving the quality of professional services in schools and community organizations* (pp. 339–350). Mahwah, NJ: Erlbaum.

Rosenfield, S. A., & Gravois, T. A. (1996). *Instructional consultation teams: Collaborating for change.* New York: Guilford.

Sandoval, J. (1996). Constructivism, consultee-centered consultation, and conceptual change. *Journal of Educational and Psychological Consultation, 7,* 89–97.

Sandoval, J. (2003). Constructing conceptual change in consultee-centered consultation. *Journal of Educational and Psychological Consultation, 14,* 231–242.

Sandoval, J. (2004). Evaluation issues and strategies in consultee-centered consultation. In N. Lambert, I. Hylander, & J. Sandoval (Eds.), *Consultee-centered consultation: Improving the quality of professional services in schools and community organizations* (pp. 391–400). Mahwah, NJ: Erlbaum.

Schoenwald, S. K., & Hoagwood, K. (2001). Effectiveness, transportability, and dissemination of interventions: What matters when? *Psychiatric Services, 52,* 1190–1197.

Sheridan, S. M. (1992). Consultant and client outcomes of competency-based behavioral consultation training. *School Psychology Quarterly, 7,* 245–270.

Sheridan, S. M., Welch, M., & Orme, S. F. (1996). Is consultation effective? A review of outcome research. *Remedial and Special Education, 17,* 341–354.

Simeonsson, R. J. (1994). *Risk, resilience, and prevention: Promoting the wellbeing of all children.* Baltimore, MD: Brookes.

Slesser, R. A., Fine, M. J., & Tracy, D. B. (1990). Teacher reactions to two approaches to school based psychological consultation. *Journal of Educational and Psychological Consultation, 1,* 243–258.

Stoiber, K. C. (2002). Revisiting efforts on constructing a knowledge base of evidence-based intervention within school psychology. *School Psychology Quarterly, 17,* 533–546.

Stoiber, K. C., & Kratochwill, T. R. (2000). Empirically supported interventions and school psychology: Rationale and methodological issues — Part I. *School Psychology Quarterly, 15*, 75–105.

Thombs, D. L. (2000). A retrospective study of DARE: Substantive effects not detected in undergraduates. *Journal of Alcohol and Drug Education, 46*, 27–40.

Truscott, S. D., Cosgrove, G., Eidle, K., & Meyers, J. (2000). The acceptability of organizational consultation with prereferral intervention teams. *School Psychology Quarterly, 15*, 172–206.

Uttal, W. R. (2001). *The new phrenology: The limits of localizing cognitive processes in the brain.* Boston: MIT Press.

Walker, H. M. (2004). Commentary: Use of evidence-based interventions in schools: Where we've been, where we are, and where we need to go. *School Psychology Review, 33*, 398–410.

Webster, L., Knotek, S. E., Babinski, L. M., Rogers, D. L., & Barnett, M. M. (2003). Mediation of consultee's conceptual development in new teacher groups: Using questions to improve coherency. *Journal of Educational and Psychological Consultation, 14*, 281–301.

Weisz, J. R., & Hawley, K. M. (1999). *Procedural and coding manual for identification of beneficial treatments.* Washington, DC: American Psychological Association, Society for Clinical Psychology, Division 12, Committee on Science and Practice.

West, D. C., Pomeroy, J. R., Park, J. K., Gerstenberger, E. A., & Sandoval, J. (2000). Critical thinking in graduate medical education: A role for concept mapping assessment? *Journal of the American Medical Association, 284*, 1105–1110.

Wetherell, M., Taylor, S., & Yates, S. J. (2001). *Discourse as data: A guide for analysis.* London: Sage.

Yin, Y., & Shavelson, R. J. (2004). *Application of generalizability theory to concept-map assessment research* (CSE Report, 640). National Center for Research on Evaluation, Standards, and Student Testing. Los Angeles: University of California.

8

Behavioral Consultation

BRIAN K. MARTENS AND FLORENCE D. DIGENNARO

Syracuse University

INTRODUCTION

The behavioral consultation (BC) model was originally developed by John R. Bergan (1977) as an extension of D'Zurilla and Goldfried's (1971) problem-solving approach to behavior therapy as well as attempts to apply behavior modification in residential schools and treatment centers (e.g., Reppucci & Saunders, 1974). With respect to the former influence on BC, D'Zurilla and Goldfried characterized problem solving and behavior modification as sharing similar goals — training behaviors that can be used across situations to increase positive consequences and avoid negative consequences. Toward these goals, the authors described a general problem-solving process to help individuals identify potentially effective solutions through problem definition and brainstorming and to select the best solution through problem analysis and outcome assessment.

With respect to the influence of attempts to apply behavior modification on BC, Tharp and Wetzel (1969) described a method for applying the principles of behavior modification in human service settings that involved three participants: (a) the *consultant*, who is anyone with knowledge and expertise in behavior analysis; (b) the *mediator*, who is anyone responsible for client behavior and therefore controls reinforcers; and (c) the *target*, who is anyone with a problem. Early attempts to train direct-care staff in the use of behavior modification procedures were met with limited success due to bureaucratic constraints, poor communication, difficulties modifying staff behavior, and limited resources at the host agencies (Erchul & Martens, 2002; Reppucci & Saunders, 1974). Bergan attempted to overcome these barriers in his BC model by incorporating strategic communication skills, collaboration between consultant and consultee, specified intervention plans, and outcome assessment into the consultation process.

As an indirect service delivery model, BC shares the same fundamental assumptions of other consultation models. Specifically, BC has been described as involving a voluntary, collaborative, and confidential relationship between co-equal professionals, the goals of which are to address clients' problems and increase the ability of consultees to address similar problems in the future (Bergan, 1977; Gutkin & Curtis, 1982). BC typically involves little or no contact between consultant and client but relies instead on face-to-face interviews with the consultee to identify and analyze client problems and to design and evaluate intervention plans. Consultees are expected to participate actively in the interview process by describing problem behavior and the conditions surrounding its occurrence and by collecting data to evaluate plan effectiveness (Bergan & Kratochwill, 1990;

Martens, Erchul, & Witt, 1992). Because BC is a voluntary process and because consultees are responsible for plan implementation, they are also viewed as having the right to reject or modify consultants' suggestions.

Unique to the BC model is its reliance on a four-stage problem-solving process derived from D'Zurilla and Goldfried (1971) that includes problem identification, problem analysis, plan implementation, and problem evaluation. The four problem-solving stages are enacted over the course of three interviews, each containing specific interviewing objectives (see Erchul & Martens, 2002, for a complete listing). During the problem identification interview (PII), the consultant and consultee are responsible for identifying a target problem behavior, estimating how often and under which conditions the problem occurs, and initiating data collection procedures for use in evaluating intervention effectiveness. During the problem analysis interview (PAI), baseline data that were collected subsequent to the PII are used to set goals for client change; the conditions surrounding problem behavior as antecedents and consequences are discussed more thoroughly; and a treatment plan is designed and put in place. Once the treatment plan has been implemented, the consultant and consultee meet for a problem evaluation interview (PEI) to decide if the goals for client change were met and whether the intervention should be continued, discontinued, or modified (Goldstein & Martens, 2000).

Although some authors have focused on BC as a problem-solving process (e.g., Kratochwill, Elliott, & Callan-Stoiber, 2002), the BC model is also unique for its reliance on the strategies and tactics of applied behavior analysis to develop interventions and to monitor their effectiveness (Erchul & Martens, 2002). At the time BC was developed, these strategies included (a) defining problem behavior in operational terms; (b) recording occurrences of behavior through systematic observation or other direct assessment methods; (c) displaying observational data collected under baseline and treatment conditions in line or bar graphs; and (d) using some form of contingency management to reinforce desired or punish undesired behavior (e.g., token economy or point system, time-out or response cost).

As noted by Gutkin and Curtis (1982), "At its most basic level, consultation is an interpersonal exchange. As such, the consultant's success is going to hinge largely on his or her communication and relationship skills" (p. 822). Given that problem identification and analysis were accomplished through interviewing and that consultees maintained responsibility for plan implementation, effective communication skills were viewed as particularly important to the BC process. Accordingly, Bergan and Tombari (1975) developed the Consultation Analysis Record (CAR) to evaluate consultant interviewing effectiveness. The CAR is the only coding system designed specifically for quantifying verbal interactions occurring during consultation (Martens et al., 1992). CAR codes are applied to independent clauses within consultant and consultee statements, and each clause is coded by *message source* (who spoke), *message content* (the topic under discussion), *message process* (the function of what was said), and *message control* (whether information was requested or presented).

Early research using the CAR was aimed primarily at obtaining indices of consultant effectiveness that could be related to indices of consultation outcome. Findings from this line of research suggested that (a) the best predictor of problem resolution is the consultant's skill in helping consultees define the problem in behavioral terms (Bergan & Tombari, 1975, 1976); (b) the consultant's use of behavioral versus medical model cues leads to higher expectations by teachers about their ability to teach children with academic problems (Tombari & Bergan, 1978); and (c) the odds are 14 times higher that a teacher will identify resources needed to carry out an intervention plan if the consultant asks instead of tells the consultee to do so (Bergan & Neumann, 1980).

EFFECTIVENESS OF BEHAVIORAL CONSULTATION AND EMERGING CHALLENGES

Early reviews of consultation research highlighted the popularity of BC and showed it to be an effective professional practice in the schools (e.g., Medway, 1982). For example, Alpert and Yammer (1983) found that 75% of all published research on consultation at that time was concerned with BC. In a more recent review, Sheridan, Welch, and Orme (1996) found that BC continued to dominate outcome research published since 1985, with 46% of articles, followed by mental health consultation (11%) and organizational consultation (4%). Sheridan et al. also found that 89% of all reported outcomes from BC studies were positive.

When implemented on a schoolwide basis, BC has been shown to decrease the number of children referred for special education placement while increasing the placement rates for children who are referred (D. Fuchs, Fuchs, & Bahr, 1990; Graden, Casey, & Bonstrom, 1985; Gutkin, Henning-Stout, & Piersel, 1988; Rosenfield, 1992). As a result, *prereferral intervention* programs based on the BC model became increasingly popular during the 1980s and 1990s. As defined by McDougal, Clonan, and Martens (2000):

> Prereferral intervention is a consultation-based approach for providing behavioral and/or instructional support to students experiencing problems before considering their eligibility for special class placement. … As such, prereferral intervention services involve consultation between a referring teacher and a team of consultants toward the common goals of specifying the referral problem in behavioral terms; analyzing maintaining variables; and designing, implementing, and evaluating one or more intervention plans. (p. 150)

Prereferral intervention services are now commonplace in school districts across the country, and some states require documented failure of an appropriate intervention before a child can be referred for special education placement (Erchul & Martens, 2002). Although the quality of services is likely to vary from district to district, research has suggested that more effective programs are actively supported by district administration, make use of consultants internal to the district, employ a team consultation approach with predefined roles for participants, and use scripts or manuals to guide the BC process and to monitor treatment integrity (D. Fuchs, Fuchs, Bahr, Fernstrom, & Stecker, 1990; McDougal et al., 2000; Rosenfield, 1992).

With consulting teams already in place in many schools throughout the country, BC was the vehicle through which school districts were expected to comply with the 1997 and 2004 amendments of the Individuals With Disabilities Education Act (IDEA). Specifically, IDEA was amended in 1997 to mandate that "if a student with disabilities exhibits problem behaviors that impede his or her learning … then the student's IEP [Individual Education Plan] team shall consider strategies including *positive behavioral interventions, strategies, and supports to address that behavior*" (emphasis added) (1414(d)(3)(B)(i)). The IDEA 1997 also mandated that, "In response to disciplinary actions by school personnel, the IEP team must … meet to develop a *functional behavioral assessment plan* to collect information. This information should be used for *developing or reviewing and revising an existing behavioral intervention plan to address such behaviors*" (emphasis added) (615(k)(1)(B)). In 2004, IDEA was amended again to allow local education agencies to evaluate a child's *response to scientific, research-based intervention* in determining eligibility for classification as learning disabled (LD). Although originally provided to teachers on an individual and voluntary basis by school psychologists working outside their normal job duties (Piersel & Gutkin, 1983), BC has evolved into a stand-alone service delivered by teams of professionals and will soon become a federally mandated decision tool for eligibility determination.

The challenges facing BC researchers and practitioners in this era of high-stakes, team-based service delivery form the structure around which the remainder of the chapter is organized. The first challenge for BC is for consulting teams to select interventions that are appropriate for presenting problems and that are supported by empirical research (Martens & Ardoin, 2002). Selecting interventions that have a theoretical relationship to variables believed to cause or maintain problem behavior is referred to as conceptual relevance (Yeaton & Sechrest, 1981). When selecting behavioral treatment programs, conceptual relevance is addressed by conducting a functional assessment or analysis of problem behavior or a brief experimental analysis (BEA) of treatment options (Iwata, Dorsey, Slifer, Bauman, & Richman, 1982/1994; Martens, Eckert, Bradley, & Ardoin, 1999; Witt, Daly, & Noell, 2000). Although these methods of treatment selection are widely used with some populations (i.e., functional analysis for individuals with severe disabilities) and for some problems (i.e., BEA for reading problems) (e.g., Daly, Martens, Hamler, Dool, & Eckert, 1999; Hanley, Iwata, & McCord, 2003), they did not yet exist when BC was first developed. As a result, it is typical for behavioral consultants to rely entirely on verbal reports by consultees during the PII and PAI to identify potential maintaining variables for problem behavior (Witt, Gresham, & Noell, 1996). This practice is not likely to be defensible in the face of recent federal mandates (Drasgow & Yell, 2001). This means that the future viability of the BC model may depend on the ability of consulting teams to supplement information gleaned from the interview process with more direct assessment methods (Sterling-Turner, Robinson, & Wilczynski, 2001; Witt et al., 2000).

When selecting interventions for a given problem, behavioral consultants are faced with a choice of a variety of alternatives. In the past, these choices were often driven by considerations such as teacher skill, familiarity with the procedure, acceptability, or perceived ease of use rather than effectiveness (e.g., Martens, Peterson, Witt, & Cirone, 1986; Ysseldyke, Pianta, Christenson, Wang, & Algozzine, 1983). However, following the IDEA amendments of 1997 and 2004 as well as passage of the No Child Left Behind (NCLB) Act, it is clear that consulting teams will need to rely primarily, if not solely, on evidence-based interventions for responding to children's learning and behavior problems.

The second challenge for BC is for teacher training programs, in-service providers, and behavioral consultants to effectively prepare teachers and other direct-care staff for the role of consultee. Both behavioral consultants and consultees (i.e., teachers) are asked to assume a higher level of accountability for client (i.e., child) outcomes. This expectation has become increasingly more apparent as services based on the BC model are used to significantly reduce the numbers of children served in special education. This means that only a small percentage of children can be identified as treatment "nonresponders" (Vaughn & Fuchs, 2003), and when this occurs, the onus will be on student assistance teams and the teachers with whom they consult to defend their consultation and intervention activities. Under these circumstances, teachers may no longer have the luxury of rejecting interventions suggested by a consulting team because the procedure is unfamiliar, inconsistent with their philosophy of teaching, or difficult to implement. Conversely, consulting teams may no longer be able to assume that a cursory verbal description of the procedure during the PAI is sufficient to train teachers in plan implementation. Consistent with research on the effectiveness of prereferral intervention programs (e.g., McDougal et al., 2000), consulting teams may need to take a more direct or prescriptive approach to plan implementation.

The third challenge for BC is how to promote lasting changes in consultee behavior to sustain intervention use over time. Research by Noell and his colleagues (e.g., Noell, Witt, Gilbertson, Ranier, & Freeland, 1997) has suggested that without ongoing support, teachers are likely to stop using an intervention after meetings with the consultant have ended. For example, Noell et al. monitored the number of intervention steps completed by three teachers each day after the procedure was explained and necessary materials were provided. All of the teachers implemented 100% of the treatment steps initially, but within 2 weeks this level had dropped to 0% for two teachers and 40% for the third teacher.

Clearly, such low levels of implementation are inadequate when BC services are used to determine a student's eligibility for special education placement. This process, referred to as *response to intervention* (RTI), involves progress monitoring and ongoing evaluation of children's responsiveness to universal followed by a sequence of increasingly intensive, evidence-based interventions as a basis for instructional intervention and eligibility decisions. Through RTI, consulting teams are expected to systematically rule out questions about basic instruction as an alternative explanation for low performance, find and apply an optimal intervention "dosage" to improve child performance or behavior, and then use this information to make eligibility decisions (L. S. Fuchs, 2003; Gresham, 2004; Heller, Holtzman, & Messick, 1982). To have decision utility in an RTI process, intervention plans must be implemented frequently enough and with sufficient accuracy to evaluate their effects on student behavior (Martens, 2004). If effective, these interventions must be implemented long enough to solve the presenting problem. In fact, for many children receiving services under an RTI model, typical instruction enriched with one or more school-based interventions actually becomes their regular education experience.

Given the challenges discussed, the present chapter begins by reviewing research in three areas deemed critical for the future effectiveness and accountability of BC services: (a) the value and feasibility of conducting functional behavior assessments (FBAs) and analyses as part of the consultation process, (b) the importance of selecting evidence-based interventions and conducting brief experimental analyses of treatment options if appropriate, and (c) preparing teachers to assume the role of consultee during both preservice and in-service training. Research concerning the effectiveness of more direct or prescriptive approaches to BC and strategies for providing implementation support to teachers are reviewed in this section. We conclude the chapter by offering suggestions for future research to promote continued evolution of the BC model in an era of high-stakes, team-based service delivery.

CRITICAL ISSUES IN THE EFFECTIVENESS OF BEHAVIORAL CONSULTATION

Conducting Functional Behavior Assessments and Analyses

Early research by Lovaas and his colleagues (e.g., Lovaas & Simmons, 1969) and Carr and his colleagues (e.g., Carr, Newsom, & Binkoff, 1976) demonstrated that severe problem behavior in children was sensitive to the presentation of social-positive reinforcement or the removal of demands (Hanley et al., 2003). Drawing on these findings, Iwata et al. (1982/1994) described a set of procedures for conducting a functional analysis of behavior (FA). These procedures involved exposing children to a series of brief (e.g., 10-minute) test conditions, each designed to mimic a different type of reinforcement contingency believed to maintain problem behavior in the natural environment. Increases in problem behavior under one of these test conditions was taken as an indicator of the operant function of such behavior at baseline. Once identified through such "miniexperiments," contingencies believed to maintain problem behavior could then be eliminated, reversed, or weakened through intervention (Martens, Witt, Daly, & Vollmer, 1999).

In the years following the study by Iwata et al. (1982/1994), functional analysis test conditions have become "the hallmark of behavioral assessment" in the treatment of severe problem behavior (Hanley et al., 2003). In fact, Hanley et al. identified 277 published articles reporting a functional analysis through the year 2000. The prevalence of functional analyses for self-injurious and aggressive behavior drew attention to the potential benefits of assessing the conditions surrounding all problem behavior. By extension, a variety of methods for conducting a functional behavior assessment (FBA) have been reported in the literature. FBA methods attempt to describe antecedent-behavior-consequence relationships in the absence of manipulation by using informant report questionnaires (Durand & Crimmins, 1988), scatterplot observations (Touchette, MacDonald, & Langer, 1985), narrative ABC recordings (Bijou, Peterson, & Ault, 1968), and systematic observations of behavior and its consequences (e.g., Lalli, Browder, Mace, & Brown, 1993). Some form of FBA has now become an integral part of the assessment process in clinical and school settings (Braddock, 1999).

IDEA 1997 stipulated that school professionals address student problem behaviors by considering various strategies and supports when a student's behavior negatively impacts his or her own learning or that of peers. FBA was among these mandated strategies and supports. Primarily, the intent of the law was to create a safe and orderly environment to promote learning within the school setting (as cited by Drasgow & Yell, 2001). An additional aim of IDEA 1997 was to encourage the development of intervention plans to teach appropriate replacement behaviors and to safeguard the rights of individuals with disabilities to a free and appropriate public education (FAPE). The law mandated that school personnel conduct FBAs when students receiving special education services are suspended from school for over 10 consecutive days, when students are removed to an interim alternative educational setting for up to 45 calendar days due to weapons or drug charges, or when a student is granted an alternative placement by a hearing officer as a result of engaging in behavior deemed dangerous to oneself or others (Drasgow & Yell, 2001).

The 2004 reauthorization of IDEA (Pub. L. 108–446) in large part mirrors IDEA 1997 regarding FBAs, but with two further distinctions. First, IDEA 2004 mandates that an FBA be conducted on determining that a student's problem behavior is a manifestation of his or her disability. The current law also requires an FBA when a student has been removed to an interim setting for 45 school days rather than 45 calendar days as specified in IDEA 1997.

There is a lack of consensus in the published literature regarding the necessary components of an FBA (Sterling-Turner, Robinson, et al., 2001). In addition, there are few data available identifying particular procedures within an FBA that have been shown to accurately identify the functions of behavior (e.g., Lerman & Iwata, 1993; Mace & Lalli, 1991) or to maximize treatment outcomes (e.g., consultee verbal report versus systematic observation of behavior-consequence relations). With respect to the first issue, Lerman and Iwata (1993) observed six adults with profound mental retardation and recorded sequences of self-injurious behavior (SIB) and staff responses using partial-interval recording. Conditional probabilities of staff responses given the occurrence of SIB were then computed and graphed. Comparing these data to the results of standard FA test conditions (Iwata et al., 1982/1994) revealed that the FBA often did not differentiate between attention or escape functions, whereas the FA did. In the absence of more extensive treatment validity data, FBA has been described as a multistep process involving a "continuum of integrated assessment procedures that may involve an array of data collection tools" (Knoster, 2000, p. 203). A prototypical FBA sequence that is believed to reflect best practices by incorporating multiple data sources involves the following steps: (a) an operational definition of a target behavior; (b) indirect assessment methods, including record reviews, teacher or student interviews, or behavior rating scales; (c) direct observation of antecedents (e.g., events, times, and situations) that likely occasion the occurrence and nonoccurrence of problem behavior; (d) direct observation of consequences for problem behavior; (e) generation of hypotheses regarding behavioral functions; and (f) hypothesis testing through experimental analysis (e.g., Drasgow & Yell, 2001; Ervin et al., 2001; Sterling-Turner, Robinson, et al., 2001; Witt et al., 2000).

Despite the minimum standards for conducting an FBA set forth in published research, the application of systematic functional assessment procedures in school settings often falls short of best practices (Drasgow & Yell, 2001). Although a paucity of research exists specifically examining how FBAs are conducted in schools, in our experience school personnel often rely on assessment procedures that lie at the lower end of the directness continuum. For example, a school psychologist may conduct a teacher interview, administer a behavior rating scale, or briefly observe a student in the classroom. Assessment practices beyond these steps are rare. In addition, hypotheses about the possible functions of problem behavior often do not relate to principles of reinforcement and are infrequently verified through experimental analysis.

Drasgow and Yell (2001) reviewed 14 due process hearings held at the state level between the time when IDEA 1997 was enacted and August 2000. In these cases, parents contested the school districts' appropriate implementation of IDEA as it pertained to the FBA mandate described in this chapter. In 13 of the 14 cases, the hearing officer deemed the districts' implementation inadequate and ruled in favor of the parents. Specifically, in 11 cases the districts failed to conduct an FBA when legally required, resulting in financial remuneration to the parents in three instances. In addition, the hearing officer determined that an inadequate FBA was conducted in 3 cases, and these consisted of an interview with the student; a single, 1-hour observation; and completion of a handwritten, fill-in-the-blank questionnaire, respectively. The authors interpreted these findings to mean that IEP teams face a major difficulty in their inability to comply with the procedural requirements of IDEA for conducting an FBA.

Several explanations may account for the discrepancy between suggested best practices and actual school-based implementation of FBAs. First, although Congress highlighted the importance of determining the purpose of problem behaviors through the IDEA regulations (OSEP Questions and Answers, 1999), it failed to specify necessary procedures for obtaining this information. Thus, decisions regarding how best to conduct an FBA are left to the states, school districts, and multidisciplinary IEP teams. Districts should ensure that multidisciplinary teams responsible for conducting FBAs and designing IEP goals have adequate training in these areas, but often they do not. Consequently, school personnel may lack the skills required to conduct and interpret FBAs as well as the expertise to design intervention plans based on data gathered through the FBA process (Nelson, Roberts, Mathur, & Rutherford, 1999). In the absence of these skills, teams may ultimately neglect their responsibility to provide a FAPE for students with disabilities (Drasgow & Yell, 2001).

Second, a core component of comprehensive FBAs is to conduct multiple direct observations of student behavior in a variety of educationally relevant settings (e.g., academic settings and subjects, varied types of instruction) (Gresham & Lambros, 1998). However, it may not be possible to conduct observations of this type if the student has been removed to an alternate placement. In these instances, school professionals may be forced to rely on retrospective interviews with teachers or parents (i.e., PAIs) and generate hypotheses regarding behavior function based on these data alone. Third, others have argued that results of FBAs often dictate changing some aspect of the child's instructional environment, which is viewed as a challenge for many schools and serves as a barrier to continued implementation of FBA procedures (Gartin & Murdick, 2001). Further, school personnel tend to focus on the topography of problem behavior as opposed to its operant function (Alberto & Troutman, 2003). Fourth, dynamics within the multidisciplinary IEP team may impede the assessment process. Jolivette, Barton-Arwood, and Scott (2000) have suggested that the varying perspectives, expertise, levels of commitment, working styles, and roles of team members may result in failure to conduct the assessment process in an effective manner consistent with the intent of IDEA and best practices.

Conducting Functional Analyses of Behavior in Naturalistic Settings

Given the described barriers to conducting a comprehensive FBA, consulting teams may consider identifying the situational determinants of problem behavior through a school-based functional analysis. As an example, a behavioral consultant might hypothesize that a student refuses to do schoolwork to gain attention from the teacher or to escape an overly difficult assignment. To determine which hypothesis is accurate, the consultant might ask the teacher to provide attention for every instance of work refusal on some occasions and to send the child to time-out for work refusal on other occasions. If work refusal increases as a result of sending the child to time-out, then the consultant might conclude that the behavior is maintained by escape from task demands (i.e., a negative-reinforcement contingency).

Several decisions must be made prior to conducting an FA in school settings (Sterling-Turner, Robinson, et al., 2001). First, one must consider the setting in which the analysis is to take place. This may occur within the classroom itself or in an analogue setting within the school building. Greater experimental control is typically afforded in analogue settings; however, the generalizability of results from these settings to the classroom may be compromised. Next, one must determine the type of experimental design or strategy that will be used to compare the various test conditions. Options reported in the literature have included the multielement or alternating treatments design with clearly specified conditions (Iwata et al., 1982/1994), contingency reversals (e.g., Sterling-Turner, Robinson, et al., 2001), brief functional analyses with test conditions lasting 5–10 minutes each, and sequential or hierarchical applications (e.g., Daly et al., 1999). Finally, the behavioral consultant must decide whether antecedent conditions, in addition to or in lieu of consequences, will also be included in the analysis.

Sterling-Turner, Robinson, et al. (2001) examined the effects of an intervention plan that incorporated data from an experimental analysis (i.e., FA) in combination with descriptive functional assessment information (i.e., FBA) on the inappropriate behavior of a 13-year-old boy with a learning disability. Based on the results of the indirect/descriptive assessments, the researchers hypothesized that his behavior (spitball throwing) was maintained by attention (social-positive reinforcement). However, it was unclear regarding whether teacher or peer attention was serving as the reinforcer. The researchers compared the conditions thought to maintain appropriate behavior with those thought to maintain inappropriate behavior using a procedure known as contingency reversal in an alternating treatments design. Specifically, the teacher provided verbal reprimands (i.e., attention) following each instance of spitball throwing. These data were compared to a condition in which the teacher provided attention on a fixed time schedule (every 2 minutes) and ignored spitball throwing. Results of this analysis revealed that the student's behavior was not affected by teacher attention. Next, the same conditions were implemented by classroom peers. That is, peers were trained to provide attention for spitball throwing in one condition and to ignore the behavior but provide attention every 2 minutes at other times. Following this contingency reversal, problem behavior increased when peer attention was provided. Thus, the researchers concluded that peer attention reinforced the inappropriate behavior. An intervention plan based on these data produced zero rates of problem behavior within 1 week.

Although results of an FA may increase our confidence in the variables maintaining problem behavior, its feasibility within school settings has been questioned. Some suggest that FA data are unnecessary for intervention planning, and that the time investment for conducting experimental analyses is a major obstacle to its utility (Axelrod, 1987; Lee & Miltenberger, 1997). Additional barriers include (a) psychologists' lack of training in the procedures; (b) efforts required to maximize experimental control; (c) failure to obtain administrative approval to devote time to this type of assessment process; and (d) varying perspectives/theoretical orientations to assessment.

Recruiting Teacher Involvement

As with FBAs, consulting teams may find it difficult to conduct school-based FAs on a regular basis. One potential solution to this problem is to recruit teacher assistance in conducting the analysis. Preliminary evidence suggests that teachers may be trained to collect and interpret FA data with a high degree of integrity (Sterling-Turner, Robinson, et al., 2001). Using a multiple-baseline-across-subjects design, Moore et al. (2002) examined the effects of two types of training on teachers' percentage of correct responses in conducting two conditions of a functional analysis (demand vs. attention conditions). Teachers initially received written and verbal information regarding conditions of the FA and then were asked to conduct a simulated FA after 1 day. Results of this phase were compared to teachers' performance in the simulation when exposed to a training package consisting of rehearsal, modeling, and performance feedback (PF). Results revealed low levels of correct responses when teachers were provided with written and verbal information alone. However, their percentage of correct responses increased during the rehearsal, modeling, and PF condition. In addition, when asked to conduct the analysis in a classroom setting with students, high levels of integrity were maintained. These data suggest that teachers are able to implement at least some conditions of an FA (i.e., attention and demand) with a high degree of accuracy.

Asmus, Vollmer, and Borrero (2002) provided a comprehensive, data-driven model that incorporated both teacher and parental involvement when conducting FBAs and FAs. The first phase of this model included a descriptive assessment during which information regarding antecedents and consequences was gathered through direct observation. They recommended that observations be conducted in the school or home for up to 5 hours or until the target behavior has been observed numerous times. The next phase included a functional analysis of problem behavior to identify reinforcers maintaining its occurrence with confidence. This phase also included a systematic analysis of potential treatments under controlled, analogue settings (i.e., a BEA) and with crisis management as needed. The final phase of this model was to communicate with the family and teacher, train individuals accordingly, and facilitate generalization of the intervention. Training during this phase included didactic instruction, role-play, modeling, corrective feedback, and follow-up. Although this model may be considered best practice, it is costly in terms of personnel, time, finances, and other resources making it difficult for school districts to replicate. Given the potential challenges of conducting FBAs in school settings, alternative approaches to identifying effective, evidence-based interventions for children's learning and behavior problems are discussed in the next section.

SELECTING EVIDENCE-BASED BEHAVIORAL INTERVENTIONS

Large numbers of children in the United States continue to have significant difficulties with basic academic skills (e.g., reading and math). The National Center for Education Statistics (2004) reported in its most recent evaluation of fourth-grade students' reading achievement that 37% of children tested read below the basic level. Percentages of African American and Hispanic children reading below basic level are even higher (60% and 56%, respectively), as is the percentage of children who qualify for free/reduced-price lunch (55%). Reading below basic level means that children lack even "partial mastery of prerequisite knowledge and skills that are fundamental for proficient work at each grade" (p. 2). Whereas 797,213 students nationwide were classified as LD in 1976–1977, this number grew to 2.8 million in 1998–1999, a 351% increase (U.S. Department of Education, 2000). Approximately 3–5% of school-age children are diagnosed with attention deficit/hyperactivity disorder (ADHD), 5–9% are diagnosed with emotional disturbance, and early school failure has been linked to peer rejection, conduct disorder, and later criminal behavior (DuPaul, Eckert, & McGoey, 1997; Patterson, Reid, & Dishion, 1992; Walker, 2004).

Many have argued that one reason for the relative ineffectiveness of the American public education system with difficult-to-teach or low-achieving students is its failure to adopt evidence-based instructional and intervention programs (Lindsley, 1992; Walker, 2004). As noted by Carnine (1992), dogma rather than science has often dictated educational reform over the years, enabling fads to cycle through the schools with no demonstrable improvements in instruction. Lindsley (1992) stated that the "fate of highly productive educational methods in public instruction is a national shame" (p. 21), citing direct instruction (DI) as a prime example. DI is an instructional program that requires the use of scripted routines by teachers to promote the sequential development of student skills according to the instructional hierarchy (i.e., acquisition, fluency, maintenance, generalization) (Becker, 1992; Begeny & Martens, 2006). DI was one of several instructional programs evaluated in Project Follow Through based on pre- and posttest scores on various measures in comparison to a control group. The data suggested that students receiving DI outperformed those receiving all other instructional programs on basic skill, comprehension, and affective measures (Becker, 1992; Watkins, 1997). Nevertheless, DI was never promoted or disseminated on a large scale, and the majority of preservice special education teachers (86%) continue to receive little or no training in the DI model (Begeny & Martens, 2006). Lindsley went on to cite philosophical differences about the value of teacher-directed learning, fluency building through practice, competition in the workplace, and the dissemination of achievement test scores as primary reasons for DI's relative obscurity.

What is meant by evidence-based practices? In the late 1990s, task forces were commissioned by separate divisions of the American Psychological Association (i.e., clinical, counseling, and school psychology) to develop criteria for use in evaluating research on psychological and educational interventions (Kratochwill & Stoiber, 2000). More recently, NCLB called on educational practitioners to use scientifically-based research to guide their decisions about which interventions to implement (U.S. Department of Education, 2003). The gold standard for such research was similar to that described by the various task forces and included statistically significant effect sizes (ESs) calculated from valid, real-world measures of children's behavior or achievement. Moreover, NCLB identified randomized controlled trials as providing the strongest evidence of intervention efficacy.

Results From Meta-Analytic Reviews

The emphasis on using evidence-based practices in both psychology and education means that behavioral consultants need to be knowledgeable about which interventions are effective and which are not (Erchul & Martens, 2002). One approach to making quantitative comparisons among treatments across large numbers of original research studies is known as meta-analysis (Smith & Glass, 1977). For each treatment study in a meta-analysis, the mean of the control group is subtracted from the mean of the treatment group, and the difference is divided by the standard deviation of the control group. The resulting ES statistic represents the change in scores for an average child in the treatment group expressed in standard deviation or z-score units of the control group. Cohen (1992) suggested that ESs be characterized as small (0.20), moderate (0.50), or large (0.80).

Literally hundreds of meta-analytic reviews of treatment research were conducted in the course of 20 years (Lipsey & Wilson, 1993). Many of these evaluated behavioral instruction or management strategies and are therefore particularly relevant to BC. For example, L. S. Fuchs and D. Fuchs (1986) reviewed 21 studies comparing the academic achievement of students whose teachers frequently monitored their progress (i.e., collected curriculum-based measures of academic performance at least twice a week) and those who did not. An overall ES of 0.70 was obtained for students whose teachers engaged in systematic formative evaluation, and this value increased to over 1.0 when a behavior modification strategy was included. DuPaul and Eckert (1997) conducted a meta-analysis of 63 studies evaluating the effects of school-based academic, behavioral, and cognitive-behavioral interventions for children with ADHD. The mean weighted ES across studies using within-subject group designs was 0.94 for behavioral interventions, 0.69 for academic interventions, and 0.19 for cognitive-behavioral interventions with this population. Erchul and Martens (2002) summarized the results of 10 common approaches to school-based intervention based on meta-analyses conducted by Kavale (1990) and Lipsey and Wilson (1993). ESs were −0.12 for special class placement for students with mild disabilities, 0.14 for modality-based instruction, 0.59 for peer tutoring, and 1.17 for reinforcement-based programs.

In terms of instructional interventions, Chard, Vaughn, and Tyler (2002) reviewed 24 studies evaluating the effectiveness of various strategies for improving oral reading fluency in children with LD. Interventions were categorized as involving repeated reading (RR) without modeling by an adult; RR with modeling (e.g., listening passage preview [LPP]); RR with multiple features (e.g., peer tutoring, comprehension strategies); RR with other intervention elements (e.g., use of instructional or mastery-level text, performance criteria) and word practice (e.g., phrase drill error correction). The average ES for RR without modeling was 0.68. For RR with modeling, ESs were larger when an adult modeled fluent reading (0.46 to 0.57) versus a peer (0.17). The average ES across studies for RR interventions with multiple features was 0.71, whereas use of mastery-level text was associated with an average ES of 1.57. Based on their review, Chard et al. (2002) concluded that RR was an effective means of increasing reading accuracy, rate, and comprehension. They went on to suggest that effective interventions for oral reading fluency should contain one or more of the following components: (a) use of instructionally matched text, (b) live modeling of fluent reading by an adult, (c) RRs of the same passage by the student, (d) corrective feedback for words missed, and (e) increases in the difficulty level of text based on a performance criterion.

Although not meta-analyses of treatment procedures per se, two additional studies evaluated aspects of BC related to issues discussed in the last section (i.e., conducting FBAs). Gresham et al. (2004) reviewed 150 school-based intervention studies published in the *Journal of Applied Behavior Analysis*. The goal of this review was to compare ESs for published school-based interventions that were or were not based on a pretreatment assessment of the operant function of problem behavior. A mean ES of 6.77 was reported for treatments in studies that did not include an FBA. A mean ES of 4.60 was reported for studies in which an FA was conducted, 0.70 for studies in which an FBA was conducted, and 2.18 for studies with combined FBA/FA procedures. Of the studies sampled, 52% did not conduct an FBA but apparently "relied on strong reinforcers and/or punishers which overrode the conditions maintaining behavior" (p. 26). Two findings from this study are worth noting. First, larger ESs were obtained for studies in which an FA rather than an FBA were conducted. Second, although a larger ES was obtained for non-FBA studies, the standard deviation of ES statistics for these studies was more than three times higher (18.69) than that of the other categories (7.62, 5.07, 1.37).

Beavers, Kratochwill, and Braden (2004) compared two approaches for selecting school-based interventions when consulting with teachers about children's reading problems. Thirty-two students across 18 teachers were randomly assigned to one of two conditions. The first condition was termed *functional assessment* and involved questions by the consultant about five common reasons why children exhibit academic performance problems (e.g., motivation problems, lack of practice, inadequate prompting and feedback, poor instructional match). The second condition was termed *empiric* and involved questions by the consultant about the topographies of reading problems that were then matched to interventions recommended in a published treatment manual. The mean ES for cases in which treatment was based on the answers to functional assessment questions by the consultant was 0.63 ($SD = 0.50$). The mean ES for cases in which treatment selection was dictated by the manual was 0.48 ($SD = 0.61$). Thus, both approaches to treatment selection produced moderate ESs, the means of which were not significantly different.

Several implications for behavioral consultants can be drawn from the meta-analytic reviews of school-based interventions described (Erchul & Martens, 2002). It is clear that some interventions are more effective on average than others, and the steps involved in implementing these procedures are readily available from multiple published and Web-based sources (e.g., Shinn, Walker, & Stoner, 2002; www.interventioncentral.org). Behavioral consultants and consulting teams, therefore, have a responsibility to be familiar with and know how to implement effective intervention strategies in their schools. Generally, interventions for children's academic problems appear to be more effective if they (a) target developmentally appropriate skills; (b) involve instructionally matched materials, frequent progress monitoring (e.g., systematic formative evaluation), and resulting instructional changes as necessary; (c) allow for brief, repeated practice opportunities with modeling, prompting, and corrective feedback (e.g., LPP and RRs); and (d) include incentives for improvements in performance such as goal setting, performance charting, and reinforcement (Daly, Witt, Martens, & Dool, 1997; Martens & Witt, 2004). For children's behavior problems, reinforcement programs tend to produce consistently large ESs with or without a pretreatment functional analysis. For children with ADHD, differential reinforcement of alternative or desired behavior appears to be more effective than cognitive-behavioral strategies on average. Although effective reinforcement-based programs can be developed without conducting an FBA, doing so appears to decrease variability in intervention effectiveness. On average, treatment programs derived from an analysis of potential maintaining variables appear to be more effective if an FA rather than a descriptive FBA was conducted.

Conducting Brief Experimental Analyses

When two or more school-based interventions seem appropriate for a given problem even after consulting the literature, it may be useful to directly compare the effectiveness of these alternatives by conducting a BEA (e.g., Daly et al., 1999). A BEA typically involves a small number of exposures (e.g., 1–3) to each of several treatment options while monitoring effects on behavior using some form of direct assessment (e.g., curriculum-based probes, systematic observations). The various treatment procedures compared may be implemented in an alternating fashion (i.e., a multielement design), sequentially beginning with the simplest or least intrusive procedure or sequentially beginning with a single component and then adding additional components (Martens, Eckert et al., 1999). When interventions are evaluated sequentially, a brief return to baseline followed by reinstatement of the most effective alternative (i.e., a mini-withdrawal) is often included to allow for stronger conclusions about treatment efficacy.

Although conducting a BEA may delay plan implementation by several days, the savings in time and resources from implementing an ineffective procedure and recycling back through the problem analysis stage may be considerable. BEAs also give behavioral consultants or consulting teams the opportunity to work through logistics related to program design and monitoring prior to full-blown implementation (Martens, Eckert et al., 1999). Involving teachers in conducting the various test conditions can be one way of familiarizing them with procedures that will later be used in treatment. Moreover, presenting data to teachers showing clear improvements in child behavior under one or more treatment conditions (i.e., demonstrating efficacy) may improve perceptions of treatment acceptability or subsequent implementation integrity.

BEAs have been used to inform treatment selection for a wide range of child problems, including oral reading fluency, spelling accuracy, off-task behavior, and compliance (e.g., Daly, Martens, Dool, & Hintze, 1998; Harding, Wacker, Cooper, Millard, & Jensen-Kovalan, 1994; Kern, Childs, Dunlap, Clarke, & Falk, 1994; Martens, Eckert et al., 1999; McComas et al., 1996). For example, Daly et al. (1999) evaluated the effects of five intervention components grouped hierarchically on students' oral reading fluency in both trained and untrained, high-content-overlap passages. Intervention components that were compared included contingent reinforcement (CR) for rapid reading, RR alone, LPP + RR, LPP + RR + instructionally matched (IM) passages, and LPP + RR + sequential modification (SM) across passages. The combinations of RR + SM, LPP + RR + SM, or LPP + RR + IM produced the largest fluency gains, more than doubling oral reading rate in the generalization passages. Daly et al. (1998) conducted a similar analysis that incorporated phrase drill (PD) error correction into the LPP component. Again, reading rate more than doubled for each participant under at least one combination of strategies. Eckert, Ardoin, Daly, and Martens (2002) compared brief exposures to LPP + RR alone and in combination with PF and/or CR. The largest gains in oral reading fluency were obtained when LPP + RR was combined with either PF or CR for five of the six participants.

Chafouleas, Martens, Dobson, Weinstein, and Gardner (2004) conducted a BEA to evaluate the effectiveness of three instructional packages for students with different reading profiles. The instructional packages consisted of practice alone via RRs, practice plus PF, and practice plus PF plus contingent reward. The two students with the highest reading and lowest error rates at baseline (i.e., the most accurate readers) showed the greatest gains in oral reading fluency under the practice alone condition. By contrast, the student with the lowest fluency and highest error rates at baseline (i.e., the least accurate reader) benefited more from the practice plus feedback and practice plus feedback plus reward conditions. The authors concluded that adding PF and reinforcement to the practice condition focused the latter student's attention on reading accuracy, thereby helping to bring fluent reading under stimulus control of the printed text. The other two readers merely needed practice to increase their fluency levels because stimulus control by the printed text had already been established.

Although BEAs can be useful in selecting among different treatment options, they require skills similar to those involved in conducting an FA (e.g., the experimental manipulation of antecedents or consequences, use of single-case design elements, measurement of behavior under different conditions). In addition, they may only be appropriate for certain types of treatments, namely, those that are expected to produce immediate changes in behavior (e.g., contingency management programs, DI). As such, BEAs may be difficult to conduct for some school personnel due to lack of training or experience or impractical for some types of treatment (e.g., systematic desensitization). The extent to which brief exposures to treatment predict outcomes after lengthier implementation is still unclear, although results from initial studies in this area have been promising (e.g., Jones & Wickstrom, 2002).

PREPARING TEACHERS FOR THE CONSULTEE ROLE

As mentioned at the outset of the chapter, the principal goal of BC is to design, implement, and evaluate school-based interventions for children's learning and behavior problems. As originally conceived (Bergan, 1977), this goal was to be accomplished within the boundaries of a consultative relationship by adhering to the four-stage problem-solving process during the PII, PAI, and PEI. To represent different, more intensive, or even special approaches to instruction and classroom management, interventions designed as part of the BC process typically rely on some form of DI (e.g., word list training with error correction) or programmed reinforcement (e.g., token economies or point systems). Consistent with the core characteristics of consultation in general, teachers are primarily responsible for implementing agreed-on plans with support from the behavioral consultant.

Teachers, parents, or other direct-care providers (e.g., hospital staff) must engage in a variety of behaviors when assuming the role of consultee. During the PII and PAI, consultees are expected to meet face-to-face with the consultant; provide detailed descriptions of the target child's problem behavior; and describe important, controllable, and causal influences on problem behavior that occur in the classroom. An explicit goal of the PII is to establish procedures for data collection to be used by teachers during baseline and intervention conditions (Erchul & Martens, 2002). To be sensitive to short-term improvements in child behavior, these procedures typically involve some form of event recording, time sampling, or curriculum-based measurement (Martens, Eckert et al., 1999). As primary treatment agents, consultees must learn how to implement agreed-on plans correctly and must conduct a sufficient number of intervention episodes to evaluate effects on child behavior (Lentz & Daly, 1996). Learning an intervention plan may mean that consultees memorize a step-by-step protocol, watch the consultant model its use, practice the procedure while the consultant looks on, implement the plan in the regular classroom during instructional periods, and correct implementation errors in response to PF (e.g., Hiralall & Martens, 1998; Noell et al., 1997). For the PEI, teachers may be asked to graph child outcome data or interpret graphs that are prepared for them. In short, assuming the role of consultee often requires that teachers engage in assessment, instructional, managerial, or data evaluation activities that differ from their typical teaching behaviors.

How much training do teachers receive in skills related to the BC process? Begeny and Martens (2006) conducted a survey of 110 preservice teachers enrolled in master-level teacher preparation programs at six universities and colleges in the Northeast. Participants included 39 teachers in elementary education programs, 35 in secondary education programs, and 36 in special education programs. Most respondents to the survey were Caucasian (96%) and female (81%), with a mean age of 28 years.

The survey itself presented teachers with descriptions of 26 different empirically supported, behavioral assessment and instruction principles, strategies, and programs. Items on the survey were derived from a content analysis of textbooks in applied behavior analysis and education (e.g., Alberto & Troutman, 1999; Wolery, Bailey, & Sugai, 1988) and included strategies such as DI, curriculum-based measurement, peer tutoring, shaping, fading, and using bar graphs to make instructional decisions. Teachers were asked to respond to each item by indicating the extent to which the skill described was trained either in course work or applied training (e.g., practica, student teaching) using a 7-point scale (0 = none, 7 = full semester or more). Results in terms of course work training for a subset of 9 items from the survey is presented in Table 8.1. Values in the table indicate the percentage of teachers in each sample who received training in that item (i.e., a full class meeting to a full semester or more). As shown in the table, most teachers in the three certification programs reported little or no training in seven of the nine items. Exceptions included varied instruction and writing objectives. Interestingly, lower percentages of preservice special education teachers reported training on 5 of the 9 items in comparison to regular education elementary teachers.

Results of Begeny and Martens (2006) suggest that teachers (both special and regular education) are likely to have received little preservice training in the assessment and intervention strategies that behavioral consultants may expect them to implement. Implications of this finding for engaging teachers in the BC process are clear. First, it is unlikely that antecedent verbal instruction by a

Table 8.1 Preservice Teachers' Training in Nine Behavioral Instruction Practices

	Percentage of Sample Reporting Training in Instructional Practice		
Item	Elementary	Secondary	Special
Standard celeration chart	5	0	3
Direct instruction	13	12	14
Line or bar graph	13	11	14
Instructional hierarchy	49	32	33
Fading	41	29	36
CBM	23	23	39
Shaping	49	29	39
Varied instruction	84	68	63
Writing objectives	56	72	83

Note: CBM = curriculum-based measurement. Abstracted from Begeny and Martens (2006).

consultant will be sufficient to teach intervention plans to teachers prior to implementation (Martens & Ardoin, 2002; Witt, 1997). Although consultant verbal behaviors during the PII and PAI may be helpful in introducing a plan and providing a rationale for its use, research reviewed in the next section reinforces the notion that some form of ongoing implementation support is critical (Erchul & Martens, 2002).

Second, behavioral consultants must take seriously the goal of increasing consultees' ability to deal with similar problems in the future (Gutkin & Curtis, 1990). Given what is required of consultees for plan implementation, the BC process provides an excellent context for skill training. A skill-training view of BC may require consultants to take a more directive or prescriptive approach when working with consultees (Sterling-Turner, Watson, & Moore, 2002), although some have argued that this is inconsistent with consultation's core characteristics (Gutkin, 1999). Along these lines, Wickstrom, Jones, LaFleur, and Witt (1998) randomly assigned 29 consultant-teacher dyads to either a collaborative or prescriptive consultation condition. Collaborative consultation consisted of the behavioral consultant asking the teacher for input on 76% of PII and PAI interviewing objectives. For the prescriptive consultation condition, teachers were not asked to provide input on any of the interview objectives. In both conditions, teachers' intervention choices included a point or chart system to increase desired behavior or a response cost procedure to decrease problem behavior. One measure of treatment acceptability and three measures of treatment integrity, or the accuracy with which teachers implemented agreed on plans, were collected for each case: (a) teacher-completed scatterplot recordings of student disruptive behavior during 10-minute intervals throughout the school day once per week, (b) the presence of intervention materials during two observations, and (c) percentage of opportunities to deliver a programmed consequence by the teacher that were actually acted on during two observations. Results indicated that both consultation conditions were viewed as equally acceptable by consultees, and there were no significant differences for any of the three integrity measures.

Sterling-Turner et al. (2002) compared the effects of indirect, didactic instruction, and direct skill training on the integrity with which teacher's implemented agreed-on treatment plans. Four dyads, each consisting of a special education teacher or aide and a student with problem behavior, participated in the study. After an initial PII and PAI, teachers were given verbal instruction in how to implement steps of the agreed-on plan. The percentage of steps implemented correctly by each teacher was then monitored using a multiple-baseline design across dyads. Once implementation levels stabilized, teachers were directly trained in how to implement the plan using a combination of role-play, rehearsal, corrective feedback, and praise for correct steps. Low levels of treatment integrity were observed for three of the four teachers following didactic instruction. Integrity levels increased for all four teachers after direct skill training. Improvements in child behavior were associated with implementation integrity for two of the four dyads. Direct training involving rehearsal and feedback was also shown to produce higher levels of integrity relative to videotape modeling and didactic instruction in a sample of 64 undergraduate educational psychology students (Sterling-Turner, Watson, Wildmon, Watkins, & Little, 2001).

As noted, because of the triadic nature of consultation, responsibility for implementing interventions developed through the BC process rests with the teacher (Gutkin & Curtis, 1999). Most intervention plans require teachers who serve as consultees to acquire new instructional and behavior management skills and incorporate these skills into their teaching repertoire (Noell & Gresham, 1993). A critical aspect of effective consultation then is ensuring that consultees have acquired these skills and that consultee behavior change has occurred (Erchul & Martens, 2002). That is, consultants must confirm that interventions are consistently and accurately implemented by consultees (Gresham, 1989; Wickstrom et al., 1998). A critical area of study in BC therefore involves examining the conditions under which consultees will continue to implement interventions with integrity (Lentz & Daly, 1996). Addressing this issue typically involves an analysis of the antecedent and consequential conditions that promote desired teacher responding, verification of consultee behavior change through direct observation of intervention episodes, and calculation of the percentage of treatment steps implemented correctly (Lentz & Daly, 1996; Noell & Witt, 1996).

Noell and his colleagues conducted a series of investigations examining the conditions under which consultees demonstrate adequate treatment integrity (Mortenson & Witt, 1998; Noell et al., 1997; Witt, Noell, LaFleur, & Mortenson, 1997). Specifically, they examined teachers' treatment integrity after initial training and following exposure to a PF package. For example, Witt et al. (1997) investigated the effects of a PF package on the integrity with which teachers implemented a reinforcement-based program in their classrooms. Four female elementary teachers were asked to implement an intervention to increase task completion by four male students. The intervention plan was initially described to each teacher, materials needed to implement the intervention were provided, and the teacher was coached in how to implement the plan in the classroom until 100% integrity was observed. After training, teachers implemented the plan independently while integrity was monitored via use of permanent products. Teacher treatment integrity was calculated as a percentage by computing the number of correct permanent products divided by total number of treatment steps multiplied by 100%. In addition, student performance was calculated as the percentage of correct items on the daily academic assignment.

A nonconcurrent multiple-baseline design was used to evaluate the effects of a daily PF package that included meetings with the consultant to review teacher integrity data, discussion of missed steps, and both positive and corrective feedback. Results indicated that teachers obtained 100% integrity during initial training but exhibited an immediate downward trend (integrity was not maintained above 80% for more than 2 days). Application of the PF package resulted in increases in teacher treatment integrity. Two of the four teachers maintained integrity at 100% for 4 consecutive days, while the remaining two teachers achieved integrity at or above 80% for 3 or more consecutive days. Further, the interventions resulted in increased student performance initially, and subsequent increases in treatment integrity produced greater gains in academic performance for three of the students.

In a related study, Mortenson and Witt (1998) used a multiple-baseline design across teachers to examine the effects of weekly PF. The authors were interested in extending previous research by examining the effects of PF provided weekly as opposed to daily. Four teachers were required to implement an academic intervention on a daily basis for a student experiencing difficulty. At the end of each school day, teachers sent a fax to the consultant consisting of answers to three questions regarding student performance. The consultant verified the accuracy of this information weekly by examining permanent products. Following initial training and reduction of treatment integrity below 70%, weekly PF was provided to the consultees during a brief meeting (i.e., 5 to 7 minutes in duration) with the consultant. During the meeting, the consultant presented data on treatment integrity and student academic performance, provided positive and corrective feedback, answered any questions or concerns, obtained continued commitment by the consultee to carry out the intervention, reminded the consultee to send data via fax daily, and arranged a meeting for the following week. Results indicated somewhat lower and more variable levels of treatment integrity when PF was provided weekly as compared to daily. Although gains in student academic performance were generally found, these were also more variable with weekly feedback.

Other studies have suggested that teachers' implementation may be affected by simple contingencies of reinforcement (Gillat & Sulzer-Azaroff, 1994; Noell et al., 1997, 2000) in much the same way that student behavior is subject to contingencies of reinforcement (see also Lentz & Daly, 1996; Martens & Witt, 1988). Although earlier research applied social-positive reinforcement through verbal praise (e.g., Gillat & Sulzer-Azaroff, 1994), some recent findings suggest that negative reinforcement may be a viable alternative (e.g., DiGennaro, Martens, & McIntyre, 2005; Noell et al., 2000).

DiGennaro et al. (2005) examined this issue by evaluating the extent to which daily PF, practice, and the opportunity to avoid meetings with a consultant influenced the treatment integrity of four teachers and reduced students' problem behaviors. Teachers were trained initially in how to implement an intervention in their classroom using procedures similar to those used by Noell et al. (1997). After they were observed implementing the intervention on their own, teachers were given daily written feedback about their implementation accuracy (i.e., PF). During this condition, teachers were able to avoid meeting with a consultant for directed rehearsal (i.e., practicing each missed step three times) by demonstrating 100% integrity, thereby establishing a negative-reinforcement contingency for correct implementation. Using a multiple-baseline design across teachers, results of the study showed that integrity increased to 100% for all teachers following implementation of the PF/negative-reinforcement package. Integrity was maintained at high levels when the package was faded to once a week and then once every 2 weeks. Moderate decreases in problem behavior were observed for all four students. These data suggest that modeling, coaching, PF, and systematic arrangement of contingencies for correct implementation of intervention plans can be used to aid teachers in their behavior change efforts.

CONCLUSIONS

Before suggesting directions for future research in BC, it might be helpful to revisit BC's core characteristics in this era of high-stakes, team-based service delivery. We believe that BC can, and perhaps should, be conceptualized differently now from when it was originally conceived. First, in light of federal and state mandates for consultation services, the proliferation of prereferral intervention programs, emphasis on evidence-based interventions, and emerging RTI models, BC can no longer be seen as strictly involving (a) voluntary participation by the consultee, (b) the right of the consultee to reject consultant suggestions, and (c) absolute confidentiality of information shared during consultative interviews (cf. Erchul & Martens, 2002). Second, although BC remains an indirect service requiring cooperation between consultant and consultee, the responsibilities of these individuals has expanded. Research reviewed in this chapter suggests that behavioral consultants or consulting teams are responsible for conducting FBAs using a continuum of direct (e.g., client observations) and indirect (e.g., consultee interview) assessment methods; selecting a conceptually relevant intervention from among various evidence-based alternatives; using modeling, practice, and corrective feedback to train teachers in how to use the intervention; providing ongoing implementation support in the form of PF and reinforcement; and evaluating effects on child behavior and recommending more intensive intervention as appropriate.

Consultees, on the other hand, are responsible for contributing information to the FBA process by providing detailed descriptions in the PII and PAI; completing behavior rating or motivation assessment scales (e.g., Durand & Crimmins, 1988); or collecting direct observational data. When necessary for treatment selection, consultees may be asked to help implement a series of FA or BEA test conditions. Once an intervention has been selected, consultees are responsible for learning the intervention protocol and implementing the plan with sufficient integrity to evaluate its effects on child behavior. If the plan is effective, then consultees are expected to sustain implementation until the problem is solved.

FUTURE RESEARCH AGENDA FOR BEHAVIORAL CONSULTATION

Several directions for future research in BC are critical for behavioral consultants and consultees to fulfill expanded responsibilities. The chapter concludes by listing these directions as research questions in the areas of FBA/FA/BEA, evidence-based intervention in an RTI framework, and teacher training and support.

Conducting School-Based Analyses

1. Although it is clear that typical FBAs in school settings fall short of best practices, how and how often do behavioral consultants conduct FBAs, FAs, or BEAs, and what are the barriers to doing so?
2. What components or combination of components in a comprehensive FBA model have the greatest treatment utility yet are still efficient in terms of time and resources?
3. If FAs produce larger ESs than FBAs on average (e.g., Gresham et al., 2004), can standard functional analysis test conditions be adapted for classroom behavior problems?
4. Although preliminary data suggest that BEAs are predictive of outcomes following extended treatment implementation, is this the case for a variety of interventions or behavior problems?
5. When compared directly, does FBA, FA, or BEA have the greatest treatment utility? Which is most acceptable to school personnel?

Incorporating Evidence-Based Interventions in a Response-to-Intervention Model

1. RTI models require the evaluation of children's responsiveness to instruction at varying intensity levels (e.g., universal instruction in large groups, selected instruction in small groups, targeted individual instruction). Interventions developed during BC, however, have typically been individualized. How can these interventions be modified or new procedures developed for use with groups of students?
2. Although meta-analytic reviews suggest that some interventions are more effective on average than others (e.g., EBIs), can these be matched reliably to student learning and behavior

problems based on topography to produce strong results (e.g., Beavers et al., 2004)? Which student characteristics moderate the effectiveness of school-based interventions?

3. Whereas it is clear that treatment integrity should be monitored during plan implementation, the logic of RTI models suggests that the dosage level of intervention also should be monitored. What constitutes higher doses of school-based interventions for learning and behavior problems (e.g., cumulative intervention time per week, number of behaviors reinforced)?

4. Related to question #3 above, do implementation accuracy (i.e., integrity) and frequency (i.e., dose) contribute equally to intervention effectiveness?

Providing Teacher Training and Support

1. Consultant-implemented positive- and negative-reinforcement contingencies have been shown to increase implementation integrity. What contingencies are available at the administrative level (i.e., building, district), and how can these be applied to promote high levels of integrity?

2. Given the increased accountability of BC in general, would public posting of either teacher or student behavior change be an effective and acceptable way to promote implementation integrity by teachers?

3. Some research suggests that prescriptive consultation is as acceptable but more effective at increasing targeted consultee skills than collaborative consultation (e.g., Wickstrom et al., 1998). How much of the BC process can be put into standard protocols before it loses its effectiveness?

4. Finally, the data are clear in suggesting that we can no longer afford the luxury of a constructivist approach to preservice teacher training. Under the current model, teachers are not receiving the skills necessary to meet the needs of difficult-to-teach or low-achieving students. In the absence of effective teaching, learning becomes a function of individual differences. With this in mind, what are the short- and long-term effects of training teachers in evidence-based behavioral instruction and managerial practices, and to what extent do these generalize to the classroom setting? How can participation in the BC process be used best to increase skill acquisition by teachers?

REFERENCES

Alberto, P. A., & Troutman, A. C. (1999). *Applied behavior analysis for teachers* (5th ed.). Upper Saddle River, NJ: Merrill Prentice Hall.

Alberto, P. A., & Troutman, A. C. (2003). *Applied behavior analysis for teachers* (6th ed.). Upper Saddle River, NJ: Merrill Prentice Hall.

Alpert, J., & Yammer, M. D. (1983). Research in school consultation: A content analysis of selected journals. *Professional Psychology, 14*, 604–612.

Asmus, J. M., Vollmer, T. R., & Borrero, J. C. (2002). Functional behavioral assessment: A school-based model. *Education and Treatment of Children, 25*, 67–90.

Axelrod, S. (1987). Functional and structural analyses of behavior: Approaches leading to reduced use of punishment procedures? *Research in Developmental Disabilities, 8*, 165–178.

Beavers, K. F., Kratochwill, T. R., & Braden, J. P. (2004). Treatment utility of functional versus empiric assessment within consultation for reading problems. *School Psychology Quarterly, 19*, 29–49.

Becker, W. C. (1992). Direct instruction: A 20-year review. In R. P. West & L. A. Hamerlynch (Eds.), *Designs for excellence in education: The legacy of B. F. Skinner* (pp. 71–112). Longmont, CO: Sopris West.

Begeny, J. C., & Martens, B. K. (2006). Assessing pre-service teachers' training in empirically-validated behavioral instruction practices. *School Psychology Quarterly, 21*, 262–285.

Bergan, J. R. (1977). *Behavioral consultation.* Columbus, OH: Merrill.

Bergan, J. R., & Kratochwill, T. R. (1990). *Behavioral consultation and therapy.* New York: Plenum.

Bergan, J. R., & Neumann, A. J. (1980). The identification of resources and constraints influencing plan design in consultation. *Journal of School Psychology, 18,* 317–323.

Bergan, J. R., & Tombari, M. L. (1975). The analysis of verbal interactions occurring during consultation. *Journal of School Psychology, 13,* 209–226.

Bergan, J. R., & Tombari, M. L. (1976). Consultant skill and efficiency and the implementation and outcomes of consultation. *Journal of School Psychology, 14,* 3–14.

Bijou, S. W., Peterson, R. F., & Ault, M. H. (1968). A method to integrate descriptive and experimental field studies at the level of data and empirical concepts. *Journal of Applied Behavior Analysis, 1,* 175–191.

Braddock, D. (Ed.). (1999). *Positive behavior supports for people with developmental disabilities: A research synthesis.* Washington, DC: American Association of Mental Retardation.

Carnine, D. (1992). Expanding the notion of teachers' rights: Access to tools that work. *Journal of Applied Behavior Analysis, 25,* 13–19.

Carr, E. G., Newsom, C. D., & Binkoff, J. A. (1976). Stimulus control of self-destructive behavior in a psychotic child. *Journal of Abnormal Child Psychology, 4,* 139–153.

Chafouleas, S. M., Martens, B. K., Dobson, R. J., Weinstein, K. S., & Gardner, K. B. (2004). Fluent reading as the improvement of stimulus control: Additive effects of performance-based interventions to repeated reading on students' reading and error rates. *Journal of Behavioral Education, 13,* 67–81.

Chard, D. J., Vaughn, S., & Tyler, B. J. (2002). A synthesis of research on effective interventions for building reading fluency with elementary students with learning disabilities. *Journal of Learning Disabilities, 35,* 386–406.

Cohen, J. (1992). A power primer. *Psychological Bulletin, 112,* 155–159.

Daly, E. J., Martens, B. K., Dool, E. J., & Hintze, J. M. (1998). Using brief functional analysis to select interventions for oral reading. *Journal of Behavioral Education, 8,* 203–218.

Daly, E. J., Martens, B. K., Hamler, K., Dool, E. J., & Eckert, T. L. (1999). A brief experimental analysis for identifying instructional components needed to improve oral reading fluency. *Journal of Applied Behavior Analysis, 32,* 83–94.

Daly, E. J., Witt, J. C., Martens, B. K., & Dool, E. J. (1997). A model for conducting a functional analysis of academic performance problems. *School Psychology Review, 26,* 554–574.

DiGennaro, F. D., Martens, B. K., & McIntyre, L. L. (2005). Increasing treatment integrity through negative reinforcement: Effects on teacher and student behavior. *School Psychology Review, 34,* 220–231.

Drasgow, E., & Yell, M. L. (2001). Functional behavioral assessments: Legal requirements and challenges. *School Psychology Review, 30,* 239–251.

DuPaul, G. J., & Eckert, T. L. (1997). The effects of school-based interventions for attention-deficit/hyperactivity disorder: A meta-analysis. *School Psychology Review, 26,* 5–27.

DuPaul, G. J., Eckert, T. L., & McGoey, K. E. (1997). Interventions for students with attention-deficit/hyperactivity disorder: One size does not fit all. *School Psychology Review, 26,* 369–381.

Durand, V. M., & Crimmins, D. B. (1988). Identifying the variables maintaining self-injurious behavior. *Journal of Autism and Developmental Disorders, 18,* 99–117.

D'Zurilla, T. J., & Goldfried, M. R. (1971). Problem solving and behavior modification. *Journal of Abnormal Psychology, 78,* 107–126.

Eckert, T. L., Ardoin, S. P., Daly, E. J., & Martens, B. K. (2002). Improving oral reading fluency: A brief experimental analysis of combining an antecedent intervention with consequences. *Journal of Applied Behavior Analysis, 35,* 271–281.

Erchul, W. P., & Martens, B. K. (2002). *School consultation: Conceptual and empirical bases of practice* (2nd ed.). New York: Kluwer Academic/Plenum.

Ervin, R. A., Radford, P. M., Bertsch, K., Piper, A. L., Erhardt, K. E., & Poling, A. (2001). A descriptive analysis and critique of the empirical literature on school-based functional assessment. *School Psychology Review, 30,* 193–210.

Fuchs, D., Fuchs, L. S., & Bahr, M. W. (1990). Mainstream assistance teams: A scientific basis for the art of consultation. *Exceptional Children, 57,* 128–139.

Fuchs, D., Fuchs, L. S., & Bahr, M. W., Fernstrom, P., & Stecker, P. M. (1990). Prereferral intervention: A prescriptive approach. *Exceptional Children, 56,* 493–513.

Fuchs, L. S. (2003). Assessing intervention responsiveness: Conceptual and technical issues. *Learning Disabilities Research and Practice, 18*, 172–186.

Fuchs, L. S., & Fuchs, D. (1986). Effects of systematic formative evaluation: A meta-analysis. *Exceptional Children, 53*, 199–208.

Gartin, B. C., & Murdick, N. L. (2001). A new IDEA mandate: The use of functional assessment of behavior and positive behavior supports. *Remedial and Special Education, 22*, 344–349.

Gillat, A., & Sulzer-Azaroff, B. (1994). Promoting principals' managerial involvement in instructional improvement. *Journal of Applied Behavior Analysis, 27*, 115–129.

Goldstein, A. P., & Martens, B. K. (2000). *Lasting change: Methods for enhancing generalization of gain.* Champaign, IL: Research Press.

Graden, J. L., Casey, A., & Bonstrom, O. (1985). Implementing a prereferral intervention system: Part II. The data. *Exceptional Children, 51*, 487–496.

Gresham, F. M. (1989). Assessment of treatment integrity in school consultation and prereferral intervention. *School Psychology Review, 18*, 37–50.

Gresham, F. M. (2004). Current status and future directions of school-based behavioral interventions. *School Psychology Review, 33*, 326–343.

Gresham, F. M., & Lambros, K. M. (1998). Behavioral and functional assessment. In T. S. Watson & F. M. Gresham (Eds.), *Handbook of child behavior therapy* (pp. 3–22). New York: Plenum.

Gresham, F. M., McIntyre, L. L., Olson-Tinker, H., Dolstra, L., McLaughlin, V., & Van, M. (2004). Relevance of functional behavioral assessment research for school-based interventions and positive behavioral support. *Research in Developmental Disabilities, 25*, 19–37.

Gutkin, T. B. (1999). Collaborative versus directive/prescriptive/expert school-based consultation: Reviewing and resolving a false dichotomy. *Journal of School Psychology, 37*, 161–190.

Gutkin T. B., & Curtis, M. J. (1982). School-based consultation: Theory and techniques. In C. R. Reynolds & T. B. Gutkin (Eds.), *The handbook of school psychology* (pp. 796–828). New York: Wiley.

Gutkin, T. B., & Curtis, M. J. (1990). School-based consultation: Theory, techniques, and research. In T. B. Gutkin & C. R. Reynolds (Eds.), *The handbook of school psychology* (2nd ed., pp. 577–611). New York: Wiley.

Gutkin, T. B., & Curtis, M. J. (1999). School-based consultation theory and practice: The art and science of indirect service delivery. In C. R. Reynolds & T. B. Gutkin (Eds.), *The handbook of school psychology* (3rd ed., pp. 598–637). New York: Wiley.

Gutkin, T. B., Henning-Stout, M., & Piersel, W. C. (1988). Impact of a district-wide behavioral consultation prereferral intervention service on patterns of school psychological service delivery. *Professional School Psychology, 3*, 301–308.

Hanley, G. P., Iwata, B. A., & McCord, B. E. (2003). Functional analysis of problem behavior: A review. *Journal of Applied Behavior Analysis, 36*, 147–185.

Harding, J., Wacker, D. P., Cooper, L. J., Millard, T., & Jensen-Kovalan, P. (1994). Brief hierarchical assessment of potential treatment components with children in an outpatient clinic. *Journal of Applied Behavior Analysis, 27*, 291–300.

Heller, K., Holtzman, W., & Messick, S. (Eds.). (1982). *Placement of children in special education: A strategy for equity.* Washington, DC: National Academy Press.

Hiralall, A. S., & Martens, B. K. (1998). Teaching classroom management skills to preschool staff: The effects of scripted instructional sequences on teacher and student behavior. *School Psychology Quarterly, 13*, 94–115.

Iwata, B. A., Dorsey, M. F., Slifer, K. J., Bauman, K. E., & Richman, G. S. (1994). Toward a functional analysis of self-injury. *Journal of Applied Behavior Analysis, 27*, 215–240. (Reprinted from *Analysis and Intervention in Developmental Disabilities, 2*, 1–20, 1982)

Jolivette, K., Barton-Arwood, S., & Scott, T. M. (2000). Functional behavioral assessment as a collaborative process among professionals. *Education and Treatment of Children, 23*, 298–313.

Jones, K. M., & Wickstrom K. F. (2002). Done in 60 seconds: Further analysis of the brief assessment model for academic problems. *School Psychology Review, 31*, 554–568.

Kavale, K. (1990). Effectiveness of special education. In T. B. Gutkin & C. R. Reynolds (Eds.), *Handbook of school psychology* (2nd ed., pp. 868–898). New York: Wiley.

Kern, L., Childs, K. E., Dunlap, G., Clarke, S., & Falk, G. D. (1994). Using assessment-based curricular intervention to improve the classroom behavior of a student with emotional and behavioral challenges. *Journal of Applied Behavior Analysis, 27*, 7–19.

Knoster, T. P. (2000). Practical application of functional behavioral assessments in schools. *Journal of the Association for Persons With Severe Handicaps, 25,* 201–211.

Kratochwill, T. R., Elliott, S. N., & Callan-Stoiber, K. (2002). Best practices in school-based problem-solving consultation. In A. Thomas and J. Grimes (Eds.), *Best practices in school psychology IV* (pp. 583–608). Bethesda, MD: The National Association of School Psychologists.

Kratochwill, T. R., & Stoiber, K. C. (2000). Diversifying theory and science: Expanding the boundaries of empirically supported interventions in school psychology. *Journal of School Psychology, 38,* 349–358.

Lalli, J. S., Browder, D. M., Mace, F. C., & Brown, D. K. (1993). Teacher use of descriptive analysis data to implement interventions to decrease students' problem behavior. *Journal of Applied Behavior Analysis, 26,* 227–238.

Lee, M. I., & Miltenberger, R. G. (1997). Functional assessment and binge eating: A review of the literature and suggestions for future research. *Behavior Modification, 21,* 159–171.

Lentz, F. E., & Daly, E. J. (1996). Is the behavior of academic change agents controlled metaphysically? An analysis of the behavior of those who change behavior. *School Psychology Quarterly, 11,* 337–352.

Lerman, D. C., & Iwata, B. A. (1993). Descriptive and experimental analyses of variables maintaining self-injurious behavior. *Journal of Applied Behavior Analysis, 26,* 293–319.

Lindsley, O. R. (1992). Why aren't effective teaching tools widely adopted? *Journal of Applied Behavior Analysis, 25,* 21–26.

Lipsey, M. W., & Wilson, D. B. (1993). The efficacy of psychological, educational, and behavioral treatment: Confirmation from meta-analysis. *American Psychologist, 48,* 1181–1209.

Lovaas, O. I., & Simmons, J. Q. (1969). Manipulation of self-destruction in three retarded children. *Journal of Applied Behavior Analysis, 2,* 143–157.

Mace, F. C., & Lalli, J. S. (1991). Linking descriptive and experimental analyses in the treatment of bizarre speech. *Journal of Applied Behavior Analysis, 24,* 553–562.

Martens, B. K. (2004). *Helping teachers with plan implementation.* Invited workshop for the Syracuse City School District SBIT Veteran Training, Syracuse, NY, December 2004.

Martens, B. K., & Ardoin, S. P. (2002). Training school psychologists in behavior support consultation. *Child and Family Behavior Therapy, 24,* 147–163.

Martens, B. K., Eckert, T. L., Bradley, T. A., & Ardoin, S. P. (1999). Identifying effective treatments from a brief experimental analysis: Using single-case design elements to aid decision making. *School Psychology Quarterly, 14,* 163–181.

Martens, B. K., Erchul, W. P., & Witt, J. C. (1992). Quantifying verbal interactions in school-based consultation: A comparison of four coding schemes. *School Psychology Review, 21,* 109–124.

Martens, B. K., Peterson, R. L., Witt, J. C., & Cirone, S. (1986). Teacher perceptions of school based interventions. *Exceptional Children, 53,* 213–223.

Martens, B. K., & Witt, J. C. (1988). Expanding the scope of behavioral consultation: A systems approach to classroom behavior change. *Professional School Psychology, 3,* 271–281.

Martens, B. K., & Witt, J. C. (2004). Competence, persistence, and success: The positive psychology of behavioral skill instruction. *Psychology in the Schools, 41,* 19–30.

Martens, B. K., Witt, J. C., Daly, E. J., & Vollmer, T. (1999). Behavior analysis: Theory and practice in educational settings. In C. R. Reynolds & T. B. Gutkin (Eds.), *Handbook of school psychology* (3rd ed., pp. 638–663). New York: Wiley.

McComas, J. J., Wacker, D. P., Cooper, L. J., Asmus, J. M., Richman, D., & Stoner, B. (1996). Brief experimental analysis of stimulus prompts for accurate responding on academic tasks in an outpatient clinic. *Journal of Applied Behavior Analysis, 29,* 397–401.

McDougal, J. L., Clonan, S. M., & Martens, B. K. (2000). Using organizational change procedures to promote the acceptability of prereferral intervention services: The school-based intervention team project. *School Psychology Quarterly, 15,* 149–171.

Medway, F. J. (1982). School consultation research: Past trends and future directions. *Professional Psychology, 13,* 422–430.

Moore, J. W., Edwards, R. P., Sterling-Turner, H. E., Riley, J., DuBard, M., & McGeorge, A. (2002). Teacher acquisition of functional analysis methodology. *Journal of Applied Behavior Analysis, 35,* 73–77.

Mortenson, B. P., & Witt, J. C. (1998). The use of weekly performance feedback to increase teacher implementation of a prereferral academic intervention. *School Psychology Review, 27,* 613–627.

National Center for Educational Statistics. (2004). *The nation's report card: Reading highlights 2003.* Washington, DC: U.S. Department of Education.

Nelson, J. R., Roberts, N., Mathur, S., & Rutherford, R. (1999). Has public policy exceeded our knowledge base? A review of the functional behavioral assessment literature. *Behavioral Disorders, 24,* 169–179.

Noell, G. H., & Gresham, F. M. (1993). Functional outcome analysis: Do the benefits of consultation and pre-referral intervention justify the costs? *School Psychology Quarterly, 8,* 200–226.

Noell, G. H., & Witt, J. C. (1996). A critical re-evaluation of five fundamental assumptions underlying behavioral consultation. *School Psychology Quarterly, 11,* 189–203.

Noell, G. H., Witt, J. C., Gilbertson, D. N., Ranier, D. D., & Freeland, J. T. (1997). Increasing teacher intervention implementation in general education settings through consultation and performance feedback. *School Psychology Quarterly, 12,* 77–88.

Noell, G. H., Witt, J. C., LaFleur, L. H., Mortenson, B. P., Ranier, D. D., & LeVelle, J. (2000). Increasing intervention implementation in general education following consultation: A comparison of two follow-up strategies. *Journal of Applied Behavior Analysis, 33,* 271–284.

OSEP Questions and Answers. (1999, March 12). 64(48) *Fed. Reg.* 12617–12632.

Patterson, G. R., Reid, J. B., & Dishion, T. J. (1992). *Antisocial boys.* Eugene, OR: Castalia.

Piersel, W. C., & Gutkin, T. B. (1983). Resistance to school-based consultation: A behavioral analysis of the problem. *Psychology in the Schools, 20,* 311–320.

Reppucci, N. D., & Saunders, J. T. (1974). Social psychology of behavior modification: Problems of implementation in natural settings. *American Psychologist, 29,* 649–660.

Rosenfield, S. (1992). Developing school-based consultation teams: A design for organizational change. *School Psychology Quarterly, 7,* 27–46.

Sheridan, S. M., Welch, M., & Orme, S. F. (1996). Is consultation effective? A review of outcome research. *Remedial and Special Education, 17,* 341–354.

Shinn, M. R., Walker, H. M., & Stoner, G. (2002). *Interventions for academic and behavior problems II: Preventive and remedial approaches.* Bethesda, MD: National Association of School Psychologists.

Smith, M. L., & Glass, G. V. (1977). Meta-analysis of psychotherapy outcome studies. *American Psychologist, 32,* 752–760.

Sterling-Turner, H. E., Robinson, S. L., & Wilczynski, S. M. (2001). Functional assessment of distracting and disruptive behaviors in the school setting. *School Psychology Review, 30,* 211–226.

Sterling-Turner, H. E., Watson, T. S., & Moore, J. W. (2002). The effects of direct training and treatment integrity on treatment outcomes in school consultation. *School Psychology Quarterly, 17,* 47–77.

Sterling-Turner, H. E., Watson, T. S., Wildmon, M., Watkins, C., & Little, E. (2001). Investigating the relationship between training type and treatment integrity. *School Psychology Quarterly, 16,* 56–67.

Tharp, R. G., & Wetzel, R. J. (1969). *Behavior modification in the natural environment.* New York: Academic Press.

Tombari, M. L., & Bergan, J. R. (1978). Consultant cues and teacher verbalizations, judgments, and expectancies concerning children's adjustment problems. *Journal of School Psychology, 16,* 212–219.

Touchette, P. E., MacDonald, R. F., & Langer, S. N. (1985). A scatter plot for identifying stimulus control of problem behavior. *Journal of Applied Behavior Analysis, 18,* 343–351.

U.S. Department of Education. (2000). *Twenty-second annual report to Congress on the implementation of the Individual With Disabilities Education Act.* Washington, DC: Government Printing Office.

U.S. Department of Education. (2003). *Identifying and implementing educational practices supported by rigorous evidence: A user friendly guide.* Washington, DC: Institute of Education Sciences.

Vaughn, S., & Fuchs, L. S. (2003). Redefining learning disabilities as inadequate response to instruction: The promise and potential problems. *Learning Disabilities Research and Practice, 18,* 137–146.

Walker, H. M. (2004). Use of evidence-based interventions in schools: Where we've been, where we are, and where we need to go. *School Psychology Review, 33,* 398–407.

Watkins, C. L. (1997). *Project Follow Through: A case study of contingencies influencing instructional practices of the educational establishment.* Concord, MA: Cambridge Center for Behavioral Studies.

Wickstrom, K. F., Jones, K. M., LaFleur, L. H., & Witt, J. C. (1998). An analysis of treatment integrity in school-based behavioral consultation. *School Psychology Quarterly, 13,* 141–154.

Witt, J. C. (1997). Talk is not cheap. *School Psychology Quarterly, 12,* 281–292.

Witt, J. C., Daly, E. J., & Noell, G. (2000). *Functional assessments: A step-by-step guide to solving academic and behavior problems.* Longmont, CO: Sopris West.

Witt, J. C., Gresham, F. M., & Noell, G. H. (1996). What's behavioral about behavioral consultation? *Journal of Educational and Psychological Consultation, 7,* 327–344.

Witt, J. C., Noell, G. H., La Fleur, L. H., & Mortenson, B. P. (1997). Teacher use of interventions in general education: Measurement and analysis of the independent variable. *Journal of Applied Behavior Analysis, 30,* 693–696.

Wolery, M., Bailey, D. B., & Sugai, G. M. (1988). *Effective teaching: Principles and procedures of applied behavior analysis with exceptional students.* Boston: Allyn & Bacon.

Yeaton, W. H., & Sechrest, L. (1981). Critical dimensions in the choice and maintenance of successful treatments: Strength, integrity, and effectiveness. *Journal of Consulting and Clinical Psychology, 49,* 156–167.

Ysseldyke, J. E., Pianta, R., Christenson, S., Wang, J., & Algozzine, B. (1983). An analysis of prereferral interventions. *Psychology in the Schools, 20,* 184–190.

9

Conjoint Behavioral Consultation
What Do We Know and What Do We Need to Know?

SUSAN M. SHERIDAN, BRANDY L. CLARKE, AND JENNIFER D. BURT

University of Nebraska-Lincoln

WHERE WE HAVE BEEN: BACKGROUND TO CONJOINT BEHAVIORAL CONSULTATION

The importance of parent involvement and home-school partnerships has been clearly established (Christenson, 2004). Research has shown unequivocally that when parents are involved in their children's educational programs, children, families, classrooms, and schools all benefit (Christenson & Sheridan, 2001). Professional organizations and the national government have also recognized the positive impact of home-school partnerships. Policy calls for schools to engage in deeper partnerships with parents and communities to meet the increasing academic, behavioral, and social needs of students (No Child Left Behind [NCLB], 2002). In fact, NCLB specifically calls for "local education agencies to assist school personnel to reach out to, communicate with, and work with parents as equal partners; implement and coordinate parent programs; and build ties between parents and the school" (Pub. L. 107-111, 1118). As a result, both the National Association of School Psychologists and the interorganizational School Psychology Futures Conference have identified the development of home-school partnership models as a top priority in the field (Christenson, 2004; Ysseldyke et al., 1997).

Strong, positive relationships between the home and school systems are essential in addressing the needs of children and families and have demonstrated positive outcomes for parents, students, and teachers alike (Haynes, Comer, & Hamilton-Lee, 1989; Masten & Coatsworth, 1998). However, few models have been specified and validated that bring families and schools together in joint problem solving and decision making within a consultation framework. Conjoint behavioral consultation (CBC) is one exception. CBC is an indirect method of service delivery that facilitates a collaborative working relationship among the key individuals in a child's life by establishing linkages between the home and school systems. Given its conceptual importance to the model, *collaboration* is defined here as a relational process between participants by which unique information, expertise, values, and goals are shared, and the insight gleaned from each party is incorporated into a joint intervention and evaluation plan for which all bear some responsibility.

Table 9.1   Overarching Goals and Objectives of Conjoint Behavioral Consultation

Goals

1. Promote academic, socioemotional, and behavioral outcomes for children through joint, mutual, cross-system planning.
2. Promote parent engagement in which parental roles, beliefs, and opportunities for meaningful participation are clear, within a developmental, culturally sensitive context.
3. Establish and strengthen home-school partnerships on behalf of children's learning and development, immediately and over time.

Outcome Objectives

1. Obtain comprehensive and functional data over extended temporal and contextual bases.
2. Establish consistent treatment programs across settings.
3. Improve the skills, knowledge, or behaviors of all parties (i.e., family members, school personnel, and the child-client).
4. Monitor behavioral contrast and side effects systematically via cross-setting treatment agents.
5. Enhance generalization and maintenance of treatment effects via consistent programming across sources and settings.
6. Develop skills and competencies to promote further independent conjoint problem solving between the family and school personnel.

Process Objectives

1. Improve communication, knowledge, and understanding about family, child, and school.
2. Promote shared ownership and joint responsibility for problem solution.
3. Promote greater conceptualization of needs and concerns and increase perspective taking.
4. Strengthen relationships within and across systems.
5. Maximize opportunities to address needs and concerns across, rather than within, settings.
6. Increase shared (parent and teacher) commitments to educational goals.
7. Increase the diversity of expertise and resources available.

Definition, Goals, and Objectives of Conjoint Behavioral Consultation

Conjoint behavioral consultation is defined as "a systematic, indirect form of service delivery, in which parents and teachers are joined to work together to address the academic, social, or behavioral needs of an individual for whom both parties bear some responsibility" (Sheridan & Kratochwill, 1992, p. 22). It is a conceptual and functional extension of a traditional approach to behavioral consultation (BC) that articulates several goals and objectives above and beyond conventional consultation practice. In CBC, a consultant facilitates a collaborative partnership through a problem-solving process designed to recognize the interconnections between the home and school settings (Sheridan & Kratochwill, 1992).

There are several goals and objectives of CBC, as summarized in Table 9.1. These goals include (a) promoting the academic, behavioral, and socioemotional outcomes for children through joint problem solving; (b) encouraging parent engagement; and (c) strengthening the relationship among systems on behalf of the child's learning and development (Sheridan & Kratochwill, in press). Within the goals of CBC are several process and outcome objectives. Process (relational) objectives are concerned with building and promoting positive, constructive partnerships among systems. Outcome objectives are directed toward the child and child-oriented results that occur through joint problem solving and planning.

Stages of Conjoint Behavioral Consultation

The goals and objectives of CBC are achieved via four stages implemented in a collaborative manner, involving formal meetings and informal contact between the consultant, parents, and teachers. These stages include (a) conjoint needs identification, (b) conjoint needs analysis, (c) cross-setting plan implementation, and (d) conjoint plan evaluation (Sheridan, Kratochwill, & Bergan, 1996). Three of the four stages are initiated in the context of a structured interview with parents and teachers. Next are guidelines that operationally depict the CBC process. Refer to Sheridan et al. (1996) and Sheridan and Kratochwill (2007) for a detailed description of CBC.

Conjoint Needs Identification

The conjoint needs identification stage (previously considered the conjoint problem identification stage) provides a framework for parents and teachers to develop a collaborative working relationship. This stage is procedurally operationalized during the Conjoint Needs Identification Interview (CNII; previously referred to as Conjoint Problem Identification Interview [CPII]). During the CNII, the consultant works with consultees to identify the child's most salient needs across home and school settings. Based on the severity and the relationship with other behaviors, the consultees jointly select a target behavior and define it in concrete, operational terms. Joint responsibility is encouraged to identify the specific settings and goals to be the focus of consultation. Consultees then collaboratively establish valid procedures for collecting baseline data across home and school settings. The goals of the CNII go beyond the identification of the target behavior and data collection procedures to include facilitating a relationship between the parents and teacher. Throughout this stage, the consultant identifies the strengths and capabilities of the child, family, and school to promote competencies in all participants. The consultant also remains in close contact with consultees to assist with data collection, answer questions as they arise, and promote the working relationship between home and school.

Conjoint Needs Analysis

In the conjoint needs analysis stage of CBC (previously known as conjoint problem analysis), the consultant assists consultees in developing solutions across settings based on baseline behavioral data. The Conjoint Needs Analysis Interview (CNAI; previously the Conjoint Problem Analysis Interview [CPAI]) provides a context for the consultant and consultees jointly to (a) identify ecological variables across settings that might influence the attainment of the behavioral goal and (b) develop a meaningful, solution-focused plan to address the target behavior across home and school. The consultant elicits information from consultees to facilitate the identification of environmental factors or functional variables that assist in understanding presenting concerns and developing meaningful plans. In addition, equal participation of parents and teachers, as well as shared ownership of plan development and problem solution, are encouraged. Baseline data are explored to identify setting events (i.e., environmental conditions that are distal in time or place from the target behavior but influence its occurrence); ecological conditions (e.g., home or classroom variables such as seating arrangement, delivery of instructions, and distractions in the environment); and cross-setting variables (e.g., consistency in expectations or management of behavioral concerns) that may have an impact on the target behavior. The focus of discussion centers on environmental conditions rather than internal causes to link assessment effectively to intervention and to promote a solution-focused, strength-based approach to plan development. Efforts are made to identify the presence of common events that occur across settings and are responsible for the presentation or maintenance of the target behavior. Hypotheses are generated around environmental conditions that contribute to the target behavior, and a joint plan then is developed to address the needs of the child across home and school settings. Throughout this stage, the consultant continues to promote the working relationship between home and school by encouraging and validating parents' and teachers' perspectives and ideas about the target behavior and plan development.

Plan Implementation

In the third stage of CBC (cross-system plan implementation), parents and teachers implement the intervention in the home and school settings. During this stage, the consultant remains in close contact with the family and school (e.g., phone calls, e-mails, and personal visits) to provide support, ensure understanding of intervention procedures, and reinforce parent and teacher efforts. Research indicates that an expanded (i.e., cross-setting) behavioral intervention base is advantageous to encourage consistency across environments (Kratochwill & Sheridan, 1990). The partnership between parents and teachers helps to ensure cross-setting consistency in treatment implementation and increases the potential for generalization and maintenance of positive outcomes.

The extent to which a treatment plan is implemented as intended is described as *treatment integrity* (Gresham, 1989; Noell, chapter 15, this volume). This variable is likely to mediate outcomes in consultation or the effectiveness of CBC. For this reason, it is critical for the consultant to use strategies to promote treatment integrity during the plan implementation phase. Treatment plans that are not implemented, or not implemented as intended, are less likely to produce positive child outcomes. Performance feedback is a particularly effective procedure to enhance treatment implementation (Noell et al., 2005). It consists of monitoring treatment implementation and providing feedback to the individual responsible for treatment delivery. Although there is little research supporting other strategies, it has been suggested that treatment integrity may also be enhanced by (a) providing consultees with specific written information regarding the plan; (b) providing training or feedback in intervention components (e.g., modeling, rehearsing, and feedback); and (c) requesting that consultees self-monitor their adherence to the treatment plan (Noell et al., 2005).

Conjoint Plan Evaluation

Conjoint plan evaluation is the final stage of CBC. The aim of the Conjoint Plan Evaluation Interview (CPEI) is to analyze the behavioral data to determine the achievement of consultation goals and the efficacy of treatment across settings. Throughout this stage, the behavioral data are used to focus the discussion around a future course of action (e.g., continuation, termination, planning for maintenance and follow-up). Additional interviews are scheduled as needed. Furthermore, the consultant encourages parents and teachers to continue to use open communication methods (e.g., home-school notes, regular phone contact, and meetings) to promote partnering and problem solving in the future. Often, systematic methods of consultee and client follow-up are necessary to ensure maintenance of positive child outcomes and the parent-teacher relationship. If positive outcomes are not maintained, then it may be necessary for the consultant to conduct future problem analysis, plan development, or consultee training.

CBC is a partnership-centered approach to service delivery. The goals and objectives of the model equally address the attainment of positive child outcomes and the establishment of a working relationship among systems. Although this process is formally operationalized via structured interviews, it is important to recognize that CBC occurs in the context of ongoing reciprocal interactions rather than simply through a series of formal interviews. Many of the objectives for each stage occur outside the formal interviews (e.g., behavioral observations and relationship building).

Further, positive outcomes for all participants are achieved in the context of a collaborative relationship with ongoing communication and dialogue vital for continued progress.

WHAT WE KNOW: THE EMPIRICAL BASE FOR CONJOINT BEHAVIORAL CONSULTATION

Along with the articulation of the principles and practice guidelines related to CBC, empirical studies of the model have been accumulating since the early 1990s. Numerous studies have focused on outcomes, communication processes, and social validation of CBC. Findings generally have (a) lent support to the efficacy of the model, (b) gleaned insights into the nature of communication patterns and relational features of practice, and (c) suggested positive perceptions by consumers of CBC services. These research areas are reviewed below.

Review of Conjoint Behavioral Consultation Outcome Research

Outcome research assessing the efficacy of CBC is growing. Numerous studies have been conducted evaluating the efficacy of CBC across home and school settings, in relation to academic, social, and behavioral outcomes, using experimental and case study methodologies. Table 9.2 presents a list of published studies summarized by authors, sample, target behavior, measures, results, methodological features (e.g., social validity assessment, fidelity information, and follow-up), and limitations.

A total of 13 studies have been published investigating the effects of CBC. The most common target concern identified in CBC research is behavioral in nature (e.g., compliance and aggression), with 6 studies addressing behavioral issues. Two studies addressed social concerns (e.g., social withdrawal), and 2 addressed academic concerns (e.g., work completion and accuracy). Common methods used to assess outcomes across studies are direct observations and behavioral rating scales. In some studies, data on acceptability and satisfaction were also reported. In these studies, common measures are the Behavior Intervention Rating Scale (BIRS) Acceptability factor (Elliott & Von Brock Treuting, 1991) revised for CBC (Sheridan, Eagle, Cowan, & Mickelson, 2001) and the Consultant Evaluation Form (CEF; Erchul, 1987). Both experimental (e.g., multiple baseline, pretest-posttest randomized control) and case study designs were used. The majority of studies assessed clinical meaningfulness and perceptions of intervention effectiveness (i.e., social validity) using scales such as the BIRS Effectiveness factor (Elliott & Von Brock Treuting, 1991) and Goal Attainment Scaling (GAS; Kiresuk, Smith, & Cardillo, 1994). In addition, most reported integrity of implementing CBC (i.e., process integrity).

In this section, we summarize three large-scale reviews of CBC research (Guli, 2005; Sheridan et al., 2001; Sheridan, Eagle, & Doll, 2006). A description of individual studies follows, organized as reviews of studies using (a) experimental outcome designs and (b) case study methods. In addition to the published studies reviewed here, a number of unpublished dissertation studies have been completed (e.g., Brown, 2004; Cagle, 2003; Colton, 1999; Finn, 2003; Illsley, 2003; Lasecki, 2001; Lepage, 1999; Morganstein, 2003; Moscovitz, 2004; Mulgia, 2001; Myers, 1997; Schnoes, 2003; Scope, 2003; Stephan, 1999). Due to space constraints, these are not be reviewed here, but interested readers are referred to relevant Dissertation Abstracts International sources for complete studies.

Reviews and Meta-Analyses

Guli (2005) conducted an extensive search of parent consultation literature using rigorous criteria specified in the *Procedural and Coding Manual of the Division 16 Task Force on Evidence-Based Interventions in School Psychology* (Kratochwill & Stoiber, 2002). The majority of the 18 studies identified used single-participant designs, including both within-participant and multiple-baseline

Table 9.2   Summary of Conjoint Behavioral Consultation Outcome Research

Authors	Sample	Target Behavior	Measures	Results	Methodological Features	Limitations
Colton and Sheridan (1998)	N = 3 males, 8–9 years old, diagnosed with ADHD	Cooperative peer interactions	Direct observations Social Skills Rating System Social validity	SSRS-P: Significant pre/post results for child 2 SSRS-T: Significant pre/post results for Child 1 and 3	Independent observations Direct observations (participants and peers) Treatment integrity Multiple-probe design across participants Social validity assessed	Participant groups not matched Objectivity of behavioral observations Lack of independent observations in home
Galloway and Sheridan (1994)	N = 6, Grades 1–3	Math completion and accuracy	Classroom math assignments (completion/accuracy) Social validity Treatment integrity	Math accuracy: Gains for home-note group ranged from 20–84% Gains for CBC group ranged from 50–144% Math completion: Gains for home-note group ranged from 14–99% Gains for CBC group ranged from 39–133%	Permanent product measures Social comparison across both groups Treatment integrity Comparison group Social validity assessed	AB design with replications, not true experiment Increasing baseline data points Lack of control over math instruction Generalizability
Gortmaker, Warnes, and Sheridan (2004)	5-year-old male kindergarten case study	Selective mutism	Direct observations Social validity Treatment integrity	Effect size = 1.60	Direct observations Treatment integrity Process integrity	No reliability data No objective treatment integrity data
Illsley and Sladeczek (2001)	N = 5	Conduct problem behavior Parenting practices and skills	Direct observations of child behavior Parental knowledge of behavioral principles Videotaped parent-child interactions	Positive change in child behavior 4/5 parents had improvements in parenting skills	Direct observations Manualized approach Parental behavior/ knowledge change measures	Significant variation between parents

Study	Sample	Target	Measures	Results	Methods	Limitations
Kratochwill, Elliott, Loitz, Sladeszek, and Carlson (2003)	N = 125 Head Start preschoolersrs	Externalizing and internalizing behavior problems	Direct observations; Child Behavior Checklist (CBCL); Treatment integrity; Responding to Children's Behavior Checklist (RCB); Social validity	Effect sizes for manual group	Direct observations; Standardized assessments; Treatment integrity; Random assignment; Control group	Statistical power low due to small group size and large variance; Two treatment groups not randomly assigned; High attrition rate
Ray, Skinner, and Watson (1999)	5-year-old male diagnosed with autistic disorder	Increase compliance with low-probability commands	Direct observations	Increased rate of compliance from 15% to 95%5%	Direct observations	Generalizability; Lack of social validity data
Sheridan, Clarke, Knoche, & Edwards (2006)	N = 50 children aged 6 and younger	Academic Social Behavioral	Direct observations; Parent-Teacher Relationship Scale-II (PTRS); Social validity	Median effect size for home = 0.97, school = 1.06; Significant improvement in parent-teacher relationship	Process integrity; Treatment integrity; Direct observation	Relability of direct observations; Quasi-experimental approach; No direct measure of treatment integrity
Sheridan and Colton (1994)	6-year-old male	Fear of sleeping in own room	Direct observations	Gradual increasing trend with treatment; No overlapping data points	Direct observations; Follow-up data	No control group; Lack of control over extraneous variables; Social validity data
Sheridan, Eagle, Cowan, and Mickelson (2001)	N = 52, K–Grade 9	Academic Social Behavioral	Direct observations; Social validity	Effect sizes for home = 1.08, school = 1.11; Total = 1.10 (n = 66)	Direct observations; Process integrity; Treatment integrity	Reliability of direct observations; Limited treatment integrity data
Sheridan, Eagle, and Doll (2006)	N = 125 students with one, more than one, or no forms of diversity	Efficacy of CBC with diverse clients; 192 different target behaviors	Direct observations; Social validity; Demographic measures of diversity	Average effect sizes for one form of diversity = 1.21; Average effect sizes for two or more forms of diversity = 1.51; Average effect sizes for no diversity = 1.35	Direct observations; Process integrity	Lack of experimental control; Nonrandom selection or group assignment; Limited sample size within groups; Diversity indicators based on parent reports

Continued

Table 9.2   Summary of Conjoint Behavioral Consultation Outcome Research (*Continued*)

Authors	Sample	Target Behavioror	Measures	Results	Methodological Features	Limitations
Sheridan, Kratochwill, and Elliott (1990)	N = 4, 8–9 years old	Social interactions (withdrawn)	Direct observations Behavioral rating scales Self-report	Home social withdrawal behaviors decreased 1–2 SD School social withdrawal/total internalizing problems decreased 1+ SD 3 parents reported that assertion/social initiation increased 1+ SD At school, assertion/social initiation increased 1+ SD	Independent observations Direct observations (participants and peers) Treatment integrity Multiple baseline design	Participant groups not matched Objectivity of behavioral observations Lack of independent observations in home
Sheridan, Warnes, Cowan, Schemm, and Clarke (2004)	4-year-old male in early childhood special education	Tantrumming	Direct observations Social validity	Length of tantrums decreased from 4 to 1.6 minutes	Case study Social validity measures	No effect size reported Generalizability
Weiner, Sheridan, & Jenson (1998)	N = 5, grades 7–9	Math homework completion Math accuracy	Permanent products Social validity	Total effect size for math completion = 0.60; accuracy = 0.67	Multiple baseline design Follow-up data Process integrity Treatment integrity	Lack of stability and variability during baseline Limited treatment integrity data

Note.   Readers are referred to Guli (2005) for additional methodological information and findings related to CBC research.

designs. Each of the studies was subjected to comprehensive and rigorous review of methodological strengths and weaknesses. CBC research was included in this review due to its emphasis on consultation as the structure for service delivery.

Within the context of the task force criteria, CBC was found to hold promise as an evidence-based parent consultation model. Specifically, relative to other parent consultation models, CBC provided the strongest evidence for producing significant school-related outcomes. Furthermore, parent consultation studies receiving the highest ratings for key methodological features were those using a model of joint parent-teacher consultation, including CBC. All but one of the highest ratings for both significant outcomes and clinical significance were received by joint models of parent-teacher (i.e., conjoint) consultation.

Sheridan et al. (2001) reported the outcomes of 4 years of federally funded CBC studies. Thirty graduate student consultants provided CBC services to parents and teachers of 52 students with disabilities (such as behavior disorders, learning disabilities, and attention deficit/hyperactivity disorder [ADHD]) or who were at risk for becoming eligible for special education services. Efficacy of CBC in terms of ameliorating target concerns was evaluated in each case by computing effect sizes (ESs) across home and school settings. In addition, a prediction model was tested based on client age, case complexity, and symptom severity. Perceptions of effectiveness, process acceptability, and consultee satisfaction with CBC services were also assessed.

Average case outcomes were favorable as determined by effect sizes at home and at school. Specifically, the average effect size for CBC case outcomes was 1.10 (SD = 1.07), with home- and school-based effect sizes averaging 1.08 (SD = 0.82) and 1.11 (SD = 1.24), respectively. Confidence intervals computed around effect sizes revealed that the true population average effect size related to CBC could be found within the range of 0.83 and 1.36, with 95% confidence.

These researchers were also concerned with identifying variables that may predict CBC outcomes. Multiple linear regression was used to examine the relationships between client age, case complexity (i.e., number of target behaviors), severity of symptoms (i.e., rated by parents and teachers prior to CBC), and individual effect sizes. A model fitting client age and symptom severity was found to predict school effect size relatively well (R^2 = .425, Adjusted R^2 = .343; P = .008). Specifically, the older client (11 years of age and older) with less-severe symptoms would be predicted to experience higher effect sizes with CBC intervention. On the other hand, the older client with more severe symptoms would be predicted to demonstrate a smaller effect size. Similarly, younger clients (age 5–7 years) with higher severity ratings prior to CBC services would be predicted to experience higher effect sizes than those experiencing less severity and than older children at all severity levels. Case complexity (i.e., number of target behaviors) was not significant in the models. Likewise, the multiple regression with home effect sizes did not result in any statistically significant model. Thus, client age, symptom severity, and case complexity were not predictive of effects in home settings.

The outcomes of CBC with a sample of diverse students (experiencing one, more than one, or no forms of diversity) was reported by Sheridan et al. (2006). Behavioral change, goal attainment, acceptability, satisfaction, and perceptions of efficacy of the CBC model were measured with 125 students representing varying levels of diversity and with 192 target behaviors. Of the clients, 44% were diverse in one or more respect. Collectively, 26% of the clients experienced one form of diversity; 18% demonstrated two or more. Approximately 23% of the sample were identified by their parents as racially diverse (non-White); 19.5% had only one adult living at home, 15.3% were living in poverty conditions, 6.9% had mothers who had not completed high school, and 4.8% spoke a language other than English in the home.

Findings indicated that CBC-mediated interventions yielded generally high effect sizes regardless of the presence of diversity or the number of diverse characteristics exhibited. Average effect sizes were 1.21, 1.51, and 1.35 for students experiencing one, two or more, and no forms of diversity, respectively. Social validity measures (i.e., perceptions of goal attainment, effectiveness, acceptability, and satisfaction) also yielded favorable results. Thus, parents and teachers of students experiencing diversity were positive regarding the CBC process and outcomes.

Experimental Studies

In the first empirical study of CBC, Sheridan, Kratochwill, and Elliott (1990) were concerned with increasing the social initiation behaviors of socially withdrawn children. Of particular interest was the demonstration of behavioral generalization to the home setting. Participants in this study were four socially withdrawn children from a rural town in the Midwest (3 girls, 1 boy; ages 8–12). There were two treatment conditions in the study (i.e., CBC and consultation with teachers only). In the CBC condition, teachers and parents worked together with a school psychologist consultant; in the teacher-only condition, parents were not included in consultation. In both conditions, children were exposed to the same behavioral treatment (i.e., goal setting, self-monitoring, and positive reinforcement). In the CBC condition, these same procedures were implemented across home and school settings.

A multiple-baseline across-participants design was used to evaluate the effectiveness of the separate consultation interventions. When consultation was undertaken with parents and teachers together, initiations increased in both home and school settings. However, when consultation was undertaken with teachers only, children's initiations increased at school only. Treatment gains at school were maintained for all children in both conditions but were most notable for those in the CBC condition. Although the traditional use of BC with teachers was found to be effective in increasing the social initiation behaviors of socially withdrawn children at school, both generalization and maintenance of treatment effects appeared to be stronger when conjoint consultation procedures were utilized. Social validity and treatment integrity measures were also included and yielded positive results.

A second outcome study evaluated the effects of CBC combined with a behavioral training and reinforcement program with three Caucasian boys between the ages of 8 and 9 diagnosed with ADHD and exhibiting performance deficits in their cooperative play behavior (Colton & Sheridan, 1998). A behavioral social skills treatment package was implemented within the context of CBC to address the children's observed social deficits. The behavioral social skills treatment program consisted of four major components: (a) social skills coaching and role-play, (b) a home-school communication system, (c) self-monitoring of recess behaviors, and (d) positive reinforcement.

Outcome measures in this study included direct observations of positive interaction behaviors and behavioral rating scales. A multiple-baseline across-participants design was used to evaluate the effects of the CBC/social skills treatment program on target children's cooperative play behaviors. All participants increased positive play behaviors with peers during treatment phases. Social comparison data (i.e., involving a comparison with same-gender classmates identified by classroom teachers as having adequate social skills) revealed that all children increased their positive interactions to a level that approached that of normal comparison peers. Parents and teachers reported that the procedures were acceptable (based on responses on the BIRS revised for consultation procedures (Von Brock & Elliott, 1987), and child responses on the Children's Intervention Rating Profile (CIRP; Witt & Elliott, 1985) suggested that they found the social skills intervention highly acceptable.

A variation of traditional, individualized CBC was evaluated by Weiner, Sheridan, and Jenson (1998), who implemented consultation services in a group format. Parents and teachers of five junior high school (eighth and ninth grade) students with homework concerns served as participants in this study. Given the age of the sample, students also participated in the CPAI and CPEI meetings. A multiple-baseline across-participants design was used to evaluate the effects of CBC on math homework completion and accuracy. A structured homework intervention program (Olympia, Jenson, & Hepworth-Neville, 1996) was used to standardize strategies across participants. The primary components of the program were self-recording, home-based structure and supervision, and positive reinforcement.

Moderate effect sizes were yielded for both homework completion (ES = 0.60) and accuracy (ES = 0.67). Parents and teachers reported satisfaction with outcomes and beliefs that the consultation goals were mostly or completely met as assessed with the BIRS Effectiveness factor (Von Brock & Elliott, 1987) and GAS (Kiresuk et al., 1994), respectively. Parents and teachers reported high levels of acceptability on the BIRS Acceptability factor, and consultees were generally satisfied with the consultant as measured by the CEF.

Kratochwill, Elliott, Loitz, Sladeczek, and Carlson (2003) conducted a study of the differential effects of CBC using two methods of consultee intervention support: manual based and video based. Using a pretest-posttest repeated-measures experimental design, the investigators evaluated outcomes of CBC-manual, CBC-video, and control group using multiple measures (Child Behavior Checklist, Achenbach, 1991a; Teacher Rating Form, Achenbach, 1991b; Social Skills Rating Scale, Gresham & Elliott, 1990). The sample was comprised of 125 Head Start children, parents, and teachers. Target behaviors included aggression, compliance, and "other" behaviors such as participating, staying on task, and joining a group. Parents' and teachers' goal attainment scores characterized students as meeting their overall behavior goals. Specifically, 75% of parents in the manual group and 95.5% of parents in the video group reported progress toward goal attainment. For teachers, 60% in the manual group and 73.1% in the video group reported similar progress. Reliable change indices (RCI; Gresham & Noell, 1993) were computed for the standardized measures to determine whether reported changes in behaviors pre- to posttest were significant. Across outcome measures, an average of 46.08% and 31.37% of RCIs were deemed statistically significant in the manual and video conditions, respectively. This is in comparison to 25.42% in the control condition. Contrary to these positive findings, effect sizes were negligible. Parents and teachers reported high rates of treatment acceptability and satisfaction with the manual and videotape treatment programs.

Case Studies

Some systematic CBC case studies have also been conducted. In a carefully controlled set of case studies, the model was evaluated with academically underachieving children (Galloway & Sheridan, 1994). Participants were six primary grade students (Grades 1–3) who often failed to complete math assignments on time and with accuracy. They all demonstrated performance rather than skill deficits. In two separate sets of case studies, the investigators evaluated the effectiveness of a standard intervention with and without the inclusion of CBC. Both studies involved the use of a manualized home note system, in which teachers recorded daily performances in math as well as process behaviors intended to help them complete work (e.g., pencil ready and papers out). The home note also included a checklist to help remind parents of what to do at home and served as a measure of treatment integrity.

The investigators used AB with replication designs to assess outcomes of the home note and CBC interventions. All three children in the home note-only case studies showed improvements in math completion and accuracy; however, their performance continued to be variable.

As in the home note condition, all children in the home note with CBC condition demonstrated improvements in math completion and accuracy, but the gains were greater and more stable. Findings in the CBC case studies also suggested enhanced treatment integrity, maintenance of treatment gains at follow-up, and consumer acceptability. Furthermore, parents in the CBC condition adhered more faithfully to the treatment regimen than did parents in the home note-only case studies, which may be one reason for the greater treatment effects.

Another case study involved a child displaying irrational fears (Sheridan & Colton, 1994). In this case, a kindergarten teacher referred a 6-year-old boy with sleep disturbances. Due to unfounded fears, the child slept in his parents' room all night, every night for more than 2 years. The goal for consultation in this case was to get the child to sleep in his own room on a consistent basis.

Treatment involved a fading of environment and positive reinforcement procedure in which positive reinforcers were delivered each time the child slept in a spot that moved successively closer to his own room. An AB changing criterion design was used, with the criterion adequate performance demonstrated over two occasions at each successive level, moving the boy closer to his own room. Dramatic, immediate improvements were observed in this case. Two weeks of baseline showed 0 occasions of sleeping in his own room and 14 occasions of sleeping on the floor of his parents' room. Six steps were identified during treatment that involved the child moving successively closer to his room. The child demonstrated immediate effects, with perfect performance at each level until he met the goal of sleeping in his bed. Likewise, he demonstrated no regression at a 1-month follow-up.

Ray, Skinner, and Watson (1999) implemented CBC in the case of a 5-year-old boy with autism, who demonstrated problem behaviors including aggression and noncompliance. Compliance behaviors appeared to be related to the person issuing the command, with greater levels of compliance associated with his mother as compared to his teacher. The intervention plan involved the issuance of high-probability command sequences (simple, easy-to-perform tasks) immediately preceding low-probability commands (those typically preceding noncompliance and problem behaviors). As part of consultation, the parent and teacher received instruction on issuing commands, which included sharing information, modeling, and practicing effective commands. Multiple phases of the intervention were instituted to allow for the transfer of stimulus control from the parent to the teacher in the classroom environment. Across eight phases of intervention and a final generalization phase, the child gradually demonstrated high rates of compliance with teacher-issued commands. Compliance with teacher commands increased from 15% during baseline to 95% and 100% during the final intervention and generalization phases, respectively.

Gortmaker, Warnes, and Sheridan (2004) reported the outcomes of a case study of a 5-year-old child with selective mutism. An AB case study with follow-up design was used to evaluate the effects of the CBC-mediated intervention. The interventions used in this case included programming common stimuli and positive reinforcement. Specifically, because school was the only setting in which the child would not speak, talking was established with the teacher in an alternative location outside the classroom. Once the child established speech with the teacher outside the classroom, reinforcers were delivered in the classroom as he gradually spoke in the classroom. On intervention implementation, a gradual positive trend was seen in the child's speaking behaviors. In addition, the child spoke to multiple persons in the school setting (e.g., different teachers and peers) and spoke in front of groups of peers with seeming comfort. Both the child's parent and teacher reported high levels of acceptability for the process on the BIRS Acceptability factor. Satisfaction with the consultant was also high, as determined by responses on the CEF.

In an article describing CBC within a context of "family-centered" services, Sheridan, Warnes, Cowan, Schemm, and Clarke (2004) described a case study of a 4-year-old male attending early childhood special education. The target concern on CBC referral was tantrumming behavior in the school, home, and public settings, with a specific goal of decreasing the duration of tantrums. The intervention designed to address the concerns of consultees was comprised of antecedent control and differential reinforcement. Specifically, the child was provided with choices for activities and was ignored when tantrumming occurred. When he responded appropriately, the child was reinforced through verbal praise and tactile stimulation. Behavioral data indicated that the goal was met quickly on intervention implementation. The child's parent and teacher both reported that their goals were completely met, as indicated via GAS. Both the parent and teacher also reported high levels of acceptability perceptions of effectiveness, as assessed with the BIRS.

Illsley and Sladeczek (2001) reported five case studies of children with significant conduct problems, including aggression, compliance, and socially inappropriate behaviors. In addition, this series of case studies sought to identify changes in parent knowledge and skill related to effective parenting practices. CBC was effective in producing positive changes in the children's conduct problems at home. All children made significant progress on behaviors targeted for intervention, with decreases in aggressive behavior and increases in compliance and socially appropriate behaviors. As a group, parents tended to demonstrate improvements in their knowledge of child management strategies, increased their use of praise, and were less critical of their children following CBC. However, much variability in parent outcomes was observed.

Review of Conjoint Behavioral Consultation Process Research

In addition to improving child outcomes related to behavioral, social, or academic targets, another primary objective of CBC is to engage parents and teachers in collaborative problem solving (see Table 9.1). The manner in which this collaborative relationship is cultivated through the verbal processes of CBC has become the focus of much-needed investigation. Next, we discuss the research investigating relational communication patterns of the CBC process. A summary of this research is in Table 9.3.

Relational Communication Patterns

Erchul et al. (1999) sought to explain, through an investigation of relational control, the relational communication patterns that occur within CBC. Analyses conducted with the use of relational coding systems emphasize the connectedness of individuals within a conversation, along with the pragmatic (i.e., control-related) aspects of messages. BC research investigating dimensions of relational control (i.e., Erchul, 1987) borrowed the terms *domineeringness* and *dominance* from previous relational communication research. In the study, Erchul and his colleagues defined domineeringness as an index of an individual's directiveness or attempt to define or structure relationships throughout consultation. Dominance was considered to be an index of an individual's demonstrated influence or success in defining the relationship.

The purpose of this investigation was to "map" the patterns of relational control that unfold throughout the CBC process by assessing who is speaking to whom and with what degree of relational control. This study was conducted using a relational coding measure known as the family relational communication control coding system (FRCCCS; Heatherington & Friedlander, 1987). This system allows for the analysis of the unique characteristics of group communication, such as statements made to multiple recipients and interruptions in reciprocity. Four CBC cases consisting of 12 interviews were audiotaped, transcribed, and coded in terms of domineeringness and dominance using the FRCCCS. Across the 12 interviews, 9,696 individual messages were analyzed.

Comparisons of the present study were made with earlier work conducted by Erchul (1987) investigating relational communication patterns in BC. The analysis revealed that consultants and teachers participating in CBC displayed similar levels of domineeringness as their BC counterparts. In addition, CBC consultants appeared to be far less dominant than BC consultants, with

Table 9.3 Summary of Conjoint Behavioral Consultation Process Research

Authors	Sample	Dependent Variable	Measures	Results	Limitations
Erchul, Sheridan, Ryan, Grissom, Killough, and Mettler (1999)	4 CBC cases 9,696 individual messages	Domineeringness Dominance	Family Relational Communication Control Coding System (FRCCCS) CBC process integrity	Domineeringness: Overall, consultants displayed higher levels than both parents and teachers Dominance: Parents and teachers displayed the same level and were somewhat higher than consultants	Small sample size Generalizability No established sense for "high" or "low" levels of domineeringness or dominance Altered standardized measures No CBC research for "optimal" relationship dynamics
Grissom, Erchul, and Sheridan (2003)	$N = 20$ CBC cases $N = 16$ consultants $N = 23$ teachers $N = 20$ parents $N = 20$ clients	Domineeringness Dominance	Family Relational Communication Control Coding System (FRCCCS) Social validity	Overall, all participants shared in the level of influence over the process No significant correlations for domineeringness and outcomes were found Teachers reported lower acceptability when parents were more dominant Parents reported lower perceived effectiveness when they were more dominant	Small sample size Low statistical power Only CPIIs were coded Self-report outcome measures Limited external validity of CBC cases
Sheridan, Meegan, and Eagle (2002)	$N = 13$ consultants $N = 19$ parents and teachers $N = 16$ students 8,848 speech acts 4,986 speech exchanges	Influence Involvement	Psychosocial Processes Coding Scheme (PPCS) Direct observations Social validity	Participants displayed higher levels of collaboration followed by obliging statements with minimal controlling or withdrawing comments No significant relationship between speech act exchanges and behavioral outcomes was found	No control of relationship or differences among participants No study of intermediary variables Small sample size All consultants trained by same researcher Lack of reliability data for direct behavioral outcomes Only CPIIs were coded Selection bias

teachers receiving similar scores across groups. Thus, teachers appeared more dominant than the consultants in CBC but not in BC. These findings suggest that within the CBC process, no single individual attempts to direct or influence the other members at disproportionate levels; rather, communication patterns tend to be more bidirectional and reciprocal. In terms of relational control theory, such evidence supports the notion that CBC is a collaborative process involving symmetrical and reciprocal relationships. The authors suggested that it may be the interpersonal dynamics of the CBC triad that lead to a greater degree of shared influence among participants, as opposed to the BC dyad. Thus, CBC appears to be more of a collaborative service delivery method that facilitates equal relationships, whereas BC may be more appropriately viewed as involving a complementary relationship.

In a similar study, Grissom, Erchul, and Sheridan (2003) investigated aspects of interpersonal control within the context of CBC in relation to case outcomes. Measures of dominance and domineeringness were assessed using the FRCCCS and compared against outcome measures of acceptability/effectiveness of CBC, consultant effectiveness, and attainment of consultation goals. CPIIs for 20 CBC cases were used in the coding of the relational control variables (as per Erchul & Schulte, 1990). It was hypothesized that there would be: (a) significant positive correlations between consultant domineeringness and dominance and parent and teacher outcome ratings; (b) significant negative correlations between teacher domineeringness and dominance and parent and teacher outcome ratings; and (c) significant negative correlations between parent domineeringness and dominance and parent and teacher outcome ratings. Correlation analysis between the relational communication variables of domineeringness and dominance and the three outcome measures failed to produce any significant relationships for the first two hypotheses. Perceptions of outcomes in CBC were not significantly related to attempts to influence (i.e., domineeringness) and demonstrated influence (i.e., dominance) by consultants and teachers. The relationship between parent domineeringness and outcome measures also was not significant; however, parent dominance was significantly related to two outcome measures. Specifically, as parents influenced the parent-consultant dyadic relationship, the acceptability/effectiveness ratings given by teachers was lower. This finding indicates that the verbal communication between a dyad is related to the perceived outcomes of the third individual. The authors speculated that teachers' lower perceptions of acceptability and effectiveness may be due to unmet expectations for the consultant to be more directive with the process.

In addition, parent dominance within the parent-consultant and parent-teacher dyad was associated with less-favorable parental goal attainment ratings. Thus, as parents demonstrated more influence in the CNII, they reported less-positive behavioral outcomes for their child. Two possible explanations for this finding were proposed. First, parents may view consultation as a means for gaining social support, with problem solving a secondary function of the process. Second, parent dominance within the CNII may interfere with problem identification, which has been identified as an important component of successful consultation (Bergan & Tombari, 1976). Previous research in BC demonstrated similar results, with teacher attempts of control over the process relating to less-positive outcomes (e.g., Erchul, 1987; Erchul & Chewning, 1990; Witt, Erchul, McKee, & Pardue, 1991). Such findings suggest that control within the consultee-to-consultee and consultee-to-consultant relationships may be an important factor influencing perceptions of case outcomes.

Both of the studies described explored relational communication patterns within the verbal exchanges of CBC. In the next section, research evaluating the social context of verbal exchanges within CBC is reviewed.

Social Context

Sheridan, Meegan, and Eagle (2002) examined the nature of the social context in CBC and its relationship to case outcomes (i.e., effect sizes, perceived effectiveness/acceptability of consultation procedures, and satisfaction with the consultant). The Psychosocial Processes Coding Scheme (PPCS; Leaper, 1991) was used to assess two dimensions of communication function within CBC: influence and involvement. *Influence* referred to the degree to which a speech act (i.e., a phrase or utterance bound by intonation, pauses, or grammar that conveyed a single message) attempts to control the task in consultation or the extent to which a statement directly or indirectly influences the process. *Involvement* referred to the degree to which a speech act facilitates or hinders the social relationship. Direct and indirect levels of these two dimensions then create four main categories of speech acts: (a) *collaborative* speech is high in both influence and involvement, (b) *controlling* speech is high on influence and low on involvement, (c) *obliging* speech is low on influence and high on involvement, and (d) *withdrawing* speech is low on both influence and involvement.

Analyses were conducted using 30-minute segments of 16 CPIIs. This sample yielded 8,848 codable speech acts and 4,986 codable speech act exchanges. Descriptive analysis of the speech acts revealed that individual speech acts among participants were highly collaborative, followed by obliging, with negligible amounts of controlling or withdrawing messages. More specifically, when consultants were not making collaborative statements, they were obliging rather than controlling. Such results indicate that the social context of CBC is conducive to the development of collaborative partnerships across home and school settings. In addition, effect sizes were found to be meaningful and positive. These findings suggest that not only were positive relationships formed, but also they were effective in addressing concerns on behalf of the child.

Up to this point, a review of outcome and process research has demonstrated that CBC is an effective, collaborative process. The following section reviews social validity findings related to participants' perceptions of the acceptability, goal attainment, and helpfulness of CBC.

Review of Social Validity Research

Social validity has been identified as an important research topic in consultation (Elliott, Witt, & Kratochwill, 1991). Kazdin (1977) and Wolfe (1978) described social validity as the social significance of the target behavior chosen for treatment, the social appropriateness or acceptability of the treatment procedures, and the resulting behavior change. Specifically, the aims of social validity research are to determine the degree to which (a) treatment goals are socially significant; (b) treatment procedures are considered socially appropriate; and (c) treatment effects are clinically meaningful.

In the consultation literature, the predominant focus of social validity research is centered on treatment acceptability. Kazdin (1980) defined treatment acceptability as "judgments of lay persons, clients, and others of whether the procedures proposed for treatment are appropriate, fair, and reasonable for the problem or client" (p. 493). GAS (Kiresuk et al., 1994) is another social validity measurement that provides a subjective account of how consultation goals have been achieved. The CBC literature has also examined social validity through parent and teacher perceptions of helpfulness. Helpfulness is characterized as (a) responsiveness to client needs, (b) promotion of competency acquisition, and (c) promotion of partnership and collaboration among systems (Dunst, Trivette, Davis, & Cornwell, 1994).

CBC is a consultation model that has been recognized as acceptable (Freer & Watson, 1999; Sheridan & Steck, 1995; Sladeczek, Elliott, Kratochwill, Robertson-Mjaanes, & Stoiber, 2001) and helpful (Sheridan, Erchul, et al., 2004) by parents, teachers, and school psychologists. Traditionally, social validity research has used survey methodology to assess hypothetical acceptability rather than actual case-specific acceptability. In the section that follows, research examining the social validity of CBC in both hypothetical and naturalistic contexts is reviewed. Specifically, CBC acceptability, goal attainment, and helpfulness research are discussed. Studies that have as their main focus the social validity of CBC are reviewed in Table 9.4.

Acceptability Research

An early study by Sheridan and Steck (1995) surveyed a national sample of school psychologists to examine their perceptions of CBC as an acceptable model of service delivery. The Consultation Questionnaire was used to assess school psychologists' acceptability of CBC. The questionnaire consisted of three sections: (a) demographic and consultant information (i.e., gender, highest degree earned, age of students served, number of years as a practicing school psychologist, and geographic locale of practice); (b) procedural acceptability of CBC (i.e., 15 items from the Acceptability factor of the BIRS); and (c) situational acceptability (i.e., acceptability of four methods of service delivery across 21 student problem situations). The purpose of their study was to (a) evaluate practicing school psychologists' perceptions of CBC, (b) investigate variables that influence its acceptability, and (c) examine the desirability of CBC with other behavioral modes of service delivery (i.e., direct intervention, parent-only, and teacher-only consultation).

The results of this study indicate practicing school psychologists find CBC is an acceptable model of service delivery. Overall, CBC was rated favorably by respondents, and ratings were positive across different problem types and in comparison to other modes of service delivery. School psychologists rated the mean procedural acceptability of CBC as 5.24 on a 6-point Likert scale, with 6 reflecting high acceptability. The overall mean logistical barriers score was 4.31 (on a 6-point Likert scale with high scores reflecting a lack of logistical barriers). Although school psychologists rated CBC as an acceptable model, they also indicated that logistical barriers, such as lack of time and administrative/ organization support, impacted the overall acceptability of the model. Age of students served, theoretical orientation, and number of years in practice had little influence on the acceptability ratings.

School psychologists also found CBC to be more acceptable than other modes of service delivery across all problem types (i.e., academic, behavioral, and social-emotional). Further, CBC was rated similarly by school psychologists across all age groups, with the exception of secondary school psychologists rating CBC and direct service as equally acceptable. These findings suggest that CBC is perceived by practicing school psychologists as more generally applicable than other modes of service delivery.

Freer and Watson (1999) examined parent and teacher acceptability of three different approaches to BC: teacher-only consultation, parent-only consultation and CBC. Participants in the study were 111 parents of elementary-aged children and 61 elementary and secondary teachers. Each participant received a packet containing the Problem Questionnaire and the Intervention Rating Profile-15 (IRP-15; Witt & Elliott, 1985). The author-developed Problem Questionnaire consisted of a list of 17 common academic (e.g., reading problems), behavioral (e.g., high distractibility), and social-emotional (e.g., trouble making friends) problems. Respondents were asked to select one consultation approach that was most appropriate for each given problem and rated the overall acceptability of each consultation model using the IRP-15.

The results of this study suggest that both parents and teachers find CBC to be a very acceptable model of BC. The respondents consistently selected CBC as the most preferred consultation approach for academic, behavioral, and social-emotional problems. Regarding overall acceptability, both parents and teachers rated CBC as the most acceptable model of BC (overall mean CBC = 78.88, parent only = 63.31, teacher only = 60.45). These results replicate the findings from Sheridan

Table 9.4 Summary of Conjoint Behavioral Consultation Social Validity Research

Authors	Sample	Dependent Variable	Measures	Results	Limitations
Freer and Watson (1999)	$N = 111$ parents $N = 61$ teachers	Acceptability ratings between teacher-only consult, parent-only consult, and CBC	Problem questionnaire (list of academic, social/emotional, behavioral problems) Intervention Rating Profile-15 (IRP-15)	CBC rated as most preferred approach for all problem types by parents and teachers CBC rated as most acceptable form of consultation by parents and teachers	Low return rate of surveys Lack of variability in characteristics of sample Bias of previous experience with consultation Differences may be explained by other variables Analogue data lacks ecological validity
Sheridan, Erchul, et al. (2004)	$N = 137$ parents $N = 122$ teachers $N = 118$ child-clients	Perceptions of helpfulness	Consultant Evaluation Form (CEF) Behavior Intervention Rating Scale — Effectiveness factor (BIRS-E) Behavior Intervention Rating Scale — Acceptability factor (BIRS-A) Goal Attainment Scaling (GAS) Direct observations Congruence between parent and teacher ratings	Nonsignificant relationship between parent and teacher helpfulness ratings Nonsignificant relationship between parent and teacher agreement and effect sizes Significant relationships between difference scores and parent acceptability, teacher acceptability, and parent effectiveness ratings	Reliability of observational data Select consultant sample
Sheridan and Steck (1995)	$N = 409$ school psychologists	Perceptions of CBC (procedural acceptability, situational acceptability)	Consultation Questionnaire	Procedural acceptability ratings were "highly acceptable" CBC acceptability was greater than other modes of service delivery (teacher consultation, parent consultation, direct service) for academic, behavioral, and social/emotional concerns	Only nationally certified school psychologists sampled Situational acceptability and process acceptability measures may assess different constructs Self-report of attitudes may differ from behavior
Sladeczek, Elliott, Kratochwill, Robertson-Mjaanes, and Stoiber (2001)	Case study 5-year-old preschool male with conduct problems	Perceptions of goal attainment	Goal Attainment Scaling (GAS) Direct observation	T score = 64.18, a score above 50 indicating performance above baseline expectations	Generalizability Case study

and Steck (1995), who also found that school psychologists reported CBC to be more acceptable than other modes of BC, clearly suggesting that school psychologists, parents, and teachers find CBC to be an acceptable model of service delivery. However, this research used survey methodology, assessing acceptability of analogue situations rather than actual cases. Thus, the results of these studies are based on hypothetical acceptability not actual experience with the model.

CBC outcome studies have extended the social validity literature base to include treatment acceptability measurements from field-based casework. A 4-year study examining the effectiveness of 52 CBC cases demonstrated parents and teachers found the CBC process to be acceptable (Sheridan et al., 2001). Specifically, parent and teacher ratings on the Acceptability factor of the Behavior Intervention Rating Scale-Revised (BIRS-R; Elliott & Van BrockTreuting, 1991) demonstrated that CBC was a highly acceptable process. These results are not unique to this outcome study as multiple CBC studies have investigated the acceptability of CBC and have found it to be rated as highly acceptable by parents and teachers alike. Refer to Table 9.2 for a complete list of outcome studies that measured social validity.

Goal Attainment

Sladeczek and colleagues (2001) investigated participants' perceptions of client goal attainment as a program evaluation procedure within the context of a CBC case study. Specifically, a kindergarten teacher referred a 5-year-old preschool boy, Anthony (fictitious name), for conduct problems. The teacher reported Anthony frequently screamed when angry, and his mother indicated that he was demanding of her attention by clinging to her. The initial goals for consultation were to decrease Anthony's inappropriate behaviors (i.e., decrease screaming behavior at school and decrease clinging behavior at home).

During the CPAI, baseline data were discussed, intervention goals were identified, and intervention strategies were developed. The GAS worksheet was used to identify clear goals for the target behaviors. Baseline data were anchored to the 0 position (i.e., no progress), the best-possible scenario for the target behavior was anchored to the +2 (i.e., goal fully met), and the worst-possible scenario was rated as a −2 (i.e., situation significantly worse). During intervention, the parent, teacher, and consultant met weekly to discuss the degree to which the intervention was effective. The GAS represented an average frequency of the target behavior over a 1-week period and provided the teacher and parent with a common language to communicate the effectiveness of the intervention.

During the last few weeks of the intervention, Anthony's parents and teacher both consistently rated his progress toward the intervention goals at +2 (goal fully met). The GAS scores can also be transformed into a T score, using the computation provided by Cardillo and Smith (1994). At the end of intervention, Anthony had a T score of 64.18, which indicated positive outcomes for the intervention package implemented within the context of CBC. Despite the positive outcomes of this case study, caution should be executed when generalizing outcomes given the single-participant design. Further, GAS may not be useful for establishing an absolute level of functioning.

Previous outcome studies have also used GAS to assess parent and teacher perceptions of consultation goals. A 4-year investigation by Sheridan et al. (2001) examined the effectiveness of 52 CBC cases. Goal attainment reports indicated that 100% of parents and 94% of teachers rated goals as partially or fully met. The following section reviews parent and teacher perceptions of helpfulness during the context of CBC.

Helpfulness Research

Sheridan, Erchul, et al. (2004) conceptualized CBC as a help-giving model and examined the congruency of parent and teacher perceptions of helpfulness in actual CBC cases. Although the literature suggests that congruence among systems increases academic performance (Hansen, 1986; Hill, 2001) and congruence between consultants' and consultees' on their respective roles is associated with positive outcomes of consultation (Erchul, Hughes, Meyers, Hickman, & Braden, 1992), no research prior to the Sheridan, Erchul, et al. study examined the degree to which congruency of perceptions between parents and teachers has an impact on consultation outcomes. Specifically, Sheridan and colleagues sought to assess (a) the degree to which parents and teachers found the CBC consultant to be helpful and (b) the relationship between parent and teacher agreement and social validity and behavioral outcomes.

Participants included 118 child clients, 137 parents, 122 teachers, and 53 graduate consultants. Measures collected at the time of consultation were used as predictor variables. The Acceptability factor of the BIRS-R was used to assess parent and teacher acceptability of CBC. GAS provided a second assessment of parents' and teachers' perceptions of efficacy through their rating of the degree to which consultation goals were achieved. In addition, the CEF (Erchul, 1987) was used to measure parents' and teachers' perceptions of the consultant's helpfulness. Individual child outcomes were measured via permanent products and direct behavioral observations throughout the implementation of CBC with effect sizes computed using a no assumptions approach (Busk & Serlin, 1992).

To assess the congruence between parents' and teachers' perceptions of helpfulness, a Pearson correlation was computed between parents' and teachers' total scores on the CEF. The resulting correlation was nonsignificant. Correlations between parent and teacher agreement scores (i.e., absolute difference score between parent and teacher CEF scores) and effect sizes were also nonsignificant. The results suggest that parents' and teachers' perspectives of the helpfulness of the consultant are not necessarily related to one another. However, negative correlations were found between parent and teacher agreement scores (i.e., CEF difference scores) and social validity outcomes (i.e., teacher acceptability, parent acceptability, and parent effectiveness ratings). These results suggest that as differences between parents and teachers regarding the helpfulness of CBC increased, the acceptability of the model decreased. For parents only, as the differences among parents and teachers increased, the perceptions of the efficacy of CBC decreased.

The acceptability and helpfulness research for the CBC model is accumulating. Although the research appears to indicate CBC is an acceptable model of service delivery for parents, teachers, and school psychologists in both hypothetical and naturalistic contexts, more research using a variety of methods is needed. Future research should utilize a combination of methods (e.g., surveys, semistructured interviews, and focus groups) to glean more detailed information on the consultees' perceptions of acceptability.

WHERE WE ARE GOING: EVOLUTION OF CONJOINT BEHAVIORAL CONSULTATION

Current conceptions of professional practice of family-based service delivery call for a family-centered approach that aims specifically at promoting competence and providing a context for empowerment. Philosophically, calls encouraging the consideration of parents as partners within educational decision making promote services that are responsive to family needs, strengths based rather than focused on deficits, and valid within a family's cultural and ecological contexts. These tenets of family-centered services have influenced the continued conceptualization and evolution of CBC within an emerging paradigm.

Family-Centered Services

The significance of the family context on child development has been established (Sheridan, Eagle, & Dowd, 2005); however, services provided to families to enhance outcomes on behalf of children have not always been delivered through a model that respects existing family strengths, values, and competencies. A family-centered philosophy of practice has been championed by family service providers (Dunst & Trivette, 1987; McWilliam, Snyder, Harbin, Porter, & Munn, 2000). The philosophy behind family-centered services emphasizes the importance of promoting positive family functioning by facilitating empowerment on behalf of family members. Such services are characterized by four guiding principles outlined in a model developed by Dunst and Trivette (1987). These principles include (a) intervention efforts must be based on family- (rather than professional-) identified needs; (b) existing strengths and capabilities of the family must be used to enhance developing competencies; (c) personal family social networks must be maximized as a source of support; and (d) helping behaviors must be used to promote new skills and abilities. In addition, family-centered services emphasize the importance of the process by which families work toward goals rather than focus solely on final outcomes.

The guiding principle advanced in this chapter states that partnerships and collaboration between these home and school systems are necessary to promote optimal outcomes for children (Christenson & Sheridan, 2001; Sheridan et al., 1996). To achieve this goal within a conjoint framework, CBC research and practice has begun to adopt a philosophy of partnership-centered practices that parallels that of family-centered practices. Within this philosophy, the strengths and capacities of both families and educators are fostered through a positive working relationship that is driven by the jointly identified goals and needs of the child. A strong emphasis is placed on the process by which a partnership between the home and school is developed, which is facilitated through collaboration and communication. In addition, an important role of the consultant is to promote enhanced skills and capacities of families and educators to facilitate empowerment. Importantly, these principles are embodied within and embellish (rather than replace) the structured, evidence-based decision-making context of the CBC model. The relevance of each partnership-centered principle within the context of CBC is explored next.

Principles of Partnership-Centered Conjoint Behavioral Consultation

Partnership-Centered Conjoint Behavioral Consultation Focuses on Jointly Identified Needs and Priorities

The focus of the CBC process is determined by the mutually identified priorities and concerns of the educators and caregivers on behalf of the child. It is assumed that these individuals are in the best position to determine the most salient needs of the child within the natural contexts of home and school. By allowing consultees to determine the priorities for consultation with the guidance of a consultant, it is likely that an effective match with the culture and values of homes and schools will be facilitated, and families and educators will be invested in the process (Sheridan, Warnes, Cowan, et al., 2004). The primary objective of the CBC process is then to ensure that these identified needs are met to help the child positively engage in his or her home and school system. To do so, consultants provide opportunities in the initial stages of CBC for consultees to identify priorities that are most salient to them, rather than focusing on the predetermined targets of the consultant (Sheridan et al., 1996). Consultants also remain flexible in meeting the needs of the parents and teachers by assisting them in developing interventions and data collection measures that fit within the context of the environment (Sheridan et al., 2005). As a result, it is expected that teachers and caregivers are more likely to be invested in the process and willing to carry out intervention plans with integrity.

Partnership-Centered Conjoint Behavioral Consultation Uses Existing Strengths and Capabilities of Consultees to Promote Developing Competencies in Addressing Concerns

The principle of using existing consultee strengths and capabilities to promote developing competencies in addressing concerns underscores the belief that all families and educators possess unique strengths and expertise. Specifically, teachers possess knowledge of child development, classroom management, and educational processes, and families have a unique understanding of the individual child and the home environment (Sheridan et al., 2005). The knowledge of the consultees is vital in understanding the distinctive needs of each child and developing culturally sensitive interventions to address concerns. Consultants are called on to assist consultees to identify and mobilize existing strengths and expertise to promote positive functioning on behalf of the child (Sheridan, Warnes, Cowan, et al., 2004). By acknowledging the abilities of the consultees, consultants are in a position to enhance the self-efficacy of parents and teachers to create positive changes in the life of the child (Dunst, Trivette, & Deal, 1988). It is the task of the consultant to establish an atmosphere that focuses on family and educator strengths and resources rather than deficits. These key components must be systematically acknowledged and utilized as a foundation for intervention planning and implementation.

Partnership-Centered Conjoint Behavioral Consultation Strives to Maximize Social Networks and Resources of Support Across Contexts

Another aim of the CBC process is to establish strong linkages across the home and school systems that foster positive support networks long after consultation is terminated (Sheridan, Warnes, Cowan, et al., 2004). Throughout the process, partnerships between home and school are fostered through joint problem solving and responsibility sharing (Sheridan et al., 2005). Both parties are provided equal decision-making opportunities, emphasizing the notion of a true "partnership." Consultants facilitate such a partnership by addressing decision making as a team, ensuring that all parties are allowed power in determining goals and intervention plans. They also attempt to provide a safe atmosphere in which parents and educators feel free to share different perspectives without fear of repercussion while still maintaining positive communication.

Partnership-Centered Conjoint Behavioral Consultation Is Delivered Through Helping Behaviors That Promote New Skills and Abilities for Consultees

An additional objective of CBC is to provide consultees with the skills and knowledge of how to address identified concerns for their child in the future (Sheridan et al., 1996). Through participation in the process, consultees are provided with the knowledge and practice of using a structured, data-based approach to systematically develop interventions designed to promote positive outcomes. As a result, families and educators are provided with the necessary tools to address future concerns and decrease their dependence on the support of the consultant, thus facilitating empowerment (Sheridan, Warnes, Cowan et al., 2004). Consultants facilitate new skill development by structuring the problem-solving process in such a way that allows consultees to focus their efforts using a systematic approach. Consultees learn to prioritize, define, monitor, and evaluate concerns in the initial stages of the CBC process. Data collected from consultees' observations are discussed with the team and used to guide the process. Consultants refer to this information to help parents and teachers select developmentally appropriate goals and interventions based on meaningful information. In addition, strategies are discussed for how to modify intervention efforts and continue assessment of ongoing treatment goals. Throughout each step of the process, consultants provide consultees with rationales for why it is important, thus giving the process away by making it overt.

Partnership-Centered Conjoint Behavioral Consultation Emphasizes the Importance of the Process in Addition to Outcomes

Although one of the main objectives of CBC has always been to effect positive change on behalf of the child, the process by which parents and educators reach this aim is important. Active engagement and collaboration among parents and teachers are essential in achieving these goals and are vital to the CBC process (Sheridan et al., 1996). Throughout CBC, consultants provide opportunities for consultees to take active responsibility by sharing information and implementing assessment and intervention strategies. Although the role of the consultant is to facilitate and support the process, consultees bear most of the responsibility for assessment and intervention.

WHAT WE NEED TO KNOW: FUTURE RESEARCH AGENDA

Despite the increasing empirical support for the efficacy and social validity of CBC, clear and important research challenges remain. In light of increasing demands for accountability and evidence of empirical support for interventions implemented in school and other practice settings, the demand for broad and rigorous research is omnipresent. In addition, new research questions related to both process and outcome are evident as the CBC model continues to evolve. As in other forms of consultation research, many of the questions at their most basic levels are concerned with interactions between participants and systems, exhibit mediating and moderating variables influencing outcomes, and require both depth and breadth in uncovering and understanding their complexity. In this section, we address new and expanding research questions in need of investigation and methodological requirements necessary to move the field of CBC research forward.

New Research Questions

As in any growing and evolving field, the proliferation of research in CBC paradoxically opens the door for even more empirical investigation covering a broad and expansive scope. Several important areas of research exist, some of which are reviewed here. Examples of research agendas presented include the (a) need to understand conditions under which CBC is effective, including the setting (where), sample characteristics (for whom), and their relationship to outcomes; (b) effects of CBC on consultee variables such as competence, role construction, and self-efficacy; (c) effects of CBC on relationships at all levels, including those between parents, teachers, and children; (d) long-term maintenance effects of CBC outcomes, including maintenance of interventions, partnerships, and relationships between participants; and (e) utility of CBC as a prevention model. New and sophisticated research designs will be required to address several of these agendas, and they are also explored.

Setting Characteristics

In practice, CBC has been implemented in multiple settings (e.g., preschool programs, Head Start settings, and elementary schools). To date, little research has systematically investigated the utility of the model in different practice arenas. There is a need to study the effects of CBC across various contexts, each with its unique challenges. Interactions between settings, samples, targets, and other case-related variables will undoubtedly influence outcomes, and these need to be examined empirically. Examples of settings where CBC should be investigated systematically include pediatric medical settings, early intervention settings, and secondary schools.

CBC has been offered as a means to integrate systems and services for children with medical and educational needs. For example, Power, DuPaul, Shapiro, and Kazak (2003) suggested that CBC "provides a framework for (a) aligning the family, school, and health systems to facilitate the integration of children with health problems into school, and (b) integrating systems of care into the problem solving process" (p. 89). They went on to indicate that the model "may be highly useful in designing strategies to prevent further health risk and promote resilience in the school context" (p. 90). Similarly, Sheridan, Warnes, Ellis, et al. (2004) offered specific procedures for the inclusion of CBC within the framework of pediatric psychological services, linking family, school, and medical systems in addressing concerns of a child. Although preliminary outcome data are encouraging, much more research is needed to understand the effects of the model within the interdisciplinary medical environment and inherent challenges linking diverse systems of care.

A second setting within which CBC may be tested empirically is early childhood settings. As identified in the early intervention literature, factors that maximize effectiveness of early intervention efforts include continuity among caregiving systems, involvement of key stakeholders, positive relationships among caregivers, and a family-centered approach (Dunst & Trivette, 1987; Early, Pianta, Taylor, & Cox, 2001). Indeed, these characteristics represent some of the main principles of CBC, suggesting the potential usefulness of the model within early intervention contexts. Important research questions within this setting include effects of CBC on young children's academic development, self-management, and social skills; the utility of CBC as a means of engaging families as defined in early childhood special education law; the role of CBC in the development of Individualized Family Service Plans; and the degree to which the structured, collaborative CBC process can be integrated into home visits and other early childhood service delivery contexts.

The majority of practice and research in CBC has focused on services within elementary school programs. The effectiveness of the model within other educational settings is virtually unknown. For example, the context and nature of secondary school programs are qualitatively and structurally distinct. School organization, staffing, and size are variables that potentially affect the manner in which CBC services can be delivered and the type of effects that can be expected. Furthermore, the age of students served in secondary settings may influence the manner in which services are delivered. For example, the inclusion of students within the CBC process may be necessary to increase ownership of the process (Schemm, Dowd, & Sheridan, 2002; Schemm & Sheridan, 2002). CBC research within secondary settings is lacking.

Sample Characteristics

Research aimed at understanding participant characteristics and their relationship to CBC outcomes has yet to be conducted. There is a clear need in consultation research generally (Ingraham, 2000), including CBC research specifically (Sheridan, 2000), to understand empirically the effects of services on diverse samples. Developments in the area of evidence-based interventions (EBIs) have sorely neglected samples of culturally diverse participants (Doyle, 1998; Kratochwill & Stoiber, 2002). Attention to the effects of consultation and interventions for specific diverse groups of children has been encouraged by leaders in the EBI movement (e.g., American Psychological Association Division 16/Society for the Study of School Psychology Task Force on EBIs), who recommend evaluation of treatments and computation of separate effect sizes for individuals demonstrating cultural diversity (Kratochwill & Stoiber, 2002).

Conceptual discussions of CBC's use with culturally diverse clients have begun to appear. Specifically, Sheridan (2000) defined multicultural CBC as "a home-school consultation relationship wherein important individual differences are present among two or more participants (i.e., parent, teacher, student, school psychologist-consultant) with respect to association with distinct cultural group(s) … includ[ing] sociodemographic (e.g., race, gender, national origin, class, language) as well as less tangible features of individuals (e.g., beliefs, attitudes, values) and schools (e.g., norms, customs)" (p. 345). Features of CBC, such as interactive and collaborative problem solving; distributed decision making; appreciation for cultural values, perspectives, and norms; and relationship building, are consonant with the principles of culturally sensitive services. Relational processes inherent within the CBC model may allow for the recognition and appreciation of individual cultural differences among consultants, consultees, and clients. However, with the exception of a non-experimental investigation by Sheridan et al. (in press), little research has been conducted that identifies the efficacy of home-school consultation services with a diverse sample.

Effects on Consultees

One of the stated goals of all forms of BC, including CBC, is enhancing the skills and competencies of consultees. The basis for this goal lies in the assumption that involvement in the CBC process instills new skills in parents and teachers, which can be transferred to their work with other children, in other settings, and exhibiting other behavioral concerns. These goals and assumptions have not been tested heretofore. There is a clear research gap related to what consultees learn as a function of their involvement and how this learning generalizes beyond the immediate CBC case.

Related to the unknown effects on consultee skill development, little is known about the degree to which involvement in active and collaborative home-school decision making affects psychological variables related to teaching and parenting. Hoover-Dempsey and Sandler (1997) offered a model articulating the importance of parents' beliefs about their own role and ability to perform that role as precursors to active and meaningful involvement. Their model also addresses the relationship between teachers' beliefs about working with parents and the importance of parent involvement in learning. Future CBC research could investigate the degree to which these variables mediate consultee practices and CBC outcomes. Similarly, an investigation of the degree to which CBC affects these consultee variables (e.g., alters parent or teacher roles or enhances self-efficacy vis-à-vis cross-system partnerships and parental engagement in education) is in need of research attention.

Relationship Effects

A unique goal of CBC is concerned with enhancing relationships at all levels, including those between parents, teachers, and children. That is, there are clear and unequivocal attempts within CBC to strengthen relationships and a partnership between parents and teachers in support of children's learning. However, to date researchers have not assessed the degree to which this goal is met in practice. The effects of CBC as a model that supports family-school partnerships, enhances parent-teacher relationships, and encourages ongoing dialogue and shared decision making among participants is unknown.

Important features implicit in positive family-school relationships include trust and open, bidirectional communication between family members and school personnel (Christenson & Sheridan, 2001). Some have suggested that the ongoing and frequent contact between consultants, parents, and teachers inherent in CBC practice are potentially useful in building trust and promoting positive communication. These assumptions have not been tested empirically and are in need of research attention.

A third area of relational research necessary for investigation concerns the effect of CBC on relationships between parents and their children. It is possible that features within CBC may enhance parent-child relationships. For example, the strength-based approach suggested in new conceptualizations of CBC, a focus on solutions rather than problems, active participation in a child's education, and opportunities to support and encourage learning and development may influence parent-child relationships in positive ways. These are important outcomes in need of research attention.

Long-Term Effects of Conjoint Behavioral Consultation Outcomes

Given the promising immediate effects found in several CBC outcome studies, it is necessary to understand the long-term effects of the model. Whereas some studies have investigated short-term follow-up of CBC (e.g., Galloway & Sheridan, 1994; Sheridan et al., 1990), no research has extended the investigation of maintenance beyond a few weeks. Research is needed to determine the lasting effects of CBC interventions and procedures by which to ensure long-term outcomes.

In addition to maintenance of treatment effects on child participants, there is a need to examine the long-term effects of CBC on parent, teacher, and relational variables. Some of the consultee variables identified in this chapter are worthy of long-term assessment, including the effects on parents' ongoing involvement in their children's educational programs and teachers' continued use of home-school partnership practices.

Conjoint Behavioral Consultation as a Prevention Model

CBC outcome research has focused historically on its effects on participants referred for intervention given challenging behaviors or intractable academic concerns. This approach characterizes the CBC process as one concerned with identified samples in a reactive (i.e., indicated) framework. However, prevention science in contemporary service delivery frameworks supports the benefits of addressing concerns in universal and selective samples as well. That is, emphasis is placed on addressing concerns through large-scale intervention efforts addressing entire groups (as in universal services) or subgroups of children at risk for unhealthy development (selective services; Power, 2003) through early identification and intervention efforts. Research on the role of CBC as an intervention model within preventive service delivery options is clearly warranted.

Design Features in Future Research

As is evident from the discussion on scope and depth of research needs, the emerging needs and complex issues facing CBC researchers present significant challenges related to the design and analysis of empirical studies. It is no longer sufficient to ask questions such as, Does CBC work? using traditional univariate or single-participant designs. To further advance the field, researchers must address the daunting issues facing consultation (and CBC) services and attempt to understand a host of methodological issues.

Randomized trials have been regarded as the hallmark of intervention science. Such designs allow researchers to randomly assign participants to experimental and control conditions to test systematically the effects of interventions. Such designs increasingly are becoming the criterion for federally funded research and require serious consideration among consultation researchers. Within such designs, interactions between variables and the identification of specific variables predicting outcomes are possible. Once consultation is demonstrated to be effective under highly controlled experimental procedures, efficacy studies can be conducted to identify factors that are necessary to bring models "to scale."

The inherent interactions among systems and participants need to be studied to understand the complex dynamics of consultation, including what works, for whom, and under which conditions. In a similar vein, the identification of predictor variables that mediate and moderate outcomes is necessary to discern the relationship between services and outcomes. Longitudinal models that address growth over time, particularly those that attend to the inherent nested nature of research conducted within classrooms and schools, are necessary to move the consultation field forward.

Despite the importance of, and press for, increasingly rigorous methodological designs, it is imperative that important qualitative features of the consultation process and relationships therein are addressed in CBC research. Mixed methods, including rigorous qualitative features of research, are necessary. Such designs will allow more depth in understanding not only what works under which conditions, but also the essential question, Why? Researchers are encouraged to embrace such complex designs with high levels of sophistication based on recommendations in sources such as Creswell (2002) and Nastasi, Moore, and Varjas (2003).

CONCLUSIONS

CBC is a structured, indirect model of service delivery by which parents, educators, and consultants work collaboratively to meet a child's developmental and learning needs, address concerns, and achieve positive outcomes by promoting the competencies of all participants (Sheridan & Kratochwill, 2007). It is operationalized via four stages aimed at (a) identifying and prioritizing a child's target behavior, (b) setting goals and selecting intervention strategies that can be used cooperatively at home and school, (c) implementing a joint plan across home and school settings, and (d) evaluating the plan and monitoring the child's progress toward goals. CBC holds promise as an evidence-based parent consultation model (Guli, 2005). Outcome research has demonstrated CBC to be an effective model for addressing the needs of children who are at risk for academic, behavioral, or social difficulties. Furthermore, research indicates the CBC process establishes a collaborative context for joint problem solving and planning. Research in CBC has also extended the previous literature on hypothetical acceptability of consultation models to include participant perceptions of acceptability from field-based casework. Parents, teachers, and school psychologists have identified CBC as an acceptable model of service delivery in both hypothetical and naturalistic settings.

Reforms within the education field call for the inclusion of family-centered principles into professional practice to promote competence and empowerment in families. CBC practices parallel and extend those of family-centered services to include a partnership-centered philosophy. Within a partnership-centered framework, the process by which goals are achieved is recognized to be as important as the achievement of positive child outcomes. Active collaboration and communication between the home and school systems are recognized as central to the achievement of positive child and relational outcomes.

This evolution of the CBC model has established the need for further empirical investigation of both outcomes and processes of CBC. Specifically, future research in this area should be expanded to include (a) conditions under which CBC is effective, (b) the effects of CBC on consultee variables, (c) the effects of CBC on relationships, (d) long-term maintenance effects of outcomes, and (e) the utility of CBC as a prevention model. To advance the field, researchers should address these complex issues through new and advanced research designs such as randomized trials and mixed-method approaches.

CBC research indicates the model is effective, acceptable, and collaborative. By its very design, CBC is positioned to address the growing demands of schools to be accountable for student outcomes and to form home-school partnerships. There is a clear need to establish and disseminate valid training guidelines to encourage school psychology training programs to embrace the CBC model. Clearly, this type of specialized training in consultation and home-school partnerships will prepare future school psychologists to address the increasing needs of children, families, and schools.

ACKNOWLEDGMENTS

Preparation of this chapter was supported in part by grants funded by the U.S. Department of Education (R305F05284 and H325D030050) and National Institutes of Health (5R01HD046135) awarded to the first author. The ideas and opinions expressed here belong to the authors and do not reflect those of the granting agencies. Appreciation is extended to Elaine Clark, Mary Haskett, Tom Kehle, Tom Kratochwill, Judy Oehler-Stinnett, Dan Olympia, and Ingrid Sladeczek, who provided information on CBC dissertations completed under their mentorship. Special gratitude is expressed toward all the graduate students, parents, teachers, and children who have participated in CBC research over the decades.

REFERENCES

Achenbach, T. M. (1991a). *Manual for the Child Behavior Checklist/4-18 and 1991 Profile*. Burlington: University of Vermont, Department of Psychiatry.

Achenbach, T. M. (1991b). *Manual for the Teacher's Report Form and 1991 Profile*. Burlington: University of Vermont, Department of Psychiatry.

Bergan, J. R., & Tombari, M. L. (1976). Consultant skill and efficiency and the implementation and outcomes of consultation. *Journal of School Psychology, 14*, 3–14.

Brown, M. S. (2004). Effects of early childhood-conjoint behavioral consultation (EC-CBC) on preschool child compliance. *Dissertation Abstracts International, 65* (08), 2894A.

Busk, P., & Serlin, R. (1992). Meta-analysis for single-case research. In T. R. Kratochwill & J. Levin (Eds.), *Single-case research design and analysis* (pp. 187–212). Hillsdale, NJ: Erlbaum.

Cagle, M. L. (2003). Conjoint behavioral consultation with parents and teachers of Hispanic children: A study of acceptability, integrity, and effectiveness. *Dissertation Abstracts International, 64* (02), 394A.

Cardillo, J. E., & Smith, A. (1994). Psychometric issues. In T. J. Kiresuk, A. Smith, & J. E. Cardillo (Eds.), *Goal Attainment Scaling: Applications, theory, and measurement* (pp. 173–241). Hillsdale, NJ: Erlbaum.

Christenson, S. L. (2004). The family-school partnership: An opportunity to promote the learning competence of all students. *School Psychology Review, 33*, 83–104.

Christenson, S. L., & Sheridan, S. M. (2001). *Schools and families: Creating essential connections for learning*. New York: Guilford Press.

Colton, D. L. (1999). Utilizing behavioral consultation services to support the inclusion of students with learning disabilities in the general education classroom. *Dissertation Abstracts International, 59* (11), 4052A.

Colton, D. L., & Sheridan, S. M. (1998). Conjoint behavioral consultation and social skills training: Enhancing the play behaviors of boys with attention deficit hyperactivity disorder. *Journal of Educational and Psychological Consultation, 9*, 3–28.

Creswell, J. W. (2002). *Research design: Qualitative, quantitative, and mixed methods approaches* (2nd ed.). Thousand Oaks, CA: Sage.

Doyle, A. B. (1998). Are empirically validated treatments valid for culturally diverse populations? In K. S. Dobson and K. D. Craig (Eds.), *Empirically supported therapies: Best practice in professional psychology* (pp. 93–103). Thousand Oaks, CA: Sage.

Dunst, C. J., & Trivette, C. M. (1987). Enabling and empowering families: Conceptual and intervention issues. *School Psychology Review, 16*, 443–456.

Dunst, C. J., Trivette, C. M., Davis, M. & Cornwell, J. C. (1994). Characteristics of effective help-giving practices. In C. J. Dunst, C. M. Trivette, & A. G. Deal (Eds.), *Supporting and strengthening families. Vol. 1: Methods, strategies and practices* (pp. 171–186). Cambridge, MA: Brookline.

Dunst, C. J., Trivette, C. M., & Deal, A. G. (1988). *Enabling and empowering families: Principles and guidelines for practice*. Cambridge, MA: Brookline.

Early, D. M., Pianta, R. C., Taylor, L. C., & Cox, M. J. (2001). Transition practices: Findings from a national survey of kindergarten teachers. *Early Childhood Education Journal, 28*, 199–206.

Elliott, S. N., & Von Brock Treuting, M. B. (1991). The Behavior Intervention Rating Scale: The development and validation of a social validity measure. *Journal of School Psychology, 29*, 43–52.

Elliott, S. N., Witt, J.C., & Kratochwill, T. R. (1991). Selecting, implementing, and evaluating classroom interventions. In G. Stoner, M. R. Shinn, & H. M. Walker (Eds.), *Interventions for achievement and behavior problems* (pp. 99–135). Silver Spring, MD: National Association of School Psychologists.

Erchul, W. P. (1987). A relational communication analysis of control in school consultation. *Professional School Psychology, 2*, 113–124.

Erchul, W. P., & Chewning, T. G. (1990). Behavioral consultation from a request-centered relational communication perspective. *School Psychology Quarterly, 5*, 1–20.

Erchul, W. P., Hughes, J. N., Meyers, J., Hickman, J. A., & Braden, J. P. (1992). Dyadic agreement concerning the consultation process and its relationship to outcome. *Journal of Education and Psychological Consultation, 3*, 119–132.

Erchul, W. P., & Schulte, A. C. (1990). The coding of consultation verbalizations: How much is enough? *School Psychology Quarterly, 5*, 256–264.

Erchul, W. P., Sheridan, S. M., Ryan, D. A., Grissom, P. F., Killough, C. E., & Mettler, D. W. (1999). Patterns of relational communication in conjoint behavioral consultation. *School Psychology Quarterly, 14*, 121–147.

Finn, C. A. (2003). Remediating behavior problems of young children: The impact of parent treatment acceptability and the efficacy of conjoint behavioral consultation and videotape therapy. *Dissertation Abstracts International, 63* (07), 2456A.

Freer, P., & Watson, T. S. (1999). A comparison of parent and teacher acceptability ratings of behavioral and conjoint behavioral consultation. *School Psychology Review, 28*, 672–684.

Galloway, J., & Sheridan, S. M. (1994). Implementing scientific practices through case studies: Examples using home-school interventions and consultation. *Journal of School Psychology, 32*, 385–413.

Gortmaker, V., Warnes, E. D., & Sheridan, S. M. (2004). Conjoint behavioral consultation: Involving parents and teachers in the treatment of a child with selective mutism. *Proven Practice, 5*, 66–72.

Gresham, F. M. (1989). Assessment of treatment integrity in school consultation and prereferral intervention. *School Psychology Review, 18*, 37–50.

Gresham, F. M., & Elliott, S. N. (1990). *Social Skills Rating System manual*. Circle Pines, MN: American Guidance Service.

Gresham, F. M., & Noell, G. (1993). Documenting the effectiveness of consultation outcomes. In J. E. Zins, T. R. Kratochwill, & S. N. Elliott (Eds.), *Handbook of consultation services for children: Application in educational and clinical settings* (pp. 249–273). San Francisco: Jossey-Bass.

Grissom, P. F., Erchul, W. P., & Sheridan, S. M. (2003). Relationships among relational communication processes and perceptions of outcomes in conjoint behavioral consultation. *Journal of Educational and Psychological Consultation, 14*, 157–180.

Guli, L. A. (2005). Evidence-based parent consultation with school-related outcomes. S*chool Psychology Quarterly, 20*, 455–472.

Hansen, D. A. (1986). Family-school articulations: The effects of interaction rule mismatch. *American Educational Research Journal, 23*, 643–659.

Haynes, N. M., Comer, J. P., & Hamilton-Lee, H. M. (1989). School climate enhancement through parental involvement. *Journal of School Psychology, 27*, 87–90.

Heatherington, L., & Friedlander, M. L. (1987). *Family Relational Communication Control Coding System coding manual*. Unpublished manuscript, Williams College, Williamstown, MA.

Hill, N.E. (2001). Parenting and academic socialization as they relate to school readiness: The roles of ethnicity and family income. *Journal of Educational Psychology, 93*, 686–697.

Hoover-Dempsey, K. V., & Sandler, H. M. (1997). Why do parents become involved in their children's education? *Review of Educational Research, 67*, 3–42.

Illsley, S. D. (2003). Remediating conduct problems in children: Examining changes in children and parents following consultation. *Dissertation Abstracts International, 64* (4-B), 1904B.

Illsley, S. D., & Sladeczek, I. E. (2001). Conjoint behavioral consultation: Outcome measures beyond the client level. *Journal of Educational and Psychological Consultation, 12*, 397–404.

Ingraham, C. L. (2000). Consultation through a multicultural lens: Multicultural and cross-cultural consultation in schools. *School Psychology Review, 29,* 320–343.

Kazdin, A. E. (1977). Assessing the clinical or applied significance of behavior change through social validation. *Behavior Modification, 1,* 427–452.

Kazdin, A. E. (1980). Acceptability of alternative treatments for deviant child behavior. *Journal of Applied Behavior Analysis, 13,* 259–273.

Kiresuk, T. J., Smith, A., & Cardillo, J. E. (Eds.). (1994). *Goal Attainment Scaling: Applications, theory, and measurement.* Hillsdale, NJ: Erlbaum.

Kratochwill, T. R., Elliott, S. N., Loitz, P. A., Sladeczek, I. E., & Carlson, J. (2003). Conjoint consultation using self-administered manual and videotape parent-teacher training: Effects on children's challenging behaviors. *School Psychology Quarterly, 18,* 269–302.

Kratochwill, T. R., & Sheridan, S. M. (1990). Advances in behavioral assessment. In T. B. Gutkin & C. R. Reynolds (Eds.), *Handbook of school psychology* (2nd ed., pp. 328–364). New York: Wiley.

Kratochwill, T. R., & Stoiber, K. C. (2002). Evidence-based interventions in school psychology: Conceptual foundations of the *Procedural and Coding Manual of Division 16 and the Society for the Study of School Psychology Task Force. School Psychology Quarterly, 17,* 341–389.

Lasecki, K. L. (2001). Normalizing blood glucose levels in children with Type I diabetes: Mystery motivators used within the context of behavioral consultation models. *Dissertation Abstracts International, 61* (10), 5231B.

Leaper, C. (1991). Influence and involvement in children's discourse: Age, gender, and partner effects. *Child Development, 62,* 797–811.

Lepage, K. M. (1999). Conjoint behavioral consultation: An evaluation of competency-based training through consultant outcomes, consumer satisfaction, and treatment effects. *Dissertation Abstracts International, 59* (7), 2363A.

Masten, A. S., & Coatsworth, J. D. (1998). The development of competence in favorable and unfavorable environments: Lessons from research on successful children. *American Psychologist, 53,* 205–220.

McWilliam, R. A., Snyder, P., Harbin, G. L., Porter, P., & Munn, D. (2000). Professionals' and families' perceptions of family-centered practices in infant-toddler services [Special issue: *Families and Exceptionality*]. *Early Education and Development, 11,* 519–538.

Morganstein, T. (2003). Peer relations and self-perceptions of boys with behavioral problems. *Dissertation Abstracts International, 63* (7), 2458A.

Moscovitz, K. (2004). The effects of group communication processes on treatment outcomes in school-based problem solving teams. *Dissertation Abstracts International, 65* (01), 69A.

Mulgia, E. N. (2001). Conjoint consultation versus the directive approach on language arts homework completion and accuracy in elementary school children. *Dissertation Abstracts International, 62* (01), 532B.

Myers, L. W. (1997). Conjoint behavioral consultation as an intervention for young children with disruptive behaviors. *Dissertation Abstracts International, 57* (12), 7714B.

Nastasi, B. K., Moore, R. B., & Varjas, K. M. (2003). *School-based mental health services: Creating comprehensive and culturally specific programs.* Washington, DC: American Psychological Association.

No Child Left Behind Act of 2001, Pub. L. No. 107-110, 115 Stat. 1425 (2002).

Noell, G. H., Witt, J. C., Slider, N. J., Connell, J. E., Gatti, S. L., Williams, K. L., et al. (2005). Treatment implementation following behavioral consultation in schools: A comparison of three follow-up strategies. *School Psychology Review, 34,* 87–103.

Olympia, D., Jenson, W. R., & Hepworth-Neville, M. (1996). *Sanity savers for parents: Tips for tackling homework.* Longmont, CO: Sopris West.

Power, T. J. (2003). Promoting children's mental health: Reform through interdisciplinary and community partnerships. *School Psychology Review, 32,* 3–16.

Power, T., DuPaul, G. J., Shapiro, E. S., & Kazak, A. E. (2003). *Promoting children's health: Integrating school, family, and community.* New York: Guilford.

Ray, K. P., Skinner, C. H., & Watson, T. S. (1999). Transferring stimulus control via momentum to increase compliance in a student with autism: A demonstration of collaborative consultation. *School Psychology Review, 28,* 622–628.

Schemm, A. V., Dowd, S. E., & Sheridan, S. M. (2002, March). *Student inclusion in dropout prevention: Utilizing conjoint behavioral consultation: A case study.* Paper presented at the annual convention of the National Association of School Psychologists, Chicago.

Schemm, A. V., & Sheridan, S. M. (2002, August). *Conjoint behavioral consultation: Providing tools for dropout prevention.* Paper presented at the annual convention of the American Psychological Association, Chicago.

Schnoes, C. J. A. (2003). *Conjoint behavioral consultation, ADHD, and homework: A combined intervention package for middle school youth with ADHD.* University Microfilms International.

Scope, C. R. (2003). The efficacy of conjoint behavioral consultation to reduce the off-task behavior of elementary school children diagnosed with Attention Deficit Hyperactivity Disorder. *Dissertation Abstracts International, 64* (6), 1975A.

Sheridan, S. M. (2000). Considerations of multiculturalism and diversity in behavioral consultation with parents and teachers. *School Psychology Review, 29,* 344–353.

Sheridan, S. M., Clarke, B. L., Knoche, L. L., & Edwards, C. P. (2006). The effects of conjoint behavioral consultation in early childhood settings. *Early Education and Development, 17,* 593–617.

Sheridan, S. M., & Colton, D. L. (1994). Conjoint behavioral consultation: A review and case study. *Journal of Educational and Psychological Consultation, 5,* 211–228.

Sheridan, S. M., Eagle, J. W., Cowan, R. J., & Mickelson, W. (2001). The effects of conjoint behavioral consultation: Results of a 4-year investigation. *Journal of School Psychology, 39,* 361–385.

Sheridan, S. M., Eagle, J. W., & Doll, B. (2006). An examination of the efficacy of conjoint behavioral consultation with diverse clients. *School Psychology Quarterly, 21,* 396–417.

Sheridan, S. M., Eagle, J. W., & Dowd, S. E. (2005). Families as contexts for children's adaptation. In S. Goldstein & R. Brooks (Eds.), *Handbook of resiliency in children* (pp. 165–179). New York: Kluwer Academic/Plenum Press.

Sheridan, S. M., Erchul, W. P., Brown, M. S., Dowd, S. E., Warnes, E. D., Marti, D. C., et al. (2004). Perceptions of helpfulness in conjoint behavioral consultation: Congruity and agreement between teachers and parents. *School Psychology Quarterly, 19,* 121–140.

Sheridan, S. M., & Kratochwill, T. R. (1992). Behavioral parent-teacher consultation: Conceptual and research considerations. *Journal of School Psychology, 30,* 117–139.

Sheridan, S. M., & Kratochwill, T. R. (2007). *Conjoint behavioral consultation: Promoting family-school connections and interventions.* New York: Springer.

Sheridan, S. M., Kratochwill, T. R., & Bergan, J. R. (1996). *Conjoint behavioral consultation: A procedural manual.* New York: Plenum.

Sheridan, S. M., Kratochwill, T. R., & Elliott, S. N. (1990). Behavioral consultation with parents and teachers: Delivering treatment for socially withdrawn children at home and school. *School Psychology Review, 19,* 33–52.

Sheridan, S. M., Meegan, S. P., & Eagle, J. W. (2002). Assessing the social context in initial conjoint behavioral consultation interviews: An exploratory analysis investigating processes and outcomes. *School Psychology Quarterly, 17,* 299–324.

Sheridan, S. M., & Steck, M. C. (1995). Acceptability of conjoint behavioral consultation: A national survey of school psychologists. *School Psychology Review, 24,* 633–647.

Sheridan, S. M., Warnes, E. D., Cowan, R. J., Schemm, A. V., & Clarke, B. L. (2004). Family-centered positive psychology: Focusing on strengths to build student success. *Psychology in the Schools, 41,* 7–17.

Sheridan, S. M., Warnes, E. D., Ellis, C., Schnoes, C., Burt, J., & Clarke, B. (2004, July). *Efficacy of conjoint behavioral consultation in developmental-behavioral pediatric services.* Paper presented at the annual conference of the American Psychological Association, Honolulu.

Sladeczek, I. E., Elliott, S. N., Kratochwill, T. R., Robertson-Mjaanes, S., & Stoiber, K. C. (2001). Application of Goal Attainment Scaling to a conjoint behavioral consultation case. *Journal of Educational and Psychological Consultation, 12,* 45–59.

Stephan, W. C. (1999). Conjoint behavioral consultation: Delivering treatment for children in the special education program of an elementary school. *Dissertation Abstracts International, 60* (3), 1292B.

Von Brock, M. B., & Elliott, S. N. (1987). Influence of treatment effectiveness information on the acceptability of classroom interventions. *Journal of School Psychology, 25,* 131–144.

Weiner, R. K., Sheridan, S. M., & Jenson, W. R. (1998). The effects of conjoint behavioral consultation and a structured homework program on math completion and accuracy in junior high students. *School Psychology Quarterly, 13,* 281–309.

Witt, J. C., & Elliott, S. N. (1985). Acceptability of classroom management strategies. In T. R. Kratochwill (Ed.), *Advances in school psychology* (Vol. 4, pp. 251–288). Hillsdale, NJ: Erlbaum.

Witt, J. C., Erchul, W. P., McKee, W. T., & Pardue, M. M. (1991). Conversational control in school-based consultation: The relationship between consultant and consultee topic determination and consultation outcome. *Journal of Educational and Psychological Consultation, 2,* 101–117.

Wolfe, M. M. (1978). Social validity: The case for subjective measurement or how applied behavior analysis is finding its heart. *Journal of Applied Behavior Analysis, 11,* 203–314.

Ysseldyke, J., Dawson, P., Lehr, C., Reschly, D., Reynolds, M., & Telzrow, C. (1997). *School psychology: A blueprint for training and practice II.* Bethesda, MD: National Association of School Psychologists.

10

Bringing Instructional Consultation to Scale
Research and Development of IC and IC Teams

SYLVIA A. ROSENFIELD, ARLENE SILVA, AND TODD A. GRAVOIS

University of Maryland

Schools in the 21st century are in transition, moving away from a focus on sorting and sifting students to accountability for positive outcomes for all students. As a result, many changes in schools have been recommended, including an increasing call for data-based decision making, evidence-based interventions, focus on prevention and early intervention, and more effective professional staff development. In line with this challenge to improve outcomes for all students, one promising approach is to enhance student outcomes through the development of support services to staff, using the framework of consultee-centered consultation.

Unlike traditional special services in the schools, where service is provided directly to students through specialists serving in an expert capacity, consultee-centered consultation is characterized by a focus on a consultee's work problem (Knotek, Kaniuka, & Ellingsen, chapter 7, this volume; Lambert, 2004). The primary task of the consultant and consultee is jointly to develop a new conceptualization of the work problem such that the consultee gains professional knowledge and skill and uses it to help not only the referred client, but also potentially other clients of the consultee. In other words, consultee-centered consultation is designed not only to help with the specific work-related problem, but also to serve as a professional development opportunity for the consultee (e.g., teacher), with the underlying assumption that the consultant (e.g., school psychologist) will have a greater impact by working with the person who is directly responsible for the academic and personal development of an entire classroom of children than providing direct service to the student.

One model of consultee-centered consultation is instructional consultation (IC; Rosenfield, 1987, 2002a). IC has a dual focus on *content* (i.e., instructional assessment, evidence-based academic and behavioral interventions) and *process* (i.e., problem-solving steps, which include data collection, and the collaborative, working relationship with the classroom teacher). Through these double lenses, IC seeks to improve, enhance, and increase student achievement through improving, enhancing, and increasing teachers' performance. It is the explicit emphasis on supporting teachers' professional capacity to develop and deliver effective instruction within the general education classroom that defines IC as a form of consultee-centered consultation. The model is based on the premise that quality instructional and management programming, matched to a student's assessed entry skills, increases student success, reduces behavioral difficulties, and avoids the need for special education evaluation and placement.

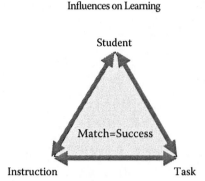

Figure 10.1   The instructional triangle.

In addition to existence as an individually delivered model of consultation service since the 1980s (Rosenfield, 1987), IC has been systematically implemented within the structure of instructional consultation teams (IC Teams; Rosenfield & Gravois, 1996). The complex innovation package of IC Teams is "characterized by three features: (a) a delivery system structured around an interdisciplinary team; (b) a collaborative instructional consultation process; and (c) an evaluation design to ensure that the innovation package has been implemented with integrity" (Gravois & Rosenfield, 2006, p. 45). The goals of the IC Team are to build a collaborative, problem-solving culture within the school by providing a core of professionals competent in the IC process. Each member of the IC Team is trained to engage in the three critical skill sets that comprise the IC process: (a) capacity to build a collaborative working relationship with the consultee to enable reflection and a reframed perspective on the concern of the consultee; (b) skill in conducting a systematic problem-solving process; and (c) knowledge and skills in instructional and behavioral assessment and intervention.

An essential characteristic of the IC and IC Team model is the focus on instructional context. The three points of the instructional triangle (Figure 10.1), central to the model, result in a framework for (a) examining the student's prior knowledge, level of skill development, and learning rate; (b) use of instructional time, classroom management procedures, instructional delivery, and assessment in conjunction with the teacher's expectations for the student; and (c) the task demands presented to the student. This differs from client-centered models, which tend to focus more on student characteristics in relative isolation from the instructional context. Instructional consultants are committed to examining the relationship between academic and behavioral problems, such that classroom problems are always examined first as potential academic concerns. Because of the salience of behavior problems to classroom teachers, underlying academic problems of the student may not be perceived as a strong contributor to the teacher's concerns about the student's behavior unless the consultant ensures that academic problems are considered as a routine part of defining the problem.

Teachers voluntarily seek out IC Team members, who are trained as instructional consultants, and work collaboratively with them through a formalized problem-solving process. IC Team members include key stakeholders in the school, namely administrators, general and special educators, school psychologists, school counselors, health care providers, and social workers. When the IC Team receives a request for assistance, a team member is assigned as consultant (i.e., a case manager) and becomes responsible for guiding the teacher through the problem-solving stages, which are tracked on the IC Student Documentation Form (SDF; Rosenfield, 2002a). The stages, which are at the heart of the IC process, include the following:

1. *Contracting*: The consultation relationship is discussed, including the teacher's expectations, time commitment, focus of problem solving, need for data collection, and non-evaluative nature of the process. The IC Team model is explained, and the case manager ensures that the teacher is committed to this form of problem solving.

2. *Problem Identification and Analysis:* This stage accounts for a considerable portion of the effort in the IC Team's process. The following information is recorded on an SDF: (a) initial description of the concerns (academic or behavioral); (b) priority of the concerns; (c) assessment of student's instructional level (whether the student has the prerequisite skills to function in the activity presented); (d) baseline data collection of the prioritized concern, graphically represented; (e) an observable and measurable statement of current performance of the prioritized concern based on the baseline data; and (f) short-term, interim, and long-term goals for achieving the expected performance.

3. *Intervention Design:* The dyad develops strategies for a plan that is feasible, research and data based, and acceptable to all concerned. A detailed description of the strategy to be implemented is documented on the SDF, including who will be responsible for each aspect of the intervention. In addition, the dyad decides how and when the effectiveness of the intervention will be evaluated.

4. *Intervention Implementation and Evaluation:* Data are collected and charted on the SDF. The dyad makes changes to the intervention as needed based on the data and teacher's use of the intervention. The student's performance is compared with the baseline data to monitor progress.

5. *Closure:* Plans for maintaining the achieved progress are discussed. A case summary form is completed, and the case is formally concluded.

IC Teams have been implemented in multiple sites across urban/rural/suburban schools, as well as districts in several states, since first appearing in the Early Intervention Project in Connecticut in the mid-1980s to address the overrepresentation of urban minority students in special education programs (see Rosenfield, 1992, for a more complete history of the origins of IC Teams). Early versions of the teaming structure were subsequently implemented in a New York State district (Kuralt, 1990) and the Project Link Pennsylvania consortium (Fudell, 1992), where the teams demonstrated promise in increasing student academic and behavioral achievement, reducing the overidentification of students in special education, and improving the quality of teaching within the general education classroom (Rosenfield, 1992). Since 1990, IC Teams have been refined and implemented in school districts in Maryland, Virginia, Delaware, North Carolina, Nevada, and Michigan. As of fall 2006, over 200 schools have or are currently implementing IC Teams, and a federally funded experimental study of the model is under way in one school district.

More than 20 years of research and design activities have resulted in the development of a conceptual model that proposes the theoretical and causal links between IC and IC Teams and specific outcomes. The causal model (Figure 10.2), proposed by Gravois and Rosenfield (2002), depicts the complex configuration of IC within a team delivery system. The process and content are designed to have an impact on both student and teacher outcomes, including special education referral patterns for both culturally and linguistically diverse (CLD) students and non-CLD students, student attainment of academic and behavioral goals, teacher satisfaction and perception of consultation effectiveness, teacher implementation of new instructional strategies, and teacher problem-solving ability and change in beliefs about problem origins. Evaluation of these outcomes within schools implementing IC Teams has been critical in guiding program refinement.

The goal of this chapter is to document not only the ongoing research and program evaluation on IC and IC Teams, but also the developmental path that created the critical elements. IC and IC Teams have evolved through a research-and-development process consistent with one presented by Tharp and Gallimore (1979), who recognized that such development "requires time ... in which ... some errors and corrections are anticipated; and in which ... the process and epistemology of

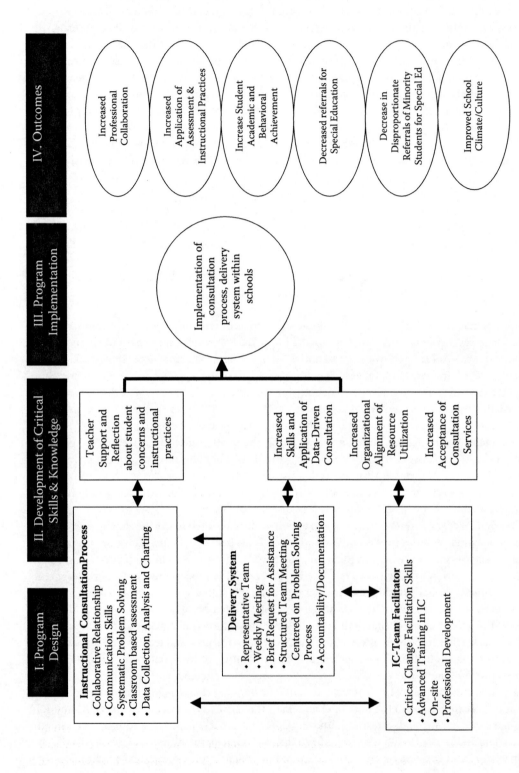

Figure 10.2   Causal model of instructional consultation teams. (From Gravois & Rosenfield, 2002.)

science governs the outcomes" (p. 39). Tharp and Gallimore's road map takes into account the complexity of the research-and-development process of complex interventions, acknowledging that "program developers cannot determine in advance which association of elements will survive the selection pressures of the succession of evaluation steps," although "this is what the typical, short-term, fixed program, summative-evaluated educational intervention must do" (p. 58). They understand that "local issues preclude generalization; feedback from data is halting and slow; conditions giving rise to an outcome change more rapidly than old solutions can even be attempted" (p. 40). What appears in its final form to be simple is actually the product of a systematic process of research and development.

In this chapter, we frame the underlying conceptual base for IC. Next, the core elements of IC are described. Then, the evolution of IC Teams as a means of scaling up IC use within schools is presented. Included is a summary of the research on and development of the implementation process for IC Teams, in this case research on training and treatment integrity. Finally, the emerging data on outcomes obtained through both program evaluation and empirical research are presented.

CONCEPTUAL BASE OF INSTRUCTIONAL CONSULTATION

IC developed from the roots of behavioral/problem-solving consultation (Kratochwill, Elliott, & Callan-Stoiber, 2002) and consultee-centered consultation (Lambert, Hylander, & Sandoval, 2004). However, several concepts from social development theory (Vygotsky, 1962, 1978) inform the IC Team model, including child in context as the unit of analysis, growth and development as a result of the zone of proximal development (ZPD), heterogeneous learning environments, mediation of functioning by language, and dynamic assessment (Knotek, Rosenfield, Gravois, & Babinski, 2003; Partanen & Wistrom, 2004; Siegler & Alibali, 2005).

Vygotsky's sociocultural theory emphasizes the importance of considering context when examining behavior. In this view, sociocultural contexts define and shape individuals and their experiences. Social development theory emphasizes the change and process of an active child within a given cultural context instead of intraindividual outcomes and performance. As such, parental guidance, teacher instruction, and language use are seen as essential to development.

Vygotsky's emphasis on the child in context as the unit of analysis is reflected in IC. Unlike traditional assessment models, the focus of problem solving in IC is on the student in the context of the environment. The instructional triangle (Figure 10.1) ensures focus on the match among the student, the task, and instruction, in order for effective learning to occur. Moreover, because two outcome goals of IC are to solve problems in the general elementary education classroom and reduce inappropriate referrals to special education (particularly for CLD students), the concept of inclusive school communities relates to Vygotsky's theory by "underscoring the importance of interactions that facilitate learning and the heterogeneous context in which they must occur" (Udvari-Solner & Thousand, 1996, p. 183).

One of Vygotsky's seminal concepts is the ZPD, which is the distance between what individuals are able to achieve alone and what they can achieve when working together with a teacher or higher-skilled peer (Siegler & Alibali, 2005) or consultant (Knotek et al., 2003; Partanen & Wistrom, 2004) who can build on existing competencies. A ZPD can be created in any situation in which an activity or interaction enables individuals to move beyond their typical level of functioning.

Within IC and IC Teams, the concept of the ZPD has been applied to both the student's and the teacher's growth and development; in the latter case, increasing the teacher's skill will lead to an increase in students' development (Partanen & Wistrom, 2004). For example, the IC process focuses on maximizing students' development by aligning the teacher's expectations, use of instructional time, classroom management procedures, instructional delivery, classroom-based assessment, and task demands to the student's prior knowledge, level of skill development, and learning rate.

Perhaps the greatest strength of Vygotsky's concept of the ZPD within IC Teams is that teachers have the opportunity to enhance their own learning and thus are able to assume added responsibility for student learning outcomes. The educator remains an important force through which instructional and other environmental conditions can be altered to achieve the students' maximum development. In this context, it challenges the notion that particular students are unable to learn due to learning disabilities, attention difficulties, poor home environments, and other factors over which the teacher has little or no control. As the support enables the teacher to work on the student's problem differently, the student's ZPD is enlarged. Although it would appear difficult for the teacher to create individual ZPDs for every student in the classroom, through systematic IC the teacher is supported in creating a ZPD for the students who are not making progress, whether in classroom environments that seem to be meeting other student needs effectively or those in which concerns exist for multiple students.

Another major concept of Vygotsky's theory is the mediation of intellectual functioning by a culture's psychological and technical tools. Psychological tools (e.g., language systems, writing, maps, strategies, and scientific concepts) transform basic mental abilities into higher mental functions, such as abstract thinking. Language is seen as the most important psychological tool because the production and comprehension of language influences thinking, behavior, representations of the past, and plans for the future.

In IC Teams, the establishment of a collaborative working relationship is seen as an important prerequisite to problem solving and a vehicle for consultee change. In this case, dialogue, problem-solving skills, and the consultation process itself become psychological tools used as part of a social process to achieve growth and higher-order learning (Knotek et al., 2003). Language and the use of effective communication skills mediate development and consideration of new ideas as supportive consultants help teachers develop professionally (Rosenfield, 2004).

Curriculum-based assessment (CBA), the classroom-based assessment technique used in IC Teams, is an example of the use of dynamic assessment, another Vygotskian concept. By performing CBA, the consultant and teacher are able to gather data on the learning process, identify specific roadblocks to learning, and match classroom-based intervention to observable and measurable identified problems (e.g., Rosenfield, 1987).

THE THREE CORE ELEMENTS OF INSTRUCTIONAL CONSULTATION

Over the course of two decades, the essential elements of the IC process have been selected and embedded in the model, as shown on Figure 10.2. To reach the desired IC outcomes, three core elements must be present: (a) a collaborative working relationship built on effective communication and interpersonal skills, (b) a systematic problem-solving process, and (c) knowledge and skills in instructional and behavioral assessment and intervention. These elements are largely drawn from consultee-centered (Lambert et al., 2004) and behavioral/problem-solving consultation (Kratochwill et al., 2002) and the knowledge base of instructional and educational psychology.

The Collaborative Working Relationship

One of the main assumptions of IC is that teachers, as professionals, are entitled to consult and collaborate around their classroom concerns, and this assumption reflects the belief that teaching is complex work best done in collaborative school cultures. The establishment of a working relationship between the consultant and consultee is seen as an important prerequisite to effective problem solving and a vehicle for consultee change, which is a focus of consultee-centered consultation. In the IC model, the collaborative working relationship is defined as "an interchange between two or more professional colleagues, in a nonhierarchal relationship, working together to resolve a problem" (Rosenfield, 1987, p. 21). The purpose of establishing and maintaining this working relationship with the consultee is to build a sense of trust, facilitate clarification of expectations for participation in the IC process, and enable consultation participants to work "shoulder to shoulder" through the stages of the process, rather than having the consultant shoulder the problem alone (Rosenfield, 1987). The collaborative relationship is reciprocal, so that, for example, data collection and analysis are most appropriately done as conjoint activities. Similarity in the manner in which the consultant and consultee perceive the process is one requirement for high implementation integrity.

The importance attached to the collaborative working relationship between professionals reflects the Vygotskian concept of the social context for learning and professional growth (Knotek et al., 2003). As such, this type of consultative relationship becomes a vehicle for expanding the ZPDs of the teacher-consultee. Supportive collaboration allows teachers to discuss perceived failures, weaknesses, and uncertainties within a nonevaluative setting (Fullan & Hargreaves, 1991). In this relationship, both participants are seen as having important contributions and areas of expertise and are actively involved in all areas of the problem-solving process.

Research on Collaboration

The element of collaboration has garnered theoretical, empirical, and real-world support and is consistent with the revisions to the Individuals With Disabilities Education Act (e.g., Allen & Graden, 2002; Fullan & Hargreaves, 1991). The benefits of a collaborative working relationship have been hypothesized to include the following (e.g., Pounder, 1998; Pugach & Johnson, 1995; Schulte & Osborne, 2003):

1. Maximization of the resources of the consultant and consultee.
2. Gain in skill and knowledge by both the consultant and consultee.
3. Increased likelihood that the consultee will take appropriate ownership and implement the intervention effectively due to investment of time, ideas, and energy to the problem-solving process.
4. Increased likelihood that the consultee will be better able to address similar problems in the future.

Although research examining the direct effect of collaboration on increased consultee intervention implementation or client outcomes is scarce, research on the traditional, expert model of consultation suggests that it is less effective in producing change in schools due to a variety of factors (Schulte & Osborne, 2003). Furthermore, research using the Consultation Preference Scale has indicated that general and special educators, administrators, and early intervention professionals prefer collaboration to traditional expert consultation (Schulte & Osborne, 2003). Based on these findings, the development of collaboration has gained increased support within most problem-solving models of consultation (e.g., Kratochwill et al., 2002).

The establishment of collaborative working relationships in IC has also been supported in a microethnographic research study examining the impact of the IC process within one school. Consultants who were specialists (e.g., school psychologists and resource teachers) reported that the collaborative working relationship "fostered flexibility in thinking and opened up unseen possibilities with which to better serve the students" (Knotek et al., 2003, p. 320). Teachers indicated that the collaborative component of the IC process was helpful in the problem-solving process. They valued the relationships they established with their consultants and felt that their perspectives were seen as integral to the IC process.

Communication Skills

Building the relationship requires that the consultant use communication skills that support the process. Language plays a central role in consultee-centered consultation practice because the process is largely mediated through verbal interactions (Rosenfield, 2004). Rosenfield (2004) provided examples from the literature on the powerful impact that language has within the various helping professions and the importance of examining what clinicians and consultants actually say in their interactions. For example, White, Summerlin, Loos, and Epstein (1992) documented in several case studies the importance of language within the context of the consultation relationship.

Language serves not only as one of the major tools needed to build the relationship, but also as the vehicle consultants use to co-construct the problem with the consultee. Rosenfield (2004) explored how meaning about problems is constructed through dialogue, with the consultant's role as an "architect of the dialogue, creating space for and facilitating the consultation conversation" (p. 139). Jones (1999) explored the process of constructing the problem within IC in a simulation study. She demonstrated how differently an initial teacher concern was constructed depending on the consultant's verbal interactions with the confederate teacher-consultee even among consultants who were in training to use the IC process. The scripted teacher role was developed to provide cues, including family problems, emotional problems, behavior problems, or academic problems, and the consultant's task was to engage with the teacher-consultee in the problem identification stage of IC. Consultants developed different types of relationships with the teacher and learned different kinds of information, depending on the specific communication strategies they used. The study results were parallel to those of Tombari and Bergan (1978), who found that the use of questions and verbal prompts was a powerful force for defining the kind of information generated and for determining whether teachers felt empowered in their ability to resolve the problems.

Benn and Rosenfield (in press) further explored how communication skills have an impact on the problem identification stage of IC. Three expert judges rated videotapes of consultant interviews with a confederate consultee as competent, partially competent, or novice, according to criteria based on IC core competencies. Six interviews were selected, two of which had been consistently rated in each category. Quantitative analysis documented that the use of clarifying questions and statements, designed to enable consultees to be more precise and specific in reflecting on and defining their student concerns, was more frequent by consultants rated as competent; other differences in types of questions were not found. This finding suggests that certain types of questions, especially clarifying questions, can be productive tools and serves to modify the original recommendation of Rosenfield (1987) to use questions sparingly. White et al. (1992) shared the perspective that questions in consultation can be helpful. For example, they found that open questions that solicit the consultee's opinion regarding the consultant's statements and hypotheses could ensure that the consultee agrees with the progression and direction of the case. It is the type of question, rather than the question structure itself, that appears to be the critical variable. In their process-outcome study of questions within behavioral consultation, Hughes, Erchul, Yoon, Jackson, and Henington (1997) noted the importance of certain types of questions (i.e., open-ended, inference, accepted questions). However, their correlational results were limited, and they concluded that future research needed to acknowledge the responsive, rather than prescriptive, use of questions within consultation.

Benn and Rosenfield's (in press) qualitative analysis expanded understanding of the role of language usage in the problem identification stage. Specifically, they showed that the content of the verbal interactions was different between the competent and less-competent IC consultants. The competent consultants, in contrast to those less competent, used the communication skills to guide problem solving along the framework of problem identification specific to IC (Rosenfield, 1987, 2002a). The substantive differences in communication across competency levels that emerged from the qualitative analysis suggest that coding schemes and quantitative analyses may not be sufficiently sensitive to capture the subtle yet important distinctions in the use of language within the IC process. These findings are also congruent with those of Gutkin (1999) and Rosenfield (2004), who both recommended examining communication skills in their context and not through coding schemes based on the category or structure of responses.

Systematic, Data-Based Decision Making

Within the problem-solving stages, IC incorporates the quality indicators of data-based decision making that have been identified in the literature (e.g., Allen & Graden, 2002). These indicators are defining problems in observable and measurable terms, setting goals, and monitoring progress, including charting and graphing. Evaluating the integrity of the indicators (i.e., treatment integrity) is also an integral part of the IC model (Rosenfield & Gravois, 1996).

Problem-Solving Stages

The use of problem-solving stages is not unique to IC or the consultation literature. Nezu and Nezu (1989) described the importance of using stages in clinical decision making for behavior therapy. They recommended the use of such stages, including problem definition and solution implementation, to reach more effective decisions and ensure that the clinical tasks of therapy are accomplished. In addition, they described how adopting such stages enables clinicians to base decisions on empirical research and minimize judgmental errors.

In IC, teachers partner with instructional consultants to work through a formalized problem-solving process (Rosenfield, 1987, 2002a). The instructional consultant is responsible for guiding the process through these stages, which were defined in the beginning of this chapter: contracting, problem identification and analysis, intervention design, intervention implementation and evaluation, and closure. During the contracting stage, the consultant obtains verbal informed consent from the teacher to engage in the process. One of the goals of contracting is to increase the consultee's awareness of the problem-solving stages. Consultee awareness of the stages of problem solving has been related to enhanced problem definition skill (Cleven & Gutkin, 1988).

Considerable focus in IC is directed toward the problem identification stage because there is evidence that accurately identifying the problem is crucial to effective problem solving (Deno, 2002). Research findings support the idea that well-defined problems lead to relevant solutions and effective decision making (Nezu & Nezu, 1989). In addition, the definition of problems in observable and measurable terms, as required in the problem identification and analysis stage of IC, significantly increases the probability of obtaining successful problem resolution (Bergan & Tombari, 1976).

Data Collection and Analysis

Data-based decision making has been cited as an underlying principle of effective, outcome-oriented practice (e.g., Allen & Graden, 2002; Stoner & Green, 1992; Ysseldyke et al., 2006). Throughout the IC stages, data are collected to help identify the problem, establish a baseline, and judge intervention effectiveness (Rosenfield & Gravois, 1996). For example, CBA data are typically collected during problem identification to determine the student's baseline skills in the area of concern and are used to develop goals and select an intervention. Postintervention data (e.g., number of known sight words) are collected on an ongoing basis to ensure that the intervention is effective in moving the student toward the goals. Goals are specifically set for each identified concern, an important aspect of progress monitoring.

Research findings also support the use of ongoing progress evaluation. In a meta-analysis investigating the effects of formative evaluation procedures on student achievement, Fuchs and Fuchs (1986) reported that using a systematic evaluation process significantly increased the school achievement of mildly handicapped students (effect size of 0.7). In addition, Telzrow, McNamara, and Hollinger (2000) found that multidisciplinary teams judged to have clearly identified goals and collected data on student responses to intervention were significantly more likely to have higher student goal attainment (although the relationship accounted for a modest 8% of the variance in outcome). Flugum and Reschly (1994) also found specific data-based components to be critical to effective early intervention procedures, including direct measurement of the student's behavior in the natural setting prior to intervention implementation (baseline data) and direct comparison of the student's postintervention performance with baseline data (assessment of change).

Charting of Data

In the IC process, the consultant and teacher chart data on the SDF (Gravois, Rosenfield, & Gickling, 2002; Rosenfield, 2002a; Rosenfield & Gravois, 1996) and compare the data to the goals set in the problem identification stage, also captured on the SDF. Maintaining a graphic record is an important component of effective intervention (Deno, 2002; Flugum & Reschly, 1994). According to Deno (2002), charting data creates a visual picture of the differences between the student's baseline performance and the desired performance, which helps determine appropriate goal setting. In addition, the graph provides continuous feedback on the student's progress toward the goal, such that changes to interventions can be dynamically monitored (Deno, 2002). In their meta-analysis of the effects of formative evaluation procedures, Fuchs and Fuchs (1986) found that graphing data led to higher effect sizes in terms of student achievement compared to simply recording data. The authors inferred that graphing data leads to more accurate and frequent analysis of student performance by teachers as well as more frequent performance feedback to students.

Instructional Assessment and Intervention

IC has a consistent, although not sole, focus on student achievement, and the instructional triangle — student, instruction, and task — is at the heart of the model. A specific type of assessment, CBA, forms the basis for deciding on the intervention if the problem is an academic one. The interventions then designed to address the identified problem reflect principles and strategies that have an evidence base.

Instructional Assessment

Central to the problem-solving conversation between the consultant and the teacher is assessment that is pertinent to the development and delivery of effective instruction. The IC process incorporates CBA (Gravois & Gickling, 2002), more recently referred to as instructional assessment. CBA has been differentiated from curriculum-based measurement (CBM) because it is designed to identify the student's instructional needs within the classroom curriculum as well as to monitor progress (see Shinn, Rosenfield, & Knutson, 1989, for a more complete discussion of the distinction between CBA and CBM). Originally developed by Gickling and colleagues (Gickling & Havertape, 1981), CBA is a dynamic form of assessment in the Vygotskian tradition, with the consultant and teacher gathering data to explore the student's entry skills, approach to curriculum tasks, and patterns of performance within an assessment process that continually manages the amount of challenge presented to the student (Gravois & Gickling, 2002).

The CBA process itself is guided by the extant research on the influence of prior knowledge on learning as well as the importance of having appropriate levels of challenge and ensuring an instructional match, even during the assessment itself (e.g., Gickling & Thompson, 1985; Gravois & Gickling, 2002). For example, prior knowledge enables students to connect existing knowledge and skills with new learning and is central to learning new tasks. Unlike many forms of norm-referenced assessment, CBA ensures that a student's prior knowledge is incorporated into the assessment task. For example, in reading, CBA identifies the appropriate level of challenge for each student (e.g., 93–97% known words in a reading passage), and errors made by students assessed at their instructional level may be quite different from those made when they are assessed in reading material at frustration level. CBA effectively creates the foundation for providing instruction that promotes good classroom performance among low-achieving children as well as children diagnosed with attention deficit/hyperactivity disorder (e.g., Gickling & Thompson, 1985).

Instructional Interventions

IC enables the delivery of carefully planned interventions to students through consultation between a teacher and consultant (Rosenfield & Rubinson, 1985). The consultant continues to support the teacher-consultee during the implementation stage of the intervention, acknowledging that few interventions work with all students, and many require adaptation during the implementation phase based on the data that are gathered to track intervention results.

The specific instructional interventions chosen during the IC process incorporate educational research and identified best practice. Some common examples of instructional principles frequently used in the IC process are presented in Table 10.1.

One example of a frequently used IC intervention for sight words uses the strategy of interspersed or incremental rehearsal of known and unknown material embedded in the folding-in strategy, sometimes also known as the *drill sandwich* (Coulter & Coulter, 1990). This technique incorporates many of the effective learning components described in the literature, such as distributed practice on rote basic skills (such as sight words or math facts) throughout the day. For example, a 7-year-old student might work with a drill sandwich that includes seven known and three unknown sight words interspersed in a sequence. By including only three unknown words of ten in the drill material, the student's age-based working memory limits are honored, and the student is ensured of some success by the presence of known material (Gravois & Gickling, 2002). The importance of managing challenge ratios (i.e., known-to-unknown ratios) has and continues to be extensively researched (see, e.g., Burns, 2004; Cooke & Reichard, 1996; Roberts & Shapiro, 1996), with refinements derived from such research incorporated into the IC process. The drill sandwich technique is quick and easy to implement by teachers, instructional assistants, and peers in the classroom, as well as by parents at home, allowing for distributed practice in a variety of settings. Regular CBA monitors that the unknown words are learned consistently (e.g., moved from working to long-term memory) and informs the composition of the drill material so that the ratio of known to unknown material is maintained.

Table 10.1   Instructional Components of Instructional Consultation Interventions

Component	Reference
Instructional match	Gickling and Thompson, 1985; Gravois and Gickling, 2002; Ysseldyke and Christenson, 1993
Academic engaged time	Harris, 1979; Ysseldyke and Christenson, 1993
Pace of instruction	Harris, 1979
Difficulty of material	Gickling and Thompson, 1985; Gravois and Gickling, 2002; Harris, 1979
Working memory limits	Pascuel-Leon, 1970, as cited in Gravois and Gickling, 2002
Instructional presentation	Ysseldyke and Christenson, 1993
Teacher expectations	Harris, 1979; Ysseldyke and Christenson, 1993
Distributed practice	Ysseldyke and Christenson, 1993
Interspersal	Neef, Iwata, and Page, 1980
Informed feedback	Ysseldyke and Christenson, 1993
Classroom environment	Ysseldyke and Christenson, 1993
Motivational strategies	Harris, 1979; Ysseldyke and Christenson, 1993

INSTRUCTIONAL CONSULTATION TEAMS: BRINGING INSTRUCTIONAL CONSULTATION TO SCALE

There is a considerable body of literature documenting the difficulty of moving research to practice and of scaling up even the most empirically sound educational programs (e.g., Rosenfield, 2000; Sarason, 1990). Among the issues related to the acceptance of consultation models in the schools, there are major problems related to effective training (e.g., Anton-LaHart & Rosenfield, 2004) and treatment fidelity (e.g., Telzrow et al., 2000) that have emerged in the scaling up of consultation models. Once the core competencies of IC for individual consultant-consultee dyads had been identified and implemented in early iterations, a scaling up process was designed that involved developing a team-based structure to ensure use of the core competencies within the existing realities of school settings. In this section, three basic issues that have been addressed in the evolution of IC within IC Teams are described: creating the organizational structure to deliver consultation services, creating effective professional development experiences, and ensuring integrity of consultation implementation.

Instructional Consultation Teams

IC is often implemented in schools within the structure of IC Teams (Rosenfield & Gravois, 1996). The goal of IC Teams, a school-based early intervention team model, is the same as for IC (i.e., to enhance, improve, and increase student and staff performance). In other words, it is not only the student who is the focus of the team, but also the staff members, reflecting the consultee-centered nature of IC. Each member of the IC Team is trained to engage in the IC process, involving the same three sets of skills described: (a) capacity to build a collaborative working relationship with the consultee to enable reflection and a reframed perspective on the concern of the consultee, (b) skill in conducting a systematic problem-solving process, and (c) knowledge and skills in instructional and behavioral assessment and intervention. However, one of the unique features of IC Teams is that the teacher does not directly come to the team for assistance. When the IC Team receives requests for assistance from teachers, a team member is assigned as a consultant (called a case manager in the IC Team model), and he or she assumes responsibility for guiding the teacher through the IC process (i.e., the formalized, data-based, problem-solving process consisting of the stages described in this chapter). It is only when the dyad becomes stuck in the problem-solving process that the teacher and case manager come to a team meeting for assistance.

The other major functions of the team structure are to support the members by providing ongoing professional development, to hold each of the team members and the team itself accountable for process integrity and outcomes through program evaluation activities, and to enhance the likelihood of building a collaborative school culture through building a core group of professionals committed to collaboration and skilled in problem solving. To ensure integrity in implementation, a design for delivering professional development (e.g., Gravois, Knotek, & Babinski, 2002) and assessing implementation integrity (Gravois & Rosenfield, 2002; Rosenfield & Gravois, 1996) has been developed.

Professional Development of Instructional Consultation Team Members

Since the 1990s, the training process for IC consultants and IC Team members has undergone extensive development. There now exists an IC Team training manual (Gravois, Rosenfield, et al., 2002), an IC Team facilitator training manual (Vail, Gravois, & Rosenfield, 1998), and a coaching manual (Gravois, Vail, & Nelson, 2004). Rosenfield (2002b) presented a model for moving individual instructional consultants from the novice to competent level on the core elements, while Gravois, Knotek et al. (2002) have described the multitier process of developing the core IC skills in IC Team members, using best practice in staff development (see also Gravois, Rosenfield, & Vail, 1999).

McKenna, Rosenfield, and Gravois (2005) documented that the training process used in developing IC Teams resulted in the ability of team members to demonstrate skill in using the IC process. A group of 20 IC consultant trainees, who worked in 12 different school districts in three states, consented to participate in the study. They received a training package, including a 20- to 25-hour training module, using the IC Team training manual, followed by coaching of a consultation case in their home schools. Participants audiotaped their consultation sessions so that they could receive online coaching from an experienced instructional consultant. The trainee mailed a tape after each consultation session to a coach, who provided feedback to the trainee via e-mail. The coaching process, documented in a detailed manual (Gravois, Vail, & Nelson, 2004), was found to be consistently applied by the coaches across all participants. The results indicated high implementation of the IC process, with each of the stages of consultation implemented by the new consultants at or above an 80% criterion level.

Treatment Integrity of Instructional Consultation Teams

The complexity of the IC process and the comprehensive training required to implement effectively the IC Team model created a need to measure and ensure integrity in use. A treatment integrity measure ensures that implementation occurred, so that the outcomes of a particular program could be attributed to the intervention. Documentation of implementation has been a priority for the IC model developers. Fudell (1992) developed a measure of implementation integrity for Project Link, a problem-solving model in the late 1980s that served as an early iteration of IC Teams. The Level of Implementation Scale Revised (LOI-R; Gravois, Fudell, & Rosenfield, 1998; Rosenfield & Gravois, 1996) is based on the earlier measure. The purpose of the instrument is both formative (providing schools with information on IC Team implementation, so that the school teams can identify training and development needs) and summative (providing data on schools' performance relative to established criteria and determining if outcomes are based on adequate treatment implementation).

The LOI-R assesses the collaborative consultation process and the service delivery system, representing the two main components of IC Teams measured by the scale; seven specific dimensions are identified as the essential characteristics for each of these two components. The LOI-R consists of interviews with case managers (consultants) and consultees (referring teachers) to document the level of implementation of the IC process. There are also document reviews, using the SDF (Rosenfield, 2002a; Rosenfield & Gravois, 1996). Analyzing interview responses and examining documentation forms determine implementation of the dimensions. Percentages of dimensions in place are then calculated.

The interrater reliability of the original LOI was assessed and initial content validity was based on expert judgment (Fudell, 1992). McKenna and colleagues (2005) conducted a validation of the LOI-R's Process Scale, the section of the LOI-R that assesses the process components of IC. In this validation study of the LOI-R, implementation scores on audiotapes of 20 completed IC consultation cases were compared to LOI-R interviews that had been completed with the teachers and consultants. The scores from coding the audiotapes were then compared to the LOI-R interviews conducted after cases were completed. Self-reports, as measured by the LOI-R interviews with the teachers and case managers, and actual behaviors, as measured by coding audiotapes of the sessions with the same critical dimensions, were significantly related. There were no significant discrepancies between the self-reported behaviors during the LOI-R interviews and the behaviors coded from the tapes. The LOI-R and audiotape scoring both indicated high levels of implementation for the seven dimensions investigated. The LOI-R was thus considered a valid measure of IC process implementation. Interrater reliability on the measures ranged from 90% to 96%.

In sum, IC training procedures have been established and evaluated. In addition, there is a process for supporting schools in the implementation of IC Teams and for evaluating the level of implementation of IC Teams. There is an emerging database to document that training results in trainees learning the process to a standard of implementation integrity, and there is evidence for the validity of the process dimensions of the LOI-R.

INSTRUCTIONAL CONSULTATION AND INSTRUCTIONAL CONSULTATION TEAM OUTCOMES

The causal model for IC Teams (Figure 10.2) reflects the interaction between the IC process and the delivery structure of IC Teams. We theorize that the core of the model is the IC process itself. However, the team structure is not considered ancillary. Instead, the team serves to broaden and deepen the acceptance of consultation services within the school setting, resulting in increased use of the IC process by staff. The team structure also serves to create a milieu that nurtures team members' continued skill development (Knotek et al., 2003). Instead of separating the effect of the IC process and IC Team structure, the logic model supports the reciprocal effect of this relationship on the outcomes that the process is designed to reach, including outcomes related to special education referral patterns, students, and teachers. The Laboratory for Instructional Consultation Teams collects program evaluation data for its project sites on an annual basis, and there have been quasi-experimental and qualitative research studies conducted by university researchers and students, as well as school districts implementing the project, much of which remains in the form of reports, conference papers, and other unpublished papers (see www.icteams.umd.edu for a complete list of documents). The evidence is further limited because of the lack of random assignment of schools to the experimental intervention (although an experimental evaluation of the IC Team model, federally funded by the Department of Education, is currently in progress). However, some research on outcomes (e.g., program evaluation data) is reported here.

Special Education Referral Patterns

As described, one of the goals of IC Teams is to help teachers resolve concerns in the general education classroom rather than refer students to special education. Gravois and Rosenfield (2002) used confirmatory program evaluation's criterion of consistency (Reynolds, 1998) to document the effect of IC Teams on overreferral and identification of students for special education. Using data from the implementation of the model in 37 schools in seven districts in one state over a period of 10 years, consistent evidence of IC Teams' positive effect on special education evaluations and placements was obtained. Although randomization was not used in these program evaluations, the results could be compared to structures then in place. Tharp and Gallimore (1979) considered this comparison of "other than program effects" a reasonable one that is based in the actual context of the schools.

A series of additional program evaluations conducted by school districts implementing IC Teams has documented the continued effect on special education referral patterns. These program evaluations document decreased student special education referral rates and increased "appropriate" special education placements corresponding with the number of years of IC Teams' implementation in a district (e.g., Coffey, 2001, 2002; Coffey, Rosenfield, & Smith, 2003; Gravois, 2004a, 2004b).

Culturally and Linguistically Diverse Student Referral Patterns

Several studies have also documented the effect of IC on CLD student referral patterns. Research comparing IC Teams to other school-based prereferral teams shows that IC Teams are effective in reducing CLD student special education referrals. The results have been demonstrated for both African American students (Gravois, 2004a, 2004b; Levinsohn, 2000; Weiner, 2002) and English language learners (Silva, 2005).

CLD students were less likely to be referred and found eligible for special education evaluation when they were served by IC Teams, as opposed to student support teams and other existing prereferral teams (Levinsohn, 2000; Silva, 2005; Weiner, 2002). Program evaluation reports from two projects in Maryland also have indicated decreased minority referral rates following IC Team implementation (Gravois, 2004a, 2004b).

Gravois and Rosenfield (2002, 2006) have documented the decrease in CLD student special education referral and placement patterns. Gravois and Rosenfield (2002) investigated IC Teams' effect on minority student special education data regarding referral and placement. For the 20 schools from which data were available, IC services, compared to current practices, led to significantly fewer African American students referred for evaluation or placed in special education. A more intensive investigation of the impact on minority referrals and placements is described by Gravois and Rosenfield (2006). Using multiple indices of disproportionality, specifically risk indexes, odds ratios, and composition indices, IC services demonstrated significant decreases in the risk of minority students referred and placed compared to nonproject schools.

Student Goal Attainment

Program evaluations across multiple districts have consistently documented that the goals set by teachers and consultants are achieved in the majority of cases when the process is followed with integrity (LaFleur & Rosenfield, 2005). Goal attainment is the metric used as the types of goals set for students depend on the individual teacher, consultant, and student concerns involved. Scoring of outcomes is based on the completed SDF, which contains baseline and intervention data as well as the goals. In such cases, students met or exceeded between 78% and 87% of the specific academic or behavioral goals set for them as a result of the consultation process (Coffey, 2001, 2002; Coffey et al., 2003; Gravois, 2004a, 2004b). An additional 3% to 19% of students made progress toward their goals. It is important to note that these results are based on data collected on these cases (e.g., mastery data on academic skills, behavioral observations) rather than teacher perceptions of goal attainment. Although the majority of students participating in IC Teams made progress toward goals seen as important by their classroom teacher, future research is needed to determine if the attainment of these goals affects student performance on high-stakes assessments.

Teacher Outcomes

Because IC is a form of consultee-centered consultation, teacher outcomes are important to assess. The effect of IC on three types of teacher variables has been studied: teacher satisfaction, teacher implementation of new instructional strategies, and teacher development of problem-solving skills.

Teacher Satisfaction

Costas, Rosenfield, and Gravois (2003) reported that the learning process resulting from IC Teams leads to high levels of teacher satisfaction. Survey and interview techniques were used to gather data from 274 teachers from six school districts implementing IC Teams over a 2-year period of data collection. Approximately 83% of teachers were reported as satisfied or very satisfied with IC Teams. Similar teacher satisfaction findings emerged from the annual program evaluations of other IC Team projects. In all cases, teacher ratings, based on a 5-point Likert scale, of their experience working with the IC Team ranged from satisfied to very satisfied (Coffey, 2001, 2002; Coffey et al., 2003; Gravois, 2004a, 2004b).

Implementation of New Instructional Strategies

In the Costas et al. (2003) study, a majority of teachers (92%) reported learning one or more skill or strategy as a result of participating in IC Teams. Equally important, half of the participants reported using strategies learned with another student or group of students. Program evaluation reports document similar findings. Teachers reported learning and implementing strategies that improved their ability to accurately assess students' skills within curriculum materials, provide individualized instruction, and generally facilitate student learning and growth (Coffey, 2001, 2002; Coffey et al., 2003; Gravois, 2004a, 2004b). These strategies included implementing data-based decision making, modifying and scaffolding instruction, building on student prior knowledge and prerequisite skills, and assessing instructional levels.

Teacher Problem Solving and Change

Over and above learning specific new instructional strategies, teachers reported higher-order learning in the problem-solving process and in their conception of classroom concerns; for example, 57% of teachers reporting learning process skills, such as how to use data to make decisions (Costas et al., 2003). In addition, most teachers reported feeling somewhat confident to very confident in their abilities to handle similar problems in the future. These findings suggest that the teachers learned to think differently about their students and their instructional planning.

Knotek et al. (2003) used a microethnographic research approach to examine how the IC Team's process supported teachers' problem solving and fostered change in their understanding of work problems over the course of an academic year in one school. Interviews, direct observations, consultation documents, and IC training documents were collected as data to support alignment with

Vygotsky's tenets of the social construction of knowledge. In particular, the researchers sought to examine development within the social context of the consultation relationship to learn how the interpersonal process enabled the participants to redefine and acquire new conceptions about the consultation problem. The unit of study was defined as consultation between a consultant and a teacher, in which one member of the school staff consulted with another member about how to improve student functioning in general education settings.

Results indicated that IC functions as a collaborative process that supports problem solving and fosters change in how both teachers and consultants conceptualize and perform within their professional roles. Specifically, effective alliance building, orderly reflection, and the generation of alternative hypotheses define IC as a constructive undertaking. Teachers valued the way consultants interacted with them. In addition, the study identified four characteristics of the process that helped facilitate the teachers' social construction of knowledge: (a) the process of reframing the problem from within-child deficits to instructional match, (b) the use of collaborative communications to enable the teacher to engage in a new form of thinking, (c) the use of data collection to represent objectively the students' functioning, and (d) the use of collaborative thinking to explore the work problems more deeply.

FUTURE RESEARCH AND PRACTICE IMPLICATIONS

The research reviewed in this chapter suggests that the IC Teams model, with the IC process embedded, holds promise as an effective problem-solving, teacher support team delivery system. The IC Team core components have been constructed based on evidence-based instructional and psychological principles and theory, first described by Rosenfield (1987). A well-developed training, technical assistance, and program evaluation design have supported scaling up of IC Teams. Consistency of findings across implementations, using confirmatory program evaluation methodology (Reynolds, 1998), has provided evidence for IC Team's effectiveness within real-world settings (Gravois & Rosenfield, 2002). Specifically, the results of the analyses suggest that IC Teams decrease special education referrals and placements and increase appropriate referrals. Program evaluation data consistently show that teachers achieve learning and behavior goals they set for their students when the process is conducted with integrity. In addition, teachers report satisfaction with IC Teams and indicate that they implement new problem-solving and instructional strategies as a result of collaborating with IC Team members. However, methodological limitations of the program evaluations require additional research be conducted that addresses some of the limitations inherent in the research conducted to date, especially that of nonrandom assignment.

The formative work to develop, implement, and evaluate IC Teams has created the foundation for an experimental study to verify the causal links between the model and its outcomes. Toward that end, a controlled, randomized study funded by the Department of Education, using schools as the unit of analysis, of the effects of IC Teams on a variety of outcome measures is currently under way to address questions related to the following variables: (a) achievement outcomes in reading and mathematics, (b) assignment of students to special education status, (c) retention in grade, (d) psychosocial adjustment, and (e) teacher efficacy and satisfaction.

Regarding further program development and refinement, some of the major issues to address include (a) determining the specific elements of the IC Team model that contribute to the outcomes (component analysis); (b) calculating the cost-benefit ratio of the program in comparison to other programs and given the resource allocation required to implement IC Teams with integrity; and (c) conducting longitudinal studies of teachers and students who have been involved in the IC process to determine more long-term outcomes on their development. On a practical level, the currently available evidence suggests that the IC Team model is a viable teacher support team model that can be scaled up because of the training and technical support structure that has been developed. In the current climate of increased standards and accountability, the results of additional and ongoing research projects will be required to determine whether the initial promise of IC is confirmed.

REFERENCES

Allen, S. J., & Graden, J. L. (2002). Best practices in collaborative problem solving for intervention design. In A. Thomas and J. Grimes (Eds.), *Best practices in school psychology–IV* (pp. 565–582). Bethesda, MD: National Association of School Psychologists.

Anton-LaHart, J., & Rosenfield, S. (2004). A survey of preservice consultation training in school psychology programs. *Journal of Educational and Psychological Consultation, 15*, 41–62.

Benn, A., & Rosenfield, S. (in press). Analysis of instructional consultants' questions and alternatives to questions during the problem identification interviews. *Journal of Educational and Psychological Consultation.*

Bergan, J. R., & Tombari, M. L. (1976). Consultant skill and efficiency and the implementation of outcomes of consultation. *Journal of School Psychology, 14*, 3–14.

Burns, M. K. (2004). Empirical analysis of drill ratio research: Refining the instructional level for drill tasks. *Remedial and Special Education, 25*, 167–175.

Cleven, C. A., & Gutkin, T. B. (1988). Cognitive modeling of consultation processes: A means for improving consultees' problem definition skills. *Journal of School Psychology, 26*, 370–389.

Coffey, M. (2001). *Instructional consultation teams: Baltimore City Public Schools and Laboratory for Instructional Consultation Teams 2000–2001 end of year progress report* (Tech. Rep. No. 9). College Park: University of Maryland, Laboratory for Instructional Consultation Teams.

Coffey, M. (2002). *Instructional consultation teams: Baltimore City Public Schools and Laboratory for Instructional Consultation Teams 2001–2002 end of year progress report* (Tech. Rep. No. 11). College Park: University of Maryland, Laboratory for Instructional Consultation Teams.

Coffey, M., Rosenfield, S., & Smith, J. (2003). *Instructional consultation teams: Baltimore City Public Schools and Laboratory for Instructional Consultation Teams 2000–2001 end of year progress report* (Tech. Rep. No. 12). College Park: University of Maryland, Laboratory for Instructional Consultation Teams.

Cooke, N. L., & Reichard, S. M. (1996). The effects of different interspersal drill ratios on acquisition and generalization of multiplication and division facts. *Education and Treatment of Children, 19*, 124–142.

Costas, L., Rosenfield, S., & Gravois, T. A., (2003, August). *Impact of instructional consultation on teacher satisfaction and skill development.* Poster session presented at the annual meeting of the American Psychological Association, Toronto.

Coulter, W. A., & Coulter, E. M. (1990). *Curriculum-based assessment for instructional design.* Unpublished training material. (Available from Directions and Resources, P.O. Box 57113, New Orleans, LA 70157.)

Deno, S. L. (2002). Problem solving as "best practice." In A. Thomas and J. Grimes (Eds.) *Best practices in school psychology–IV* (pp. 37–55). Bethesda, MD: National Association of School Psychologists.

Flugum, K. R., & Reschly, D. J. (1994). Prereferral interventions: Quality indices and outcomes. *Journal of School Psychology, 32*, 1–14

Fuchs, L. S., & Fuchs, D. (1986). Effects of systematic formative evaluation: A meta-analysis. *Exceptional Children, 53*, 199–208.

Fudell, R. (1992). Level of implementation of teacher support teams and teachers' attitudes toward special needs students. *Dissertation Abstracts International, 53* (05), 1399A. (UMI No. AAC-9227463)

Fullan, M. G., & Hargreaves, A. (1991). *What's worth fighting for? Working together for your school.* Andover, MA: Regional Laboratory for Educational Improvement of the Northeast and Islands.

Gickling, E. E., & Havertape, J. F. (1981). Curriculum-based assessment. In J. A. Tucker (Ed.), *Non-test based assessment* (pp. 189–410). Minneapolis: The National School Psychology Inservice Training Network, University of Minnesota.

Gickling, E. E., & Thompson, V. P. (1985). A personal view of curriculum-based assessment. *Exceptional Children, 52*, 205–218.

Gravois, T. A. (2004a). *Instructional Consultation Team Consortium: Eastern Shore IC Team Consortium phases 1 and 2 progress report, July 1, 2003–June 30, 2004* (Tech. Rep. No. 13). College Park: University of Maryland, Laboratory for Instructional Consultation Teams.

Gravois, T. A. (2004b). *Instructional Consultation Team Consortium: Western Maryland IC Team Consortium phases 1 progress report, July 1, 2003–June 30, 2004* (Tech. Rep. No. 14). College Park: University of Maryland, Laboratory for Instructional Consultation Teams.

Gravois, T. A, Fudell, R., & Rosenfield, S. (1998). *The instructional consultation team level of implementation scale-revised.* Unpublished manuscript.

Gravois, T. A., & Gickling, E. E. (2002). Best practices in curriculum-based assessment. In A. Thomas and J. Grimes (Eds.), *Best practices in school psychology–IV* (pp. 885–898). Bethesda, MD: National Association of School Psychologists.

Gravois, T. A., Knotek, S., & Babinski, L. (2002). Educating practitioners as instructional consultants: Development and implementation of the IC Team Consortium. *Journal Educational and Psychological Consultation,13,* 113–132.

Gravois, T. A., & Rosenfield, S. (2002). A multi-dimensional framework for the evaluation of instructional consultation teams. *Journal of Applied School Psychology, 19,* 5–29.

Gravois, T. A., & Rosenfield, S. (2006). Impact of instructional consultation teams on the disproportionate referral and placement of minority students in special education. *Remedial and Special Education, 27,* 42–52.

Gravois, T. A., Rosenfield, S. A., & Gickling, E. (2002). *Instructional consultation teams training manual.* College Park, MD: Laboratory for Instructional Consultation Teams.

Gravois, T. A., Rosenfield, S., & Vail, P. L. (1999). Achieving effective and inclusive school settings: A guide for professional development. Special Services in the Schools, *15,* 145–170. (Copublished simultaneously in S. I. Pfeiffer & L. A. Reddy, Eds., *Inclusion practices with special needs students: Theory, research, and application,* pp. 145–170. Binghamton, NY: Haworth Press)

Gravois, T. A., Vail, P. L., & Nelson, D. (2004). *Instructional consultation team coaching manual.* College Park, MD: Laboratory for Instructional Consultation Teams.

Gutkin, T. B. (1999). Collaborative versus directive/prescriptive/expert school-based consultation: Reviewing a false dichotomy. *Journal of School Psychology, 37,* 161–190.

Harris, A. J. (1979). The effective teacher of reading, revisited. *The Reading Teacher, 33,* 135–140.

Hughes, J., Erchul, W., Yoon, J., Jackson, T., & Henington, C. (1997). Consultant use of questions and its relationship to consultee evaluation of effectiveness. *Journal of School Psychology, 35,* 281–298.

Jones, G. (1999). Validation of a simulation to evaluate instructional consultation problem identification skill competence. *Dissertation Abstracts International, 60* (12A), 4317.

Knotek, S. E., Rosenfield, S. A., Gravois, T. A., & Babinski, L. M. (2003). The process of fostering consultee development during instructional consultation. *Journal of Educational and Psychological Consultation, 14,* 303–329.

Kratochwill, T. R., Elliott, S. N., & Callan-Stoiber, K. (2002). Best practices in collaborative problem solving for intervention design. In A. Thomas & J. Grimes (Eds.), *Best practices in school psychology–IV* (pp. 583–608). Washington, DC: National Association of School Psychologists.

Kuralt, S. K. (1990). *Collaboration in the classroom: Implementing consultation-based prereferral intervention as the service delivery system of five elementary multidisciplinary teams.* Unpublished doctoral dissertation, Fordham University, New York, NY.

LaFleur, A., & Rosenfield, S. (2005, April). *Student goal attainment and implementation integrity in instructional consultation teams.* Poster presented at the National Association of School Psychologists Meeting, Atlanta.

Lambert, N. M. (2004). Consultee-centered consultation: An international perspective on goals, process, and theory. In N. M. Lambert, I. Hylander, & J. H. Sandoval (Eds.), *Consultee-centered consultation: Improving the quality of professional services in schools and community organizations* (pp. 3–19). Mahwah, NJ: Erlbaum.

Lambert, N. M., Hylander, I., & Sandoval, J. H. (Eds.). (2004). *Consultee-centered consultation: Improving the quality of professional services in schools and community organizations.* Mahwah, NJ: Erlbaum.

Levinsohn, M. R. (2000). *Evaluating instructional consultation teams for student reading achievement and special education outcomes.* Unpublished doctoral dissertation, University of Maryland, College Park.

McKenna, S. A., Rosenfield, S., & Gravois, T. A. (2005, August). *Validity of the Instructional Consultation Teams (IC-Teams) Level of Implementation Scale-Revised (LOI-R)*. Poster presented at the annual meeting of the American Psychological Association, Washington, DC.

Neef, N. A., Iwata, B. A., & Page, T. J. (1980). The effects of interspersal training versus high-density reinforcement on spelling acquisition and retention. *Journal of Applied Behavior Analysis, 13,* 153–158.

Nezu, A. M., & Nezu, C. M. (Eds.). (1989). *Clinical decision making in behavior therapy: A problem-solving perspective*. Champaign, IL: Research Press Company.

Partanen, P., & Wistrom, C. (2004). Promoting student learning by consultee-centered consultation with a Vygotskian framework. In N. M. Lambert, I. Hylander, & J. H. Sandoval (Eds.), *Consultee-centered consultation: Improving the quality of professional services in schools and community organizations* (pp. 313–322). Mahwah, NJ: Erlbaum.

Pounder, D. G. (1998). *Restructuring schools for collaboration*. Albany: State University of New York Press.

Pugach, M. C., & Johnson, L. J. (1995). *Collaborative practitioners, collaborative schools*. Denver, CO: Love.

Reynolds, A. J. (1998). Confirmatory program evaluation: A method for strengthening causal inference. *American Journal of Evaluation, 19,* 203–221.

Roberts, M. L., & Shapiro, E. S. (1996). Effects of instructional ratios on students' reading performance in a regular education program. *Journal of School Psychology, 34,* 73–91.

Rosenfield, S. (1987). *Instructional consultation*. Hillsdale, NJ: Erlbaum.

Rosenfield, S. (1992). Developing school-based consultation teams: A design for organizational change. *School Psychology Quarterly, 7,* 27–46.

Rosenfield, S. (2000). Crafting usable knowledge. *American Psychologist, 55,* 1347–1355.

Rosenfield, S. (2002a). Best practices in instructional consultation. In A. Thomas & J. Grimes (Eds.), *Best practices in school psychology–IV* (pp. 609–623). Bethesda, MD: National Association of School Psychologists.

Rosenfield, S. (2002b). Developing instructional consultants: From novice to competent to expert. *Journal of Educational and Psychological Consultation, 13,* 97–111.

Rosenfield, S. (2004). Consultation as dialogue: The right words at the right time. In N. M. Lambert, I. Hylander, & J. H. Sandoval (Eds.), *Consultee-centered consultation: Improving the quality of professional services in schools and community organizations* (pp. 337–347). Mahwah, NJ: Erlbaum.

Rosenfield, S. A., & Gravois, T. A. (1996). *Instructional consultation teams: Collaborating for change*. New York: Guilford.

Rosenfield, S., & Rubinson, F. (1985). Introducing curriculum-based assessment through consultation. *Exceptional Children, 52,* 282–287.

Sarason, S. B. (1990). *The predictable failure of educational reform*. San Francisco: Jossey-Bass.

Schulte, A. C., & Osborne, S. S. (2003). When assumptive worlds collide: A review of definitions of collaboration in consultation. *Journal of Educational and Psychological Consultation, 14,* 109–139.

Shinn, M. R., Rosenfield, S., & Knutson, N. (1989). Curriculum-based assessment: A comparison of models. *School Psychology Review, 18,* 299–316.

Siegler, R. S., & Alibali, M. W. (2005). *Children's thinking* (4th ed.). Upper Saddle River, NJ: Pearson.

Silva, A. E. (2005). *English Language Learner special education referral and placement outcomes in instructional consultation teams schools*. Unpublished master's thesis, University of Maryland, College Park.

Stoner, G., & Green, S. K. (1992). Reconsidering the scientist-practitioner model for school psychology practice. *School Psychology Review, 21,* 155–166.

Telzrow, C. F., McNamara, K., & Hollinger, C. L. (2000). Fidelity of problem-solving implementation and relationship to student performance. *School Psychology Review, 29,* 443–462.

Tharp, R. G., & Gallimore, R. (1979). The ecology of program research and evaluation: A model of evaluation succession. In L. B. Sechrest (Ed.), *Evaluation studies review annual* (Vol. 4, pp. 39–60). Beverly Hills, CA: Sage.

Tombari, M. L., & Bergan, J. R. (1978). Consultant cues and teacher verbalizations, judgments, and expectancies concerning children's adjustment problems. *Journal of School Psychology, 16,* 212–219.

Udvari-Solner, A., & Thousand, J. S. (1996). Creating a responsive curriculum for inclusive schools. *Remedial and Special Education, 17,* 182–193.

Vail, P. L., Gravois, T. A., & Rosenfield, S. (1998). *IC-team facilitator training manual*. College Park, MD: Laboratory for Instructional Consultation Teams.

Vygotsky, L. (1962). *Thought and language*. Cambridge, MA: Harvard University Press.

Vygotsky, L. V. (1978). *Mind in society: The development of higher psychological processes.* Cambridge, MA: Harvard University Press.

Weiner, R. K. (2002). *A comparison of IC-teams to IEP teams on special education referral and eligibility rates of minority students.* Unpublished master's thesis, University of Maryland, College Park.

White, L. J., Summerlin, M. L., Loos, V. E., & Epstein, E. S. (1992). School and family consultation: A language-systems approach. In M. Fine & C. Carlson (Eds.), *The handbook of family-school intervention: A systems perspective* (pp. 347–362). Boston: Allyn & Bacon.

Ysseldyke, J. E., & Christenson, S. L. (1993). *The instructional environment system (TIES)–II.* Longmont, CO: Sopris West.

Ysseldyke, J., Burns, M., Dawson, P., Kelly, B., Morrison, D., Ortiz, S., et al. (2006). *School psychology: A blueprint for training and practice III.* Bethesda, MD: National Association of School Psychologists.

11

Organization Development and Change in School Settings
Theoretical and Empirical Foundations

ROBERT J. ILLBACK AND MARGARET A. PENNINGTON

REACH of Louisville

Psychologists who practice in schools conduct their work in complex social systems and have been encouraged both to conceptualize problems from organizational perspectives (Illback & Maher, 1984) and to become active in facilitating planned organizational and systems-level change (Curtis & Stollar, 2002; Illback & Zins, 1995). Historical antecedents for such involvement by school psychologists are long-standing (see, e.g., Bardon & Bennett, 1974; Gallessich, 1973; Sarason, 1971) and cut across diverse lines of school psychology practice and research. In this context, school psychologist organization-level consultative activities might include program evaluation, team building, education and training, supervisory practices, conflict management, administrative-level consultation and coaching, and information systems design (Borgelt & Conoley, 1999; Huebner, Gilligan, & Cobb, 2002; Illback & Fields, 1992; Illback, Maher, & Zins, 1999; Rosenfield & Gravois, 1999; Sheridan, Napolitano, & Swearer, 2002). By the early 1980s, the term *organizational school psychology* began to appear in the literature, suggesting the need to consider this area as a practice subspecialty that could be delineated and systematized (Illback & Maher, 1984; Maher & Illback, 1982a, 1982b; Maher, Illback, & Zins, 1984).

Organizational and systems perspectives offer the prospect of integrating professional roles and activities by recognizing intricate relationships between embedded social systems in schools and communities (Bronfenbrenner, 1977). These complex social systems must work together in a cohesive and effective manner for student performance to be maximized. Psychologists who work in schools are in a unique position to engage in system-strengthening activity because they routinely cross physical, temporal, and normative boundaries in school, family, and community systems, helping people individually and in groups to function effectively. In the language of organizational psychology, school psychologists are organizational boundary role professionals to a greater extent than most education professionals (Illback & Maher, 1984).

Although the school psychology literature is replete with examples of systems-level activities and strategies, research on the efficacy and effectiveness (Seligman, 1995) of these consultative approaches in the service of student learning and achievement is varied and diffuse. This suggests the need for an examination of the current state of knowledge (i.e., the evidence base) for consultation-based organization development strategies. The present chapter begins with a review of organization development (OD)[1] as a consultation-oriented, multidisciplinary practice specialty with an evolving research base. Initially, OD relied almost exclusively on idiographic (e.g., case study) research strategies but has gradually expanded to include a broader range of investigative approaches. The chapter further describes how OD has moved from concentrating on improving components of organizational functioning and effectiveness (i.e., aspects of process and structure) toward a broader focus on the management of change processes. This general discussion of OD theory, research, and practice concludes with a brief review of the relatively limited research base related to systems-level consultant effectiveness.

The knowledge base for educational OD is considered, beginning with the pioneering work of Schmuck, Runkel, Arends, and Arends (1977) and continuing with the theoretical and empirical efforts of Fullan and Stiegelbauer (1991). Numerous reviews of research related to school change and reform initiatives over the past several decades provide ample evidence of the challenges inherent in creating sustainable change in schools (Berends, Bodilly, & Kirby, 2002; Cuban, 1988; Fullan, 1993; Hall & Hord, 1987; Sarason, 1990). Following this, a prominent exemplar of a current research-based educational change initiative (i.e., positive behavior supports, PBS) is discussed in some detail to illustrate both the complexity of comprehensive change efforts and the OD features of this state-of-the-art organizational change initiative. A concluding section discusses the challenges associated with evidence gathering and knowledge generation in educational OD and provides suggestions for research and evaluation paradigms that can enhance the available body of knowledge about consultation-based OD interventions.

ORGANIZATIONAL DEVELOPMENT AS PRACTICE

Organizational development has been variously defined as (a) a "change strategy for organizational self-development and renewal" (Fullan, Miles, & Taylor, 1980, p. 121); (b) "planned and sustained effort to apply behavioral science for system improvement using reflexive, self-analytic methods" (Miles & Schmuck, 1971, p. 2); (c) "a theory, a method and a value system (often hidden) for improving the human side of organizational life and thereby improving the task-goal accomplishments of their complex organizations"(Derr, 1976, p. 11); (d) "a pastiche of techniques developed in the behavioral sciences which focus on problems of organizational learning, motivation, problem solving, communications, and interpersonal relations" (Kimberly & Nielsen, 1975, p. 191); and (e) a field "concerned with helping managers, plan change in organizing and managing people that will develop requisite commitment, coordination and competence. Its purpose is to enhance both the effectiveness of organizations and the well-being of their members through planned interventions in the organizations' human processes, structures, and systems, using knowledge of behavioral science and its intervention methods" (Beer & Walton, 1990, p. 154).

As Worley and Feyerhorn (2003) noted, most OD definitions focus on planned change for entire systems; emphasize human and social processes within organizations; conceptualize systems at individual, group, and system (e.g., cultural) levels; and seek to improve organizational ability to adapt, renew, and thrive.

Some attribute the beginnings of OD to the work of the National Training Laboratories, which emerged from the work of Kurt Lewin (1947) in group relations and social psychology during the 1940s and was characterized by T groups (sensitivity training) and related laboratory human relations approaches. However, Kleiner (1996) noted that the focus on these human relations processes was also in reaction to concern that scientific management and bureaucratic approaches to organization were "dulling" the human spirit. As a practical matter, OD emerged from a synthesis of ideas and technologies in fields as diverse as psychology, sociology, anthropology, scientific management, military science, and business. It is closely aligned with the related disciplines of organizational science, industrial-organizational psychology, and management science and tends to focus on the application of empirically derived methods and strategies of organizational effectiveness. Although diffuse and lacking a central or unified theory (Piotrowski, Vodanovich, & Armstrong, 2001), OD is held together by a core of shared values that emphasize the relationship of organizational effectiveness to goal attainment and the well-being of employees, consumers, and the community at large.

OD practitioners tend to apply an admixture of concepts, theories, and ad hoc (i.e., cobbled together) approaches in their work, and these often reflect more about the problem at hand than the systematic application of a body of knowledge with demonstrated efficacy (Fitzgerald, 1987). In a study of members of the International Registry of Organization Development Professionals, Piotrowski et al. (2001) found that most OD practitioners cite multiple theorists as informing their work. A partial list of major theorists cited include Schein (process consultation), Lewin (field theory), Argyris (intervention theory), Maslow (needs hierarchy), Drucker (management by objectives), Deming (total quality management), Skinner (reinforcement theory), Levinson (leadership), Bandura (social learning), Locke (goal setting, leadership), Gibb (communication), and French and Raven (organizational power). Their results document the multidisciplinary nature of the field, as well as the heterogeneity and diversity of theories employed. OD practitioners commonly use both micro and macro approaches in various combinations. In general, OD is characterized by what Lazarus (1992) called *technical eclecticism*, a belief that practice should be guided by what works (practical utility) but nonetheless be informed by well-grounded theory.

Although there is some concern in OD that lack of theoretical cohesion can be a weakness, more often the emphasis on what works is described as a strength. As opposed to applying techniques in a doctrinaire manner based on a narrow theoretical framework, OD practitioners tend to use multiple theoretical frameworks in a complex and creative fashion (Norcross & Prochaska, 1988). The complex interplay among theory, knowledge, and practice in OD reflects a heuristic approach that can serve to generate new ideas and applications and therefore serves a self-renewal function.

The methods and strategies employed by consultants who engage in OD work have evolved to encompass wide-ranging, change-oriented strategies and activities, including executive coaching, organizational restructuring, change management, leadership development, team building, total quality management, culture change, and development of learning organizations. Similar to psychology in the schools, the strength of OD as a field is derived from its diversity, but it has also been prone to frequent discussions about identity, evolution, boundaries, and fragmentation. In a sense, the field of OD is claimed by many disciplines but "owned" by none. OD has gone through several transformations in its history, as reflected by current debates within the field regarding the relevance of traditional approaches such as team building, conflict management, diversity awareness, and the like. Concepts of organizational health, employee satisfaction, and communitarian concerns, all of which are grounded in traditional OD values and beliefs, have taken a back seat to management-oriented approaches that enable business organizations to survive and thrive in highly competitive environments. In part, this has been driven by the emphasis within business and industry on outcomes and the bottom line as opposed to process-oriented explorations of human interaction (Church, Burke, & Van Eynde, 1994). Thus, much of the growth within OD has occurred in areas such as change management and leadership development. In fact, some have argued that the name OD is obsolete and should be changed to *change management*.

ORGANIZATION CHANGE AND TRANSFORMATION

A widely cited article in *Harvard Business Review* (Kotter, 2001) parallels the emerging focus of the field, which has moved from OD consultation that enhances organizational effectiveness (through effective management practices) toward managing change (through leadership development).

> Management is about coping with complexity. Its practices and procedures are largely a response to one of the most significant developments of the twentieth century: the emergence of large organizations. Without good management, complex enterprises tend to become chaotic in ways that threaten their very existence. Good management brings a degree of order and consistency to key dimensions like the quality and profitability of products. ... Leadership, by contrast, is about coping with change. (p. 4)

Thus, for many OD practitioners, facilitating the ability of organizations to adapt to and self-renew during periods of rapid change (which have become the norm), has become the primary task (D. K. Carr, Hard, & Trahant, 1996).

Weick and Quinn (1999) reviewed the organizational change and development research literature, and provided a useful framework for organizing extant research findings and theorizing about change and transformation. They posited that organizational change (and OD intervention) should be understood within parallel processes: (a) change that is episodic, discontinuous, and intermittent; and (b) change that is continuous, evolving, and incremental.

Episodic Change

Beginning with the research literature on organizations that are most prone to stability characterized by inertia and unresponsiveness (and for which change is most often discontinuous and intentional), the image that emerges is one of *punctuated equilibrium* (Tushman & Romanelli, 1985). Maintaining the status quo is often at the expense of adaptation to changes in the external environment. As the environment changes dramatically, pressure increases to change, and a short period of significant changes ensue, followed by a return to equilibrium. Most change is of the *first order*, in which minor alterations in current beliefs occur (Watzlawick, Weakland, & Fisch, 1974). *Second-order change* (when one belief system replaces another) occasionally occurs in periods of "revolution." In this regard, a metaphor that will resonate with school-focused OD practitioners is the description of *bounded instability* experienced by these organizations, defined as "operating at the edge of chaos" (McDaniel, 1997).

Within the episodic framework, the change process is infrequent, slower, less complete, more deliberate and formal, and more disruptive to routines. Changes are primarily governed by the external environment, and the primary task of the organization is to return to a state of equilibrium (Lewin, 1947). The sequence of change in these settings is (a) unfreeze (disconfirmation of expectations, learning anxiety, provision of psychological safety); (b) transition (cognitive restructuring, semantic definition, conceptual enlargement, new standards of judgment); and (c) refreeze (create supportive social norms, make change congruent with personality). Change agents (internal or external consultants) are essentially "prime movers" who create change by focusing on inertia, finding points of central leverage, changing systems of meaning, and building coordination and commitment to the desired change.

It is not difficult to see school systems and educational OD within this framework. As complex systems, schools clearly operate at the edge of chaos, continuously seek stability and equilibrium, and are slow to change. Internal or external OD consultants seek to create a felt need for change and to produce second-order change through the explication of an alternative schema presented clearly and persistently (Bartunek, 1993). Educational OD consultants tend to conceptualize their interventions within a systems framework, craft interventions that involve alterations in management systems to enable better adaptation to changes in the external environment, recognize that change must account for all elements of these complex systems, gather data from the environment and make it available within the school organization, utilize participative approaches at various levels, and combine pro-cessual and structural interventions (Bunker & Alban, 1992; Illback & Zins, 1995).

Continuous Change

The change process looks and behaves much differently in organizations that update social inter-action and work processes continuously in response to perceived goodness of fit between orga-nizational functioning and the external environment (Brown & Duguid, 1991; Tsoukas, 1996). Typically, these types of organizations are seen as more healthy, well-developed, and able to sustain their focus and direction. They tend to make adaptations and accommodations through alert reac-tions to daily exigencies at all levels, keeping a focus on the long view. They are self-organizing, distribute authority broadly as opposed to maintaining positional power, and are not so embedded in routine as to be rigid. Thus, continuous change organizations achieve a sense of stability in the face of disequilibrium and uncertainty through small, frequent, and targeted adaptations, rather than the large, infrequent, and disruptive adaptations seen in episodic organizations.

Typically, the research that underlies these approaches is based on findings from case studies of highly successful firms. Weick and Quinn (1999) noted that successful firms are not mechanistic in the application of bureaucracy but rather have clear management-based priorities while allowing for improvisation and flexibility at the unit level. They also have deep and redundant communica-tion systems and place a high value on cross-activity interaction. They strike a functional balance between order and disorder and link current work with future directions, thereby coping with inherent bounded instability and preserving a sense of direction (without becoming doctrinaire). In a sense, continuous change organizations are able to encompass both episodic and ongoing change within one process and are therefore less vulnerable to overrigidity and nonresponsiveness.

An empirical analysis of core management practices of organization design that characterize successful business organizations (and are no less relevant to schools and other human service organizations) includes features such as perceived employment security, selective hiring, self-man-aged teams and decentralization, extensive training, reduction of status differences, sharing of information, and high and contingent compensation (Pfeffer, 1998). Clearly, many of these features are not present in school organizations, although attempts to foster one or more are present in vari-ous school reform initiatives.

The sequence of change in continuous change of organizations (as articulated originally by Lewin, 1947, and elaborated by Weick and Quinn, 1999) is (a) freeze (take note of emerging pat-terns); (b) rebalance (reinterpret, relabel, resequence, empower self and others); and (c) unfreeze (resume improvisation and organizational learning). These activities are seen as occurring at high rates (as miniepisodes) and are enabled by organizational cultures that legitimize variation from the norm in the service of adaptability (Kotter & Heskett, 1997). In this regard, *culture* is defined as cognitive and affective structures that people within organizations use to perceive, explain, eval-uate, and construct reality (Choo, 1998). Increasingly, OD consultations are framed to facilitate changes in organizational culture to enable precisely these types of behaviors.

An explosion of books in the popular press describing the latest organizational theory, research, or management approach has made "gurus" out of a number of academicians and senior leaders. Prominent examples of this literature include *The 1-Minute Manager* (Blanchard & Johnson, 1983); *Good to Great* (Collins, 2001); *The Seven Habits of Highly Effective People* (Covey, 2004); *The Fifth Discipline* (Senge, 1990); and *Managing in a Time of Great Change* (Drucker, 1998). Much of this literature involves translating OD theory and research into practice, but there is also a faddish quality to much of it. The almost-evangelical organizational change "industry" has been criticized by Mickelthwait and Woolrich (1996), whose primary criticisms focus on the incoherence and confusion that ensues when complex and conflicting messages about what works emerge from this literature.

EMPIRICISM AND ORGANIZATION DEVELOPMENT

Some within OD (e.g., Macy & Izumi, 1993) are highly critical of the state of methodological sophistication in OD research, citing Kahn's (1974) statement that: "A few theoretical propositions are repeated without additional data or development; sturdy empirical observations are quoted with reverence but without refinement or explication" (p. 487). Without question, the literature is replete with theoretically driven interventions that are not well specified. In particular, OD research studies often provide limited information about implementation variables and are evaluated with no clear logic model (Fetterman, 1996) to link processes with outcomes. In effect, much of OD "research" is not research at all, at least in the sense of having much empirical rigor. Early work in OD consisted of individual case studies in organizations that described business problems, OD consultation processes, and some outcomes that were observed and agreed on by those involved (but not necessarily derived from formal measurement).

Historically, experimental designs involving randomization, contrast conditions, or other methods common to the positivist tradition have not been employed routinely. In fact, a backlash against such designs has been seen among OD researchers and practitioners. For example, Bullock and Svyantek (1987) argued that traditional research methods run counter to the fundamental assumptions of OD, which rely on full collaboration and participation in change processes. Relatedly, Eden (1986) argued that experimental designs aimed at controlling for alternative explanations of change (e.g., expectancy effects) can actually reduce intervention efficacy because these variables are important to the intervention.

By the 1990s, an important change seemed to have occurred within the OD research literature, corresponding with the advent of qualitative research and evaluation methods (Patton, 2002). OD research began to employ a higher degree of rigor with respect to theory and intervention specification, implementation assessment, and outcome measurement. This was consistent with Woodman's (Woodman & Pasmore, 1989) utilization-focused emphasis on "thick" description, generalizable propositions, and a combined paradigm approach (i.e., integrating qualitative and quantitative methods in OD projects). During the same time frame, the emerging field of program planning and evaluation began to view utilization and organizational change as its core objects. The confluence of these ideas has enriched both fields, in terms of both experimental methodology and utilization (i.e., relevance) of findings.

For example, these concepts have coalesced in an approach called *appreciative inquiry* championed by Cooperrider and Srivasta (1987). In this approach, researchers (often in participant-observer roles) take note of the areas within which an organization is effective and then engage people within the organization in collaborative inquiry focusing on growth and renewal. In this regard, the approach does not seek to "pathologize" organizations but rather to improve practice and theory within a strengths-based model. Another evaluative technology that has led to growth in the field is *logic modeling*, which grew out of the early work of Wholey (1979) and more recent work in empowerment evaluation (Fetterman, 1996). In this approach, organizational members are encouraged to specify linkages between needs, goals, activities, and short- and long-term outcomes as a means toward improving planning, design, management, and quality of services. In a related method, Porras (1987) conceived of *stream analysis* as a graphic tool to map organizational problems within four domains: organizational arrangements (e.g., goals, strategies, structures, policies, procedures, reward structures); social factors (e.g., values, norms, language, rituals, interaction processes, networks, communication, management style); technology (e.g., equipment, job design, work flow, technical expertise); and the physical setting (e.g., space, physical ambiance, interior design, architectural design).

OD has also grown considerably in the use of measurement-based quantitative methodologies. An example is the occasional use of factorial analyses within structural equation models to examine change in relation to complex relationships within a proposed model (Babakus, Yavas, Karatepe, & Avci, 2003; Koberg, Boss, Senjem, & Goodman, 1999; Millsap & Hartog, 1988). In addition, it has become more common to see literature reviews that seek to draw generalizations from prior studies through meta-analysis, typically generalizing about effect sizes by aggregating across case studies (Bullock & Tubbs, 1987; Bushe & Coetzer, 1995; Porras & Silvers, 1999).

One of the key challenges to researching OD is the need to reach agreement within the field regarding the core outcomes of organizational change efforts (Porras & Silvers, 1999). Porras and Silvers suggested consideration of the earlier research by Porras and Hoffer (1986), who surveyed organizational consultants and derived nine indicators (targets) of change: communicating openly, collaborating, taking responsibility, maintaining a shared vision, generating participation, leading by vision, functioning strategically, promoting information flow, and developing others. Lack of agreement regarding the best indicators of change continues to hamper efforts toward meta-analysis and improvement of measures.

In sum, Weisbord's (1977) critique of the current status of the evidence base of OD is no less relevant at present than it was 31 years ago:

> Depending on who you talk to and what you read you will learn that OD works, doesn't work, is extremely complex, scientific and mysterious, defies description, can't be evaluated, should always be evaluated, risks becoming professionalized, risks not becoming professionalized, doesn't really exist, once existed but is becoming extinct, is metamorphosing into something else which also works, doesn't work, is extremely complex, scientific and mysterious, defies description, etc., etc., etc. (p. 2)

What is notable, of course, is that despite these issues of rigor and relevance, the field of OD remains vibrant and in high demand — especially in business and industry.

ORGANIZATION DEVELOPMENT CONSULTATION EFFECTIVENESS

Wooten and White (1989) noted that a major impediment to understanding the active ingredients of OD is the lack of attention paid to the actual behavior of OD consultants. There have been few research investigations of OD consultation behavior, although the field certainly draws heavily from the general literature on consultation practice (Gallessich, 1973). Some early theoretical work in the area of consultation effectiveness was accomplished by Warwick and Donovan (1979), who delineated a classification scheme to describe 40 skills presumed to determine OD consultant effectiveness. These included four broad categories of competence: knowledge, consulting, conceptual, and human skills. A similar scheme by Neilsen (1984) added project management skills to the mix. Self- and interpersonal awareness; conceptual, analytic, research; and change and influence skills were suggested as the crucial domains by Carey and Varney (1983). Esper (1990) reported on core practitioner competencies that emerged from interviews of key informants, including process skills (individual, group, and organizational dynamics) and conceptual ability, communication, and management of the consulting process.

In an attempt to delineate the foundational and more advanced competencies and skills OD practitioners should be trained to perform, Varney (Varney et al., 1999; Worley & Varney 1998) surveyed practitioners and academics in the fields of OD and organizational behavior. Entry-level knowledge and skills (i.e., those learned in the first years of academic study) were identified as including group dynamics; management and organizational theory; research methods and statistics; business management principles; and development of interpersonal communication, collaboration, coaching, and teamwork skills. This work suggested that more advanced skills included organizational design, organization-level research, system dynamics, process consultation, and change management.

In the context of information technology (IT) projects, Kendra and Taplin (2004) sought to explore the manner in which OD practitioners support IT change efforts, including their role as change agents and the knowledge, skills, and competencies required. Their work suggests a pyramid comprised of four levels of professional development for OD change agents and project managers. The *foundation* level is comprised of the basic knowledge base; the *skill* level has to do with proficiencies that are acquired through practice; *competency* implies habitual use of skills; and *mastery* connotes continuous learning through feedback, observation, and education. Six common trajectories of professional development for OD practitioners are then described: communication, teamwork, process management, training, leadership, and continuous learning.

With this paucity of research as backdrop, O'Driscoll and Eubanks (1993) studied a sample of 45 OD-experienced consultants from the United States and Canada. To participate, consultants had to have conducted an intervention with an organization, and two or three members of that organization were also solicited to provide information (including a top executive and another person who had extensive contact with the consultant). Thus, in addition to the 45 consultants, 89 clients participated in the study. A critical incident scale (validated in earlier work) was employed within which six clusters of behavioral competence were assessed: contracting, using data, implementing the intervention, displaying interpersonal skills, managing group processes, and maintaining client relations. Respondents (clients and consultants) were asked about the extent to which consultation and intervention goals were specific, measurable, and timely and by whom they were set (e.g., consultant, management, collaboratively). They also completed questionnaires that sought to estimate the impact of the consultation on salient processes (e.g., communication, leadership, power distribution) and outcomes (e.g., organizational effectiveness, profitability, satisfaction). Finally, they rated the flexibility of the OD program, amount of support and acceptance it received from management, extent of collaboration evident, and relative value of the program in terms of time and money.

There were a number of fascinating results, some of which were predictable (O'Driscoll & Eubanks, 1993). For example, to a moderate degree, consultants tended to rate themselves more favorably than clients. A higher level of agreement was achieved on the goal-setting questions, on which both agreed that goals were set mostly by management or jointly. In general, most consultant interventions were judged to have been worthwhile. Stepwise multiple regression was employed to relate consultant competencies to outcomes, and the results showed that, for consultants, data utilization and goal-setting skills accounted for the most variance (56%). This same pattern held true for client perceptions, but with the additional components of measurable goals, interpersonal skills, and group process management, 76% of the variance could be taken into account.

In discussing these findings (O'Driscoll & Eubanks, 1993), the authors hypothesized that (a) data collection is a proxy for the initial gathering and interpretation of information about the organization, which includes learning the language and culture of the group; (b) listening to and understanding the client's perspective, providing feedback, and breaking problems down into manageable elements are core skills of the consultation process; and (c) setting specific and measurable goals in collaboration with management sets the stage for effective OD consultation.

Although the O'Driscoll and Eubanks (1993) study has some obvious methodological problems, it suggests that the core competencies described in the general consultation literature (e.g., displaying interpersonal skills, using data, managing the change process) are essential in organizational consultation as well. In all probability, the OD consultant must also be able to deal with multiple levels of change processes and higher levels of ambiguity and complexity. This point was reinforced by Whelan-Berry, Gordon, and Hinings (2003), who found that successful OD consultants actually conceptualize and manage at least three nested change processes (i.e., individual, group, organizational). In this regard, they proposed a model of planned change to facilitate such conceptualization (see Figure 11.1).

EDUCATIONAL ORGANIZATION DEVELOPMENT

Educational systems present unique challenges for the OD practitioner interested in facilitating sustainable change, in part because of the manner in which they are constructed and also because of the complex role they play in society. The unique features of schools led Derr (1976) to write an article, "OD Won't Work in Schools," in which he argued that the fundamental assumptions of OD work are not present because (a) schools have no common indicators of performance and therefore cannot sense their problems; (b) schools are monopolies that are guaranteed to survive while at the same time are driven by crises (and therefore incapable of reflection); (c) schools are not organized to enable collaborative endeavors in that their core employees (teachers) are highly autonomous; (d) schools are not oriented to working together and are unwilling (or unable) to pay for the "cost" of collaboration; (e) schools are dominated by a civil service mentality that makes participants impervious to change and innovation; and (f) schools have insufficient resources to support change initiatives.

With Derr's apparent exasperation as background, Fullan et al. (1980) published a seminal review of educational OD in the *Review of Educational Research*, taking the view that, although these issues are accurate, the issue is not that OD in schools is untenable but rather that educational OD needs to take these and related issues (e.g., overpermeable boundaries, lack of accountability) into account in framing interventions. They discovered a fairly large number of projects that could be loosely classified as involving OD interventions and suspected that there were many more unpublished initiatives with a focus on organizational improvement and some experimental rigor (which remains true at present). In particular, they reviewed the work of Schmuck and Runkel (1994) from the University of Oregon, who for many years coordinated a program of research on OD in schools and action research.

Since the publication of Fullan et al. (1980), there has been a virtual explosion of change initiatives related to school reform efforts, but few of these make specific reference to OD as a guiding framework for change, and surprisingly few articles in the OD research literature are based in schools. At the same time, the language and concepts of OD have infused much of the discussion about school reform, especially through the ongoing writing and research of Michael Fullan, who remains a major contributor to the school change literature.

School Reform and Organizational Change

Most agree that the "tipping point" for the dramatic expansion of school restructuring and reengineering activity was the publication of *A Nation at Risk: The Imperative for School Reform* by the

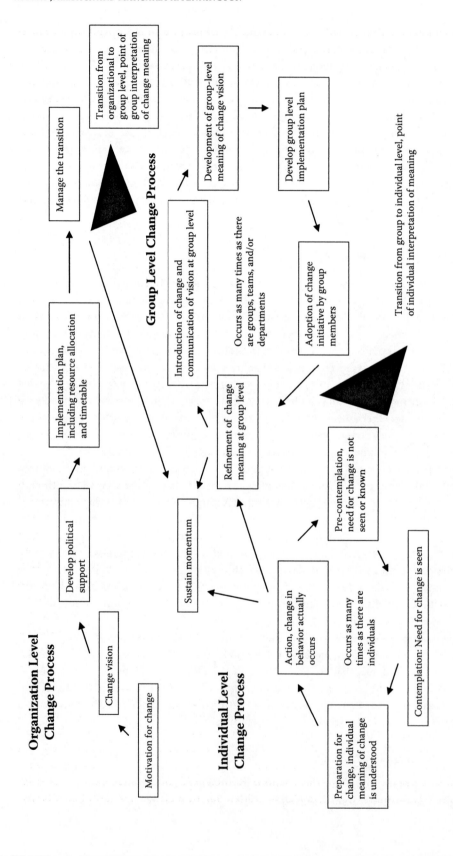

Figure 11.1   Nested change processes in OD. (From Whelan-Berry, Gordon, and Hinings (2003). Reprinted with permission.)

National Commission on Excellence in Education (1983), which altered the landscape by stimulating a national discussion about school improvement. Since that time, there have been numerous reports about school change, recommendations for specific types of reforms, state-level initiatives to promote reform, a far-reaching national initiative (i.e., No Child Left Behind Act, U.S. Department of Education, 2001), and evaluation projects to demonstrate the effects of reform on school efforts (although most of these do not have OD as their explicit focus).[2] In this regard, the Northwest Regional Educational Laboratory (2000) catalogued at least 26 whole-school education reform approaches, many of which have been funded by foundations.[3]

Much of school reform is based on the notion that by changing the manner in which schools are organized, teaching and learning processes will be transformed in ways that increase student opportunities for learning. Newman (1993) provided a useful summary of the logic of school restructuring plans (reforms) in the service of changing the school environment and improving achievement, many of which he believes lack a unified theory of change. The most prominent reforms include one or more of the following components: parental choice of school, school competition for funding, autonomous school decision making, teacher and parent decision making, increased accountability, heterogeneous grouping strategies, year-round schools, coordinating community social services with schools, national certification, ladders of professional advancement for teachers, increased teacher planning time, individualized instruction, and competency-based advancement. Each of these components implies major alterations to the organizational functioning (i.e., structure and process) of schools.

Despite the plethora of expert recommendations for how schools should be restructured, much of the educational reform movement has failed to achieve its aims (Chatterji, 2002; Elmore, 1991; Sarason, 1990). Fullan and Stiegelbauer (1991) noted that much of the change in school reform is of the first order, in which goals are altered, different materials are used, and new behaviors are imitated, but what is lacking is a fundamental understanding of the principles and rationale behind the recommended change. The result is that the intended change is not sustained.

The inability of many school reforms to take hold may relate (at least in part) to a limited understanding of organizational change as it relates to both organizational culture and structure. But, some have argued that organization-level reforms are essentially unrelated to teaching and learning in a direct fashion. In this regard, Peterson, McCarthey, and Elmore (1996) analyzed restructuring experiments in three elementary schools over a 2-year time frame using observation and case study methodology. The focus of the change project was writing skills, and they found that all of the schools did restructure, as evidenced by changes in grouping and time allocation, teacher collaboration, shared decision making, and access to new ideas. On closer examination, however, the researchers found that all teachers were struggling to integrate what they were learning into instructional practices. They concluded that changing the structure can provide opportunities for changes in teaching practices, but that teacher learning is the critical variable for instructional changes to occur. In their words, "Teachers who see themselves as learners work continuously to develop new understandings and improve their practices" (Peterson et al., 1993, p. 148). Thus, school structure follows good practice. Changing the school structure, by itself, did not result in meaningful change.

The idea that school organizational change is less critical than altering the processes of teaching and learning was reinforced by a controversial (but highly influential) article by Wang, Haertel, and Walberg (1993). These authors synthesized 270 research reviews and meta-analyses using content analysis, expert opinion, and meta-analytic techniques. The 228 identified variables found to influence learning were categorized into 30 scales within six broad categories, based on distance from the actual teaching and learning transaction in the classroom. In this model, state and school district policies (e.g., reform guidelines) were considered the most distal, and time on task, discipline, and other classroom variables were the most proximal. The presumed strength of association with learning outcomes was then assessed, leading to a model of influence on learning that suggested that proximal variables are more closely associated with learning than more distal variables. The order of influence that resulted was (a) program design (e.g., curriculum and instruction); (b) out-of-school contextual variables (e.g., home environment, out-of-school use of time); (c) classroom instruction and climate (e.g., classroom management); (d) student variables (e.g., motivation, placement); (e) school-level variables (e.g., parent involvement policy); and (f) state and district variables (e.g., state-level policy). A subsequent analysis identified the scales with the strongest and weakest associations with learning. The five strongest were classroom management, metacognitive processes, cognitive processes, home environment/parental support, and student-teacher social interactions. The scales receiving the lowest mean ratings were district demographics, school policies, state-level policies, school demographics, and program demographics.

Does this argue for discarding organization-level change or school restructuring in favor of concentrating resources on teacher training? Elmore (1993) argued persuasively that it does not and stated that school change will need to account for district-level (organizational) dynamics. This view was seconded by Sarason (1990):

> The failure of educational reform derives from a most superficial conception of how complicated settings are organized: their structure, their dynamics, their power relationships, and their underlying values and axioms. (pp. 2–3)

Rather than concentrating on either the teaching-learning process or the functioning of the organization, a consensus seems to have emerged that OD consultants planning school reform initiatives must do both, with particular attention paid to changing fundamental aspects of the culture of schools. "I came to see what should have been obvious: the characteristics, traditions and organizational dynamics of school systems were more or less lethal obstacles to achieving even modest, narrow goals" (Sarason, 1971, p. 12).

Similarly, Fullan and Stiegelbauer (1991) discussed the significance of educational change research in terms of combining three *stories*: the *inside story* (what happens in the classroom), the *inside-out story* (complex relationships between the school and its immediate environment), and the *outside-in story* (influence of the more distal policy environment). These insights serve to frame a more concrete discussion about an educational OD initiative (i.e., PBSs) in the following section.

Organization Development Elements in Positive Behavior Supports Initiatives

Curtis and Stollar (1996) summarized the core elements of OD interventions as they relate to school change and reform, including collaborative interaction (whether as an external or internal consultant); team development (capitalizing on the energy, creativity, and ideas of members of the organization); and group problem solving (situational analysis, goal identification, strategy development and implementation, and evaluation). All of these are evident in the emerging literature on PBS, an organizational-level change initiative well known to psychologists who work in schools. The case of PBS can serve as a useful platform for a closer examination of educational OD theory and research, leading to a discussion about the need for programmatic research on change management and OD consultation approaches in schools.[4]

PBS refers to a collection of efforts evident across the country that seek to strengthen individual-, group-, and organization-level systems that influence student behavior. The approach and accompanying technology is based on theoretical and empirical foundations delineated by Sugai, Horner, and their colleagues at the University of Oregon. PBS emphasizes change activities that acknowledge the need to create school environments in which positive behaviors are encouraged, norm-violating behaviors are reduced, and student success is enhanced. It addresses the need for schoolwide (i.e., organization-level) responses that are relevant for all children, in combination with more targeted responses for students who exhibit more complex needs (e.g., histories of disruptive behaviors, family dysfunction). PBS is informed by theory and research that support the notion that individual interventions are essential but insufficient to change problematic learning and behavior. In essence, PBS-related activities represent the introduction of a set of new ideas and technologies (innovations) into school environments, necessitating systematic needs assessment through data collection, planning, collaboration, and supportive consultation (both internal and external). Individuals who seek to organize or guide such interventions can be seen as engaging in educational OD.

Although school-specific implementations vary, PBS solutions typically involve the creation and ongoing work of a planning team; proactive identification of appropriate and inappropriate behaviors among individuals and among groups; data-based decision making; teaching all students school rules, and teaching identified students new skills; imposing limits that make the problem behavior unproductive for the student; redesigning features of the school/classroom environment to help students be more successful; and investing resources to continue to provide the required support to reinforce the positive behaviors, including activities that communicate schoolwide policies and that recognize and celebrate appropriate behavior (Lohrmann-O'Rourke et al., 2000; Todd, Horner, Sugai, & Sprague, 1999; Walker et al., 1996).

In this regard, Todd and her colleagues have identified four embedded systems that comprise the teaching-learning environment: (a) schoolwide systems; (b) classroom systems; (c) nonclassroom systems, such as cafeterias, hallways, and gymnasiums; and (d) individual student support systems (Todd et al., 1999). Effective PBS strategies involve integrated planning to address patterns of behavior in each of these systems. Similarly, Sugai and Horner (1999) identified four targets for intervention that characterize PBS: (a) change of systems (policies, structures, routines); (b) change of environments; (c) change of student and adult (parent, teacher, staff) behavior; and (d) change in appreciation of appropriate behavior in all involved individuals (e.g., student, staff, family).

Essential to PBS is the systematic use of data for decision making. Measurement of change within PBS occurs at both organizational and individual levels. Although surveys and observations can document change in many of these areas, most PBS programs also use archival data on attendance and disciplinary referrals.

In addition to maintaining a systems perspective and a comprehensive focus on the interactions of the overlapping systems, the behavior consultant (in effect, the OD consultant) often plays a key role in gathering and analyzing data to inform decisions at all levels of planning and intervention. The behavioral/OD consultant also provides technical assistance and training by identifying antecedent conditions that precipitate negative behaviors, identifying strategies for reinforcing positive behaviors, and training faculty and nonclassified personnel in techniques for extinguishing behaviors that are negative and reinforcing those that are positive. Thus, PBS programs benefit from the ability of the internal or external OD consultant to serve as boundary spanner and multilevel intervention coordinator.

Numerous empirical studies document both the efficacy (through controlled research) and effectiveness (assessment of successful outcomes) of PBS in facilitating change at all levels, at least over brief periods of time (e.g., 1–3 years). Many of these PBS evaluations are framed as case studies in particular school districts or buildings, and they vary in specificity and level of analysis (see, e.g., the *Journal of Positive Behavior Interventions*, which regularly includes such case studies). For instance, Warren et al. (2006) demonstrated decreases in aversive methods and variable changes in behavior patterns (based on direct observation and analysis of archival data) in an urban middle school. Putnam, Luiselli, and Jefferson (2002) implemented a districtwide PBS strategy in two suburban communities in north central Massachusetts, focusing on initial data gathering about costs associated with out-of-district placement, the content of Individual Education Plans, and teacher perspectives on service delivery. These data served as the springboard for subsequent planning about needed change. Similarly, a team of consultant researchers has assisted an urban middle school to address behavioral and academic objectives through implementation of a continuous systems-level assessment as part of a PBS initiative (Freeman, Smith, & Tieghi-Benet, 2003; Smith & Freeman, 2002).

Todd et al. (1999) studied a behavioral support team in operation for 4 years in an Oregon elementary school setting. In close collaboration with these University of Oregon researchers, the faculty at this elementary school mounted a comprehensive school improvement plan coordinated by an effective behavior support team. This team was comprised of the administrator, certified staff from each grade level, classified staff, and a site council. A second component of the change initiative was termed the schoolwide self-manager program, aimed at facilitating student self-management through a number of mechanisms. Finally, the behavioral teacher assistance team was designed to support the needs of individual students. At least over the 4 years of the project, evidence of intervention impact has been positive in that changes in allocation of faculty resources, teaching/monitoring of student expectations, and capacity for teacher assistance have been associated with reductions in the number of referrals for office discipline and a decrease in the number of youth referred by teachers to alternative placements.

There have been some studies of PBS that have employed quasi-experimental designs. For example, Gottfredson (1988) studied two junior high schools, one of which used an OD approach that encompassed the key elements of behavioral approaches for reducing student behavior disorders later formulated as PBS. Two junior high schools with similar demographics in Baltimore, Maryland, were selected for organizational intervention due to high rates of behavior problems. Following a detailed needs assessment and planning process, the intervention school began to implement assertive discipline and reality therapy strategies schoolwide, coupled with student team learning (a motivational approach to increase academic engaged time). Ancillary strategies included a parent communication system, a community support program, extracurricular activities, a policy review followed by establishment of consistent school rules, a revised disciplinary referral system, and a career exploration program. In contrast to no changes in the control school, evidence suggested positive improvements in organizational health and student engagement as well as lower rates of behavior problems in the intervention school. A subsequent expansion of this design (Gottfredson, Gottfredson, & Hybl, 1993) implemented similar schoolwide changes in several intervention middle schools and found variability in performance, but overall changes of a greater magnitude than in control schools with respect to classroom organization and rule clarity.

In sum, a meta-analysis by E. G. Carr, Carlson, Langdon, Magito-McLaughlin, and Yarbrough (1999), which reviewed over 100 empirical studies related to PBS published between 1985 and 1996, found at least an 80% reduction in inappropriate behaviors for approximately two thirds of the behavioral outcomes that were studied.

Given the weight of the extensive empirical work completed to date on PBS, is it then reasonable to conclude that PBS as an OD consultative intervention is efficacious? Safran and Oswald (2003) pointed to a glaring omission in the available PBS research literature when they concluded that:

In research zest to evaluate intervention effectiveness, they have yet to examine process and leadership factors, including team decision-making practices, how staff consensus for intervention priorities are developed, and the role of school leadership. As in all large organizations, efforts at meaningful change can hit many institutional roadblocks. Without strong leadership, staff ownership, and commitment to the PBS process, these research-validated practices may go by the wayside. (p. 370)

Unfortunately, most PBS-related studies neither delineate the consultation processes that facilitate change nor hypothesize about the consultant behaviors that are necessary and sufficient to conduct these processes. For example, many of the local initiatives described in the PBS literature indicate that one or more external consultants (typically university-based consultant researchers) collaborated extensively in the work. Most commonly, reference is made to a vital internal consultant (e.g., principal, school psychologist) who coordinates, integrates, and champions the PBS change process. Rarely do these case studies articulate the precise nature of these consultation activities (e.g., implementation features) but rather focus on the content of the intervention.

How important is it to have access to external consultants with certain skills and knowledge? Can the approach be fully replicated without such access? What competencies and access must an internal OD consultant possess to be effective? When there is evidence of positive systems change, is there any accompanying evidence that specific consultation processes played an enabling role? What are the facilitators and barriers to implementation of PBS processes? Is there any evidence that the sustainability of PBS interventions may relate to ongoing consultation processes? These and similar questions have yet to be addressed to any extent in the PBS literature.[5]

TOWARD A RESEARCH AGENDA FOR ORGANIZATION DEVELOPMENT-ORIENTED EDUCATIONAL CONSULTATION

What should be clear at this juncture is that the field of OD consultation in schools is alive and well, but the evidence base for such practice remains weak. Throughout the literature, there are numerous examples of school-based initiatives that can be construed as OD consultation, prominent examples of which include Adelman and Taylor's (1999) work on integrated services, Rosenfield's (1987) approach to the development of instructional support teams as mechanisms for improving instructional practices, and Elias, Zins, Graczyk, and Weissburg's (2003) research on promotion of social competence. Similar to Sugai and Horner's work with respect to PBSs, these and similar initiatives seek to alter fundamental aspects of the schooling experience through changes in the way the school organization functions. Although some evidence of program effectiveness (e.g., goal attainment) is often available for school-based systems change programs, the explicit consultation activities that enable changes in organizational functioning have not always been thoroughly described or researched. When available, such material is often in the form of a case study, with a focus more on the content of the change than the underlying consultation processes.

The evidence base for educational OD would be greatly enhanced by fuller and more detailed descriptions of school consultation processes using both quantitative and qualitative methods. Along those lines, Patton (2002) provided a guide for inquiry of a qualitative nature. For example, in the context of an organization-level consultation, process studies of consultant behavior and decision making could illuminate how people engage with each other (and in particular, with the school-based consultant) and what the critical decision points may be to move the consultation forward. Implementation evaluations of the school consultation process could serve to demonstrate whether organizational interventions succeed or fail as a function of the extent to which the consultation was implemented as intended. This may be especially important given the prospect that an efficacious change program (i.e., an innovation) could be introduced in an organization that was ready to change, but the necessary and sufficient support processes to adopt the change (i.e., consultation) were not properly implemented. Similarly, studies of school consultant logic models (theories of action) for their work at the organizational level could help differentiate effective from ineffective consulting activities.

Another line of research that could prove fruitful would be to more closely examine school sites (e.g., buildings, districts) that did or did not respond to the consultative intervention. Clearly, organization-level school consultation is a highly complex and interactive activity, making the goodness of fit between consultant skills and key characteristics of the school as an organization an important target for further study. Patton (2002) suggested sampling strategies that are relevant to such investigations, including intensity sampling (studying school organizations that make for information-rich case studies), outlier sampling (studying schools that are unique or unusual), criterion sampling (studying schools that meet some objective criterion as exemplars), and snowball sampling (studying school sites recommended by exemplars as having similar characteristics). Each approach relies on a slightly different method as a function of the issues to be investigated.

School organizational readiness for consultation is a related area ripe for investigation. An example of such an approach is provided by a study on organizational readiness for a PBS program (Robbins, Collins, Liaupsin, Illback, & Call, 2004). In the context of a large-scale system of care initiative, an organizational assessment was piloted in three regions of southeastern Kentucky to determine which schools were most ready to engage in a comprehensive OD consultative process. Beginning with a readiness framework derived from the organizational change literature, practitioner focus groups comprised of 28 school and mental health administrators with extensive PBS experience delineated indicators of readiness. These indicators were then used to construct a screening tool in consultation with a panel of experts. With the readiness indicators guiding the effort, applications for funding and related documentation were rated, and follow-up site visits and structured interviews were conducted. Follow-up debriefing indicated that the approach had promise as a means to ensure that limited resources were distributed efficiently and effectively.

Finally, as suggested, there is a need to move beyond $n = 1$ case study methodology toward experimental and quasi-experimental designs that allow for meaningful contrasts. For example, implementation of diverse consultative approaches in schools that have similar characteristics and that are ready for the innovation could help to determine what level of consultation is required for success and sustainability. Similarly, a contrast of internal versus external consultation processes could be accomplished in this manner. In the case of PBS, it might be interesting to look at whether university-based consultants are core or ancillary with respect to achieving maximum outcomes. There are limits to the use of the positivist paradigm, however, and it is improbable that high levels of experimental control to achieve well-defined contrasts (and greater certainty) can be achieved given cost and practicality. Creative use of statistical controls and meta-analytic technology can help ameliorate these limitations to some extent.

For heuristic purposes, a sampling of focusing questions for school psychologists interested in systems-level consultative intervention research is as follows:

1. What building- and district-level readiness is necessary to create the conditions for successful organizational consultation? Can these be reliably assessed?
2. How are change processes perceived in different school environments? How are they perceived for various types of problems?

3. Are there qualitative differences in entry and site preparation processes for internal and external school consultants? Do these vary as a function of the type of problem? Magnitude of change desired? Are they related to consultation effectiveness?

4. What types of consultative activities are most essential for consultation effectiveness and efficacy in various systems change initiatives? At what dosage and frequency?

5. What organizational assessment methods are most likely to yield reliable and meaningful information to guide consultative intervention?

6. What long-term involvement on the part of the school consultant is necessary and sufficient to sustain change? Can first-order (transitory) and second-order (lasting) change be reliably determined?

7. What does effective organizational consultation look like in schools? Can specific organizational consultant behaviors be described and related to organizational change? Can these skills be taught to (and applied by) relatively inexperienced practitioners, or should they be emphasized at more advanced levels of training (e.g., doctoral or subspecialty level)?

In sum, the need for greater research activity related to OD consultation in schools is apparent. As qualitative methodology becomes more widely accepted, it is hoped that the evidence base for educational OD will expand. As generalizability of case study findings and adoption/adaptation processes become more salient, the creative use of comparative methods can, at least to a limited extent, also grow. Certainly, the need for validated school change approaches is as great as it has ever been.

NOTES

1. For the purpose of efficiency, the term *organizational development* (OD) is used henceforth as a general rubric to denote the broad range of organizational and system-level activities under discussion.

2. The following link provides access to an annotated summary of a wide range of educational reform initiatives: http://www.library.uiuc.edu/schoolreform/nsri.htm

3. See http://www.nwrel.org/scpd/catalog/modellist.asp

4. It should be noted that there are many other examples of system-level intervention programs and approaches in the school psychology literature that could also be reviewed in this manner, space permitting. These include, but are not limited to: (a) consultation on curricular and instructional practices (Rosenfield & Gravois, 1999); (b) inclusion of pupils with special needs and disabilities (Fuchs & Fuchs, 1988); (c) school restructuring and reform (Harris, 2000); (d) school mental health and integrated services (Adelman & Taylor, 2000); (e) school health services (Carlson, Tharinger, Bricklin, DeMers, & Paavola, 1996); (f) home-school collaboration (Christenson, & Conoley, 1992; Sheridan et al., 2002); and (g) social competence promotion (Elias et al., 2003).

5. It is not our intent here to imply that PBS proponents have been less than diligent in researching their approach. In fact, just the opposite is true. We view the need to conduct PBS-related OD research as developmental and most salient when generalizability and replicability are of concern.

REFERENCES

Adelman, H. S., & Taylor, L. (1999). Mental health in schools and system restructuring. *Clinical Psychology Review, 19,* 137–163.

Adelman, H. S., & Taylor, L. (2000). Shaping the future of mental health in schools. *Psychology in the Schools, 37,* 49–60.

Babakus, E., Yavas, U., Karatepe, O., & Avci, T. (2003). The effect of management commitment to service quality on employees' affective and performance outcomes. *Journal of the Academy of Marketing Science, 31,* 272–286.

Bardon, J. I., & Bennett, V. C. (1974). *School psychology.* Englewood Cliffs, NJ: Prentice-Hall.

Bartunek, J. M. (1993). The multiple cognitions and conflicts associated with second order organizational change. In J. K. Murnighan (Ed.), *Social psychology in organizations: Advances in theory and research,* 322–349.

Beer, M., & Walton, E. (1987). Organization change and development. *Annual Review of Psychology, 38,* 339–367.

Beer, M., & Walton, E. (1990). Developing the competitive organization: interventions and strategies. *American Psychologist, 45*(2), 154–216.

Berends, M., Bodilly, S., & Kirby, S. N. (2002). Looking back over a decade of whole-school reform: The experience of New American Schools. *Phi Delta Kappan, 84,* 168–175. Retrieved October 25, 2005, from http://www-writing.berkeley.edu/tesl-ej/.

Blanchard, K., & Johnson, S. (1983). *The 1-minute manager.* New York: Penguin Putnam.

Borgelt, C. E., & Conoley, J. C. (1999). Psychology in the schools: Systems intervention case examples. In C. R. Reynolds & T. B. Gutkin (Eds.), *The handbook of school psychology* (3rd ed., pp. 1056–1076). New York: Wiley.

Bronfenbrenner, U. (1977). Toward an experimental ecology of human development. *American Psychologist, 32,* 513–531.

Brown, J. S., & Duguid, P. (1991). Organizational learning and communities-of-practice: Toward a unified view of working, learning, and innovation. *Organizational Science, 2,* 40–57.

Bullock, R. J., & Svyantek, D. J. (1987). The impossibility of using random strategies to study the organization development process. *Journal of Applied Behavioral Science, 23,* 255–262.

Bullock, R., & Tubbs, M. (1987). A case meta-analysis of gain sharing plans as organization development interventions. *Journal of Applied Behavioral Science, 26,* 383–404.

Bunker, B., & Alban, B. (1992). Conclusion: What makes large group interventions effective? *Journal of Applied Behavioral Science, 28,* 579–591.

Bushe, G., & Coetzer, G. (1995). Appreciative inquiry as a team-development intervention: A controlled experiment. *Journal of Applied Behavioral Science, 31,* 13–30.

Carey, A., & Varney, G. (1983). Which skills spell success in OD? *Training and Development Journal, 37*(4), 38–40.

Carlson, C., Tharinger, D., Bricklin, P., DeMers, S., & Paavola, J., (1996). Health care reform and psychological practice in schools. *Professional Psychology: Research and Practice.* 14–23.

Carr, D. K., Hard, K. J., & Trahant, W. J. (1996). *Managing the change process.* New York: McGraw Hill.

Carr, E. G., Carlson, J. I., Langdon, N. A., Magito-McLaughlin, D., & Yarbrough, S. C. (1999). Two perspectives on antecedent control: Molecular and molar. In J. K. Luiselli & M. J. Cameron (Eds.), *Antecedent control: Innovative approaches to behavioral support* (pp. 3–28). Baltimore, MD: Brookes.

Chatterji, M. (2002).Models and methods for examining standards-based reforms and accountability initiatives: Have the tools of inquiry answered pressing questions on improving schools? *Review of Educational Research, 72,* 345–386.

Christenson, S. L., & Conoley, J. C. (Eds.). (1992). *Home-school collaboration: Enhancing children's academic and social competence.* Silver Spring, MD: NASP.

Choo, C. W. (1998). *The knowing organization: How organizations use information to construct meaning, create knowledge, and make decisions.* New York: Oxford University Press.

Church, A., Burke, W., & Van Eynde, D. (1994). Values, motives, and interventions of organization development practitioners. *Group and Organization Management, 19,* 5–50.

Collins, J. (2001). *Good to great: Why some companies make the leap ... and others don't.* New York: Harper Business.

Cooperrider, D. L., & Srivasta, S. (1987). Appreciative inquiry in organizational life. In R. W. Woodman (Ed.), *Research in organizational change and development* (pp. 129–169). Greenwich, CT: JAI Press.

Covey, S. R. (2004). *The seven habits of highly effective people* (14th ed.). New York: Free Press.

Cuban, L. (1988). A fundamental puzzle of school reform. *Phi Delta Kappan, 69,* 341–344.

Curtis, M. J., & Stollar, S. A. (1996). Applying principles and practices of organizational change to school reform. *School Psychology Review, 25,* 409–417.

Curtis, M. J., & Stollar, S. A. (2002). Best practices in system-level change. In A. Thomas & J. Grimes (Eds.), *Best practices in school psychology IV* (pp. 223–234). Bethesda, MD: National Association of School Psychologists.

Derr, C. B. (1976). OD won't work in schools. *Education and Urban Society, 8,* 227–241.

Drucker, P. (1998). *Managing in a time of great change.* New York: Plume Books.

Eden, D. (1986). OD and self-fulfilling prophecy: Boosting productivity by raising expectations. *Journal of Applied Behavior Science, 22,* 1–13.

Elias, M. J., Zins, J. E., Graczyk, P. A., & Weissburg, R. P. (2003). Implementation, sustainability, and scaling up of social-emotional and academic innovations in public schools. *School Psychology Review, 32,* 303–319.

Elmore, R. (1991). *Paradox of innovation in education: Cycles of reform and the resilience of teaching.* Unpublished manuscript, Harvard University, Cambridge, MA.

Esper, J. (1990). Organizational change and development: Core practitioner competencies and future trends. *Advances in Organization Development, 1,* 277–314.

Fetterman, D. M. (1996). *Empowerment evaluation: Knowledge and tools for self-assessment and accountability* (pp. 161–187). Thousand Oaks, CA: Sage.

Fitzgerald, T. H. (1987). The OD practitioner in the business world: Theory versus reality. *Organizational Dynamics, 16,* 20–33.

Freeman, R. L., Smith, C. L., & Tieghi-Benet, M. (2003). Promoting implementation success through the use of continuous systems-level assessment strategies. *Journal of Positive Behavior Interventions, 5*(2), 66–70.

Fuchs, D., & Fuchs, L. S. (1988). Mainstream assistance teams to accommodate difficult-to-teach students in general education. In J. Graden, J. E. Zins, & M. J. Curtis (Eds.), *Alternative educational delivery systems* (pp. 49–70). Washington, DC: National Association of School Psychologists.

Fullan, M. G. (1993). *Change forces: Probing the depths of educational reform.* Bristol, PA: Falmer Press.

Fullan, M., Miles, M. B., & Taylor, G. (1980). Organizational development in schools: The state of the art. *Review of Educational Research, 50,* 121–183.

Fullan, M., & Stiegelbauer, S. (1991). *The new meaning of education change.* New York: Teachers College Press.

Gallessich, J. (1973). Organizational factors influencing consultation in the schools. *Journal of School Psychology, 11,* 57–65.

Gottfredson, D. C. (1988). An evaluation of an organization development approach to reducing school disorder. *Evaluation Review, 11,* 739–763.

Gottfredson, D. C., Gottfredson, G. D., & Hybl, L. G. (1993). Managing adolescent behavior: A multi-year, multi-school study. *American Educational Research Journal, 30,* 179–215.

Hall, G. E., & Hord, S. M. (1987). *Change in schools: Facilitating the process.* Albany: State University of New York Press.

Harris, A. (2000). What works in school improvement: Lessons from the field and future directions. *Education Research, 42,* 1–11.

Huebner, E. S., Gilligan, T. D., & Cobb, H. (2002). Best practices in preventing and managing stress and burnout. In A. Thomas & J. Grimes (Eds.), *Best practices in school psychology IV* (pp. 173–182). Bethesda, MD: National Association of School Psychologists.

Illback, R. J., & Fields, T. (1992). Building effective teams and groups: Common themes and future directions. *Special Services in the Schools. 6,* 195–205.

Illback, R. J., & Maher, C. A. (1984). The school psychologist as an organizational boundary role professional. *Journal of School Psychology, 22,* 63–72.

Illback, R. J., Maher, C. A., & Zins, J. E. (1999). Program planning and evaluation. In T. B. Gutkin & C. R. Reynolds (Eds.), *Handbook of school psychology* (3rd ed.) (pp. pp. 907–932). New York: Wiley.

Illback, R. J., & Zins, J. E. (1995). Organizational intervention in educational settings. *Journal of Educational and Psychological Consultation, 6,* 217–236.

Kahn, R. L. (1974). Organizational development: Some problems and proposals. *Journal of Applied Behavior Science, 10,* 485–502.

Kendra, K. A., & Taplin, L. J. (2004). Change agent competencies for information technology project managers. *Consulting Psychology Journal: Practice and Research, 56,* 20–34.

Kimberly, J. R., & Nielsen, W. (1975). Organizational development and change in organizational performance. *Administrative Science Quarterly, 20,* 191–206.

Kleiner, A. (1996). *The age of heretics.* New York: Doubleday.

Koberg, C., Boss, R., Senjem, J., & Goodman, E. (1999). Antecedents and outcomes of empowerment: Empirical evidence from the health care industry. *Group and Organization Management, 24,* 71–91.

Kotter, J. P. (2001). *What leaders really do: Best of HBR.* Boston: Harvard Business School.

Kotter, J. P., & Heskett, J. L. (1997). *Corporate culture and performance.* New York: Free Press.

Lazarus, A. A. (1992). Multimodal therapy: Technical eclecticism with minimal integration. In J. C. Norcross & M. R. Goldfried (Eds.), *Handbook of psychotherapy integration* (pp. 231–263). New York: Basic.

Lewin, K. (1947). Frontiers in group dynamics. *Human Relations, 2,* 5–41.

Lohrmann-O'Rourke, S., Knoster, T., Sabatine, K., Smith, D., Horvath, B., & Llewellyn, G. (2000). School-wide application of PBS in the Bangor area school district. *Journal of Positive Behavior Interventions, 2,* 238–240.

Macy, B. A., & Izumi, H. (1993). Organizational change, design, and work innovation: A meta-analysis of 131 North American field studies: 1961–1991. *Research in Organizational Change and Development, 7,* 235–313.

Maher, C. A., & Illback, R. J. (1982a). Considerations for education and training in organizational school psychology. *Psychology in the Schools, 19,* 194–199.

Maher, C. A., & Illback, R. J. (1982b). Organizational school psychology: Issues and considerations. *Journal of School Psychology, 20,* 244–253.

Maher, C. A., Illback, R. J., & Zins, J. E. (Eds.). (1984). *Organizational psychology in the schools: A handbook for professionals.* Springfield, IL: Charles C. Thomas.

McDaniel, R. R., Jr. (1997). Strategic leadership: A view from quantum and chaos theories. *Health Care Management Review, Winter,* 21–37.

Micklethwait, J., & Wooldridge, A. (1996). *The witch doctors.* New York: Times Books.

Miles, M. B., & Schmuck, R. A. (1971). Improving schools through organizational development: An overview. *Organization development in schools.* Palo Alto, CA: National Press.

Millsap, R. E., & Hartog, S. B. (1988). Alpha, beta, and gamma change in evaluation research: A structural equation approach. *Journal of Applied Psychology, 73,* 574–584.

National Commission on Excellence in Education. (1983). *A nation at risk: The imperative for school reform.* Washington, DC: U.S. Government Printing Office.

Neilsen, E. (1984). *Becoming an OD practitioner.* Englewood Cliffs, NJ: Prentice-Hall.

Newman, F. M. (1993). Beyond common sense in educational restructuring: The issues of content and linkage. *Educational Researcher, 22*(2), 4–13.

Norcross, J. C., & Prochaska, J. O. (1988). A study of eclectic (and integrative) views revisited. *Professional Psychology: Research and Practice, 19,* 170–174.

Northwest Regional Educational Laboratory. (2000). *Evaluating whole-school reform efforts.* Retrieved October 25, 2005, from http://www.nwrac.org/whole-school/index.html.

O'Driscoll, M. P., & Eubanks, J. L. (1993). Behavioral competencies, goal settings, and OD practitioner effectiveness. *Group and Organizational Management, 18,* 308–327.

Patton, M. Q. (2002). *Qualitative research and evaluation methods.* Thousand Oaks, CA: Sage.

Peterson, P. L., McCarthey, S. J., & Elmore, R. F. (1993). Learning from school restructuring. *American Educational Research Journal, 33,* 119–153.

Pfeffer, J. (1998). *The human equation.* Boston: Harvard Business School.

Piotrowski, C., Vodanovich, S. J., & Armstrong, T. (2001). Theoretical orientations of organizational practitioners. *Social Behavior and Personality, 29,* 307–312.

Porras, J. (1987). *Stream analysis: A powerful new way to diagnose and manage change.* Reading, MA: Addison-Wesley.

Porras, J., & Hoffer, S. (1986). Common behavior changes in successful OD efforts. *Journal of Applied Behavioral Science, 22,* 477–494.

Porras, J. I., & Silvers, R. C. (1999). Organization development and transformation. *Annual Review of Psychology, 42,* 51–78.

Putnam, R. F., Luiselli, J. K., & Jefferson, G. L. (2002). Expanding technical assistance consultation to public schools: District-wide evaluation of instructional and behavior support practices for students with developmental disabilities. *Child & Family Behavior Therapy, 24,* 113–128.

Robbins, V., Collins, K., Liaupsin, C., Illback, R. J., & Call, J. (2004). Evaluating school readiness to implement positive behavioral supports. *Journal of Applied School Psychology, 20,* 47–66.

Rosenfield, S. (1987). *Instructional consultation.* Hillsdale, NJ: Erlbaum.

Rosenfield, S., & Gravois, T. A. (1999). Working with teams in the school. In C. R. Reynolds & T. B. Gutkin (Eds.), *Handbook of school psychology* (3rd ed., pp. 1025–1040). New York: Wiley.

Safran, S. P., & Oswald, K. (2003). Positive behavior supports: Can schools reshape disciplinary practices? *Exceptional Children, 69,* 361–373.

Sarason, S. (1971). *The culture of the school and the problem of change.* Boston: Allyn & Bacon.

Sarason, S. B. (1990). *The predictable failure of educational reform.* San Francisco: Jossey-Bass.

Schmuck, R., & Runkel, P. (1994). *The handbook of organization development in schools and colleges.* Prospect Heights, IL: Waveland Press.

Schmuck, R., Runkel, P., Arends, J., & Arends, R. (1977). *The second handbook of organization development in schools.* Palo Alto, CA: Mayfield.

Seligman, M. E. P. (1995). The effectiveness of psychotherapy: The *Consumer Reports* study. *American Psychologist, 50,* 965–974.

Senge, P. (1990). *The fifth discipline.* New York: Doubleday.

Sheridan, S. M., Napolitano, S. A., & Swearer, S. M. (2002). Best practices in school-community partnerships. In A. Thomas & J. Grimes (Eds.), *Best practices in school psychology IV* (pp. 321–336). Bethesda, MD: National Association of School Psychologists.

Smith, C. L., & Freeman, R. L. (2002). Using continuous system level assessment to build school capacity. *American Journal of Evaluation, 23,* 307–319.

Sugai, G., & Horner, R. H. (1999). Discipline and behavioral support: Practices, pitfalls, and promises. *Effective School Practices, 17,* 10–22.

Todd, A. W., Horner, R. H., Sugai, G., & Sprague, J. R. (1999). Effective behavior support: Strengthening school-wide systems through a team-based approach. *Effective School Practices, 17*(4), 23–37.

Tsoukas, H. (1996). The firm as a distributed knowledge system: A constructionist approach. *Strategic Management Journal, 17,* 11–26.

Tushman, M., & Romanelli, E. (1985). Organizational evolution: A metamorphosis model of convergence and reorientation. *Research in Organizational Behavior, 7,* 171–222.

U.S. Department of Education. (2001). Pub. L. 107-110 (No Child Left Behind Act of 2001), 115 STAT. 1425–2094 (January 8, 2002) [unbound].

Walker, H. M., Horner, R. H., Sugai, G., Bullis, M., Sprague, J. R., Bricker, D., et al. (1996). Integrated approaches to preventing antisocial behavior patterns among school-age children and youth. *Journal of Emotional and Behavioral Disorders, 4,* 193–256.

Wang, M., Haertel, G., & Walberg, H. (1993). Toward a knowledge base for school learning. *Review of Educational Research, 63,* 249–294.

Warren, J. S., Edmonson, H. M., Turnbull, A. P., Sailor, W., Wickham, D., Griggs, S. E. & Beech, S. E. (2006). Schoolwide positive behavior support: Adressing behavior problems that impede student learning. *Educational Psychology Review, 2,* 187–198.

Warwick, D., & Donovan, T. (1979). Surveying organization development skills. *Training and Developmental Journal, 33*(9), 22–25.

Watzlawick, P., Weakland, J. H., & Fisch, R. (1974). *Change: Principles of problem formation and problem resolution.* New York: Norton.

Weick, K. E., & Quinn, R. E. (1999). Organizational change and development. *Annual Review of Psychology, 50,* 361–386.

Weisbord, M. (1977). How do you know it works if you don't know what it is? *OD Practitioner, 9*(3), 1–9.

Whelan-Berry, K., Gordon, J., & Hinings, C. (2003). Strengthening organizational change processes: Recommendations and implications from a multilevel analysis. *Journal of Applied Behavioral Science, 39,* 186–207.

Wholey, J. S. (1979). Evaluability assessment: Developing program theory. In L. Bickman (Ed.), *Using program theory in evaluation* (New Directions for Program Evaluation, No. 33). San Francisco: Jossey-Bass.

Woodman, R. W., & Pasmore, W. A. (1989). *Research on organizational change and development.* Greenwich, CT: JAI Press.

Wooten, K., & White, L. (1989). Toward a theory of change role efficacy. *Human Relations, 42,* 651–669.

Worley, C. G., & Feyerhorn, A. E. (2003). Reflections on the future of organization development. *The Journal of Applied Behavioral Sciences, 39,* 91–115.

Worley, C., & Varney, G. (Winter, 1998). A search for a common body of knowledge for master's level organization development and change programs. *Academy of Management OD Consultants Newsletter,* pp. 1–4.

12

Section Commentary
An Integrative View of Process/Outcome Research From Selected Models of Consultation

EMILIA C. LOPEZ

Queens College, City University of New York

BONNIE K. NASTASI

Walden University

In the past several decades, a number of different consultation models have emerged to address educational and psychological issues in schools and mental health settings (Brown, Pryzwansky, & Schulte, 2006). Each of the major models discussed in this volume — mental health consultation (MHC) (i.e., consultee-centered consultation [C-CC] approach), behavioral consultation (BC), conjoint behavioral consultation (CBC), instructional consultation (IC), and organizational development consultation (ODC) — has its own distinct history and features, but they also share several important characteristics. These common characteristics, to some extent, facilitate the process of examining issues relevant to consultation process and outcome.

The first common characteristic is that each model has accumulated a significant amount of literature that is helpful in conceptualizing research on consultation processes and outcomes. Multiple literature sources between the 1970s and today have explored consultation process and outcome issues that have helped researchers, practitioners, and trainers (a) identify process and outcome research variables and questions, (b) examine the available empirical research in those areas, and (c) prioritize a future process and outcome research agenda (e.g., Fuchs, Fuchs, Dulan, Roberts, & Fernstrom, 1992; Gresham & Noell, 1993).

The second shared characteristic is that they are typically and frequently taught in school psychology programs and practiced in the field (Costenbader, Swartz, & Petrix, 1992; Meyers, Wurtz, & Flanagan, 1981). In a survey of training programs, Anton-Lahart and Rosenfield (2004) found that the BC model was most frequently taught (91%), followed by MHC (59%), IC (53%), and ODC (52%). As these consultation models are taught in training programs, graduates such as school psychologists put into practice the consultation knowledge and skills they learned (Costenbader et al.). Because these models are frequently taught and used in practice, we need to bridge the practice-and-research gap by generating research that will inform our understanding of process and outcome issues in consultation, which will in turn improve our consultation practices and training (Froehle & Rominer, 1993).

The third shared characteristic is that all five models are couched within clearly conceptualized theoretical frameworks, and several of the models actually share theoretical foundations. Caplan (1970) developed the MHC model and framed it within a psychodynamic theoretical orientation with strong foci on mental health prevention and intervention. The most recent model for C-CC, as described in the chapter by Knotek, Kanuika, and Ellingsen (chapter 7, this volume), proposes a constructivist framework to guide the consultants' work with consultees (Knotek & Sandoval, 2003). ODC was originally based on industrial and organizational psychology, group process theory, and systems theory; the organizational change (OC) framework discussed by Illback and Pennington (chapter 11, this volume) shares those conceptual theories (Schmuck, 1990). Behavioral theory is at the core of the BC, IC, and the IC teams (ICT) approach and CBC models of consultation (Martens & DiGennaro, chapter 8, this volume; Sheridan, Clarke, & Burt, chapter 9, this volume; Rosenfield, Silva, & Gravois, chapter 10, this volume). The IC/ICT model also emphasizes educational and instructional psychology and instructional implementation (Rosenfield, 1987). The CBC model integrates elements of ecological theory through its emphasis on home-school collaboration and partnerships (Sheridan et al.). Because these models were developed using sound theoretical principles, they have generated a plethora of research hypotheses as well as a wealth of future process and outcome research questions that reflect how much we yet have to learn about the complexity of the consultation process.

The fourth characteristic that these models share is that they emphasize common structural elements that include an indirect system of service delivery, a focus on prevention, and an emphasis on consultant and consultee relationship issues (e.g., coordinate relationship, voluntary participation on the part of the consultee, confidentiality, and a collaborative relationship) (Gutkin & Curtis, 1999). The fifth shared characteristic is that consultants navigate the problem-solving process via sequential stages that include problem identification and analysis, intervention planning and implementation, and process and outcome evaluation. These common elements "unify the various consultation models" (p. 601) and provide researchers with shared process and outcome that can be examined across the models.

Despite the aforementioned commonalities across the various consultation models, there are also major differences between and among these models as well as some challenges that these differences pose. Reschly (1976) identified major differences between some of these selected models in the areas of theoretical orientation, definitions of consultation, goals of consultation, and intervention methods. As discussed in this chapter, the five models of consultation do not share the same theoretical orientations and thus reflect differences in how consultation is approached and implemented. These models also define consultation somewhat differently. For example, the CBC model emphasizes the collaboration between the consultant and several consultees (e.g., parent and teacher) who relate to the client in different contexts (e.g., home and school); the organizational consultation model highlights the relationships between many individuals within organizations (e.g., parents, administrators, teachers, students).

The specific goals of consultation also vary across models. For example, in BC and IC, the primary goal is typically to improve the behaviors of an individual client, whereas in ODC the goal is to improve social systems and relationships between groups of individuals within organizations (Reschly, 1976). Because the theoretical orientations of the models frame how consultants view the problems and the interventions are directly connected to the problems identified, intervention techniques and approaches also vary from model to model. In the BC model, changes are made to the environment in terms of antecedents and consequences, whereas in the ODC model interventions are targeted toward the organizational system and groups of individuals within those systems. Models that are inherently different will most likely approach process and outcome issues in different ways and will frame process and outcome research questions from different perspectives.

Using the reviews provided in the five chapters and previous literature reviews, the next section discusses what we know about process and outcome issues in consultation. Recommendations for future process and outcome research are also provided.

WHAT WE LEARN ABOUT CONSULTATION FROM THE FIVE SELECTED MODELS

The five chapters reviewing BC, CBC, IC/ICT, MHC, and ODC summarize the major findings to date for each model and provide substantive recommendations for future research in consultation. The content of the chapters can be summarized using themes that emerged from the discussion of the various authors. Each of the themes is summarized here within the contexts of the existing knowledge base and future research recommendations.

Process Research

Process has been defined in diverse ways in past research reviews. For example, Medway (1982) defined process research as focusing on "characteristics of consultation participants" and "content and parameters of treatment approaches" (p. 426). In his review of the literature, Medway discussed process research that investigated the characteristics of effective consultants (e.g., warmth, empathy) and responsive consultees (e.g., younger, less experienced), the effectiveness of various consultation models, and consultants' verbal behaviors. Meade, Hamilton, and Yuen (1982) framed process in terms of investigating the stages of consultation and the relationship between consultants and consultees. Gresham and Kendell (1987) discussed process research in the context of teacher expectancies, communication, issues with an impact on the acceptability of interventions, theme interference, and consultee beliefs about the causes of clients' difficulties. Heron and Kimball (1988) examined interpersonal and communication issues between consultants and consultees. Polsgrove and McNeil (1989) defined process in consultation as "the methods and procedural sequence consultants may employ to help consultees ameliorate learning and behavioral problems in youngsters" (p. 7).

Several subthemes related to consultation process emerge across the five models: (a) common processes across models (i.e., communication and collaboration), (b) distinct elements and measurement approaches, and (c) the way in which the process of change is characterized. A discussion of the subthemes follows.

Common Processes: Communication and Collaboration

Collaboration is prominently discussed in most of the models as a central aspect of the consultative practice. The CBC, BC, IC/ICT, and C-CC models examine collaboration within the context of patterns of communication. For example, the CBC and BC research studies examine relational patterns of communication and report data showing that consultants and consultees join in the communication and participate without efforts to dominate interactions as possible evidence of collaboration. Similarly, the IC/ICT model, which incorporates a C-CC approach, uses discourse analysis methodology to examine patterns of communication within teams to find evidence of collaboration.

The CBC model seems promising in terms of promoting mutual and collaborative patterns of communication between consultants and parent-teacher consultees (Erchul et al., 1999; Sheridan, Meegan, & Eagle, 2002). Similar conclusions can be drawn from the ICT research (e.g., Knotek, Rosenfield, Gravois, & Babinski, 2003). Research suggesting that behavioral consultants appear to be more dominant in their interactions with consultees merits future attention as patterns of communication may vary across consultation models.

Given the lack of consensus regarding how to define, operationalize, and measure collaboration in consultation (Schulte & Osborne, 2003; Sheridan, 1992), it seems premature to compare and contrast models in terms of their collaborative attributes. The collaborative consultation research is at the early stages of development, and what we now know about collaboration in consultation is limited (Witt, 1990).

Distinctions: Elements and Measurement of Communication and Collaboration

Despite the common focus on communication and collaboration, the models address distinct elements and use different measurement approaches to examine those processes. For example, in the CBC and BC models, communication is examined within the context of relational patterns via the use of structured and quantitative oriented tools that quantify who leads and follows, and how much reciprocity there is in communication patterns between consultants and consultees (e.g., see discussion in Martens & DiGennaro [chapter 8, this volume] regarding seminal research using the Consultation Analysis Record [CAR; Bergan & Tombari, 1975] to analyze verbal interactions in consultation). In contrast, the IC/ICT and C-CC models use qualitative discourse analysis methods to examine how "the problem" is constructed in problem identification (Rosenfield, 2004), and how language (e.g., types of questions asked) shapes the type of information obtained from consultees.

Process of Change

Research on selected models focuses on the process of change. The IC/ICT and C-CC models highlight the importance of conceptual change in terms of how consultees view clients' problems and evolve toward resolutions of those problems. The ODC literature has explored types of change in organizations (e.g., episodic, continuous) outside school settings (e.g., business organizations).

Research is needed to examine change at the levels of consultation participants (i.e., consultants and consultees). Conceptual change in consultees can be explored across models to compare and contrast how consultants using those different models conceptualize change and actualize conceptual changes in consultees. Research suggests that providing specific feedback to consultees about treatment integrity results in greater adherence to treatment integrity (Noell, chapter 15, this volume; Noell et al., 2000; Sterling-Turner, Watson, & Moore, 2002; Witt & Elliott, 1985). However, we have little information about conceptual changes that are needed and how to achieve those changes so that consultees also change their behaviors toward clients and within the context of intervention implementation (e.g., treatment integrity). Illback and Pennington (chapter 11, this volume) recommend identifying indicators of change in schools and point to the lack of research examining "underlying consultation processes" in ODC (p. 239). They recommend studies that provide detailed descriptions of school consultation processes such as consultants' decision making, effective and ineffective consultation activities, and organizational readiness for consultation.

Thus far, research on conceptual change focuses solely on consultees (Knotek et al., chapter 7, this volume). However, consultation is an interactive process between consultants and consultees and shining a light on half of that dyad ignores questions such as: Are there consultation situations in which consultants' conceptualizations change as a result of working with particular consultees or targeting particular clients? How do those conceptual changes have an impact on how consultants work with future consultees? How do changes in consultants' perceptions evolve, and which variables lead to consultants' conceptual changes? How do changes in the consultants' conceptualizations have an impact on consultees? When consultants' conceptualizations are more or less aligned with the consultees' perceptions of the consultation issues, how does that have an impact on collaboration in consultation?

In general, process research across the five models focuses on areas such as collaboration and communication. However, those variables are examined using divergent approaches and multiple definitions that prohibit drawing clear conclusions about those processes.

OUTCOME RESEARCH

The extent to which specific consultation models have been subject to empirical validation via outcomes research varies. BC and CBC have strong empirical support, IC/ICT is gaining support via various methodological approaches (e.g., field cases, program evaluations), and MHC and ODC have minimal support. In recent years, the two latter models have evolved into newer versions, C-CC and organizational change (OC), respectively. These newer versions are beginning to accumulate necessary empirical evidence, particularly through specific applications. This section summarizes the empirical evidence on outcome research as reflected in the respective chapters for the five consultation models and addresses future research needs.

Martens and DiGennaro (chapter 8, this volume) cite research evidence from individual studies and meta-analytic reviews that show strong support for the effectiveness of BC for improving academic and behavioral outcomes and reducing referrals to special education. Indeed, as the authors noted, BC is the most extensively researched of the consultation models, with outcome studies showing consistently strong support for its efficacy and effectiveness. One source of evidence comes from meta-analytic reviews of treatment outcomes. As the authors stated, these reviews consistently show the strongest effects for interventions employing behavioral strategies compared to other intervention approaches (e.g., cognitive-behavioral, peer tutoring, special education placement). In particular, the authors cited strong support for use of behavioral interventions to improve academic performance (e.g., reading), with effect sizes of 1.0 or above.

Given the extensive research supporting BC, researchers are turning their attention to examining other issues considered critical to the effectiveness and accountability of BC, namely functional behavior assessment (FBA) and functional analysis (FA), brief experimental analysis (BEA) of treatment options, and teacher training in the consultee role (Martens & DiGennaro, chapter 8, this volume). Minimal attention has been paid to the specific role of FBA and FA in determining treatment effectiveness, and the findings are equivocal (Martens & DiGennaro), with research showing stronger effect sizes for FA compared to FBA and strongest effect sizes (although with greater standard deviations) for non-FBA approaches. Initial evidence on the effectiveness of BEA for facilitating selection of behavioral treatment options is positive. What remains to be determined is the extent to which the brief exposures in BEA can predict effectiveness of lengthier implementation of the interventions. The role of teacher training in ensuring effective implementation leading to effective outcomes has been minimally researched. The few available studies (cited in Martens & DiGennaro's chapter) suggest that behavioral intervention strategies applied to teacher training (e.g., systematic arrangement of reinforcement contingencies and performance feedback) are effective for training teachers in the use of behavioral interventions. Although promising, this area needs more extensive research.

Research on CBC provides strong support for its effectiveness in addressing academic, behavioral, and social difficulties (Sheridan et al., chapter 9, this volume). Consistent with BC, research on CBC has yielded average effect sizes of 1.0 or above. These strong effects have been documented for both home and school outcomes. Furthermore, in comparison with other parental consultation models, CBC has been shown to be most effective for producing school-related outcomes (Sheridan et al.).

Chapter 10 by Rosenfield et al. (this volume) summarizes the 20-year history of programmatic research supporting the conceptual foundations and effectiveness of IC/ICT. (Note that these authors consider IC process and ICT structure to be integrated and reciprocal in function and thus do not separately document effects of IC vs. ICT.) The intended outcomes of IC/ICT include those related to students (e.g., special education referrals, attainment of academic and behavioral goals) and teachers (e.g., satisfaction, perception of effectiveness, strategy implementation, problem-solving ability, and change in beliefs about problem origin). An extensive research program using confirmatory program evaluation methodology has shown strong support for the effectiveness of IC/ICT in achieving student and teacher outcomes in real-world settings (Rosenfield et al.). This research supports the effectiveness of IC/ICT for student outcomes, including decreasing special education referrals and placements, increasing appropriate special education referrals, and attaining student academic or behavioral goals set by teacher and consultant. Furthermore, research supports the effectiveness of IC/ICT for achieving the following teacher outcomes (based primarily on teacher reports): (a) learning and implementing new instructional strategies with the target students and other students; (b) improving the assessment of student skills with curriculum materials; (c) providing individualized instruction and facilitating student growth through strategies such as utilizing data-based decision making and assessing instructional levels and by scaffolding instruction based on students' prior knowledge and skills; (d) learning to think differently regarding conceptualizing and solving student and classroom problems; (e) gaining confidence in handling similar student and classroom problems; and (f) indicating their satisfaction with ICT. The support for the effectiveness of IC/ICT comes from a program of research by the developers of the model, thus necessitating additional research to confirm these findings. As Rosenfield et al. state, this formative work provides the foundation for future experimental research to confirm the causal links between IC/ICT and student and teacher outcomes.

MHC is the perhaps the least well researched consultation model. As Knotek et al. (chapter 7, this volume) note, much of the literature on MHC is theoretical in nature, and most research has focused on interpersonal or process variables without sufficient attention to questions regarding efficacy or effectiveness. The authors cite one meta-analysis that provides weak support for client outcomes; however, the findings for consultee outcomes (e.g., changing consultee behavior) are more promising.

Perhaps as a response to the weak evidence base for MHC and the difficulties inherent in transferring an approach originally intended for clinic settings to schools, the MHC model has evolved into the contemporary C-CC model. The C-CC model is focused more specifically on the impact of consultation on the consultee. According to Knotek et al. (chapter 7, this volume), micrographic studies have documented the effectiveness of using questions to facilitate the consultee's understanding of the problem and development of solutions. In the absence of a strong evidence base for CC-C, the authors advocate for programmatic research conceptualized with the framework set forth by the Task Force on Evidence-Based Interventions in School Psychology (Kratochwill & Stoiber, 2002).

With the exception of positive behavior support (PBS) initiatives, research supporting the effectiveness of ODC and OC is sparse. The primary research findings reported by Illback and Pennington (chapter 11, this volume) are drawn from retrospective interviews or surveys of consultants' self-reported behaviors within organizational development or change experiences. As the authors note, much of the work in ODC/OC is theoretically driven, and organizational models have not been subjected to empirical validation. In their chapter, Illback and Pennington provide recommendations for future research to remedy this situation.

In contrast to ODC/OC in general, PBS has received considerable research attention as an educational organizational/system reform approach (Illback & Pennington, chapter 11, this volume). Empirical support comes from experimental and quasi-experimental research, organizational case studies, and meta-analyses of over 100 experimental studies. This research supports the effectiveness of PBS for effecting individual and organizational change. Regarding student outcomes, PBS has been shown to reduce inappropriate student behavior, increase student engagement, and decrease referrals for office discipline and alternative placement. At the organizational level, documented changes include improvements in classroom organization, clarity of rules, teaching and monitoring of student expectations, allocation of faculty resources, and organizational capacity for teacher assistance.

CONTENT RESEARCH

A discussion of process and outcomes research would be incomplete without addressing content issues in consultation because content has a direct impact on both process and outcome issues in consultation. Rosenfield et al. (chapter 10, this volume) refer to content within the IC/ICT models as pertaining to "instructional assessment, evidence-based academic and behavioral interventions" (p. 203). As such, content refers to assessment and intervention processes and products. For example, consultants and consultees need to collect problem identification data in natural environments using tools that are designed to answer the specific consultation referral questions. Those data are then analyzed and utilized for problem validation. When planning and implementing interventions, consultants and consultees also need to specify intervention goals, choose interventions that are evidence based and directly related to the identified problems, and monitor intervention integrity as well as outcomes. In addition, content refers to specific assessment and intervention processes and products, as in the application of specific interventions that are linked to the clients' difficulties. For example, if a student is having difficulties with out-of-seat behavior, the consultant may use behavioral interventions (e.g., positive reinforcement, response cost) to target the out-of-seat behavior. In the IC/ICT model, consultants addressing instructional problems apply curriculum-based methods (e.g., curriculum-based assessment and curriculum-based measurement) to identify and analyze instructional problems.

Empirical evidence is available showing a direct relationship between the implementation of assessment and intervention practices that follow quality indicators for problem identification and intervention implementation in the behavioral literature (see Upah & Tilly, 2002). However, Martens and DiGennaro (chapter 8, this volume) refer to the "lack of consensus in the published literature regarding the necessary components of an FBA" (p. 152) and point out the gap between research and practice in this area. Similar concerns have been raised in the IC/ICT literature regarding curriculum-based assessment (Burns, 2004). Content variables related to assessment and interventions within the C-CC model of consultation are poorly defined, and research within the proposed constructivist C-CC framework will be needed. The proposed research agenda in ODC by Illback and Pennington (chapter 11, this volume) focuses on identifying problems and implementing change in systems. Those authors specifically identify organizational change in schools as an area that needs future investigation. Among the content questions that can be investigated are, Which tools can be used to identify problems with creating change within organizations (e.g., organizational readiness to change)? Which tools can be used to measure systemic change in school settings? Which interventions are effective to achieve short- and long-term change in schools? Which support systems are needed to support short- and long-term changes in schools?

Finally, the authors of the five chapters direct our attention toward evidence-based intervention (EBI) and response-to-intervention (RTI) initiatives that will have an impact on the content of consultation as well as process and outcome issues. These initiatives have underscored the challenges we face in consultation within the contexts of intervention planning and implementation, and those intervention issues are addressed next.

FOCUS ON INTERVENTION IMPLEMENTATION

The literature in education, school psychology, and mental health currently reflects much emphasis on the implementation of EBIs (e.g., Christenson, Carlson, & Valdez, 2002; Cook & Cook, 2004; Mufson, Pollack, Olfson, Weissman, & Hoagwood, 2004). The implementation of RTI initiatives is also under discussion in school psychology as well as special education (e.g., Fuchs & Fuchs, 2006; Mastropieri & Scruggs, 2005).

Intervention planning and implementation are emphasized by all the authors of the five chapters. Knotek et al. (chapter 7, this volume) plot a course for research in intervention efficacy and effectiveness that is relevant to all the selected models of consultation. Several of the chapters also refer to consultation as a service delivery model that can facilitate efforts to plan and implement EBI and RTI initiatives in schools.

The chapter focusing on BC provides provocative and challenging forecasts about the direction that consultative practices will take in an era of EBI and RTI. Martens and DeGennaro (chapter 8, this volume) suggest that consultants may find themselves working in situations in which consultees do not have the options of participating voluntarily, maintaining confidentiality, or freely rejecting or accepting interventions. For example, RTI will require evidence related to treatment integrity and outcomes, possibly precluding consultees' rights to confidentiality. A number of research questions can be identified within this new era of consultation: How do we create school organizational cultures that value EBI and RTI within the context of ODC? Which organizational supports do we need in schools to implement EBI and RTI initiatives? What are the organizational barriers to implementing EBI and RTI within consultation frameworks in schools? How can consultation, as a service delivery model, support the implementation of EBI and RTI initiatives? How do the emphases on EBI and RTI have an impact on the processes (e.g., collaboration, communication, conceptual change) and outcomes of consultation (e.g., client and consultee behavior and attitudes, acceptability of consultation) across the different models? Research is not available at this point examining how the application of EBI and RTI has an impact on the consultation process. The development of that line of research will provide an important step toward understanding the implementation of interventions within consultative practices.

RESEARCHING CONTENT, PROCESS, AND OUTCOME RELATIONSHIPS

Although less well researched than outcome, process, or content alone, the relationships among these three constructs have received some attention within the context of the selected models of consultation. In this section, we summarize those relationships.

Regarding BC, Martens and DiGennaro (chapter 8, this volume) identify several variables that have empirical support as predictors of consultation outcome. These include consultants' skills and behaviors, conditions within school districts, and specific features of behavioral intervention plans. First, research supports the link between treatment outcomes and consultant skill in facilitating problem definition in behavioral terms, using behavioral (e.g., vs. medical) cues, and voicing questions rather than directive statements to identify solutions. Second, the following conditions within the school have been shown to lead to effective behavioral intervention programming: (a) active administrative support; (b) internal (vs. external) consultants; (c) team consultation approach with predefined roles; and (d) use of scripts or manuals for planning, implementation, and monitoring. Third, the authors identify the following components of behavioral interventions as critical to effectively address academic problems: (a) developmentally appropriate target skills and instructionally matched materials; (b) use of frequent progress monitoring with adaptations as needed; (c) intervention strategies with brief repeated practice, modeling, prompting, and corrective feedback; and (d) use of incentives (e.g., reinforcement for improvements in performance).

Sheridan et al. (chapter 9, this volume) address the role of several predictor or process variables related to CBC outcomes. In particular, researchers have examined student characteristics, parent-consultant and parent-teacher relationship variables, and differential perceptions of parents and teachers regarding the social validity of the intervention. Examination of student characteristics yielded differential relationships to school and home outcomes. Whereas student age and symptom severity predicted school outcomes, these variables were not predictive of home outcomes. Furthermore, Sheridan et al. cite their own research findings regarding the effectiveness of CBC for working with diverse student populations. They found consistently high average effect sizes (i.e., greater than 1.0) regardless of presence of diversity or number of diverse characteristics (i.e., race, language, poverty, parental education, and number of adults in household). Examination of relationships within the consultation triad yielded the following findings across studies: (a) parental dominance or control within the parent-consultant or parent-teacher relationship was associated with less-favorable parent and teacher ratings of acceptability and perceived behavioral outcomes; (b) collaborative relationships, established via consultant's facilitation, were linked to effective outcomes; and (c) parental perceptions of outcomes were negatively correlated with differences in parent and teacher views of intervention acceptability.

The extensive formative research supporting outcomes of IC/ICT provides evidence for the links between outcomes and three core elements: the collaborative team relationship, systematic problem-solving process, and knowledge and skills in instructional and behavioral assessment and intervention (Rosenfield et al., chapter 10, this volume). The research cited in the chapter supports the relationship between student outcomes and the following variables: (a) instructional assessment, (b) systematic ongoing (formative) evaluation using data-based procedures (behavioral observation and graphing), and (c) observable and measurable behavioral definitions.

Other factors have been linked to teacher outcomes (Rosenfield et al., chapter 10, this volume). For example, the use of coaching, documented in a detailed manual, was linked to effective skill demonstration by ICT members and subsequent intervention integrity. Microethnographic research supports the relationship between teacher and consultant outcomes (e.g., problem conceptualization, learning, and role performance) and a collaborative process characterized by building effective alliances, generating alternative hypotheses in a constructive manner, using orderly reflection, reframing problems to focus on instructional match, using collaborative communications and thinking, and collecting data to represent student functioning.

As noted, the research evidence on MHC and C-CC is sparse and has focused primarily on process variables. The lack of well-documented outcomes precludes a discussion of process-outcome research. Knotek et al. (chapter 7, this volume), however, identify IC as an example of C-CC. Readers are therefore referred to the section on IC/ICT for evidence supporting process-outcome links.

The lack of documented outcomes for ODC/OC (with the exception of PBS), as described in this summary, also precludes examination of process-outcome links. Furthermore, the research on PBS has neither examined process variables nor provided sufficient information about the consultation processes involved to conduct such analyses. Illback and Pennington (chapter 11, this volume) cite evidence, drawing from a research review and meta-analysis by Wang, Haertel, and Walberg (1993), to support the relationship of multiple sets of variables to the effectiveness of school organizational change efforts. In order of influence, these variable sets included program design, out-of-school variables (e.g., home environment), classroom instruction and climate, student variables, school-level variables (e.g., policy), and state and district variables (policy). Further analysis indicated that learning and teaching process variables (e.g., classroom management, cognitive and meta-cognitive processes, home environment, and parental support) were more strongly correlated with outcomes than were organizational factors (e.g., school and state policy; program, school, and district demographics). Clearly, there is a need for additional research on the link between process and outcome variables related to school ODC and the process of change (OC).

RESEARCH ON SUSTAINABILITY AND TRANSPORTABILITY

Perhaps the least-researched area in consultation concerns the sustainability of consultation outcomes and transportability of evidence-based strategies to real-life settings. Some of these issues also pertain to facilitating research to practice, which is explored in the Research-to-Practice Gap in Consultation section on page 259. In this section, research related to sustainability and transportability is summarized regarding the five consultation models. In addition, future research directions are discussed.

Sustainability

Sustainability refers to the extent to which student, consultee, and organizational outcomes are maintained over time. At a minimum, sustainability research needs to address the question of long-term maintenance of outcomes. In addition, ensuring sustainability requires attention to intervention acceptability, intervention integrity, and the conditions that support maintenance of effects (e.g., what training is necessary to ensure that teachers continue to apply newly learned strategies; what organizational conditions are necessary for maintaining newly adopted procedures).

Research related to sustainability of BC outcomes, presented by Martens and DiGennaro (chapter 8, this volume), focuses on conditions that facilitate treatment integrity and continued implementation of intervention strategies by consultees. As one might expect, BC researchers have examined the effectiveness of behavioral strategies for increasing treatment integrity (i.e., consistent and accurate implementation). The research reviewed by Martens and DiGennaro demonstrates the effectiveness of performance feedback and systematic arrangement of contingencies for increasing intervention integrity. For example, more frequent performance feedback (daily vs. weekly) to teachers results in more consistent accurate implementation of interventions. In addition, use of simple reinforcement contingencies, such as positive social reinforcement, can facilitate correct implementation of interventions. Furthermore, this research has documented that gains in intervention integrity are reflected in gains in student outcomes. Thus, BC research provides excellent examples of the application of theoretically and empirically based strategies to the training of consultees as a way to enhance intervention integrity and subsequent student outcomes.

As Sheridan et al. (chapter 9, this volume) note, research on sustainability of CBC outcomes is sparse, with no research documenting maintenance of effects beyond a few weeks. Drawing on BC research on integrity, these authors also cite the effectiveness of performance feedback (i.e., monitoring plus feedback) for enhancing treatment implementation.

The programmatic research and development related to IC/ICT has directly addressed questions related to implementation integrity and sustainability in the context of scaling up (i.e., transporting IC/ICT to multiple schools and districts; Rosenfield et al., chapter 10, this volume). In particular, these researchers have focused on designing strategies to facilitate an organizational structure to support IC/ICT, support professional development of team members, and ensure implementation integrity. Their programmatic research supports the use of a coaching model to facilitate consistent application of the IC process across team members (Rosenfield et al.). The coaching process includes 20–25 training modules (supported by a training manual) and follow-up performance feedback through the use of videotaping and online coaching by an experienced instructional consultant as team members attempt to implement IC in school settings. These researchers also have developed a self-report measure of implementation that incorporates data consistent with that gained through videotaped observation, which provides a valid and more efficient approach to documenting integrity. Rosenfield and colleagues thus present an excellent model for ensuring and documenting intervention integrity and sustainability.

Given the current status of outcome research for MHC and C-CC (Knotek et al., chapter 7, this volume), questions related to sustainability are premature. At the current time, the programmatic research and development of IC/ICT (identified as an example of C-CC; Knotek et al.) can provide a model for planning research related to integrity and sustainability of C-CC process and outcome.

The sparse empirical basis for ODC/OC also precludes a discussion of sustainability. The focus on changes at both individual and systemic levels suggests that OC models have the potential for sustainable change; however, the extent to which OC programming can achieve long-term outcomes in schools remains to be seen. Illback and Pennington (chapter 11, this volume) offer a list of relevant questions for guiding future research, including questions regarding the role of the consultant in facilitating sustainable change. The international development work of Oxfam (Eade, 1997; Eade & Williams, 1995) also provides a model for building capacity for sustainable change in communities that might help to guide our work in school-based organizational change. An application of these principles to school-based mental health programming can be found in Nastasi, Moore, and Varjas (2004).

Transportability

Transportability refers to the extent to which empirically supported consultation strategies and related intervention techniques can be applied outside of experimental conditions in natural settings. Related research questions include the extent to which evidence-based practice can be applied consistently under diverse natural conditions, the universality of empirically supported practices, and the conditions necessary for effective implementation.

As reflected in the five chapters reviewed here, questions about transportability are only beginning to be addressed. Across the five models, no research on transportability issues is reported. The authors of the respective chapters, however, pose questions that provide direction for future research. This section summarizes the respective questions and future directions for each model. (See also the Research-to-Practice section of this commentary.)

Martens and DiGennaro (chapter 8, this volume) discuss issues of transportability in the context of considering BC as the solution to federal mandates for EBIs (e.g., Individuals With Disabilities Education Act amendments of 1997 and 2004; No Child Left Behind Act). They pose several challenging issues that consultants are likely to face in implementation of BC within naturalistic school settings. For each challenge, we propose relevant research questions:

1. *Issue*: Skill level of consultants and consultees in communication and selection and implementation of evidence-based assessment and intervention strategies; related implications for pre-service and in-service training of school psychologists and teachers. *Research Questions*: Which skills are necessary for application of BC within context of school settings outside experimental conditions? How do we best prepare consultants and consultees to apply BC?

2. *Issue*: Availability of necessary resources such as time, personnel, and finances. *Research Questions*: What are the minimal resources necessary for effective application of evidence-based BC process and assessment/intervention strategies? How can consultants facilitate acquisition of these resources?

3. *Issue*: Organizational barriers related to school psychologists' and teachers' roles. *Research Questions*: What are the role barriers to active engagement in application of BC within school settings? How can consultants and consultees negotiate role change to incorporate BC activities?

4. *Issue*: Changing nature of the consulting relationship within a mandatory process. *Research Questions*: What are the implications of mandatory participation in consultation process for consultees? What are the effects of mandatory participation for intervention integrity and outcomes?

5. *Issue*: Experimental control in natural settings. *Research Questions*: What level of experimental control is necessary to achieve acceptable outcomes? What are the alternative research designs (e.g., quasi experimental; program evaluation) that can be employed in natural settings to achieve acceptable outcomes?

Issues of transportability were not addressed in the chapter by Sheridan et al. (chapter 9, this volume). However, the issues raised above related to BC would be applicable to CBC as well. In addition, issues relevant to the involvement of parents in the consultation process and the triadic (consultant-teacher-parent) relationship would need to be addressed.

Rosenfield et al. (chapter 10, this volume) have given considerable attention to transportability within the programmatic efforts related to scaling of IC/ICT model within schools. (These issues are discussed in the section on Sustainability.) The 20 years of research with repeated applications across multiple schools and school districts have provided the opportunity for these researchers to develop a transportable model of consultation. This programmatic approach to research and development can serve as a prototype for the scaling up and transportability of other consultation models.

As Knotek et al. (chapter 7, this volume) note, the application of MHC to school settings has been limited by theoretical (i.e., reliance on psychodynamic theory) and practical (i.e., reliance on external consultant) barriers and a lack of empirical evidence to support its use in schools. The emergence of C-CC is thus a response to these limitations. The nascent research base in C-CC has not yet considered the issue of transportability, with the possible exception of IC/ICT. Knotek and colleagues, however, do provide guidance in addressing issues of transportability in the context of "professional development needs, adaptation to the school's unique ecological context, a workable evaluation process, and a means to encourage system buy-in" (p. 135). The current status of this emerging model provides an opportunity for researchers to engage in a systematic approach to addressing transportability within the context of programmatic research and development (e.g., such as that employed within IC/ICT).

As indicated by Illback and Pennington (chapter 11, this volume), transportability issues in educational ODC/OC have not been addressed through research. This is understandable given the limited evidence base supporting effectiveness of ODC/OC. In addition, descriptions of successful educational organizational change or school reform efforts typically focus on content of the interventions rather than process of consultation (Illback & Pennington). Such examples, often presented as case studies, fail to provide sufficient description of the conditions and processes to facilitate transfer to other settings. Illback and Pennington have identified a number of issues that need to be addressed in subsequent educational ODC/OC research, several of which have direct relevance to transportability. These issues include school/district readiness for OC, the necessary components of effective OC, the necessary competencies of organizational consultants, and organizational facilitators and barriers.

RESEARCH METHODOLOGY

An examination of the status of process and outcome research in consultation is incomplete without attention to research methodology. A review of the five chapters in the section reveals a range of existing research approaches. Research on BC is characterized by single-subject design and meta-analyses, with a strong focus on outcomes. CBC research has included single-subject experimental designs, meta-analyses, and case studies. MHC/CC-C research methodology is microethnographic and meta-analytic, with a primary focus on process rather than outcome. OC/ODC research historically has been characterized by qualitative evaluation research methods (e.g., appreciate inquiry, logic modeling, stream analysis), with recent attention given to the role of quantitative methods such as structural equation modeling and meta-analysis. The exception is PBS research, which has employed experimental and quasi-experimental designs, use of archival data, case studies, and meta-analysis. Research on IC/ICT reflects a systematic program of mixed-methods research and development. IC/ICT research methods include confirmatory program evaluation, microethnographic (i.e., qualitative) methods, case studies, survey research, and meta-analyses.

The scope of research methods specific to each consultation model is reflective of the status of research. Whereas BC has the most extensive evidence base resulting from systematic application of single-subject designs and subsequent meta-analyses, issues of transportability have not been adequately addressed. In contrast, IC/ICT research, with its use of a systematic program of mixed-methods research, provides the most solid basis for transportability to real-life settings. To facilitate the application of research to practice, it is imperative that consultation research move beyond the focus on outcomes and limited array of process variables to more effectively address questions concerning critical processes relevant to sustainable outcomes and effective implementation across diverse settings (e.g., preschools, pediatric medical settings), situations, problems, and participants (e.g., diverse in terms of ethnicity, culture, and race).

RESEARCH-TO-PRACTICE GAP IN CONSULTATION

Gutkin (1993) argued that consultation research was not keeping up with consultation practice, thus creating a schism between research and practice. That statement is also true today because, as evidenced in the five chapters reviewed, although we know much more about consultation, what we do not know remains vast.

This schism between research and practice also is evident in terms of how practitioners integrate research-based recommendations into their daily practices. Doll et al. (2005) recently asked members of prereferral consultation teams why they did not follow research-based recommendations for team consultation practices. The team members indicated that (a) they lacked the knowledge and skills to implement the research-recommended practices, (b) the practices required extensive time demands, (c) the practices were too complicated and irrelevant to the children's success, and (d) they had limited resources for intervention implementation and limited administrative support.

Gutkin (1993) recommended that we start by conducting research about how consultation is taking place in real settings because this type of research will expand our knowledge base of the actual gap between research and practice. Druckman (2000) proposed "bridge building" (p. 1568) by emphasizing research that addresses practical issues and has practical applications and by creating opportunities for practitioners and researchers to collaborate on research projects. Gresham (1991) advised following a scientist-practitioner model in which practitioners conduct practice-based research such as single-case studies. Simultaneous clinical replications also may be useful within a scientist-practitioner paradigm. In simultaneous clinical replications, researchers are able to examine data from multiple single cases that can be conducted by one practitioner or by multiple practitioners (Cancelli et al., 1989).

The authors of the five chapters also make multiple recommendations regarding the research-to-practice gap. Sheridan et al. (chapter 9, this volume) suggest conducting research using actual cases instead of analogue-based studies. Rosenfield et al. (chapter 10, this volume) recommend looking at goal attainment in consultation within the context of the realities faced by schools, such as high-stakes assessment. Knotek et al. (chapter 7, this volume) focus their recommendations on conducting efficacy and effectiveness research to lessen the divide between research and practice. The next section provides recommendations for new directions in how to conceptualize the five models.

NEW DIRECTIONS IN CONSULTATION PROCESS AND OUTCOME RESEARCH

Consultation Models of the Future: From Multiple Models to Meta-Model

An examination of the similarities and differences across the five major models in school-based consultation raises questions about the continued need for multiple models with distinct research agendas. The authors of the CBC and IC/ICT models acknowledge the importance of organizational variables and their impact on consultation processes and outcomes. Illback and Pennington (chapter 11, this volume), in their discussion of ODC/OC, also acknowledge that ODC has applications at the microlevel in terms of classroom systems and organizations. Particularly as we move toward questions of sustainability and transportability, the differences across models begin to blur. For example, as we consider sustainability and transportability of BC, CBC, and IC/ICT, we need to address questions relevant to organizational change. Each of the models also addresses multiple systems that target the many factors that can have an impact on how children function in schools. For example, the BC model targets individual children and the immediate school setting (e.g., classroom), the CBC model targets the classroom as well as the family system, the C-CC model targets the consultant-consultee relationship, and the ODC model targets larger systems components. Within a systemic framework, each of these models is complementary and enhances consultants' abilities to meet the multiple and complex needs of children in schools. Viewing these models from a more systemic framework generates a number of research questions that are more generic across the models, discussed next.

What Are the Consistencies Across Models?

Knotek et al. (chapter 7, this volume) suggest that C-CC, with a primary focus on the consulting relationship, collaborative problem solving, and conceptual change, could serve as a meta-intervention in which the C-CC could be applied across a wide range of problems and intervention strategies. Indeed, the foundation of all five models is the consulting relationship that relies on effective communication, mutual respect, a problem-solving collaborative process conducted jointly by consultant and consultee, and the facilitation of conceptual change for the consultee (e.g., changing how teachers conceptualize student problems).

What Are the Distinctions Across Models?

An apparent distinction across models is the theoretical basis. BC, for example, is based on behavioral theory and applies behavioral principles to effecting both client and consultee outcomes. CBC, drawing on the foundations of BC, integrates behavioral and ecological theories with a family-centered partnership framework. The extension of BC to include school and family reflects a more systemic approach. C-CC, the contemporary interpretation of MHC, has adopted a constructivist framework for characterizing the consultation process. The foundation of IC/ICT is Vygotsky's social-cultural theory, which guides both process and content. Finally, ODC/OC has a systemic theoretical foundation (e.g., Bronfenbrenner's [1989] ecological theory).

In addition to the theoretical distinctions, though closely tied to theory, are differences regarding focus of the interventions. BC, for example, focuses on the individual student (client) and teacher (consultee) with the goal of effecting change in the client through the consultee. CBC extends the focus beyond the school/teacher to include home/family, thus bridging the relationship between two systems and broadening the focus of change to include client and multiple consultees. C-CC and IC are focused on effecting change in the consultee, with the assumption that such change will affect multiple clients in the future. ICT extends the focus to include systemic change through creation of sustainable consultation teams. ODC/OC focuses on change at multiple levels within the system or organization (e.g., student, teacher, administrator, organizational structure).

Is a Meta-Model Feasible? What Would Constitute an Appropriate Meta-Model?

Clearly, the commonalities across the five consultation models suggest a consistent process for engaging in consultation. The distinctions, however, raise questions about the feasibility of a comprehensive meta-model to guide consultation research and practice. We contend that the current emphasis on sustainability and transportability of consultation and related interventions requires a broader conceptual framework for all models of consultation. A higher-level framework may also help to facilitate communication and collaboration across models so that consultants and consultees can draw on the strengths of various models. Ultimately, those meta-model efforts can advance the scientific foundations of school-based consultation and intervention.

Gutkin and Curtis (1999) suggested the term *ecobehavioral consultation* to emphasize a union between the BC model and the ecological framework. They argued that an ecobehavioral consultation model would facilitate targeting proximal environmental variables (e.g., antecedents, consequences) and distal variables (e.g, parent-child relationship, organizational issues in school).

Given our argument that the models have much in common and are complementary in many ways, we propose that Bronfenbrenner's (1989) ecological model could constitute a meta-model for consultation for a number of reasons. This recommendation is in line with Anderson's (1983) application of an ecological framework when working with families. First, an ecological perspective provides a framework for facilitating change at multiple levels within a particular system (e.g., school). Second, an ecological perspective addresses the connections across systems (e.g., school-home). Third, an ecological perspective addresses the reciprocal nature of human interaction (e.g., reciprocity of teacher-student or consultee-consultant) as a foundation for assessment and intervention. Within the ecological meta-model, professional preparation of consultants and consultees (e.g., school psychologists and teachers) can initially address the common processes related to the consultation relationship, problem-solving process, and conceptual change. This foundation in ecological theory and consultation processes would then provide the basis for examination of the multiple models of consultation and development of an integrated framework for guiding consultation and intervention practice.

In addition to guiding professional development and practice, an ecological meta-model can guide future research agendas across models. Addressing questions regarding outcomes, process, process-outcome links, and sustainability and transportability requires a focus on multiple levels of the ecological systems and connections across those systems.

Several integrative models of consultation are emerging in the literature. Rosenfield et al. (chapter 10, this volume) refer to integrating C-CC as a means of strengthening the consultant-consultee relationship and processes. Erchul and Martens (2002) also proposed a BC and MHC integrative model of consultation that emphasizes consultee-centered issues, emotional and instrumental (collaborative) support for consultees, a problem-solving framework, and social influence issues. Integrative models may provide us with a road map toward developing a meta-model of consultation. The conceptual bases for these integrated models are in development, but much more research will be needed to validate them. Research also will be needed to clearly explore process and outcome findings within these integrative formats.

Which Research Methodologies Can We Utilize to Investigate Consultation Within an Ecological Framework?

As suggested in the five chapters in this section, answering current and future research questions requires expanding the repertoire of research methodology to include a range of quantitative, qualitative, and mixed-methods research and evaluation designs. Integrating multiple methods within the context of programmatic research and development will require consideration of an overarching framework for conceptualizing research, such as those proposed in contemporary social science research texts (see Creswell, 2003; Tashakkori & Teddlie, 2003). As noted, the work of Rosenfield et al. (chapter 10, this volume) provides an excellent example of programmatic research and development within a mixed-methods framework. An additional illustration can be found in Nastasi et al. (2004).

CONCLUSION

The five major consultation models are clearly "works in progress" as they trace the evolution of their past research accomplishments and plot a course for future research efforts. Many questions remain related to process and outcome issues in consultation. Practice in consultation is still ahead of research, and future research efforts will hopefully lessen that divide. A cyclical pattern of research informing practice and practice informing research will contribute toward diminishing the gap between research and practice in consultation.

Consultation research that reflects the complexity of the consultation process in practice will be particularly important (Gresham & Noell, 1993). In the practice of consultation, children have multiple problems that may include behavioral difficulties as well as learning problems, social deficits, and mental health needs. Schools, classrooms, and families are complex systems that present multiple consultation facilitators as well as barriers. Consultees work under multiple stressors and pressures and exhibit strengths as well as weaknesses in terms of their knowledge, skills, and attitudes. We agree with Gresham and Noell, who stated that consultation service delivery will be better understood when researchers use research methods that reflect as well as embrace those complexities.

Consultation research will need to continue to evolve in the future, especially as consultation practice continues to respond to changing times. The models have evolved over time because social conditions, educational guidelines and regulations, and schools in general have changed over time (Truesdell & Lopez, 1995). These changes will mean that our research foci will necessarily expand. The authors of these five chapters clearly foresee numerous changes that will be reflected in the future consultation research.

The models complement each other as each focuses on different systemic factors (e.g., home, classroom, school, community) that have an impact on students' behavioral, instructional, social, and mental health functioning. The similarities and differences across the five major models and their complementary elements provide a rationale for an ecological meta-model of consultation that will enhance opportunities to target consultants', consultees', and clients' complex needs. As consultation practice changes in response to social conditions, educational regulations, and school demands, the research will need to be directed toward the implications of those changes to sustain the science, applicability, and relevancy of consultation practice.

REFERENCES

Anderson, C. (1983). An ecological developmental model for a family orientation in school psychology. *Journal of School Psychology, 21*, 179–189.

Anton-LaHart, J., & Rosenfield, S. (2004). A survey of preservice consultation training in school psychology programs. *Journal of Educational and Psychological Consultation, 15*, 41–62.

Bergan, J. R., & Tombari, M. L. (1975). Consultant skill and efficiency and the implementation and outcomes of consultation. *Journal of School Psychology, 14*, 3–14

Bronfenbrenner, U. (1989). Ecological systems theory. In R. Vasta (Ed.), *Annals of child development* (Vol. 6, pp. 187–249). Greenwich, CT: JAI Press.

Brown, D., Pryzwansky, W. B., & Schulte, A. C. (2006). *Psychological consultation and collaboration: Introduction to theory and practice* (6th ed.). Boston: Allyn & Bacon.

Burns, M. K. (2004). Using curriculum-based assessment in consultation: A review of three levels of research. *Journal of Educational and Psychological Consultation, 15*, 63–78.

Cancelli, A. A., Lange, S. M., Lopez, E., Kerwin, C., Matalon, T., Perlman, L., et al. (1989). A study of guidelines for the conduct and analysis of simultaneous clinical replications. *Professional School Psychology, 4*, 295–305.

Caplan, G. (1970). *The theory and practice of mental health consultation.* New York: Basic Books.

Christenson, S. L., Carlson, C., & Valdez, C. R. (2002). Evidence-based interventions in school psychology: Opportunities, challenges, and cautions. *School Psychology Quarterly, 17*, 466–474.

Cook, B. G., & Cook, L. (2004). Bringing science into the classroom by basing craft on research. *Journal of Learning Disabilities, 37*, 240–247.

Costenbader, V., Swartz, J., & Petrix, L. (1992). Consultation in the schools: The relationship between preservice training, perception of communicative skills, and actual time spent in consultation. *School Psychology Review, 21*, 95–108.

Creswell, J. W. (2003). *Research design: Qualitative, quantitative, and mixed methods approaches* (2nd ed.). Thousand Oaks, CA: Sage.

Doll, B., Haack, K., Kosse, S., Osterloh, M., Siemers, E., & Pray, B. (2005). The dilemma of pragmatics: Why schools don't use quality team consultation practices. *Journal of Educational and Psychological Consultation, 16*, 127–156.

Druckman, D. (2000). The social scientist as a consultant. *American Behavioral Scientist, 43*, 1565–1577.

Eade, D. (1997). *Capacity-building: An approach to people-centered development.* Oxford, England: Oxfam.

Eade, D., & Williams, S. (1995). *The Oxfam handbook of development and relief.* Oxford, England: Oxfam.

Erchul, W. P., & Martens, B. K. (2002). *School consultation: Conceptual and empirical bases of practice* (2nd ed.). New York: Kluwer Academic/Plenum.

Erchul, W. P., Sheridan, S. M., Ryan, D. A., Grissom, P. F., Killough, C. E., & Mettler, D. W. (1999). Patterns of relational communication in conjoint behavioral consultation. *School Psychology Quarterly, 14*, 121–147

Froehle, T. C., & Rominer, III, R. L. (1993). Directions in consultation research: Bridging the gap between science and practice. *Journal of Counseling and Development, 71*, 693–700.

Fuchs, D., & Fuchs, L. S. (2006). Introduction to response to intervention: What, why and how valid is it? *Reading Research Quarterly, 41*, 92–99.

Fuchs, D., Fuchs, L. S., Dulan, J., Roberts, H., & Fernstrom, P. (1992). Where is the research on consultation effectiveness? *Journal of Educational and Psychological Consultation, 3*, 151–174.

Gresham, F. M. (1991). Moving beyond statistical significance in reporting consultation outcome research. *Journal of Educational and Psychological Consultation, 20*, 1–13.

Gresham, F. M., & Kendell, G. K. (1987). School consultation research: Methodological critique and future research directions. *School Psychology Review, 16*, 306–316.

Gresham, F. M., & Noell, G. H. (1993). Documenting the effectiveness of consultation outcomes. In J. E. Zins, T. R. Kratochwill, & S. N. Elliott (Eds.), *Handbook of consultation services for children: Applications in educational and clinical settings* (pp. 249–273). San Francisco: Jossey-Bass.

Gutkin, T. G. (1993). Conducting consultation research. In J. E. Zins, T. R. Kratochwill, & S. N. Elliott (Eds.), *Handbook of consultation services for children: Applications in educational and clinical settings* (pp. 227–248). San Francisco: Jossey-Bass.

Gutkin, T. B., & Curtis, M. J. (1999). School based-consultation theory and practice: The art and science of indirect service delivery. In C. R. Reynolds & T. B. Gutkin (Eds.), *Handbook of school psychology* (3rd ed., pp. 598–637). New York: Wiley.

Heron, T. E., & Kimball, W. H. (1988). Gaining perspective with the educational consultation research base: Ecological considerations and further recommendations. *Remedial and Special Education, 9*, 21–28.

Knotek, S. E., Rosenfield, S. A., Gravois, T. A., & Babinski, L. M. (2003). The process of fostering consultee development during instructional consultation. *Journal of Educational and Psychological Consultation, 14*, 303–328.

Knotek, S. E., & Sandoval, J. (Eds.). (2003). Consultee-centered consultation [Special issue]. *Journal of Educational and Psychological Consultation, 14*(3&4).

Kratochwill, T. R., & Stoiber, K. C. (2002). Evidence-based interventions in school psychology: Conceptual foundations of the *Procedural and Coding Manual of Division 16 and the Society for the Study of School Psychology Task Force. School Psychology Quarterly, 17*, 341–389.

Mastropieri, M. A., & Scruggs, T. E. (2005). Feasibility and consequences of response to intervention: Examination of the issues and scientific evidence as a model for the identification of individuals with learning disabilities. *Journal of Learning Disabilities, 38*, 525–531.

Meade, C. J., Hamilton, M. K., & Yuen, R. K. (1982). Consultation research: The time has come, the walrus said. *The Counseling Psychologist, 10*, 39–51.

Medway, F. J. (1982). School consultation research: Past trends and future directions. *Professional Psychology, 13*, 422–430.

Meyers, J., Wurtz, R., & Flanagan, D. (1981). A national survey investigating consultation training occurring in school psychology programs. *Psychology in the Schools, 18*, 297–302.

Mufson, L. H., Pollack D., K., Olfson, M., Weissman, M. M., & Hoagwood, K. (2004). Effectiveness research: Transporting interpersonal psychotherapy for depressed adolescents (IPT-A) from the lab to school-based health clinics. *Clinical and Child Family Psychology Review, 7*, 251–261.

Nastasi, B. K., Moore, R. B., & Varjas, K. M. (2004). *School-based mental health services: Creating comprehensive and culturally specific programs.* Washington, DC: American Psychological Association.

Noell, G. H., Witt, J. C., LaFleur, L. H., Mortenson, B. P., Ranier, D. D. & Le Velie, J. (2000). A comparison of two follow-up strategies to increase teacher intervention implementation in general education following consultation. *Journal of Applied Behavior Analysis, 33*, 271–284.

Polsgrove, L., & McNeil, M. (1989). The consultation process: Research and practice. *Remedial and Special Education, 10*(1), 6–13.

Reschly, D. J. (1976). School psychology consultation: "Frenzied, faddish, or fundamental?" *Journal of School Psychology, 14*, 105–113

Rosenfield, S. A. (1987). *Instructional consultation.* Hillsdale, NJ: Erlbaum.

Rosenfield, S. (2004). Consultation as dialogue: The right words at the right time. In N. M. Lambert, I. Hylander, & J. H. Sandoval (Eds.), *Consultee-centered consultation: Improving the quality of professional services in schools and community organizations* (pp. 337–347). Mahwah, NJ: Erlbaum.

Schmuck, R. (1990). Organization development in schools: Contemporary concepts and practices. In T. B. Gutkin & C. R. Reynolds (Eds.), *The handbook of school psychology* (2nd ed., pp. 899–919). New York: Wiley.

Schulte, A. C., & Osborne, S. S. (2003). When assumptive worlds collide: A review of definitions of collaboration in consultation. *Journal of Educational and Psychological Consultation, 14,* 109–138.

Sheridan, S. M. (1992). What do we mean when we say "collaboration"? *Journal of Educational and Psychological Consultation, 3,* 89–92.

Sheridan, S. M., Meegan, S. P., & Eagle, J. W. (2002). Assessing the social context in initial conjoint behavioral consultation interviews: An exploratory analysis investigating processes and outcomes. *School Psychology Quarterly, 17,* 299–324.

Sterling-Turner, H. E., Watson, T. S., & Moore, J. W. (2002). The effects of direct training and treatment integrity on treatment outcomes in school consultation. *School Psychology Quarterly, 17,* 47–77.

Tashakkori, A., & Teddlie, C. (2003). *Handbook of mixed methods in social and behavioral research.* Thousand Oaks, CA: Sage.

Truesdell, L. A., & Lopez, E. (1995). An introduction to consultation models revisited. *Journal of Educational and Psychological Consultation, 6,* 1–5

Upah, K. R. F., & Tilly, W. D., (2002). Best practices in designing, implementing and evaluating quality interventions. In A. Thomas & J. Grimes (Eds.), *Best practices in school psychology IV* (pp. 483–516). Bethesda, MD: National Association of School Psychologists.

Wang, M., Haertel, G., & Walberg, H. (1993). Toward a knowledge base for school learning. *Review of Educational Research, 63,* 249–294.

Witt, J. C. (1990). Collaboration in school-based consultation: Myth in need of data. *Journal of Educational and Psychological Consultation, 1,* 367–370.

Witt, J. C., & Elliott, S. N. (1985). Acceptability of classroom intervention strategies. In T. Kratochwill (Ed.), *Advances in school psychology* (Vol. 4, pp. 251–288). Hillsdale, NJ: Erlbaum.

D

WHAT WE KNOW: PROCESS/OUTCOME FINDINGS FROM SELECTED RESEARCH PERSPECTIVES

13

Studying Multicultural Aspects of Consultation

Colette L. Ingraham

San Diego State University

INTRODUCTION TO MULTICULTURAL ASPECTS IN SCHOOL-BASED CONSULTATION

Today's schools, universities, and communities are composed of increasingly culturally diverse populations, and contemporary researchers and practitioners are challenged to demonstrate the efficacy of their work within multicultural settings. There is a growing body of literature that informs the study of multicultural aspects of consultation. The purpose of this chapter is to summarize current research findings, methods, and literature and to propose future directions for studying the multicultural aspects of school consultation. The chapter begins with conceptual foundations about culture and the multicultural aspects of consultation, followed by an examination of research methods used to study these aspects, a summary of extant research findings, and an integration of what we know about the processes and outcomes attained through multicultural approaches to consultation. The chapter concludes with a summary of available evidence regarding the multicultural aspects of consultation and sets a research agenda for future investigations to contribute to this area of consultation research and practice.

There are many ways that multicultural aspects are embedded within consultation, the members of the consultation system, the process of consultation, and research about consultation. Tarver Behring and Ingraham (1998) proposed that culture influences all aspects of consultation, and that it should be a central component of consultation theory, research, training, and practice. This chapter examines some of the issues and methods for studying cultural influences on consultation.

Inquiry regarding multicultural aspects of consultation begins with an understanding of what culture is and how it influences various processes. *Culture* has been defined in a variety of ways, typically involving a set of beliefs, values, behaviors, and traditions. Within the consultation literature, culture is defined broadly and includes "an organized set of thoughts, beliefs, and norms for interaction and communication, all of which may influence cognitions, behaviors, and perceptions" (Ingraham, 2000, p. 325). Culture may be influenced by a whole host of factors that serve to shape one's worldview. The depth of one's experiences with these factors and the importance they play in determining a person's thinking, values, and behaviors influences the extent to which they shape one's cultural identity. Culture may be partially shaped by race, ethnicity, language, socioeconomic status, age, educational attainment, sexual orientation, spirituality, professional role, level of acculturation, and worldview or operational paradigm. In addition, ecosystemic factors such as geographic location, institutional culture, and professional perspectives can affect one's cultural identity. When the consultant, consultee, and client hold different belief systems, paradigms, or philosophies, they are operating from different frames of reference. Soo-Hoo (1998) explained that understanding a person's frame of reference includes attending to influences of their cultural, sociopolitical, and psychological contexts. Often, when one is a member of the dominant or prevailing culture, a person may not be as aware of their cultural frame of reference as one whose culture is in the minority. When people interact with members of different cultures, they more readily learn the characteristics of their own culture (Lynch & Hanson, 2004).

When one or more members of the consultation system is visibly culturally different from the others, such as by virtue of a different language, race, or ethnicity, consultants may realize that there are potential cultural aspects to the consultation process. The first situation that may occur to school psychologists is when the client is culturally different from the consultant and school-based consultee. For example, a school psychologist might consult with a teacher regarding a student who has a different cultural background from the teacher and consultant. In many school consultation situations, the consultant and teacher consultee are from middle-class European American mainstream U.S. backgrounds, and the parent consultee and client are from a lower socioeconomic status ethnic minority background. The consultant and teacher seek to develop interventions that are appropriate for the client based on their understanding of the client's culture and psychoeducational needs. Training programs attempting to prepare students for working with diversity may begin with this level of thinking and include readings about service delivery to culturally diverse populations. Similarly, researchers attempting to include cultural features into their investigations often refer to the cultural composition of their participants or consultation clients. Although situations with culturally different clients may be the easiest to identify, these represent only a small part of the multitude of multicultural aspects of consultation. Focusing on the client's culture is a preliminary step in approaching the multicultural aspects of consultation. Consultants and consultees also bring their cultural perspectives to the consultation system.

The most basic and readily apparent cultural influences occur when one or more members of the consultation system (consultant, consultee, or client) is culturally different from the other members. Ingraham (2000) described and diagrammed five ways that culture might be distributed among the members of the consultation process: consultant-client similarity, consultant-consultee similarity, consultee-client similarity, three-way cultural diversity, and contextual cultural differences. In these constellations, the consultees may be educators, families, or both. Ingraham used the term *consultation constellation* to refer to the ways that cultures are distributed among members of the consultation system. Different cross-cultural consultation dynamics occur, depending on the consultation constellation and where the cultural similarities and differences reside. Given the current demographics of the school psychology and teaching professions (predominantly European American white middle class and female), the most prevalent of consultation constellations is consultant-teacher similarity with a culturally different family and student. As the ethnic diversity of school psychologists and teachers increases, more consultation constellations arise involving the consultant or teacher consultee who may be culturally different from the mainstream culture as well. Specific consultation strategies for such cross-cultural situations were detailed by Ingraham (2000, 2003, 2007), Nastasi, Moore, and Varjas (2004), and Tarver Behring, Cabello, Kushida, and Murguia (2000). Thus, when any member of the consultation system differs culturally from one or more of the other members, multicultural aspects can influence the consultation processes and outcomes.

Cultural issues are influential in the development of consultation theories and research studies as well. The paradigm and worldview of researchers influences the questions asked, the definitions developed, the tools used for gathering evidence, and the interpretation and reporting of results (Ingraham & Oka, 2006; Ingraham, Oka, & Nastasi, 2004, 2005; Matsumoto, 2000; Quintana, Troyano, & Taylor, 2001). Ingraham et al. (2004, 2005) developed coding criteria for evidence-based interventions (EBIs) in school psychology that address more fully issues of cultural validity and the myriad ways that culture affects research on EBIs. Ingraham (2003), Sue (1999), and Wampold, Licktenberg, and Waehler (2002) have recommended that researchers need to identify their own cultural lenses and report these in their publications so that the cultural perspectives of the researchers are more transparent to readers. Thus, the theories about consultation, the researchers who study it, the selection of tools and methods to investigate consultation processes and outcomes, and those individuals who practice consultation are all influenced by cultural assumptions, paradigms, and lenses for perceiving.

In sum, many issues are involved with studying multicultural aspects of consultation. One must understand what culture is, how it is expressed through human thought and action, and how it is integral to the paradigm, worldview, perspective, and experiences from which one functions. Culture is not a variable or something that one has or does not have; rather, culture is a complex set of influences and relationships that shapes the thoughts and behaviors of individuals, groups, and institutions. Studying the multicultural aspects of consultation involves developing an understanding of how culture permeates all aspects of our conceptualization, interaction, problem solving, and interpretations. The next section discusses research methods used to study multicultural aspects of consultation.

RESEARCH METHODS USED TO STUDY MULTICULTURAL ASPECTS OF CONSULTATION

A variety of research methods has been used to study the multicultural aspects of consultation. Some of the earliest publications about sociocultural, ethnic, and racial issues in consultation were descriptions by consultants working with different populations within organizations and international consultation (e.g., Pinto, 1981) or consultant training within community psychology (e.g., Gibbs, 1980, 1985). The authors of these publications proposed differing orientations to help consultants understand the different ways consultees may be thinking of and perceiving the consultation experience. They outlined stages of consultation at which the consultants' relationships with the consultees were influenced by culturally distinct orientations or interpersonal patterns. These early descriptions of different ways of interacting and developing consultative relationships laid the foundations for the analogue studies that emerged in the following decade.

Within the field of school psychology, there is growing recognition that there is a variety of appropriate and needed research methods for the study of EBIs (Kratochwill & Stoiber, 2002). The national Task Force on Evidence-Based Interventions in School Psychology, a group of scholars across several domains of school psychology research and practice, spent approximately 5 years generating a coding manual that includes specific criteria for developing and evaluating studies using group designs, single-case designs, qualitative designs, and mixed-methods research designs. Each of these designs has merits and relative advantages for investigating the efficacy of interventions within school psychology, depending on the paradigm of the researcher, the purposes of the research, and the interventions studied. At the request of the Task Force, Nastasi (cochair of the task force's Qualitative Research Committee), Oka, and Ingraham (cochairs of the task force's Multicultural Considerations Committee) worked to integrate the perspectives and methods of qualitative research paradigms and multicultural issues into a revision of the coding manual so that it would be inclusive of a broad range of valued research methods. They (Ingraham et al., 2004, 2005) operationalized and expanded the cultural validity work of Quintana et al. (2001) and developed a revision of the manual that attends to different methodologies and multicultural issues within school psychology. At the time of this writing, this proposed revision is in press by the task force. Also, Ingraham and Oka (2006) discussed cultural considerations necessary to responsibly adopt an EBI perspective in diverse contexts. The following discussion of research methods used in studying multicultural aspects of consultation research is informed by this work. It is recommended that future research consider the quality standards advanced by the task force and the cultural considerations in Ingraham and Oka (2006) in the development, design, and application of consultation intervention research.

Quantitative Methods

Both quantitative and qualitative methods have been used to study multicultural aspects of consultation. This section describes research using analogue studies and issues regarding external, social, and cultural validity as they relate to multicultural research of consultation.

Analogue Studies

In the 1990s, analogue studies were used to investigate the influences of race (Duncan & Pryzwansky, 1993; Naumann, Gutkin, & Sandoval, 1996; Rogers, 1998); gender (Harris, Ingraham, & Lam, 1994); and consultee perspectives (Conoley, Conoley, Ivey, & Scheel, 1991). These studies typically used a written, audiotaped, or videotaped scenario describing a consultation situation and asked participants to rate the consultants on different dimensions of consultant effectiveness, attentiveness to the values and perspectives of consultees, and in some cases, multicultural sensitivity. The race or gender of the consultant was varied in the cases available to the participants.

There are both advantages and drawbacks to using analogue studies to investigate multicultural aspects of consultation. A major advantage of analogue studies is that researchers can vary key variables to isolate specific aspects of the cultural differences and similarities, such as the race of the consultant, consultee, or client; gender of consultant or consultee; and level of experience of the consultant or consultee. Participants who read, view, or hear a standardized consultation exchange can be asked to rate the exchange and its participants along a host of dimensions and characteristics. In this way, the researchers can control participant access to information and cultural cues to study the relative impact of different variables in multicultural consultation on the perceptions of raters. Rogers (1998) developed an eloquent study to investigate the effects of consultant race and race-sensitive consultation content on the perceptions of African American and Caucasian preservice teachers. She used a $2 \times 2 \times 2 \times 2$ multivariate analysis and univariate follow-up tests to investigate the influences of consultee and consultant race, consultant verbal behaviors, and race of raters. Rogers's study is an excellent example of the benefits of using a carefully designed analogue study. Rogers's findings are described in more detail in the section Racial Influences Among Consultants and Consultees. Briefly, she found that the discussion of racial topics during the consultation sessions, not the race of the consultant, was most influential in determining ratings of consultant effectiveness and multicultural sensitivity.

A criticism of analogue studies is that they are contrived scenarios in which raters speculate about their feelings and thoughts regarding the members of the consultation system. It is difficult to assess the degree to which political correctness, stereotypes, and other potential biases influence their observations and ratings. Similarly, it is difficult to demonstrate that a respondent's ratings during hypothetical situations are indicative of how they would think or feel if they were actually involved with a consultation relationship with real presenting problems. When it comes to the feelings (e.g., trust, frustration, empathy, or judgment) that may surface during real cross-cultural consultation cases, it is not clear that analogue studies can fully capture the range of influences that actually determine multicultural consultation processes and outcomes.

Concepts of External, Social, and Cultural Validity

Evidence-based research about consultation, like other types of interventions, must address three central questions: (a) Which interventions are effective? (b) For whom are these interventions effective? and (c) Under which circumstances or contexts are they effective? Answering these questions allows policymakers and interventionists to evaluate the potential transferability of specific EBIs for given populations and contexts. In making decisions about transferability, readers need to look for evidence of three types of validity: external, social, and cultural (Ingraham & Oka, 2006).

Sue (1999) stressed the critical importance of external validity in developing an understanding of human beings in all of their diversity. Unless research includes details about the ethnic diversity of its participant samples and the cultural context in which the interventions are delivered, it is difficult to reach conclusions regarding its applicability to other samples and settings. Researchers need to provide adequate information about the cultures and ethnicities of the participants to enable evaluations of the external validity of the findings.

Social validity is central to answer the questions, Who cares? and So what? (Kazdin 1977). Typically, *social validity* refers to the judgments regarding the importance of intervention goals, appropriateness of their procedures, and importance of the outcomes. *Intervention acceptability*, a subset of social validity, refers to the participants' perceptions of the value and appropriateness of a given intervention. Within consultation research, measures of social validity are frequently used to document the effectiveness of consultation services.

Barnett et al. (1995) advocated for the notion of *ethnic validity*, an extension and application of social validity, as a key concept in cross-cultural professional competence in school psychology. They defined ethnic validity as "the degree to which problem definition and problem-solving are acceptable to the client in respect to the client's belief and value systems, as these are associated with the client's ethnic/cultural group" (p. 221). They recommended that future research verify the construct of ethnic validity and explore its value in understanding different conceptualizations of problem situations and their sociocultural origins. Researchers have expanded the notion of ethnic validity and are using the construct of *cultural validity* to encompass a range of facets that includes external validity, social validity, and ethnic validity (Ingraham & Oka, 2006; Ingraham et al., 2004, 2005; Quintana et al., 2001).

Within consultation research in school psychology, Ramirez, Lepage, Kratochwill, and Duffy (1998) outlined a series of questions about multicultural issues in school-based consultation that could be addressed through quantitative methods. They proposed using an adaptation of the treatment utility of assessment approach, which they called *utility of cultural variable investigations*, to investigate ways that information regarding cultural variables assists in problem solving. In this conceptualization, they described that "utility of a cultural variable refers to the degree to which consideration/inclusion of the cultural variable/issue is shown to contribute to successful consultation outcome(s)" (p. 497). The work of Ramirez et al. helps to highlight some of the literature in multicultural counseling and psychotherapy that relates to consultation and ways that cultural considerations affect each stage in the typical problem-solving consultation models. Despite their specificity in the research questions and methods that could be used to explore a range of cultural influences in the consultation process, unfortunately little empirical research has resulted from their recommendations.

One controversial approach to studying multicultural aspects of consultation and other EBIs suggests comparing the effect sizes of intervention outcomes with different cultural populations. Kratochwill and Stoiber (2002) posited that this might be a way to explore the EBIs across different cultural populations. Following Kratochwill and Stoiber's suggestion for comparing effect sizes for different cultural groups, Sheridan, Eagle, and Doll (2006) compared the effect sizes and social validity ratings of students with differing numbers of diversity indicators in an exploration of the utility of conjoint behavioral consultation with diverse students and their families. Others (e.g., Ingraham & Oka, 2006; Quintana et al., 2001) have noted that comparing the effect sizes is insufficient to address issues of cultural validity and a broader interpretation and integration of cultural validity criteria is warranted.

Despite the recommendations of Ramirez et al. (1998) and others, there has been little published research on the use of quantitative methods to study cultural aspects of consultation. One reason for this dearth of quantitative studies may be that researchers with expertise in multicultural issues are electing qualitative methods to address the complexities and richness of consultation among diverse consultees, clients, consultants and settings. For those who believe that culture is a paradigm or worldview and not a single variable (e.g., Ingraham, 2000, 2003; Nastasi et al., 2004; Soo-Hoo, 1998; Tarver Behring & Ingraham, 1998), research designs that treat culture as one among a series of demographic variables may be perceived as inadequate to express the diverse dimensions and influences of culture on human thought and behavior.

Qualitative and Naturalistic Methods

Several scholars have called for naturalistic studies of consultation (e.g., Pryzwansky & Noblit, 1990), specifically for studying cultural aspects of consultation (Henning-Stout & Meyers, 2000; Ingraham, 2000a; Ingraham & Meyers, 2000; Nastasi, Vargas, Berstein, & Jayasena, 2000; Tarver Behring & Ingraham, 1998), to more fully capture the realities and complexities of multicultural consultation. In the 1990s, and more extensively since the year 2000, naturalistic inquiry, qualitative methods, and case studies have been used to study multicultural aspects of consultation. Scientist-practitioners have presented cases describing their consultation work in real school and community settings with people of different ethnic and linguistic groups (Goldstein & Harris, 2000; Harris, 1991, 1996; Hernández, Bunyi, & Townson, in press; Lopez, 2000; Tarver Behring et al., 2000) and across differing cultural and international contexts (Maital, 2000; Nastasi, Vargas, Berstein, et al., 2000). Scholars are using formalized methods of qualitative research, employing grounded theory (Hylander, 2003; Nastasi, Vargas, Berstein, et al., 2000), multiple-case study analysis with embedded units of analysis (Ingraham, 2003), ethnographic methods (Nastasi et al., 2004), and other qualitative methods (Goldstein & Harris, 2000; Lopez, 2000; Tarver Behring et al., 2000).

Case Studies

For numerous reasons, case studies are an important type of qualitative research in the study of multicultural issues in consultation. Case studies provide a richness of information, called *thick descriptions*, that gives readers a more complete perspective of the context for the study, the various components and how they work together, and the relationships that evolve among those involved in the interventions (Lincoln & Guba, 1985). This offers the reader a wealth of information for evaluating the potential transferability across contexts (i.e., how applicable the findings of a particular study might be to other contexts). Case studies are recommended for emic inquiry, a focus on the reconstruction of the participant's conceptualizations (Erlandson, Harris, Skipper, & Allen, 1993), which is an important emphasis in studying the multicultural aspects of consultation (Ingraham, 2003, 2004).

Qualitative case studies have been proposed as an excellent method for developing systematic studies of consultation procedure and for helping consultants learn to work effectively in a content area that is not well understood. According to Pryzwansky and Noblit (1990), "Qualitative case studies have a unique strength in providing a format to understand the dynamics of a situation, linking context, processes, and outcomes" (p. 297). They advocated for the use of case studies as a means to understand and improve consultation practice, and they described guidelines for conducting qualitative case studies to support the training and practice of consultation.

Within the literature on multicultural issues in consultation, case studies have been used in several investigations across diverse geographic and cultural regions and problem situations. Case studies of cross-cultural consultation were used in both illustrative (e.g., Hernández et al., in press; Soo-Hoo, 1998; Tarver Behring & Ingraham, 1998) and formalized qualitative studies (e.g., Goldstein & Harris, 2000; Ingraham, 2003; Lopez, 2000; Nastasi, Vargas, Berstein, et al., 2000). Tarver Behring and Ingraham (1998) offered two cases to compare school consultation with and without multicultural consultation training. Lopez (2000) employed a case study methodology to examine five instructional consultation cases in New York in which interpreters were used to support communication between English language learner students, their parents, consultants, and consultees. In addition, case study methods were used to compare school consultant practices within two different Latino communities (Goldstein & Harris, 2000). Tarver Behring et al. (2000) analyzed 28 cases to investigate the cultural modifications made by African American, Asian American, Latino, and European American beginning consultants working with teachers and culturally diverse students and families. Using case studies and comparisons across and within cases, Ingraham (2003) studied the approaches used by beginning consultants seeking to raise cultural hypotheses with experienced teachers. Hernández et al. (in press) used case study methods to report the processes and results of cross-cultural consultation with a community agency specializing in service to African refugees in the United States.

Case studies such as these serve to advance the research and theory development regarding consultation within a variety of multicultural contexts. In addition, as Pryzwansky (200) pointed out in his commentary on a qualitative study about multicultural consultation, such investigations "should be invaluable to trainers of consultants, either at the preservice or inservice levels, when multicultural matters are present" (p. 367). Thus, case studies are contributing to the development of multicultural consultation theory, research, training, and practice.

Grounded Theory

Grounded theory is an alternative to the deductive theory-testing model of research and an excellent method when the researcher seeks to explore a new field or offer a novel perspective on an established theory or aspect of research, as in the change process of consultation research (Hylander, 2003). With this method, the researcher begins with a question or topic of study and develops the theories through an iterative process of working with the data and constructing meaning. Hylander used this method successfully to study the turning points in the consultation process where the consultee gains a new conceptualization of a problem and its potential solutions. Hylander's work with grounded theory methods has explored the process of consultation among psychologists consulting with staff in preschool and child care centers in Sweden and neighboring countries. Her research has become a central focus of international consultee-centered consultation research and training.

Ethnography

Perhaps the most well-known systematic use of ethnography to study cultural issues in consultation is Nastasi and colleagues' work with the participatory culture-specific intervention model (PCSIM; Nastasi et al., 2004; Nastasi, Vargas, Berstein, et al., 2000; Nastasi, Vargas, Schensul, et al., 2000). With detailed ethnographic studies, Nastasi and her colleagues demonstrated skillful use of qualitative methods and participatory action research to advance the mental health interests of the children and communities. Originating through a binational, multiyear project in Sri Lanka, this work led to the evolution of a new method of consultation and intervention. In this method, psychologists work across cultures, through the support of cultural brokers, and project participants are active in the construction of the questions, methods of inquiry, and interpretation of findings. The use of ethnographic methods allows readers to more fully understand the cultural context for the research and the richness of its processes and findings. The PCSIM principles for developing culture-specific consultation and intervention methods are applicable to settings within a wide range of school and community contexts (see Nastasi et al., 2004, for details of implementation).

WHAT IS KNOWN ABOUT MULTICULTURAL ASPECTS OF CONSULTATION

The use of quantitative, qualitative, and mixed-methods research is producing an emerging body of literature regarding cultural issues in consultation. In addition, several authors have reported on their own experiences as consultants in ways that have advanced the understanding of the multicultural issues and aspects of consultation. Based on the available literature, there are some consultation approaches that appear to be successful with differing populations, and these involve the use of specific models of consultation, interpersonal communication approaches, and different consultation dynamics that can arise in multicultural consultation. For the purposes of presenting some of the relevant research findings in this chapter, research is grouped into the following domains: (a) consultant interpersonal styles and orientations, (b) racial influences among consultants and consultees, (c) culture-specific findings, and (d) cross-cultural findings.

Consultant Interpersonal Styles and Orientations

Several findings relevant to consultation within multicultural and cross-cultural contexts have resulted from researchers who have integrated research from related disciplines with school consultation research. Drawing from the literatures in organizational development, cross-cultural and community psychology, interpersonal communication, and family therapy, among others, scholars have expanded the understanding of multicultural aspects of consultation in school and community settings.

Pinto (1981) described four cross-cultural consultant styles that vary according to different "combinations of relationships among value orientations, perceptions of client systems, congruence with a developed or underdeveloped sociocultural universe, and techniques for intervention" (p. 67). These consultant styles are differentiated by the ways the consultant perceives the client as similar to or different from oneself, one's cultural values, and the primary focus of the organizational or institutional consultation (e.g., technical assistance, policy development, management).

Gibbs's (1980) model of interpersonal orientation described five stages paired with five consultant behaviors in the consultee's approach to the entry phase of consultation. Through her description of five critical incidents, she illustrated the differences between black and white consultees in an inner-city school setting in California.[1] She reported that black consultees working with a black consultant tended to focus more on interpersonal aspects of the consultation relationship, as contrasted with instrumental aspects more common among white consultees. She speculated that this pattern is the result of historical, social, and cultural factors and is reflected in differences in the development of trust and sociopolitical assessments. Similar to other descriptions of the relationship among black peoples, Gibbs posited that interpersonal competence must be demonstrated to black consultees before they engage in task-focused, problem-solving processes of consultation. The five entry stages described in Gibbs's interpersonal orientation to consultation are appraisal, investigation, involvement, commitment, and engagement. She described how black consultees use these stages to evaluate a consultant's authenticity, egalitarianism, identification (within social and cultural group identities), acceptance, and performance. White consultees working with black consultants tended to demonstrate more task orientation earlier in the relationship, focusing more on the topic of consultation rather than the development of the relationship with the consultant. Over time, if at all, white consultees developed a relationship with the consultant. Black consultees, on the other hand, initially responded in a more personal and non-task-oriented way and then moved into task orientation over time.

Application of frame-of-reference and reframing techniques can enhance consultation in multicultural schools. Specifically, according to Soo-Hoo (1998), "Frame of reference primarily refers to ways in which a person views the problem at hand; it does not focus on every aspect of the individual's background or characteristics" (p. 329). He described three ways that frame of reference applies to school consultation in multicultural contexts: (a) one's cultural context, (b) a sociopolitical economic context, and (c) an individual psychological context. These three contexts affect a person's perceptions about one or more problems that are explored in consultation. Soo-Hoo reported a case in which he was asked to provide consultation for a school case involving an African American school psychologist consultee working with a Filipino mother and her son's elementary school teacher. The school psychologist consultee expressed frustration with what she interpreted as the mother's passive-aggressive behavior. The case description explicates the differing frames of reference of the school psychologist, mother, and teacher. It also demonstrates how the author articulated and demonstrated empathy for these frames of reference, beginning with the consultee's perspective, to convey understanding of each perspective and then used reframing to help the consultee understand the cultural, sociopolitical, and psychological aspects of the mother's perspective. This deepened the school psychologist's conceptual understanding and supported an alternative hypothesis regarding why the mother was agreeing with the stated intervention and then not following through with its implementation. Using frame-of-reference and reframing techniques, the author demonstrated how cross-cultural consultation was used to achieve positive consultee and client outcomes.

Another approach to understanding individuals' perspectives and frames of reference comes from the communication literature. The term *context communication* refers to the types and amount of contextual cues provided during communication. Ingraham (2003, 2006) discussed two communication styles within the literature on context communication that are related to multicultural consultation: direct and indirect. Through a series of exercises, Ingraham (2002) demonstrated that consultants who are attentive to and congruent with the communication style of their consultees develop and maintain more positive consultation relationships than consultants who use a style that conflicts with that of the consultee's. Ingraham noted that people who prefer a more indirect communication style respond best to a gentle and indirect style of consultation that matches their own interpersonal communication style. People who prefer a direct style respond best when the consultant is direct, uses shorter sentences, and is task oriented. A person's preference for indirect or direct communication is not bound by one's ethnic identity or other group identity but seems more related to the intersection of personal and cultural styles (Ingraham, 2002). In a study by

Conoley et al. (1991), acceptability of the intervention increased when consultants offered a rationale for the intervention congruent with the consultee's perspectives. Specifically, teachers in a summer program rated interventions with a rationale that matched their self-perceived strengths as more acceptable than those that were mismatched or included no rationale.

Preliminary data suggest that a consultee's epistemology and values about multicultural education may influence his or her responsiveness to multicultural consultation. In a study of experienced teachers and novice consultants, Ingraham (2003) noted that the teacher consultees supporting a color-blind approach to educational intervention were more resistant to consultant attempts to explore cultural hypotheses than those who acknowledged cultural differences among their students.

Grounded in four years of consultations with an early education program for Ethiopian immigrant children in Israel, Maital (2000) proposed a reciprocal distancing model to explain the interpersonal processes she observed that led to persistent problems. The model involves a sequence of progressive disengagement that leads to chronic problems in cross-cultural relations between the client and consultee. As the consultees became more frustrated with their efforts to teach their culturally different students, the teachers increasingly attributed the difficulty to stable characteristics within the clients and felt hopeless in their efforts to effect change. This reduced the teachers' motivation, commitment, and effort in delivering interventions and widened the barriers between the consultees and students. Successful interventions and more positive perceptions resulted when consultees were able to appreciate the students' culture, focus on the students' competencies and strengths, and examine the mismatch between the students' needs and the curriculum.

In another interdisciplinary study, Hernández et al. (in press) bridged between family therapy and cross-cultural consultation in their research and consultation with a nonprofit community agency working with refugee children, primarily from Africa. Their work used concepts of critical consciousness and Hernández's (2003) model of cultural context. The consultants employed notions of social location and cultural context to identify and deconstruct issues of gender, ethnicity, privilege, power, and empowerment that were embedded within the consultation system.

Racial Influences Among Consultants and Consultees

Some studies have examined how race or the inclusion of racial content affects consultation processes and outcomes. Gibbs (1980, 1985), one of the first to describe racial issues in consultation, wrote about her experiences with black consultant teams working with white and black consultees in urban schools. She reported racially distinct patterns among consultees during the entry phase of consultation that she attributed to racial differences in the process of building a professional relationship. Subsequent investigations used quantitative methods to study racial factors in consultation (Duncan & Pryzwansky, 1993; Naumann et al., 1996; Rogers, 1998). Rogers (1998) specifically tested the influence of consultant race and inclusion of racially related consultation content on ratings of consultant effectiveness and multicultural sensitivity. Her study systematically varied the race of consultant, race of consultee, verbal behaviors of consultant, and race of rater. Rogers concluded that when the videotaped consultation session involved race-sensitive, compared with race-blind, communication, consultants of either race were rated as more competent. This finding was consistent for both African American and Caucasian female preservice teacher raters. Consultants were rated as more multiculturally sensitive when they attended to racial issues, compared to consultants who did not attend to racial issues in the session content. In other words, it appeared that it was not the race of the consultant but their inclusion of racial issues in the context of their consultation session that was associated with ratings of consultant effectiveness and multicultural sensitivity. This is an important finding given the preponderance of U.S. school consultants who identify as Caucasian (Ingraham, 2000).

Culture-Specific Findings

Tarver Behring and Ingraham (1998) defined multicultural consultation as "a culturally sensitive, indirect service in which the consultant adjusts the consultation services to address the needs and cultural values of the consultee, the client, or both" (p. 58). Research about consultation with specific cultural groups can serve as a guide to consultants working with particular populations, informing them about which adjustments to make so that the consultation services are culturally compatible. To date, culture-specific consultation research has explored consultation with educators and culturally diverse parents and families (Brown, 1997; Miranda, 1993; Nastasi et al., 2004; Tarver Behring et al., 2000; Tarver Behring & Gelinas, 1996). Tarver Behring and Gelinas (1996) discussed some of the cultural values of Asian Americans and studied school consultation with Asian American children and families. They found that traditional Asian American consultees tended to prefer that consultants take a directive, expert role and focus on academic achievement, in contrast to the prevalent egalitarian problem-solving models of consultation. Consultants of Asian American cultural heritage made modifications to contemporary consultation models and included some cultural practices that are appropriate for working with Asian American families. For example, the consultants focused more on the students' academic achievement and less on mental health issues as they built the consulting relationship with Asian American parents. They also accepted gifts of thanks from the families, such as dinner in the family's home, as a culturally acceptable way for the family to thank and "repay" the consultant for support with the child, both practices that are not recommended in European American notions of professionalism in consultation.

In a subsequent study, Tarver Behring et al. (2000) investigated the modifications to current consultation approaches made by beginning consultants of four different ethnic identities. Current consultation approaches were defined as "consultation components defined by the literature without reference to culture" (p. 356). Consultants of European American, African American, Asian American, and Latino ethno-cultural backgrounds consulted with teachers and families of similar and ethnically different groups. Twenty-eight beginning consultants were involved in the qualitative study. The findings revealed that consultants to ethnically similar families used the most cultural modifications, such as making home visits; speaking in the family's language; allowing additional time to develop rapport; demonstrating respect for the parents' cultural style, gender roles, and values; finding community services; and providing follow-up after the consultation ended. Although consultants of European American ethnicity were aware of the need to adjust the consultation approaches to match the family's cultural values, Tarver Behring et al. reported that they were less knowledgeable about which cultural modifications to make. For example, the European American consultants working with cases with African American students worked with the students' teachers, but none succeeded in involving an African American parent. The researchers concluded that culturally sensitive consultation approaches might necessitate the consultant making modifications to traditional consultation approaches when working with students and families from non-European American backgrounds. Tarver Behring and colleagues noted that the exact nature of the modifications might differ depending on the family's culture.

Nastasi and colleagues (2004) developed a model for creating comprehensive and culturally specific school-based mental health programs and services. The PCSIM is a "participatory process for creating or facilitating the development of acceptable, socially valid, effective, and sustainable programs" (p. 3). PCSIM is designed as a model for developing interventions that can be used within a wide range of settings, populations, and target problems. The model includes numerous methods for ensuring that the intervention services are congruent with the specific cultural values and beliefs of the participating groups. Thus, PCSIM represents an ideal model for developing culturally specific systemic intervention. Participatory culture-specific consultation (Nastasi, Vargas, Berstein, et al., 2000) is an approach that combines collaborative consultation with ethnography and action research, focusing on identifying and addressing the culture-specific needs of individuals and systems. Supported by a substantial body of research (see Nastasi et al., 2004, for a review) and field tested in an international project between consultants and researchers working in Sri Lanka and the United States, the model has the potential for use within a variety of school cultures and communities within the United States. In this model, consultants involve members of the designated cultural group in forming partnerships; identifying the problems and goals for intervention; generating culture-specific hypotheses; designing, implementing, and evaluating interventions; and interpreting the results.

Cross-Cultural Findings

As schools, families, and professionals working in schools become more culturally diverse, the opportunities for cross-cultural consultation increase. Scholars have identified important theoretical and conceptual aspects of cross-cultural consultation (e.g., Brown, 1997; Duncan, 1995; Gibbs, 1980, 1985; Ingraham, 2000, 2007; Nastasi et al., 2004; Pinto, 1981; Soo-Hoo, 1998), and studies are beginning to investigate research questions empirically within cross-cultural consultation (e.g., Ingraham, 2003; Lopez, 2000; Nastasi, Vargas, Berstein, et al., 2000; Tarver Behring et al., 2000).

Ingraham and Meyers (2000a) reviewed literature regarding cultural issues in consultation and organized a special issue of the *School Psychology Review* to focus on conceptual and empirical study of multicultural and cross-cultural consultation in schools (see Ingraham & Meyers, 2000b). This issue was designed to bring together research of scholars from across the nation who are engaged in and conducting research using multicultural and cross-cultural consultation. Grounded in naturalistic research with cross-cultural consultation cases, these articles offer a wealth of information about cross-cultural consultation research in geographically and culturally diverse school settings. The findings of this research are discussed in more detail in this section.

The articles in the special issue presented a conceptual model of multicultural consultation, advanced the study of culture in school psychology inquiry, grounded consultation inquiry in naturalistic paradigms, and contributed to the understanding of cross-cultural consultation competencies (Rogers, 2000). Rogers summarized the ways cross-cultural consultation competencies converge on six themes: understanding one's own and others' culture, developing cross-cultural communication and interpersonal skills, examining the cultural embeddedness of consultation, using qualitative methodologies, acquiring culture-specific knowledge, and applying understanding and skill in work with interpreters. The themes transcend consultation work and are consistent with many of the recommendations for cross-cultural school psychology (Rogers et al., 1999; Rogers & Lopez, 2002), multicultural counseling (Arredondo et al., 1996), and psychological practice (American Psychological Association, 1993).

In a presentation of a comprehensive framework for multicultural school consultation, Ingraham (2000) conceptualized five components essential for culturally competent consultation: consultant learning and development, consultee learning and development, cultural variations in the consultation constellations, types of contextual and power influences, and methods for supporting consultee and client success. Table 13.1 depicts these five components in Ingraham's framework.

Table 13.1   Five Components of Ingraham's (2000) Multicultural School Consultation Framework

1. Domains of consultant learning and development for multicultural school consultation competence

    a. Understanding one's own culture

    b. Understanding the impact of one's own culture on others

    c. Respecting and valuing other cultures

    d. Understanding individual differences within cultural groups and multiple identities

    e. Cross-cultural communication and multicultural consultation approaches for rapport development and maintenance

    f. Understanding cultural saliency and how to build bridges across salient differences

    g. Understanding the cultural context for consultation

    h. Multicultural consultation and interventions appropriate for the consultees and clients

2. Domains of consultee learning and development

    a. Knowledge

    b. Skill

    c. Perspective and decreasing:

        (1) Filtering perceptions through stereotypes

        (2) Overemphasizing culture

        (3) Taking a color-blind approach

        (4) Fear of being called a racist

    d. Confidence

        (1) Preventing intervention paralysis

        (2) Avoiding reactive dominance

3. Cultural variations in the consultation constellation

    a. Consultant-consultee similarity

    b. Consultant-client similarity

    c. Consultee-client similarity

    d. Three-way diversity: tricultural consultation

4. Contextual and power influences

    a. Cultural similarity within a differing cultural system

    b. Influences by the larger society

    c. Disruptions in the balance of power

5. Methods for supporting consultee and client success

    a. Framing the problem and the consultation process

        (1) Value multiple perspectives

        (2) Create emotional safety and motivational support

        (3) Balance affective support with new learning

        (4) Build on principles for adult learning

        (5) Seek systems interventions to support learning and development

    b. Potential multicultural consultation strategies for working with the consultees

        (1) Support cross-cultural learning and motivation

        (2) Model bridging and processes for cross-cultural learning

Continued

Table 13.1   Five Components of Ingraham's (2000) Multicultural School Consultation Framework (*Continued*)

(3) Use consultation methods matched with the consultee's style
(4) Work to build consultee confidence and self-efficacy
(5) Work to increase knowledge, skill, and perspective
c. Continue one's professional development and reflective thinking
(1) Continue to learn
(2) Engage in formal and informal continuing professional development
(3) Seek feedback
(4) Seek cultural guides and teachers

Note. From "Consultation Through a Multicultural Lens: Multicultural and Cross-Cultural Consultation in Schools," by C. L. Ingraham, 2000, *School Psychology Review, 29*, p. 327. Copyright 2000 by the National Association of School Psychologists. Reprinted with permission of the publisher.

Within each of these areas are types of knowledge and competence for effective practice of multicultural and cross-cultural school consultation.

Cross-cultural consultation is a component of multicultural consultation in which one or more members of the consultation systems are culturally different from the others. In Ingraham's multicultural consultation framework, the consultant uses knowledge and skill across eight competence domains (see the first component of Table 13.1, consultant learning and development) to assess and intervene in the consultee's knowledge, skill, perspective (originally called objectivity), and confidence and to build bridges of understanding across salient cultural differences among members of the consultation system. In cross-cultural consultation, specific threats to consultee (and consultant) perspective relate to the cultural lenses, or lack of cultural perspectives, the individual takes with respect to problem definition, interpretation, intervention development, and implementation. Culturally competent consultants can offer support in developing culturally or cross-culturally appropriate consultee knowledge, skill, perspective and confidence in working with students and other clients (Ingraham, 2000).

Cultures can be distributed in different ways among the members of the consultation system. Table 13.1 shows the four cultural variations in the consultation constellation. The consultant, consultees (e.g., parents, teachers), and clients each can represent a culture similar to or different from the others. There are specific issues that can arise among the members of the consultation system, and the framework suggests consultant strategies for working through these issues. For example, when the consultant and client are of the same ethnic minority and the teacher is culturally different from both consultant and client, the teacher consultee may try to shift responsibility for the intervention onto the consultant, saying that the consultant, culturally similar to the client, understands that culture better. Consultants can use one-downsmanship (Caplan, 1970) to empower the teacher to stay involved in the intervention and mentoring or sharing of information to ensure that the teacher has the tools to intervene in culturally appropriate ways. Consequently, a more lasting intervention is developed as the teacher expands his or her intervention repertoire and learns strategies to intervene in similar cases in the future. Other issues that arise between consultant, consultee, and client are discussed and presented as they correspond to different combinations of cultures among the members of the consultation system (see Ingraham, 2000).

Due to sociocultural positioning or social location and variances in interpersonal power, each member of the consultation system can come to the consultation with differing levels of power. For example, one who is a member of the dominant, mainstream culture has a degree of privilege simply because of his or her social positioning within the larger culture, compared to one who is of a minority culture operating in a mainstream context. Other factors such as level of experience and personal power also influence the power dynamics that operate within the consultation system (see Erchul & Raven, 1997). These power differentials and the emotions they invoke can have more pronounced influences on the consultation relationship in cross-cultural consultation (Ingraham, 2000, 2002). Cross-cultural consultants need to be aware of how both culture and power are distributed among the members of the consultation system to understand the potential impact of power imbalances, privilege, oppression, and the intensity of feelings, both spoken and unspoken, that they may involve.

Effective cross-cultural consultants also engage in continuing professional development to further their own and their consultees' learning and development. Ingraham (2000) recommended that consultants seek to develop knowledge and learning across eight different areas (see the first component of Table 13.1): their own culture, the impact of one's culture on others, respecting and valuing of different cultures, understanding individual differences and variations within cultural groups and multiple cultural identities, cross-cultural communication and approaches to develop and maintain cross-cultural rapport, cultural saliency and methods for bridging across salient differences, the cultural context for consultation, and multicultural consultation interventions appropriate for the cultures of both consultees and clients. Consultants can support consultee learning and development in these same eight areas. Consultants can support consultee and client success through their framing of the problem and the consultation process, use of multicultural consultation strategies, reflective practice, and modeling of continuing learning (see Ingraham, 2000, for further discussion).

In a qualitative investigation of the multicultural consultation framework, Ingraham (2003) reported findings of naturalistic cross-cultural consultation case studies between novice consultants and experienced teachers who were working with culturally diverse students. This investigation found that even novice consultants, with multicultural consultation training, can deliver cross-cultural consultation and achieve positive student and consultee outcomes when consultees are open to the notion that cultural knowledge and skill can inform their professional work. The study demonstrated that consultants who use self-disclosure about their own cross-cultural learning experiences and who use approaches in Ingraham's (2000) multicultural consultation framework can achieve significant consultation outcomes. For example, two consultants who were culturally different from their teacher consultees used multicultural consultation techniques, instructional consultation, and aspects of mental health consultation to (a) reframe the teacher's conceptualization of the problem, (b) expand teacher understanding of the cultural issues that were influencing the students' progress, (c) support the teachers in engaging in culturally appropriate socioemotional and instructional strategies to build more effective teacher-student relationships, and (d) increase the competence and confidence of the teachers. Concurrently, student outcomes included increases in student participation, academic achievement, and targeted classroom behaviors. In one case when positive consultation outcomes were not achieved, hypotheses explored the potential influences of teacher attitudes about the value of cultural understanding and the complexities when consultants are confronted with teachers who maintain beliefs that a color-blind approach is paramount. Ingraham (2003) concluded, among other things, that consultant educators may need to develop specific approaches to prepare prospective consultants for the range and intensity of values and attitudes that they may encounter in cross-cultural consultation.

Some authors have written about cross-cultural consultation with parents and families. Although not yet supported by empirical research, Brown (1997) discussed how Pinto's (1981) advice for cross-cultural consultants has implications for cross-cultural consultation with families. Building on Pinto's recommendations and the guidelines for multicultural counselors (e.g., Arredondo et al., 1996), Brown advocated for developing understanding of one's own values and cultural empathy as a foundation for cross-cultural consultation with families. According to Brown (1997), "Cultural values are the foundation of people's biases, including perceptions of how parenting should be conducted" (p. 29). Brown has drawn from the work of several others in his list of traditional values of five major cultural groups in the United States: Eurocentric, Hispanic, American Indian, African American, and Asian American. In assessing one's own values, Brown proposed that consultants determine their own perspectives with respect to self-control, time orientation, activity, social relationships, and achievement, and he has used these dimensions to compare and contrast the values of these five cultural groups. This perspective of learning about one's own culture is reflected more fully in the work of Brown, Pryzwansky, and Schulte (2006).

When consultees and clients are culturally different from each other, several processes can challenge the success of cross-cultural consultation. Maital (2000) described a process by which the consultees feel increasingly frustrated in their efforts to work with culturally different clients. When success does not result, the consultees begin to attribute the failure to stable internal characteristics within the clients, resulting in consultees labeling the clients and withdrawal from the relationship by both consultees and clients. Maital reported the results of a 4-year project with Israeli teachers working with Ethiopian immigrant children in preschool and kindergarten classes. She used group consultation meetings to explore differing beliefs about acculturation and diversity. Maital concluded that the group consultation approach allowed her to support the development of a pluralistic perspective necessary for multicultural tolerance.

Hernández et al. (in press) reported a study in which a culturally diverse consultant team was involved with a community agency led by European American males working with U.S. immigrant children from Africa. In this consultation system, all parties were of differing cultural backgrounds. The authors referred to issues of social location related to social class, gender, and ethnic privilege as they engaged in cross-cultural consultation. The consultees were unaware of their own biases toward culturally different consultants and clients, and their reactions toward one of the consultants was used to illustrate how these biases can interfere with the development of effective cross-cultural relationships and the disempowerment of consultants and clients.

There are times when the consultant must work across languages, as well as across cultures. Lopez (2000) investigated how the use of school interpreters influenced the process of instructional cross-cultural consultation with students, families, teachers, and consultants in New York high schools. Using a detailed qualitative case study methodology, she focused on the voices of the consultees and clients who interacted with the interpreters. The use of interpreters led to a slower pace of the instructional consultation process, improved the clarity of communication between consultation participants, and both facilitated and hindered the establishment of trust and rapport. One of the implications of the study was that important information may be distorted or lost during problem identification when working through an interpreter. Lopez concluded the article with valuable recommendations for training and working with interpreters to increase consultation effectiveness.

Cross-cultural consultation does not appear to be limited to a single consultation model. Studies report on the successful use of instructional (e.g., Ingraham, 2003; Lopez, 2000), consultee-centered (Ingraham, 2003), conjoint behavioral (Sheridan et al., 2006), participatory culture-specific (Nastasi, Vargas, Berstein, et al., 2000), and team consultation (Goldstein & Harris, 2000). Cultural perspectives can become central in the use of a variety of models of consultation as long as consultants are respectful and inclusive of the cultural values of members of the consultation system (Ingraham, 2000).

FUTURE DIRECTIONS FOR EMPIRICALLY SUPPORTED
MULTICULTURAL ASPECTS OF CONSULTATION

Compared with other areas of consultation research, investigations of the multicultural aspects of consultation are relatively new. Research derived from consultation experiences and analogue studies of race and gender composed the bulk of the multicultural consultation literature until recently. Qualitative methods using naturalistic procedures are beginning to document the range of conditions, processes, and outcomes resulting from research with a multicultural perspective. Clearly, there is much that remains empirically unexplored and untested; thus, there is room for researchers using a variety of research methods and questions to contribute to our understanding of relationships between culture and consultation. Within the movement toward identifying and developing EBIs, there is recognition that new research approaches are needed. According to Kratochwill and Stoiber (2002), "A research perspective that examines the role of cultural diversity to EBIs will also likely require a rethinking of research design and interpretations" (p. 31). Thus, the future directions for empirically supported multicultural aspects of consultation are integrally connected to the recommendations emerging from the Task Force on EBIs in School Psychology and those who have been studying these issues within the profession (e.g., Ingraham & Oka, 2006; Ingraham et al., 2004, 2005; Nastasi et al., 2004).

As a first step in developing future research, I encourage an epistemological consideration of how people approach consultation research and practice. The ways we understand and interpret events are culture bound (Henning-Stout 1994a, 1994b; Kratochwill & Stoiber, 2002; Matsumoto, 2000; Tarver Behring & Ingraham, 1998). Researchers need to be mindful that the questions they ask, the research methods and forms of data collection they employ, and the interpretations they form are all culture bound (Henning-Stout & Meyers, 2000; Ingraham & Oka, 2006; Matsumoto, 2000). Ponterotto (2005) presented a valuable guide to research paradigms and philosophy of science conceptualizations that includes a discussion of epistemology and other constructs that have applications to studying multicultural aspects of consultation. If researchers are truly considering the multicultural aspects of consultation, then they will understand that their thinking and research methods are influenced by their own cultural beliefs and the paradigms from which they work.

Traditional methods of assessing intervention acceptability may be unintentionally biased by the cultural frames of reference of the researcher and the measurement methods used to collect the data. Simply computing effect sizes for different cultural groups may be an ethnocentric strategy, and it does not address the differing perspectives, worldviews, or social location of these groups. There are numerous reasons why participants in consultation may not reveal their true thoughts and feelings about consultation, and researchers need to find ways to be acutely sensitive to the power they have to shape the data and the results. Consultants, consultees, and clients, particularly those who feel less privileged or empowered within mainstream culture or in interaction with the researchers, may not challenge the paradigms from which the research questions emerge or the "fit" within their own culture.

Different approaches for managing these realities have been proposed within the consultation literature. Henning-Stout and Meyers (2000) advised researchers to consider the voices of those most marginalized within the mainstream as a way to further the inquiry about multicultural issues in consultation. They proposed using Sandra Harding's notion of strong objectivity (Harding, 1991, as cited in Henning-Stout & Meyers, 2000) as a way "to extend the theoretical basis from which human diversity and consultation are considered" (p. 420) and to consider research investigating multicultural issues in consultation. For example, they emphasized the importance of inviting the perspectives of those marginalized or typically omitted from the discourse. Seeking the perspectives and voices of consultation participants, and even the children for whom our consultation services are designed to serve, would be a way to use the concept of strong objectivity to enhance the relevance and value of empirically validated practices. Henning-Stout and Meyers suggested that both quantitative and qualitative research methods offer greater promise *if* primary consideration is given to perspectives situated at the margins of the mainstream, employing strong objectivity and seeking the perspectives from those who may hold differing beliefs and worldviews. Referring to the five areas of research on multicultural issues in consultation (Ramirez et al., 1998), they concluded that "when the perspectives of people most marginal to a school or any other system are brought into primary consideration in the development and testing of consultation theory and practice each of these questions can be addressed more fully" (Henning-Stout & Meyers, 2000, p. 423).

Ramirez et al. (1998) posed five general areas that are important for future work and suggested a variety of quantitative methods to examine the questions within a "utility of cultural variable" framework. They listed research questions that can be investigated through single-case and group designs that use post hoc, a priori, single-case, and multiple-dimensional studies. For example, they asked the question: "What is the effect of different uses of available cultural data on the consultation process/outcome?" (p. 499). They proposed that this question could be addressed through an a priori single-dimension study with random assignment of two or more cultural groups and the same level of availability of cultural data but differing levels of data usage. They gave the example of consultation in which "cultural data about the degree of assimilation are used for only one of two groups" (p. 499). The study could then examine if different outcomes occurred for the two comparisons of cultural data used and cultural data not used.

Despite thoughtful conceptualization of research questions and methods by which to investigate them, it is difficult to understand why more empirical research has not resulted from research questions and methods posed by Ramirez et al. (1998). One thought, from my perspective, is that perhaps the attempt to put cultural influences into a variable that is coded as one point of data may seem limiting to some researchers. Although some of the research questions help expand our understanding of how culture might influence consultation processes and outcomes, some of the methods appear to be situated within a positivistic paradigm of research that seeks to determine the "objective reality" by systematically varying selected variables or conditions and studying the results. For example, Ramirez et al.'s (1998) first question is, "In what ways is information regarding cultural variables helpful in problem-solving consultation?" (p. 496). This question seems to presume that culture is a variable or category of variable rather than a paradigm or worldview that permeates one's thoughts and actions. It does not reflect an understanding that the types of quantitative research methods recommended are embedded within a particular cultural framework. Despite these potential limitations, there are numerous research questions and proposed methods included in the work of Ramirez et al. (1998) that could inform the development of quantitative and single-case studies to further our understanding of ways that culture may influence consultation processes and outcomes. It would be helpful to have empirical studies in this area to move the profession forward.

Perhaps a broader set of research methods would allow for an expanded view of culture and its influences within school-based consultation. Tarver Behring and Ingraham (1998) called for culture to become a central component of consultation theory, research, and practice, not just a consideration or variable to include. Nastasi and colleagues (Nastasi et al., 2004; Nastasi, Vargas, Berstein, et al., 2000; Nastasi, Vargas, Schensul, et al., 2000) used methods of ethnography, participatory action research, and cultural brokers to involve participants in the conceptualizations that shape the research process and interpretation of outcomes. This method of involving participants in the conceptualization of the research process has the potential to approach a culturally compatible process of cross-cultural research in school psychology and school consultation.

When researchers attempt to include cultural aspects in their research, several questions may emerge. From the initial description of participants to the intricate details of how various aspects of culture manifest during the consultation process, there are countless decisions about culture that may be made. Even in the initial articulation of what cultures are relevant to a particular study, several questions need attention. Some examples are as follows:

1. How is information about cultural perspectives and affiliations obtained?
2. Who determines which aspects of culture are most salient in one's identity and worldview?
3. How does a researcher determine the relative influence of one cultural descriptor compared with another?
4. If the researcher is attempting to document the culture of participants, then how does one know, for example, the relative importance participants place on their race, religion, ethnicity, sexual orientation, age, economic status, profession, gender, level of acculturation, or belief systems? Many have had the experience of categorization by one or more "diversity factors" that they may not have considered influential and to be unseen by another factor that they perceive as critical in shaping their own perspectives and worldview.
5. Similarly, how do researchers work with participants who are bicultural, sharing multiple identities within differing group affiliations? For example, is a heterosexual Baptist woman with a middle-class background and African American/Filipino heritage considered as having the same worldview as a lesbian woman of a middle-class economic background and Latino/indigenous Native American heritage? Both might be "coded" as biracial middle-class women, but would that accurately represent their potentially differing worldviews?

Another set of questions refers to the study of the processes and means by which the cultural context influences consultation processes and outcomes.

Researchers need to provide readers with information regarding the cultural perspectives of study participants that is as complete and rich as possible (Ingraham & Oka, 2006; Sue, 1999). Brief characterizations of participants' cultures and beliefs can offer more information than is typically available in research publications, but whatever words are used to describe ethnicity, culture, and identity give preference to some aspects of one's culture and leave other aspects unseen (Ingraham, 2003). In general, the more fully participants are able to describe themselves and not be subjected to researcher categorizations of their culture, the more readers will have access to relevant cultural information that may influence the transferability and interpretation of the results.

Some scholars have posed research questions associated with multicultural and cross-cultural issues of consultation that are in need of investigation. For purposes of discussion, these can be grouped into the six ways of considering culture in consultation research, shown in Table 13.2. They involve careful selection of the research paradigm, methods, data collection, and analyses that are appropriate for multicultural research. They also involve providing thorough discussion and inclusion of the cultural perspectives of the participants (including researchers and those collecting the data) and the cultural context and setting in which the research is conducted.

Future research studying the multicultural aspects of consultation needs to address each of these six areas. If such investigation includes consideration of these six areas and thorough discussion of how they are addressed in the study, it will make a much-needed contribution to our emerging

Table 13.2   Some Ways for Bringing Cultural Perspectives Into Consultation Research

Consideration	Recommendation
1. Research paradigm and methods of inquiry	Consider how the methods are appropriate for the complexities of multicultural and cross-cultural inquiry
2. Questions asked and by whom	Consider and articulate from whose frame of reference and inclusive of which perspectives research questions are posed
3. Methods of data collection and analysis	Provide evidence, specific to the given cultural group or population, of the validity and reliability of methods employed
4. Thorough descriptions of participants and researchers	Provide rich and thorough discussion of the cultural perspectives of researchers, consultants, consultees, and clients
5. Inclusion of diverse perspectives	Include attention to diverse perspectives, including the perspectives of those most marginalized by traditional methods
6. Full description of context and setting	Describe the features of the naturalistic setting, with full description of the cultural context of the school or setting

understanding. More specific and accurate information will be available regarding the specific consultation approaches that are that effective with identified types of consultees and clients, within particular conditions or contexts. Some (Ingraham & Oka, 2006; Kratochwill & Stoiber, 2002) have advocated against accepting the hypothesis that EBIs are equally effective across all cultural groups. In contrast, they have promoted operating from the assumption of cultural specificity, presuming that intervention effectiveness differs across different cultural groups, until we have evidence to the contrary. This approach applies to the study of cultural issues within consultation. Evidence about consultation efficacy or effectiveness is not presumed to be universally applicable to diverse individuals and groups. Instead, with careful descriptions of the participants and their role in conceptualizing research, readers should have valuable information to make decisions about the applicability and transferability of specific research findings to related contexts.

Research methods needed to advance the profession must include a range of designs and paradigms beyond traditional empirical hypothesis testing. Investigations using qualitative and mixed methods are making valuable contributions. Consideration of the six areas described in Table 13.2 may enhance the value of carefully designed quantitative, qualitative, and mixed-methods forms of research. Future directions in the study of multicultural aspects of consultation may be informed by research methods that allow for investigation of intriguing research questions. In a special issue of the *Journal of Counseling Psychology* (April 2005), scholars have presented numerous articles about new methods for research that attend to context, culture, and perspective more effectively than some of the more traditional methods. Many of these approaches appear to offer direction for researchers studying the multicultural aspects of consultation.

NOTE

1. Consistent with the racial and ethnic terminology used at the time, Gibbs referred to participants as black or white; thus, these terms are used here in the review of her study.

REFERENCES

American Psychological Association. (1993). Guidelines for providers of psychological services to ethnic, linguistic and culturally diverse populations. *American Psychologist, 48,* 45–48.

Arredondo, P., Toporek, R., Brown, S. P., Jones, J., Locke, D. C., Sanchez, J., et al. (1996). Operationalization of the multicultural counseling competencies. *Journal of Multicultural Counseling and Development, 24*, 42–78.

Barnett, D. W., Collins, R., Coulter, C., Curtis, M. J., Ehrhardt, K., Glaser, A., et al. (1995). Ethnic validity and school psychology: Concepts and practices associated with cross-cultural professional competence. *Journal of School Psychology, 33*, 219–234.

Brown, D. (1997). Implications of cultural values for cross-cultural consultation with families. *Journal of Counseling and Development, 76*, 29–35.

Brown, D., Pryzwansky, W. B., & Schulte, A. C. (2006). *Psychological consultation and collaboration: Introduction to theory and practice* (6th ed.) Boston: Pearson Education.

Caplan, G. (1970). *The theory and practice of mental health consultation.* New York: Basic Books.

Conoley, C. W., Conoley, J. C., Ivey, D. C., & Scheel, M. J. (1991). Enhancing consultation by matching the consultee's perspectives. *Journal of Counseling and Development, 69*, 546–549.

Duncan, C. F. (1995). Cross-cultural school consultation. In C. Lee (Ed.), *Counseling for diversity* (pp. 129–139). Boston: Allyn & Bacon.

Duncan, C., & Pryzwansky, W. B. (1993). Effects of race, racial identity development, and orientation style on perceived consultant effectiveness. *Journal of Multicultural Counseling and Development, 21*, 88–96.

Erchul, W. P., & Raven, B. H. (1997). Social power in consultation: A contemporary view of French and Raven's bases of power model. *Journal of School Psychology, 35*, 137–171.

Erlandson, D. A., Harris, E. L., Skipper, B. L., & Allen, S. D. (1993). *Doing naturalistic inquiry: A guide to methods.* Newbury Park, CA: Sage.

Gibbs, J. T. (1980). The interpersonal orientation in mental health: Toward a model of ethnic variations in consultation. *Journal of Community Psychology, 8*, 195–207.

Gibbs, J. T. (1985). Can we continue to be color-blind and class-bound? *The Counseling Psychologist, 13*, 426–435.

Goldstein, B. S. C., & Harris, K. C. (2000). Consultant practices in two heterogeneous Latino schools. *School Psychology Review, 29*, 368–377.

Harris, K. C. (1991). An expanded view on consultation competencies for educators serving culturally and linguistically diverse exceptional students. *Teacher Education and Special Education, 14*, 25–29.

Harris, K. C. (1996). Collaboration within a multicultural society. *Remedial and Special Education, 17*, 2–10.

Harris, A. M., Ingraham, C. L., & Lam, M. K. (1994). Teacher expectations for female and male school-based consultants. *Journal of Educational and Psychological Consultation, 5*, 115-142.

Henning-Stout, M. (1994a). Consultation and connected knowing: What we know is determined by the questions we ask. *Journal of Educational and Psychological Consultation, 5*, 5–21.

Henning-Stout, M. (1994b). Thoughts on being a white consultant. *Journal of Educational and Psychological Consultation, 5*, 269–273.

Henning-Stout, M., & Meyers, J. (2000). Consultation and human diversity: First things first. *School Psychology Review, 29*, 419–425.

Hernández, P. (2003). The cultural context model in supervision. *Journal of Feminist Family Therapy, 15*, 1–18.

Hernández, P., Bunyi, B., & Townson, R. (in press). Interweaving ethnicity and gender in consultation: A case study. *Family Psychotherapy.*

Hylander, I. (2003). Toward a grounded theory of the conceptual change process in consultee-centered consultation. *Journal of Educational and Psychological Consultation, 14*, 263–280.

Ingraham, C. L. (2000). Consultation through a multicultural lens: Multicultural and cross-cultural consultation in schools. *School Psychology Review, 29*, 320–343.

Ingraham, C. L. (2002, February). *Multicultural consultation in schools: Strategies for supporting teacher and student success.* Presentation at a workshop for the National Association of School Psychologists, Chicago, IL. Audiotape set available through NASP.

Ingraham, C. L. (2003). Multicultural consultee-centered consultation: When novice consultants explore cultural hypotheses with experienced teacher consultees. *Journal of Educational and Psychological Consultation, 14*, 329–362.

Ingraham, C. L. (2004). Multicultural consultation: A model for supporting consultees in the development of cultural competence. In N. M. Lambert, I. Hylander, & J. H. Sandoval (Eds.), *Consultee-centered consultation: Improving the quality of professional services in schools and community organizations* (pp. 133–148). Mahwah, NJ: Erlbaum.

Ingraham, C. L. (2006). Context communication. In Y. Jackson (Ed.), *Encyclopedia of multicultural psychology* (pp. 110–111). Thousand Oaks, CA: Sage.

Ingraham, C. L. (2007). Focusing on consultees in multicultural consultation. In G. B. Esquivel, E. C. Lopez, & S. Nahari (Eds.), *Handbook of multicultural school psychology* (pp. 99–118). Mahwah, NJ: Erlbaum.

Ingraham, C. L., & Meyers, J. (2000a). Introduction to multicultural and cross-cultural consultation in schools: Cultural diversity issues in school consultation. *School Psychology Review, 29,* 315–319.

Ingraham, C. L., & Meyers, J. (Guest Eds.). (2000b). Multicultural and cross-cultural consultation in schools: Cultural diversity issues in school consultation [Special issue]. *School Psychology Review, 29*(3).

Ingraham, C. L., & Oka, E. R. (2006). Multicultural issues in evidence-based intervention. *Journal of Applied School Psychology, 22,* 127–149.

Ingraham, C. L., Oka, E. R., Nastasi, B. (2004, August). *Developing cultural and methodological diversity in EBIs in school psychology.* Poster presented at the annual meeting of the American Psychological Association, Honolulu, Hawaii.

Ingraham, C. L., Oka, E. R., & Nastasi, B. (2005, January). *Infusing cultural validity criteria into the SP EBI scoring manual.* Poster presented at the National Multicultural Summit and Conference, Hollywood, CA.

Kazdin, A. E. (1977). Assessing the clinical or applied importance of behavior change through social validation. *Behavior Modification, 1,* 427–452.

Kratochwill, T. R., & Stoiber, K. C. (2002). Evidence-based interventions in school psychology: Conceptual foundations of the *Procedural and Coding Manual of Division 16 and the Society for the Study of School Psychology Task Force. School Psychology Quarterly, 17,* 341–389.

Lincoln, Y. S., & Guba, E. G. (1985). *Naturalistic Inquiry.* Beverly Hills: Sage.

Lopez, E. C. (2000). Conducting instructional consultation through interpreters. *School Psychology Review, 29,* 378–388.

Lynch, E. W., & Hanson, N. J. (Eds.). (2004). *Developing cross-cultural competence: A guide for working with children and their families* (3rd ed.). Baltimore, MD: Brookes.

Maital, S. L. (2000). Reciprocal distancing: A systems model of interpersonal processes in cross-cultural consultation. *School Psychology Review, 29,* 389–400.

Matsumoto, D. (2000). *Cultural influences on research methods and statistics.* Prospect Heights, IL: Waveland Press.

Miranda, A. H. (1993). Consultation with culturally diverse families. *Journal of Educational and Psychological Consultation, 4,* 89–93.

Nastasi, B. K., Moore, R. B., & Varjas, K. M. (2004). *School-based mental health services: Creating comprehensive and culturally specific programs.* Washington DC: American Psychological Association.

Nastasi, B. K., Vargas, K., Berstein, R., & Jayasena, A. (2000). Conducting participatory culture-specific consultation: A global perspective on multicultural consultation. *School Psychology Review, 29,* 401–413.

Nastasi, B., K. Vargas, K., Schensul, S. L., Silva, K. T., Schnesul, J. J., & Ramayake, P. (2000). The participatory intervention model: A framework for conceptualizing and promoting intervention acceptability. *School Psychology Quarterly, 15,* 207–232.

Naumann, W. C., Gutkin, T. B., & Sandoval, S. R. (1996). The impact of consultant race and student race on perceptions of consultant effectiveness and intervention acceptability. *Journal of Educational and Psychological Consultation, 7,* 151–160.

Pinto, R. F. (1981). Consultant orientations and client system perceptions: Styles of cross-cultural consultation. In R. Lippitt & G. L. Lippitt (Eds.), *Systems thinking: A resource for organizational diagnosis and intervention* (pp. 57–74). Washington, DC: International Consultants.

Ponterotto, J. G. (2005). Qualitative research in counseling psychology: A primer on research paradigms and philosophy of science. *Journal of Counseling Psychology, 52,* 126–136.

Pryswansky, W. B. (2003). Finally, a contemporary treatment of consultee-centered consultation. *Journal of Educational and Psychological Consultation, 14* (3 & 4), 363–368.

Pryswansky, W. B., & Noblit, G. W. (1990). Understanding and improving consultation practice: The qualitative case study approach. *Journal of Education and Psychological Consultation, 1* (4), 293–307.

Quintana, S. M., Troyano, N., & Taylor, G. (2001). Cultural validity and inherent challenges in quantitative methods for multicultural research. In J. G. Ponterotto, J. M. Casas, L. A. Suzuki, & C. M. Alexander (Eds.), *Handbook of multicultural counseling* (2nd ed., pp. 604–630). Thousand Oaks, CA: Sage.

Ramirez, S. Z., Lepage, K. M., Kratochwill, T. R., & Duffy, J. L. (1998). Multicultural issues in school-based consultation: Conceptual and research considerations. *Journal of School Psychology, 36,* 479–509.

Rogers, M. R. (1998). The influence of race and consultant verbal behavior on perceptions of consultant competence and multicultural sensitivity. *School Psychology Quarterly, 13,* 265–280.

Rogers, M. R. (2000). Examining the cultural context of consultation. *School Psychology Review, 29,* 414–418.

Rogers, M. R., Ingraham, C. L., Bursztyn, A., Cajigas-Segredo, N., Esquivel, G., Hess, R., et al. (1999). Providing psychological services to racially, ethnically, culturally, and linguistically diverse individuals in the schools: Recommendations for practice. *School Psychology International, 20,* 243–264.

Rogers, M. R., & Lopez, E. C. (2002). Identifying critical cross-cultural school psychology competencies. *Journal of School Psychology, 40,* 115–141.

Sheridan, S. M., Eagle, J., & Doll, B. (2006). An examination of the efficacy of conjoint behavioral consultation with culturally diverse clients. *School Psychology Quarterly, 21,* 396–417.

Soo-Hoo, T. (1998). Applying frame of reference and reframing techniques to improve school consultation in multicultural settings. *Journal of Psychological and Educational Consultation, 9,* 325–345.

Sue, S. (1999). Science, ethnicity, and bias: Where have we gone wrong? *American Psychologist, 54,* 1070–1077.

Tarver Behring, S., Cabello, B., Kushida, D., & Murguia, A. (2000). Cultural modifications to current school-based consultation approaches reported by culturally diverse beginning consultants. *School Psychology Review, 29,* 354–367.

Tarver Behring, S., & Gelinas, R. T. (1996). School consultation with Asian American children and families. *The California School Psychologist, 1,* 13–20.

Tarver Behring, S., & Ingraham, C. L. (1998). Culture as a central component of consultation: A call to the field. *Journal of Educational and Psychological Consultation, 9,* 57–72.

Wampold, B. E., Licktenberg, J. W., & Waehler, C. A. (2002). Principles of empirically supported interventions in counseling psychology. *The Counseling Psychologist, 30,* 197–217.

14

Studying Interpersonal Influence Within School Consultation
Social Power Base and Relational Communication Perspectives

WILLIAM P. ERCHUL, PRISCILLA F. GRISSOM,
AND KIMBERLY C. GETTY

North Carolina State University

The idea that it is not only feasible but also often advisable to view school consultation as an interpersonal influence process has gained greater currency over the past two decades. Discussions of social power and interpersonal influence within school psychology (e.g., Hughes, 1992; Lambert, 1973; Martin, 1978) have led to the empirical study of these phenomena within school consultation (e.g., Erchul, 1987; Erchul, Raven, & Whichard, 2001; Martens, Kelly, & Diskin, 1996). Visibly linked to the emergence of this line of research has been the advancement of the paradox of school psychology, which contends that school psychologists must focus their attention and professional expertise primarily on adults in order to serve children and adolescents most effectively (Conoley & Gutkin, 1986; Gutkin & Conoley, 1990). Working with other adults to deliver psychological services in schools requires a careful consideration of social psychological and organizational factors and, in particular, interpersonal influence processes because "effective indirect service ... depend[s] to a large extent on psychologists' abilities to influence the behavior of third-party adults" (Conoley & Gutkin, 1986, p. 403).

Interestingly, this view acknowledging the value of social power and influence to explain processes and outcomes of school consultation comprises one side of what has been termed the *collaboration debate* (Erchul, 1999; Gutkin, 1999a, 1999b). It is beyond the scope of this chapter to delineate the nuances of this debate; however, central to our purpose is a point made by Schulte and Osborne (2003) when tracing the history of collaboration within consultation. In citing early organizational research on the role of factory supervisors' participation in reducing their resistance to change (i.e., Coch & French, 1948; Marrow & French, 1945), Schulte and Osborne noted that "collaboration was seen as a way for a consultant to exert influence and induce change without eliciting ... resistance from the consultee because there was no attempt to directly or overtly change consultee beliefs or actions" (p. 121). Thus, inviting consultee participation — one way to operationalize collaboration — has been acknowledged as a successful means to achieve social influence in consultation for over 60 years.

Before proceeding further, it is critical that we define the terms social (i.e., interpersonal) influence and social power. *Social influence* is the demonstrated change in the beliefs, attitudes, or behavior of Person B (i.e., target of influence) that can be attributed to Person A (i.e., influencing agent). *Social power* is the influencing agent's potential to effect such change in a target of influence using available resources (French & Raven, 1959). Social power, then, constitutes one necessary basis for the exercise of social influence.

Erchul and his colleagues (Erchul, Raven, & Whichard, 2001; Erchul, Raven, & Wilson, 2004) have delineated six reasons why the study of social power and social influence is important to furthering our understanding of school consultation:

1. As noted already, scholars increasingly have recognized the utility of viewing consultation as an interpersonal influence process.
2. In line with the paradox of school psychology, the effective delivery of indirect services is linked to the application of social power and influence.
3. Power and influence are integral to all human relationships, so their relevance to consultation is without question.
4. Despite their lack of formal position power or authority, school psychologist consultants are routinely depicted as having the ability to influence others.
5. The systematic examination of power and influence can inform the collaboration debate.
6. Increased knowledge of power and influence are relevant to understanding specific issues in consultation (e.g., consultee follow-through with baseline data collection, consultee implementation of an intervention, treatment integrity/fidelity, the success or failure of consultation).

Given this backdrop, the primary purpose of this chapter is to describe and critique selected research studies that have (a) considered school consultation as a social influence process and (b) been conducted within two specific research perspectives. These perspectives are the bases of social power (French & Raven, 1959; Raven, 1965, 1992, 1993) and relational communication (Parks, 1977; Rogers & Escudero, 2004; Rogers & Farace, 1975). To appropriately delimit and concentrate this presentation, other clearly related lines of research are not addressed. (See, for example, O'Keefe & Medway, 1997, for a review of persuasion research applied to school consultation, and the Evidence-Based Intervention [EBI] Work Group, 2005, for a review of other theories of change applied to the adoption of EBIs in practice settings.).

Social psychologist Bertram Raven's typology of social power bases is the best-known framework for studying interpersonal power (Mintzberg, 1983) and one that recently has witnessed a modest surge in research activity within organizational and school psychology. Relational communication, which has its roots in fields as diverse as anthropology, systems theory, and cybernetics, has been a mainstay topic within speech communication since the late 1960s. Relational communication emphasizes the importance of form and process, as opposed to the verbal content, of messages and the changing nature of these messages over time (Rogers & Escudero, 2004).

Although the social power base and relational communication perspectives represent two different research traditions, a strong case may be made for their complementarity. Key to understanding this connection is Olson and Cromwell's (1975) specification of three domains of social power: (a) *power base*, viewed as the resources Person A can potentially use to change the behavior of Person B; (b) *power process*, seen as the face-to-face interactions in which influence is exerted by A and accepted or rejected by B; and (c) *power outcome*, regarded as the consequences of influence attempts, such as which person benefited more from the interaction. The complementarity of the two chosen perspectives becomes apparent when one sees that Raven's (1992, 1993) social power base typology directly illustrates the power base domain, and relational communication provides a means to assess the power process domain (Erchul, 1992b).

Our approach to this chapter is to outline each perspective in turn, first offering some background information and then describing and evaluating research studies within school consultation that have employed the perspective. There is an explicit focus on what is currently known and which questions/issues need to be explored in the future. For organizational clarity, we have retained Olson and Cromwell's (1975) three domains as major headings within the chapter.

THE SOCIAL POWER BASE PERSPECTIVE

Foundations and Background

The concept of social power has its roots within social psychology, a field devoted to understanding and explaining how the "thought, feeling, and behavior of individuals are influenced by the actual, imagined, or implied presence of others" (Allport, 1985, p. 3). Accordingly, French and Raven's (1959) theory of social power is based on the processes of psychological change and social influence as they relate mainly to a dyadic relationship. Within this conceptualization, *psychological change* is defined as any change in an individual's behaviors, beliefs, attitudes, or other psychological function, and *social influence* occurs when the influencing agent successfully changes the beliefs, attitudes, or behaviors of a target of influence. In other words, social influence occurs when the agent induces psychological change in the target. *Social power*, then, is a means of potential influence (French & Raven, 1959).

The original version of the French and Raven (1959) power base typology advanced five power bases that individuals may use in their attempts to influence others: reward, coercive, legitimate, expert, and referent power. The premise behind *reward power* is that a target may change his or her behavior if he or she perceives that an agent is capable of and willing to provide tangible rewards for such a change. *Coercive power* is based on a target's perception that an agent may punish him or her in some way for noncompliance. *Legitimate power* is predicated on a target's sense of an obligation to comply with an agent, often due to the agent's status or organizational position. *Expert power* is based on a target's perception that an agent is knowledgeable or has expertise in a specific area. *Referent power*, the final original power base, is rooted in a target's sense of similarity with the agent or the desire to identify with the agent (French & Raven, 1959).

Raven (1965) added a sixth power base — *informational power*. The idea behind informational power is that a target of influence may comply with an influencing agent because he or she perceives the information contained within the agent's message to be relevant to the situation at hand. Although it appears at first to be the same as expert power, informational power is different in that it is the target's judged relevance of the agent's message — not the agent's expertise — that influences the target (Raven, 1992, 1993).

Since their inception, these six power bases (French & Raven, 1959; Raven, 1965) have been used to help understand interpersonal relationships in a variety of settings, including within the family, among children, between teachers and students, and among supervisors/supervisees in organizational settings. This wide application has led to substantial modification and revision of the original social power base model, the most recent version of which is Raven's (1992, 1993) power/interaction model of interpersonal influence. For the purposes of this chapter, it is sufficient to note that this comprehensive model incorporates six stages describing the process and decision making an agent goes through to select, implement, and evaluate the use of social power bases to influence a target.

Table 14.1   Definitions of Raven's (1992, 1993) Social Power Bases

Social Power Base	Definition
Positive expert	Person A does what Person B says because Person B is perceived to be an expert in a particular area.
Negative expert	Person A does the opposite of what Person B says because he or she believes that Person B is thinking of his or her own best interests.
Positive referent	Person A does what Person B wants because he or she wants to be similar to or associated with Person B.
Negative referent	Person A does the opposite of what Person B says because he or she does not want to be similar to or associated with Person B.
Impersonal reward	Person A complies with Person B because he or she perceives that Person B can give some form of tangible reward for complying.
Personal reward	Person A complies with Person B because he or she believes Person B will like or approve of him or her for complying.
Impersonal coercion	Person A complies with Person B because he or she perceives that Person B has the ability to tangibly punish him or her for noncompliance.
Personal coercion	Person A complies with Person B because he or she believes that Person B will dislike or disapprove of him or her for noncompliance.
Direct information	Person A complies with Person B because the information provided by Person B makes logical sense.
Indirect information	Person A complies with Person B because he or she overhears from a third party that a certain course of action worked well in a similar situation.
Formal legitimate/position	Person A feels obligated to comply with Person B because Person B occupies a position of status or authority.
Legitimacy of reciprocity	Person A feels obligated to comply with Person B because Person B has done something positive for him or her in the past.
Legitimacy of equity	Person A feels obligated to comply with Person B as a way of compensating for Person B's previous hard work.
Legitimacy of dependence	Person A feels obligated to comply with Person B because Person B is unable to accomplish a certain action without his or her help.

Note: From "The Relationship Between Gender of Consultant and Social Power Perceptions within School Consultation" by W. P. Erchul, B. H. Raven, and K. E. Wilson, 2004, *School Psychology Review, 33*, p. 584. Copyright 2004 by National Association of School Psychologists, Bethesda, MD. Adapted with permission of the publisher.

In addition, Raven's (1992, 1993) updated model has expanded to include 14 social power bases, each of which stems from the original 6 bases (French & Raven, 1959; Raven, 1965). Specifically, reward and coercive power each have been differentiated into personal and impersonal forms, and expert and referent power each have positive and negative forms. Informational power has been divided into direct and indirect forms, and finally, legitimate power has been divided into four forms: formal legitimate, legitimacy of reciprocity, legitimacy of equity, and legitimacy of dependence (Raven, 1992, 1993). Table 14.1 provides a summary of these 14 expanded social power bases.

The Measurement of Social Power Bases

Over time, the widespread application of the initial five social power bases outlined by French and Raven (1959) led to the development of several instruments to measure these bases. However, many of these early measures were limited in a psychometric sense as some failed to define French and Raven's power bases operationally or used a single item to represent an entire social power base (Podsakoff & Schriesheim, 1985).

In an attempt to address these psychometric limitations as well as to create an instrument to define and measure Raven's (1992, 1993) expanded set of power bases operationally, Raven, Schwarzwald, and Koslowsky (1998) created the Interpersonal Power Inventory (IPI). Building on previously developed scales (e.g., Hinkin & Schriesheim, 1989) and specific definitions of the power bases provided in Raven's (1992, 1993) model, Raven et al. (1998) developed items for 11 of the 14 power bases. Because expert power, negative referent power, and indirect informational power are more difficult to conceptualize concretely and thus more difficult to measure, these 3 power bases were excluded from the IPI. Four items were eventually constructed for each of the 11 power bases measured in the IPI, resulting in a total of 44 items (Raven et al., 1998).

The IPI is a critical-incident instrument having two forms: the subordinate form and the supervisor form. Instructions for the subordinate form ask respondents to think of an instance when they were told by their supervisor to do their job somewhat differently, and although initially reluctant, they did exactly as requested. Respondents are then asked to rate how likely each of the 44 items would be a reason for their compliance using a 7-point scale, with 1 indicating the item was *definitely not a reason* and 7 indicating the item was *definitely a reason* for complying. Instructions for the supervisor form are nearly identical; the only difference is that respondents are asked to think of a similar work situation in which they were the supervisor, not the subordinate. On this form, respondents are asked to indicate how likely each item was a reason why the subordinate would have complied, and the form uses the same 7-point scale (Raven et al., 1998).

Having constructed the IPI, Raven et al. (1998) then conducted two studies to examine its psychometric properties and underlying factor structure. Our attention now turns to a review of these two studies as their results established the IPI as a reliable and valid instrument for measuring the social power bases.

In their first study, Raven et al. (1998) administered the IPI to 317 American college students. The researchers calculated the intercorrelations among the four items hypothesized as belonging to each power base and eliminated the item that had the greatest effect on reducing the reliability of the factor, resulting in a total of 33 items. Coefficient alphas for bases ranged from .67 to .86, indicating moderate to very good internal consistency. Next, a principal components analysis was performed on the 33 items, which resulted in 7 factors with eigenvalues greater than 1. Alphas for the seven factors ranged from .72 to .90, again indicative of moderate to very good internal consistency. Finally, Raven et al. factor analyzed the mean scores of the 11 power bases, which resulted in a two-factor solution; Factor I explained 34.6% of the variance and included *soft* bases, which are more relational in nature, and Factor II explained 24.7% of the variance and included *harsh* bases, which represent more heavy-handed forms of power (Erchul, Raven, & Whichard, 2001).

In Raven et al.'s (1998) second study, 101 workers in an Israeli hospital each completed the 33-item IPI (translated into Hebrew). Similar to the American version of the IPI, coefficient alphas for each scale on the Hebrew version ranged from .63 to .88. In addition, a two-factor solution indicating a harsh/soft distinction among the power bases was identified, which was similar to that found in Raven et al.'s first study. The first factor explained 39.8% of the variance and was comprised of the harsh bases, and the second factor explained 20.3% of the variance and consisted of the soft bases.

In sum, Raven et al. (1998) demonstrated that the IPI is a reliable/internally consistent and valid instrument for assessing how Raven's (1992, 1993) social power bases are attributed to supervisors when attempting to influence subordinates. Their results not only showed very good internal consistency for IPI items that comprised each of the 11 power bases, but also indicated a robust harsh/soft power structure present among the 11 bases.

Subsequent to the work of Raven et al. (1998), other researchers have demonstrated the applicability of the IPI in measuring the social power bases in alternate organizational settings. For example, Koslowsky, Schwarzwald, and Ashuri (2001) administered both forms of the IPI to nurses to examine the relationship between subordinates' reasons for compliance and variables of job satisfaction, organizational commitment, and professional distance. Schwarzwald, Koslowsky, and Agassi (2001) investigated compliance to social power bases in relation to leadership style using a sample of police captains and officers. Schwarzwald, Koslowsky, and Ochana-Levin (2004) studied whether situational determinants (i.e., organizational settings in which either complex or routine tasks dominate) would have an effect on social power usage. In a study of Italian medical personnel, Pierro, De Grada, Raven, and Kruglanski (2004) found that leadership style interacted with the use of interpersonal power strategies.[1] Specifically, individuals concerned about promotion and advancement prefer a forceful style that requires a harsher strategy, whereas those concerned with assessment orientation prefer an advisory style represented by the softer power strategies. In addition to the various significant relationships found between perceptions of social power and certain organizational variables, each of these studies also replicated the findings of Raven et al. (1998) that identified a clear harsh/soft power base distinction.

Applying the Social Power Base Perspective to School Consultation Research: What We Know

Having provided the background for the social power base typology (French & Raven, 1959; Raven, 1965, 1992, 1993), including its development, measurement, and relevance within organizational settings, we now examine the application of a social power base perspective to school consultation research.

Phase I Studies (1980–1991)

The first wave of research in this area, which we call Phase I studies, stemmed from an influential article by Martin (1978). Martin emphasized the importance of power and influence in the school consultation process and was the first school psychologist to apply French and Raven's (1959) original five power bases to consultation. In considering each of these power bases, Martin (1978) concluded that school consultants had access to, or could be attributed, only expert and referent power. He posited that because school psychologists occupy staff rather than line positions, they do not possess the authority or right to dictate behavior, and thus coercive, reward, and legitimate power are essentially irrelevant to their role as consultants.

Based on Martin's (1978) conclusion, seven empirical studies were conducted between 1980 and 1991 that examined the relationship between the positive forms of expert and referent power and outcomes in school consultation (see Table 14.2, reprinted from Erchul & Raven, 1997). Despite methodological shortcomings and a somewhat mixed set of results, the Phase I studies do represent an important first step in establishing the relevance of social power to school consultation. Following are highlights of these seven investigations.

Three Phase I studies found clear support for the value of expert and referent power within school consultation. Martin and Curtis (1980) examined the impact of school consultants' and teachers' age and experience on consultation outcomes, and the analysis of 164 school psychologists' responses documenting their most and least successful teacher consultation experiences led to two key results. First, psychologists reported outcomes as *most* successful when the psychologist

Table 14.2   Empirical Studies of Expert and Referent Social Power Bases in School Consultation (Phase I Studies)

Study	Participants	Methodology	Key Results and Conclusions
Martin and Curtis (1980)	164 school psychologists	Responses generated to actual consultations using critical incident technique	(a) Successful consultation outcomes were related to the similarity of ages and amount of professional experience of consultant and teacher, suggesting the importance of referent power for consultants. (b) Unsuccessful consultation outcomes were related to a teacher who was older and more experienced than the consultant, suggesting the importance of expert power for consultants.
Cienki (1982)	68 schoolteachers	Ratings made relative to a simulated, videotaped consultation	Several measures of consultant effectiveness were highly correlated with indicators of expert and referent power, suggesting that both bases are important and a mixture of the two is preferable for consultants.
Crowe (1982)	231 college students	Ratings made relative to a simulated, written consultation scenario	No significant relationships were found between indicators of consultant expert and referent power and participants' ratings of consultation process and outcome.
Kruger (1984)	74 schoolteachers	Ratings made relative to a simulated, videotaped consultation	No significant relationships were found between indicators of consultant expert and referent power and participants' ratings of consultation process and outcome.
Kinsala (1985)	45 graduate student consultants	Data from 503 actual consultation sessions examined relative to indicators of expert and referent power	Although indicators of consultant expert and referent power correlated significantly with three outcome measures, multiple regression analyses revealed that each accounted for negligible amounts of variance in the outcome measures. Some support for the value of referent power was found.
Roberts (1985)	15 educators	Ratings made relative to an actual consultant	Indicators of consultant expert and referent power correlated significantly with outcome measures of consultee satisfaction and problem resolution.

Continued

Table 14.2   Empirical Studies of Expert and Referent Social Power Bases in School Consultation (Phase I Studies) (*Continued*)

Study	Participants	Methodology	Key Results and Conclusions
Short, Moore, and Williams (1991)	153 schoolteachers	Ratings made relative to a simulated, videotaped consultation	(a) The consultant described as having a doctoral degree was rated high on expertness.
			(b) The consultant described as experienced was rated high on expertness and trustworthiness. Results support the value of expert power but not referent power in school consultation.

Note. From "Social Power in School Consultation: A Contemporary View of French and Raven's Bases of Power Model," by W. P. Erchul and B. H. Raven, 1997, *Journal of School Psychology, 35*, p. 149. Copyright 1997 by Elsevier. Reprinted with permission from Elsevier.

and teacher were similar in age and level of experience, suggesting that referent power contributes to the effective delivery of consultative services. Second, psychologists reported outcomes to be *least* successful when the teacher was older and more experienced than the psychologist. Not only does this second result provide further support for referent power, but also it reinforces the value of expert power in its suggestion that consultation will be more successful when psychologists are more experienced — and perhaps seen as more credible — than teachers.

Further support for the role of expert and referent power was found by Cienki (1982), who examined teacher perceptions of school consultant expert and referent power-related behaviors and their link to various indicators of consultant effectiveness. Teachers viewed one of three videotaped analogues portraying an initial consultation session between a school consultant and teacher, each of which was prefaced by the same written description of the consultant's qualifications. In the first session, the consultant demonstrated expert power by displaying specialized skills, and in the second, the consultant evidenced referent power by emphasizing similarities with the teacher. In the third session, the consultant portrayed both expert and referent characteristics. Results indicated that characteristics of consultant effectiveness were significantly correlated with indicators of both expert and referent power, suggesting that both power bases are important within school consultation.

Roberts (1985) also examined the relationship between expert and referent power on various consultation outcome measures, including consultee satisfaction and problem resolution. Serving as a school consultant, Roberts consulted with 15 teachers, after which they filled out several questionnaires providing information regarding their perceptions of the consultation experience. Results based on questionnaire responses as well as measures of expert and referent power indicated that, overall, both expert and referent power were positively related to consultation outcomes, thereby supporting the findings of Martin and Curtis (1980) and Cienki (1982).

As noted, results of the Phase I studies are not entirely consistent. In two of the seven studies, for instance, support was found for either expert or referent power, but not both. Specifically, using methodologies similar to those presented already, Short, Moore, and Williams (1991) found only expert power to be associated with perceptions of consultant effectiveness, and Kinsala (1985) found only referent power to be related to perceptions of successful consultation outcomes. The remaining two Phase I studies (i.e., Crowe, 1982; Kruger, 1984) did not uncover any significant relationships between expert and referent power and school consultation outcomes.

Taken together, the seven Phase I studies examining the French and Raven (1959) social power bases within school consultation broke new ground in terms of furthering our understanding of key relational elements of consultation. However, the methodological limitations inherent to these investigations (e.g., analogue designs, biased participant sampling procedures, unvalidated instruments) serve to diminish their overall contribution (Erchul & Raven, 1997). Fortunately, a second wave of research that attempts to improve on these limitations has developed, and our attention now turns to a presentation of three empirical investigations of social power within school consultation, termed the Phase II studies.

Phase II Studies (2001 to Present)

This second phase of research was prompted by an article by Erchul and Raven (1997), who after examining Raven's (1992, 1993) expanded set of social power bases and the power/interaction model of interpersonal influence, provided an updated view of the relevance of social power bases to school consultation. Specifically, Erchul and Raven emphasized that the power model is meant to apply to any interpersonal situation in which social power and influence are involved. Because of the growing acknowledgment that school consultation is an interpersonal influence process, Erchul and Raven concluded that school consultants have the potential to access, or to be attributed, types of *all* forms of social power and not just expert and referent power as suggested by Martin (1978).

Consequently, drawing from the research agenda proposed by Erchul and Raven (1997), each of the Phase II studies investigates the expanded set of social power bases in relation to school consultation, leading to a more comprehensive understanding of this application of social power. Furthermore, each study used a modified version of the original IPI to measure 11 of the current 14 social power bases, an aspect that has improved the quality of research in this area by allowing for consistent measurement of power bases and enabling researchers to more easily compare results across studies.

The first of the Phase II studies was conducted by Erchul, Raven, and Ray (2001), who examined school psychologists' perceptions of social power within consultation. Specific areas of interest included (a) which social power bases school psychologists would perceive as most effective in helping an initially reluctant teacher to follow a consultant's specific request and (b) the similarity between social power base rankings within the school consultant/consultee relationship and the rankings found within organizational relationships demonstrated in previous research. To address these areas, 101 school psychologists completed a modified version of the original, 44-item IPI, termed the IPI-Form CT (i.e., "consultant"). Alterations included changes to individual items and to the overall directions for completion such that the wording was appropriate for school psychologists rather than supervisors in an organizational setting. Similar to the original version of the IPI, respondents were asked to think of a time when they were consulting with a teacher about a situation and the teacher was initially reluctant to comply with their requests (e.g., start an intervention on a particular day). Respondents then rated each item in terms of how likely it might be to influence that teacher to comply with their requests.

After examining the intercorrelations among the 4 items hypothesized as belonging to each of the 11 power bases, Erchul, Raven, and Ray (2001) eliminated the item with the lowest correlation within each power base, resulting in a total of 33 items. Next, the mean rankings of the 11 power bases were compiled, and these results indicated that, in terms of perceived effectiveness, 5 of the 6 highest ranked power bases were soft bases according to Raven et al.'s (1998) classification. Rankings based on high-to-low effectiveness ratings were informational, expert power, impersonal reward (a harsh base according to Raven et al.), referent, legitimate dependence, and personal reward power, respectively.

In addition, a principal components analysis revealed a two-factor solution among the 33 items within the IPI-Form CT, which corresponded highly to the harsh/soft power base distinction identified by Raven et al. (1998). The harsh factor, accounting for 23.5% of the variance, consisted of impersonal coercion, impersonal reward, legitimate equity, personal coercion, and legitimate reciprocity. The soft factor, accounting for 22.9% of the variance, consisted of legitimate dependence, direct informational, referent, personal reward, expert, and legitimate position power. These findings indicate that the harsh/soft power base distinction is meaningful within the field of school consultation (Erchul, Raven, & Ray, 2001).

Overall, results of Erchul, Raven, and Ray (2001) support the contentions of other researchers and are in line with findings of previous empirical studies. Not only are the high rankings of expert and referent power consistent with Martin's (1978) position that school consultants have access to these power bases, but also the high rankings of informational, legitimate dependence, and personal reward power lend support to Erchul and Raven's (1997) belief that certain forms of all social power bases are relevant to school consultation. Finally, the emergence of a harsh/soft, two-factor solution suggests that this distinction is meaningful within school consultation as well as other organizational contexts.

In the second Phase II study, Erchul, Raven, and Whichard (2001) addressed a research direction posed by Erchul, Raven, and Ray (2001), which was to examine teachers' perceptions of social power bases as well as those of school consultants. Erchul, Raven, and Whichard (2001) used two modified forms of the IPI to examine school psychologist consultants' and teachers' perceptions of the effectiveness of social power bases when used by psychologists to gain compliance from initially reluctant teachers. They advanced three research questions pertaining to psychologists consulting with teachers who are initially reluctant to comply with requests: (a) How do teachers perceive the relative effectiveness of power bases used by school psychologists? (b) how similarly do psychologists and teachers perceive the relative effectiveness of power bases used by psychologists? and (c) do teachers perceive psychologists' use of soft bases as more effective than harsh bases?

Modified versions of the IPI-Form CT (Erchul, Raven, & Ray, 2001) were administered to 134 school psychologists and 118 teachers using a survey-by-mail methodology. For each item, participants were asked to rate their responses on a 7-point scale, with 1 indicating *much more likely to comply* and 7 indicating *much less likely to comply*.

The IPI-Form CT also was edited to create a second instrument, termed the IPI-Form CE (i.e., "consultee"). The IPI-Form CE is identical to the IPI-Form CT except that the directions and items are worded to allow for assessment of teachers' perceptions of the effectiveness of social power bases as used by consulting school psychologists. Teachers rated each item using the same 7-point Likert scale described for the IPI-Form CT. Internal consistency estimates based on the teacher sample are moderately high, with coefficient alphas derived from principal components analysis ranging from .82 to .92 (Erchul, Raven, & Whichard, 2001).

Results indicated that teachers rated informational, expert, legitimate dependence, and referent power — all soft power bases — as the top four bases that would be most effective for school psychologists to use to increase their own compliance. Psychologists rated direct informational, expert, referent, and personal reward power — also all soft power bases — as the top four power bases most likely to be effective to gain teacher compliance. Interestingly, both teachers and psychologists rated informational and expert power as the two power bases most likely to result in teacher compliance, and the overall rank order of power bases provided by psychologists and teachers was significantly correlated ($r_s = .73$, $p < .05$). These findings suggest that teachers and psychologists generally share similar views regarding the effectiveness of social power bases in gaining compliance from teachers.

Additional results indicated that both teachers and psychologists rated soft power bases as significantly more effective than harsh power bases within consultation. Not only are these findings consistent with those of Erchul, Raven, and Ray (2001), who also found that psychologists believed soft power bases rather than harsh power bases would result in greater teacher compliance, but also they indicate that teachers themselves perceive soft power bases as likely to be more effective than harsh bases in gaining their compliance to psychologists' requests.

In the third Phase II study, Erchul et al. (2004) delved more deeply into the Erchul, Raven, and Whichard (2001) data set by examining how similarly male and female school psychologists perceive the effectiveness of social power when consulting with teachers described as initially reluctant to comply with requests. Based on research examining gender and the use of language and power strategies, Erchul et al. (2004) hypothesized that female school psychologists would perceive soft power bases as more effective in consulting with teachers than would male school psychologists. A research question they posed related to how male and female school psychologists would compare with respect to their perceptions of the effectiveness of individual social power bases during teacher consultation.

Results comparing the effectiveness ratings of the harsh and soft power bases by gender of respondent were significant, indicating that female school psychologists rated both harsh and soft power bases as more likely to result in teacher compliance during consultation than male school psychologists. In addition, a more conservative effect size (ES) analysis was conducted with an a priori criterion of 0.50 established to indicate real-world significance. The ES for soft bases was 0.50, and the ES for harsh bases was 0.42. Based on these ESs, Erchul et al. (2004) concluded that female school psychologists regard soft power bases — but not harsh bases — as more effective than male school psychologists.

Finally, the effectiveness ratings of the 11 individual power bases were compared by participants' gender, which addressed Erchul et al.'s (2004) research question. The overall multivariate analysis of variance results were not significant, suggesting that male and female school psychologists do not have significantly different perceptions regarding the effectiveness of the 11 individual power bases measured by the IPI-Form CT.

Taken together, the three Phase II studies (summarized in Table 14.3) have contributed to our understanding of the application of Raven's (1992, 1993) social power base typology to school consultation, providing clear support for its utility in explaining relational processes within consultation. Furthermore, this research has repeatedly demonstrated that the harsh/soft power base distinction initially identified within organizational field research is also meaningful within school consultation, as evidenced by psychologist and teacher perceptions that soft power bases are more effective than harsh bases. Finally, we know that this distinction is meaningful in relation to gender, in that female consultants perceive the soft power bases to be more effective than male consultants, leading to the suggestion that female school psychologists may employ different methods and techniques (including their implementation of social power) when consulting with teachers.

A Critique of the Social Power Base Perspective as Applied to School Consultation Research

There are several notable strengths associated with the social power base perspective. First, the French and Raven (1959) typology, updated by Raven (1965, 1992, 1993), is well known in social and organizational psychology. It has been used to study many types of social relationships, and its research literature spans nearly 50 years. Second, with the development of the IPI (Raven et al., 1998), the measurement of power bases now has greater psychometric integrity. Third, the application of a social power base

Table 14.3   Summary of Phase II Studies Examining Raven's (1992, 1993) Social Power Bases Within School Consultation

Study	Participants	Purpose	Key Results
Erchul, Raven, and Ray (2001)	101 school psychologists	Determine if the IPI is useful in examining social power bases in school consultation; determine which power bases psychologists perceive as most likely to be effective in gaining teacher compliance; examine similarity in social power rankings between those in organizational relationships and in psychologist-teacher relationships	Psychologists ranked direct informational power and expert power as the two social power bases most likely to gain teacher compliance; five of the six highest ranked social power bases were soft bases; two-factor solution identified a harsh/soft power base distinction; social power rankings consistent with previous research in organizational settings
Erchul, Raven, and Whichard (2001)	134 school psychologists and 118 teachers	Determine teachers' perceptions of effectiveness of social power bases when used by school psychologists; examine how similarly teachers and school psychologists perceive effectiveness of social power bases; determine if teachers view soft power bases as more effective than harsh bases	The top four power bases rated by teachers and psychologists as most effective in gaining teacher compliance were soft bases, and this rank order correlation was significant; both teachers and psychologists perceived soft power bases as more effective than harsh bases
Erchul, Raven, and Wilson (2004)	134 school psychologists	Examine the relationship between gender and perceived effectiveness of social power bases	Female school psychologists perceived soft power bases as more effective than male psychologists; no differences between male and female psychologists regarding effectiveness of the 11 individual power bases

perspective to school consultation has brought with it a much-needed relational or interpersonal focus, in contrast to earlier consultation research that emphasized the measurement of individual consultant behavior only (e.g., Knoff, Hines, & Kromrey, 1995). The net gain has been effectively to document selected aspects of the consultant/consultee relationship. Finally, results of the three Phase II studies offer school psychologist consultants several implications for practice, perhaps the most fundamental of which is to encourage them to reflect on how their attitudes toward soft power bases affect interpersonal communication styles when consulting with teachers (Erchul et al., 2004).

There are also several weaknesses with respect to applying a social power base perspective to school consultation. First, the self-report/survey methodology used in IPI-based research is a liability, and the standard limitations of this approach certainly apply. Second, although the social power base perspective clearly contributes to our further understanding of consultation, it alone may explain a small portion of the variance in client outcomes. Third, and in a related way, to date no social power base research has documented a clear impact on client behavior change in consultation, thereby currently limiting the contributions of this research perspective to discussions of EBIs (e.g., Kratochwill & Stoiber, 2002). Finally, maybe the most severe limitation of the social power base perspective is its controversial nature. As noted in the beginning of this chapter, there is growing consensus on the importance of viewing consultation as an interpersonal influence process (e.g., the paradox of school psychology). However, it remains difficult for many to accept that a helping relationship such as consultation can involve the concepts of social power and influence to explain relevant interpersonal processes and outcomes (Erchul, 1992a, 1999).

Future Research Agenda: What We Need to Know

Updating Erchul and Raven's (1997) research agenda, we pose the following questions for future investigations:

1. What are the relationships between a school consultant's use of Raven's (1992, 1993) power bases and (a) teacher follow-through with baseline data collection; (b) treatment integrity of a teacher-implemented intervention; (c) teacher judgments of intervention acceptability; and (d) the overall efficacy/effectiveness of school consultation, particularly with respect to client outcomes?
2. Does a consultant's choice of consultation model (e.g., behavioral vs. conjoint behavioral consultation [CBC]) lead to differential use of social power bases? *rural areas*
3. How do myriad issues of consultant, consultee, and client <u>diversity play into a social</u> *vs.* power base/social influence perspective? (See, for example, Wosinka, Cialdini, Barrett, & *urban areas* Reykowski, 2001.)
4. Moving beyond the consultant/consultee dyad, how can a social power base perspective be applied to better understand the functioning of school-based problem-solving groups (e.g., student support teams, intervention assistance teams)?
5. Are harsh power bases essentially irrelevant to the practice of school consultation? Should future research in this area consider only soft power bases? If so, what finer distinctions between and among soft power bases can be made relative to the specific context of school consultation?
6. Where does a social power/interpersonal influence framework intersect with a "collaboration" framework within school consultation? For example, using different language, both frameworks acknowledge the importance of fostering relationship development (i.e., positive referent power vs. rapport building). What other points of commonality exist?
7. Do school consultants have ethical concerns with respect to applying a social power/social influence perspective? If so, what specific concerns do they have?
8. Do consultees recognize their use of power bases to influence consultants? On which ones do they rely most frequently and to what end? How do consultees typically react to consultant influence attempts?

Having addressed the social power base perspective, we continue by describing power process: the face-to-face exchanges during which Person A (agent) makes an influence attempt and Person B (target) either accepts or rejects it (Olson & Cromwell, 1975). The perspective chosen to illustrate power process is relational communication (Rogers & Escudero, 2004).

THE RELATIONAL COMMUNICATION PERSPECTIVE: POWER PROCESS

Foundations and Background

Relational communication generally refers to the way in which a speaker defines his or her position relative to the position of another speaker. In addition, relational communication emphasizes the

(a) relational control (process) analysis as opposed to the verbal content analysis of interpersonal communication; (b) examination of paired sequential messages (i.e., transactions) rather than single, isolated messages; and (c) analysis of the changing nature of these messages over time (Millar & Rogers, 1976; Rogers & Farace, 1975).

theoretical roots The theoretical roots of relational communication derive mainly from the contributions of anthropologist Gregory Bateson (1935, 1958). Bateson's thinking is regarded as a major influence in shifting the field toward a consideration of the processes and relationships within face-to-face communication (Watzlawick, Beavin, & Jackson, 1967). In particular, Bateson's (1935) observations of the Iatmul tribe of New Guinea formed the basis for his (a) theory of schismogenesis and (b) the distinction between report and command meanings of spoken messages. Both concepts later would lay the groundwork for relational communication (Rogers & Escudero, 2004).

refers to the style of comm. The theory of schismogenesis (Bateson, 1935, 1958) is predicated on the concepts of symmetrical and complementary relationships; *symmetrical* relationships exist when speakers evidence similar interactional styles, and *complementary* relationships are characterized by opposite styles. *Schismogenesis* occurs when an interaction becomes unbalanced, demonstrating extreme symmetry (similarity) or complementarity (difference). To combat schismogenesis, *reciprocity*, the process of balancing the relationship, must occur to prevent eventual termination of the relationship (see Table 14.4, reprinted from Erchul et al., 1999).

Why do you think this is important in comm? The difference between report (content) and command (relational) meanings of messages is central to understanding relational communication. Bateson (1935, 1958) noted that every message has two simultaneously conveyed levels of meaning: (a) a *report* or content level that transmits information and (b) a *command* or relational level that defines the relationship between speakers. The essence of this distinction is that, "We do not relate and then talk, but we relate in talk" (Duncan, 1967, p. 249). Relational communication concerns itself with the study of command or behavior-imposing functions of messages (Parks, 1977).

The original applications of relational communication may be traced to the field of psychiatry about 20 years after Bateson's initial writings. An example of an early clinical application is the double-bind theory of schizophrenia (Bateson, Jackson, Haley, & Weakland, 1956). As elements of relational communication gained clinical utility among practitioners (e.g., Ruesch, 1973), those in nonclinical settings recognized the need for objective, psychometrically defensible ways to measure relational communication. This recognition led to the development of several speech act coding schemes having this purpose. Although relational communication may be conceptualized more broadly and encompass many different dimensions (e.g., trust, inclusion-exclusion), nearly all relational communication verbal interaction coding systems advanced to date have emphasized almost exclusively the dominance-submission dimension, with a narrowed focus on relational control (Erchul, 1999).

RCCCS The most widely researched relational communication coding system was developed by Rogers and Farace (1975) in an effort to operationalize the constructs associated with Bateson's theory. The Rogers and Farace relational communication control coding system (RCCCS) relies on a pair of sequential messages as the basis for examining an interaction between two speakers, and the initial research using this system focused on marital dyads. Within the RCCCS, a message is considered both a response to the preceding message and a stimulus for the message that follows. Each message is assigned a three-digit code, with each digit representing one of three categories: (a) speaker, (b) grammatical form of message, and (c) response mode or metacommunicational function the message serves relative to the message that preceded it. Then, using the second and third digits (i.e., grammatical form of message and response mode), one of three possible control codes is assigned to each message: *one-up* ($\uparrow$), signifying an effort to gain control

Table 14.4   Definitions of Key Terms Used in Relational Communication Theory and Research

Terms From Bateson's (1958) Theory of Schismogenesis	
Term	**Definition**
Symmetry	A relationship type characterized by a minimization of differences between individuals (e.g., A and B both attempt to seek control or give up control to the other); symmetry becomes dysfunctional, or schismogenic, when escalation or competition occurs
Complementarity	A relationship type characterized by a maximization of differences between individuals (e.g., Person B usually complies with Person A's demands); complementarity becomes dysfunctional, or schismogenic, when these relational differences become too rigid or exaggerated, thus polarizing individuals
Reciprocity	A relationship type that is balanced with respect to symmetry and complementarity; represents the best way to avoid schismogenesis
Schismogenesis	A process triggered by extreme types of symmetry or complementarity that results in poor relational outcomes; can be corrected through the development of a reciprocal relationship

Terms From Rogers and Farace's (1975) RCCCS and Heatherington and Friedlander's (1987) FRCCCS Coding Systems	
Term	**Definition**
Assertion	A completed referential statement, either declarative or imperative in form
Closed question	A direct question that limits a person's answer to a small set of response options
Open question	An open-ended question that is phrased to permit a range of possible answers
Talkover	An interruption, used by a speaker to enter a conversation
Incomplete	A message that is started but not finished
Intercept	In conversations involving three or more speakers, an interruption of an ongoing dyadic message exchange by a third person
Support	A message that gives or seeks agreement, assistance, acceptance, or approval
Nonsupport	A message indicating disagreement, rejection, or challenge
Extension	A message that continues the flow or theme of the preceding message
Disconfirmation	A message that ignores another speaker's request for information, action, opinion, etc.
Topic change/topic shift	A message that introduces a new idea immediately after some discussion of a different idea
One-up ($\uparrow$)	A control code assigned to a message indicating an attempt to assert definitional rights and to control the relationship by directing the communication process
One-down ($\downarrow$)	A control code assigned to a message indicating an acceptance of, or request for, another person's definition of the relationship
One-across ($\rightarrow$)	A control code assigned to a message indicating a nondemanding, nonaccepting, leveling movement that has no implications for relational control

Terms From Courtright, Millar, and Rogers-Millar's (1979) and Rogers-Millar and Millar's (1979) Research Studies	
Term	**Definition**
Domineeringness	A monadic, or individually defined, measure of a person's attempts to control or define a relationship; operationally defined as the number of a person's one-up ($\uparrow$) messages divided by the total number of his or her messages; in consultation research, domineeringness may be considered more appropriately as a measure of directiveness

Continued

Table 14.4   Definitions of Key Terms Used in Relational Communication Theory and Research (*Continued*)

Terms From Courtright, Millar, and Rogers-Millar's (1979) and Rogers-Millar and Millar's (1979) Research Studies

Term	Definition
Dominance	A dyadic measure of complementarity and, more specifically, relational control; for Person A, operationally defined as the proportion of one-down ($\downarrow$) messages given by Person B to all one-up ($\uparrow$) messages offered by A; in consultation research, dominance may be considered more appropriately as a measure of one's demonstrated influence over another, thereby indicating the presence of a give-and-take pattern of cooperation (Erchul & Chewning, 1990), teamwork (Erchul et al., 1992), cooperative partnership (Zins & Erchul, 1995), partnership (Gutkin, 1996), or collaboration (Gutkin, 1997)

Note: From "Patterns of Relational Communication in Conjoint Behavioral Consultation," by W. P. Erchul, S. M. Sheridan, D. A. Ryan, P. F. Grissom, C. E. Killough, and D. W. Mettler, 1999, *School Psychology Quarterly, 14*, pp. 124–125. Copyright 1999 by Division 16, American Psychological Association. Reprinted with permission.

or assert definitional rights; *one-down* ($\downarrow$), a request or acceptance of the other speaker's control; and *one-across* ($\rightarrow$), an indication of neither an attempt to gain nor request/accept control. Once the control code is assigned, sequential messages and their respective codes are paired to indicate the transactional control present within the interaction. Symmetrical transactions are evidenced by directionally identical codes ($\uparrow\uparrow$, $\downarrow\downarrow$, or $\rightarrow\rightarrow$), complementary transactions are characterized by directionally opposite codes ($\uparrow\downarrow$ or $\downarrow\uparrow$), and transitory transactions include a one-across code ($\uparrow\rightarrow$, $\downarrow\rightarrow$, $\rightarrow\uparrow$, or $\rightarrow\downarrow$) (Rogers & Farace, 1975).

Critical to an advanced understanding of research using the RCCCS are two additional indices of relational control: domineeringness and dominance (Courtright, Millar, & Rogers-Millar, 1979; Rogers-Millar & Millar, 1979). *Domineeringness* refers to the number of one-up messages for Person A divided by A's total messages. As an individual variable, domineeringness measures bids for control by A without consideration of Person B's responses. *Dominance*, in contrast, refers to the number of Person A's one-up messages that are responded to with a one-down message by Person B. As a relational variable, dominance relies on the interaction between Persons A and B to define the nature of control within the relationship. Within consultation research, domineeringness has been characterized more recently as one's attempts to structure or define relationships, whereas dominance is one's demonstrated influence or success in defining relationships (Erchul et al., 1999).

Applying the Relational Communication Perspective to School Consultation Research: What We Know

There is a 20-year history of published research that has applied relational communication concepts and coding systems to study the links between interpersonal processes and outcomes of school consultation. Nearly all of this research has been conducted on behaviorally based consultation (e.g., Bergan & Kratochwill, 1990) because of this model's series of structured interviews as well as its explicit focus on consultant verbalizations and "strategic interpersonal communication" (Daly & Wiemann, 1994). In this section, we review eight such investigations; Table 14.5 summarizes major points of these studies.

Table 14.5   Summary of Process and Process/Outcome Studies Examining Relational Communication Within School Consultation

Study	Participants/Interviews	Purpose	Model of Consultation Used	Coding System(s) Used	Key Results
Erchul (1987)	8 graduate student consultants; 8 consultees (PII, PAI, PEI)	Examine the nature of interpersonal control within behavioral consultation (BC)	Behavioral	Rogers and Farace (1975)	(a) Consultants demonstrated higher domineeringness and dominance than consultees (b) Consultant dominance associated with higher consultant effectiveness ratings by consultees (c) Consultee domineeringness negatively associated with consultant perceptions of consultee willingness to collect baseline data
Erchul and Chewning (1990)	10 graduate student consultants; 10 consultees (PII, PAI, PEI)	Examine the nature of interpersonal control within BC by analyzing requests (i.e., bids) and responses to requests	Behavioral	Folger and Puck (1976)	(a) Consultants made significantly more requests than consultees (b) During the PII, consultee requests associated with less-favorable consultation outcomes.

Continued

Table 14.5   Summary of Process and Process/Outcome Studies Examining Relational Communication Within School Consultation (*Continued*)

Study	Participants/Interviews	Purpose	Model of Consultation Used	Coding System(s) Used	Key Results
Witt, Erchul, McKee, Pardue, and Wickstrom (1991)	8 graduate student consultants; 8 consultees (PII, PAI, PEI)	Examine the relationship between topic determination and outcomes	Behavioral	Tracey and Ray (1984)	(a) Consultant topic determination associated with consultant and consultee perceptions of favorable outcomes (b) Consultee topic determination less positively linked to outcome measures
Martens, Erchul, and Witt (1992)	4 graduate student consultants; 4 consultees (PII only)	Compare utility of four verbal interaction coding systems, three of which derive from principles of relational communication	Behavioral	Bergan and Tombari, (1975); Rogers and Farace (1975); Folger and Puck (1976); Tracey and Ray (1984)	(a) Consultants appeared to control process of consultation by asking questions and changing topics while consultees appeared more passive (b) General consistency found among coding systems suggest they are reliable and useful in studying consultation
Erchul, Covington, Hughes, and Meyers (1995)	26 graduate student consultants; 26 consultees, primarily regular education teachers (PII only)	Examine the nature of interpersonal control within school consultation by analyzing requests (i.e., bids) and responses to requests	Behavioral and more generic problem-solving consultation	Folger and Puck (1976)	When isolating the 14 BC cases: (a) Consultant use of dominant requests associated with less-favorable effectiveness ratings (b) Consultant use of dominant-affiliative requests associated with more favorable effectiveness ratings

Study	Participants	Purpose	Model	Measure	Findings
Hughes, Erchul, Yoon, Jackson, and Henington (1997)	41 graduate student consultants; 41 consultees, primarily general education teachers (PII only)	Study the relationship between consultant use of different types of questions and consultee evaluations of consultant effectiveness	Behavioral	A researcher-devised, question-centered coding system that examined open vs. closed questions; elicitors; and acceptance or nonacceptance of consultant questions by consultee	(a) Using frequency (rather than percentage) data, consultee evaluations of consultant effectiveness positively correlated with the number of consultee accepted questions and consultant inference questions (b) The few significant findings were attributed to the fact consultants need to be responsive rather than prescriptive
Erchul et al. (1999)	4 graduate student consultants; 4 teacher consultees; 4 parent consultees (all mothers) (CPII, CPAI, CTEI)	Examine the patterns of relational communication within CBC	Conjoint behavioral	Heatherington and Friedlander (1987)	Consultants and consultees demonstrated similar levels of domineeringness and dominance
Grissom, Erchul, and Sheridan (2003)	16 graduate student consultants; 23 teachers (primarily regular education); 20 parents, (primarily mothers) (CPII only)	Examine the relationship between relational control and outcomes of CBC	Conjoint behavioral	Heatherington and Friedlander (1987)	Parent dominance associated with less-favorable outcomes

Dyadic Behavioral Consultation With Teachers

Erchul (1987) utilized a modified version of the Rogers and Farace (1975) coding system in an investigation of the nature of interpersonal control within behavioral consultation (BC). Erchul studied eight BC cases, each of which was comprised of three interviews: problem identification interview (PII), problem analysis interview (PAI), and problem evaluation interview (PEI). Domineeringness and dominance scores for each consultant and consultee were calculated based on the RCCCS control codes assigned to each message. Consultees completed the Consultant Evaluation Form (CEF) at the conclusion of consultation, which assessed their perceptions of consultant effectiveness. With respect to the nature of interpersonal control, results indicated that (a) consultants demonstrated higher domineeringness and dominance scores across the three interviews than did consultees, (b) consultee domineeringness scores correlated −.81 with consultant perceptions of consultee willingness to collect baseline data, and (c) consultant dominance scores correlated .65 with CEF scores. (This last result, marginally significant at $p < .08$, was found to be significant at a conventional alpha level of .05 in 1990 by Erchul and Schulte, who used a larger sample that afforded greater statistical power.) From these findings, Erchul concluded that (a) consultants were in control of the process of BC; (b) consultees with high levels of domineeringness were perceived by consultants as less willing to participate in baseline data collection, an important BC activity; and (c) consultants with high levels of dominance were rated as more effective by consultees.

A second study examining interpersonal control within BC was conducted by Erchul and Chewning (1990) using the Folger and Puck (1976) request-centered relational communication coding system. The Folger and Puck system analyzes the requests made by Person A (e.g., questions, instructions) and the nature of the response by Person B (e.g., acceptance, rejection). Based on the results of Erchul (1987), the authors hypothesized that consultants would make more requests than consultees, thus appearing more in control of the process of consultation; consultees were hypothesized to be accepting and cooperative as related to the nature of their requests and responses. The authors coded 30 BC interviews (i.e., 10 BC cases, each consisting of the PII, PAI, and PEI) by assigning the following codes: Bids (or requests) were coded as dominant, dominant-affiliative, or submissive; responses were coded as accepted, rejected, or evaded. Following the PEI, consultees completed the CEF. The results supported Erchul and Chewning's hypotheses for both consultant and consultee verbal behavior. With respect to the nature of requests, consultants averaged 93.5 requests across the three BC interviews, compared with an average of 15 requests for consultees. The results also indicated that, during the PII, consultee bids were moderately and negatively correlated with consultation outcomes (e.g., CEF) in 11 of 12 correlations. The authors noted that although only two of the correlations were statistically significant, a consistent pattern was evident that linked consultee requests to less-positive outcomes. Erchul and Chewning concluded that the relationship between consultants and consultees should be considered cooperative instead of collaborative, as characterized by consultees following the lead of consultants.

In a third study, Witt, Erchul, McKee, Pardue, and Wickstrom (1991) extended this line of research by examining the relationship between topic determination and outcomes of BC. The researchers were specifically interested in analyzing whether consultants and consultees exhibited equal control when determining topics during consultation, a pattern that would appear to support the presence of collaboration in consultation. The data consisted of eight BC cases, each comprised of the three BC interviews. The interviews were transcribed, and each message was coded as either topic following or topic initiation. Two additional variables were further derived for each participant: topic determination and topic continuation. *Topic determination* is an indicator of a person's success in changing the topic, and *topic continuation* is a person's acceptance of the topic without attempts to change it. The three outcome measures used were the CEF (Erchul, 1987); a single-item consultant rating of the consultee's willingness to collect baseline data; and a single-item consultant rating of the consultee's willingness to implement the treatment plan.

The results indicated that, with respect to topic determination, consultants successfully changed the topic 78% of the time, and consultees successfully changed the topic 58% of the time. To assess whether the statistical difference in topic determination had an effect on outcomes, the researchers conducted a series of correlational analyses. These analyses indicated that consultant topic determination was positively associated with both consultant and consultee perceptions of favorable outcomes, whereas consultee topic determination demonstrated less-positive associations with outcome measures.

Martens, Erchul, and Witt (1992) compared four verbal interaction coding systems used within school consultation research. The coding systems studied were Bergan and Tombari's (1975) Consultation Analysis Record (CAR), Folger and Puck's (1976) request-centered coding system, Rogers and Farace's (1975) RCCCS, and Tracey and Ray's (1984) topic following-topic initiation coding system. Because the origin of each of these coding systems (with the exception of the CAR) was in an area other than consultation, the authors' purpose was to describe the use of these coding systems within school consultation research. To generate transcripts, four consultants completed BC cases with consultees. The PII for each case was then coded using all four coding schemes.

Before summarizing Martens et al.'s (1992) results, a brief description of each coding system is presented. The CAR (Bergan & Tombari, 1975) was developed as a content coding system to assess consultant effectiveness. Four coding categories are used: content (e.g., background environment, plan); process (e.g., summarization, validation); source (speaker); and control (elicitor, emitter). Each message is coded independently of other messages; therefore, the CAR is considered nonrelational in nature. As described in this chapter, the second coding system, the RCCCS, was originally developed within the field of speech communication to research relational control within marital dyads. Paired messages are studied in an effort to reveal the form and process, rather than the content, of the communication across time. The third coding system, Folger and Puck's (1976) request-centered relational coding system, was also developed by speech communication researchers. Within this system, only messages that are requests (i.e., bids) and responses to these requests are relevant. As noted in the Erchul and Chewning (1990) study description, requests are coded as (a) dominant or submissive and (b) affiliative or hostile; responses are coded as accepted, rejected, or evaded. The fourth coding system was Tracey and Ray's (1984) topic following-topic initiation coding system, which involves coding each message as either following the preceding topic or initiating a new topic. As noted, the relational aspect is revealed when these descriptors are translated into two variables: (a) topic determination, which indicates the success of a speaker in changing topics; and (b) topic continuation, which indicates that neither speaker is seeking control of the topic.

Martens et al.'s (1992) results of the comparisons among the four coding systems were generally consistent in describing the interpersonal processes occurring during school consultation. Specifically, the coding systems indicated that consultants successfully control the consultative relationship by asking questions that are polite and mainly focus on the child. Consultants also are more likely to initiate topic changes while also offering additional statements that summarize or validate consultee input. Consultee participation during consultation was described as passive, based on the infrequency of questions posed and lower frequency of successful topic changes. The authors concluded that these coding systems provide a reliable and useful means to study interpersonal communication within school consultation.

Erchul, Covington, Hughes, and Meyers (1995) extended the work of Erchul and Chewning (1990) by again using the Folger and Puck (1976) request-centered relational coding system. However, they included a larger set of consultants and studied the verbal processes occurring only during the initial consultation interview. Based on the findings reported by Erchul and Chewning, the authors hypothesized that (a) consultee requests (bids) would be associated with negative consultation outcomes, and (b) consultant requests would be associated with positive outcomes. The initial interviews completed by 26 consultants were coded using the Folger and Puck (1976) coding system. The consultation outcome measure was the CEF (Erchul, 1987). No significant correlations were found when analyzing the complete data set, and the authors offered two hypotheses for the lack of significant findings. First, compared to Erchul and Chewning's consultants and consultees, both consultants and consultees in this study were more controlling. Therefore, consultees may have relinquished control by using submissive bids rather than completely refraining from using bids, a pattern that would result in a more controlling style.

Second, the consultants received their training from one of three different university programs, which may have affected the manner in which a problem-solving model of school consultation was implemented. To address this possible explanation, Erchul et al. (1995) isolated 14 cases for which consultants reported using the BC model, either mostly or exclusively. Analyzing this subset of cases, the authors reported two key findings. First, the percentage of consultant dominant bids (characterized mostly by instructions) was negatively associated with CEF scores, $r = -.67$, $p = .008$, suggesting that consultees may have considered consultants who told them what to do as less effective. Second, the percentage of consultant dominant-affiliative bids was positively associated with CEF scores ($r = .52$, $p = .027$), which provided support for the authors' hypothesis that consultant requests would be associated with positive outcomes. Erchul et al. noted that the results pertaining to this subset of self-identified behavioral consultants suggest that consultant effectiveness and its relation to verbal behavior may differ among consultation models. Based on their overall findings (i.e., all 26 cases), the authors concluded that consultation "appears to involve a cooperative, give-and-take type of relationship" (p. 630).

Although they did not use a recognized relational communication coding scheme, Hughes, Erchul, Yoon, Jackson, and Henington (1997) were clearly influenced by relational communication principles in their study of consultant questioning and its association with consultation outcomes. Recognizing that asking questions is a primary way that behavioral consultants direct the problem-solving process, Hughes et al. developed a system that codes only consultant questions and consultee responses to them. Specifically, their coding system categorizes questions as (a) open versus closed (format); (b) specific types of elicitors (cf. Bergan & Tombari, 1975) (process); and (c) accepted or nonaccepted by consultee (response) (cf. Folger & Puck, 1976). The researchers hypothesized that consultee positive evaluations of consultant effectiveness would be related to the occurrence of three consultant question types: open ended, inference (a specific CAR category), and accepted.

Drawing on a database of 41 PIIs conducted by graduate student consultants, Hughes et al. (1997) found no support for their hypotheses when correlations based on percentage data were computed. Using frequency data, however, consultee evaluations of consultant effectiveness were significantly correlated with the number of (a) consultant questions accepted by consultees ($r = .32$) and (b) consultant inference questions ($r = .35$), thus lending support to two of their hypotheses. The authors concluded that much verbal process-outcome school consultation research has produced relatively small and inconsistent correlations between variables of interest, in part because consultants need to be responsive to consultees' needs rather than prescriptive in an absolute sense to be effective in their role. Hughes et al.'s explanation argues strongly for the use of a dyadic or interpersonal research perspective (Erchul, Hughes, Meyers, Hickman, & Braden, 1992), which is embodied in relational communication approaches (e.g., consultant dominance is dependent on how a consultee responds to a consultant on a message-by-message basis).

Conjoint Behavioral Consultation With Teachers and Parents

As CBC (Sheridan et al., 1996) became more prominent during the 1990s, a logical research direction was to examine the verbal processes within CBC. CBC is similar in format to BC but involves adding a parent or guardian to the consultation process. Unlike BC, the goals of CBC extend beyond invoking immediate client change to enhancing relationships between parents and teachers and supporting home-school partnerships. Two CBC studies that have applied concepts of relational communication are briefly reviewed here (for more information, see Sheridan, Clarke, & Burt, chapter 9, this volume).

Erchul et al. (1999) conducted the initial study investigating patterns of relational communication within CBC. The coding system employed was the family relational communication coding system (FRCCCS; Heatherington & Friedlander, 1987), which was developed for use with a group of speakers and is an extension of the Rogers and Farace (1975) coding system. Four CBC cases were conducted, and the three conjoint interviews (CPII, CPAI, CTEI [conjoint treatment evaluation interview]) for each case were coded with the FRCCCS. Domineeringness and dominance scores were calculated for each consultant and consultee (i.e., teacher, parent) to measure the nature of relational control within CBC. The results suggested the consultants and consultees demonstrated similar levels of domineeringness and dominance during CBC, which differed from results of previous teacher-only BC research that included more controlling consultant verbal behavior (cf. Erchul, 1987). As the authors noted, this study presented only a description of relational communication within CBC and did not attempt to link verbal processes to outcomes.

Grissom, Erchul, and Sheridan (2003) furthered the work of Erchul et al. (1999) by examining the relationship between relational control and CBC outcomes. Twenty CPIIs were coded using the FRCCCS, and domineeringness and dominance scores were calculated for consultants and consultees. The outcome measures used were the Behavior Intervention Rating Scale (Elliott & Von Brock Treuting, 1991; Von Brock & Elliott, 1987); CEF (Erchul, 1987); and Goal Attainment Scaling (Kiresuk, Smith, & Cardillo, 1994). Results indicated that parent dominance was associated with less-favorable outcomes of CBC. The authors noted that future CBC research may benefit from further examining the nature of parental control within CBC interviews.

In summary, research examining relational communication within school consultation has provided a unique perspective on the verbal processes of this professional helping relationship. The results of studies that have focused on dyadic BC with teachers have generally demonstrated that consultants control or direct the process of consultation. Furthermore, this pattern of consultant relational control has been associated with more favorable social validity outcomes (e.g., consultant effectiveness as measured by the CEF). Interestingly, the patterns of relational communication within CBC are somewhat different, though less research exists that documents these phenomena. The results of the extant literature suggest that consultants within CBC appear less dominant than consultants in teacher-only BC, and consultee verbal behavior appears to be an important area of interest for future research.

Before moving on, it is important to acknowledge that this relational communication-based consultation research has been the major impetus for the "collaboration debate" within consultation (Erchul, 1999; Gutkin, 1999a, 1999b; Schulte & Osborne, 2003). In particular, Gutkin (1999b) has offered alternative explanations of the results of studies conducted by Erchul and his colleagues by reinterpreting the results to describe relationships within consultation as "collaborative." However, as noted by Erchul (1999), variables associated with relational communication (e.g., domineeringness, dominance) are well operationalized, while other terminology introduced into this debate (e.g., collaboration itself) has yet to be defined sufficiently for the purpose of conducting scientific research or is defined in different ways by different researchers (Schulte & Osborne, 2003). The subtleties associated with this debate clearly highlight the complex and challenging nature of this research.

what do you think are strengths? limitations?

A Critique of the Relational Communication Perspective as Applied to School Consultation Research

strengths Several strengths can be noted with respect to applying a relational communication perspective to school consultation research. First, this perspective is rooted in theory and concepts that have been the objects of considerable study by researchers in social science disciplines as varied as anthropology and communication. This cross-pollination of ideas is beneficial to a field such as school psychology, which some regard as insular. Second, the relational communication literature supplies well-defined constructs that allow for the microanalysis of actual behaviors occurring during consultation. In particular, this perspective operationalizes influence attempts on a message-by-message level, a characteristic unmatched by any other methodology used to date in consultation research. Third, the relational communication coding systems that have been applied to study consultation interviews present excellent reliability and adequate validity (Martens et al., 1992). Fourth, as stated with respect to the social power base framework, a relational communication perspective succeeds in taking the focus off the individual and places it on dyadic (i.e., BC) and small group (i.e., CBC) contexts. The net gain is that an interpersonal research perspective is then realized (Erchul et al., 1992).

limitations Several limitations in applying a relational communication perspective to school consultation research also are apparent. First, it is a somewhat obscure perspective that is not well known outside the field of speech communication. Perhaps this is the main reason why some contributors to the consultation literature have found the constructs of domineeringness and dominance to be unacceptable in their original form (cf. Erchul et al., 1999). Second, the relational communication perspective focuses exclusively on how verbal behavior unfolds, which is just one of several aspects of interpersonal communication that is relevant to school consultation. Third, Erchul and Schulte's (1990) finding that the PII represents a psychometrically defensible sampling of verbal behavior when one is studying relational communication within consultation may have had the unintended effect of limiting the focus of consultation research to its early stages (e.g., problem identification). Obviously, other stages are important and require research attention. Fourth, given its anthropological roots, the nature of a relational communication research perspective lends itself more readily to correlational rather than experimental designs, which results in a lowered ability to draw firm conclusions about causal relationships. A final weakness parallels one mentioned regarding the social power base perspective — with the inclusion to date of only social validity outcomes, relational communication-based consultation research has yet to make a significant contribution to the EBI literature.

Future Research Agenda: What We Need to Know

The second half of this chapter has presented a brief history of relational communication as well as a detailed review and critique of its current application to school consultation research. The initial work of Erchul and his colleagues in traditional BC (Bergan & Kratochwill, 1990) demonstrated that the verbal behavior of consultants differs from that of consultees, with consultants displaying greater control of the process of BC. These research studies further documented that consultant control is associated with more positive social validity outcomes (e.g., consultant effectiveness), with additional (but more limited) evidence indicating that consultee relational control is associated with more negative social validity outcomes. As this work extended to CBC (Sheridan et al., 1996), new patterns of relational control emerged, suggesting that the addition of parents as consultees changes the nature of relational communication within consultation.

We pose the following issues for future investigations of school consultation that employ a relational communication perspective:

1. As noted, the relational communication coding systems that have been applied to consultation thus far have focused nearly exclusively on the dominance-submission/control dimension, yet relational communication encompasses more than this single dimension. For instance, trust and intimacy (Millar & Rogers, 1976) as well as similarity/dissimilarity, formality/informality, and task orientation/social orientation (Hale, Burgoon, & Householder, 2005) are regarded as themes within an expanded view of relational communication and could form the basis for future research in school consultation.

2. Because of the historical focus on the control dimension, consultation studies that have employed the RCCCS or FRCCCS have analyzed only one-up ($\uparrow$) and one-down ($\downarrow$) messages. Escudero and Rogers (2004), however, have indicated the value of one-across ($\rightarrow$) messages in forming "conflict regulators" and "mechanisms for introducing solutions in therapeutic situations" (p. 72). In particular, they have highlighted one-across, one-down ($\rightarrow\downarrow$) transactions as potentially representing episodes in which Person A offers information about a conflict or relational issue in a leveling, neutralizing way, and then Person B accepts this idea or suggestion. Thus, the study of these one-across, one-down leveling negotiation episodes within school consultation may prove to be fruitful.

3. Although consultation studies that draw on a relational communication framework have done well in documenting paired message sequences (e.g., dominance), they have not attempted to map transactional patterns that unfold over longer periods of time. Consequently, it will be important for future consultation researchers to consider using computer programs such as the Sequential Data Interchange Standard-Generalized Sequential Courier (SDIS-GSEQ; Bakeman & Quera, 1995) to analyze longer streams of data to better understand the relational dynamics of school consultation.

4. It has been over 30 years since the CAR (Bergan & Tombari, 1975) was first published, and it is perhaps the most well-known system for coding verbal interactions in school consultation. Because the CAR has a nonrelational orientation (i.e., each message is coded independently of other messages), it may be worthwhile to take the CAR's best features and merge them with a relational communication coding system (e.g., RCCCS) to form a more comprehensive tool to assess verbal interactions in consultation.

5. Despite the past and present emphasis on the application of quantitative methods to study relational communication, we agree with Escudero and Rogers (2004), who noted that qualitative and mixed-method approaches reflect a valuable research direction. As a result, many of the ideas proposed by Meyers, Truscott, Meyers, Varjas, and Collins (chapter 5, this volume) are important to consider with respect to future work in this area.

Ultimately, both perspectives reviewed in this chapter are concerned with making sense of human relationships. Therefore, borrowing from Conoley and Conoley's (1981) notion of "prescriptive consultation," we advance one overarching question: What relational dynamics that develop in consultant/consultee relationships result in the most favorable outcomes for all participants in consultation? Addressing this question within social power base and relational communication perspectives, and employing quantitative, qualitative, and mixed-method designs, will keep consultation researchers active for many years to come.

CONCLUSION: POWER OUTCOME AND THE SECOND PARADOX OF SCHOOL PSYCHOLOGY

The reason school consultants should strive to understand and incorporate social power and relational communication concepts into their daily practice is to make consultees more powerful and influential in dealing with their clients (Erchul & Martens, 2002). Consequently, in terms of power outcome (Olson & Cromwell, 1975), the overall aim of the two perspectives reviewed here is to make consultees the "ultimate victors" (Erchul, 1992b, p. 442). In so doing, consultees — be they parents, teachers, or other school staff — will be better equipped to positively effect change in the academic and social behaviors of the child and adolescent clients they directly serve.

As Martin (1978) pointed out, however, endorsing a social power/influence perspective often creates cognitive dissonance for school consultants because it appears antithetical to their professional training, which often has promoted a consultation approach emphasizing concepts such as "helping" and "collaboration" more than effecting consultee behavior change. For a variety of reasons, others (e.g., Brown, 1993; Gutkin, 1999b; Henning-Stout, 1993) have voiced objections to a conceptualization of school consultation that explicitly promotes an awareness of social power and interpersonal influence. Standing in stark contrast to these opinions are findings of empirical investigations that indicate successful consultation outcomes do not just magically occur; rather, positive results are often achieved when the consultee is regarded as a target of behavior change. Research studies illustrating this point include the impact of (a) consultant performance feedback given to consultees on treatment implementation and client outcomes (e.g., Noell et al., 2005) and (b) consultant negative reinforcement given to consultees on treatment implementation (DiGennaro, Martens, & McIntyre, 2005). Given this emerging research literature, it is clear that the modern practice of school consultation requires one to look more closely at how adult (i.e., consultee) behavior can be changed to implement EBIs with integrity.

We began this chapter by mentioning the paradox of school psychology (Conoley & Gutkin, 1986), noting how it led to the conduct of much of the research subsequently reviewed. Taking stock of the field 22 years later, we conclude by proposing the second paradox of school psychology:

> Although school psychologists have the potential to influence and thereby change the behavior of consultees, many are reluctant to recognize and exercise this influence, and as a result the effectiveness of consultation is not maximized.

Given the reality of delivering school consultation services under the Individuals With Disabilities Education Act 2004 (Pub. L. 108-446) — especially with its response-to-intervention component — a traditional, passive consult-and-hope approach is naïve and no longer defensible. However, we are confident that school psychologists and other school-based consultants will act to resolve the second paradox, resulting in the delivery of effective school consultation services in this new era of practice.

ACKNOWLEDGMENT

We wish to thank Bertram H. Raven and L. Edna Rogers for reviewing this chapter prior to publication. It was an honor to have Professors Raven and Rogers, pioneers in the areas of social power bases and relational communication, respectively, examine our application of concepts from these literatures to school consultation research. Any remaining errors of fact or interpretation are clearly ours.

NOTE

1. When interpreting social power bases through the lens of Raven's (1992, 1993) power/interaction model of interpersonal influence, it is more accurate to refer to individual power bases as power strategies (B. H. Raven, personal communication, February 18, 2004). However, to maintain consistency with related work in the school psychology literature, we have chosen to use the term *bases* throughout this chapter.

REFERENCES

Allport, G. W. (1985). The historical background of social psychology. In G. Lindzey & E. Aronson (Eds.), *The handbook of social psychology* (3rd ed., Vol. 1, pp. 1–46). New York: Random House.

Bakeman, R., & Quera, V. (1995). *Analyzing interaction: Sequential analysis with SDIS and GSEQ.* New York: Cambridge University Press.

Bateson, G. (1935). Culture contact and schismogenesis. *Man, 35,* 178–183.

Bateson, G. (1958). *Naven* (2nd ed.). Stanford, CA: Stanford University Press.

Bateson, G., Jackson, D. D., Haley, J., & Weakland, J. (1956). Toward a theory of schizophrenia. *Behavioral Science, 1,* 251–264.

Bergan, J. R. & Kratochwill, T. R. (1990). *Behavioral consultation and therapy.* New York: Plenum.

Bergan, J. R., & Tombari, M. L. (1975). The analysis of verbal interactions occurring during consultation. *Journal of School Psychology, 13,* 209–226.

Brown, D. (1993). Defining human service consultation. In J. E. Zins, T. R. Kratochwill, & S. N. Elliott (Eds.), *Handbook of consultation services for children: Applications in educational and clinical settings* (pp. 46–64). San Francisco: Jossey-Bass.

Cienki, J. A. (1982). Teachers' perception of consultation as a function of consultants' use of expert and referent power (Doctoral dissertation, University of Pennsylvania). *Dissertation Abstracts International, 43* (3-A), 725.

Coch, L., & French, J. R. P. (1948). Overcoming resistance to change. *Human Relations, 1,* 512–532.

Conoley, J. C., & Conoley, C. W. (1981). Toward prescriptive consultation. In J. C. Conoley (Ed.), *Consultation in schools: Theory, research, procedures* (pp. 265–293). New York: Academic Press.

Conoley, J. C., & Gutkin, T. B. (1986). School psychology: A reconceptualization of service delivery realities. In S. N. Elliott & J. C. Witt (Eds.), *The delivery of psychological services in schools: Concepts, processes, and issues* (pp. 393–424). Hillsdale, NJ: Erlbaum.

Courtright, J. A., Millar, F. E., & Rogers-Millar, L. E. (1979). Domineeringness and dominance: Replication and expansion. *Communication Monographs, 46,* 179–192.

Crowe, D. S. (1982). Effects of expert and referent power in the consultation process (Doctoral dissertation, University of Georgia). *Dissertation Abstracts International, 43,* 1887A.

Daly, J. A., & Wiemann, J. M. (Eds.). (1994). *Strategic interpersonal communication.* Hillsdale, NJ: Erlbaum.

DiGennaro, F. D., Martens, B. K., & McIntyre, L. L. (2005). Increasing treatment integrity through negative reinforcement: Effects on teacher and student behavior. *School Psychology Review, 34,* 220–231.

Duncan, H. D. (1967). The search for a social theory of communication in American sociology. In F. E. X. Dance (Ed.), *Human communication theory* (pp. 236–263). New York: Holt, Rinehart & Winston.

Elliott, S. N., & Von Brock Treuting, M. (1991). The Behavior Intervention Rating Scale: Development and validation of a pretreatment acceptability and effectiveness measure. *Journal of School Psychology, 29,* 43–51.

Erchul, W. P. (1987). A relational communication analysis of control in school consultation. *Professional School Psychology, 2,* 113–124.

Erchul, W. P. (1992a). On dominance, cooperation, teamwork, and collaboration in school-based consultation. *Journal of Educational and Psychological Consultation, 3,* 363–366.

Erchul, W. P. (1992b). Social psychological perspectives on the school psychologist's involvement with parents. In F. J. Medway & T. P. Cafferty (Eds.), *School psychology: A social psychological perspective* (pp. 425–448). Hillsdale, NJ: Erlbaum.

Erchul, W. P. (1999). Two steps forward, one step back: Collaboration in school-based consultation. *Journal of School Psychology, 37*, 191–203.

Erchul, W. P., & Chewning, T. G. (1990). Behavioral consultation from a request-centered relational communication perspective. *School Psychology Quarterly, 5*, 1–20.

Erchul, W. P., Covington, C. G., Hughes, J. N., & Meyers, J. (1995). Further explorations of request-centered relational communication within school consultation. *School Psychology Review, 24*, 621–632.

Erchul, W. P., Hughes, J. N., Meyers, J., Hickman, J. A., & Braden, J. P. (1992). Dyadic agreement concerning the consultation process and its relationship to outcome. *Journal of Educational and Psychological Consultation, 3*, 119–132.

Erchul, W. P., & Martens, B. K. (2002). *School consultation: Conceptual and empirical bases of practice* (2nd ed.). New York: Kluwer Academic/Plenum.

Erchul, W. P., & Raven, B. H. (1997). Social power in school consultation: A contemporary view of French and Raven's bases of power model. *Journal of School Psychology, 35*, 137–171.

Erchul, W. P., Raven, B. H., & Ray, A. G. (2001). School psychologists' perceptions of social power bases in teacher consultation. *Journal of Educational and Psychological Consultation, 12*, 1–23.

Erchul, W. P., Raven, B. H., & Whichard, S. M. (2001). School psychologists and teacher perceptions of social power bases in school consultation. *Journal of School Psychology, 39*, 483–497.

Erchul, W. P., Raven, B. H., & Wilson, K. E. (2004). The relationship between gender of consultant and social power perceptions within school consultation. *School Psychology Review, 33*, 582–590.

Erchul, W. P., & Schulte, A. C. (1990). The coding of consultation verbalizations: How much is enough? *School Psychology Quarterly, 5*, 256–264.

Erchul, W. P., Sheridan, S. M., Ryan, D. A., Grissom, P. F., Killough, C. E., & Mettler, D. W. (1999). Patterns of relational communication in conjoint behavioral consultation. *School Psychology Quarterly, 14*, 121–147.

Escudero, V., & Rogers, L. E. (2004). Analyzing relational communication. In L. E. Rogers & V. Escudero (Eds.), *Relational communication: An interactional perspective to the study of process and form* (pp. 51–79). Mahwah, NJ: Erlbaum.

Evidence-Based Intervention Work Group. (2005). Theories of change and adoption of innovations: The evolving evidence-based intervention and practice movement in school psychology. *Psychology in the Schools, 42*, 475–494.

Folger, J. P., & Puck, S. (1976, April). *Coding relational communication: A question approach*. Paper presented at the meeting of the International Communication Association, Portland, OR.

French, J. R. P., & Raven, B. H. (1959). The bases of social power. In D. Cartwright (Ed.), *Studies in social power* (pp. 150–167). Ann Arbor, MI: Institute for Social Research.

Grissom, P. F., Erchul, W. P., & Sheridan, S. M. (2003). Relationships among relational communication processes and perceptions of outcomes in conjoint behavioral consultation. *Journal of Educational and Psychological Consultation, 14*, 157–180.

Gutkin, T. B. (1996). Patterns of consultant and consultee verbalizations: Examining communication leadership during initial consultation interviews. *Journal of School Psychology, 34*, 199–219.

Gutkin, T. B. (1997, August). *Collaborative versus directive/expert school-based consultation: Reviewing and resolving a false dichotomy*. Paper presented at the annual convention of the American Psychological Association, Chicago, IL.

Gutkin, T. B. (1999a). The collaboration debate: Finding our way through the maze: Moving forward into the future: A response to Erchul (1999). *Journal of School Psychology, 37*, 229–241.

Gutkin, T. B. (1999b). Collaborative versus directive/prescriptive/expert school-based consultation: Reviewing and resolving a false dichotomy. *Journal of School Psychology, 37*, 161–190.

Gutkin, T. B., & Conoley, J. C. (1990). Reconceptualizing school psychology from a service delivery perspective: Implications for practice, training, and research. *Journal of School Psychology, 28*, 203–223.

Hale, J. L., Burgoon, J. K., & Householder, B. (2005). The Relational Communication Scale. In V. L. Manusov (Ed.), *The sourcebook of nonverbal measures: Going beyond words* (pp. 127–139). Mahwah, NJ: Erlbaum.

Heatherington, L., & Friedlander, M. L. (1987). *Family Relational Communication Control Coding System coding manual*. Unpublished manuscript. Williams College, Williamstown, MA.

Henning-Stout, M. (1993). Theoretical and empirical bases of consultation. In J. E. Zins, T. R. Kratochwill, & S. N. Elliott (Eds.), *Handbook of consultation services for children: Applications in educational and clinical settings* (pp. 15–45). San Francisco: Jossey-Bass.

Hinkin, T. R., & Schriesheim, C. A. (1989). Development and application of new scales to measure the French and Raven (1959) bases of social power. *Journal of Applied Psychology, 74*, 561–567.

Hughes, J. N. (1992). Social psychological foundations of consultation. In F. J. Medway & T. P. Cafferty (Eds.), *School psychology: A social psychological perspective* (pp. 269–303). Hillsdale, NJ: Erlbaum.

Hughes, J. N., Erchul, W. P., Yoon, J., Jackson, T., & Henington, C. (1997). Consultant use of questions and its relationship to consultee evaluation of effectiveness. *Journal of School Psychology, 35*, 281–297.

Kinsala, M. G. (1985). An investigation of variables affecting perceived consultation outcome: A utilization of expert and referent power theory (Doctoral dissertation, Texas Women's University). *Dissertation Abstracts International, 45*, 3922B.

Kiresuk, T. J., Smith, A., & Cardillo, J. E. (1994). *Goal attainment scaling: Applications, theory, and measurement.* Hillsdale, NJ: Erlbaum.

Knoff, H. M., Hines, C. V., & Kromrey, J. D. (1995). Finalizing the Consultant Effectiveness Scale: An analysis and validation of the characteristics of effective consultants. *School Psychology Review, 24*, 480–496.

Koslowsky, M., Schwarzwald, J., & Ashuri, S. (2001). On the relationship between subordinates' compliance to power sources and organizational attitudes. *Applied Psychology: An International Review, 50*, 455–476.

Kratochwill, T. R., & Stoiber, K. C. (2002). Evidence-based interventions in school psychology: Conceptual foundations of the *Procedural and Coding Manual of Division 16 and the Society for the Study of School Psychology Task Force. School Psychology Quarterly, 17*, 341–389.

Kruger, R. H. (1984). The effects of problem-related stress, consultant's approach, and consultant's source of social power on teacher reactions to behavioral consultation (Doctoral dissertation, University of Cincinnati, 1983). *Dissertation Abstracts International, 44*, 3637A–3638A.

Lambert, N. M. (1973). The school psychologist as a source of power and influence. *Journal of School Psychology, 11*, 245–250.

Marrow, A. J., & French, J. R. P. (1945). Changing a stereotype in industry. *Journal of Social Issues, 2*, 33–37.

Martens, B. K., Erchul, W. P., & Witt, J. C. (1992). Quantifying verbal interactions in school-based consultation: A comparison of four coding schemes. *School Psychology Review, 21*, 109–124.

Martens, B. K., Kelly, S. Q., & Diskin, M. T. (1996). The effects of two sequential-request strategies on teachers' acceptability and use of a classroom intervention. *Journal of Educational and Psychological Consultation, 7*, 211–221.

Martin, R. (1978). Expert and referent power: A framework for understanding and maximizing consultation effectiveness. *Journal of School Psychology, 16*, 49–55.

Martin, R., & Curtis, M. (1980). Effects of age and experience of consultant and consultee on consultation outcome. *American Journal of Community Psychology, 8*, 733–736.

Millar, F. E., & Rogers, L. E. (1976). A relational approach to interpersonal communication. In G. R. Miller (Ed.), *Explorations in interpersonal communication* (pp. 87–103). Beverly Hills, CA: Sage.

Mintzberg, H. (1983). *Power in and around organizations.* Englewood Cliffs, NJ: Prentice Hall.

Noell, G. H., Witt, J. C., Slider, N. J., Connell, J. E., Gatti, S. L., Williams, K. L., et al. (2005). Treatment implementation following behavioral consultation in schools: A comparison of three follow-up strategies. *School Psychology Review, 34*, 87–106.

O'Keefe, D. J., & Medway, F. J. (1997). The application of persuasion research to consultation in school psychology. *Journal of School Psychology, 35*, 173–193.

Olson, D. H., & Cromwell, R. E. (1975). Power in families. In R. E. Cromwell & D. H. Olson (Eds.), *Power in families* (pp. 3–11). Beverly Hills, CA: Sage.

Parks, M. R. (1977). Relational communication: Theory and research. *Human Communication Research, 3*, 372–381.

Pierro, A., De Grada, E., Raven, B. H., & Kruglanski, A. W. (2004). Fonti, antecedentie conguenti del potere organizzativi: l'Interpersonal Power/Interaction Model. In A. Pierro (Ed.), *Potere e leadership* (pp. 33–58). Rome: Carocci.

Podsakoff, P. M., & Schriesheim, C. A. (1985). Field studies of French and Raven's bases of power: Critique, reanalysis, and suggestions for future research. *Psychological Bulletin, 97*, 387–411.

Raven, B. H. (1965). Social influence and power. In I. D. Steiner & M. Fishbein (Eds.), *Current studies in social psychology* (pp. 371–382). New York: Holt, Rinehart & Winston.

Raven, B. H. (1992). A power/interaction model of interpersonal influence: French and Raven 30 years later. *Journal of Social Behavior and Personality, 7*, 217–244.

Raven, B. H. (1993). The bases of power: Origins and recent developments. *Journal of Social Issues, 49,* 227–251.

Raven, B. H., Schwarzwald, J., & Koslowsky, M. (1998). Conceptualizing and measuring a power/interaction model of interpersonal influence. *Journal of Applied Social Psychology, 28,* 307–332.

Roberts, L. A. (1985). School psychological consultation outcomes and perception of consultant power base (Doctoral dissertation, University of Connecticut, 1984). *Dissertation Abstracts International, 46,* 382A.

Rogers, L. E., & Escudero, V. (Eds.). (2004). *Relational communication: An interactional perspective to the study of process and form.* Mahwah, NJ: Erlbaum.

Rogers, L. E., & Farace, R. V. (1975). Analysis of relational communication in dyads: New measurement procedures. *Human Communication Research, 1,* 222–239.

Rogers-Millar, L. E., & Millar, F. (1979). Domineeringness and dominance: A transactional view. *Human Communication Research, 5,* 238–246.

Ruesch, J. (1973). *Therapeutic communication.* New York: Norton.

Schulte, A. C., & Osborne, S. S. (2003). When assumptive worlds collide: A review of definitions of collaboration in consultation. *Journal of Educational and Psychological Consultation, 14,* 109–138.

Schwarzwald, J., Koslowsky, M., & Agassi, V. (2001). Captain's leadership type and police officers' compliance to power bases. *European Journal of Work and Organizational Psychology, 10,* 273–290.

Schwarzwald, J., Koslowsky, M., & Ochana-Levin, T. (2004). Usage of and compliance with power tactics in routine versus nonroutine work settings. *Journal of Business and Psychology, 18,* 385–402.

Sheridan, S. M., Kratochwill, T. R., & Bergan, J. R. (1996). *Conjoint behavioral consultation: A procedural manual.* New York: Plenum.

Short, R. J., Moore, S. C., & Williams, C. (1991). Social influence in consultation: Effect of degree and experience on consultees' perceptions. *Psychological Reports, 68,* 131–137.

Tracey, T. J., & Ray, P. B. (1984). Stages of successful time-limited counseling: An interactional examination. *Journal of Counseling Psychology, 31,* 13–27.

Von Brock, M. B., & Elliott, S. N. (1987). Influence of treatment effectiveness information on the acceptability of classroom interventions. *Journal of School Psychology, 25,* 131–144.

Watzlawick, P., Beavin, J. H., & Jackson, D. D. (1967). *Pragmatics of human communication: A study of interactional patterns, pathologies and paradoxes.* New York: Norton.

Witt, J. C., Erchul, W. P., McKee, W. T., Pardue, M. M., & Wickstrom, K. F. (1991). Conversational control in school-based consultation: The relationship between consultant and consultee topic determination and consultation outcome. *Journal of Educational and Psychological Consultation, 2,* 101–116.

Wosinka, W., Cialdini, R. B., Barrett, D. W., & Reykowski, J. (Eds.). (2001). *The practice of social influence in multiple cultures.* Mahwah, NJ: Erlbaum.

Zins, J. E., & Erchul, W. P. (1995). Best practices in school consultation. In A. Thomas & J. Grimes (Eds.), *Best practices in school psychology-III* (pp. 606–623). Washington, DC: National Association of School Psychologists.

15

Research Examining the Relationships Among Consultation Process, Treatment Integrity, and Outcomes

GEORGE H. NOELL

Louisiana State University

Consultation in schools can serve a diverse array of functions, including providing organizational development, staff development, professional support, and intervention development for students (Erchul & Martens, 2002; Kratochwill, Bergan, Sheridan, & Elliott, 1998; Zins, Kratochwill, & Elliott, 1993). However, even modest scrutiny of either practice or the empirical literature suggests that the predominant function of consultation in schools is to address the concerns of parents and educators regarding individual or small groups of children who are not functioning well (e.g., Fuchs & Fuchs, 1989; Sheridan, Eagle, Cowan, & Mickelson, 2001). In short, we consult primarily to intervene on behalf of students. In these cases, consultation is a vehicle for the treatment of students' academic, behavioral, and emotional concerns. A tremendous number of variables are known or hypothesized to influence the efficacy of treatments provided in educational, psychological, and social service settings. Although many variables are thought to influence treatment efficacy, one variable appears to be most definitive in its impact on treatment efficacy: treatment integrity. Treatment integrity is the degree to which an independent variable or treatment is implemented as planned (Gresham, 1989; Moncher & Prinz, 1991; Yeaton & Sechrest, 1981). To state the obvious, treatment plans that are not implemented have little chance of benefiting anyone.

Case-centered consultation focused on the treatment of referral concerns is the psychological activity, both within and outside schools, for which treatment integrity is perhaps most paramount. Due to the indirect nature of service delivery within consultation, the consultant is not the person who delivers the treatment. Thus, the efficacy of consultation as a treatment modality is dependent on the efficacy of consultants in causing others to implement effective treatments. Both surprisingly and interestingly, what is known about both causal and mediating variables for treatment integrity in school-based consultation is limited (Noell, Duhon, Gatti, & Connell, 2002; Sheridan & Gutkin, 2000). This chapter focuses on what is known and what remains unknown regarding treatment integrity within consultation.

The study of treatment integrity within consultation is a complex process that requires the clear specification of a number of conceptual distinctions. Unfortunately, our professional and scientific language has not yet developed widely accepted terms to connote these distinctions. For example, *treatment integrity* in consultation can refer to at least three different processes. First, treatment integrity can refer to the degree to which the consultant adheres to an established consultation model (e.g., Bergan & Kratochwill, 1990). Second, treatment integrity can refer to the degree to which one or more specific procedures embedded within an established consultation model (i.e., behavioral consultation) are implemented as designed by the consultant (e.g., Noell et al., 2005). In this sense, an experimental procedure is embedded in and studied within the context of an established practice. Researchers may be particularly concerned about the implementation of a performance feedback or social influence procedure as the experimental variables of interest in a study of consultation. Finally, treatment integrity can be the degree to which the consultee delivers the treatment to the client. In each of these instances, some behavior is assumed to be operationally defined, and integrity refers to the extent to which actual behavior matches this definition. In each instance, the behavior about which the match to definition (i.e., integrity) is of concern is thought to be a treatment that may in turn influence some other behavior that is also of concern.

Discussions of the implementation of independent variables and treatments within the professional literature can and have become quite clouded as a result of the use of overlapping terms such as procedural reliability, treatment integrity, and treatment fidelity. The conventions regarding terms for describing treatment integrity described next are roughly based on the work of Noell and colleagues (2005) and are used throughout this chapter. Specification of these terms at the outset is intended to facilitate clarity and simple prose. *Treatment integrity* is used to refer to the accuracy of implementation of the independent variable in an experimental study. It is also used to describe the broader professional literature focused on treatment integrity that typically is not specific to consultation. It is not used to refer to any specific process within consultation or consultation research due its conceptual ambiguity in this application. *Consultation procedural integrity* (CPI) is used to refer to the degree to which consultation procedures were implemented as designed in both practice and research contexts. In research contexts, CPI should commonly refer to the independent variable that is directly manipulated by the research team.

Treatment plan implementation (TPI) is used to describe the degree to which a treatment plan developed within consultation is implemented as designed. TPI is not an independent variable in the experimental sense of the term because it is not under the control of the experimenter in consultation research. TPI is an outcome of the consultation process, and as such it is a dependent variable. It can be argued that TPI is the most immediate and direct outcome of consultation. It often has been conceptualized as the independent variable causing child behavior change; however, that may not be the most productive or accurate conceptualization. Rather, it may be more appropriate to describe child behavior change as a second-order effect in consultation that may be moderated by a number of variables, including TPI. It is critical to remember that variables beyond TPI will influence child behavior change. For example, the degree to which the treatment plan matches the child's needs and phenomena such as regression toward the mean may influence outcome to a similar or greater extent than TPI. The general conceptualization of consultation that is discussed in this chapter is presented in Figure 15.1. This model is elaborated on in subsequent sections. In summary, in this chapter treatment integrity is used to refer to general experimental concerns, CPI is used to refer to integrity of the consultation process, and TPI refers to implementation of the treatment plan.

EMERGENCE OF TREATMENT INTEGRITY AS A PROFESSIONAL AND SCIENTIFIC CONCERN

General concern regarding treatment integrity as an epistemological issue in science occurred long before the emergence of consultation or psychological services. The central concern regarding treatment integrity in the broader scientific literature is that degradations in treatment integrity

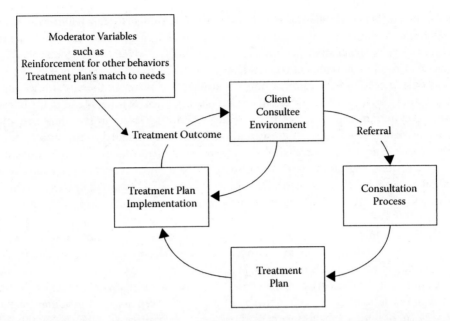

Figure 15.1   A graphic representation of the consultation process indicating major relationships that are proposed to exist and depicting the cyclical nature of many consultation cases. Hypothetically, a direct link could exist between the consultation process and child outcome if a direct service (e.g., anger management training) were part of the consultation process.

create substantial threats to the internal validity of any conclusions regarding the effect of the independent variable on the dependent variable (Gresham, 1989; Moncher & Prinz, 1991). If the independent variable did not occur or did not occur as planned, nothing can be concluded about the relationship between changes in the dependent variable and the independent variable. For example, if the dosage of gamma-radiation, fertilizer, or medication is measured and applied inaccurately in physics, agriculture, or medicine, conclusions reached regarding the effect of the independent variable on the dependent variable are likely to be spurious.

Beginning notably with Peterson, Homer, and Wonderlich (1982), a number of authors have observed the emergence of a "curious double standard" (p. 478) regarding the specification and measurement of the independent and dependent variables. More rigorous standards have been applied to the operational definition and measurement of dependent variables than independent variables. Behavioral researchers routinely provide specific operational definitions of dependent variables and reliability or observer agreement data for the measures employed. This level of precision has been extensively adopted in field-based research in psychology and behavior analysis to at least partially reduce confounds associated with fieldwork as compared to laboratory settings (Billingsley, White, & Munson, 1980). The types of mechanical and electrical recording devices that are characteristic of laboratory research are infrequently practical or relevant to field-based research. Concern regarding the precision of the measurement of dependent variables has led to an extensive scientific literature examining issues such as observer training, observational drift, reactivity, expectancy, and methods of calculating observer agreement (Haynes & O'Brien, 1999).

In contrast to dependent measures, the specification of the independent variable and assessment of its reliability have been much more limited. For example, Peterson et al.'s (1982) review of research published in the *Journal of Applied Behavior Analysis* found that 10% to 50% of articles published each year between 1968 and 1980 failed to provide an operational definition of independent variables, and that only 20% of studies assessed the integrity of treatment implementation. Two meta-analyses by Gresham and colleagues covering the years 1980 to 1990 found that the rate of operational definition of treatment was low (35% and 34.2%) and that approximately 15% (14.9% and 15.8%) of studies assessed treatment integrity in the child behavior therapy studies analyzed (Gresham, Gansle, & Noell, 1993; Gresham, Gansle, Noell, Cohen, & Rosenblum, 1993). It is worth noting that no programmatic research has emerged examining issues in the implementation of independent variables that parallels the research related to observational data collection. For example, implementation drift and the effects of expectancy on implementation have not been studied.

The classic epistemological concerns regarding treatment integrity within behavioral research are based on two fundamental concerns. First, as treatments are changed their effects are likely to change. Second, to the extent that the degree of treatment integrity is unknown, potential threats to the internal validity of any conclusions drawn from a study emerge (Billingsley et al., 1980; Peterson et al., 1982). These concerns have direct parallels in the treatment of psychological concerns, and these concerns are most pronounced in the domain of consultation because implementation of the treatment is not controlled by the consulting psychologist. At a practical level, different concerns arise regarding treatment integrity in the context of a treatment that is conducted by a trained therapist (e.g., a social skills group conducted by a psychologist) versus a treatment implemented by a parent, teacher, or both. In the former case, the issue is one of professional responsibility and an individual practicing in a controlled setting. In the latter case, the issue may be one of a novice carrying out new behaviors in complex environments with many simultaneous competing demands.

The importance of TPI in applied contexts, frequently referred to as treatment integrity, has been a focus of increasing concern in the psychological treatment literature (e.g., Lentz & Daly, 1996; Mueller, Edwards, & Trahant, 2003; Rhymer, Evans-Hampton, McCurdy, & Watson, 2002; Riley-Tillman & Chafouleas, 2003). This interest has been particularly pronounced in the treatment of childhood concerns (e.g., education, school psychology, clinical child psychology). The dominant and most strongly empirically supported treatments for childhood concerns typically require that someone other than the psychologist implement the treatment (DuPaul & Eckert, 1997; Swanson & Hoskyn, 1998; Weiss & Weisz, 1995; Weisz, Weiss, Alicke, & Klotz, 1987). These common treatments frequently have a number of components that occur throughout the day over many occasions per day or week and can be described as ecological. In these contexts, parents, teachers, or other care providers are likely to be the primary treatment agents. Numerous reports from both practice and research demonstrate that developing a plan and providing training is not sufficient to ensure accurate sustained TPI for either student-focused or classwide concerns (Happe, 1982; Noell, Witt, Gilbertson, Ranier, & Freeland, 1997; Taylor & Miller, 1997). Although the empirical literature examining TPI could be better described as emerging than well established, observations from diverse settings and types of treatments have contributed to increasing interest in TPI as a problem worthy of study.

Much of the early work focused on TPI grew out of the treatment acceptability literature. It has been argued previously and extensively that treatment acceptability is or should be related to treatment integrity (Eckert & Hintze, 2000). This conceptual linkage spawned an era of active investigation of the acceptability of treatments by varying potential consumers (Eckert & Hintze, 2000; Nastasi & Truscott, 2000). However, the hypothesized relationship, while much discussed, was not demonstrated. Although it appeared logical that high acceptability might lead to implementation, data have not emerged demonstrating this to be the case. More recent research has demonstrated that high acceptability may not be sufficient to ensure treatment implementation (Noell et al., 2005). In fact, the acceptability ratings of common psychological interventions for children may be so uniformly high and similar that acceptability has no relationship to TPI for those treatments that naturally occur.

This recent research may help clarify that TPI, like all human behavior, is a multiply determined phenomenon in which the correspondence between prior statements and subsequent behavior may not be strong. Evaluating a treatment as acceptable is unlikely to be sufficient to ensure its use. Although many, if not most, individuals would describe exercise and a moderate diet as acceptable, health problems associated with obesity and inactivity remain widespread (Bray, 2004). Similarly, low acceptability may not always be a substantial barrier to implementation. If the environmental supports are sufficiently strong, then teachers may implement interventions despite having reservations. For example, if a teacher is overtly accountable to parents and a principal who are actively concerned about the implementation of the plan, these environmental supports may be sufficient to ensure implementation (e.g., Noell et al., 2000). Diverse issues such as competing time demands, resources provided to support implementation, monitoring of implementation, and accountability for implementation may all influence implementation. Issues related to the interaction of variables that may play either a causal or moderating role in the degree of implementation of intervention plans are discussed in more detail in the following section.

In addition to the emerging literature focused on how to improve TPI, another line of investigation relating TPI to outcomes has emerged. This line of research has focused on how changes in TPI change outcomes (e.g., Greenwood, Terry, Arreaga-Mayer, & Finney, 1992; Rhymer et al., 2002). Rather than asking how to ensure TPI, this line of research has investigated how decreased TPI influences outcomes. Research examining the relationship between TPI and student outcomes has not emerged as a clear, coherent, or sustained line of empirical inquiry. The limited studies have yielded disparate results, with some studies suggesting that degradations in TPI lead to poorer outcomes (e.g., Greenwood et al., 1992; Henggeler, Melton, Brondino, Scherer, & Hanley, 1997; Taylor & Miller, 1997) and others suggesting that at least some imperfections in TPI are not related to differential outcomes (e.g., Gansle & McMahon, 1997; Rhymer et al., 2002). Examining the issues related to linking TPI to child outcome in any systematic manner across diverse interventions does not appear to be a promising line of inquiry at this point in time.

The relationship between TPI and treatment outcome is likely to be so complex that meaningful generalizations are likely to be difficult to achieve. For example, if one measures TPI as the percentage of steps completed, then it may be the case that all steps are not equally important, and as a result substantial error is introduced if appropriate weighting is not included. However, there are no treatments of which I am aware for which an empirical basis for weighting of components is available. In addition, critical issues in TPI may be issues of quality rather than quantity in some cases. It may be less important that praise be provided each time that the student achieves a behavioral goal than that the praise be specific and genuine. It is also likely that some individuals targeted for intervention may be better able to tolerate decreased treatment integrity than others. For example, treatment integrity may be more critical for initial skill establishment than for building fluency. Finally and obviously, some treatments may be more robust in that they remain effective despite incomplete TPI, while others might be described as brittle (small deviations in TPI resulting in an ineffective treatment).

BARRIERS TO A SCIENCE AND TECHNOLOGY OF TREATMENT PLAN IMPLEMENTATION

Despite the central role of TPI in successful consultation, educators and psychologists know more about how to devise effective interventions than we do about how to ensure TPI (Noell, Duhon et al., 2002; Sheridan & Gutkin, 2000). This reality exists despite the substantial number of scholars who have devoted considerable portions of their careers to consultation and the numerous publications related to consultation in schools. Although the study of any human behavior in an applied context is challenging, the study of consultation processes possesses a number of unique challenges that may have attenuated our progress toward a scientific understanding of TPI. A number of barriers specific to the study of TPI within consultation are particularly salient at the conceptual, methodological, and pragmatic levels.

Conceptual Barriers

Perhaps the most salient barriers to the scientific understanding of TPI have been conceptual. The indirect connection between what consultants do and the ends they typically seek to achieve may have limited the extent to which TPI has been studied. For example, a consultant in a school typically will be consulting for the purpose of improving a child's functioning. However, the consultant rarely will provide a treatment designed to improve the student's functioning. The intervention will commonly be provided by the consultee. The actions of the consultant are typically designed to change the behavior of the consultee. However, changing the behavior of the consultee is not the end goal of consultation; it is improving the functioning of the child. So much of the consultation research has focused on child outcomes, either measured directly or by adult report, with TPI commonly assumed to occur.

An alternative conceptualization of consultation might be more productive in developing a scientific understanding of TPI. In this conceptualization, consultation is an adult behavior change process with the target of change being the consultee. As such, consultation procedures are successful to the extent that they can bring about behavior change in adults (Noell & Witt, 1998). This change in consultee behavior may in turn effect positive changes for the student, but that is a separate issue that is moderated by diverse variables such as resistance to intervention, competing responses for the child, match of the intervention to child needs, and artifacts such as regression toward the mean. This suggests that effective consultation at some level includes at least two distinct but complementary components. First, does the consultation assessment and analysis model identify an intervention that has a high probability of success? Second, does the consultation model provide supports that lead to implementation of interventions? A consultation model can be successful on either front without being successful on the other. However, for consultation to consistently produce positive effects, it will need to do both.

Conceptualizing consultation as a procedure to change adult behavior clarifies another conceptual barrier to developing a scientific understanding of TPI. Focus on child outcomes contributes to ambiguity regarding the independent variable (consultation process vs. the treatment). In some consultation studies, the independent variables that were manipulated are child-focused procedures such as social skills training (Colton & Sheridan, 1998). It can be argued that studies that manipulate the treatment that is delivered to the child are not consultation studies per se but are treatment outcome studies in a consultation context. To study consultation experimentally, the consultation process must be manipulated in a single-subject or group experimental design. In addition, much of the consultation research is focused on broad complex conceptualizations of consultation such as behavioral consultation (Bergan & Kratochwill, 1990) or school consultation (Erchul & Martens, 2002). Although either approach can provide a framework within which to study specific procedures (e.g., Noell et al., 2005; Wickstrom, Jones, LaFleur, & Witt, 1998), these complex procedures in and of themselves are unlikely to permit isolation of critical procedural variables that support or inhibit TPI. Although models are available examining procedural variations within existing consultation models, it may be the case that the wide acceptance of particular

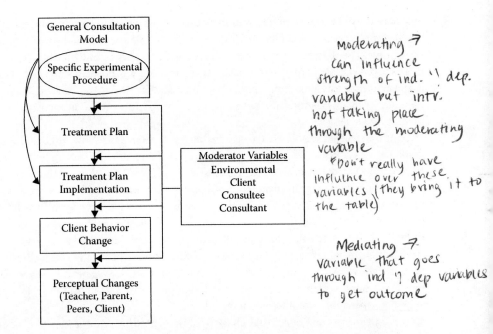

Handwritten margin notes:

moderating →
can influence
strength of ind. ': dep.
variable but intr.
not taking place
through the moderating
variable
• Don't really have
influence over these
variables (they bring it to
the table)

Mediating →
variable that goes
through ind ': dep variables
to get outcome

Figure 15.2   A linear representation of the consultation process highlighting the importance of environmental, client, consultee, and consultant variables in moderating each step in the process. For example, the development of the treatment plan may be influenced by the consultant's knowledge base, implementation of the plan may be influenced by the competing demands on the consultee's time, child behavior change may in turn be influenced by its history of reinforcement, and perceptual changes may in turn be influenced by consultee expectations.

models has had a chilling effect on TPI research by suggesting that the correct method for consultation has been developed.

A second major conceptual barrier to a science of TPI has been the limited consideration of moderating and mediating variables. A moderating variable is a variable that influences the nature *[margin note: Moderators]* or strength of the relationship between an independent variable and a dependent variable (Jensen et al., 2001). For example, parental resources and engagement with their children's education may moderate the efficacy of school-home note programs. School-home note programs may be generally effective, but more so with families that are engaged with schooling and that have abundant resources. A mediating variable is a variable that controls the apparent relationship between the independent variable and the dependent variable (Jensen et al.). For example, the apparent benefit *[margin note: Mediators]* of instructional consultation regarding reading problems may be dependent on TPI occurring. If that were the case, then instructional consultation would only be effective when TPI occurred (i.e., mediated by TPI).

A conceptualization of consultation, TPI, and child outcome that identifies the consultation process as the independent variable and a treatment plan and TPI as consultation's direct outcomes is presented in Figure 15.2. Figure 15.2 also acknowledges that a considerable number of moderating or mediating relationships are likely to exist. For example, development of the treatment plan is likely to be mediated by the knowledge and skills of the consultant and consultee. The degree of TPI might be moderated by the competing demands on the consultee's time and the complexity of treatment. The degree of client behavior change may in turn be mediated or moderated by the degree of TPI and the degree of fit between the treatment plan and the client's needs. Finally, perceptual changes may be mediated or moderated by the degree of client behavior change, the degree of remaining deviance from peers, and the duration of concerns prior to consultation. Study of these relationships is clearly a promising area of research. However, a more mature and complete empirical database describing the link between consultation and TPI may be needed before substantial progress is possible on the subtle issues of moderating and mediating variables.

Examination of the published research that has studied TPI following consultation within schools demonstrates substantial variation in the degree of TPI across teachers (e.g., Jones, Wickstrom, & Friman, 1997; Mortenson & Witt, 1998; Noell et al., 1997). Although the general phenomenon of poor and deteriorating implementation appears to be reasonably consistent across studies, this pattern is not characteristic for all teachers or to the same degree for all teachers. It is reasonable to assume that this variability is not a random phenomenon but is moderated by a number of individual and contextual variables. It certainly appears to be a promising area of investigation to study which variables mediate or moderate TPI following provision of a well-established consultation procedure. At present, however, we know far less than we need to know about the extent to which teachers implement interventions following consultation and even less about which variables determine the extent to which they do so.

In addition to the conceptual challenges presented in parsing out the independent, dependent, and moderating/mediating variables in consultation research, school consultation research is uniquely challenged by its context. The traditional emphasis on collaborative work, equal relationships, and consultee ownership of concerns (Zins & Erchul, 1995) may have created a perception of the consultee as a coinvestigator rather than the participant who is studied. This thinking seems a natural outgrowth of the reasonable desire to treat other professionals respectfully. This role and relationship challenge is particularly salient in consultation because the person who is the target of TPI research, the consultee, is frequently not conceptualized as having the problem. The collaborative nature of the relationship, the reality that the problem is frequently conceptualized as residing with the child, and the fact that the consultee is commonly another educator working in a professional role may have combined to create a chilling effect on interest in conducting TPI research.

An additional conceptual barrier to a scientific understanding of TPI may lie in part within the publication patterns regarding consultation in the schools. There are a great many reasoned and thoughtful analyses of how things might work or should work within consultation. In some instances, these analyses have drawn on relatively well-established literatures in other areas to develop hypotheses and guide studies regarding how constructs from other domains may play out within consultation (e.g., Erchul, Grissom, & Getty, chapter 14, this volume; Erchul & Raven, 1997). However, for some interesting and important issues within consultation we may have more discussion than data regarding the issue (e.g., variables mediating TPI). Some of these thoughtful analyses have on occasion been subsequently cited as if they were findings. For example, Gresham (1989) advanced a number of reasonable hypotheses regarding how a number of variables such as the number of steps involved in a treatment and perceived effectiveness may influence TPI. Although the ideas advanced by Gresham appear to make sense, 17 years after their publication they remain largely untested, and some of the evidence indirectly touching on these issues suggests they many not play out in schools as was assumed. However, some discussions of consultation cite this and other classic discussion papers as if they were findings rather than hypotheses. In some cases, the literature suggests that we know more about TPI and consultation than we do.

Methodological Barriers

One of the most enduring substantive challenges to the study of TPI is the measurement of TPI. This arises from the diversity of treatments that exist, the diversity of components, and variation in how TPI is defined. Treatment plans typically will have a number of steps, but most psychologists reasonably assume they are not equally important. However, no empirical basis exists for weighting the components. In the face of this challenge, the most reasonable approach appears to be an improper linear model (Dawes, 1979). An improper linear mode requires assigning equal weights to all variables. Although this may be the only practical solution at present, it may not be optimal.

Another methodological issue that arises in the measurement of treatment integrity is the operational definition that is employed. This area of research is so new that well-developed standards have not emerged. An example of the importance of this may help to illustrate. Suppose that a simple treatment for disruptive behavior included one antecedent element (e.g., a prompt), a contingent consequence for a behavior (e.g., redirecting), and a cumulative consequence that occurred at the end of the day based on behavior that day (e.g., a reward for no severe disruptive behavior). Then, suppose that data demonstrate the teacher never implemented the antecedent or cumulative consequence but implemented the redirection at 9 of 10 opportunities. Would the "correct" TPI score be 30% (the mean implementation of each step: $[0 + 0 + 90\%]/3$) or 43% (responses implemented divided by response opportunities $[0 + 0 + 9]/21$) or 82% (treatment occasions in which treatment was provided at least in part divided by opportunities: 9/11)? These different values may lead to substantively differing conclusions regarding the independent variable under study or the relationship between TPI and outcome.

An additional methodological issue related to the assessment of TPI is that treatments may occur at diverse times throughout the day (e.g., Jones et al., 1997; Witt, Noell, LaFleur, & Mortenson, 1997). This can quickly lead to severe data collection problems. If the researcher chooses to do a direct observation at some specific points in time (e.g., Jones et al.), then those observations are likely to represent a small sample of TPI. Given both the potential for reactivity to the observation and the limited size of the sample, it is quite reasonable to have concerns that the data will not be representative (Hintze & Matthews, 2004). An alternative strategy is to use permanent products of TPI. This will be a practical strategy for many, but certainly not all, treatment plans in schools. This strategy is relatively desirable because it samples all occasions and may reduce reactivity by adopting an unobtrusive strategy (Foster & Cone, 1986). However, unlike observations, the evidence regarding implementation is subject to confounds such as faking data and failing to represent treatment steps that have no physical product. A final strategy is to assess treatment integrity by some form of self-report by the treatment agent. At present, this appears to be the least satisfactory solution. The limited evidence available to date suggests that self-reports are severely upwardly biased and are not statistically related to either direct observation or permanent product recording (Noell et al., 2005; Wickstrom et al., 1998).

A final methodological confound is that in consultation research of a reasonably large scale, treatment plans will vary across participants. Although it is possible to consult regarding a number of cases, identify a subset for whom a particular intervention is appropriate, and then study TPI in these roughly equivalent cases (see Jones et al., 1997, or Noell, Duhon et al., 2002), this is only a viable strategy with small-n studies. Larger studies in which the treatment plans are developed within consultation will inevitably lead to heterogeneity of treatment plans. That is part of the purpose of consulting (Erchul & Martens, 2002). However, this leads to enormous complexity in devising a systematic measure of TPI that can be applied to all cases. At present, no empirically supported standards exist for accomplishing this.

The remaining methodological challenges to TPI research in consultation are linked to the conceptual complexity of studying consultation. One of the critical challenges to consultation research is that it inevitably involves nested independent variables, not all of which may be the focus of study. For example, one might be interested in the effect of a social influence manipulation on TPI (Erchul & Raven, 1997). However, it is not possible to study those in a vacuum. They will have to be embedded in a comprehensive consultation model. Social influence bids would then be manipulated within a broader consultation model that might be described as behavioral or instructional and is held constant across conditions (e.g., Noell et al., 2005). However, the efficacy of the social influence bids may change depending on the consultation model. In addition, researchers are likely to be interested in student outcomes, which will complicate matters enormously. In evaluating student outcomes, diverse interventions with varying degrees of implementation will in turn be nested within differing consultation conditions that were devised to change consultee behavior rather than student behavior. In this instance, the student effects may be better described as second order or generalized effects for the primary study rather than direct effects themselves.

Contextual artifacts, confounds, and moderating variables are inevitable challenges to consultation research. Baseline TPI may vary across school sites due to characteristics of the school leadership, students, parents, teachers, or school environment. Interestingly, these same potential threats to internal validity are also an exciting area of potential study. However, at present little is known about the direction or magnitude of these effects or which variables are important. The only prudent course of action in the study of TPI at present is to use random assignment to conditions within schools rather than random assignment of schools to conditions. Although that will on average equate the conditions on these confounds, it can also be exceedingly challenging pragmatically to manage multiple conditions within the same school simultaneously. A final methodological challenge for the study of TPI is that for some, but not all, teachers the effects of some procedures to improve TPI will be irreversible (see Noell et al., 1997). Once they master a procedure and it is firmly established as a part of their routine, withdrawing the consultative support may not lead to a return to baseline levels. For those researchers examining TPI in a small-n or single-subject design, this suggests the desirability of a multiple-baseline design, which itself creates additional coordination challenges in conducting the study.

Pragmatic Barriers

The bulk of the pragmatic barriers to conducting consultation research are those that emerge as the result of doing treatment outcome research. It is expensive, complex, subject to influences beyond the researcher's control, creates ethical challenges, and takes a long time. To state the obvious, substantive treatment outcome research is difficult to conduct. Researchers in schools examining consultation face a few additional and unique challenges in conducting consultation-TPI research. First, unlike working in a university clinic, a consultation researcher does not control the environment (the school). The sheer complexity of coordinating the study within an active professional culture with a mission that does not include conducting research is a different enterprise from conducting a study through a university-affiliated setting.

An additional challenge may be more subtle and specific to the culture of schools. At schools, educators are professionals who carry out their roles within the organization. Generally, they are not assumed to have a problem or be in need of some service. This is a different situation from a patient who seeks treatment at a clinic. At some times and in some places, there appears to be reluctance to study the behavior (rather than opinions) of teachers. The extent to which this is true and the extent to which these issues are related to contracts, traditions, or just a sense of propriety is likely to vary across settings. Within the culture of schools, it is frequently more comfortable and acceptable to study students than it is to study teachers.

An additional challenge that may be somewhat specific to consultation research in schools is the diversity of concerns that emerge. In an outpatient context, one can advertise for participants who are seeking treatment for disfluent reading or phobia. In the context of studying consultation in schools, the interest is more commonly in consultation as a general case problem-solving model for diverse concerns (Sheridan, Welch, & Orme, 1996). The school-based researcher can choose to focus on a specific type of concern, such as attention deficit/hyperactivity disorder or can take the range of naturally emerging referrals. In the former case, the research team will have to handle a number of cases that will be disqualified and will have to be available to more children to identify a sufficient number of appropriate participants. In addition, the external validity of conclusions reached will be attenuated by the selective nature of the sample. In contrast, researchers can choose to permit students with diverse concerns to participate in the study. However, that will create substantial demands for rather elaborate experimental procedures. Plus, effect sizes may be somewhat smaller in the heterogeneous sample situation due to the increased within-group variability. However, the external validity would be strengthened in describing consultation as a general case problem-solving model.

Summary

When one examines the challenges confronting consultation researchers, it is not surprising that our understanding of TPI is limited. The conceptual articulation that is needed to support programmatic TPI research is complex and has not been widely accepted at present. In addition, consultation is like an onion; it has layers, many layers. As a result, within any case in a study there is layering of multiple independent variables, moderating variables, and possibly one or more mediating variables. A conceptual and empirical basis is needed for establishing some limited set of known relationships that serve as a basis for exploring some of the more complex and potentially interesting relationships. Most of the methodological issues uniquely confronting consultation researchers derive from the complexity of consultation. Perhaps the unique challenge confronting TPI researchers is the measurement of the dependent variable. It is complex, has many potential solutions, and little practical empirical work is available to guide choices. Finally, the primary pragmatic barriers to consultation research are those that apply to all treatment outcome research. School-based consultation researchers are confronted with additional challenges emerging from conducting research within school cultures that have their own missions, values, and routines. In addition, the researcher's ability to control the environment in schools may be limited.

EMERGENCE OF RESEARCH EXAMINING TREATMENT PLAN IMPLEMENTATION

Three substantive questions appear to be most salient and pressing for developing a science of TPI. First, what are meaningful and practical methods for assessing TPI? Second, how does TPI influence treatment outcome? Third, what variables influence TPI to a substantive degree? This section of the chapter will provide a focused review of the existing literature relevant to each of these questions.

What Are Meaningful and Practical Methods for Assessing Treatment Plan Implementation?

The short answer to the question of meaningful and practical TPI assessment methods is that school-based researchers have developed little specialized knowledge in this regard. Generally, the issues of defining and assessing TPI will be the same as those related to assessing any behavior.

Specifically, the issues of operationally defining the target behaviors, devising a measurement net, and selecting measurement methods are not unique. Two unique issues do arise in assessing treatment integrity. First, treatments are almost always complex, multistep behaviors. Researchers and clinicians have a natural inclination to create a summary index of overall performance. There is no comparative literature examining different means of summarizing TPI. In the face of this uncertainty, an improper linear model (see Dawes, 1979) appears to be most appropriate, but research is certainly needed to examine the adequacy of this approach.

A second measurement issue is the agreement between assessment methods. TPI can and has been assessed by direct observation (Jones et al., 1997), permanent products (Mortenson & Witt, 1998), and teacher reports (Colton & Sheridan, 1998). No empirical literature examining agreement between permanent products and direct observation has yet emerged. The limited data regarding the agreement between teacher self-reports and either direct observation or permanent products suggests that teacher self-report results in dramatically higher estimates of implementation, and these estimates are nearly uniformly high, with no substantive relationship to the variability in more direct assessments (Noell et al., 2005; Wickstrom et al., 1998). If one accepts that direct observation and permanent product recording are more direct lower inference assessments, then the use of self-reports does not appear to be supported. It is worth noting that neither Noell et al. nor Wickstrom et al. specifically focused on agreement between self-report and direct assessment. These were secondary issues in larger studies. It may be the case that it is possible to devise a self-report system that achieves higher agreement with a criterion measure.

How Does Treatment Plan Implementation Influence Treatment Outcome?

The short answer to the question of how TPI influences treatment outcome appears to be that as TPI deteriorates, the probability that a child will respond favorably to treatment decreases. However, this is not an entirely satisfactory answer as it is vague and general. The problem with achieving more specific and useful answers has to do with the number of treatments that are used in schools, the number of elements they can contain, and the number of different ways in which those elements can be degraded. A broad science linking TPI to treatment outcome may not be possible because there simply may be too many types of treatments that can be degraded in too many ways.

Despite the substantive challenges confronting researchers linking TPI to treatment outcome, a few published studies have examined this link. Studies have examined the impact of TPI in the context of providing treatment for disruptive behavior (Gansle & McMahon, 1997); treatment for anxiety disorders (Vermilyea, Barlow, & O'Brien, 1984); classwide peer tutoring (Greenwood et al., 1992); social skills training (McEvoy, Shores, Wehby, Johnson, & Fox, 1990); constant time delay instruction (Holcombe, Wolery, & Snyder, 1994); differential reinforcement (Vollmer, Roane, Ringdahl, & Marcus, 1999); strategy instruction (Noell, Gresham, & Gansle, 2002); and multisystemic therapy for juvenile offenders (Henggeler et al., 1997). The number of studies and investigators examining how TPI mediates treatment outcome might suggest substantive progress toward understanding the relationship. However, that does not appear to be the case.

No programmatic research exists in which a series of related studies have built on prior findings in this area. In each instance, a single study examining either manipulated levels of TPI (Gansle & McMahon, 1997; Noell, Duhon et al., 2002; Vollmer et al., 1999) or provided descriptive data regarding TPI that was then linked to outcome (Greenwood et al., 1992; Henggeler et al., 1997; Vermilyea et al., 1984). In each study, one or more links between TPI and treatment outcome were either demonstrated or presented descriptively. Across all of the studies, degradations in TPI were generally associated with poorer treatment outcomes. These poorer outcomes included fewer participants responding positively to the treatment, poorer outcomes on some specific measures, or a diminished size of treatment effect. However, this finding was not uniform. In some instances, decreases in TPI had no appreciable effect on some outcome measure or for some participants (Gansle & McMahon, 1997; Holcombe et al., 1994; Vollmer et al., 1999).

The difficulties in synthesizing and summarizing these studies is that (a) none of them examined the same treatment, (b) they share little in how they measured TPI, and (c) they vary substantially in the treated population. Although specific and differentiated findings are available in each study individually, collectively they suggest conceptualizing the relationship between TPI and treatment outcome as a probabilistic function. As TPI decreases, it becomes more likely that the treatment effect will decrease or fail outright. The greater the degree of TPI degradation, the greater the risk is. However, the treatment effect will not always decrease with some decrease in TPI, and this is especially true when the decrease in TPI is small.

In theory, it should be possible to summarize an educational/psychological treatment by describing the effect size, the degree to which treatment integrity can be decreased before it will begin to become less effective, and the degradation point at which it is likely to fail entirely. In addition, to accommodate slight unmeasured variations in treatment implementation, individual differences, and environmental confounds, all of these values could be put into confidence ranges with probability of degradation and probability of failure statements. The challenge for consultation researchers is that the number of ways in which TPI can be degraded may be too numerous and functionally dissimilar to fit into a simple function. For example, we might like to know that TPI from 80% to 100% will rarely fail and from 50% to 79% will commonly result in reduced outcomes, and TPI below 50% is rarely beneficial. The challenge is that to reach these types of conclusions it matters what the elements of treatment are that are not occurring and how they are measured. At present, the literature regarding the relationship between TPI and treatment outcome would support only the following broad conclusion: Assuming an effective treatment, decreasing TPI in one or more elements increases the risk that the treatment will become less effective or fail entirely. As the degree of TPI decreases, the risk of treatment failure increases. However, some individuals do tolerate poor implementation of one or more elements of treatment plans with no adverse effects. No means currently exist for identifying these resilient individuals.

What Variables Influence Treatment Plan Implementation to a Substantive Degree?

One of the fascinating aspects of examining the variables that may influence TPI in schools is the realization that diverse views are readily available from colleagues about what should influence TPI. In contrast to what practitioners and researchers believe may be important, we know little about what is important. This section provides a brief focused review of what has been learned thus far with a particular emphasis on the substantive conclusions rather than an exhaustive consideration of the details of each study. Interested readers should consult the original sources.

One of the recurrent issues in the consultation literature has been the extent to which additional or specific training would be sufficient to enhance TPI (Watson & Robinson, 1996). Two studies have touched on this issue. Taylor and Miller (1997) demonstrated that implementation of a time-out procedure following a didactic training procedure was low. Implementation improved following an intensive and extensive in vivo training procedure. During training, teachers implemented the intervention with 100% accuracy in the classroom with the consultant observing over three sessions. A subsequent investigation also demonstrated superior implementation following direct instruction in intervention implementation (modeling or rehearsal with feedback) versus didactic instruction (Sterling-Turner, Watson, Wildmon, Watkins, & Little, 2001). It is worth noting that in the Taylor and Miller study the extent of the training greatly exceeded what would commonly occur in consultation and included training to a rigorous criterion. In addition, the degree to which teachers sensitized to the presence of observers, creating reactivity, following this extensive training procedure is unknown. The Sterling-Turner et al. study has questionable external validity because it studied undergraduate volunteers in a simulation. In sum, although these studies provide some basis for hypothesizing that training that includes enacting the treatment may contribute to improved TPI, the limited number of studies and the methodological issues preclude any definitive conclusions.

One of the enduring points of discussion in the consultation literature has been the degree to which consultation should be a collaborative, co-equal exchange versus one in which the consultant takes a more directive role. To avoid the problem of creating a false dichotomy, it appears that the scholars who have contributed to this discussion are focused on relative degrees, with some favoring greater consultee control and some favoring greater consultant control (Gutkin, 1999). Only one study has been published thus far that has examined the impact of adopting a more collaborative than prescriptive approach to consultation (Wickstrom et al., 1998). The collaborative procedures required the consultant to make more supportive statements and seek teacher input at a number of specified points during interviews. The prescriptive procedure provided fewer supportive statements and fewer prompts to obtain teacher input. Teachers in both conditions collected approximately half of the progress-monitoring data called for and implemented the programmed consequences on approximately 4% of relevant occasions. No statistically significant differences were found between the collaborative and prescriptive consultation groups in the degree of plan implementation.

The bulk of the data relating consultation procedures in schools to TPI has focused on performance feedback as a follow-up procedure for ensuring and sustaining TPI. A fairly considerable number of studies are now available supporting the efficacy of performance feedback to improve and maintain TPI (Jones et al., 1997; Martens, Hiralall, & Bradley, 1997; Mortenson & Witt, 1998; Noell, Duhon, et al., 2002; Noell et al., 1997, 2000, 2005; Witt et al., 1997). The initial studies in this area demonstrated the efficacy of performance feedback in improving TPI for academic interventions and teacher delivery of praise across diverse populations (Jones et al.; Martens et al.; Witt et al.). These initial positive findings have been followed up with a series of subsequent studies that have examined procedural variations and extended the research to additional referral concerns and interventions.

The first follow-up study (Noell et al., 1997) was a systematic replication of the work of Witt et al. (1997). This study replicated the Witt study in providing a relatively complex reinforcement-based treatment for students exhibiting academic performance deficits. The replication differed from the original study in that intervention training was only provided didactically in the consultation session, and the teacher was not provided the intervention materials. Initial implementation in the replication was similar to TPI in the earlier Witt study, and performance feedback was similarly effective. This study suggested that the provision of the intervention materials and the relatively extensive training that had been provided in the original study were not necessary for performance feedback to remain effective. This is not to suggest that in vivo training and providing teachers with intervention materials are not desirable professional practices.

Mortenson and Witt (1998) extended the previous consultation, TPI, and performance feedback literature by examining weekly rather than daily feedback. They found weekly feedback to be effective but less consistently so than daily feedback. The subsequent Noell et al. (2000) study examined the efficacy of brief follow-up meetings in which the consultant inquired about implementation and outcome but did so without a formal data review. The study found that follow-up meetings in the absence of data review were effective for two of five teachers. Performance feedback was effective for four of five teachers, with one teacher's implementation not improving until performance feedback was combined with discussion of the follow-up meeting with the principal and parents. A subsequent study extended the research to a behavior management intervention and examined the importance of providing a graph showing student outcome and TPI to the teacher as part of performance feedback (Noell, Duhon et al., 2002). This study found that although performance feedback without graphing was effective, the addition of the graphs resulted in much more consistent effects.

The most recent study in this line of research (Noell et al., 2005) extended the previous studies in a number of ways. First, it was the first study to include students with diverse concerns in the same study. It was the first randomized clinical field trail examining performance feedback, and it examined an alternative approach to improving TPI: antecedent social influence and planning. The control condition consisted of a brief weekly interview structured similarly to a problem evaluation interview. The key findings were that performance feedback was associated with superior TPI in comparison to either of the other two conditions, which did not differ at a statistically significant level. Performance feedback was also associated with superior child outcome. Performance feedback was provided approximately twice during the first week of implementation and then faded to weekly feedback. It is also worth noting that the data from this study suggested the need for additional research examining commitment emphasis and self-management procedures. Teacher ratings of consultants and treatment acceptability were similar across conditions. A moderate statistically significant correlation between treatment integrity and child behavioral outcome was obtained.

In summary, across these eight studies five key conclusions appear tenable. First, performance feedback regarding treatment implementation following consultation leads to improved TPI. Second, constructing a graph either in the feedback session or prior to meeting with the teacher increases the consistency of the effect. Third, meetings in the absence of review of objective data appear to be inconsistent in their effectiveness. Fourth, for the types of common educational interventions that have been studied, extensive prior training does not appear to be sufficient to sustain implementation and does not appear to be necessary for performance feedback to work. This is not to suggest that training is not needed or that extensive training might not be needed if the intervention were very dissimilar to common educational practices. Finally, the general phenomenon of problematic integrity and positive response to performance feedback is evident across interventions ranging from simple to complex.

SUMMARY AND DIRECTIONS FOR THE FUTURE

A reasonable argument can be made that studying and understanding TPI is or should be a central concern of psychologists working with children as we begin the 21st century. Support for this assertion comes from three observations. First, psychologists and educators spent a great deal of the 20th century developing and studying diverse interventions for children's academic, social, emotional, and behavioral needs. Most of these require some implementation in part or whole by parents and teachers. If we do not know how to support intervention implementation, then much of the prior work, though laudable as scholarship, will have little value in improving the lives of children in need. A second argument in favor of TPI research is the current and increasing emphasis on the provision of intervention services in general education (Reschly & Tilly, 1999). Of particular note is the increasing interest in response to intervention as at least part of the entitlement process in schools (see Fuchs, 2003). Simply put, a response to an intervention-based entitlement process that does not ensure and document accurate implementation of the intervention is fatally flawed.

Response to a planned, but never implemented consistently, intervention is not an approach that any reasonable scholar or policymaker would support. Finally, the development of a treatment plan and the subsequent TPI are the most direct and immediate outcomes of consultation. In that case, it seems reasonable that, as a scholarly community, we should strive to understand this most direct outcome of a major professional practice.

Assuming that TPI is a major need for schools, at least four broad lines of inquiry seem readily apparent. First, how should we measure TPI? The dominant methods that are evident in the literature are self-report, direct observation, and permanent products. We have little information about how these methods compare to one another. There are specific needs that could be addressed regarding each. For example, how large a sample is needed to assess TPI by direct observation? Alternatively, to what extent do permanent product and direct observation measurements agree? Finally, can the methodology of self-report be improved such that it yields results that are more similar to direct measures?

Second, how do variations in TPI moderate or mediate treatment outcome? This appears to be the most daunting line of inquiry related to TPI. There are simply so many variations in treatments, children, and contexts that it will be extremely difficult to develop systematic and broadly useful principles. The most productive approach at present might be to focus on a few well-established and extensively researched interventions and begin by systematically varying TPI to observe its effect within a well-controlled experimental design. To provide scientists and practitioners with useful information, research linking TPI to treatment outcomes will need to be sustained, of considerable volume, and systematic.

Third, which variables influence TPI following consultation using a widely accepted model such as behavioral consultation? At present, we do not know which environmental variables, teacher attributes, student characteristics, or intervention characteristics influence TPI. This is a potentially fascinating line of research. The critical challenge for this sort of research is that it will likely require a large-n design due to its descriptive nature. For some potential mediator variables (e.g., time required to implement treatment), it may be possible to manipulate them and achieve clear results with a modest n; for others (e.g., years teaching experience), manipulation of the variable clearly is not possible. The possibilities for different mediating relationships and their interactions could consume at least one additional chapter.

Finally, what can consultants do to support and sustain TPI by consultees? This is by far the most practical pressing question. At present, it appears that performance feedback works. By no means does that mean that performance feedback is the only thing that may work. It is the only evidence-based practice at present. A number of alternative approaches merit examination. Specifically, social influence strategies, self-management procedures, peer collaboration and accountability, and procedures incorporating parents all appear worthy of study. However, it is worth noting that what both practice and science need are sustained programmatic lines of research that develop well-established relationships.

In summary, we know that teachers sometimes, perhaps frequently, do not implement interventions following consultation or do not sustain them. The literature suggests that as TPI deteriorates the chances that treatment outcome will deteriorate or break down completely increases. Performance feedback has been repeatedly demonstrated to increase TPI. Little is known about how a host of variables such as the teacher's years of experience, the complexity of the treatment, or the acceptability of treatments influences implementation. The critical consideration is relatively straightforward. If consultation does not lead to intervention implementation, then no service is delivered to the student. With the apparent and increasing emphasis on intervention in education, viable technologies for ensuring treatment implementation are badly needed.

REFERENCES

Bergan, J. R., & Kratochwill, T. R. (1990). *Behavioral consultation and therapy.* New York: Plenum.

Billingsley, F., White, O. R., & Munson, R. (1980). Procedural reliability: A rationale and an example. *Behavioral Assessment, 2,* 229–241.

Bray, G. A. (2004). The epidemic of obesity and changes in food intake: The fluoride hypothesis. *Physiology and Behavior, 82,* 115–121.

Colton, D. L., & Sheridan, S. M. (1998). Conjoint behavioral consultation and social skills training: Enhancing the play behaviors of boys with attention deficit hyperactivity disorder. *Journal of Educational and Psychological Consultation, 9,* 3–28.

Dawes, R. (1979). The robust beauty of improper linear models in decision making. *American Psychologist, 34,* 571–582.

DuPaul, G. J., & Eckert, T. L. (1997). The effects of school-based interventions for attention deficit hyperactivity disorder: A meta-analysis. *School Psychology Review, 26,* 5–27.

Eckert, T. L., & Hintze, J. M. (2000). Behavioral conceptions and applications of acceptability: Issues related to service delivery and research methodology. *School Psychology Quarterly, 15,* 123–148.

Erchul, W. P., & Martens, B. K. (2002). *School consultation: Conceptual and empirical bases of practice.* New York: Kluwer Academic/Plenum.

Erchul, W. P., & Raven, B. H. (1997). School power in school consultation: A contemporary view of French and Raven's bases of power model. *Journal of School Psychology, 35,* 137–171.

Foster, S. L., & Cone, J. D. (1986). Design and use of direct observation. In A. R. Ciminero, K. S. Calhoun, & H. E. Adams (Eds.), *Handbook of behavioral assessment* (pp. 253–324). New York: Wiley.

Fuchs, D., & Fuchs, L. S. (1989). Exploring effective and efficient prereferral interventions: A component analysis of behavioral consultation. *School Psychology Review, 18,* 260–283.

Fuchs, L. (2003). Assessing intervention responsiveness: Conceptual and technical issues. *Learning Disabilities Research & Practice, 18,* 172–186.

Gansle, K. A., & McMahon, C. M. (1997). Component integrity of teacher intervention management behavior using a student self-monitoring treatment: An experimental analysis. *Journal of Behavioral Education, 7,* 405–419.

Gresham, F. M. (1989). Assessment of treatment integrity in school consultation and prereferral intervention. *School Psychology Review, 18,* 37–50.

Gresham, F. M., Gansle, K. A., & Noell, G. H. (1993). Treatment integrity in applied behavior analysis with children. *Journal of Applied Behavior Analysis, 26,* 257–264.

Gresham, F. M., Gansle, K. A., Noell, G. H., Cohen, S., & Rosenblum, S. (1993). Treatment integrity of school-based behavioral intervention studies: 1980–1990. *School Psychology Review, 22,* 254–272.

Greenwood, C. R., Terry, B., Arreaga-Mayer, C., & Finney, R. (1992). The classwide peer tutoring program: Implementation factors moderating students' achievement. *Journal of Applied Behavior Analysis, 25,* 101–116.

Gutkin, T. B. (1999). Collaborative versus directive/prescriptive/expert school-based consultation: Reviewing and resolving a false dichotomy. *Journal of School Psychology, 37,* 161–190.

Happe, D. (1982). Behavioral intervention: It doesn't do any good in your briefcase. In J. Grimes (Ed.), *Psychological approaches to problems of children and adolescents* (pp. 15–41). Des Moines: Iowa Department of Public Instruction.

Haynes, S. N., & O'Brien, W. H. (1999). *Principles and practice of behavioral assessment.* New York: Kluwer.

Henggeler, S. W., Melton, G. B., Brondino, M. J., Scherer, D. G., & Hanley, J. H. (1997). Multisystemic therapy with violent and chronic juvenile offenders and their families: The role of treatment fidelity in successful dissemination. *Journal of Consulting and Clinical Psychology, 65,* 821–833.

Hintze, J. M., & Matthews, W. J. (2004). The generalizability of systematic direct observations across time and setting: A preliminary investigation of the psychometrics of behavioral observation. *School Psychology Review, 33,* 258–270.

Holcombe, A., Wolery, M., & Snyder, E. (1994). Effects of two levels of procedural fidelity with constant time delay on children's learning. *Journal of Behavioral Education, 4,* 49–73.

Jensen, P. S., Hinshaw, S. P., Swanson, J. M., Greenhill, L. L., Conners, C. K., Arnold, L. E., et al. (2001). Findings from the NIMH Multimodal Treatment Study of ADHD (MTA): Implications and applications for primary care providers. *Journal of Developmental and Behavioral Pediatrics, 22,* 60–73.

Jones, K. M., Wickstrom, K. F., & Friman, P. C. (1997). The effects of observational feedback on treatment integrity in school-based behavioral consultation. *School Psychology Quarterly, 12*, 316–326.

Kratochwill, T. R., Bergan, J. R., Sheridan, S. M., & Elliott, S. N. (1998). Assumptions of behavioral consultation: After all is said and done more has been done than said. *School Psychology Quarterly, 13*, 63–80.

Lentz, F. E., & Daly, E. J., III. (1996). Is the behavior of academic change agents controlled metaphysically? An analysis of the behavior of those who change behavior. *School Psychology Quarterly, 11*, 337–352.

Martens, B. K., Hiralall, A. S., & Bradley, T. A. (1997). A note to teacher: Improving student behavior through goal setting and feedback. *School Psychology Quarterly, 12*, 33–41.

McEvoy, M. A., Shores, R. E., Wehby, J. H., Johnson, S. M., & Fox, J. J. (1990). Special education teachers' implementation of procedures to promote social interaction among children in integrated settings. *Education and Training in Mental Retardation, 25*, 267–276.

Moncher, F. J., & Prinz, R. J. (1991). Treatment fidelity in outcome studies. *Clinical Psychology Review, 11*, 247–266.

Mortenson, B. P., & Witt, J. C. (1998). The use of weekly performance feedback to increase teacher implementation of a prereferral academic intervention. *School Psychology Review, 27*, 613–627.

Mueller, M. M., Edwards, R. P., & Trahant, D. (2003). Translating multiple assessment techniques into an intervention selection model for classrooms. *Journal of Applied Behavior Analysis, 36*, 563–573.

Nastasi, B. K., & Truscott, S. D. (2000). Acceptability research in school psychology: Current trends and future directions. *School Psychology Quarterly, 15*, 117–122.

Noell, G. H., Duhon, G. J., Gatti, S. L., & Connell, J. E. (2002). Consultation, follow-up, and behavior management intervention implementation in general education. *School Psychology Review, 31*, 217–234.

Noell, G. H., Gresham, F. M., & Gansle, K. A. (2002). Does treatment integrity matter? A preliminary investigation of instructional implementation and mathematics performance. *Journal of Behavioral Education, 11*, 51–67.

Noell, G. H., & Witt, J. C. (1998). Toward a behavior analytic approach to consultation. In T. S. Watson & F. M. Gresham (Eds.), *Handbook of child behavior therapy* (pp. 41–57). New York: Plenum.

Noell, G. H., Witt, J. C., Gilbertson, D. N., Ranier, D. D., & Freeland, J. T. (1997). Increasing teacher intervention implementation in general education settings through consultation and performance feedback. *School Psychology Quarterly, 12*, 77–88.

Noell, G. H., Witt, J. C., LaFleur, L. H., Mortenson, B. P., Ranier, D. D., & LeVelle, J. (2000). A comparison of two follow-up strategies to increase teacher intervention implementation in general education following consultation. *Journal of Applied Behavior Analysis, 33*, 271–284.

Noell, G. H., Witt, J. C., Slider, N. J., Connell, J. E., Gatti, S. L., Williams, K. L., et al. (2005). Treatment implementation following behavioral consultation in schools: A comparison of three follow-up strategies. *School Psychology Review, 34*, 87–106.

Peterson, L., Homer, A. L., & Wonderlich, S. A. (1982). The integrity of independent variables in behavior analysis. *Journal of Applied Behavior Analysis, 15*, 477–492.

Reschly, D., & Tilly, W. D. (1999). Reform trends and system design alternatives. In D. Reschly, W. D. Tilly, & J. Grimes (Eds.), *Special education in transition: Functional assessment and noncategorical programming* (pp. 19–48). Longmont, CO: Sopris West.

Rhymer, K. N., Evans-Hampton, T. N., McCurdy, M., & Watson, T. S. (2002). Effects of varying levels of treatment integrity on toddler aggressive behavior. *Special Services in the Schools, 18*, 75–82.

Riley-Tillman, T. C., & Chafouleas, S. M. (2003). Using interventions that exist in the natural environment to increase treatment integrity and social influence in consultation. *Journal of Educational and Psychological Consultation, 14*, 139–156.

Sheridan, S. M., Eagle, J. W., Cowan, R. J., & Mickelson, W. (2001). The effects of conjoint behavioral consultation: Results of a 4-year investigation. *Journal of School Psychology, 39*, 361–385.

Sheridan, S. M., & Gutkin, T. B. (2000). The ecology of school psychology: Examining and changing our paradigm for the 21st century. *School Psychology Review, 29*, 485–502.

Sheridan, S., Welch, M., & Orme, S. (1996). Is consultation effective? A review of outcome research. *Remedial and Special Education, 17*, 341–354.

Sterling-Turner, H. E., Watson, T. S., Wildmon, M., Watkins, C., & Little, E. (2001). Investigating the relationship between training type and treatment integrity. *School Psychology Quarterly, 16*, 56–67.

Swanson, H. L., & Hoskyn, M. (1998). Experimental intervention research on students with learning disabilities: A meta-analysis of treatment outcomes. *Review of Eduational Research, 68*, 277–321.

Taylor, J., & Miller, M. (1997). When timeout works some of the time: The importance of treatment integrity and functional assessment. *School Psychology Quarterly, 12,* 4–22.

Vermilyea, B. B., Barlow, D. H., & O'Brien, G. T. (1984). The importance of assessing treatment integrity: An example in the anxiety disorders. *Journal of Behavioral Assessment, 6,* 1–11.

Vollmer, T. R., Roane, H. S., Ringdahl, J. E., & Marcus, B. A. (1999). Evaluating treatment challenges with differential reinforcement of alternative behavior. *Journal of Applied Behavior Analysis, 32,* 9–23.

Watson, T. S., & Robinson, S. L. (1996). Direct behavioral consultation: An alternative to traditional behavioral consultation. *School Psychology Quarterly, 11,* 267–278.

Weiss, B., & Weisz, J. R. (1995). Relative effectiveness of behavioral versus nonbehavioral child psychotherapy. *Journal of Consulting and Clinical Psychology, 63,* 317–320.

Weisz, J. R., Weiss, B., Alicke, M. D., & Klotz, M. L. (1987). Effectiveness of psychotherapy with children and adolescents: A meta-analysis for clinicians. *Journal of Consulting and Clinical Psychology, 55,* 542–549.

Wickstrom, K. F., Jones, K. M., LaFleur, L. H., & Witt, J. C. (1998). An analysis of treatment integrity in school-based consultation. *School Psychology Quarterly, 13,* 141–154.

Witt, J. C., Noell, G. H., LaFleur, L. H., & Mortenson, B. P. (1997). Teacher usage of interventions in general education: Measurement and analysis of the independent variable. *Journal of Applied Behavior Analysis, 30,* 693–696.

Yeaton, W. H., & Sechrest, L. (1981). Critical dimensions in the choice and maintenance of successful treatments: Strength, integrity, and effectiveness. *Journal of Consulting and Clinical Psychology, 49,* 156–167.

Zins, J. E., & Erchul, W. P. (1995). Best practices in school consultation. In A. Thomas & J. Grimes (Eds.), *Best practices in school psychology III* (pp. 609–624). Washington, DC: National Association of School Psychologists.

Zins, J. E., Kratochwill, T. R., & Elliott, S. N. (Eds.). (1993). *The handbook of consultation services for children.* San Francisco: Jossey-Bass.

16

Empirical and Theoretical Support for an Updated Model of Mental Health Consultation for Schools

JAN N. HUGHES, LINDA LOYD, AND MICHELLE BUSS

Texas A&M University

INTRODUCTION

Mental health consultation, defined as an indirect model for the delivery of mental health services, has been a major role for school psychologists since the specialty's beginning (Mannino & Shore, 1975; Medway & Updyke, 1985). Gerald Caplan, who is widely recognized as the founder of mental health consultation, articulated the basic tenets of consultation in his seminal 1970 text, *The Theory and Practice of Mental Health Consultation*. He described an indirect model of providing mental health services that was prevention oriented and population focused (see Knotek, Kaniuka, & Ellings, chapter 7, this volume). Caplan sought to decrease the prevalence and incidence of psychopathology and to enhance mental health functioning through the provision of mental health consultation to professionals who were not trained in mental health but whose interactions with community clients in natural contexts had an impact on the mental health of clients. The consultant attempted to increase the capacity of professional caregivers and of organizations that provide care to children to promote the mental health of the communities they served.

Caplan's emphasis on population-focused mental health prevention through consultation with community-based, professional caregivers is every bit as relevant to school psychology practice today as it was in 1970. Several reports have documented the magnitude and range of risk conditions that children and youth confront in their daily lives (Annie E. Casey Foundation, 2004). Nearly one in five children live in poverty and experience the multiple, layered risks associated with poor homes and poor communities (Evans, 2004; U.S. Census Bureau, 2002). As a result of widespread risk conditions and low access to preventive or remedial mental health services, approximately 20% of children have a diagnosable mental disorder, and 9–13% of children have severe emotional disorders that impair their functioning at home or school (Friedman, Katz-Leavy, Manderscheid, & Sondheimer, 1996). Consequently, at least 25% of adolescents in the United States are at serious risk of not achieving "productive adulthood" (National Research Council, 1993).

These statistics on population-level risk among youth, combined with a rapidly expanding array of empirically supported mental health prevention programs, have led to renewed calls for an increased emphasis on deploying empirically supported prevention programs into children's

343

natural settings. The Surgeon General's National Action Agenda for Children's Mental Health (U.S. Public Health Service, 2002) has recommended that prevention programs be embedded into schools and other child-serving institutions, and the National Institute of Mental Health has targeted significant resources toward efforts to disseminate such programs into schools and other community settings.

Despite strong theoretical and empirical arguments for population-focused, prevention-oriented, and indirect models for the delivery of school psychological services and repeated calls in the literature for such a model since the 1960s (Alpert, 1985; Curtis, Hunley, Walker, & Baker, 1999; Durlak, 1995; Elias & Branden, 1988; Felner & Felner, 1989; Gray, 1963; Hoagwood & Johnson, 2003; Weissberg, 1990; Wonderly, 1979; Zins, Conyne, & Ponti, 1988), this model is rare in contemporary practice (Bramlett, Murphy, Johnson, Wallingsford, & Hall, 2002; Reschly, 2000). Individual child assessment, diagnosis, and remediation continue to be the primary roles for school psychologists, followed by consultation with teachers (Bradley-Johnson & Dean, 2000; Reschly, 2000; Reschly & Wilson, 1995).

Based on surveys of school psychologists (Bramlett et al., 2002), descriptions of training in consultation (Kratochwill, Elliott, & Busse, 1995), and published literature on school consultation (Hughes, 2000; Sheridan, Welch, & Orme, 1996), school consultation practice commonly involves the application of operant procedures to modify an individual child's targeted problem behaviors. Furthermore, consultation research rarely examines whether consultation effects last beyond the end of consultation. For example, none of the 46 studies on consultation reviewed by Sheridan et al. (1996) assessed cross-year changes in children's social, emotional, or academic functioning. Because published studies evaluating behavior consultation make no attempt to assess the impact of consultation on functioning beyond the year of the consultative intervention, any claims that behavior consultation is a preventive approach are based on "consult and hope" rather than empirical evidence.

Felner et al. (2001) observed that current models of school psychology practice focus on changing children rather than on changing schools. In light of extensive evidence that school contexts are often inconsistent with children's developmental needs, they recommended the following:

> Approaches that seek to change the environmental side of the equation to improve student adaptation should be emphasized to at least an equal degree as those that seek to change the individuals to fit the settings. Indeed, if we take the stance that schooling should have as its goals both the promotion of positive developmental outcomes and the prevention of negative ones, then the alteration of environmental conditions rather than individual change efforts becomes a preferred approach. (p. 179)

The fact that teacher consultation accounts for a significant portion of school psychologists' time suggests the possibility that this time could be re-deployed to realize a population-focused, prevention-oriented model of mental health consultation. Realization of that vision, however, will require significant changes in school psychology training, practice, and research. As past efforts to reinvent school psychology illustrate, change will not come easy. School psychology practice is certainly shaped by a variety of factors, many of which exist at the "macrosystem" (Bronfenbrenner, 1979) or societal level. Among such changes that offer a unique opportunity for the specialty to reinvent itself and narrow the gap between reality and aspirations are legislated mandates that hold schools accountable for the success of all students, accumulated evidence that social and emotional competencies contribute to academic achievement (Brand, Felner, Seitsinger, Shim, & Dumas, 2005; Elias, Zins, Graczyk, & Weissberg, 2003), and an array of empirically supported prevention interventions (Greenberg, Domitrovic, & Bumbarger, 2001).

CHAPTER GOALS

This chapter has three goals. First, we review the current outcome research on school consultation, relying on extant reviews of the literature and our own review of outcome studies published between 1994 and 2004. Our review focuses on the characteristics of consultation research in light of calls for a more population-focused, prevention-oriented model of school psychology. Second, we articulate an updated model of mental health consultation that is consistent with Caplan's vision of consultation as a service delivery model that promotes the well-being of populations. Third, we discuss implications of an updated model for training, practice, and research.

REVIEW OF OUTCOME RESEARCH IN CONSULTATION

Summary of Previous Reviews of the Outcome Research on School Consultation

Reviews of consultation outcome studies have appeared in the published literature every few years since the early 1970s, with the occurrence of studies peaking in the years 1975 to 1988 (Gresham & Kendell, 1987; Mannino & Shore, 1975; Medway, 1979, 1982; Medway & Updyke, 1985; Sheridan et al., 1996; West & Idol, 1987). Although studies differ in coding schemes and criteria for study inclusion, their results are remarkably similar in most respects. Importantly, all reviews document that the majority of consultation studies report at least some positive outcomes. For example, in a review of studies conducted through 1979, Medway (1982) reported that 84% of school-based consultation studies reported at least some positive outcomes. In a review of consultation studies published between 1984 and 1995, Sheridan et al. (1996) reported that 76% of school consultation studies resulted in at least one positive outcome. Behavior consultation is found to be the most common model evaluated and to produce superior outcomes relative to alternative models, a conclusion that holds whether the comparison is based on effect sizes (Medway & Updyke, 1985) or the percentage of positive outcomes (Gresham & Kendell, 1987; Mannino & Shore, 1975; Medway, 1982; Sheridan et al., 1996).

Reviewers also concur in assessment of limitations of consultation research. Prominent among these limitations are reliance on nonexperimental designs, lack of data on long-term effects of consultation, absence of data on generalization of findings, reliance on subjective measures of teacher attitudes or ratings of improvement, and inadequate assessment of consultation integrity (both the integrity of the consultation procedures and the integrity of the client's implementation of recommendations). In comparing results of studies published between 1984 and 1995 with studies published prior to 1984, Sheridan et al. (1996) determined that more recent studies were more likely to use experimental designs (primarily single-case designs) and to use multiple methods to assess outcomes, including direct observation.

Review of Recent (1994–2004) Outcome Research on School Consultation

The primary purpose of this review is to characterize recently published outcome literature in school consultation to detect possible changes in response to calls for prevention-oriented school psychology practice (Elias & Branden, 1988; Felner & Felner, 1989; Zins et al., 1988). We conducted an online computer search through PsycInfo using the terms *consultation* or *consult* and *student* or *teacher* or *school*. The search was limited to journal articles published in English. We also conducted a hand search of four journals that publish a majority of research on school consultation: *Journal of School Psychology, School Psychology Review, School Psychology Quarterly,* and *Journal of Educational and Psychological Consultation.*

For this review, *consultation* was defined as an indirect model of delivering mental health services to students in kindergarten to Grade 12 in which the consultee participated in defining the problem and in selecting the intervention approach. Thus, studies that included teacher consultation as a component of a curriculum adopted by a school and implemented on a schoolwide basis were excluded unless teachers had significant responsibility for deciding how the curriculum would be implemented in their classrooms. Additional criteria for inclusion were (a) the consultant was a mental health expert, such as a psychologist, social worker, psychiatrist or counselor; (b) one of the consultees was a teacher, administrator, or other credentialed school professional; (c) the study employed either a quasi-experimental or experimental design (if group based) or single-case design that minimized threats to internal validity (e.g., multiple-baseline design or AB design replicated across cases); and (d) outcome assessment included measures of students' social, emotional, or behavior functioning or of teachers' skills, knowledge, or beliefs relevant to promoting students' social, emotional, or behavioral functioning. Studies that only obtained measures of consultee attitudes toward or satisfaction with consultation were excluded. Studies that involved only training of teachers or administrators in the absence of ongoing consultation were also excluded. The search terms initially yielded 223 articles on consultation published between 1994 and 2004. Each of us reviewed the abstracts to determine whether each met the criteria for inclusion. Disagreements were resolved by discussion. Of these 223 articles, only 16 met all inclusionary criteria.

The second and third authors served as primary raters in this review, with differences resolved by discussions with the first author. Table 16.1 presents coding categories and definitions, and Tables 16.2 and 16.3 provide coding results for each article. The full citations for these 16 empirical studies of consultation outcomes are included in the list of references. Some studies used a design that met the criteria for inclusion in the review but reported some outcomes that did not result from one of the qualifying designs (i.e., experimental or quasi-experimental group or single case). In these cases, we only considered outcomes that were evaluated with one of the qualifying designs. For example, for a study reporting outcomes both for student behavior assessed in a multiple-baseline design and for teacher satisfaction with consultation, only the student behavior outcome was included in the analysis.

As reported in Table 16.2, for 12 (75%) of the articles, all consultants were trainees, and for 15 (94%), the consultant's discipline was school psychology. Each study involved teacher consultation, with 7 (44%) also involving parents. No study involved consultation with administrators. Fourteen studies presented data on the median time elapsed between the initiation and termination of consultation. For 9 (64%) of these studies, the median duration was under 7 weeks. Table 16.3 reports that 6 (37.5%) studies employed objective outcome assessment measures (i.e., archival records, such as achievement test scores or absences or observations by individuals blind to students' treatment status). Of the 4 (25%) studies using group-based designs, only one used random assignment to treatment conditions. With respect to the direction of outcome effects, no study reported negative outcomes, and all but 1 study reported more positive than neutral (i.e., no treatment effect) results.

Only one study, published in the *American Journal of Orthopsychiatry* (Goldman, Botkin, Tokunaga, & Kuklinski, 1997), assessed cross-year effects of consultation. This study assessed both student and teacher outcomes. Given the rarity of consultation outcome studies that assess long-term changes, this study deserves special attention. Mental health consultation services provided by a clinical social worker were available on a voluntary basis to teachers in three schools (the experimental condition). Three similar schools served as control schools. A measure of teacher utilization of consultation was collected in the experimental schools. Baseline measures of student cognitive self-concept and academic achievement were obtained from all students, and teachers completed measures of teacher self-efficacy. Results showed that teacher use of consultation was positively

Table 16.1   Coding Categories and Definitions

Category	Coding Abbreviations and Definitions
Consultant	SP = School Psychologist
	O = Other psychologist/mental health specialist
Consultant educational level	S = Student/trainee
	PR = Professional
Consultee	T = Teacher
	P = Parent
	A = Administrator
	O = Other (e.g., school counselor)
Focus of study	PG = Program
	C = Case
Length of consultation	Number of weeks (if only the number of sessions was reported, then we translated number of sessions into weeks, i.e., 3 sessions was coded as 3 weeks)
	NR = Not reported
	CY = Cross-year (if outcomes were assessed during the year or grade following that in which consultation occurred)
Designs	Gr:Exp = Experimental group design (random assignment)
	Gr:Q = Quasi-experimental group design
	SC = Single-case experimental design
Targeted outcome	SED = Student educational
	SB = Student behavioral
	SS = Student social/emotional
	CS = Consultee skill/knowledge
	CA = Consultee attitude (e.g., self-efficacy, mental health, stress)
	SAT = Satisfaction with evaluation of consultation
Source of outcome data	CT = Consultant
	CE = Consultee
	OB = Blind observer
	ON = Nonblind observer
	CHSR= Child self-report (e.g., questionnaire)
	CHP = Child performance (e.g., measures of achievement)
Number and direction of outcomes	+ = Positive outcome
	n = Neutral outcome
	− = Negative outcome; in group designs, each outcome was coded as positive, neutral, or negative based on statistical tests and P values < .05, e.g., the Dunson, Hughes, and Jackson (1994) study evaluated four outcomes, two of which demonstrated positive effects and two of which demonstrated no effect; for single-case studies that reported observational data for multiple cases or multiple outcomes, a single outcome was recorded based on whether the majority of targeted variables improved, deteriorated, or remained the same

Table 16.2   Descriptions of Studies

Authors and Year	Consultant	Education Level	Consultee	Focus	Length
Bonner and Barnett, 2004	SP	S	T, P	C	NR
Busse, Kratochwill, and Elliott, 1999	SP	S	T	C	3
Colton and Sheridan, 1998	SP	S	T, P	C	4
Draper, White, O'Shaughnessy, Flynt, and Jones, 2001	SP, O	PR	T, O	PG	6
Dunson et al., 1994	SP	S	T	C	3
Galloway and Sheridan, 1994	SP	PR	T, P	C	7
Goldman et al., 1997	O	PR	T	PG	CY
Hughes, Hasbrouck, Serdahl, Heidergerken, and McHaney, 2001	SP, O	S	T, P	C	6
Kratochwill et al., 1995	SP	S	T	C	14
Noell, Duhon, Gatti, and Connell, 2002	SP	S	T	C	NR
Riley-Tillman and Eckert, 2001	SP	S,PR	T	C	3
Robbins and Gutkin, 1994	SP	S	T	C	7
Schill, Kratochwill, and Elliott, 1998	SP	S	T, P	C	8
Sheridan, Eagle, Cowan, and Mickelson, 2001	SP	S	T, P	C	4
Weiner, Sheridan, and Jenson, 1998	SP	S	T, P	C	2
Wickstrom, Jones, LaFleur, and Witt, 1998	SP, O	S	T	C	3.5

Table 16.3   Experimental Designs and Outcomes

Authors and Year	Design	Source of Data	Outcome	Dir. of Outcome
Bonner and Barnet, 2004	SC	CE, CT, ON	SB	1+
Busse, Kratochwill, and Elliott, 1999	SC	CE	SB	1+
Colton and Sheridan, 1998	SC	OB	SB	1+
Draper, White, O'Shaughnessy, Flynt, and Jones, 2001	Gr: Q	CE, S, ON	SB, SS, CS	3+
Dunson et al., 1994	Gr: Exp	CE, OB	SB, CS	2+, 2n
Galloway and Sheridan, 1994	SC	CHP	SED	1+
Goldman et al., 1997	Gr: Q	CE, CHP, CHSR	SED, CA	2+, 1n
Hughes, Hasbrouck, Serdahl, Heidergerken, and McHaney, 2001	SC	CE	SB	1+
Kratochwill et al., 1995	SC	CE, CT	SB	1+
Noell, Duhon, Gatti, and Connell, 2002	SC	CT, ON	SB	1+
Riley-Tillman and Eckert, 2001	SC	CT, ON	CS	1+
Robbins and Gutkin, 1994	SC	CE, OB	SB, CS	1+, 2n
Schill, Kratochwill, and Elliott, 1998	Gr:Q, SC	CT, CE, ON	SB, SAT	1+, 2n
Sheridan, Eagle, Cowan, and Mickelson, 2001	SC	CE, ON	SB	1+
Weiner, Sheridan, and Jenson, 1998	SC	CHP	SED	1+
Wickstrom, Jones, LaFleur, and Witt, 1998	SC	CT	SB	1+

associated with improvements in teacher self-efficacy, which predicted changes in student achievement. Although design limitations, including a high teacher attrition rate, suggest these results should be considered as tentative, the longitudinal nature of the study and assessment of consequential outcomes for teachers and for their students illustrate design features needed to build empirical support for consultation as a prevention model.

In terms of study design and outcomes, results of this review are strikingly similar to those of Sheridan et al.'s (1996) review of studies published in the preceding decade. The typical published study on consultation outcomes involves relatively brief consultation with a single teacher concerning some aspect of a student's classroom behavior and utilizes single-case methodology to assess consultation outcomes. Consultation reliably produces short-term improvements in targeted student classroom behaviors.

Consultation outcome research continues to be largely silent regarding the effectiveness of consultation in preventing problems or in creating school contexts that promote children's competencies. This finding is not surprising given that these are not the stated goals of most published consultation studies. Before consultation outcome research can address preventive and system change goals, new models of consultation are needed. Next, we present principles underlying an updated model of consultation designed to achieve the population-focused and preventive goals that Caplan (1970) thought was consultation's primary contribution to a public mental health agenda.

PRINCIPLES UNDERLYING A PUBLIC HEALTH MODEL OF CONSULTATION

Public health models of school consultation are based on certain principles about the impact of classroom and school context on children's learning and development. These principles are consistent with a developmental system perspective, the dominant framework within contemporary child development (Lerner, 1998). This perspective holds that development is a result of the dynamic interplay of factors at multiple levels of analysis, including factors within and outside the developing individual, and that risk and protective mechanisms are located within the child's interactions within and across these systems (Cicchetti, 1989; Sameroff, 1975, 1989).

Schools Are Contexts for Development

Developmental psychologists have long studied children in the context of families and peer groups. However, the classroom has not received the attention it deserves as a context that shapes children's social, emotional, and cognitive competencies, as well as their character, values, and core beliefs about themselves and others. Pianta (2005) reminded us that schools are designed to change development. Children spend a large part of their waking hours in school, where they interact and form relationships with peers and adults, learn skills that promote competence and autonomy, and relate to cultural values, beliefs, and mores that may or may not be similar to those of their family. In their day-to-day experiences at school, children confront social and academic challenges, relate to diverse individuals, cope with their own and others' emotions, conform their behavior to group norms and expectations, experience bullying as well as compassionate styles of relating, function as members of a community, coordinate their actions with those of others, and encounter discrimination as well as fair and respectful treatment. These naturally occurring interactions have more influence on children's mental health than any program or intervention. Indeed, the success of preventive interventions depends on their ability to change the day-to-day experiences of classrooms (i.e., the contexts for development). For these reasons, the Surgeon General's "action agenda" for children's mental health (U.S. Public Health Service, 2002) recommended that prevention programs be embedded in schools.

Research on the contexts of classrooms has highlighted the tremendous variability across classrooms on nearly every dimension studied (National Institute of Child Health and Human Development Early Child Care Research Network, 2002, 2003; Pianta, La Paro, Payne, Cox, & Bradley, 2002). For example, Pianta et al. (2002) observed 223 public kindergarten and first-grade classrooms. They found that there was no typical kindergarten or first grade classroom. Classrooms were distributed across the entire range of possible scores on type of instruction (group based or individual), emotional supportiveness, teacher-managed versus child-managed instructional strategies, and organization and structure. In a study of 179 first- and second-grade classrooms, Hughes, Zhang, and Hill (2005) also found great variability in normative levels of classroom warmth. Additional studies have documented classroom differences in normative levels of aggression, safety, teacher support, clarity of rules and expectations, student commitment to achievement, and support for cultural pluralism (Brand, Felner, Shim, Seitsinger, & Dumas, 2003; Stormshak et al., 1999).

School Contexts Matter

Importantly, differences in classroom contexts matter to children's development. Several studies using multilevel modeling have demonstrated that dimensions of classroom contexts make unique contributions to children's development of social, emotional, and academic competencies, above the influence of child and family characteristics. That is, these differences have consequences for children's development of academic and social and emotional competencies. Children in classrooms where aggression is common are more likely to increase their levels of aggression than are children in classrooms low in aggression (Kellam, Ling, Merisca, Brown, & Ialongo, 1998; Silver, Hops, & Davis, 2005). Peer approval for aggression may be one of the mechanisms responsible for this effect. In classrooms characterized by high levels of normative aggression, student aggression is positively related to peer acceptance, which is contrary to the usual finding that aggressive children are not well liked (Stormshak et al., 1999). Children in classrooms that are well managed, relative to children in poorly managed classrooms, achieve more and behave better (National Institute of Child Health and Human Development Early Child Care Research Network, 2003). Children in classrooms where teachers are warm are more engaged in the classroom, enjoy higher levels of peer acceptance, and exhibit higher levels of academic and social competence relative to children in low-warmth classrooms (Hughes, Zhang et al., 2005; Pianta et al., 2002).

Too often, educational practices serve to amplify rather than to minimize differences in students' backgrounds. For example, in a dissertation study, Gibbs (2002) reported on the relations between an index of teacher monitoring on the playground, school poverty, and observed levels of aggression on the playground in a sample of 14 elementary schools in a midsize city in the southwestern United States. As predicted, he found a statistically significant and positive relation between school poverty (i.e., the percentage of students receiving free or reduced lunch) and observed aggression on the playground ($r = .60$). He also found a statistically significant and negative relation ($r = -.68$) between school poverty and a measure of teacher density on the playground and a negative relationship between teacher density and observed playground aggression ($r = -.54$). Importantly, teacher density mediated the relation between school poverty and observed aggression, such that the relation between school poverty and observed aggression was no longer statistically significant when teacher density was included in model.

It is important to note that the correlation between the index of school poverty and percentage of minority students in Gibb's study was high ($r = .98$), and that the large majority of teachers in the study were Caucasian. Gibbs concluded that Caucasian teachers in high-poverty, minority-serving schools may not feel responsible for what occurs on the playground. Thus, rather than serving as an ameliorative influence, teacher practices in this study amplified differences in student backgrounds.

Classroom context variables affect children differently. For example, an emphasis in first-grade classrooms on explicit literacy instruction is beneficial to children with low entering literacy skills, whereas an emphasis on implicit literacy instruction is beneficial to children with high entering literacy skills (Connor, Morrison, & Petrella, 2004). Normative level of classroom aggression has a more negative effect on future aggression levels of children who have a previous history of aggressive behavior, relative to children without such a history (Kellam et al., 1998; Silver et al., 2005). Because school contexts differ in ways that shape children's development of competencies, consultation that focuses on improving school contexts has the possibility of affecting the social, emotional, and academic performance of many children.

School context also moderates the effectiveness of prevention programs. For example, the Positive Alternative Thinking Skills (PATHS; Kusche & Greenberg, 1995) program, an empirically supported universal prevention program that promotes children's social and emotional competencies, was found to be differentially effective in different school contexts. Specifically, the program was least effective in improving disruptive behavior in classrooms that were poorly managed (Bierman, 2005). Hughes, Cavell, Meehan, Zhang, and Collie (2005) found that two mentoring programs for aggressive children were differentially effective in schools that differed in levels of school adversity. These findings underscore the need to consider school contexts in selecting prevention interventions.

Teachers Matter

The principle that "teachers matter" is self-evident. However, efforts to disseminate prevention programs that target school and classroom contexts often give scant attention to how the teacher implements the program. Elias et al. (2003) made this point: "School innovations are fully dependent on human operators for their design, implementation, and continuation" (p. 314). Several research findings underscore the validity of this observation. First, despite the fact that a number of prevention programs have been proven to be "efficacious," schools rarely adopt these programs (National Advisory Mental Health Council Workgroup, 2001; National Institute of Mental Health, 1996). When adopted, the fidelity of program implementation is often poor, and quality of program implementation is highly predictive of program effects. Programs that are adopted and implemented are often not sustained over time in schools (Greenberg et al., 2001; Kam, Greenberg, & Walls, 2003).

It is generally recognized that some level of adaptation to local context, including resources, other programs at the school, and characteristics of students, will be necessary when introducing an intervention. However, the optimal balance between implementation fidelity and program adaptation to the local context is a hotly contested issue (Dusenbury, Brannigan, Falco, & Hansen, 2003). In our view, missing from this discussion is a consideration of the teacher as collaborator in the prevention effort. The view that a prevention program is a "thing" that can be placed in classrooms with minimal impact on "nonprogram" aspects of the classroom is inconsistent with the fact that classrooms are incredibly complex and dynamic contexts. We believe a *program mentality* to innovation diffusion (i.e., thinking about programs as things rather than as ways of interacting with students) on the part of consultants, administrators, and teachers is a major contribution to poor implementation and sustainability. The power of prevention programs resides not in a program but in how a program produces changes in children's everyday interactions in the classroom. Consultants should work with teachers to assist them in applying a specific program to their natural interactions such that the developmental value of their interactions with children is enhanced (Pianta, 2003, p. 334).

When teachers understand and agree with the rationale for a program, perceive a need that the program addresses, receive adequate professional development and ongoing support in integrating the program into their classrooms, and are involved in reviewing and analyzing data about program implementation and effectiveness, the chances that the program will produce sustained changes in classroom interactions are greatly increased. In a large, multisite, applied research program on reforming middle schools (Felner et al., 2001), research staff members work closely with school administrators and teachers in every step of program implementation, from adapting evidence-based innovations to fit the local situation to using data for revising innovations. A series of longitudinal studies demonstrate the effectiveness of this collaborative and systematic approach to creating developmentally responsive contexts (Brand et al., 2005; Felner et al., 2001; Seitsinger, Felner, Shim, Brand, & Dumas, 2005).

The goal of introducing prevention programs in schools should be that they change normal practices in the schools in such a way that teachers and administrators do not think of their practices as part of a program but as "just what we do here" (Biglan, 2004, p. 19). Consultants have an important role to play in helping administrators and teachers select prevention programs and in engaging teachers as collaborators in the process of incorporating empirically supported practices into the everyday interactions in the classroom. Caplan (1970) provided much guidance to consultants in how to establish coordinate-interdependent relationships with consultees that result in consultees accepting "ownership" of changes resulting from the consultation:

> The fundamental goals in … all types of mental health consultation are for the consultant to stimulate the development of a coordinate relationship of mutual trust and respect. This must be based upon the consultees' perceiving him [sic] as a reliable professional who has specialized knowledge and skills that he is prepared to put at their disposal to enhance their working capacity, without infringing on their authority and responsibility and without endangering their occupational status and personal self-respect. (p. 271)

IMPLICATIONS OF PRINCIPLES FOR AN UPDATED MODEL OF MENTAL HEALTH CONSULTATION

Caplan believed the preventive goal of consultation was best achieved by enhancing the professional functioning of individuals embedded in clients' everyday lives. A key contribution of Caplan's model to consultation practice was his emphasis on the consultee as the agent of change. He realized that this goal often involved changing how consultees think about their role, their abilities, and the problem for which consultation is sought. Thus, consultees' thinking about the problem was often the focus of consultation.

Caplan's emphases on prevention and on changing clients' everyday contexts are consistent with current calls for public health roles for school psychologists. However, Caplan's model pre-dated recent scientific advancements concerning developmental processes and the role of school context on children's development. In this section, we draw on these scientific developments in articulating an updated model of mental health consultation.

Incorporate Knowledge of Developmental Processes Into Consultation

In response to Sheridan and Gutkin's (2000) assertion that school psychology is not sufficiently ecological, Pianta (2000) stated that, "Fundamentally, the ecological model in school psychology is not fully informed; it is not sufficiently developmental or systematic in nature" (p. 503). Developmental psychopathology views the development of competence and dysfunction as a result of multiple factors at multiple levels of analysis (e.g., genetic, constitutional, physiological, behavioral, psychological, environmental, and sociological) that are in dynamic transaction with one another (Cicchetti, 1989). Risk and protective mechanisms are viewed as located within the child's interactions within these systems (e.g., parent-child relationship, teacher-child relationship, child's relationship with siblings and the peer group) and interactions occurring across these systems (e.g., home-school relationship).

The developmental psychopathology framework has propelled longitudinal research on risk and resiliency factors at various levels and how these factors interact to deflect children from maladaptive developmental pathways. The result of this research paradigm is the accumulation of a wealth of information about how children's transactions with their environments (e.g., peer group interactions, parent-child interactions, interactions with academic tasks at school) influence development. This information should inform the selection of intervention outcomes in both individual and program consultation. In recognition of the fact that the same process differs in impact at different developmental periods (Vellutino, Scanlon, & Tanzman, 1998), it should also inform the timing of interventions intended to bring about improved trajectories.

Focus on School Contexts

The advent of accessible statistical methods for analyzing the unique contribution of classroom and school context, above individual student variables, has led to a miniexplosion of research on the influence of school context on the development of academic, social, and behavioral competencies and academic motivation and engagement (Kellam et al., 1998; Silver et al., 2005). For example, using multilevel modeling approaches, Brand et al. (2005) reported that a number of school climate factors assessed by a variety of methods predict changes in student growth trajectories for academic aspirations and motivation in Grades 6 to 8. Interestingly, most of these climate factors involve social processes (teacher support, positive peer interactions, sense of safety at school), suggesting the importance of universal interventions that target these processes in school reform. Given the pressure exerted on schools to demonstrate improved learning outcomes for all students, it is especially noteworthy that positive growth trajectories for academic achievement from Grades 6 to 8 were predicted by the following school climate factors: higher levels of perceived emotional support from peers and teachers, higher levels of student commitment to achievement, and lower levels of normative disruptive behavior. Furthermore, these researchers reported that school climate factors mediated the impact of individual- and school-level poverty, such that positive learning climates protected youth with low socioeconomic status from normative declines in academic motivation, educational aspirations, and achievement in the middle school years.

RECOMMENDATIONS FOR CONSULTATION TRAINING AND RESEARCH

Historically, the majority of consultation research in school psychology has been conducted in the context of consultation training. In our review, all 15 studies in which the consultant's discipline was school psychology involved student consultants. Because research and training have been inextricably linked, changes in one necessitate changes in the other. We begin by focusing on changes in training and then turn our attention to changes in research on consultation.

Recommendations for Consultation Training

Data on curricular emphasis in school psychology programs are meager (Fagan, 2005). If other programs in school psychology accredited by the American Psychological Association are similar to the one at Texas A&M University, programs devote much more curriculum time (in terms of credit hours) to direct service roles (i.e., assessment and remediation of within-child factors) than to prevention, developmental processes, and system-level consultation skills. We recommend a decrease in courses and supervised experiences related to child assessment and counseling and an increase in courses in development, organizational psychology, prevention science, and program evaluation. School mental health consultants need to understand the theories of risk and resiliency that underlie prevention programs, know how to evaluate evidence not only of a program's efficacy but also of a program's effectiveness, and understand processes involved in organizational change. The new mental health consultant should be well versed in the literatures on school reform, organizational change, and educational policy.

Trainees need instruction and supervised experience in helping schools and teachers implement empirically supported practices. Too often, programs fail because teachers do not implement the program (Gottfredson, Jones, & Gore, 2002). Because quality of program implementation predicts outcomes, authors have underscored the importance of ensuring program fidelity (Greenberg et al., 2001). However, an emphasis on treatment fidelity may be counterproductive to sustained change because the program remains outside, or disconnected from, the day-to-day realities of the classroom. That is, the emphasis on programs comes at the expense of a more organic, holistic approach to change. The fact that successful programs are often discontinued after funding for clinical trials ends draws attention to the limitations of a focus on the program as the change agent rather than altered interactions among students, teachers, and the curriculum. Elias et al. (2003) noted limitations of a strong emphasis on implementing evidence-based programs:

> These efforts are limited in that they need to be adapted to the circumstances in which they are currently being implemented. Too often, it is assumed that evidence-based programs can be "plugged in" and then work effectively. How academic and social-emotional development programs fit with one another and with the rest of the school day matters a great deal to learners. Creating this fit takes more time to work out than one might infer from written accounts or presentations. (p. 310)

Trainees need experience in helping schools and teachers strike an optimal balance between treatment fidelity and "fitting" the program into particular, local contexts (reinvention). Reinventions are inevitable and not necessarily bad, but they should be the result of a deliberate decision-making process based on a consideration of resources, constraints, and possibilities in the setting and an understanding of the rationale and empirical support for program elements. Teachers and administrators who have a conceptual understanding of how a program brings about change will be able to accommodate a treatment to particular setting realities and student characteristics in ways that increase the probability of success. Ideally, this discussion will be informed by prevention science research that has identified the proximal processes that are responsible for a program's effectiveness. However, it is more likely that such data do not exist. It is still important to articulate the model of change (e.g., personalized learning environments provide students with a sense of school belonging and connection, which increases their motivation to become positively engaged in the learning environment of the classroom) so that the teacher can select, generalize, or design transactions in the classroom that are likely to promote those processes.

Trainees also need instruction and supervised experience in providing training and ongoing support to teachers engaged in adopting empirically supported practices. One factor in dilution of effects from clinical trials to community settings is the lack of resources for training and support. Too little attention has been paid to the infrastructures and delivery system characteristics that most effectively allow schools and communities to implement empirically based programs with high fidelity over sustained periods in ways that are locally and culturally appropriate and serve a majority of those in need (Bierman, 2005). As part of their consultation to schools regarding evidence-based social and emotional learning programs, consultants should help schools determine if they have, or can obtain, the resources needed to be successful.

The knowledge base relevant to the formation and modification of attitudes is also highly relevant to the consultant's role (Erchul, Grissom, & Getty, chapter 14, this volume; Hughes, 1992; Petty, Heesacker, & Hughes, 1997). As psychologists become more concerned with changing teachers' day-to-day interactions in the classroom, their focus will shift to teachers not as deliverers of packaged interventions, but as developing professionals whose attitudes, beliefs, knowledge, and motivation to change have implications for how they interact with students and how they respond to recommended practices. The paradox of school psychology — that we strive to improve children's well-being by changing how caregiving adults think about and interact with children — has long been recognized (Gutkin & Conoley, 1990).

Implications for Research

Random clinical trials are widely recognized as the gold standard in intervention outcome research. However, because identification of the problem to be addressed in consultation is an essential phase of individual consultation, randomized clinical trials have not been employed in school consultation. Randomized group experimental designs are essential to answering the critical question, Does the provision of consultation (model to be specified) to a school improve the social, emotional, and academic functioning of students? An affirmative answer to this question supports the consultation model for the provision of school psychological services. Studies on school-based reform efforts that employ random assignment of schools to conditions have been used successfully to evaluate the efficacy of a variety of school-based mental health interventions, including programs focusing on students' social and emotional competencies (Collaborative for Academic, Social, and Emotional Learning, 2003; Conduct Problems Prevention Research Group, 1999), motivation and engagement in learning (Battistich, Schaps, Watson, & Solomon, 1996), and conflict resolution skills (Aber, Jones, Chaudry, & Samples, 2002).

The Fort Bragg study (Bickman, 1996; Bickman et al., 1995) provides a particularly salient model for evaluating consultation as a service delivery option. The Fort Bragg study compared a traditional system of care with a system of care based on the continuum-of-services model (e.g., single point of entry, multidisciplinary assessments, case management, and full range of services) for children who had access to insurance through CHAMPUS, the insurer of dependents of persons in the uniformed services. Surprisingly, the much more expensive coordinated continuum of care model for children did not result in improved clinical outcomes above the benefits of the traditional system of care. This large, federally sponsored study on service delivery models reminds us that one's most cherished assumptions may be wrong. Although much has been written arguing for benefits of consultative model of psychological services delivery over a direct services model, the consultative model has not been subjected to a rigorous empirical test. Evidence that the mental health consultation model provides added value to schools' efforts to develop children's academic, social, and emotional competencies would go a long way toward establishing policy and local supports for this model.

CONCLUSION

The challenge for consultation researchers is to conduct a new generation of outcome research on consultation as a service delivery model. Large-scale studies in which schools are assigned to consultation or to an alternative mental health service delivery model (e.g., counseling services for referred students) are needed to determine whether consultation results in improved student outcomes on a variety of measures, including measures of achievement, psychological functioning, academic motivation, and attitude toward school. Such studies will need to grapple with ways of defining consultation intervention in ways that permit an assessment of treatment fidelity while allowing the consultant to be responsive to the unique aspects of different schools, teachers, and students. Research on multisystemic therapy (Henggeler, Schoenwald, Borduin, Rowland, & Cunningham, 1998), a highly effective intervention for delinquent youth, provides a model of balancing the need for treatment integrity with the need to be flexible in responding to clients that may be relevant to school consultation.

Despite the challenges involved in conducting research capable of answering questions about the effectiveness of consultation in addressing the mental and emotional needs of students, some optimism is warranted. Our optimism is based on recent macro-level changes that impinge on schools (No Child Left Behind and other educational policy mandates; rapid shifts in population demographics unparalleled since the turn of the century; Hernandez & Denton, 2005) as well as scientific advancements in the developmental and prevention sciences. Thus, we are experiencing a fortuitous juncture when external demands for relevance are met with a scientifically credible (and rapidly evolving) knowledge base to guide prevention-oriented consultation research.

REFERENCES

Aber, J. L., Jones, S. B., Chaudry, N., & Samples, F. (2002). Resolving conflict creatively: Evaluating the developmental effects of a school-based violence prevention program in neighborhood and classroom context. *Development and Psychopathology, 10,* 187–213.

Alpert, J. L. (1985). Change within a profession: Change, future, prevention, and school psychology. *American Psychologist, 40,* 1112–1121.

Annie E. Casey Foundation. (2004). *Kids count 2004 data book online.* Retrieved April 7, 2005, from http://www.aecf.org/kidscount/databook

Battistich, V., Schaps, E., Watson, M., & Solomon, D. (1996). Prevention effects of the Child Development Project. *Journal of Adolescent Research, 11,* 12–35.

Bickman, L. (1996). A continuum of care: More is not always better. *American Psychologist, 51,* 689–701.

Bickman, L., Guthrie, P. R., Foster, E. M., Lambert, E. W., Summerfelt, W. T., Breda, C. S., et al. (1995). *Evaluating managed mental health services: The Fort Bragg experiment.* New York: Plenum Press.

Bierman, K. L (2005, April). *Elementary school characteristics, classroom peer communities, and student social-emotional development.* Paper presented at the biennial meeting of the Society for Research in Child Development, Atlanta, GA.

Biglan, A. (2004). Contextualism and the development of effective prevention practices. *Prevention Science, 5,* 15–21.

Bronfenbrenner, U. (1979). *The ecology of human development.* Cambridge, MA: Harvard University Press.

Bonner, M. & Barnett, D. W. (2004). Intervention-based school psychology services: Training for child-level accountability; preparing for program-level accountability. *Journal of School Psychology, 42,* 23–43.

Bradley-Johnson, S., & Dean, V. J. (2000). Role change for school psychology: The challenge continues in the new millennium. *Psychology in the Schools, 37,* 1–5.

Bramlett, R. K., Murphy, J. J., Johnson, J., Wallingsford, L., & Hall, J. D. (2002). Contemporary practices in school psychology: A national survey of roles and referral problems. *Psychology in the Schools, 39,* 327–335.

Brand, S., Felner, R., Seitsinger, A., Shim, M., & Dumas, T. (2005, April 10). *Longitudinal influence of school climate and social organization on trajectories of development during early adolescence.* Paper presented at the biennial meeting of the Society for Research on Child Development, Atlanta, GA.

Brand, S., Felner, R., Shim, M., Seitsinger, A., & Dumas, T. (2003). Middle school improvement and reform: Development and validation of a school-level assessment of climate, cultural pluralism, and school safety. *Journal of Educational Psychology, 95,* 570–588.

Busse, R. T., Kratochwill, T. R., & Elliott, S. N. (1999). Influences of verbal interactions during behavioral consultations on treatment outcomes. *Journal of School Psychology, 37*, 117–143.

Caplan, G. (1970). *The theory and practice of mental health consultation.* New York: Basic Books.

Cicchetti, D. (1989). Developmental psychopathology: Some thoughts on its evolution. *Development and Psychopathology, 1*, 1–4.

Collaborative for Academic, Social, and Emotional Learning. (2003). *Safe and sound: An education leader's guide to evidence-based social and emotional learning (SEL) programs.* Retrieved September 10, 2005, from http://www.casel.org

Colton, D. L., & Sheridan, S. M. (1998). Conjoint behavioral consultation and social skills training: Enhancing the play behaviors of boys with attention deficit hyperactivity disorder. *Journal of Educational and Psychological Consultation, 9*, 3–28.

Conduct Problems Prevention Research Group. (1999). Initial impact of the Fast Track prevention trial for conduct problems: II. Classroom effects. *Journal of Consulting and Clinical Psychology, 67*, 648–657.

Connor, C. M., Morrison, F. J., & Petrella, J. N. (2004). Effective reading comprehension instruction: Examining Child × Instruction interactions. *Journal of Educational Psychology, 96*, 682–698.

Curtis, M. J., Hunley, S. A., Walker, K. J., & Baker, A. C. (1999). Demographic characteristics and professional practices in school psychology. *School Psychology Review, 28*, 104–116.

Draper, K., White, J., O'Shaughnessy, T. E., Flynt, M., & Jones, N. (2001). Kinder training: Play-based consultation to improve the school adjustment of discouraged kindergarten and first grade students. *International Journal of Play Therapy, 10*, 1–29.

Dunson, R. M., Hughes, J. N., & Jackson, T. W. (1994). Effect of behavioral consultation on student and teacher behavior. *Journal of School Psychology, 32*, 247–266.

Durlak, J. A. (1995). *School-based prevention programs for children and adolescents.* Thousand Oaks, CA: Sage.

Dusenbury, L., Brannigan, R., Falco, M., & Hansen, W. B. (2003). A review of research on fidelity of implementation: Implications for drug abuse prevention in school settings. *Health Education Research, 18*, 237–256.

Elias, M. J., & Branden, L. R. (1988). Primary prevention of behavioral and emotional problems in school-aged populations. *School Psychology Review, 17*, 581–592.

Elias, M. J., Zins, J. E., Graczyk, P. A., & Weissberg, R. P. (2003). Implementation, sustainability, and scaling up of social-emotional and academic innovations in public schools. *School Psychology Review, 32*, 303–319.

Evans, G. W. (2004). The environment of childhood poverty. *American Psychologist, 59*, 77–92.

Fagan, T. K. (2005). The 50th anniversary of the Thayer conference: Historical perspectives and accomplishments. *School Psychology Quarterly, 20*, 224–251.

Felner, R. D., Favazza, A., Shim, M., Brand, S., Gu, K., & Noonan, N. (2001). Whole school improvement and restructuring as prevention and promotion: Lessons from STEP and the project on high performance learning communities. *Journal of School Psychology, 39*, 177–202.

Felner, R. D., & Felner, T. Y. (1989). Primary prevention programs in the educational context: A transactional-ecological framework and analysis. In L. A. Bond & B. E. Compas (Eds.), *Primary prevention and promotion in the school* (pp. 13–49). Newbury Park, CA: Sage.

Friedman, R. M., Katz-Leavy, J. W., Manderscheid, R. W., & Sondheimer, D. L. (1996). Prevalence of serious emotional disturbance in children and adolescents. In R. W. Manderscheid & M. A. Sonnenschein (Eds.), *Mental health: United States* (pp. 71–89). Rockville, MD: Substance Abuse and Mental Health Services Administration.

Galloway, J. & Sheridan, S. M. (1994). Implementing scientific practices through case studies: Examples using home-school interventions and consultation. *Journal of School Psychology, 32*, 385–413.

Gibbs, M. C. (2002). *The role of school context is the development of aggressive behavior in children.* Unpublished doctoral dissertation, Texas A&M University, College Station, TX.

Goldman, R. K., Botkin, M. J., Tokunaga, H., & Kuklinski, M. (1997). Teacher consultation: Impact on teachers' effectiveness and students' cognitive competence and achievement. *American Journal of Orthopsychiatry, 67*, 374–384.

Gottfredson, G. D., Jones, E. M., & Gore, T. W. (2002). Implementation and evaluation of a cognitive-behavioral intervention to prevent problem behavior in a disorganized school. *Prevention Science, 3*, 43–56.

Gray, S. W. (1963). *The psychologist in the schools.* New York: Holt, Rinehart & Winston.

Greenberg, M. T., Domitrovic, C., & Bumbarger, B. (2001). The prevention of mental disorders in school-aged children: Current state of the field. *Prevention and Treatment, 4,* Article 1. Retrieved March 15, 2002, from http://Journals.apa.org/prevention/volume4/pre0040001a.html

Gresham, F. M., & Kendell, G. K. (1987). School consultation research: Methodological critique and future research directions. *School Psychology Review, 16,* 306–316.

Gutkin, T. B., & Conoley, J. C. (1990). Reconceptualizing school psychology from a service delivery perspective: Implications for practice, training, and research. *Journal of School Psychology, 28,* 203–223.

Henggeler, S. W., Schoenwald, S. K., Borduin, C. M., Rowland, M. D., & Cunningham, P. B. (1998). *Multisystemic treatment of antisocial behavior in children and adolescents.* New York: Guilford Press.

Hernandez, D. J., & Denton, N. A. (2005, April). *Resources and challenges for young children in immigrant families.* Paper presented at the biennial meeting of the Society for Research on Child Development, Atlanta, GA.

Hoagwood, K., & Johnson, J. (2003). School psychology: A public health framework: I. From evidence-based practices to evidence-based policies. *Journal of School Psychology, 41,* 3–22.

Hughes, J. N. (1992). Social psychology of consultation. In F. J. Medway and T. P. Cafferty (Eds.), *School psychology: A social psychological perspective* (pp. 269–303). Hillsdale, NJ: Erlbaum.

Hughes, J. N. (2000). The essential role of theory in the science of treating children. Beyond empirically supported treatments. *Journal of School Psychology, 38,* 301–330.

Hughes, J. N., Cavell, T. A., Meehan, B. T., Zhang, D., & Collie, C. (2005). Adverse school context moderates the outcomes of selective interventions for aggressive children. *Journal of Consulting and Clinical Psychology, 73,* 731–736.

Hughes, J. N., Hasbrouck, J. E., Serdahl, E., Heidgerken, A. & McHaney, L. (2001). Responsive systems consultation: A preliminary evaluation of implementation and outcomes. *Journal of Educational and Psychological Consultation, 12,* 179–201.

Hughes, J. N., Zhang, D., & Hill, C. (2005). *Peer assessments of normative and individual teacher-student support predict social acceptance and engagement among low-achieving children.* Unpublished manuscript. (Available from Jan Hughes, 4225 TAMU, College Station, TX 77843-4225; jhughes@tamu.edu)

Kam, C. M., Greenberg, M. T., & Walls, C. T. (2003). Examining the role of implementation quality in school-based prevention using the PATHS curriculum. *Prevention Science, 4,* 55–63.

Kellam, S. G., Ling, X., Merisca, R., Brown, C. H., & Ialongo, N. (1998). The effect of the level of aggression in the first grade classroom on the course and malleability of aggressive behavior into middle school. *Development and Psychopathology, 10,* 165–186.

Kratochwill, T. R., Elliott, S. N., & Busse, R. T. (1995). Behavior consultation: A 5-year evaluation of consultant and client outcomes. *School Psychology Quarterly, 10,* 87–117.

Kusche, C. A., & Greenberg, M. T. (1995). *The PATHS curriculum.* Seattle, WA: Developmental Research and Programs.

Lerner, R. (1998). Theories of human development: Contemporary perspectives. In W. Damon & R. M. Lerner (Eds.), *Handbook of child psychology* (5th ed., pp. 1–24). New York: Wiley.

Mannino, F. V., & Shore, M. F. (1975). The effects of consultation: A review of the literature. *American Journal of Community Psychology, 3,* 1–21.

Medway, F. J. (1979). How effective is school consultation? A review of recent research. *Journal of School Psychology, 17,* 272–282.

Medway, F. J. (1982). School consultation research: Past trends and future directions: *Professional Psychology, 13,* 422–430.

Medway, F. J., & Updyke, J. F. (1985). Meta-analysis of consultation outcome studies. *American Journal of Community Psychology, 13,* 489-5-5.

National Advisory Mental Health Council Workgroup on Child and Adolescent Mental Health Intervention Development and Employment. (2001). *Blueprint for change: Research on child and adolescent mental health.* Rockville, MD: National Institute of Mental Health.

National Institute of Child Health and Development Early Child Care Research Network. (2002). The relation of global first grade classroom environment to structural classroom features, teacher, and student behaviors. *Elementary School Journal, 102,* 367–387.

National Institute of Child Health and Development Early Child Care Research Network. (2003). Social functioning in first grade: Associations with earlier home and childcare predictors and with current classroom experiences. *Child Development, 74,* 1639–1662.

National Institute of Mental Health. (1996). *A plan for preventive research for the National Institute of Mental Health* (NIH Publication No. 96–4093). Rockville, MD: Author.

National Research Council. (1993). *Losing generations: Adolescents in high-risk settings.* Washington, DC: National Academy Press.

Noell, G. H., Duhon, G. J., Gatti, S. L., & Connell, J. E. (2002). Consultation, follow-up, and implementation of behavior management interventions in general education. *School Psychology Review, 31,* 217–234.

Petty, R. E., Heesacker, M., & Hughes, J. N. (1997). The elaboration likelihood model: Implications for the practice of school psychology. *Journal of School Psychology, 35,* 107–136.

Pianta, R. C. (2000). Commentary: Sheridan and Gutkin's vision of the future: Information will help us get there. *School Psychology Review, 29,* 503–504.

Pianta, R. C. (2003). Commentary: Implementation, sustainability, and scaling up in school contexts: Can school psychology make the shift? *School Psychology Review, 32,* 331–335.

Pianta, R. C. (2005, April). *Models of schooling and development: Transactions and multilevel systems.* Paper presented at the biennial meeting of the Society for Research in Child Development, Atlanta, GA.

Pianta, R. C., La Paro, K. M., Payne, C., Cox, M. J., & Bradley, R. (2002). The relation of kindergarten classroom environment to teacher, family, and school characteristics and child outcomes. *Elementary School Journal, 102,* 225–238.

Reschly, D. J. (2000). The present and future status of school psychology in the United States. *School Psychology Review, 29,* 507–522

Reschly, D. J., & Wilson, M. S. (1995). School psychology practitioners and faculty: 1986–1992 Trends in demographics, roles, and satisfaction, and system reform. *School Psychology Review, 24,* 62–80.

Riley-Tillman, T. C., & Eckert, T. L. (2001). Generalization programming and school-based consultation: An examination of consultees' generalization of consultation-related skills. *Journal of Educational and Psychological Consultation, 12,* 217–241.

Robbins, J. R., & Gutkin, T. B. (1994). Consultee and client remedial and preventive outcomes following consultation: Some mixed empirical results and directions for future researchers. *Journal of Educational and Psychological Consultation, 5,* 149–167.

Sameroff, A. J. (1975). Transactional models in early social relations. *Human Development, 18,* 65–79.

Sameroff, A. J. (1989). Principles of development and psychopathology. In A. Sameroff & R. Emde (Eds.), *Relationship disturbances in early childhood* (pp. 17–32). New York: Basic Books.

Schill, M. T., Kratochwill, T. R., & Elliott, S. N. (1998). Functional assessment in behavioral consultation: A treatment utility study. *School Psychology Quarterly, 13,* 116–140.

Seitsinger, A., Felner, R., Shim, M., Brand, S., & Dumas, T. (2005, April). *Family contexts and adolescent development: Engaging parents in learning.* Paper presented at the biennial meeting of the Society for Research on Child Development, Atlanta, GA.

Sheridan, S. M., & Gutkin, T. B. (2000). The ecology of school psychology: Examining and changing our paradigm for the 21st century. *School Psychology Review, 29,* 485–503.

Sheridan, S. M., Eagle, J. W., Cowan, R. J., & Mickelson, W. (2001). The effects of conjoint behavioral consultation: Results of a 4-year investigation. *Journal of School Psychology, 39,* 361–385.

Sheridan, S. M., Welch, M., & Orme, S. F. (1996). Is consultation effective? *Remedial and Special Education, 17,* 341–354.

Silver, R. B., Hops, H., & Davis, B. (2005, April). *The classroom context and aggression: Contributions from peer relationships, teacher interactions, and classroom aggression level.* Paper presented at biennial meeting of the Society for Research in Child Development, Atlanta, GA.

Stormshak, E. A., Bierman, K. L., Bruschi, C., Dodge, K. A., Coie, J. D., & The Conduct Problems Prevention Research Group. (1999). The relation between behavior problems and peer preference in different classroom contexts. *Child Development, 70,* 169–182.

U.S. Census Bureau. 2002. American community survey. Percent of people below poverty level: Retrieved August 14, 2004, from http://www.census.gov/acs/www/Products/Ranking/2002/R01T050.htm

U.S. Public Health Service. (2002). *Report of the Surgeon General's Conference on Children's Mental Health: A national action agenda.* Washington, DC.

Vellutino, F. R., Scanlon, D. M., & Tanzman, M. S. (1998). The case for early intervention in diagnosing specific reading disability. *Journal of School Psychology, 36,* 367–397.

Weiner, R. K., Sheridan, S. M., & Jenson, W. R. (1998). The effects of conjoint behavioral consultation and a structured homework program on math completion and accuracy in junior high students. *School Psychology Quarterly, 13,* 281–309.

West, J. F., & Idol, L. (1987). School consultation (part 1): An interdisciplinary perspective on theory, models, and research. *Journal of Learning Disabilities, 20,* 388–408.

Weissberg, R. P. (1990). Support for school-based social competence promotion. *American Psychologist, 45,* 986–988.

Wickstrom, K. F., Jones, K. M., LaFleur, L. H., Witt, J. C. (1998). An analysis of treatment integrity in school-based behavioral consultation. *School Psychology Quarterly, 13,* 141–154.

Wonderly, D. M. (1979). Primary prevention in school psychology: Past, present, and proposed future. *Child Study Journal, 9,* 163–179.

Zins, J. E., Conyne, R. K., & Ponti, C. R. (1988). Primary prevention: Expanding the impact of psychological services in schools. *School Psychology Review, 17,* 542–549.

17

Section Commentary
Evidence-Based Consultation: The Importance of Context and the Consultee

SUSAN G. FORMAN

Rutgers, The State University of New Jersey

JOSEPH E. ZINS

University of Cincinnati

The four chapters in this section addressing process/outcome findings indicate the importance of understanding contextual and consultee-related issues in school consultation. Improving our understanding in these areas will be essential prerequisites to increasing the success of consultation and thereby developing effective practices, programs, and environments that support learning and emotional/social health for child and adolescent clients.

In chapter 13, Ingraham points to the fact that the context for school consultation is increasingly multicultural and explores what we know about the multicultural aspects of consultation, the process of studying this, and implications for future research and practice in this arena. She states that unless consultation research includes details about the ethnic diversity of its participant samples and the cultural context in which the consultation process and intervention was delivered, it is difficult to reach conclusions about applicability to other samples and settings. The importance of establishing the cultural validity of interventions recommended during consultation is emphasized in this chapter. The importance of an individual's frame of reference and its potential effects on the consultation process is also advanced.

In a consultation process, the cultural context of the consultant, consultee, and client may differ. Ingraham points out that focusing on the cultural context of the client is a first step in approaching multicultural consultation, but that the consultant and consultee also bring cultural perspectives to the consultation process that must be considered. Those who have worked to identify evidence-based interventions have recognized the need to ensure that evidence-based interventions are in fact evidence based for members of a particular culture or in diverse contexts. However, differences in frame of reference due to cultural differences between the consultant and the consultee are also significant issues that need to be addressed to maximize the probability of successful consultation, as such differences can lead to lack of implementation of interventions recommended during the consultation process.

Ingraham calls for additional research on cultural aspects of the consultation process using qualitative and naturalistic methods. However, she cautions that researchers in this area need to understand that their research questions, research methods, and interpretations are all culture bound. She advances the need for *multicultural consultation*, which is defined as a consultation process in which the consultant adjusts the services to address the needs and cultural values of the consultee, the client, or both.

In chapter 14, Erchul, Grissom, and Getty view consultation as an interpersonal influence process and focus on the role that social power and interpersonal influence play within school consultation. The authors point out that working with other adults, such as consultees, requires consideration of social psychological and organizational factors such as the interpersonal influence process. Interpersonal influence processes are important because effective indirect service, such as consultation, depends on the psychologist's abilities to influence the behavior of "third-party adults." The authors underscore the significance of the paradox of school psychology: that school psychologists must focus on adults in order to serve children and adolescents (Gutkin & Conoley, 1990).

Erchul et al. describe and critique research studies that have considered school consultation as a social influence process, and that have been conducted from the perspective of the bases of social power and relational communication. Social power is an individual's potential to effect change in a target of influence. Relational communication describes the way a speaker defines his or her position relative to another speaker. Relational communication focuses on the importance of form and process, as opposed to the verbal content of messages, and the changing nature of these messages over time.

Studies on social power in consultation have demonstrated that teachers rate informational, expert, legitimate dependence, and referent power as the top four bases of power that would be most effective for use by school psychologists; psychologists rate direct informational, expert, referent, and personal reward power as the top four bases of power likely to be effective. Both rate soft power bases as more effective than harsh power bases. Erchul and his colleagues state that because school consultation is an interpersonal influence process, school consultants have the potential to access all forms of social power and should be aware that social power is an important contextual variable within consultation.

Studies on relational communication have provided information on the verbal processes of school consultation. Work in behavioral consultation has indicated that verbal behavior of consultants differs from that of consultees, with consultants displaying greater control of the process of behavioral consultation. Consultant control within behavioral consultation has been associated with more positive social validity outcomes. The authors suggest that school consultants should understand social power and relational communication and their implications for practice to make consultees more effective in dealing with their clients.

Positive results in consultation are often achieved when the consultee is regarded as a target of behavior change (Erchul et al.). However, school psychologists' professional training, which has emphasized concepts such as helping and collaboration, has prevented some from serious consideration of interpersonal influence and social power in professional functioning. They advance the second paradox of school psychology: "Although school psychologists have the potential to influence and thereby change the behavior of consultees, many are reluctant to recognize and exercise this influence, and as a result the effectiveness of consultation is not maximized."

In chapter 15, Noell focuses on the issue of treatment integrity. He starts with the premise that the function of school consultation is to address concerns of educators and parents regarding children. Extant literature on school consultation indicates that the purpose of consultation is to intervene regarding student problems. Treatment integrity is the one variable that appears to be most definitive in its impact on treatment efficacy. *Treatment integrity* is defined as the degree to which a treatment is implemented as planned. Noell contends that treatment plans that are not implemented will not be beneficial. In this chapter, he describes what is known and unknown about treatment integrity within consultation.

Noell uses the term *treatment plan implementation* to describe the degree to which a treatment plan in consultation is implemented as designed. He states that treatment plan implementation is the most direct outcome of consultation and that the efficacy of consultation depends on whether consultants can cause others to implement treatments. He suggests that child behavior change in consultation can be considered a second-order effect that may be moderated by treatment plan implementation. Noell's review of the literature indicates that, within a consultation context, developing a plan and providing training are not sufficient to ensure accurate and sustained treatment plan implementation. As part of training and technical assistance, performance feedback has been shown to improve and maintain implementation. He also contends that even if a treatment is acceptable to a consultee, issues such as competing time demands, lack of resources, monitoring of implementation, and accountability for implementation may influence whether a consultee implements a treatment plan.

Noell concludes that we know more about how to devise effective interventions than we do about how to ensure treatment plan implementation. He offers an alternative conceptualization of consultation in which consultation is an adult behavior change process with the consultee as the target of change. The model has two components. The first focuses on assessing the problem and identifying an intervention that has a high probability of success. The second focuses on providing supports that lead to the implementation of the intervention. In this model, consultation procedures are considered successful if they can bring about behavior change in adults. Noell contends that we know less than we need to know about the extent to which teachers implement interventions following consultation and even less about the variables that determine the extent of implementation.

In the final chapter in this section, Hughes, Loyd, and Buss call for the use of an updated model of mental health consultation, originally developed by Caplan (1970). They cite evidence of high risk in the general child and adolescent population and indicate that despite repeated calls in the literature for population-focused, prevention-oriented, indirect models of school psychological service delivery, in practice they rarely exist. They further state that current school consultation practice typically involves application of operant procedures to modify an individual child's problem behaviors. Current school psychology practice focuses on changing children, rather than changing schools, despite our current knowledge about the effects of school and classroom context on learning and emotional/social development, and on the effectiveness of interventions and prevention programs.

In a review of consultation outcome studies, the authors find that the majority of consultation studies report some positive outcomes; that behavioral consultation is the most common model of consultation examined in these studies; and that behavioral consultation produces the best results. The chapter reviews recent outcome research (1994–2004), finding that a study typically involves a relatively brief consultation with a teacher concerning a student's classroom behavior, using single-case methodology, and showing short-term results. Consultation outcome research was found to be generally silent regarding preventing problems or developing supportive school contexts. The authors contend that new models of consultation are needed to address preventive and system change goals.

The updated model of mental health consultation described by the authors emphasizes enhancing the functioning of individuals embedded in clients' lives and focuses on the consultee as the agent of change. The model also incorporates knowledge of developmental processes. In addition, it focuses on the importance of school context in healthy development, academic achievement, behavior, and mediating the effects of poverty. The authors point out that schools rarely adopt evidence-based prevention programs, and that when they do, fidelity is often poor. They suggest that assisting schools in selection of evidence-based prevention programs and incorporation of these programs in classrooms should be a significant role for the school consultant. They also emphasize the importance of working with teachers to assist them in applying specific programs to their natural interactions with students in classrooms.

EVIDENCE-BASED CONSULTATION: THE IMPORTANCE OF IMPLEMENTATION

The need to focus on the consultee, on context, and on implementation and sustainability issues is highlighted by the four chapters in this section. The chapters converge on the notion that in consultation research and practice it is time to move from a focus on determining the content of an intervention program to suggest to the consultee, and from the assumption that the consultee will implement a practice if it is evidence-based, to a focus on how to ensure effective implementation of that practice or program by the consultee so that it leads to effective outcomes for the client. As Noell suggests, an evidence-based practice or program that is discussed during consultation but not implemented, or not sustained, will not lead to improved client outcomes.

We contend that it is essential to develop information on evidence-based consultation to complement existing literature on evidence-based interventions. Evidence-based consultation is the process through which consultants not only bring client-appropriate evidence-based practices and programs to the attention of the consultee, but also use consultation strategies and consultant behaviors that have been shown empirically to lead to effective implementation and sustainability of those practices and programs by the consultee. A body of literature on evidence-based consultation will address questions about how characteristics of the consultant, the consultee, the client, the proposed client intervention, and the social/environmental/organizational context of the consultee and the client interact to influence the outcomes of consultation.

As Noell points out in chapter 15, we lack knowledge about the extent to which teachers implement interventions discussed during consultation and about the variables that influence implementation. Supporting this contention, in chapter 16 Hughes and her colleagues indicate that consultation research has typically failed to examine if effects continue beyond the end of consultation. In her review of recent consultation research, a typical study involves a relatively brief consultation and shows only short-term client improvements. As Erchul and his colleagues contend in chapter 14, a consult-and-hope approach is no longer defensible. We need to bring science and professional effort to the issue of supporting the consultee in implementation. And, as all four chapters imply, we will need to increase our attention to context and to the consultee to accomplish this.

WHAT DO WE KNOW ABOUT EFFECTIVE IMPLEMENTATION?

What do we know about implementation and sustainability issues, and how can this information help us develop the science and practice of evidence-based consultation? In the past, implementation was thought to be an event that would happen automatically when information was made available about a practice or program of good quality. Recent literature informs us that implementation is a complex process in which a practice or program is put in use in a particular context with a particular population. There are several areas of literature in psychology and related disciplines that can help inform the development of evidence-based consultation and effective consultee implementation of program and practice plans. Following is a review of some of the areas of literature that may form the basis for future work in this area.

Treatment Acceptability

The area of treatment acceptability is a good place to start when examining literature that can inform school consultation implementation issues. This is a body of literature that is fairly well developed in school psychology. Acceptability is the extent to which individuals describe themselves as liking interventions and consists of consumer judgments about intervention procedures. It is assumed that individuals are more likely to implement interventions that they like. Research on treatment acceptability in school psychology has focused on acceptability of behavioral interventions by teachers, parents, and students. A number of factors have been found to influence acceptability of school-based interventions (Eckert & Hintze, 2000). These include provision of information regarding the effectiveness of the intervention; the severity of the problem behavior (interventions for more severe behavior are rated as more acceptable than when applied to mild behavior problems); and use of jargon in treatment description (pragmatic descriptions are best). Acceptability has also been found to be higher for positive rather than reductive treatment procedures. However, as noted by Noell, high treatment acceptability may not be sufficient to ensure treatment implementation and additional research in this area should examine the role of treatment acceptability, among the other variables discussed in this section, in determining treatment implementation. Additional investigations of consultant behaviors and school setting characteristics that may influence treatment acceptability are also needed.

Training and Professional Development

Other literature that provides useful information in formulating a plan of action regarding implementation comes from the area of training and professional development. This literature, which is known and contributed to by school psychologists, tells us that to teach knowledge and skill in a new practice, training activities should be multisession, should include written materials, and should include goal setting, modeling, practice, feedback, and follow-up "booster sessions" or technical assistance after the initial training (Joyce & Showers, 2002). Despite the fact that this literature is known among school psychologists, it has generally not been applied to the practice of consultation. As Noell indicates in chapter 15, developing a plan during consultation and providing initial short-term training is not sufficient to ensure effective implementation of those plans. The studies cited by Noell regarding the importance of performance feedback in maintaining treatment integrity have made a substantial contribution to our knowledge of the components of effective professional development. Additional research in this area specific to the consultation process would be useful as the existing knowledge on training generally comes from studies of group training, and consultation tends to occur with one consultee rather than a group. Within the consultation context, necessary components of effective training, in addition to performance feedback, need to be determined.

Stages of Innovation Diffusion

Literature on innovation diffusion provides an important starting point for broadening our thinking about implementation issues and evidence-based consultation because a major goal of consultation is to initiate new consultee behaviors that will in turn lead to positive outcomes in the client. The literature on diffusion of innovations tells us that there are unique but related phases to this process, including innovation development, innovation adoption, and innovation implementation. Rogers (1995) identified five characteristics of innovations that influence *adoption*, the decision to use a new practice or program: *relative advantage*, the degree to which the innovation is perceived to provide a greater advantage than what is currently used; *compatibility*, the degree to which an innovation is compatible with the current state of the individual or organization; *complexity*, the degree to which an innovation is perceived to be easy to understand or use; *trialability*, the degree to which an innovation may be implemented on an experimental or limited trial basis; and *observability*, the degree to which an individual can see the results of the innovation. Additional key attributes of innovations that explain variance in adoption rates in service organizations (Greenhalgh, Robert, Macfarlane, Bate, & Kyriakidou, 2004) include risk (if the innovation is perceived as risky, then it is less likely to be adopted) and task issues (if the innovation is relevant to the performance of the user's work and improves task performance, then it is more likely to be adopted).

This literature points to the potential importance of these factors during the initial phases of consultation, defining practice and program characteristics that may facilitate or impede consultee decisions to use recommendations of consultants. However, this literature also tells us that innovation adoption, or the decision to use a new program or procedure, will not necessarily lead to successful implementation of that practice or program (McGrew, Bond, Dietzen, & Salyers, 1994).

Research related to the concerns-based adoption model, a model of innovation in schools (Hall & Hord, 1987), indicates that in the preadoption stage, it is important that potential adopters are aware of the innovation, have information about what it does and how to use it, and understand how the innovation will affect them personally. During early use of an innovation, success is more likely if implementers have continuing access to information about what the innovation does and to sufficient training and support on how to fit the innovation to their daily tasks. Later in implementation, success is more likely if adequate feedback is provided about the consequences of implementation and if the implementer has sufficient opportunity and support to adapt the innovation. Thus, it may be important for the consultant to spend time in the consultation process working out how the consultee will fit the recommended practice or program with their existing daily routine, in addition to addressing details concerning how the new practice or program should be implemented and might be adapted without losing effectiveness. Additional research related to this area should focus on determining how consultant behaviors can effectively support implementation, with the understanding that effective support may be different in the early implementation stage, in later implementation, and in the sustainability stage.

Consultee Characteristics

In a review of the literature on innovation in service organizations, Greenhalgh et al. (2004) emphasized the fact that focusing on the attributes of the innovation obscures the importance of human perception. Individuals may judge the attributes of an innovation differently from one another, and what is easy to use for one person may be difficult for another. Thus, consultee characteristics, perceptions, attitudes, and beliefs also have an impact on implementation. In chapter 13 of this volume, Ingraham underscores the importance of attending to the cultural needs and values of the consultee as well as the client.

Greenhalgh et al. (2004) pointed out that the meaning attached to an innovation has a strong influence on the adoption decision. However, they have further indicated that this meaning is generally not fixed and can be reframed through discourse. This implies the importance of thorough discussion of the consultee's perceptions, attitudes, and beliefs regarding a proposed practice or program during consultation sessions and indicates that a major task of the consultant may be to change the meaning attached to a practice or program for the consultee. The effectiveness of consultant methods of reframing or changing consultee perceptions, beliefs, and attitudes about interventions will be an important avenue of research in this area.

Decision Making

The literature on the factors that influence people's decisions (Plous, 1993) also provides some direction on influencing adoption decisions and facilitating effective implementation. Research on loss aversion (the tendency for individuals to attempt to avoid losses or situations in which change is negative) tells us that losses loom larger than gains. That is, in making a decision, a possible loss will be considered more than a possible gain. This points to the potential importance of emphasizing the negatives of not using a new practice or program, as well as the positives of using it, when discussing why to adopt and implement a new procedure during consultation sessions. Research on vividness (the perceived intensity of information) tells us that decisions are affected by the degree to which the information is emotionally interesting. Thus, using anecdotes rather than only data and statistics to develop a rationale and make a case for a new practice or program may be important. The phenomenon of cognitive dissonance (Festinger, 1957) occurs when people try to reduce inconsistency when they have two thoughts that are psychologically inconsistent. Having the consultee involved in selection and development of the practice or program to be used with the client may therefore be useful to build a solid base for implementation effectiveness. The practice implications advanced here are extrapolated from studies that were neither school based nor consultation focused. The importance of discussing the negatives of not using an intervention, of using anecdotes in presenting the intervention, and of involvement of the implementer in intervention selection should be examined in future research within the school consultation context.

Social Influences Theory

Social influences theory and social comparison research tell us that people compare themselves to others, and the results of those comparisons influence their decisions (Bandura, 1974). Some people exert influence through their authority and status, and some exert influence through their representativeness and credibility. Although consultation tends to be a dyadic process, in the case of school personnel, the opinions of others working in the school regarding the course of action recommended during consultation may be an important factor in decisions to adopt and implement. In the case of parents, the opinions of extended family, community, or religious organization members regarding approaches discussed during consultation may have important effects. Chapter 14 by Erchul, Grissom, and Getty in this volume describes a series of studies that directly link issues of social influence to consultation effectiveness. In particular, they review the importance of using informational, expert, legitimate dependence, and referent social power, and relational communication involving consultant verbal control of the consultation process, as important to positive consultation outcomes with teachers. Ingraham in chapter 13 also emphasizes the importance of the social network of the consultee. Both chapters specify a number of suggestions for a research agenda in this area converging on the importance of examining how social relationships influence implementation decisions and behavior of consultees and how consultant behaviors can influence this.

Organizational Influences

When the consultee is a teacher or other school staff member, work setting factors may also influence implementation. In literature on innovation implementation in the business workplace, implementation effectiveness is seen as a function of two factors (Klein & Sorra, 1996). The first factor is the organization's climate for the implementation of the innovation. This refers to staff members' perceptions of the extent to which the innovation is rewarded, supported, and expected. The other factor is organizational members' perception of the fit of the innovation to their values. Staff members who perceive the innovation to be consistent with their values are more likely to be committed and enthusiastic in their use. This model is based on a number of case studies of business organizations that have identified factors that influence innovation implementation in the workplace, including adequate training, adequate user support services, support from supervisors, financial incentives, lack of budgetary constraints, user-friendliness of the innovation, staff members' belief that they are capable of using the innovation, and time to experiment with the innovation.

Thus, extrapolating to the school setting, although the school consultation process typically involves interactions between the consultant and an individual consultee (usually a teacher), the organizational context within which the teacher operates is likely to influence whether and how a teacher implements practices and programs discussed during consultation. Although interventions suggested during consultation may only target one student client, the consultant needs to consider if and how the proposed intervention fits with the general philosophy of the school about learning and dealing with student problems and should recognize that the likelihood of implementation may be decreased if the recommended practice or program is seen as interfering with other programs or work that is deemed important by the consultee. An additional role of the consultant should be to garner administrative support (e.g., support from the principal) for the proposed intervention; to ensure that administrators make teachers aware of their support through overt actions; and to make sure that any needed space, equipment, materials, or extra staff are identified and procured before implementation is attempted.

Greenhalgh et al. (2004) reviewed literature on system readiness for innovation and found essential elements included tension for change (staff perception that the current situation is intolerable); innovation-system fit (the innovation fits with the organization's existing values, norms, strategies, goals, skill mix, supporting technologies and ways of working); assessment of implications (potential effects of the innovation are fully assessed and anticipated); support and advocacy (supporters outnumber and are more strategically placed than opponents); dedicated time and resources (budget and other resources should be adequate and continuing); and capacity to evaluate (the organization will be able to monitor and evaluate the impact of the innovation). These elements, which predict the readiness for an organization to implement an innovation may have implications for elements that are important regarding readiness of individuals working within systems (such as teachers) to implement innovative practices and programs as a result of consultation.

As Hughes et al. indicate in chapter 16, school context has been found to moderate the effectiveness of prevention and intervention programs. Hoagwood and her colleagues have pointed out that a number of aspects of school context influence the ability of schools (and school staff) to adopt and implement new practices (Ringeisen, Henderson, & Hoagwood, 2003). Individual-level factors for consideration include professional training, skills, and ongoing infrastructure needed by the implementer and the perception of the implementer of the helpfulness of the practice or program. Organizational-level factors include school resources (staff, structure, funding) needed for implementation of the new program, whether allocation of these resources to the new program will affect existing programs, and organizational climate features. State- and federal-level factors include service eligibility criteria, academic accountability standards, and state and national education priorities. Again, although consultation typically involves a consultant working with an individual teacher, the consultant should recognize that the organizational context of that teacher may have an important influence on implementation, and the consultant may need to intervene at an organizational level to support individual teacher implementation of plans generated in consultation. Additional school consultation research is needed in this area to determine which school organizational factors influence intervention implementation in the consultation context and whether these factors can be influenced by the consultant in attempts to support program implementation.

Implementation Fidelity

Many researchers believe that we should expect positive outcomes only if effective practices and programs are fully implemented (Fixsen, Naoom, Blasé, Friedman, & Wallace, 2005). *Implementation fidelity*, also referred to as treatment integrity, refers to how well the practice or program is implemented in comparison with the original design of the practice or program as used in efficacy studies. In chapter 15, Noell emphasizes the importance of treatment plan implementation for effective consultation. Yet, we also know that when individuals and organizations can adapt, refine, or modify an innovation to suit their own needs, it will be adopted, implemented, and sustained more readily (Berman & McLaughlin, 1978; Greenhalgh et al., 2004; Rogers, 1995). This adaptation is sometimes referred to as *reinvention*. In general, the degree of reinvention that can be tolerated with a given program or practice without losing effectiveness is not known. What we do know is that attention to fidelity and the adaptation are both important, and that a balance between the two is probably necessary. Finding this balance will include attention to (a) the theory base behind the program, including the core values and assumptions; (b) the core components of the program; and (c) adaptations that may be necessary for particular target population, environment, political, and funding circumstances (Dane & Schneider, 1998). Future research in this area should examine how consultees typically change programs and practices recommended by consultants and the extent to which programs and practices recommended during consultation can be altered without compromising effectiveness.

IMPLICATIONS FOR PRACTICE

As the chapters in this section indicate, we know little about whether teachers, parents, or other consultees actually implement and sustain the plans developed during consultation. And, as these chapters and the literature reviewed in this chapter indicate, attention to the conditions that surround the delivery of the practice or program recommended during consultation, specifically to the consultee and the consultee's organizational and social context, will be essential for success in implementation. Most school consultants currently address their time and effort to the development of an appropriate treatment plan for the client. However, the chapters in this section and the literature reviewed here indicate that planning and action regarding the context for the treatment plan are as important and will likely require as much or more time and effort than will developing the content of the treatment plan. In addition to development of a treatment plan with effective content, targets for planning and action related to treatment plan context should include variables such as (a) the process of selecting the recommended intervention; (b) training and technical assistance; (c) the infrastructure and resources needed for the intervention; (d) implementer attitudes and beliefs related to the consultation process and to the intervention and the attitudes and beliefs of those in their social network; (e) the relationship of the intervention to the mission, goals, programs, and practices of the school; (f) administrative support for the intervention; and (g) the reward and support system of the school.

A number of the authors in this section raise questions about the collaboration issue. The issue concerns whether school consultants can incorporate knowledge and skill related to changing the behavior, attitudes, and beliefs of consultees within a collaborative process. It is not an either/or issue. We believe it is possible for consultation to proceed within a collaborative framework in which both the consultant and consultee understand the fact that context and the success of the consultee in implementing and sustaining the intervention plan will ultimately influence client outcomes. Recognition of knowledge regarding how the process of successful implementation in consultation can occur and sharing of that knowledge with the consultee so that the process is understood by both parties can strengthen the collaborative nature of the relationship. Collaboration should not be viewed as a condition under which "sameness" among the participants is of importance, and the consultant and consultee must be equal in all respects. Rather, collaboration can be viewed as a way of interacting in which the participants in the relationship have different areas of knowledge and skill and in which both contribute to move toward the attainment of mutually defined goals (i.e., the improvement in learning or social-emotional functioning of students through implementation of an intervention plan).

IMPLICATIONS FOR TRAINING AND RESEARCH

If we conceptualize the incorporation of new interventions into daily professional practice as innovation and change and understand the importance of context in change efforts, then we see that success in the implementation phase of consultation will require knowledge and skill in a number of areas that traditionally have not been considered core areas of knowledge and skill for school consultation. These areas include organizational psychology, systems change, adult learning, judgment and decision making, group dynamics, and program planning and evaluation. The traditional foundational area of social psychology also takes on renewed importance. Knowledge and skill in these areas will provide a foundation for school consultation practice that supports consultee implemention of intervention plans in addition to the traditional emphasis on developing an effective intervention plan for the client.

However, substantial new knowledge is needed to develop a more comprehensive and definitive understanding of the process of effective implementation in school consultation. It is essential for researchers to recognize that consultee and context variables are essential components of the study of school consultation. In addition, it is essential to extend the temporal focus of consultation research to the longer-term implementation and sustainability phases of the consultation process.

Significant bodies of literature regarding perceptions of the acceptability of school-based interventions and the process of training and professional development for school staff have been developed. However, additional information about how organizational and other social context variables influence school personnel is needed, as is information about how consultants can effectively engage the diversity of organizational and social environments of consultees to bring about successful implementation of intervention plans. Much of the existing work on effects of organizational context on innovation implementation is based on research carried out in business organizations, in which frequently decision making is conducted in a more linear fashion than is the case in schools.

Many questions need to be answered in efforts to build this knowledge base. For example, which school organizational/social context factors most influence consultees' decisions to use (adopt) intervention plans, and are these the same factors that most influence consultee's success in implementation and sustainability? Which organizational/social context factors are identified by consultees as barriers to implementation and sustainability for various types of intervention plans? Which type of technical assistance is needed to support successful implementation? Which type of technical assistance is needed for longer-term sustainability? How do various administrative behaviors affect implementation of intervention plans for individual student clients and student client groups? How do the attitudes of other school staff influence the implementation success of teacher consultees? How does the practice of reinvention occur in the consultation process? How does the consultee change an intervention plan to fit the school or classroom context, and how does that affect client outcomes? What are the reasons for discontinuance of use of intervention plans?

Which strategies can a consultant use to deal effectively with organizational barriers to consultee implementation of intervention plans? Both qualitative and quantitative approaches to answering these questions will be needed to develop the depth of information necessary to move us from the consult-and-hope approach to the practice of evidence-based consultation.

REFERENCES

Bandura, A. (1974). Behavior theory and the models of man. *American Psychologist, 29,* 859–869.

Berman, P., & McLaughlin, M. W. (1978). *Federal program supporting educational change. Volume 8: Implementing and sustaining innovations.* Santa Monica, CA: Rand.

Caplan, G. (1970). *The theory and practice of mental health consultation.* New York: Basic Books.

Dane, A. V., & Schneider, B. H. (1998). Program integrity in primary and early secondary prevention: Are implementation effects out of control? *Clinical Psychology Review, 18,* 23–45.

Eckert, T. L., & Hintze, J. M. (2000). Behavioral conceptions and applications of acceptability: Issues related to service delivery and research methodology. *School Psychology Quarterly, 15,* 123–148.

Festinger, L. (1957). *A theory of cognitive dissonance.* Stanford, CA: Stanford University Press.

Fixsen, D. L., Naoom, S. F., Blasé, K. A., Friedman, R. M., & Wallace, F. (2005). *Implementation research: A synthesis of the literature.* Tampa: University of South Florida.

Greenhalgh, T., Robert, G. Macfarlane, F., Bate, P., & Kyriakidou, O. (2004). Diffusion of innovations in service organizations: Systematic review and recommendations. *The Milbank Quarterly, 82,* 581–629.

Gutkin, T. B., & Conoley, J. C. (1990). Reconceptualizing school psychology from a service delivery perspective: Implications for practice, training, and research. *Journal of School Psychology, 28,* 203–233.

Hall, G. E., & Hord, S. M. (1987). *Change in schools: Facilitating the process.* Albany: State University of New York Press.

Joyce, B., & Showers, B. (2002). *Student achievement through staff development* (3rd ed.). Alexandria, VA: Association for Supervision and Curriculum Development.

Klein, K. J., & Sorra, J. S. (1996). The challenge of innovation implementation. *Academy of Management Review, 21,* 1055–1080.

McGrew, J. H., Bond, G. R., Dietzen, L., & Salyers, M. (1994). Measuring the fidelity of implementation of a mental health program model. *Journal of Consulting and Clinical Psychology, 62,* 670–678.

Plous, S. (1993). *The psychology of judgement and decision making.* Philadelphia: Temple University Press.

Ringeisen, H., Henderson, K., & Hoagwood, K. (2003). Context matters: Schools and the "research to practice gap" in children's mental health. *School Psychology Review, 32,* 153–168.

Rogers, E. M. (1995). *Diffusion of innovations.* New York: Free Press.

E

EPILOGUE

18

Epilogue
Final Comments on School Consultation Research

SUSAN M. SHERIDAN AND WILLIAM P. ERCHUL

"But all endings are also beginnings. You just don't know it at the time."

Mitch Albom, 2003, p. 1

Writing an epilogue (i.e., an ending) to a text as forward-thinking as this one is a bit of an oxymoron. Indeed, it has been the intent of the coeditors to encourage authors not only to provide "state of the science" relative to consultation research in key areas, but also to look ahead and carve out important research agendas still facing the field. It was our hope that the ideas presented herein would stimulate and invigorate new research directions and agendas and spur researchers to tackle new and challenging issues to move the field forward. Many themes have been offered in relation to the research discussed in the preceding chapters. Thus, this concluding chapter synthesizes the issues presented across chapters and offers some predictions about the future of school consultation research and its potential to guide practice.

If one thing is certain, it is that the research undertakings required to bolster new understandings in consultation will be neither simple nor straightforward. Virtually all of the authors in the handbook reflected on what is known and concluded that much more needs to be known. In one way or another, each lamented that we are ill-prepared to draw firm conclusions about processes or outcomes of consultation practice. This assessment is predicated on the fact that previous research has largely used imprecise or incomplete tools, improper methods, and limited samples. To make advances, we must improve our understanding of the mechanisms by which consultation works; interactions among relevant variables; and effects on broader, more salient outcomes. Whereas this account of limitations may appear rather daunting, we suggest that it represents exciting directions and opportunities for consultation researchers to expand and energize research efforts for the future. In this chapter, we explore questions that, if addressed, may accelerate the future progress of consultation research.

WHAT IS OUR METRIC?

The first question concerns the tools available to consultation researchers to measure the things that we believe to be important. Indeed, our understanding of what is known about consultation is limited by the measures we have to assess the variables of interest. Several authors addressed the "measurement issue" in this text. Schulte (chapter 3, this volume) devoted an entire chapter to the topic of measurement in consultation. Others discussed the importance of (and challenges surrounding) the measurement of related variables, including treatment plan implementation (Noell, chapter 15, this volume); culture and context (Ingraham, chapter 13, this volume; Meyers, Truscott, Meyers, Varjas, & Smith Collins, chapter 5, this volume; Sheridan, Clarke, & Burt, chapter 9, this volume); relational communication and social influence within consultation practice (Erchul, Grissom, & Getty, chapter 14, this volume); and cost-effectiveness of consultation practice (Rosenfield, Silva, & Gravois, chapter 10, this volume; Schulte, chapter 3, this volume). Indeed, psychological and educational measurement is a science unto itself with rigorous standards that should be adopted by consultation researchers. Awareness of what needs to be measured is just the start; systematic and directed research is also needed to investigate the unique and important variables in a reliable and valid manner. This will undoubtedly involve the development of measures with concomitant scrutiny of their psychometric properties to be useful in the long term. Exciting research collaborations with psychometric and measurement experts are both indicated and potentially fruitful to consultation scholars.

How Do We Know What We (Need to) Know?

Methods used to understand and interpret the information we collect (i.e., our research designs) present both strengths and challenges. Whereas single-subject designs have proliferated our literature for several decades (see Gresham & Vanderwood, chapter 4, this volume) and yielded important preliminary findings, they are no longer sufficient. Authors across chapters (e.g., Hughes, Loyd, & Buss, chapter 16, this volume; Sheridan et al., chapter 9, this volume; Knotek, Kanuika, & Ellingsen, chapter 7, this volume; Rosenfield et al., chapter 10, this volume) have challenged researchers to go beyond single-case methods and "ramp up" the investigation of outcomes on a much larger scale. Randomized clinical trials are the gold standard for intervention research, and if we are offering consultation as an intervention (cf. Frank & Kratochwill, chapter 2, this volume) with empirical evidence, we need to go well beyond our current small-n methods. Although consultation outcome research (in particular, behavioral consultation; see Martens & DiGennaro, chapter 8, this volume; Sheridan et al., chapter 9, this volume) has demonstrated positive and consistent effects on the individual client level, research is in its infancy in terms of demonstrating effects in a large-scale, generalized sense.

An inherent challenge in consultation research concerns the reality of school contexts as the setting for empirical study. Beyond the extensive realities of ecological variables in school settings (e.g., school norms, culture), the fact that children are situated within classrooms where curricula and social climates are controlled by one teacher, whose actions and decisions are influenced by the school within which he or she teaches, presents highly unique experimental challenges. Whether the interest is on child or teacher outcomes, school-based consultation research requires methodological designs that take into account the fact that services are delivered in contextualized, nested settings that are by nature interdependent. This theoretical elegance raises methodological complexities that must be addressed in future consultation research. That is, research studies that attempt to answer questions concerning the effects of consultation must use multilevel, hierarchical designs that consider the realities of the structure of schools within which services are provided.

Certain (in fact, many) questions within consultation cannot be answered with purely quantitative methods. Across many chapters (e.g., Erchul et al., chapter 14, this volume; Illback & Pennington, chapter 11, this volume; Ingraham, chapter 13, this volume; Knotek et al., chapter 7, this volume; Lopez & Nastasi, chapter 12, this volume; Meyers et al., chapter 5, this volume; Sheridan et al., chapter 9, this volume), the call for mixed methods combining the strengths of empirically rigorous quantitative and qualitative approaches was clear. As questions become increasingly complex and consultation researchers venture into new and necessary arenas, methods will need to be broadened and expanded. It is our belief that a prudent and scientifically responsible approach is one that uses the most defensible and systematic procedures integrated across quantitative and qualitative paradigms, with an eye toward uncovering important answers to spur additional, deeper investigations.

Who?

A common theme across the chapter contributions, and one that we simply can no longer ignore, concerns the individual characteristics of participants in consultation. A much clearer understanding of participant characteristics is necessary to understand the effects of consultation. The question that needs to be explored — and one that several authors touched on — is, For whom and under which conditions is consultation effective? At a basic level, this requires attention to characteristics of the child, including gender, age, ethnicity, culture, religion, language, presenting concerns, classification status, physical presentation, psychiatric issues, and a host of other within-child features.

Equally important, and possibly less visible in the consultation literature, are discussions of consultee and consultant characteristics that relate to or interact with consultation outcomes. (An exception is the consultee-centered consultation model, which considers characteristics of the consultee directly, with this individual serving as a primary target of research. See Knotek et al., chapter 7, this volume, for a review.) The indirect, triadic nature of consultation service delivery involves a consultant exerting direct influence on the consultee to encourage him or her to alter his or her behavior vis-à-vis a client. The unique and critical role that is assumed by consultees in the consultation relationship requires attention to both demographic factors (such as background experience, training, educational level) and cognitive and affective features such as beliefs, attitudes, and role construct. Understanding issues related to the consultee and personal or interpersonal factors that predict his or her interpretation of target concerns, willingness or readiness to change, ability to deliver alternative intervention plans, or engage in unique roles are important areas for research (see Forman & Zins, chapter 17, this volume).

Sorely little research on characteristics of consultants has made its way into the literature base, yet this seems germane to our understanding of the processes undergirding effective practice. VanDerHeyden and Witt (chapter 6, this volume) specified some features that appear to "make an effective consultant" based on anecdotal experience. Early research by West and Cannon (1988) characterized consultant competencies based on perceptions of interdisciplinary team members. Others have discussed the importance of interpersonal skill on the part of the consultant (e.g., Sheridan & Kratochwill, 2007). However, no research has empirically identified constitutional factors within the consultant that predict effectiveness. Indeed, from an outcomes perspective, the vast majority of research has used graduate student consultants to deliver and evaluate services, which is quite removed from generalizable service delivery in the field. Scale-up research will require the delivery of consultation by professional consultants in naturalistic, authentic field settings; these consultants may vary greatly in terms of training, background, experience, workload, job demands, attitudes, and a host of other critical features. Understanding how these characteristics may affect the consultation experience, and hence outcomes, is an important research direction.

How and How Much?

The question of what explains the outcomes that we find in consultation services is perhaps the most vexing. Heretofore much of the research across models (including behavioral and conjoint behavioral consultation; mental health and consultee-centered consultation; and instructional and organizational consultation) has addressed questions of which effects one might expect through the delivery of consultation. The mechanisms by which change occurs are not at all understood. Indeed, many variables can serve to *mediate* the relationship between consultation services and outcomes. Various authors touched on this critical issue. In his chapter on treatment implementation and integrity, Noell (chapter 15, this volume) suggested that variations in treatment plan implementation may mediate treatment outcomes and convincingly argued that identifying those variations that produce the strongest relationship is daunting. Consultation may have a direct effect on factors inherent in the consultee system (e.g., practices, skills, beliefs, and attitudes), which may serve to mediate treatment outcomes (see Erchul et al., chapter 14, this volume; Knotek et al., chapter 7, this volume; Sheridan et al., chapter 9, this volume). Likewise, and as implied in the previous section on sample characteristics, several variables within participant, setting, system, and context may *moderate* treatment outcomes, and these need to be better understood to characterize effects with greater specificity. Indirectly, Martens and DiGennaro (chapter 8, this volume) suggested that treatment acceptability and intervention complexity may moderate consultation effects. Likewise, consultee characteristics (e.g., years of experience, cognitions, and personal attributes) were raised by Knotek et al. and Noell as variables that may interact with consultation services to determine outcomes.

Related to the issue of "how" is the question of "how much?" As indicated in various chapters throughout the handbook, the cost-effectiveness of consultation has yet to be determined but will be an increasingly important issue to service settings and funding agencies alike. Schulte (chapter 3, this volume) described a need to refine techniques to assess process integrity and determine the necessary or sufficient aspects of consultation practice that determine outcomes. Similarly, Rosenfield et al. (chapter 10, this volume) indicated a need to understand the unique and combined contributions of components of the instructional consultation team model that predict consultation effects. Martens and DiGennaro (chapter 8, this volume) questioned the effects of dosage, and this issue concerns both intervention dosage (the density of a treatment plan) and consultation dosage (the extensiveness of the process features).

What Else Is There?

As has been repeated across several chapters in reviews of consultation research and meta-analyses, the systematic and empirical investigation of consultation has focused largely on effects of services at the client level, within a behavioral consultation paradigm. Several authors addressed the need to understand the influence of consultation at diverse and sometimes broader levels, including those that relate to each ecological level (i.e., child, consultee, immediate setting, and system).

Consultation researchers generally have done an adequate job assessing the effects of consultation at the individual child level. Outcomes related to academic performance and behavioral functioning are common in consultation intervention studies. It is critical to understand effects of services at the individual level; however, it is now recognized as insufficient to assess only immediate outcomes without concern for the long-term implications for child development, learning, and functioning. As we intervene to alter a child's behaviors, careful attention to effects that are both proximal and distal to the target is necessary, including effects that permeate time and setting.

The sheer structure of consultation practice (i.e., one in which the intervention is delivered through an intermediary — the consultee) implicates the need to pay much closer attention to the effects of services on the individual with whom the consultant has most direct contact. Rosenfield et al. (chapter 10, this volume) discussed three types of teacher outcomes that have been studied in relation to instructional consultation teams: consultee (in this case, teacher) satisfaction, implementation of new instructional strategies, and development of problem-solving skills. At times, change in the consultee may be the overall goal and primary outcome of consultation. At other times, consultee variables may in fact moderate the relationship between consultation services and client outcomes but have rarely been the subject of systematic or empirical study.

The effects of consultation at the environmental (setting) and systemic levels are also worthy of investigation. With the exception of organizational consultation, surprisingly little research has attempted to identify empirically the effects of consultation on the instructional or affective environments within which children live. Illback and Pennington (chapter 11, this volume) provided a series of questions that address the implementation, maintenance, and study of organizational development consultation within educational organizations, which both support and advance research questions asked at the individual and consultee levels.

Where Does Consultation Fit?

Decades ago, the paradox of school psychology was offered as a paradigm for the field (Conoley & Gutkin, 1986; Gutkin & Conoley, 1990), and more recently Sheridan and Gutkin (2000) argued that school psychology is primarily an indirect profession. Thus, consultation is inherent in many of the services that define the profession. Furthermore, advances in research and policy have altered the manner in which mental health and educational prevention and intervention services are delivered by psychologists. Large-scale (e.g., schoolwide) models including positive behavior support (PBS) and three-tier (universal, targeted, intensive) prevention programs are prominent and create roles for psychologists that require indirect influence on children through individual mediators and reformed systems. Illback and Pennington (chapter 11, this volume) described research on PBS as an organizational development consultation intervention. They have rightly concluded that much more research is needed on specific consultation elements in the delivery of schoolwide reform efforts such as PBS and not simply attention to content elements of the models. Response-to-intervention (RTI) approaches to assessment and academic intervention are becoming increasingly common, and these methods place emphasis on the development and implementation of effective interventions by teachers or other providers. Although the process by which interventions are chosen, delivered, and evaluated in RTI models is largely consultative in nature, specific consultation processes and their relationship to outcomes are not at all understood (see Martens & DiGennaro, chapter 8, this volume). Similar issues are apparent with three-tier prevention models (see Hughes et al., chapter 16, this volume), in which data-based decision making and access to interventions are based on a client's response to an intervention, with little empirical research on the effectiveness of consultative decision making and how treatment plan modifications affect outcomes. School consultation researchers have unprecedented opportunities to advance understandings of processes inherent in PBS and RTI and to make important contributions to the consultation knowledge base.

CONCLUDING COMMENTS

We started this chapter by indicating that endings are also beginnings. Thus, we consider this ending chapter a beginning for renewed enthusiasm and energy for consultation research. We trust this chapter maps out important directions for establishing a meta-agenda for future empirical work. It is our hope that this roadmap provides direction for researchers toward areas of critical need, exciting opportunities, and extensive impact. To realize this opportunity, it will be essential that researchers view the challenges and needs in a systematic and rigorous manner. In the words of the late John Belushi (n.d.) "Nothing is over until we decide it is." Indeed, school consultation research is far from over.

REFERENCES

Albom, M. (2003). *The five people you meet in heaven.* New York: Hyperion.

Conoley, J. C., & Gutkin, T. B. (1986). School psychology: A reconceptualization of service delivery realities. In S. Elliott & J. Witt (Eds.), *Delivery of psychological services in schools: Concepts, processes, issues* (pp. 393–424). New York: Erlbaum.

Gutkin, T. B., & Conoley, J. C. (1990). Reconceptualizing school psychology from a service delivery perspective: Implications for practice, training, and research. *Journal of School Psychology, 28,* 203–223.

Sheridan, S. M., & Gutkin, T. B. (2000). The ecology of school psychology: Examining and changing our paradigm for the 21st century. *School Psychology Review, 29,* 485–502.

Sheridan, S. M., & Kratochwill, T. R. (2007). *Conjoint behavioral consultation: Promoting family-school connections and interventions.* New York: Springer.

West, J. F. & Cannon, G. S. (1988). Essential collaborative consultation competencies for regular and special educators. *Journal of Learning Disabilities, 21,* 56–63.

Author Index

Subject Index

Handbook of
Research in
School Consultation

Edited by

William P. Erchul • Susan M. Sheridan

Routledge
Taylor & Francis Group
New York   London

First published by
Lawrence Erlbaum Associates,
10 Industrial Avenue
Mahwah, New Jersey 07430

Reprinted 2009 by Routledge

Routledge
Taylor & Francis Group
270 Madison Avenue
New York, NY 10016

Routledge
Taylor & Francis Group
2 Park Square
Milton Park, Abingdon
Oxon OX14 4RN

© 2008 by Taylor & Francis Group, LLC

Printed in the United States of America on acid-free paper
10 9 8 7 6 5 4 3 2

International Standard Book Number-13: 978-0-8058-5336-0 (Softcover) 978-0-8058-5335-3 (Hardcover)

No part of this book may be reprinted, reproduced, transmitted, or utilized in any form by any electronic, mechanical, or other means, now known or hereafter invented, including photocopying, microfilming, and recording, or in any information storage or retrieval system, without written permission from the publishers.

Trademark Notice: Product or corporate names may be trademarks or registered trademarks, and are used only for identification and explanation without intent to infringe.

Library of Congress Cataloging-in-Publication Data

Handbook of research in school consultation / editors, William P. Erchul, Susan M. Sheridan.
    p. cm.
  Includes bibliographical references and index.
  ISBN-13: 978-0-8058-5336-0 (alk. paper)
  ISBN-10: 0-8058-5336-7 (alk. paper)
  ISBN-13: 978-0-8058-5335-3 (alk. paper)
  ISBN-10: 0-8058-5335-9 (alk. paper)
  1. Educational consultants--United States. 2. School psychology--United States. I. Erchul, William P. II. Sheridan, Susan M.

LB2799.2.H36 2008
371.4--dc22
                                                             2007014055

Visit the Taylor & Francis Web site at
http://www.taylorandfrancis.com